D0205715

PUBLIC
ADMINISTRATION
IN THE
THIRD WORLD

PUBLIC ADMINISTRATION IN THE THIRD WORLD

AN INTERNATIONAL HANDBOOK

Edited by
V. Subramaniam

Greenwood Press
New York • Westport, Connecticut • London

LIBRARY
OF
MOUNT ST. MARY'S
COLLEGE
EMMITSBURG, MARYLAND

WITHDRAWN

Library of Congress Cataloging-in-Publication Data

Public administration in the Third World : an international handbook /
  edited by V. Subramaniam.
     p. cm.
  Bibliography: p.
  Includes index.
  ISBN 0–313–24730–7 (lib. bdg. : alk. paper)
    1. Public administration—Developing countries. 2. Developing
countries—Politics and government. 3. Dependency.
  I. Subramaniam, Venkateswarier.
  JF60.P86   1990
  350′.0009172′4—dc19   88–7706

British Library Cataloguing in Publication Data is available.

Copyright © 1990 by V. Subramaniam

All rights reserved. No portion of this book may be
reproduced, by any process or technique, without the
express written consent of the publisher.

Library of Congress Catalog Card Number: 88–7706
ISBN: 0–313–24730–7

First published in 1990

Greenwood Press, Inc.
88 Post Road West, Westport, Connecticut 06881

Printed in the United States of America

The paper used in this book complies with the
Permanent Paper Standard issued by the National
Information Standards Organization (Z39.48–1984).

10 9 8 7 6 5 4 3 2 1

CONTENTS

PUBLIC
ADMINISTRATION
IN THE
THIRD WORLD

INTRODUCTION

V. Subramaniam

The earliest academic studies of the Third World countries concentrated on a general overview and emphasized colonialism, nonalignment and development. Later, studies became more specialized geographically, focusing on Black Africa, the Middle East, or Latin America, or ideologically, using, for example, an economic development approach or a neo-Marxist analysis. This introduction presents a critical survey of this literature as a background to our inquiry and briefly explains the outline and method of this study.

The term *Third World* was popularized by the Western media in the 1960s.

The concept has been the subject of considerable research by U.S. and West European scholars, followed later by Soviet, East European, and Afro-Asian intellectuals. Initially, work concentrated on political regimes and ideologies or on economic development and societal impediments; later, work focused on public administration as an instrument of development. This brief introduction cannot provide a detailed survey of the growing literature, but it can give a general background of that literature to distinguish and explain the theme, scope, and approach of this study. This introduction offers a limited but critical review of recent Western research interests in the Third World, earlier mappings, and then a brief explanation of the three major research perspectives that have developed as a result—namely, general studies of economic development and development administration; dependency theories regarding nondevelopment and stagnation; and theories as well as empirical studies in comparative administration. These three strands of research are usually intertwined in studies of development administration and comparative administration.

GENERAL SYNOPTIC STUDIES OF THE THIRD WORLD

The conscious identification of "three worlds of development" belongs to the early 1960s, but this was the final result of a longer historical process.[1] There had indeed been considerable interaction between different parts of the world through trade, cultural contact, missionary effort, war, and conquest in the centuries gone by, but it was the European commercial and colonial expansion of the nineteenth century that made this globe irretrievably interrelated. The Second World War, and its aftermath, put an end to the colonial empires as such but ultimately generated the overall basis for the three worlds, interrelated and interacting but still separate and specific. The end of the war also witnessed the open and total rivalry between the United States and the Soviet Union as superpowers with their search for satellites, allies, and areas of influence. Most of the newly independent countries of Asia and Africa, liberated from colonialism, wanted to keep out of the vortex of this rivalry and to promote their own economic development in peace and to receive aid without strings. This movement toward nonalignment, started by India's first prime minister, Jawaharlal Nehru, took hold after the Bandung Conference in 1954 and developed a wider basis for countries identifying with the Third World.[2]

A. J. Toynbee was one of the earliest scholars to identify this postcolonial world as developing a separate identity with its own bundle of sociohistorical characteristics, but the credit for using the term *Third World* consistently and popularizing it is generally given to Frantz Fanon, the French intellectual from Martinique who worked in Algeria during the final pangs of its liberation from French colonialism.[3] He was more passionately insightful than logically consistent, but he was among the earliest to notice that Third World postcolonial countries had developed a number of related characteristics, some good and some less than admirable.[4] Most of his thunderbolts were hurled against the Francophone African middle class, which he called the "Wretched of the Earth." Since then, much academic research and energy has been devoted to studying the Third World as a viable and consistent entity with interrelated sociohistorical, economic, and political characteristics from all possible angles. A considerable literature has grown up as a result.[5]

To most people the Third World consists of Black Africa, the Middle East including Muslim North Africa, Asia minus Japan and China, and Latin America. This group is clearly distinguished from the First World which consists of Western Europe, the United States, Canada, Australia, and Japan and the Second World, which consists of the Soviet Union, Eastern Europe, and China.[6] Whereas some apply the term *Fourth World* to the oil-rich Middle Eastern countries, others, namely, the U.N. agencies, use it to refer to the poorest countries. This confusing usage will not concern us here.

Third World countries vary markedly in terms of race and religion, demography and geography, political regime and ideology, economic development and international policies. However, they can be grouped together on the basis of certain common characteristics. This clustering has been promoted by dependency theorists who exchange and evaluate concepts such as "bureaucratic bourgeoisie" or "overdeveloped state," transferring them from Africa to Asia to Latin America.[7] To a lesser extent, the "modernization school" has used liberal economic ideology for the same end.[8] But studies based on detailed empirical work and quantitative comparisons that establish such clusters are infrequent and fragmentary. This is not intended as a rejection either of the overall concept of the Third World or of efforts to find common characteristics, but rather to state a position against overdrawn conclusions about the Third World.

Two of the earliest critical-synoptic works in the field, namely, Peter Worsley's *The Third World* and Irving Louis Horowitz's *Three Worlds of Development*, were clearly based on relating a number of sociohistorical and politico-economic factors to one another to build up the identity of the subject. This method has guided later studies, with some variations.[9] Peter Worsley's general approach was sociohistorical and related the three major facets of European colonialism— the economic facet of ruining the local economy, the political facet of subordination by force, and the psychological one of inflicting an image of inferiority on the colonized—to nationalist responses of imitation, reform, and revolution and to the postcolonial responses to the opportunities and challenges of independence. The study analyzed populism, one-party states, the problems of economic nondevelopment, and the Third World in international relations.

Irving Horowitz used an integrated multidisciplinary approach to analyze and compare a comprehensive list of economic, political, social, and military characteristics found in the three worlds. He established a single international stratification system and a single criterion of development. Starting with the economic underdevelopment of Third World countries, their low level of industrialization, and their dependence on their primary agricultural production, the study discussed the centralization of political authority resulting in a one-party state, the effort to integrate the nation from competing ethnic loyalties, and the nonalignment of the Third World in the context of Soviet-American rivalries. The work also provided a general theory of development and a point of reference for quite some time in discussions of the Third World. For example, David E. Schmitt followed Horowitz's comprehensive approach closely.[10] The same tendency to identify the Third World in terms of a comprehensive list of mutually related social, economic, and political factors has persisted for two decades, as evidenced by Robert G. Wesson's recent text, *Modern Governments: Three Worlds of Politics*.[11]

A considerable amount has also been written on the politics of the Third World. Anthony D. Smith's *State and Nation in the Third World*[12] clearly concentrates on the political situation in Africa, discussing European colonialism, African nationalism, and the problems of nation building, including ethnicity and class, and the intelligentsia, all as a set of mutual relationships. Paul E. Sigmund's *Ideologies of the Developing Nations*[13] details the ideologies of Third

World leaders in their own words, while Harry Goulbourne's *Politics and State in the Third World* brings together a number of country studies with a Marxist underpinning.[14] *The Rise and Fall of Democracies in the Third World*[15] by Vinson H. Sutlive et al. is another collection of somewhat pessimistic country studies on the general failure of democratic institutions in the Third World. John H. Kautsky's *Political Change in Underdeveloped Countries*[16] with the subtitle *Nationalism and Communism* is true to its title in concentrating on political movements, ideologies, and structures in relation to socioeconomic factors, with special attention given to the intellectuals and intelligentsia of Third World countries. Clifford Geertz's *Old Societies and New States* on political socialization or the political integration of different primordial groups is based on the premise of the close interrelation of the political, economic, and cultural realms.[17] Edward Shils' *Political Development in the New States* ties political development to structure, culture, and personality factors and explores "alternative courses of political development."[18] From the late 1970s onward, however, much of the Western analysis of Third World societies in general and their political systems in particular has been challenged on several counts by those rejecting such analysis as culturally Eurocentric and misleading and by others criticizing it from a neo-Marxist point of view.[19]

Political, economic, social, and cultural factors began to be viewed as more closely interrelated in the Third World than in the First and Second Worlds partly in response to a general tendency toward interdisciplinary work in the West in 1950s. An even more important influence was the frustration following earlier Western academic efforts to analyze African or Asian political systems of behavior in isolation in the same terms as in the West. Thus, there was an advantage in gaining some insights through the interrelation of numerous social, economic, and political factors in the emerging synoptic literature on the Third World and some disadvantage in terms of suggesting far-fetched correlations. Rarely was any serious effort made to identify factors as dependent, independent, or interdependent.[20]

Another common feature of these studies is the enormous stress placed on the legacy of European colonialism, even though several noncolonial countries are included in the Third World. The common urge in all these countries to achieve economic development similar to the Western industrial countries and to build up a similar educational system, modern professions, and bureaucracies justifies the aggregation of postcolonial and noncolonial nations into the Third World and calling them all developing countries. Particularly from our viewpoint of public administration, such aggregation is most fruitful for comparative study. They all have enough similarities and dissimilarities from the viewpoint of the "modernization school" in their efforts to replicate and adapt Western institutions and from the perspective of the dependency school and Marxist political economy in terms of their analytical categories which define the "dependent economies" of the Third World.

All of these studies lean strongly toward the practical and focus on the trio of the state, the political and intellectual elite, and the desperate urge for development.[21] However, the bureaucracy as a group and public administration as institution and process receive only minimal attention. This may be partly because the state is treated as inclusive of the bureaucracy or because the bureaucracy is regarded as merely one of the instruments of development along with other factors. Thus, from our viewpoint, these pioneering synoptic studies simply provide the background and open up the field.

DEVELOPMENT ADMINISTRATION VERSUS DEPENDENCY THEORY

Development administration, dependency theory, and comparative public administration are related to each other and to the study of public administration in the Third World in positive as well as negative ways. Development administration took shape as a term and concept in the mid–1950s in the United States and was gradually fleshed out through numerous practical and academic studies of actual field and project administration in several Third World countries.[22] Its main concern was with public administration as an instrument of economic development in the poor Third World countries, euphemistically called developing countries. Most of the research in this genre published in books or in journals such as *Public Administration and Development* has been empirical and devoted to specific projects in the field, sectors, or issues, such as agricultural extension or fisheries development.[23] With regard to this approach, faith in administration has been the crucial factor in economic development.

The perceived massive failure of the development decade of the 1960s brought into prominence its most relentless opponent, dependency theory. In spite of many internal variations and conflicts and the recent confrontation with ultra-critical neo-Marxist political economists, dependency theorists generally agree on the unimportance, or irrelevance, of public administration to the whole issue of development. According to dependencists, this issue is governed totally by the Third World's dependent economic position, generated by colonialist exploitation and entrenched by neo-colonialism and the international capitalist system through its local allies, the *comprador** bourgeoisie. The strict corollary to this position is that the study of public administration in the Third World and the analysis of underdevelopment through dependency theory are mutually irrelevant and even incompatible. However, the dependencists have more recently concerned themselves more with the "overdeveloped state" and the "bureaucratic bourgeoisie," and these concerns are indirectly related to public administration.[24]

Academic reaction to the lack of development in the Third World actually

---

*Comprador according to the Oxford English dictionary means "chief native servant in European house of business." In Portuguese, it means buyer. In dependency theory, it includes the pejorative undertones of OED and means a mediating subordinate bourgeoisie.

emerged in two opposite directions. The dependency theorists blamed it on external factors such as international capitalism and neo-colonialism, whereas another group, mainly economists, attributed it directly or indirectly to anti-developmental factors inherent in the local culture.[25] This second view led first to a wider definition of development and the study of noneconomic factors,[26] and later to the consistent application of system concepts to the study of all the interrelated aspects of developing societies. Thus, Fred W. Riggs' theory of the "prismatic society" rejuvenated the burgeoning study of comparative public administration, and it developed in tandem with the study of developing societies in the 1960s and 1970s.[27]

Development administration openly began with an instrumental bias that tried to modify and adapt public administration structures and processes away from law and order administration toward economic development,[28] mainly because the people of the newly independent countries expected some quick and even dramatic economic development following independence. Hence, most of the literature on development administration consisted of hundreds of plans, project outlines, and field administration reports, which included some reasonably good empirical work, a certain amount of homiletic theorizing on the fundamental distinction between law and order colonial administration in the past, and development administration in the future, and some expressions of frustration about local impediments and poor results. Some studies discussed various management theories relating to productivity in general or specific sectors such as agriculture, social welfare, or industry.[29] There was little concern with rigorous theoretical underpinning, but, by implication, development administration was allied to theories, models, and stages of economic growth on the one hand and modernization theories on the other. A general pattern of Western institutions and diversified economic development served as the basis for most of the literature generated by Western scholars who avoided studying the socialist growth models of the Soviet Union or China. The study of development administration was thus tied to the modernization school and to Rostowian and related theories of economic growth.[30]

On the other hand, dependency theory claims a firmer theoretical base derived from two sources: Latin America's experience in the Great Depression of the 1930s and subsequent economic stagnation; and a general revision of Marxist theory leading to the broad stream of neo-Marxism and the New Left.[31] At first, the theory developed rather independently and separately from development administration which was still holding sway in Afro-Asian studies in the 1950s. A confrontation became inevitable, however, with the obvious failures of the development decade of the 1960s.

The Latin American origins of the theory can be understood in the context of political sovereignty there for decades and economic stagnation, which could not be explained in terms of colonialism and imperialism. The discussion among Latin American economists, particularly Raul Prebish, in meetings of the Economic Commission for Latin America supplied one stream of thought. In some circles there was also considerable disillusionment with orthodox Marxist thinking, culminating in Che Guevara's writings on peasant revolutions and successful guerrilla war. Later, Paul Baran's *Political Economy of Growth* explained that industrial capitalism, far from spreading naturally from the center to the periphery, kept the colonized countries from such development by draining away the "surplus."[32] This explication was followed by A. G. Frank's more elaborate thesis on the "development of underdevelopment" in his *Capitalism and Underdevelopment in Latin America* and his later works.[33] Since that time, the dependency school has branched out in various, sometimes contradictory, directions.

Interest in explaining underdevelopment burgeoned in Africa in the 1960s when disillusionment with the slow rate of development set in. Dar-es-Salaam in Tanzania became the Mecca of African dependencists. African underdevelopment under colonialism was explained on a neo-Marxist basis in Walter Rodney's *How Europe Underdeveloped Africa*.[34] Continuing underdevelopment was seen in nearly the same terms as in Latin America: exploitation through a local *comprador* class and through multinationals by international capitalism. Thus, in spite of various internal differences, the dependencists shaped a fairly consistent theory until the 1970s when they were challenged by the remarkable economic growth of certain Third World countries. Several orthodox Marxists saw this development as proof of the Marxist prediction of the ultimate universalization of capitalist production; some dependency theorists offered a modified "political economy" explanation.[35] Some liberal economists pointed out that the very Third World countries which were closely involved with international capitalism and did not pursue "disengagement" showed the highest growth rates. Others criticized the poverty of the straitjacket universalistic approach of dependency theory in failing to explain specific cases of success and failure of individual countries.[36] Dependency theory still holds a prominent place in Third World studies, but in an important sense, it is irrelevant to our inquiry in concentrating mainly on worldwide economic factors. However, it has focused on the state and the bureaucracy while establishing a connection with the emerging Marxist interest in the capitalist state. Thus, it merits further attention here.

In the newly independent postcolonial states of Africa, the objective of quick economic development and nation building was coupled with lack of capital, technology, management, education, or national cohesion. As a result the leaders were virtually forced to use the state for all tasks, through public enterprises, one-party rule, and politicized bureaucracies. This gave the appearance of an "overdeveloped state"—provoking much theorizing and controversy about the postcolonial state.[37] Actually, the state was underdeveloped and prematurely overused. At about the same time, Nicos Poulantzaas, Ralph Miliband, and other mainstream neo-Marxists in the 1960s sought to explain the survival of the capitalist state, particularly the "relative autonomy" of the state apparatus from "classes" and "class struggle." In this endeavor they drew some inspiration from Marx's *18th Brumaire* and *Class Struggles in France*.[38] Left-wing Africanists in East Africa described the "overdevelopment" of the postcolonial state as a "fluid situation" without distinct classes, linking their theories to dependencist research on the postcolonial states in Asia.[39]

Of more relevance to this study is the Tanzanian dependencist debate on bureaucracy in the African postcolonial state. Dependencists and East European economists maintain that bureaucracy is not a "class" in the Marxist sense of having a specific function and a specific relation to the modes of production, but perhaps represents class interest. In another view, Issa Shivji argued that it was a class in itself and for itself fully class conscious of its interests.[40] Neither view seems to be sustained by available empirical evidence. However, we explore the triangular relationship of state, bureaucracy, and class independently in later chapters.

DEVELOPMENT ADMINISTRATION AND COMPARATIVE ADMINISTRATION

Development administration studies provoked confrontation from dependencists but encouraged an interest in comparative public administration. The case for comparisons based on scientific inquiry was made by Robert Dahl and others,[41] but it was really the U.S. and Western academicians who went out in good numbers to work with aid agencies or to do research in Third World countries who started the comparative movement. Frustrated by their inability to transfer Western techniques and institutions to Afro-Asian countries, they looked around for theoretical explanations and practical remedies. An important byproduct of this search was the "comparative administration group" supported by the Ford and other foundations. A leading member of this group, F. W. Riggs, outlined the theory of the prismatic society in his *Ecology of Public Administration* and developed it in greater detail in his *Administration in Developing Countries*. In addition, several other researchers have summarized it.[42] The main inspiration came from Talcott Parsons' social systems theory. This theory states that every society can be understood holistically as consisting of numerous interrelated and complementary subsystems, and any aspect can be grasped only in relation to the other subsystems and their characteristics. Following Max Weber, Parsons also developed two extreme ideal types of the traditional and modern society with pairs of opposite characteristics.

Riggs focused on the intermediate society which he thought was characteristic of Third World countries or developing nations. He described institutions or subsystems in traditional societies as "fused" because each system performed several related or even unrelated functions. In his view modern society was diffracted (like white light which has passed through a prism into separate colors), with each subsystem or institution having a clearly defined function. Developing societies were seen as light within the prism halfway between fused and diffracted, that is, prismatic, with no clear institutional division of function, some performing several functions and some functions being performed by several together. Riggs then presented an elaborate analysis of the "diffuse" features in society and its administration. He argued for a "nomothetic" approach of applying general models and deriving general conclusions, and he advocated an effort to identify a cluster of sociocultural factors affecting public administration quantitatively in terms of "which factor, how much." In this regard, Riggs followed the example of the synoptic works discussed earlier. Riggs' prismatic theory has been criticized severely for presenting negative descriptions of Third World administration, for ignoring the prismatic features of modern Western administration, and for laying a theoretical foundation that leads to vague superstructures.[43]

Ferrel Heady offered another general basis of relating administrative systems to independent controlling factors in a less theoretical way in his *Public Administration: A Comparative Perspective*. He classified Third World administrative systems in terms of the political characteristics of the regimes.[44] But in view of some recently published research, regime type is seen to be a rather uncertain determinant of bureaucratic structure or behavior in the Third World.[45]

We have noted only two major attempts to generate an overall correlative classification in the study of public administration in Third World countries. Several more modest studies of individual countries or groups of related countries have been done with some attempts at middle-level generalization. Thus, sub-Saharan Africa has received considerable academic attention in terms of politics or class formation and more recently in terms of policy making and planning. But the self-imposed regional isolationism of academicians into several groups did not promote the growth of macrocomparisons.[46] Macrocomparative administration collapsed with the downgrading of development administration partly owing to the attack of dependencists. Unfortunately, both of them took extreme positions, both were indirectly tied to a closed system concept, and both heaped all the blame for poor development and sala-administration on the "developing" countries themselves, while the dependencists pointed to external factors such as multinationals and world capitalism.[47] (Riggs uses the term *sala* to denote an informal disorganized meeting hall as against a disciplined regulated bureau. Sala-administration thus denotes an informal unregulated bureaucracy.)

The early synoptic works were not deeply concerned with administration, although they recognized the importance of the state and the intelligentsia. Development administration research was too project-oriented, management-centered, and prescriptive, even when its proponents attempted some integration through the clustering of related studies into a book. Dependencists were generally not concerned enough with bureaucracy, except for giving some attention recently to the bureaucratic bourgeoisie. Macrocomparativists, attempting a macrotheoretical explanation, focused on the overall subject matter of public administration but with disappointing results.

Thus, each of these approaches suffered some deficiency in regard to the study of public administration in the Third World. In this study we make a fresh attempt to provide an overview of the public administration of a representative group of Third World countries by different authors. All the authors are insiders in a deep sense. Some are citizens working or teaching in their own country; others are Third Worlders teaching for long periods in another Third World country. The editor himself has taught, researched, or served on seminars in most of the countries under survey. Countries have been chosen to represent all important variations in the Third World; geographically, the study includes significant countries in Africa, South and East Asia, the Middle East, and Latin America. The countries vary in size from large and populous India to the comparatively smaller Ghana. Postcolonial states like India or Nigeria, and states that were never under Western colonialism such as Turkey and Saudi Arabia, represent very different sociohistorical characteristics. In addition, federal as well as unitary states are included. The chapters follow a general format; starting with a historical introduction, they discuss the political executive, administrative structures, such as departments and public enterprises, and processes, such as personnel, financial, regional, and local administration. Depending on the varying importance of different factors in the countries studied, some uniformity as well as some variety is used in handling different chapters. For example, the salaried middle class is examined more carefully as a stagnating politico-administrative factor in Latin America; bureaucratic continuity, along with changes in regimes, is stressed in the analysis of the Indian subcontinent, and in Saudi Arabia, the secularization of administration is treated as significant.

The work that follows is a fairly detailed, updated, and objective empirical account of the evolution, structure, and processes of public administration in all these countries without theoretical presuppositions. The last chapter discusses the major common features of their public administration systems, such as the dominance of public enterprises, the persistence of colonial legacies, or the unrepresentativeness of their bureaucracies. Finally, we attempt to build up a theoretical explanation inductively from the empirical material relating these common features to the sociohistorical characteristics of a derivative middle class. We hope that this balancing of the empirical accounts with some inductive theorizing will lead to a deeper understanding of public administration in the Third World.

Notes

1. This has been asserted by several writers but most forcefully by A. J. Toynbee, *Civilization on Trial* (New York: Oxford University Press, 1948); Peter Worsley, *The Third World* (London: Weidenfeld and Nicolson, 1964), pp. 1–20, 50–51.

2. Peter Worsley, *The Third World*, Chapter 2, takes note of nonalignment, postcolonialism, and commitment to develop. Irving Louis Horowitz's *Three Worlds of Development* (New York: Oxford University Press, 1966), Chapter 2, gives a more detailed definition starting with a succinct statement more or less restating Worsley's viewpoint.

3. Frantz Fanon, *The Wretched of the Earth* (London: McGibbon and Kee, 1965).

4. For a critical account of Frantz Fanon's characterization, see V. Subramaniam,

Tranplanted Indo-British Administration (New Delhi: Ashish Publishing House, 1977), Appendix II.

5. The following general works are also referred to frequently: David E. Schmitt, *Dynamics of the Third World* (Cambridge, Mass.: Winthrop Publishers, 1974); John H. Kautsky. (ed.), *Political Change in Underdeveloped Countries, Nationalism and Communism* (New York: John Wiley, 1962); Harry Goulbourne (ed.), *Politics and State in the Third World* (London: Macmillan, 1979); Anthony D. Smith, *State and Nation in the Third World* (Brighton: Wheatsheaf Books, 1983); Paul E. Sigmund (ed.), *The Ideologies of the Developing Nations* (New York: Praeger, 1963). Several journals are devoted to modern African and Asian Studies; the *Third World Quarterly* (London), expressly uses the term *Third World*.

6. See Worsley, *The Third World*, Chapter 7; Horowitz, *Three Worlds of Development*, Chapter 1; Schmitt, *Dynamics of the Third World*, Introduction; Goulbourne, *Politics and State*, Section Two, Chapters 4, 5 and 6. Worsley, after discussing the middle stance of France and New Zealand and the Asian location of China, finally excludes them.

7. For a discussion of how the concept of the ''overdeveloped state'' bridges discussions on Asia and Africa, see Hamza Alavi, ''The State in Post-Colonial Societies: Pakistan and Bangladesh,'' and J. S. Saul, ''The State in Post-Colonial Societies: Tanzania,'' in Goulbourne, *Politics and State*.

8. The ''modernization school'' is a loose term and embraces a variety of approaches, but there is an overarching unity of understanding. See Atul Kohli (ed.), *The State and Development in the Third World* (Princeton, N.J.: Princeton University Press, 1986), Introduction.

9. Horowitz, *Three Worlds of Development*, Appendix A to Chapter 1, ''A Digest of Factors Defining the Three Worlds.''

10. *Dynamics of the Third World*, pp. 4–31.

11. Robert G. Wesson, *Modern Governments: Three Worlds of Politics* (Englewood Cliffs, N.J.: Prentice-Hall, 1981), Chapter 7.

12. Smith, *State and Nation*, Chapters 2, 3, 4, and 5 in particular.

13. Sigmund, *Ideologies*. Each chapter includes extracts from the speeches or documents of an African leader.

14. Goulbourne, *Politics and State*, Chapters 1 and 2, are extracted from Marx and Engels, respectively, and Chapter 3 by Goulbourne himself bears the title ''Some Problems of Analysis of the Political in Backward Capitalist Social Formations,'' thus proclaiming the Marxist basis of his analysis.

15. Vinson H. Sutlive et al., *The Rise and Fall of Democracies in the Third World* (Williamsburg: Studies in the Third World Series, 1984).

16. Kautsky, *Political Change*.

17. Clifford Geertz (ed.), *Old Societies and New States: The Quest for Modernity in Asia and Africa* (New York: Free Press, 1963).

18. Edward Shils, *Political Development in the New States* (The Hague: Mouton, 1968).

19. For a brief sympathetic account of the criticisms of scholars from developing countries of Western methodologies, see A. H. Somjee, *Political Capacity in Developing Societies* (London: Macmillan, 1982), Chapter 1, and also A. H. Somjee, ''Parallels and Actuals of Political Development,'' *Politics, Administration and Change* 12, 1 (Dhaka).

20. Schmitt, *Dynamics of the Third World*, raises this question on p. 4 but does not pursue it.

21. In particular, see Horowitz, *Three Worlds of Development*, pp. 21–38, also Appendix A.

22. George F. Gant, *Development Administration: Concepts, Goals, Methods* (Madison: University of Wisconsin Press, 1979). See Chapter 1, "The Concept of Development Administration," regarding the development of the concept.

23. About 50 percent of the articles in *Public Administration and Development* (London: Royal Institute of Public Administration) are on specific projects or specific areas. More importantly, when the foundation of the journal as successor to the *Journal of Administration Overseas* was being discussed, efforts were made to keep it out of the hands of theoretically oriented institutes, so that it could preserve its overall empirical development orientation.

24. J. S. Saul, "The State in Post-Colonial Societies," in Goulbourne, *Politics and State*, is a typical piece on the "overdeveloped state" theme, a theme discussed frequently in the *Review of African Political Economy* (London), in the mid–1970s. Issa Shivji's, *The Silent Class Struggle* (Dar-es-Salaam: Tanzania Publishing House, 1973), sets out his theory of the bureaucratic bourgeoisie.

25. A leading example of this is Gunnar Myrdal's *Asian Drama*, 3 vols. (New York: Pantheon Books, 1968).

26. After the failure of the "Development Decade" by 1969, the teaching of development administration in North American universities began to include practically all the social sciences. At Carleton University, Ottawa, Canada, in the mid–1970s, the Development Seminar was addressed by a different social scientist every week.

27. F. W. Riggs, *The Ecology of Administration* (Bombay: Asia Publishing House 1961), and *Administration in Developing Countries* (Boston: Houghton Mifflin, 1964).

28. Gant, *Development Administration*, Chapter 1.

29. Agriculture in particular attracted much managerial initiative. See Gant, *Development Administration*, Chapter 2, "Administration for Agricultural Production." This writer was in touch with the considerable amount of managerial research into the Agricultural Extension schemes in Kenya from 1968 to 1974.

30. Books and articles on development administration rarely refer to any theory of economic growth or modernization as such. But almost every researcher and author in this area rubs shoulders with members of the modernization school and growth model economists. Their influence is therefore felt by the second remove.

31. Magnus Blomstrom and Bjorn Hettne, *Development Theory in Transition* (London: Zed Books, 1984), pp. 1–2.

32. Paul Baran, *Political Economy of Growth* (New York: Monthly Review Press, 1957).

33. A. G. Frank, *Capitalism and Underdevelopment in Latin America* (New York: Monthly Review Press, 1967).

34. Water Rodney, *How Europe Underdeveloped Africa* (Dar-es-Salaam: Tanzania Publishing House, 1972).

35. Blomstrom and Hettne, *Development Theory in Transition*, Chapter 8.

36. For an example of criticism, see Anthony Smith, "The Underdevelopment of Development Literature: The Case of Dependency Theory," in Kohli, *The State and Development in the Third World*.

37. The *Review of African Political Economy* from 1975 to 1980 contained several

articles on the concept and reality of the overdeveloped state. In Chapter 15, I argue that the term itself is misleading since "developed" implies capacity, whereas these states were just overambitious, without capacity.

38. These two sources are used extensively by all neo-Marxists. For a typical application, see Colin Leys, *Underdevelopment in Kenya: The Political Economy of Neo-Colonialism* (London: Heinemann, 1975), Chapter on 18th Brumaire. Marx analyzes Napoleon's success as the product of an open-ended situation, in which the bourgeois was weak but the working class was not strong enough. Thus power devolved to a relatively independent dictator and a bureaucracy, partly divorced from any class basis of power.

39. Indeed, Saul's article on Tanzania and Alavi's article on Pakistan and Bangladesh together provided some meeting point and mutual reinforcement. See note 7 above.

40. Leon Trotsky held the orthodox Marxist view that bureaucracy could not be a class in itself, even though he was one of the strongest critics of Soviet bureaucracy. This requirement for being recognized as a Marxist was held so sacred that as soon as James Burham was edging toward identifying managers as the real controllers in his *Managerial Revolution*, he declared: "By no stretch of terminology can I regard myself nor permit others to regard me as a Marxist." For a discussion of this matter see V. Subramaniam, "Western Marxist Approaches to Management and Organization Theory," *Indian Journal of Public Administration* 28, 4 (New Delhi).

41. Robert Dahl, "The Science of Public Administration: Three Problems," *Public Administration Review* 7, 1 (Washington, D.C.). This article is credited with having ignited interest in comparative administrative research.

42. Riggs, *The Ecology of Public Administration* and Riggs, *Administration in Developing Countries*. A good, detailed summary of Riggs' theory is provided in Richard A. Chapman, "Prismatic Theory in Public Administration: A Review of Theories of Fred W. Riggs," *Public Administration* (Winter, 1966, London).

43. The comparative administration group as a whole was severely criticized by Warren Ilchman for failing to make any theoretical advance, for theorizing about theories, and for producing no practical result of value. See Warren Ilchman, *Comparative Public Administration and Conventional Wisdom* (Beverly Hills, Calif.: Sage Publications, 1971). For other criticisms, see Subramaniam, *Transplanted Indo-British Administration*, Introduction.

44. Ferrel Heady, *Public Administration: A Comparative Perspective* (Englewood Cliffs, N.J.: Prentice-Hall, 1986) (latest edition). The last chapter spells out his regime-type correlation thesis.

45. Muhammad A. Hakim's "The Colonial Legacy in the Administrative System of a Post-Colonial State: The Case of Bangladesh, 1971–85" (Ph.D. diss., Carleton University, Ottawa, 1987), concludes after detailed research that in the case of Bangladesh regime type had very little to do with bureaucratic behavior and performance. Colonial legacy was the real determinant. Hakim also refers to Metin Heper, Chong Lim Kim, and Seong-Tong Pai, "The Role of Bureaucracy and Regime types: A Comparative Study of Turkish and South Korean Higher Civil Servants," *Administration and Society* 12, 2, in which the authors come to the same conclusion as Hakim. The experience of bureaucratic performance with changing regimes in Nigeria also leads me to a similar conclusion.

46. For example, the Latin Americanists and Africanists got together for a combined conference for the first time in Canada only in 1984. A simple comparison of the post-colonial state in Africa and Asia did not appear in any journal until the 1970s. Journals of African studies rarely have an article on Latin America or Asia. Such topics as the

context of indirect rule in Africa as a possible consequence of British disillusionment with a rebellious Indian middle class were rarely pursued by Africanists, and my efforts to discuss it were initially met with much apathy. Worse still, not a single English-speaking African university had a course comparing Francophone and Anglophone Africa until I instituted one at the University of Zambia, two years after taking up the chair of public administration there.

47. The stress on internal factors by Fred W. Riggs and his group and the modernization school was based partly on Western ethnocentrism and more on a rigid application of a closed system theory which emphasizes mutually interacting internal factors to the exclusion of all external factors. That explanation became unacceptable to an increasing number of Third World scholars, quite independently of the criticisms of dependency theorists.

PART I

ASIA

2

BANGLADESH

Syed Giasuddin Ahmed
and Mohammad Mohabbat Khan

HISTORICAL BACKGROUND

The administrative history of Bangladesh is that of India as a whole. In the centuries before the British arrived, India had already developed sophisticated administrative structures and practices, under Hindu and Muslim rulers in regional or district administration, land revenue, and justice.[1] When the East India Company took over the revenue administration (Diwani) of Bengal from the Mughal emperor in 1865, the Mughal system of administration was already well established there. The British thereafter developed their own system of district administration by modifying Indian practices, with modern education, recruitment, and legal systems. The British system was a unitary form of government, with centralized control first vested in the Court of Directors of the East India Company and later in the secretary of state for India who acted through the viceroy and governor-general. The basic objective of British rule was to develop a military and civil framework capable of maintaining law and order, collecting land revenue, and establishing local institutions, which would preserve their imperial interests. However, the degree of centralization was gradually reduced in the wake of nationalist movements, beginning around the turn of the twentieth century.

From 1947 when the partition of India into India and Pakistan was formalized, to 1971, Bangladesh (East Pakistan) was part of Pakistan. From the beginning, Pakistan encountered problems stemming from the geographic and linguistic division of East and West Pakistan, the lack of unified leadership, and the population's low capacity for political participation. As a result, Pakistan experienced a succession of political crises. The most tragic episode was the brutal army crackdown in East Pakistan in early 1971, which led to armed resistance by the people of East Pakistan. The outbreak of war with India in late 1971 resulted in the disintegration of Pakistan and the emergence of former East Pakistan as the sovereign state of Bangladesh in December 1971. Bangladesh thus inherited the British Indian system of administration, which Pakistan carried on with some minor modifications for over twenty-four years.

Even though firmly based on long and accepted tradition, the government machinery and the constitutional and administrative norms of Bangladesh were subjected to tremendous stresses following liberation. The first such stress was the extraordinary trauma of the birth of Bangladesh, and from the beginning it had to face problems of law and order, political disunity, persistent economic stringency, and grave political crises. At liberation in December 1971, the new political leaders adopted a liberal democracy with socialist trappings. This was changed to one-party rule in January 1975. Eight months later, a brutal coup overthrew and killed Sheikh Mujibur Rahman (Sheikh Mujib), the "father of the nation." From August 1975 to early 1979, the country was ruled by the military with the help of the civil bureaucracy. Following the national parliamentary elections in February 1979, a gradual transition to a somewhat controlled democracy took place, but it did not last very long. A little over five years after Sheikh Mujib was assassinated, his effective successor, General Ziaur Rahman, was also gunned down by a faction of the Bangladesh army in May 1981. On 24 March 1982, that is, two days before the national holiday marking Bangladesh's split from Pakistan eleven years before, army Chief of Staff Lieutenant General H. M. Ershad successfully led a lightning coup and ousted President Abdus Sattar, who had been installed in place of fallen President General Ziaur Rahman.

It was the fourth time in a troubled decade that a president was overthrown, albeit bloodlessly on this occasion.[2] General Ershad declared martial law, suspended the Constitution, and installed himself as chief martial law administrator. He soon set up a largely military-bureaucratic Council of Advisers, which was subsequently euphemized as Council of Ministers. Within a week after the coup, Ershad tapped a retired Supreme Court judge to become the president of Bangladesh succeeding Abdus Sattar. But Ershad himself took over the presidency on 11 December 1983, that is, less than two years after the coup. Thus, he held three crucial offices of the government of Bangladesh for several years; president, chief martial law administrator, and army chief of staff, as well as the supreme commander of the armed forces. Gradually, he legitimized his position in 1986 and 1987. After lifting the ban on political activities in January 1986, he arranged parliamentary elections in May in which his own new party Jatiyo won a majority. In the presidential elections of October 1986, he won a landslide victory after giving up his post as chief of staff. His regime was challenged by widespread strikes in January and February 1988, but in spite of opposition boycott parliamentary elections were held as scheduled on 3 March 1988, with his party winning a clear majority. His government has thus legitimized itself and retained its incongruous civil and military combination.

This strange combination of mass politics with military civil administration can be best understood in the general demographic and occupational context of the country. Bangladesh is primarily an agricultural country with an estimated population of 98 million for a relatively small area, mostly Muslim, 80 percent of whom are dependent on agriculture.[3] The average annual per capita income is Taka 2,087 (U.S. $135). About 60 million of the total population are employed (a large number being self-employed), including a 32 million labor force, of which only 1 million is in public employment. An estimated 3 percent of the total working population is in the organized sector, while agricultural workers constitute the bulk of the working population in the traditional sector. The organized sector includes a large number of industries and factories nationalized immediately after liberation. They constitute almost 70 percent of the industries and factories in the public sector. Thus, the government is considered to be the single largest employer in the country.

Working conditions within the industries and factories are regulated by the (Indian) Companies Act of 1913 as amended from time to time. The act prescribes a forty-eight hour week for adult workers and forbids employment of children under fourteen. There were about 3,000 trade unions functioning in the country in 1977 with total membership over 1 million. The Department of Labor determines collective bargaining agents in organizations where more than one union exists.

Bangladesh's development experiences since liberation have been generally disappointing. The common people still live in shanty houses and are uneducated and ill fed. Only about two-thirds of children five to eleven years of age are enrolled in the primary schools. The dropout rate among the enrolled children is very high. The present population growth rate is estimated at about 2.5 percent. Food deficits have increased over the years owing to the high population growth against low agricultural growth. As a result, the country is heavily dependent on foreign aid.[4]

ADMINISTRATIVE STRUCTURE

Formative Phase and Development

Until December 1971, Bangladesh, then East Pakistan, was a province of federal Pakistan. At that time the provincial government was virtually a small replica of the central government. It had a secretariat, similar to that of the center, consisting of several departments, headed by ministers when there was a popular government. The secretariat departments based their respective attached directorates and subordinate offices on the pattern of the central government, exactly as in India. But the main distinguishing feature of the provincial administrative structure was that it had several field administration units that were organized hierarchically on a geographic basis: division, district, subdivision, and thana (which literally means a police station, the lowest unit of administration, enforcing governmental authority).

Therefore, immediately after liberation, the main concern of the new government in Bangladesh was to devise appropriate measures to transform the structure of the provincial administration into a national government administration. What seems to have happened, however, was that overnight (i.e., after liberation on 16 December 1971) the old provincial secretariat became the central secretariat of a national government, while the existing attached directorates and subordinate offices remained much as before, and no change whatsoever was made in the field administration units.

A serious problem arose with regard to the offices of the former central government of Pakistan based in East Pakistan and the Bengali officials and employees recruited and controlled directly by the central government. On 27 December 1971, the Awami League (the party that had spearheaded the liberation struggle) announced the formation of a committee called the Civil Administration Restoration Committee which was charged with suggesting ways of restoring the civil administration at various levels of administration. Among the problems it examined was the absorption of the officials and employees of the various ministries and departments of the central government of Pakistan and the amalgamation of the offices of the central government with comparable ministries and departments of the new government of Bangladesh built on what had previously been parts of a provincial government.[5]

According to the Laws Continuance Enforcement Order, issued on 10 April 1971, all laws that were in force in Bangladesh (East Pakistan) on 25 March 1971 (i.e., the date on which the exiles proclaimed Bangladesh to be an independent state at Mujib Nagar) were to continue in force even after the Proclamation of Independence. Similarly, all existing government officials and employees, who would take allegiance to the new government of Bangladesh, were to continue in office on their existing terms and conditions of service.[6]

At Mujib Nagar (Calcutta) the Bangladesh government-in-exile (April-December 1971) had built up some sort of national government. On the basis of the Proclamation of Independence, a provisional government was set up at Mujib Nagar on the date of the proclamation, with Sheikh Mujib as president, although he was then under detention in West Pakistan. Syed Nazrul Islam, vice president, was made acting president, and a cabinet of four ministers, with Tajuddin Ahmed as prime minister, was formed.[7] An improvised secretariat was also reported to have been established with some top-level officials to assist the cabinet in transacting its business.[8]

The officials took over their charges in liberated Bangladesh effective 18 December 1971. On 28 December 1971, Acting President Syed Nazrul Islam and all cabinet members, including many other important political leaders holding administrative posts at Mujib Nagar, formally returned to Dhaka. Immediately, the cabinet was enlarged with five new ministers.[9] However, on 12 January 1972 (i.e., two days after Sheikh Mujib's return to Bangladesh), the interim Bangladesh government was dissolved in order to establish a parliamentary form of government, with Sheikh Mujib as prime minister, under the Provisional Constitution of Bangladesh Order (1972).[10] A new cabinet was formed comprising all the previous members. By late January 1972, the total number of cabinet members stood at fifteen, with nineteen ministerial portfolios distributed among them.[11] In January 1975, the Constitution was amended to provide a presidential form of government with all executive power vested in the president.

In late 1975, the secretariat of the government of Bangladesh consisted of twenty-nine ministries and forty-seven divisions.[12] However, a major administrative reorganization took place in January 1976, and the number of ministries and divisions was reduced to twenty-four and thirty-nine, respectively. Similar steps were also taken with regard to attached departments, autonomous bodies, and public corporations, as their number had also proliferated unnecessarily during the period 1972 to 1975.[13]

After the parliamentary elections held in February 1979 under General Zia's leadership, a new cabinet was installed in April 1979 with one prime minister, two deputy prime ministers, twenty-six cabinet ministers, eleven state ministers, and two deputy ministers. By that time, there were as many as thirty-one ministers and forty-one divisions. In addition, there was a president's secretariat, consisting of two divisions, and the cabinet secretariat, consisting of three divisions. Some of the ministries consisted of only one division, for example, the Ministry of Food-Food Division, while some comprised more than one division, such as the Ministry of Finance-Finance Division, Implementation Division, Inspection Division, and External Resources Division.[14] This structure has continued with minor changes under General Ershad.

The Executive

The government of Bangladesh comprises the executive, legislature, and judiciary.

The president is the head of both state and government and is elected for a five-year term by direct election on the basis of universal adult franchise. The executive authority of the government is entirely vested in his hands, an authority that is exercised either directly or through subordinate officers in accordance with the provisions of the Constitution. All executive actions of the government are expressed in the president's name. He specifies by rules the manner in which the orders and other instruments made in his name are to be attested or authenticated. The president is also duly empowered to make rules for the allocation and transaction of the business of the government.[15] The vice president is appointed by the president. Unless removed from office by the president, he also holds office for a five-year term.[16]

Article 58 of the Constitution provides for a Council of Ministers, consisting of a prime minister, one or more deputy prime ministers, and other ministers to aid and advise the president in the discharge of his executive functions. The president appoints as prime minister the member of Parliament who appears to command the support of the majority of the members of Parliament. The deputy prime ministers and other cabinet ministers, including the state ministers and deputy ministers, are appointed by the president from among the members of Parliament. A saving clause empowers the president to appoint up to one-fifth of the ministers from among persons other than the members of Parliament. All ministers hold office at the pleasure of the president; he can remove any minister from office at any time without assigning any reason for the removal.[17]

The Legislature

The Parliament in Bangladesh works within a system in which the president is an elected omnipotent chief executive. It consists of 330 members, of whom 300 are elected directly on the basis of universal adult franchise and the remaining 30 are exclusively women. The directly elected 300 members themselves constitute an electoral college for electing the 30 women members.[18]

The constitutional provisions relating to Parliament in Bangladesh were kept under suspension in pursuance of the promulgation of martial law on 24 March 1982. The first Bangladesh Parliament constituted immediately after liberation comprised members elected in 1970 from East Pakistan to the National Assembly of Pakistan and to the Provincial Assembly of East Pakistan. It worked mainly as a Constituent Assembly. The second Parliament was formed in March 1973 following the fresh general elections held in March 1973. The third Parliament was elected in February 1979 during the regime of General Zia, a fourth in May 1986, and a fifth in February 1988 under the regime of General Ershad.[19]

Parliament was "independent" and "sovereign" since it had the power to enact laws, approve budgets, and impeach the president. The president could not veto a bill passed by Parliament for the second time. However, the Parliament's inability to remove a minister through a nonconfidence vote, the provision under which one-fifth of the ministers could be taken from outside the Parliament, and the repeated practice of bypassing Parliament when it was not in session reflected how in reality the sovereignty of Parliament was infringed. According to one interpretation, the Parliament was merely a "rubber stamp"[20] and had no direct bearing on the administration and control of public personnel. Although most ministers were members of Parliament, they were constitutionally not answerable to that body for their actions as administrative heads of ministries and divisions. Nor did the president have any obligation before Parliament to account for the discharge of his executive functions.[21]

The Judiciary

The Constitution now under suspension ensures the separation of the judiciary from the executive. The highest court of law is the Supreme Court, which comprises the High Court Division and the Appellate Division. The Supreme Court consists of the chief justice and a number of other judges. The chief justice and the judges appointed to the Appellate sit only in that division whereas other judges sit in the High Court Division.[22] The chief justice and other judges are appointed by the president. A judge holds office until he attains the age of sixty-two.[23]

The High Court Division has original, appellate, and other jurisdictions and powers, including enforcement of the fundamental rights as guaranteed under the Constitution. It has superintendence and control over all other courts subordinate to it. The Appellate Division has jurisdiction to hear and determine appeals against judgments, decrees, orders, or sentences of the High Court Divisions. It can hear appeals in cases involving a substantial question of law as to the interpretation of the Constitution or in cases of capital punishment confirmed by the High Court Division. It also acts as a legal advisory body to the president.[24]

One important measure that the Ershad military regime has taken is to decentralize the judiciary. Separate High Court benches have been set up in six district towns in addition to the main bench in Dhaka, and civil courts have been taken down to the *upazila* levels. (*Upazila*, which means subdistrict, is in practice an upgraded version of the *thana*, now abolished.) At the district level, the court is headed by the district judge, who is assisted by one or more additional district judges and other subordinate judges. At the upazila levels, civil and criminal courts have begun to function. While it is expected to make justice cheaper and swifter, unemployed or underemployed rural lawyers might also benefit from the measure.[25]

The Central Secretariat and Ministries

Immediately before the promulgation of martial law on 24 March 1982, the secretariat of the government of Bangladesh consisted of thirty-six ministries and forty-nine divisions. In addition, both the president's secretariat and the cabinet secretariat had each comprised three divisions. The military government reduced the number of ministries to twenty and that of divisions to thirty-five. By 1985, the number of cabinet ministers rose to twenty-six, which is less than the number of ministries and divisions. The president as the chief martial law administrator retained two ministries (i.e., Ministry of Defense and the Ministry of Establishment) under his direct jurisdiction.[26]

A ministry and each of its constituent divisions are primarily responsible for formulating government policies within its assigned jurisdiction. It plays an important role in supervising and reviewing the execution of its policies. Structurally, a ministry or its division is divided into several wings, branches, and sections in order to ensure efficient disposal of its business. It is normally headed by a senior official with the rank and status of a secretary to the government who acts as the principal adviser to the minister on all matters of policy and administration. In this capacity, these senior officials are responsible for the proper conduct of business allocated to their ministry under the Rules of Business and for careful observance of all relevant instructions included in the Secretariat Instructions concerning their ministry. They also act as the principal accounting officers of their respective ministry and division.[27]

A number of executive agencies normally carry out the government policies of a ministry and constituent divisions. These agencies are generally designated as attached departments and subordinate offices—as in India's administrative system. Attached departments provide executive direction in the implementation of policies laid down by the ministry and divisions to which they are attached. They also serve as the repository of technical information and advise their respective ministries and divisions on technical aspects of business. Subordinate offices generally function as field establishments or as agencies responsible for detailed execution of government policies. They are normally under the direction of attached departments. Some of the subordinate offices are also placed directly under the concerned ministries or divisions inasmuch as the volume of executive work in such offices is not considerable.[28] In addition, other types of public organizations, for example, autonomous and semiautonomous bodies or public corporations, have been set up to perform certain specialized public functions or to implement specific development tasks. They are normally freed from ministerial control in the spheres of their personnel management and financial administration.[29]

The principal officers (other than the secretaries) who work in the secretariat are the additional or joint secretaries, deputy secretaries, and section officers. The additional or joint secretaries, unless they are in charge of a ministry or division, are entrusted with a well-defined sphere of duty. They assume full responsibility within their sphere and submit all cases directly to the minister for orders. Ministerial orders are normally returned to them through the secretary. The deputy secretaries are normally in charge of a branch and are responsible for disposing of all cases within their jurisdiction in which no major question of policy is involved. Section officers, in charge of a section, dispose of all cases in which there are clear precedents, no question is involved that would imply deviation from such precedents, or which under the existing rules or standing orders, they are competent to handle. They must seek instructions from their immediate superior officers in case of any doubt.[30] The officers who work in attached departments and subordinate officers are designated variously according to the nature of the work they perform and the job specification fixed for each position in those departments and offices.[31]

Local Administration

The administrative structure in Bangladesh below the national level consists of a large number of field units that are geographically spread throughout the country. These field units are organized hierarchically in the following main tiers:

Division

District

Upazila

The whole of Bangladesh is divided into four divisions for administrative purposes each of which is again divided into several districts. Divisions are the immediate units of local administration below the national level. Their main role is to guide and supervise the district administration units, coordinate certain development activities at the district level, and hear appeals on the decisions of district revenue officials regarding revenue matters.[32]

There are sixty-four districts in Bangladesh. It should be noted here that the administrative units at district levels were always considered the core of state administration in both British India and United Pakistan. In fact, the genesis of the system of district administration can be traced back to what the Mauryas devised in the fifth century B.C. and what the Mughals in India continued in their bid to sustain a large empire and, in particular, to collect land revenue, conduct general administration, and maintain law and order at the basic units of administration (i.e., *sarkar* and *parganah*).[33] The district administration in Bangladesh continues to play a crucial role in such important spheres as collecting land revenue, maintaining law and order, stimulating economic development, coordinating all government activities relating to "nation building," and encouraging and collaborating with local self-government initiatives.[34]

Until November 1982, each district in Bangladesh consisted of several subdivisions, and each subdivision was in turn divided into a number of *thanas*. But in pursuance of an administrative reform introduced by the martial law regime beginning in November 1982, all the subdivisions in Bangladesh have been upgraded as districts, and the thanas have been renamed upazilas (subdistricts). At present, there are 460 upazilas in Bangladesh. The upazila administration is considered to be an important tier of field administration and is widely claimed as an important measure of decentralization.[35]

The administrative system at the upazila level is organized under two categories—reserved and transferred. The national government has direct responsibility for both national and regional regulatory functions and major development activities under the "reserved" heading. These functions include the civil and criminal judiciary, administration and management of central revenue, maintenance of law and order, maintenance of essential supplies including food, generation and distribution of electric power, irrigation schemes involving more than one district, technical and general education above the primary level, flood control, and development of water resources. The elected chairmen and chief

LIBRARY
OF
MOUNT ST. MARY'S
COLLEGE
EMMITSBURG, MARYLAND

of the *upazila parishads* are in charge of the transferred category. (The *upazila parishad* is a council of the upazila which performs a number of executive functions.) Most members of an upazila parishad are also elected chairmen of union parishads within the upazila. The chairman of an upazila parishad (1) conducts day-to-day administration; (2) supervises and controls staff; (3) coordinates all development activities; (4) initiates, formulates, and identifies development projects and ensures their timely implementation, monitoring and evaluation; and (5) and initiates the annual confidential report of the *upazila nirbhahi*, or the chief administrative officer. Although the services of the officers who deal with transferred subjects have been placed at the disposal of the upazila parishads and the concerned officers have been made responsible for their actions to the upazila parishads, the national government has retained total control over these officers. The appointment, transfer, promotion, discipline, and remuneration of these officers, as well as most of those who deal with reserved subjects, continue to be the responsibility of the national government. In effect, an upazila parishad has been given responsibility of, but no control over, the civil servants involved in transferred subjects in that upazila.[36]

Each upazila consists of a number of unions, and there are 4,400 unions in all. A union in turn comprises several villages, and there are as many as 68,000 villages throughout the country. An elected body called the union parishad is the statutory self-governing body entrusted with some nominal functions relating to local administration and development. It consists of an elected chairman, nine elected members, and three nominated women members. Union parishads are basically the village-based local self-government bodies, but the government retains a great measure of control over them.[37]

A separate local self-government body called the *pourashava* (municipality) operates exclusively in a specified urban area. At present there are seventy-eight pourashavas in the country. In addition, two municipal corporations—one for Dhaka (the capital city) and the other for Chittagong (the port city)—also exist. Both of these corporations operate under exclusive government control.[38] A pourashava consists of an elected chairman and such number of elected commissioners and nominated woman commissioners as may be fixed by the government. It performs functions relating to local administration and development in an urban area. But the government maintains constant surveillance over its functioning.[39]

Financial Administration

In Bangladesh, the Finance Division of the Ministry of Finance and Planning is the central department concerned with financial administration. The Ministry of Finance and Planning consists of five full-fledged divisions, namely, the Finance, Internal Resources, External Resources, Planning, and Statistics Divisions.[40]

Specifically, the Finance Division drafts the annual budget in the light of the overall state finances and the priority of expenditure needs throughout the government machinery. It also pilots the annual budget through Parliament (when a civil government exists), supervising its implementation by the various ministries and divisions and giving advice to the ministries and divisions; it exercises financial control generally, and it collects state revenue. In other words, the Finance Division acts as the national exchequer of the government.[41]

The division ensures that the establishment costs incurred by the various ministries and divisions and their attached departments and subordinate offices are in conformity with budgetary provisions and established rules. In effect it has substantial power over the organization of the bureaucracy in Bangladesh. It oversees its own cadres of finance services, controls the strength of other service cadres, performs personnel management functions for many other services, publishes service rules affecting all the services, and determines the overall salary policy. The Rules of Business (1975) specify that no ministry or division can, without previous consultation with the Finance Division, authorize any orders that will either directly or indirectly affect the finance of the state or that involve (1) expenditure for which no previous sanction exists in the budget; (2) change in the terms and conditions of service of all government servants (including employees of public corporations) which have financial implications; and (3) interpretation of service rules made by the Finance Division.[42]

Nevertheless, the ministries and divisions, other than the Finance Division, have been given wide range financial powers under a plan called the financial advisers' scheme (FAS). This plan is the continuation of a radical reform introduced in the financial administration system in United Pakistan in the early 1960s. In essence, FAS is designed to replace the dilatory system of multiple clearances from the Finance Division for incurring expenditure against appropriated funds. It purports to ensure a smooth functioning of the overall administration in the country and, in particular, to facilitate expeditious and timely implementation of the various development programs under different ministries and divisions and their attached departments.[43]

In March 1977, a major change was introduced into FAS with a view to improving the working of the scheme and to liberalizing further the delegation of financial powers to the various ministries and divisions.[44] Specifically, the new change provided for the delegation of extensive financial powers to the ministries and divisions relating to a wide variety of matters, including powers to create and retain temporary posts against development schemes, to grant traveling allowances and leave pay, and to sanction pensions.[45] By and large, the modified FAS ensures efficient management of funds and effective control of establishments, as well as reduces references to the Finance Division by other ministries and divisions.

Personnel Administration

The entire framework of personnel administration in Bangladesh is a unified process. Structured hierarchically, the Ministry of Establishment (central personnel agency) of the government of Bangladesh is attached to the highest level of executive authority. Its official head (the Establishment secretary) is responsible to the president.

The Ministry of Establishment (ME) lays down the broad policies, principles, and regulations for managing the civil bureaucracy and initiates measures for employee welfare and for improvement of procedures and techniques relating to personnel administration. It is also responsible for initial recruitment to all the cadre services and for disciplinary action and welfare in respect of all senior officials in the secretariat and outside.[46]

Although ME initiates and develops policy guidelines in respect of all major personnel matters and oversees their implementation by other ministries and divisions, its jurisdiction in routine management of the civil servants is not all-pervasive. ME directly manages the Senior Service Pool (SSP), Administrative Cadre, and Secretariat Cadre of the Bangladesh Civil Service (BCS). Other service cadres, such as Audit and Accounts, Customs and Excise, Taxation, Education, Agriculture, and Public Works, are controlled by the respective ministries and divisions. Yet, there is a persistent pattern that the general rules and regulations governing the civil servants emanate mainly from one source, that is, the ME.[47]

The Public Service Commission (PSC) in Bangladesh is a constitutional body. It is the other central personnel agency with a constitutional responsibility to conduct tests and examinations for the selection of certain categories of civil servants and to act as a "watchdog" on the government's dealings with civil servants and their conditions of service. In essence, the powers and functions of the PSC in Bangladesh are advisory based on the tradition and pattern followed and adopted in the other two countries in the Indian subcontinent.[48]

Civil Service

After liberation in December 1971, several official attempts were made to ascertain the magnitude of total public employment in Bangladesh. The National Pay Commission (1972) found that 650,615 persons were working for the government of Bangladesh at that time. This figure included 48,000 armed personnel and 205,778 employees who were previously not considered civil servants inasmuch as their salaries and allowances were not paid from the annual civil budgets. In addition, 650,615 officials and employees were shown in ten service grades matching ten comparable national scales of pay, ranging from the lowest (Taka 130) to the highest (Taka 2,000), as recommended by the National Pay Commission of 1972.[49]

In 1972, the Establishment Division of the government of Bangladesh also conducted a survey to determine the total number of civilians working in the government offices (including the central secretariat) and autonomous and semi-autonomous bodies. Total civilian public employment was estimated to be about 454,450. The breakdown of the figures according to class divisions (I, II, III,

IV) that had existed in Pakistan shows that the total number of Class I officials*
was 11,130, including 5,000 officials who belonged to various autonomous and
semiautonomous bodies. The total Class I officials included 180 members of the
erstwhile Civil Service of Pakistan (CSP) and 724 members of the former East
Pakistan Civil Service (EPCS).[50] The total number of civilians in government
offices, including the attached departments and subordinate offices, was 290,850
as compared with 163,600 in the autonomous and semiautonomous bodies.

By February 1977, the total number of civilians in the ministries and divisions,
including their attached departments and subordinate offices, rose to 470,540.
This was about 31,842 less than the sanctioned strength of 502,382 and about
0.6 percent of the total population (78.7 million) of Bangladesh in 1976. The
number of Class I civilian officials was 17,621 compared with a sanctioned
strength of 20,393. This number (17,621) included about 13,098 officials who
belonged to the various cadre services under both central and provincial governments.[51] According to a survey conducted in 1981, the total number of civilian
employees in Bangladesh was estimated at 599,278, almost 0.8 percent of the
population (89 million) of Bangladesh in that year.[52] General Ershad's military
government also conducted a survey in 1984 which revealed that 1,054,116 civil
employees were working in that year as against a sanctioned strength of 1,197,312
(see Table 2.1).

Several trends emerge when we analyze the data pertaining to the size of the
civil bureaucracy in Bangladesh. First, the number of people on the public payroll
continued to increase with the passage of time. This increase can be explained
in two ways. The size of the civilian workforce in government was small during
the early years because a large number of Bengali employees of the then central
government were stranded in West Pakistan until the middle of 1973. As soon
as those employees returned to Bangladesh, the size of the public bureaucracy
increased. In addition, in Bangladesh the government is the biggest and the most
generous source of employment. Sociopolitico-economic realities compelled successive governments to induct unnecessary and sometimes useless persons into
the civil service. In fact, the bulk of government employees belongs to Class
III and Class IV whose services are least required and can be easily dispensed
with.

Structure of Services

Bangladesh inherited civil servants belonging to both the former Central and
Provincial Services. They were all grouped horizontally into four class divisions—I, II, III, IV—on the basis of levels of responsibility, educational requirements, and admissible pay range. The civil services in Pakistan were also
classified vertically into three main categories: (1) generalist-administrative services; (2) functional services; and (3) specialist service—focusing on the type

---

*Class I officers are the equivalent of the British administrative class doing policy advising work.

Table 2.1
Civil Employees of the Government of Bangladesh (as of June 1984)

Category	Ministries/Divisions (Secretariat)		Departments/Directorates (Subordinate offices)		Public Statutory Corporations		Total	
	Sanctioned strength	Posted strength	Sanctioned strength	Posted strength	Sanctioned strength	Posted strength	Sanctioned strength	Posted strength
Class I	1,531	1,509	50,324	31,724	37,673	30,380	89,528	63,613
Class II	56	82	10,934	8,241	23,696	20,587	34,686	28,910
Class III	3,440	5,111	532,329	466,589	129,211	109,530	644,980	581,230
Class IV	1,732	2,571	144,129	122,221	83,633	75,805	229,494	200,597
Others	-	-	-	-	192,624	179,766	192,624	179,766
Total:	6,759	9,273	737,716	628,775	466,837	416,068	1,191,312	1054,116

Source: Bangladesh, Ministry of Establishment, O & M Wing, Statistics and Research Branch, 1984.

of work performed. The Central and Provincial Class I Services (including part of Class II Services) were once again divided into cadre and noncadre services. Cadre services were constituted under law with a number of positions, a distinct hierarchy, and well-defined functions for each step in the hierarchy. Recruitment to the cadre services was normally made through the public service commissions on the basis of open competitive examinations and interviews. On the other hand, noncadre services were based largely on positions with no definite structure of mobility either horizontally or vertically. Members of the cadre services could move from one department to another, whereas the noncadre personnel had to serve in the particular department to which they were originally recruited.[53] All government employees were also broadly divided into "gazetted" and "non-gazetted" categories. All Class I and some Class II employees were treated as gazetted since their appointment, posting, transfer, promotion, and retirement were to be reported in the official gazettes. Civil services in Bangladesh are still classified both horizontally and vertically along similar lines, as was the case during the days of United Pakistan.

Efforts to Reform the Civil Service

The administrative reform measures of successive governments in Bangladesh have brought significant, though not fundamental, changes in the civil service system, including its structure. In a recent fourteen-year period (1971–1985), successive governments in Bangladesh appointed six major administrative reform commissions and committees.[54] The Awami League government of Sheikh Mujib (1972–1975) appointed two high-powered bodies: the Administrative Services Reorganization Committee (ASRC) and the National Pay Commission (NPC). General Zia (1975–1981) appointed the Pay and Services Commission (PSC). The Ershad military government also appointed three major reform bodies—the Martial Law Committee for Examining the Organizational Setup of Ministries/Divisions, Departments, Directorates, and other organizations under them (MLC), the Committee for Administrative Reorganization and Reform (CARR), and the National Pay Commission (NPC II).

All the reform bodies made painstaking and detailed recommendations to recast and revamp the civil service system of the country. Two of them (ASR and CARR) went beyond the domain of the traditional civil service system and pleaded for democratization of administration and devolution of power to elected local governments. But the key recommendations of some of these bodies (ASRC and NPC) were not accepted by the government of the day, and the major recommendations of some others (PSC, MLC, and CARR) were implemented in radically modified forms. In spite of limitations in the reform process, the recommendations led to the creation of twenty-eight services under fourteen main cadres, the constitution of an apex service called Senior Services Pool (SSP), the introduction of a New National Pay Scale (NNPS), and the "decentralization" of administration.[55]

Cadre Services. On 1 September 1980, the government formally announced the introduction of a new civil service system termed the unified career service with fourteen functional cadres and fourteen subcadres (see Table 2.2). This new civil service system, based largely on the recommendations of the Pay and Services Commission (PSC), was designed primarily to create a "classless bureaucracy." All the twenty-eight cadres and subcadres were to be treated as equal, and one cadre would not be superior to any other. Equal opportunity for going up the service ladder was to be ensured, with a view to enabling the best talent in all cadres to reach the highest echelons of the civil service. All cadres were to be recruited on the basis of open competitive examination to be conducted by the Public Service Commission. There would be only one unified level of entry into the various cadre services in the New National Scale of Pay of Taka, 1,650–100–2250–EB–110–3020. The maximum age limit for entry was fixed at twenty-seven and the retirement age for all government officials would continue to be fifty-seven. All fresh recruits were to undergo a five-month training period and successfully complete the probationary period covering assignment at both the secretariat and field level.[56]

Senior Services Pool. The Senior Services Pool (SSP) formally came into being on 1 March 1979. Based on the recommendations of the Pay and Services Commission (PSC), it has been designed to constitute a new apex cadre of senior officials of proven quality drawn from all branches of the civil service on the basis of merit and ability to be tested in an objective manner. The SSP consists of posts requiring diversified experience, administrative leadership, and high-level coordination functions. Members of the SSP would ultimately fill all posts of deputy secretary, joint secretary, additional secretary, and secretary in the secretariat except for two ministries—the Ministry of Foreign Affairs and the Ministry of Law. Selection of SSP officers is to be made by the government through the Public Service Commission in accordance with certain competitive examinations or interviews.[57]

The SSP has been designed as an open structure system consisting of important administrative posts in the secretariat, as well as a certain percentage of administrative posts in the executive departments and district offices. But clearly, the constitution of the SSP has favored generalist civil servants, especially those belonging to the Civil Service of Pakistan (CSP) and the East Pakistan Civil Service (EPCS). They got into SSP automatically. This automatic induction of such a large number of generalist officers belonging to former elitist services has effectively nullified the purpose of creating this "open" structure. Instead, a superelite cadre of generalist policy makers has emerged.[58]

New National Pay Scales. The New National Pay Scales have been in effect since 1 June 1985 and emanated from the recommendations of the National Pay Commission (NPC II). The number of scales for civil employees has been kept to twenty. The minimum and maximum pay have been fixed at Taka 500 and Taka 6,000 per month, respectively. The pay scale covers almost all the em-

Table 2.2
List of Twenty-eight Cadre Services

1. Bangladesh Civil Service (Administrative: Administrative)
2. Bangladesh Civil Service (Administrative: Food)
3. Bangladesh Civil Service (Agriculture: Agriculture)
4. Bangladesh Civil Service (Agriculture: Forest)
5. Bangladesh Civil Service (Agriculture: Fisheries)
6. Bangladesh Civil Service (Agriculture: Livestock)
7. Bangladesh Civil Service (Education: General Education)
8. Bangladesh Civil Service (Education: Technical Education)
9. Bangladesh Civil Service (Economic and Trade: Economic)
10. Bangladesh Civil Service (Economic and Trade: Trade)
11. Bangladesh Civil Service (Economic and Trade: Statistical)
12. Bangladesh Civil Service (Engineering: Public Works)
13. Bangladesh Civil Service (Engineering: Public Health)
14. Bangladesh Civil Service (Engineering: Roads and Highways)
15. Bangladesh Civil Service (Engineering: Tele-Communication)
16. Bangladesh Civil Service (Finance: Audit and Accounts)
17. Bangladesh Civil Service (Finance: Customs and Excise)
18. Bangladesh Civil Service (Finance: Taxation)
19. Bangladesh Civil Service (Foreign Affairs)
20. Bangladesh Civil Service (Health and Family Planning)
21. Bangladesh Civil Service (Information)
22. Bangladesh Civil Service (Judicial)
23. Bangladesh Civil Service (Postal)
24. Bangladesh Civil Service (Enforecement: Police)
25. Bangladesh Civil Service (Enforcement: Ansar)
26. Bangladesh Civil Service (Railway: Transportation & Commercial)
27. Bangladesh Civil Service (Railway: Engineering)
28. Bangladesh Civil Service (Secretariat)

Source: Bangladesh, Establishment Division, Cabinet Secretariat,
Notication no. SRO 1-L/81/ED(R-70/80, January 1, 1981, published in
The Bangladesh Gazette (Extraordinary), January 1, 1981.
The Cadres still remain the same in 1988.

ployees within the civil service system, including those who work in various
corporations, autonomous bodies, banks, and financial institutions.[59]

Decentralization of Administration. The Ershad military government publicly
vowed to decentralize governmental activities and operations. Keeping this objective in view, the government appointed a high-powered body called the Committee for Administrative Reorganization and Reform (CARR) in April 1982.
As a result of CARR's recommendations, a representational system has been
introduced at the subnational level (the upazila level) by upgrading the former
thanas into upazilas and vesting some administrative, executive, and financial
powers in the hands of the elected upazila chairman and upazila parishads, elected
by the people at the union level with the chairman having a five-year term of
office.[60] But a look at various laws, regulations, ordinances, and resolutions
governing upazilas indicates that the national government has contrived a number
of mechanisms to control almost every aspect of upazila government in the name
of coordination.[61] Moreover, as explained earlier, the upazila chairman and
members have no control over the hierarchy of centrally recruited officials who
implement their policies quite apart from the limited number of "transferred"
functions at the upazila level.

Recruitment and Selection

In Bangladesh, the responsibilities of public personnel administration are
vested in two bodies—the Public Service Commission (PSC) and the Ministry
of Establishment (ME). Although the PSC is a constitutional body with defined
powers and functions, it is the ME which, in reality, controls the public personnel
system in the country. Rules, regulations, and instructions concerning recruitment
and selection (R & S) emanate from ME, which also ensures their proper observance by other agencies or personnel in government and the PSC. The ME
serves as a link between the government and the PSC. The personnel and financial
administration of the PSC itself are also guided by the career civil servants of
ME. Its chairman and members are appointed by the president on the advice of
the ME, which also approves its budget. Operationally, the Regulation Wing of
the ME prepares and examines the recruitment rules for cadre services before
they are sent to the PSC for approval. The annual reports of the PSC have to
be presented to the Council of Ministers through ME. The supposedly autonomous character of PSC is thus greatly diluted by the influence of civil servants
at the higher echelons of ME. Thus, the PSC's constitutional position has been
reduced to a great extent, and it has been made to play the role of a subordinate
recruiting agency of the government.[62]

The R & S process in Bangladesh is characterized by lack of a clear-cut and
well-defined recruitment policy; the practice of making ad hoc appointments and
allowing such appointees to continue for years with regularization; provision for
reservation of posts (popularly known as the quota system) for different categories
of public officials on the basis of region, sex, and participation in the country's

liberation struggle; lack of objectivity and archaic form and content of tests; lack of serious research for improving the existing situation; and relegation of the status of PSC vis-à-vis ME. All these problems have not only created anomalies, contradictions, confusions, and deficiencies in the recruitment and selection process of the country, but have also helped undermine the people's trust in the recruitment process.[63]

The Ershad military government appointed a Committee for Examination of Irregularities in Appointment and Promotion of Officers and Staff in the government in September 1982. The committee submitted its recommendations in April 1983. It made a number of recommendations to streamline the appointment and promotion of civil servants such as (1) framing new recruitment rules where such rules did not exist, modifying existing rules where necessary, and modifying recruitment rules by 31 August 1983; (2) strictly adhering to relevant rules and regulations in appointing and promoting people; (3) regularizing all irregular and ad hoc appointments by 30 September 1983 by amending the Bangladesh Civil Service Composition and Cadre Rules of 1980 and the Bangladesh Civil Service Recruitment Rules of 1981; (4) strengthening the Public Service Commission by appointing more members; and (5) enabling the Establishment Division to act as both the coordinating and supervising national personnel agency of the government.[64]

Although the government has not formally accepted the committee's recommendations, it has already initiated several implementing steps such as upgrading the Establishment Division to a full-fledged ministry known as the Ministry of Establishment and framing recruitment rules for Bangladesh civil service examinations.

Promotion

Promotion in the civil service of Bangladesh is based on seniority and annual confidential reports (ACRs). The cadre officer's first promotion to the senior scale falls due after he completes seven years of service, passes a promotion test conducted by the PSC, and obtains a favorable ACR from his superior officer. Subsequent promotions of cadre officers are determined by their performance in examinations or tests and training. Training for various cadre services is conducted by the Public Administration Training Center (PATC).

Promotion in cadre services is governed by the Bangladesh Civil Service (BCS) Recruitment Rules, 1981, and BCS Composition and Cadre Rules, 1980. Departmental Promotion Committees in ministries and departments recommend candidates for promotion, but promotion, posting, and transfer of officers connected with general administration in the districts are within the jurisdiction of the Ministry of Establishment. As a result, the promotion of candidates belonging to BCS (administration) and BCS (secretariat) is decided by the recommendations of ME's Promotional Committee, but the cases must be sent to the PSC for final approval.

All cases of supersession and promotion of officers of the level of joint secretary and above, including heads of departments and autonomous bodies and corporations, must be duly processed by the Superior Selection Board (SSB). The SSB's recommendations are then placed before the Council Committee on Senior Appointment, Promotion and Service Structure (CCSAPS) for its approval. The SSB is composed of key permanent secretaries to the government and is chaired by the cabinet secretary. The CCSAPS is headed by the deputy chief martial law administrator and chief of the naval staff. Its members include ministers of finance, establishment, home, food, energy and mineral resources, and the concerned minister (whose officer's case is being reviewed).[65]

Discipline

Successive governments in Bangladesh have enacted legislation and have framed rules to combat inefficiency, insubordination, misconduct, and corruption of civil servants. Some of these are President's Order No. 9 of 1972, Government Servants Conduct Rules, 1979, Public Servants (Special Provisions) Ordinance, 1979, and Government Servants (Discipline and Appeal) Rules, 1984. These rules and ordinances make provisions for maintaining discipline among civil servants through penalties including dismissal from the service, discharge from service, and reduction in rank and pay. The disciplinary measures usually take the shape of departmental proceedings and are quasi-judicial in nature. A penalized civil servant has the right to appeal against any order to an authority immediately superior to the appointing authority, the president being the highest appellate authority.[66]

Nonetheless, most of the disciplinary measures have failed to deal effectively with inefficiency, indiscipline, and corruption in the civil service. The failure has compelled governments to take recourse to more stringent measures like instituting special commissions and committees and enacting screening procedures to check inefficiency and corruption in the civil service.[67]

Unionization

In the traditional sense, the cadre civil servants of Bangladesh are not unionized. Civil servants (Class I and Class II) are prohibited from becoming members of trade unions, but they are allowed to form service associations to protect their interests. These associations act as vehicles for submitting representations and memoranda when opportunities arise. They become very active with the constitution of pay and service commissions, as their members' interests may be affected by the recommendations of such bodies. Although they can pressure the government not to implement certain recommendations of a committee or commission, they have no bargaining rights to negotiate their members' conditions of service.[68]

CHECKS AND CONTROL OF ADMINISTRATION

In Bangladesh two types of control mechanisms—internal and external—are available to keep the civil service under surveillance and in check. The internal mechanisms include provision for disposal of public business within a specified time depending on the level of the officer concerned, inspection, supervision, and ACR. All these mechanisms pinpoint the responsibility of a particular officer at a particular level as well as provide guidelines about how he is to discharge his duties. But internal mechanisms have failed miserably to make any impact on the indifferent and arrogant attitude that most civil servants hold toward citizens in general.[69]

The external mechanisms include control by the legislature and the judiciary, the office of ombudsman, the role of the press and citizen groups, and the role of the executive. The provision of parliamentary control was incorporated in the Rules of Procedure of Parliament of the People's Republic of Bangladesh during the Awami League regime and General Zia's presidential government (1979–1981). The rules provide for a Standing Committee on Public Accounts and a Committee on Estimates. But Parliament, instead of becoming an effective instrument to control the excess of bureaucratic action, was gradually turned into a rubber stamp in the hands of the all-usurping executive.

The judicial system in Bangladesh provides a strong guarantee that the individual's rights and interests must not be encroached upon. The constitutional guarantees and executive decrees allowed the judiciary to exercise its authority freely not only to protect the fundamental rights of the citizens, but also to contain and penalize wrongful acts of civil servants through issuance of directions, orders, or writs. The obvious limitation of the judicial system is that judges cannot initiate action on their own and have to wait for someone to bring an issue or a case to them. This acts as a significant damper as most people in Bangladesh tend to avoid the courts for fear of being drawn into a long-drawn-out, costly legal battle, even when they feel aggrieved by the actions of civil servants.

In April 1980, Parliament passed the Ombudsman Act in pursuance of Article 77 of the Constitution. This article provided for establishment of an office to deal with citizens' grievances against the administration, but the office of ombudsman has not yet been formally constituted. The press has always played a valuable role in publicizing administrative irregularities, mismanagement, inefficiency, and corrupt practices of civil servants. In addition, concerned citizens have formed groups from time to time to represent the cases of poorer and disadvantaged sections that have been discriminated against by the actions of the civil servants.

The political executive has been relatively more successful in controlling the bureaucracy. General Zia and Sheikh Mujib attempted to control bureaucrats by creating new institutions with political people to oversee the activities of the civil servants. Zia's district development committees, envoy pool, divisional development boards, *swanirvar gram sarkar* (village self-government), and Mujib's district governor's scheme are some of the examples. In fact, under Presidential Order No. 9 Mujib sacked many civil servants by withdrawing their constitutional protection. During his very brief tenure as an elected president after Zia's death, President Abdus Sattar set up administrative tribunals to try cases of corruption and mismanagement.

The military regime of General Ershad has already taken a number of actions to make civil servants accountable for their actions. For example, it has issued martial law orders, formed vigilance teams, set up summary martial law courts, arranged surprise visits from the chief martial law administrator, deputy chief martial law administrators, and zonal martial law administrators to various government offices and development projects, and instructed civil servants to fill out regularly printed forms showing in specific detail their targets and achievements. As a result of the military regime's punitive actions, many civil servants have lost their jobs.

CONCLUSION

Our focus in this chapter has been on formal structure, but gaps between formal structure as reflected in legal instruments and regulations, and "real world" operations of such structures, are commonplace in the politics of most nations. In Bangladesh, the gap is especially wide because of the political environment in which public administration has had to function since the liberation of Bangladesh. In particular, during the Awami League (AL) regime (1972–1975), a deliberate attempt was made to penalize the civil bureaucracy. Immediately after liberation many senior Bengal civil servants were removed or downgraded for alleged collaboration with the Pakistan army during the liberation war. Inexperienced and even corrupt officials took over high positions through political patronage. The established rule of seniority was violated by giving high administrative posts to midlevel and junior officers, whose only qualification was that they had joined the government-in-exile in Calcutta. Many senior Bengali officers who had been in detention in Pakistan until 1974 did not receive due positions when they returned to Bangladesh. As a result, frustration simmered in the upper echelons of the bureaucracy.[70]

Alienation of the civil bureaucracy was also caused by the enormous concentration of power in the hands of AL chief Sheikh Mujib. Nothing was possible in the administration without clearance from him, even in regard to routine matters. Senior officials spent more time waiting in line for his clearance than in implementing the policies. The inexperienced political appointees who flourished under the AL regime created a barrier between the senior bureaucrats and Sheikh Mujib, which unnecessarily complicated the decision-making process.[71]

After the downfall of the AL regime in August 1975, the new regime headed by General Zia took stern action against those guilty of subverting administration and indulging in corruption, but it could not completely rid itself of the evils flowing from nepotism and interference in the civil administration. Against established rules, General Zia appointed many military officers to high civil posts. In effect, it was he who initiated the process of militarization of the civil administration in Bangladesh. The process gained further momentum under the regime of General Ershad.

In the final analysis, the system of public administration in Bangladesh still bears a striking resemblance to what evolved and was devised in British India and United Pakistan. It retains all its characteristic features such as centralization, military-bureaucratic dominance, passion for rank, caste differentiation of officials, and lack of subsystem autonomy.

NOTES

1. For a general sociohistorical background to public administration in the Indian subcontinent, see Chapter 3, "India" by S. R. Maheshwari.

2. The general historical account of political and administrative developments in Bangladesh is drawn from A. M. M. Shawkat Ali, "Decentralization for Development: Experiment in Local Government Administration in Bangladesh," *Asian Survey*, 27, 7 (July 1987); Syed Serajul Islam, "Bangladesh in 1986: Entering a New Phase," *Asian Survey* 27, 2, (1987); and Mohammad Mohabbat Khan, "Politics of Administrative Reform and Reorganization in Bangladesh," *Public Administration and Development* 7 (1987), pp. 351–62.

The most recent developments in 1988 are drawn from issues of the *Far Eastern Economic Review* (Hong Kong), particularly 18, 25 February and 3, 10 March 1988, and issues of *Tide* and *Holiday Dhaka* for February and March 1988.

3. Bangladesh Bureau of Statistics, *Statistical Pocket Book of Bangladesh, 1983* (Dhaka, 1981), pp. 189–90. See also Planning Commission, *The Second Five Year Plan, 1980–85* (Dhaka: Bangladesh Government Press [BGP], 1983), pp. 13–14.

4. Planning Commission, *The Second Five Year Plan, 1980–85*, pp. 1–5.

5. See *Report of the Civil Administration Restoration Committee*, Part 1 (Dhaka: BGP, 1972), pp. 9–10.

6. See *The Bangladesh Gazette* (Extraordinary) (Dhaka: BGP, 23 May 1972).

7. A. M. A. Muhith, *Bangladesh: Emergence of a Nation* (Dhaka: Bangladesh Books International, 1978), pp. 243–44.

8. Ibid., pp. 254–57.

9. See *The Bangladesh Observer*, 29 December 1971.

10. See *The Bangladesh Gazette* (Extraordinary) (Dhaka: BGP, 11 January 1972).

11. S. G. Ahmed, "Ten Years of the Bangladesh Polity," *The Dhaka University Studies* 41, Part-A (December 1984), p. 133.

12. Ibid., p. 134.

13. See H. M. Zafarullah, "Public Corporation in Bangladesh," *Indian Journal of Public Administration (IJPA)* 24, 4 (1978), pp. 990–98.

14. Ahmed, "Ten Years of the Bangladesh Polity," p. 135.

15. *The Constitution of the People's Republic of Bangladesh* (hereafter cited as *Constitution of Bangladesh*), art. 56.

16. Ibid., art. 51 (2).

17. Ibid., art. 58.

18. Ibid., art. 65.

19. See M. M. Khan and H. M. Zafarullah, "The 1979 Parliamentary Election in Bangladesh," *Asian Survey* 19, 10 (1979), pp. 1023–36.

20. A. Hoque, "Bangladesh 1979: City for a Sovereign Parliament," *Asian Survey* 20, 1 (1980), p. 221.

21. See *Constitution of Bangladesh*, art. 56.

22. Ibid., arts. 94–113.

23. Ibid., art. 95.

24. Ibid., arts. 102–13.

25. See N. Chanda, "The March to Democracy," *Far Eastern Economic Review* (1 September 1983), p. 22.

26. See *The Bangladesh Observer*, 19 August 1985.

27. See Ahmed, "Ten Years of the Bangladesh Polity," p. 135.

28. Ibid., p. 136.

29. Ibid.

30. See Organization and Management Division, *Secretariat Instructions* (Dhaka: BGP, 1976), p. 4.

31. E. Ahamed, *Development Administration: Bangladesh* (Dhaka: Centre for Administrative Studies [CENTAS], 1981), p. 32.

32. S. G. Ahmed, "District Administration in Bangladesh," *Local Government Quarterly* 3, 3 and 4 (1974), p. 3.

33. S. G. Ahmed, "A Typological Study of the State Functionaries under the Mughuls," *Asian Profile* 10, 4 (1982), pp. 334–39.

34. Ahmed, "District Administration in Bangladesh," pp. 4–10.

35. See K. Siddiqui (ed.), *Local Government in Bangladesh* (Dhaka: National Institute of Local Government, 1984), pp. 43–60.

36. See M. M. Khan, "Process of Decentralization in Bangladesh" in Hasnat Hye (ed.), *Decentralization, Local Government Institutions and Resource Mobilization* (Comilla: Bangladesh Academy for Rural Development, 1985), pp. 241–62.

37. See Siddiqui, *Local Government in Bangladesh*, pp. 75–86.

38. Ibid., pp. 61–74.

39. See S. G. Ahmed, "The Emergent Leadership Pattern in Pourashavas of Bangladesh," *South Asian Studies* 10, 1 and 2 (1975), pp. 1–32.

40. See S. G. Ahmed, "Framework of Personnel Administration in Bangladesh," *IJPA* 31, 1 (1985), pp. 50–56.

41. Ibid., p. 50.

42. Cabinet Division, *Rules of Business, 1975* (Dhaka: BGP, 1980), pp. 2–3.

43. See Ahmed, "Framework of Personnel Administration in Bangladesh," p. 54.

44. Ministry of Finance, *Modification of the Financial Advisers' Scheme Along with Delegation of Financial Powers* (Dhaka: BGP, 1977), pp. 1–7.

45. Ibid., pp. 9–25.

46. Ahmed, "Framework of Personnel Administration in Bangladesh," pp. 47–48.

47. Ibid., p. 48.

48. Ibid.

49. See Bangladesh Government, *Report of the National Pay Commission* (hereafter cited as *Report of NPC*), 1 (Dhaka: BGP, 1973), pp. 88, 192.

50. See S. G. Ahmed, "Composition and Structure of Services in Bangladesh," *IJPA* 30, 1 (1984), pp. 184–85.

51. Ibid., p. 187.

52. Ibid.

53. Ibid., pp. 187–88.

54. See M. M. Khan, "Major Administrative Reform and Reorganization Efforts in Bangladesh: An Overview," *IJPA* 31, 3 (1985), pp. 1016–40; M. M. Khan, "Major Administrative Reform and Reorganization Efforts in Bangladesh, 1971–1985," in Colin Campbell, S. J. and B. Guy Peters, *Organizing Governance: Governing Organizations* (Pittsburgh: University of Pittsburgh Press, 1988), pp. 345–68.

55. See Ahmed, "Composition and Structure of Services in Bangladesh," pp. 9–12.

56. Ibid., p. 17.

57. Ibid., pp. 14–15.

58. Ibid., p. 16.

59. The twenty new scales start with Taka 500–(20)–860 at the bottom and Taka 6,000 (fixed) at the top, with the tenth mid-scale being Taka 1,350–(90)–2,250–(100)–2,750. Figures in brackets denote annual increments.

60. See Siddiqui, *Local Government in Bangladesh*, pp. 45–46.

61. See M. M. Khan, "Reform for Decentralized Development: Bangladesh's Experiment with Major Administrative Reforms/Reorganization in the '80s," in M. M. Khan and J. P. Throp (eds.), *Bangladesh: Society and Bureaucracy* (Dhaka: CENTAS, 1984), pp. 146–67; M. M. Khan, "Politics of Administrative Reform and Reorganization in Bangladesh," *Public Administration and Development* 7, 3 (1987).

62. See M. M. Khan and H. M. Zafarullah, *Recruitment and Selection in the Higher Civil Services in Bangladesh: An Overview*, SICA Occasional Papers Series, Second Series, no. 6 (Washington, D.C., 1984), p. 8.

63. See H. M. Zafarullah and M. M. Khan, "Staffing the Higher Civil Services in Bangladesh: An Analysis of Recruitment and Selection Processes," *Public Administration and Development* 3, 1 (March 1983), p. 132.

64. CMLA's Secretariat, Establishment Division, Government of Bangladesh, *Report of the Committee for Examination of Irregularities in Appointment and Promotion of Officers and Staff in the Government* (CEIAPOSG), April 1983, pp. ii, iv, 19.

65. See S. G. Ahmed, *Public Personnel Administration in Bangladesh* (Dhaka: University of Dhaka, 1985), pp. 245–56.

66. Ibid., pp. 265–70.

67. See M. M. Khan and H. M. Zafarullah, "Public Bureaucracy in Bangladesh," in Krishna K. Tummala (ed.), *Administrative Systems Abroad* (Washington, D.C.: University Press of America, 1982), p. 179.

68. See K. A. Zaman, "The Civil Service System in Bangladesh," in A. Kaksasataya and H. Siedentopf (eds.), *Asian Civil Services* (Kuala Lumpur: APDAC, 1980), p. 31.

69. See M. M. Khan, "Administrative Accountability in Bangladesh," *IJPA* 29, 3 (1983), pp. 682–89.

70. M. Rashiduzzaman, "Changing Political Patterns in Bangladesh: Internal Constraints and External Fears," *Asian Survey* 17, 9 (1977), p. 794.

71. Ibid., pp. 794–95.

3

INDIA

Shriram Maheshwari

THE SOCIOHISTORICAL BACKGROUND

India is the largest country in the Third World and has the greatest diversity and the longest continuous history in terms of culture and administration. In order to understand present-day administration in South Asia as well as Africa, it is necessary to take into account this administrative legacy of twenty-five centuries. The British East India Company took its ideas and practices regarding colonial administration from the Indian context, and British colonial administrators later transplanted them to all other British possessions in Africa, Southeast Asia, and the Caribbean. The administrative structures and processes of all the three successor states, India, Pakistan, and Bangladesh, retain a large part of this British administrative legacy.

The history of Indian administration is as long as China's Mandarinate—going back to the Mauryan Empire of Chandragupta in the fourth century B.C.—but it is far less continuous.[1] The great Indian classic handbook of imperial administration and diplomacy, *Kautilya's Arthasastra,* is the oldest text on public administration; it deals with the hierarchy of officials, the merits and failings of bureaucracy including corruption, geographical divisions of the empire, field administration through an all-purpose coordinating district overlord, land revenue, and the taxation of mines and minerals.[2] India never achieved lasting imperial unity, however, mainly because the necessary compact between the intellectuals and the rulers never emerged in the early centuries of Indian history, as it did in China.

Indeed, Indian empires disintegrated into smaller kingdoms and for brief periods even into total anarchy. However, the ideas of *Kautilya's Arthasastra* were kept alive by Brahmin scholars right until the eighteenth century and found their way into the works of liberal Muslim thinkers like Abul Fazl. During the 1760s when the British East India Company was beginning to organize its administration of Bengal, northern India was going through a period of anarchy. The highly centralized Moghul administration, based on a total concentration of revenue, executive, magistral, and military functions in the hands of the Mansabdars, had broken down completely. The East India Company's administrators laid the foundation of Indian administration, reinstituting the district overlord (without the Mansabdari military control) while improving and adapting his role for field administration. They reunified India by reshaping the Indian Civil Service in the 1850s and modernized that old institution at a most opportune moment when the British Utilitarians were ruthlessly trying to streamline state, law, and administration. India reaped some fruits of their efforts in the creation of the Western educated middle class and the modernization of the old institution of the district overlord, through competitive selection and the elegant codification of laws for administrative purposes.

British administration performed only a limited range of functions—those relating to law and order and regulation—but at the same time, projected a paternalistic image of government. The Congress party which took over the reins of government at independence was already committed to a welfare state and development through a planned economy, quite apart from integrating a populous nation with great diversities of religion, caste, culture, and language.

INDEPENDENCE

The administrative system, designed by the British to suit their own requirements, was inherited by independent India in 1947. The achievement of independence through mostly nonviolent, constitutional means fostered a climate of continuity, in spite of the country's partition, the reshuffling of a sizeable part of the population, law and order problems, and the depletion of the administrative cadres by the premature retirement of a large number of British and Muslim officers, with the "steel-frame" Indian Civil Service dwindling from 932 to 422.[3] Independent India nevertheless inherited an ongoing administrative system to cope with the emerging functions inherent in, or incidental to, statehood. The widespread backwardness of the country, the consequence of centuries of neglect, was slated to be eliminated as fast as possible, with the state as the only instrument of development. As a result governmental responsibilities expanded considerably, even when it was absorbed in assimilating the shocks of partition, communal disturbances, and other dislocations.

The Central Government had nearly 1.2 million employees on its payroll in 1950 when the present Constitution came into force and the First Five-Year Plan was formulated and put into operation. The machinery of public administration and the size of the public bureaucracy began to expand soon after, under the simultaneous impact of plan execution and allied influences. The number of ministries in the Central Government rose rapidly from eighteen in 1947 to twenty in 1952 to fifty-three in 1979 and sixty in 1985.[4] Similarly, the size of the public bureaucracy also increased from 1.5 million in 1951 to 2.094 million in 1961 to 2.920 million in 1971 to over 3.4 million in 1985. Similarly, the State bureaucracies increased from 4.74 million in 1975 to 6.3 million in 1985, and quasi-governmental employment rose from 3.2 million to 5.5 million and local government employment from 1.9 to 2.14 in the same period.

The Central Government employs over 3.4 million persons, the bulk of whom are in railways (1.5 million) and posts and telecommunications (0.5 million).[5] In a thirty-five-year period, 1950 to 1985, the central public bureaucracy thus increased its strength by nearly 250 percent. India attained statehood in the welfare era after the Second World War which led the government to assume responsibilities in many new areas of activity unknown during British colonial administration with its restricted functions. The Indian Constitution also obliged the government to take up a number of new functions, but it was planning which led to the greatest expansion of the administrative machinery at all levels of governance. Agencies and institutions in the field of development were created, and many existing ones were expanded. The expansion was both vertical and horizontal and most prominent at the field level. Moreover, planning integrated the autonomous levels of government which are so characteristic of a federation and placed a continuing emphasis on coordination between various parts, creating new coordinating roles. Again, with the dawn of independence, the poor had come to expect a great deal from the government, and the consequential increased workload caused further expansion of the bureaucracy. Finally, widespread unemployment in the country forced an excess of persons onto the government's payrolls.

ADMINISTRATIVE STRUCTURE AND ORGANIZATION

The Constitution of India is a comprehensive document containing provisions for the political organization of the Central and State governmental system. It also enumerates administrative arrangements and lays down broad guidelines for the socioeconomic structuring of society. The Constitution confers fundamental rights on the citizens in regard to equality, freedom of speech, of association, of movement, of religion, and so on, which are enforceable in courts of law. Public administration must respect these rights while dealing with the citizens. The directive principles of state policy enshrined in the Constitution also require that the state make positive efforts to improve the social, economic, and cultural conditions of society and create an order based, as the Preamble says, on justice, liberty, equality, and fraternity.

The Constitution provides for a federation in which each level of government has a parliamentary form of democracy based on the Westminister model. It enumerates the powers and functions of both levels of government in a detailed way (Union List ninety-seven items, State List sixty-six, and the Concurrent List forty-seven items). Most substantive functions like agriculture, animal husbandry, education, cooperation, public health as well as law and order are the direct responsibility of the constituent states, the Central Government's major direct responsibilities being defense, external affairs, communication, and currency. Notwithstanding the detailed enumeration of functions in the three lists, the Constitution puts the State governments under a firm obligation to so exercise their executive power as to ensure compliance with the laws made by Parliament. To this end the Center is empowered to issue necessary directions to them. Besides, financial resources are so divided as to make the States acutely dependent on the Center. The imbalance between functions and resources is so grave that it is sometimes said that the Constitution has given functions to the States and finances to the Center. What is more, the "emergency" provisions of the Constitution confer extraordinary powers on the Central Government, which has the virtual effect of negating the federal arrangement. The Indian Constitution provides for a federation that rests largely on the Center's terms.

THE POLITICAL EXECUTIVE

The government is modelled on the Westminster form. The head of state is the president of India who is elected to a five-year term by an electoral college consisting of the elected members of Parliament and of the legislative assembly of each state. Each member of Parliament has a certain number of votes according to a defined formula. The president is ordinarily a titular head of state, but where no political party commands a majority in the lower house of Parliament or does not have an elected leader, his discretion becomes decisive. For example, Zail Singh as president of India invited Rajiv Gandhi to form the government within hours of Indira Gandhi's assassination on 31 October 1984, even though Rajiv Gandhi was not yet formally elected as the leader of the Congress Parliamentary party. The president's decision is final and cannot be questioned in a court of law.

The Council of Ministers with the prime minister at its head is the real executive which is made accountable to the Lok Sabha, the lower house of the Indian Parliament. Until the mid–1970s, the constitutional nature of the office of president was left to be governed by conventions, but a recent amendment makes such a relationship explicit: "There shall be a Council of Ministers with the Prime Minister at the head to aid and advise the President who shall, in the exercise of his functions, act in accordance with such advice."[6] The Council of Ministers is firmly bound by the principle of joint responsibility and includes cabinet ministers, ministers of state, and deputy ministers. A cabinet minister is normally the political head of the ministry assigned to him, but in theory at least, his responsibilities extend to the entire field of central administration. There may be cabinet ministers without portfolios too. A minister of state may either be made head of a ministry or, as is generally done, be attached to an individual cabinet minister, but he is not a member of the cabinet and attends its meetings only on invitation. A deputy minister never holds an independent charge of a ministry, restricting himself to such functions as are entrusted to him by the minister concerned.

In any parliamentary democracy, the real repository of power is the cabinet, which consists solely of ministers of the first (or cabinet) rank. Its meets regularly under the chairmanship of the prime minister to decide national policies and matters of concern to more than one ministry. The real effectiveness of the cabinet in relation to the prime minister depends on factors like the prime minister's own personality and stature, the political weight of other members, the uniparty or biparty character of the ministry, and the like. During Indira Gandhi's prime ministership, the cabinet did not generally carry enough influence, and was content to function like a ratifying organ rather than a top-level decision-making body. But under the Janata party government (1977–1979) under Morarji Desai, which was characterized by collegiate leadership, the cabinet emerged as a forum for active discussion, Desai functioning more in the style of a chairman rather than a prime mover.

To relieve the cabinet of some of its preliminary work, cabinet committees are set up, some of which are standing ones. Ten cabinet committees are of a standing nature, of which the Political Affairs Committee and the Appointments Committee are the most powerful. Generally, the prime minister presides over a cabinet committee, which includes the senior ministers nominated by the prime minister.

The Constitution does not prescribe the size of the Council of Ministers, but it has expanded over a period of time.[7] In 1947, the council had fourteen members, but in 1985 the number stood at fifty-five and in February 1988 it rose to sixty, including sixteen cabinet ministers, thirty-seven ministers of state, and seven deputy ministers. The work of the government has, of course, increased considerably; the size of the ministry is also determined by representational compulsions in a large and diverse nation and again by political expediency and considerations of patronage.

MACHINERY OF GOVERNMENT: SECRETARIAT, ATTACHED AND SUBORDINATE OFFICES

The Constitution of India does not speak about the machinery of administration but says that the executive action of the Central Government "shall be expressed to be taken in the name of the President" and the president "shall make rules for the more convenient transaction of business of the Government of India and for the allocation among ministers of the said business."[8] The last-named provision paves the way for the promulgation of the "Allocation of Business Rules" among the ministries and departments, which are collectively known as the secretariat, the nerve center of the government. It consists of a number of ministries and departments, the number depending on the volume and variety of work, work priorities, valuational orientation, or political expediency. A ministry may be made up of one or more allied departments or may not have any separate department as such. It is headed by a minister, assisted by a career bureaucracy headed by a secretary who has under him additional secretaries, joint secretaries, directors, deputy secretaries, under secretaries, and the section officer who heads a section comprising assistants, upper and lower division clerks, typists, and so on. This secretariat structure assists the minister in policy making, the overseeing of policy execution, and the evaluation of plans and programs, and undertakes activities necessary for performing these functions. It also assists the minister in his parliamentary, legislative, and public activities. It prepares the budget of the government and exercises control over its expenditure. The number of ministries was eighteen in 1947, but by 1987 it had increased to sixty, which is a broad measure of the increase of work and, to an extent, of Parkinson's law at work. Thus, the number of secretaries increased from 9 in 1937 to 23 in 1954 to 102 in 1985; additional secretaries increased from 8 to 106, joint secretaries from 7 to 374, deputy secretaries from 13 to 538, and under secretaries from 16 to over 1,000 (approximately) in the same period.[9]

The major ministries in the government of India as of 1986 numbered thirty-one with an additional eight organizations equivalent to ministries. Some ministries have three to five departments under them, whereas others have none, the total of departments being sixty. As mentioned earlier, the secretariat is primarily a policy-making organ of the government, leaving execution of policies and programs to another set of organizations, the attached and subordinate offices. These offices were an outgrowth of a belief in the dichotomy of policy and administration. An attached office is a repository of technical knowledge on a particular subject that a ministry utilizes in its tasks. Under the Ministry of Education, for instance, is the Directorate-General of Archaeological Survey of India, which is an attached office. There are nearly seventy attached offices under various ministries in the Central Government. Below the attached offices are over 200 subordinate offices; these field establishments execute the policies and programs of the government of India. The National Archives of India, for example, is a subordinate office under the Ministry of Education.

The machinery of government at the Center (and also in the States) is designed on the basis of two important administrative principles. An overriding belief in the desirability of structural separation of policy making and administration has led to the creation of an organization that is concerned exclusively with policy making and another that is charged with implementing responsibilities. As a result, the machinery of the government of India is a three-tiered one in which the policy-making organ is the secretariat, and implementation is the responsibility of the attached and subordinate offices.

But sound policy making requires first-hand knowledge and experience of the conditions of implementation. This belief underlies the second administrative philosophy that the policy-making organ of the government of India must have no permanent cadre of officers but must instead be manned by personnel who are taken on fixed-term deputation from implementational levels so as to project field realities fully into the process of policy making. The middle- and senior-level positions in the secretariat are filled by public personnel drawn from the all-India and the central services, members of which generally work under the State governments or the field agencies of the Central Government. These personnel come to the Center for a fixed term varying from three to six years, depending on the level of appointment. They return to their parent organizations upon completion of their term, after which their positions are filled by another set of officers.

The principal argument advanced in favor of this arrangement is that higher civil servants engaged in policy making and advising ministers must possess first-hand as well as fresh experience of working in the field to keep the actions and decisions of the Central Government as close to reality and as meaningful to the people as possible. This is precisely what this "tenure principle" seeks to do. In fact, the complexity of most problems dealt with in the secretariat cannot be appreciated in a vast and diversified country like India unless the public servants concerned have direct experience of working in the States and field agencies. The civil servants who work in the secretariat are directly acquainted with the objectives underlying policies and programs, and the process of implementation does not lose sight of the objectives of the given program, thereby contributing to its success. In addition, through this arrangement each level of government gains direct insight into each other's constraints and concerns.

The discipline expected of this mode of staffing has become considerably lax over a period of time. As a result, those members of the secretariat who had an advantage of early deputation are generally reluctant to go back to their State cadre. A typical civil servant of today is not prepared to take postings quietly and instead makes all kinds of efforts to prolong his stay in the capital. Even when an extension is not granted, he endeavors to find a place in one of the government-run organizations in Delhi to get "cooled off" before he becomes formally qualified for another deputation. Therefore, there are few officers with fresh experience. Indeed, a very large number of officers who would otherwise be eligible for secretariat postings remain excluded. It is significant that (as of 1985) 1,591 IAS officers and 768 IPS officers (other than those belonging to the Uttar Pradesh cadre) with more than five years' service to their credit have not been able to gain positions with the Central Government.[10]

Postings in the secretariat are governed by the Central Staffing Scheme under which the doors are theoretically open to all higher civil services. In practice, however, a group of officers in the IAS have developed an inordinate liking for central postings, in ministries and agencies that manage economic affairs, with the ultimate aim of moving on to an international organization.

PUBLIC UNDERTAKINGS

The creation and expansion of public undertakings is the most conspicuous development in Indian public administration since independence. Starting with 5 in the year 1951, their number increased to over 200 in the mid–1980s. In

1985, public investment was of the order of Rs. 300 billion, which means that every Indian citizen has a stake of nearly Rs. 368 in their success. They employ about 1.95 million persons, out of which no fewer than 150,000 belong to the managerial cadres,[11] thus constituting a much bigger managerial group than the 35,000 or so in the ministries and departments. Apart from the strategic areas of national economy like life insurance and banking under public ownership, public undertakings also cover fields such as manufacturing, mining, petroleum, chemicals, pharmaceuticals, developmental, and financial services.

Public undertakings are organized in four forms: the department, company, public corporation, and holding company. The department form is the oldest one and has all the advantages and disadvantages associated with the regular government departments. It is used for railways, posts and telecommunications, broadcasting, and ordnance factories. The most widely used form is the company. It has gained wider acceptance because it has greater flexibility in terms of the already accumulated experience of its working and its well-defined and well-understood legal terminology, leaving little room for legal wrangles. The Fertilizer Corporation of India, the Heavy Engineering Corporation of India, and the National Mineral Development Corporation are among the one hundred-odd public undertakings organized as companies under the Company Act of 1956.[12] The public corporation form was made possible by an act passed by Parliament. India's important corporations are Air India, Indian Airlines, Damodar Valley Corporation, and the Industrial Finance Corporation. This form has not proved to be popular for three reasons. First, the way in which some of the established corporations like the Damodar Valley Corporation and the Industrial Finance Corporation were functioning in their formative years was not considered satisfactory, and this was attributed to the defective nature of the organizational form itself. Second, the corporation form of organization is inherently rigid in the sense that only a formal amendment of the concerned statute can effect the desired changes in structure and procedure. Third, the parliamentary timetable was generally too crowded to enact the legislation necessary to create more than a few public corporations.

The holding company is the newest organizational form. It was first tried in 1973 when the Steel Authority of India Limited (SAIL) was set up as the apex organization, with all the public sector steel plants like the Hindustan Steel and the Bokaro Steel as its subsidiaries. It coordinates, controls, and guides the functions of all its subsidiaries, without involving the Central Government, ascertains their budgetary requirements, and submits a consolidated budget to the government for approval. Loans and equity capital from the government are channeled through SAIL, which exercises financial discipline in the utilization of these resources, levying a small service charge on the loans advanced to its subsidiaries. SAIL consists of one chairman, three functional, and ten part-time directors. The National Textile Corporation and the Coal Authority of India Ltd. are other holding companies.

Each public undertaking, regardless of whether it is a public corporation or a company, is managed by a board of directors, appointed by the government, one of whom is nominated as the chairman of the board, full-time or part-time. The board is the policy-making organ of the undertaking, subject only to the control of the administrative ministry of the government. Until recently, the secretaries and additional secretaries of the government were appointed as chairmen of the boards of directors. Although this practice has been discontinued in the face of persistent criticism, the secretariat personnel continue to be nominated on the boards as members. This situation creates a conflict of interest: it is difficult for the secretariat personnel to act as neutral policy advisers to the minister when they also get involved in the execution of policies as board members. Moreover, they are busy with their normal assignments and can hardly do justice to the undertaking's heavy work schedule. The practice also detracts from the total sense of involvement in the board of directors and throttles its initiative, even though the daily administration of the undertaking rests in the hands of a full-time managing director.

The recruitment practices in public undertakings are both centralized and decentralized, as well as varied, including direct recruitment, recruitment by promotion, or deputation from government or other public undertakings. An analysis of recruitment made in 1980–1981 showed that direct recruitment of personnel with pay scales of Rs. 700–1,300 and above accounted for 36.5 percent, recruitment by promotion 57 percent, deputation from other public undertakings 2 percent, and deputation from government 4.5 percent.[13] Some public undertakings still get their personnel through deputation from the government, but these deputationists are now needed only in special situations. Some public undertakings have their own system of recruiting management trainees for induction at the junior level, thus initiating a move toward the creation of a cadre of professional managers. In 1958–1959, the government of India constituted the Indian Management Pool to fill the senior and top positions in public undertakings, but this pool was neither properly constituted nor effectively utilized, largely because of resistance from below in the undertakings themselves and was eventually disbanded in 1973.[14] In 1974, the Public Enterprise Selection Board (PESB) was set up to select personnel for top- and second-level positions, but the board is a purely recommendatory body, and the power of appointment still lies with the government. Many top-level positions in public undertakings are still filled on grounds of patronage or remain unfilled for long periods, thus weakening their functioning. Frequent, ill-planned transfers of personnel are not uncommon, which tends to diffuse accountability and inject confusion into the unit. The rapidity with which the chief executives of some public undertakings are moved in and out is again particularly harmful, for every time the top person is removed, the entire style of operation undergoes revision and change.

Training of managerial personnel in public undertakings does not receive much attention in India. Unlike the National Academy of Administration which provides institutional training for new recruits to the higher civil services, there is no exclusive institute for the centralized education and training of personnel in public undertakings. The Indian Institutes of Management of Ahmedabad, Calcutta, and Bangalore and the Administrative Staff College (Hyderabad) do offer training facilities to public enterprise managers, but generally they teach techniques and skills based on experience gleaned from free market economies which need considerable recasting in the case of the public sector. Ironically, the graduates of the Indian Institutes of Management prefer employment in the private sector, although these have been set up with public funds and their graduates are expected to join the public sector—in reasonable numbers. The managerial personnel of public undertakings thus receive training at various institutes without any systematic organization. Nor have most public undertakings drawn up rules about other personnel matters such as promotion, discipline, and other service conditions.

Public undertakings follow diverse practices because of the absence of centralized or overall thinking about an appropriate personnel system. To improve management, recommendations have often been made about setting up an all-India management service to fill the 400-odd posts of full-time chief executives and directors in public undertakings. The need to revamp practices in public undertakings in order to infuse a greater measure of purposiveness, goal orientation, and productivity-orientation among the managerial hierarchy is also realized, as is the need to develop software for monitoring and measuring enterprise-level productivity. But little consistent action has been taken in these regards.

Public undertakings have now been in existence for over thirty years, long enough to create a broad collective image in the society. Nevertheless, the public enterprise managerial class has not attained a distinctive sharpness. This is the case even though public undertakings in India have had many successes. The public sector has been the pioneer in introducing professional management in India, and public undertakings are engaged in producing items that constitute the infrastructure for the economy.

There are, of course, well-managed units in the public sector, and managerial effectiveness naturally varies from unit to unit. Moreover, the managers have to function within vastly more complex and varied parameters than their counterparts in the private sector. Quite often, a public undertaking is given multiple objectives, many of which are even mutually inconsistent; to further add to the complexity, they are all couched in qualitative terms. These factors, along with continuous public and parliamentary criticism, have made them appear as inveterate losers. However, it is claimed that they safeguard the Indian economy from all adverse international economic pressure. This claim was borne out by the total insulation of the economy from the ill effects of the New York stock market crash of 19 October 1987.[15]

THE CIVIL SERVICES

The Indian Constitution is unique in its detailed provisions relating to the civil services, covering matters like recruitment and conditions of service, including termination and demotion as well as the institution of the all-India services and public service commissions. Parliament is empowered to regulate the recruitment and conditions of service of civil servants, subject, of course, to the Constitution. Civil servants hold office at the "pleasure" of the president of India, but they cannot be removed or dismissed by an authority subordinate to that by which they were appointed. Moreover, before such an action is taken, they must have been given a "reasonable opportunity" of showing cause against the action proposed against them.

The government of India employs 3.4 million persons, an overwhelming number of whom are in lower level jobs; only 2.6 percent of them are engaged in positions entailing supervisory and policy-making responsibilities.[16] Corresponding, in descending order, to the differences in the level of responsibility of the work performed and qualifications required, the civil service is classified into Group A, Group B, Group C, and Group D (earlier known as Class I, II, III, and IV). Group A constitutes the service of higher civil servants in India and includes the all-India services and the Central services, numbering three and thirty-three, respectively.[17] The generalist all-India and Central services are recruited from the common competitive examination, but once service-allocation is completed the officers remain in their respective services for the rest of their career with little interservice mobility. The emolument patterns, career prospects, and other terms of service also differ from service to service and are the most favorable for the Indian Administrative Service (IAS). A member of the IAS can reach the rank of joint secretary in his sixteenth year of service, whereas a member of the Indian Police Service requires more than twenty years to reach this level. Group B is basically a class of first-line supervisor, and, like Group A, includes a number of services, each separate and distinct with little intercommunication. Group C includes clerical jobs, whereas Group D comprises messengers, peons, cyclostyling machine operators, and others doing inferior jobs. The layer of supervisory and managerial personnel is thin; in 1980, out of every one hundred central employees, 1.30 were in Group A, 2.20 in Group B, 54.79 in Group C, and the remaining in Group D.

The all-India service, common to both the Central and State Government with ultimate control vested in the Center, is a remarkable administrative innovation in Indian federalism. It was originally an arrangement made by the British colonial government in India in the early period of its rule. It was deliberately retained by independent India and was recognized in its Constitution, which mentions the Indian Administrative Service and the Indian Police Service as two all-India services, and lays down a procedure for creating additional all-India services.

Although other federal systems have followed the policy of administrative dualism with the Center and the Units recruiting their own civil services independently, India constitutionally entrenched the practice of central recruitment of these all-India services and placed them in charge of district administration and the top ranks of the administration of the State secretariats, for important historical and political reasons.

Apart from the British administrative centralization of India, the Indian National Congress was also shaping itself as a centralized organization as part of the tactics of its struggle for freedom. The climate of opinion at the time of freedom with partition in 1947 was also in favor of a strong Center. It was against this background that India's deputy prime minister, Sardar Patel, created the all-India services and entrenched them in the Constitution.[18] It was also a clear act of deliberate choice and not just a continuation of the British ICS tradition by inertia. Throughout the Congress's history, Patel had been a quiet but committed centralizer and advocated a strong Center, once partition was agreed on. Moreover his brief experience as home minister in 1946 and 1947 convinced him of the dedication of Indian members of the ICS, the usefulness of the all-India type of service, and the overall importance of administration.

Patel went about the job methodically, first gaining the consent of the (provincial) premiers at the Conference of Premiers in October 1946 with his quiet advocacy. Having obtained this necessary support, Patel advocated the creation and entrenchment of all-India services in the Constitution to the Constituent Assembly somewhat passionately, while he generously mixed his tributes to the ICS with the need for an IAS to keep the country together in the new "federal" Constitution.

The all-India services have flourished in spite of occasional strong criticisms, for reasons such as their own supraregional middle-class background, the dominance of the Congress party, and the nonvisibility of any workable alternative. In the first place, the direct recruits to the IAS are drawn from an Indian urban middle-class background, with a pronounced supraregional all-India leaning. A very high proportion (well over 60 percent) of the recruits have a supraregional character in more than one sense.[19] Many of them speak at home a language different from the language of the state they were born in; many were born in one state and domiciled and educated in another; and practically all the successful recruits took their competitive examinations far away from their birth-state. While this does not amount to the kind of group consciousness produced in Britain by a public school and Oxford education, the administrators of the all-India services have a deeper all-India character than elected politicians in the State Assemblies, owing to the sociohistorical origins and evolution of the Indian middle class. British rule generated a derivative middle class through Western education, with many of the characteristics of the Western professional middle class. This class, more than a century old by the time of independence, had developed recognizably supraregional characteristics.

State-level politicians, both Congress and non-Congress, and various other groups have severely criticized the all-India services for their dominance over State services and their centralist orientation. But in its report released in February 1988 the Sarkaria Commission on Center-State relations came out strongly in their defense.[20] It is likely that they will survive and flourish for at least some decades to come.

With an annual intake of over 125 and a total membership of over 4,000 by the year 1987, the Indian Administrative Service is the elite service of India. It easily represents the most coveted career for bright university graduates, even though private business and industry also have recently started attracting a sizeable share of the nation's talent. As a rule, its members fill top-level policy-making positions in both Central and State governments. Even after retirement (which is fixed at the age of fifty-eight), some of them are appointed as governors of states or to similar high positions.

Recruitment to the all-India and Central services is through a combined competitive examination held annually by the Union Public Service Commission, the independent recruiting body set up under the Constitution. Eligible for nearly 700 vacancies are university graduates between twenty-one and twenty-six years of age. The top-ranking candidates are assigned to the services of their choice. Indeed, in terms of the candidate's preferences, the IAS has always stood at the top, but the relative attractiveness of other services has not remained steady. For instance, the Indian Foreign Service is no longer the first or second choice of most competing graduates. Services like Income Tax, Central Excise, Railways, Audit, and Account have become more attractive to applicants and are preferred to many other services. Each candidate gets three chances to compete, and some of the successful candidates placed in other services will reappear at the competitive examination to improve their performance and thus qualify for the IAS, the successor to the world-renowned Indian Civil Service.

The newly recruited candidates to the various generalist services, both all-India and central, are required to undergo a five-month "foundational" training at the government-run National Academy of Administration at Mussorie. There all the candidates are given an understanding of the constitutional, economic, and social framework within which they all have to function. All the recruits are housed under one roof in order to promote a measure of camaraderie among them which can facilitate coordinated efforts in their subsequent career. The residential arrangements and course pattern are designed to provide opportunity for making cross-service friendships. This fraternity is ephemeral, however, and does not survive the training period at Mussorie, inasmuch as the disparity between different services extends from the pay-structure to service conditions. At the end of five months, the members of other services leave the academy to undergo further specialized training at their respective training institutions, while members of the IAS continue to stay there for professional training of a sandwich character. The institutional training is followed by on-the-job training in the district, at the end of which they reassemble at Mussorie to attend the second training phase. This phase lasts seven months, and the emphasis is on the practical problems and difficulties they have encountered or observed in the field.

Upon completion of the institutional training, the new recruit goes to the state of his allotment which he is to serve for the rest of his life, punctuated by periods of service at the Center. The emphasis in the earlier years of his career is on postings in the district where he is assigned to a variety of jobs to prepare him for the post of district collector, in the fifth year or so of his service. He rotates from one job to another and is even brought to the State secretariat where he learns how policies and programs are prepared in consultation with the Center and is assigned to the Central Government Secretariat for periods of service. A member of the IAS thus rotates between the Center and the State, and when he enters the sixteenth year or so of his service he reaches the rank of joint secretary in the Central Government. At this stage, he enters senior management. From then on competition for senior jobs becomes intense, and not all IAS officers succeed in rising to the post of secretary to the government, which is their ambition.

The higher civil servants in India are generally drawn from the urban middle class, even though 77 percent of the country's population lives in villages and only 15 percent or so of the entire society falls in the middle-class category. There are more than one hundred universities in the country, but most of the successful candidates in the competitive examination come from a small number of universities: the universities of Delhi, Allahabad, Punjab, Madras, Calcutta, and Patna, followed by five other universities—Agra, Lucknow, Meerut, Rajasthan, and Utkal.[21] A proportion of higher civil servants, particularly those belonging to the IAS, are the offspring of civil servants, and a substantial percentage of them come from families engaged in learned professions. Over a period of time the socioeconomic base of the recruits has widened as a result of a steady expansion of education in society and the adoption of various egalitarian measures by the government. The most consistent of these is the positive discrimination in favor of the members of Scheduled Castes and Scheduled Tribes sanctioned by the Constitution. Fifteen percent of government posts are presently reserved for Scheduled Castes and 7.5 percent for Scheduled Tribes. All these vacancies are gradually getting filled up as members of these castes and tribes are taking advantage of modern education and are applying for jobs. Since 1968, the reservation system has been extended to promotion as well, a provision that has sparked controversy about its propriety. Affirmative action by the state has inducted hitherto neglected sections of the society into bureaucracy, thus broadening its social base. A more representative distribution of the speakers of various Indian languages is also taking place. Yet, no great attitudinal changes are manifested by the civil servants coming from the newly opened social groups, the young being socialized in the values of their seniors.[22]

The civil service in India is designed to confer an undisguisedly hegemonic role to the generalist Indian Administrative Service. The emoluments of this service are the best, promotional prospects the brightest, service conditions the most satisfactory, and fringe benefits enviable. The developmental activities initiated since independence have resulted in the recruitment of a large number of specialists in various areas of administration, but the status accorded to them in the government is not commensurate with their contribution, both actual and potential. Although a large percentage of the IAS members is found in the higher ranges of the pay scale, the reverse is the case with medical doctors and engineers in India, a large number of whom fall in the lower income-band of their respective pay scale, seriously affecting their motivation and morale. Thus, the civil service in India consists of a number of unequal services with little interservice communication or mobility. The Administrative Reforms Commission (1966–1970), seeking to open the road to the top to all with merit, recommended a unified grading structure but this proposal was rejected.

The civil service of the country has become politicized over a period of time. Matters like postings, transfers, and promotions are decided by the executive, and as such the politically appointed ministers increasingly look to these as handy devices of reward and punishment. Careerism in the civil service makes its members receptive to the signals of ministers. As a result, there is growing political interference in administration and, as often as not, both the civil servant and the politician have learned to accommodate each other in a wide variety of matters.[23] Consequently civil service ethics in India is under heavy stress, one manifestation of which is rather widespread corruption in administration. Not long ago, a civil servant of impeccable integrity blamed not only the politicians, but also his own colleagues for the deteriorating administrative standards, bluntly observing: "The politicians use the officers only because the officers allow themselves to be used."[24]

STATE GOVERNMENTS

India is a federation, its constituent units being the twenty-five states and seven union territories. The State governments[25] have been entrusted with a large number of functions, including both regulatory and development administration, such as police and internal security, agriculture, animal husbandry, public health, cooperatives, education, and minor irrigation.[26] Indeed, most "line" functions, which are of direct concern to the citizens, are with the State governments. In addition, they constitute the instrument for carrying out many of the Center's policies and programs. Being the implementing agencies of New Delhi, they hold the key to their success. This explains why the political party in power in the Center is ever keen to gain power in the States as well, especially the larger ones.

The Constitution provides the same form of government for the States as for the Center, even though there are some important differences between the two. Each State is headed by a governor who is appointed by the president, but the term of office is not specified. He may be removed from office by the president by simple notification. Indeed, one governor, Prabhudas Patwari, of Tamilnadu was dismissed by President Sanjeeva Reddy in 1981, and two others were at least forced to resign, namely, Ram Lall in Andhra Pradesh in 1983 and Khurana in Tamilnadu in 1988. The governor may be transferred to another State (a practice first adopted in 1967); of late such transfers have become increasingly common. But he enjoys some discretionary power and has some say in the management of public affairs in the state. His position has been the subject of political and constitutional debate for over two decades. The Sarkaria Commission report of February 1988 recommended some reforms, the most important of which is mandatory consultation with the State Government before appointment.[27]

The real executive is, of course, the Council of Ministers with the chief minister at its head. In practice, however, one may discern an unmistakable shift of power toward the chief minister, particularly in states governed by the Congress party. The party's style of making the ministry is highly centralized, and invariably the prime minister nominates the chief minister who is then dutifully elected by the party's State legislators and sworn in by the governor. The chief minister does not enjoy much freedom in the appointment or dropping of other ministers which, again, is done strictly in prior consultation with the Central leadership. But he is much more powerful in matters of day-to-day administration except as head of a coalition as in West Bengal or Kerala.

As a result of its legislative majority, the Congress party has generally been forming the government in most States most of the time, but Congress ministries have often been plagued by factions and have sometimes fallen as a result of floor-crossing by legislators. In addition, the Congress party culture encourages short terms for chief ministers. Even when the party continues to enjoy legislative support, it changes this functionary in midstream, often at the behest of central leadership, contributing to political instability in the State. This is in sharp contrast to the practice at the Center where the Congress party has reelected the same person to the office of prime minister as long as he has been available.

Below the political executive is the State secretariat which is staffed, in descending order of authority, by secretaries, additional secretaries, joint secretaries, deputy secretaries, under secretaries, and other clerical personnel. As at the Center, the top officers are "birds of passage" so to speak, coming for fixed tenures from either field positions or from the Central Government. Officers who have gained first-hand experience in the field are, as a rule, preferred for policy-making positions. A special feature of State administration is the office of the chief secretary held by a very senior civil servant who coordinates the work of the State secretariat as a whole. This legacy from the British period is reviled by some critics as undemocratic and defended by others as ensuring greater efficiency and coordination.

As in the case of the Central Government, the secretariat is concerned with the broader aspects of administration, including the initiation and formulation of policies while the responsibility for their execution rests with directorates and their field staff. Thus, a separate department exists for every important activity of the State, which provides executive direction required in the implementation of policy laid down by the secretariat. These departments also serve as repositories of technical expertise and advise the secretariat on technical aspects of questions with which they have to deal. The field offices of these departments function as agencies responsible for detailed execution of the policies and decisions of the State Government. The directorates are manned by technical personnel as against the generalist composition of the secretariat, but they do not enjoy adequate power and authority, which handicaps their functioning.

DISTRICT ADMINISTRATION

The district is the cutting edge of administration where citizens come in contact with it every day. With an area ranging from 1,500 to 7,000 square miles and a population of approximately 2 million, it is the unit of administration and nearly all departments of the government have their branch offices at this level. Thus, the district superintendent of police, the chief medical officer, the assistant registrar of cooperative societies, and the district agricultural officer are all located in the district, along with their staff, to implement their departmental programs. But its uniqueness lies in the appointment of a district officer, or an area coordinator, called the district collector or deputy commissioner who represents the State Government as such and is the head of district administration. His main responsibility is the maintenance of internal security and the integration of various programs in terms of the area under his charge. He is appointed from the IAS, and is a legally powerful functionary, but the efficiency of this office has been eroded by the relative inexperience of the incumbent, his frequent transfer and increasing political interference in his affairs, as well as by restrictive departmental loyalties which frustrate his coordinational efforts.[28]

Each State also has its own civil service, consisting, as in the Central pattern, of a number of technical and generalist services, recruited through the State public service commission, while members of the all-India services as a rule occupy senior positions in the government. The State services are constituted department-wise and are divided, as at the Center, into Group A, Group B, Group C, and Group D, corresponding to the responsibility of the work performed and the qualifications required. The most prestigious Group A service is the generalist State administrative service, a certain percentage of whose members are annually promoted into the IAS. However, the State services are generally rated as inferior to the Central services because their pay scales are less competitive and promotion prospects are limited. The number of civil servants under the different State governments, varies from State to State according to size and population.[29] The largest, Uttar Pradesh, had well over half a million on its payroll in 1980 and the smallest, Tripura, about 26,000.

LOCAL GOVERNMENT

Local government, or local self-government as it used to be called during the colonial era, is government at the grassroots level entrusted with performing functions that concern day-to-day public needs such as roads, water supply, and sanitation. It is not included in the Constitution but is founded on statutes enacted by various State governments. However, it is an old institution dating back to the year 1687 when a municipal corporation was set up in Madras. It was introduced on an all-India basis by Lord Ripon's landmark Resolution of 1882. Here we will focus not on its history in ancient or medieval India or on its vicissitudes under British rule but rather on its existing organization, functions, and problems.[30]

Local government in India is organized on the basis of a rural-urban dichotomy. Rural government, called *panchayatraj,* is a hierarchically integrated government consisting of *panchayat* (village council), *panchayat samiti* (block level council), and the *zila parishad* (district level council). These elective bodies enjoy defined civic and developmental powers and are vertically integrated. In terms of the level of ultimate executive power, two broad patterns of organization have emerged. State governments like Maharashtra and Gujarat—and Karnataka from 1987 onward—vest the executive authority in the district level body, the zila parishad, with the subsidiary organ at the block level exercising only delegated powers. In most other States, on the other hand, powers are vested in the intermediate body at the block level, the panchayat samiti, with a mere coordinating role vested in the zila parishad.

Urban local government is organized in one of the following ways: municipal corporations for big cities, municipal boards for medium-sized cities, cantonment boards for military stations, notified area committees and town area committees for nascent small towns and other urban areas, and townships for a newly established industrial complex. The corporation form of urban local government has traditionally enjoyed more power and autonomy than others. Being a prestige symbol, this status is cherished by an increasingly large number of cities.

The number of various local governmental bodies is shown in the accompanying table. The figures for panchayat raj are for 1984 and those for corporations and cantonments for 1985.

Rural Local Government
(Panchayat raj)

Zila Parishads	297
Panchayat Samities	4,526
Village Panchayats	217,319

Urban Local Government

Municipal Corporations	68
Municipal Boards	1,493
Cantonment Boards	62
Notified Area Committees	202
Town Area Committees	385

Local government, urban and rural alike, has never been in sound health in India and may at best be regarded as only a marginal participant in the management of local public affairs. The dominant centralist ethos of Indian administration characterizes the State Government's attitude toward local government.[31] Its resource base is very weak and vulnerable, and it depends heavily on the State Government for finance, much as the State Government is obliged to look to the Center for assistance and to a much higher degree. The State Government's control and supervision of local government bodies is excessive and unimaginative; even municipal corporations do not enjoy any significant measure of autonomy. The original statute setting up the Bombay Municipal Corporation did not contain any provision for its dismissal, but the law was hurriedly amended in 1984. As a result the Bombay Corporation, the historical symbol of civic pride in India, was superseded on 1 April 1984. Such dissolution of local bodies is frequent and at any moment of time, more municipal corporations are to be found in a state of supersession than in a functioning position. A large number of local bodies have remained either superseded or dissolved for long periods, and elections, which have a legitimizing effect on democratic institutions, have been postponed indefinitely. In addition, the State Government tends to take away one function after another and create single-purpose agencies, leading to fragmentation of local government.

CONCLUDING REFLECTIONS

An administrative system originally designed by the British to perform regulatory functions in a dependent country was taken over lock, stock, and barrel by independent India. It is being utilized for tasks of state building and development, with some modifications in the context of parliamentary democracy and federalism, as enshrined in the Indian Constitution. By itself, this is an achievement as well as a continuing problem. It has expanded spectacularly in all directions, more so in economic, welfare-oriented, and developmental fields, and has become vastly more complex, just as the society itself has become increasingly diversified. New forms of organizations have been set up, and new skills and specialties, modern management aids, and techniques have been adopted by public administration, with more emphasis on in-service training.

India's public administration, unlike that of other federal systems, is a highly integrated one with its all-India services reinforced by successive five-year plans and the single-party dominance system, especially under the dynamic leadership of prime ministers like Jawaharlal Nehru and Indira Gandhi. This system has its obvious merits in its ability to counter centrifugal forces in a country of such great diversity as India and to keep intact the chain of command vital for swift action. The Constitution itself sought to foster a sense of unity by making the lower level of government dependent on the higher one for finance and for administrative control through the all-India services as well as other provisions. Indian administration is thus centralized, and the concentration of authority at the top can reduce the initiative and drive of personnel working in the field. The Center-strengthening federal formula enshrined in the Constitution has also come increasingly under adverse criticism, and today the State governments are making a demand for greater autonomy, particularly in financial terms.

The Sarkaria Commission (1982–1987), after five years of evidence and cogitation, has recommended only minimum changes in Center-State relations.[32] It has strongly supported the continuation, expansion, and strengthening of the all-India services, with regular consultation on the management of these services between the Center and the States, through an advisory council under the cabinet secretary for this purpose. In regard to the imposition of the president's rule on a State, the commission has acknowledged the need for that provision but has suggested several modifications concerning the conditions and the nature of the parliamentary proclamation. Regarding the Planning Commission and the planning process, the commission has made a number of suggestions involving the States in both. On the general problem of revenue sharing, the Sarkaria Commission has recommended the sharing of taxes such as corporation taxes and a levy on advertisements, apart from suitable adjustments to the sharing of income tax and other sources of revenue. In general, the commission has affirmed that "under Indian conditions, a strong center is necessary not only to protect and preserve the independence, integrity and unity of the country but also to coordinate a uniform integrated policy on basic issues of national concern."[33]

Apart from such major commissions like the Sarkaria Commission, the Central Government has set up as many as twenty-one committees on administrative reform since 1947 to revamp the administrative system of the country.[34] For example, these committees have examined various issues ranging from simple improvements in work procedures, senior staffing policies, or the elimination of corruption on basic questions concerning coordination of plans between Center and State or the overall machinery of government. Quite a few of the recommendations have been implemented. As a result, public administration in India has absorbed many changes, but the apparent conflict between the needs of development in all spheres of life and the colonial attributes of an overly cautious bureaucracy continues to plague the system.

In the course of implementing various schemes and programs in the field of development, administrative inadequacies have come to light with increasing vividness. There is still considerable overstaffing which acts as a drag on efficiency in administration, and work ethics, generally, is not high. According to civil service gossip, nearly 20 percent of public employees in the government are believed to be superfluous. Work procedures are antiquated, and more often than not the edict of the baboo (clerical personnel) prevails consequent to an unwillingness of higher level functionaries to take risks and apply their minds to the items of work coming before them for decision making. Corruption is still rampant in administration despite the vigilance agencies that have been set up to deal with the problem. What is more, there even appears to be acceptance of it, pursuant to a realization that corruption is a worldwide phenomenon. Citizen orientation on the part of the bureaucracy is weak, and people's grievances generally remain unredressed. A demand for a strong ombudsman institution is of long standing, but the ruling elite is lukewarm to its functioning. Ombudsmen, called Lokayuktas, have been set up by most State governments, but the functionary is generally kept idle without too much work.[35]

Although these and other problems are serious, some at least are the result of development itself. Some of the earlier solutions have, over a period of time, themselves become problems, putting the administration under stress. For example, an attempt was made to solve the backwardness of certain sections of the society by reserving government posts for their members. Three decades of practicing positive discrimination, while benefiting these classes, have also created certain vested interests in the system, and the process has produced a backlash effect.[36] Today, powerful lobbies of reservationists and antireservationists have arrayed against each other, and considerable public time and energy is spent on sorting out such problems. Indian public administration is presently trying to devise solutions to what are basically second-generation problems.

We must also note that public administration is the acknowledged instrument of development in India which imparts special significance to it in the society. It has made many achievements, the most impressive one being democracy, and the simultaneous and sustained promotion of development. In combining both, and shaping an independent and virile economy, Indian public administration is unique.

NOTES

1. For a more detailed comparative historical account, see V. Subramaniam, "Status and Function of Intellectuals in State and Society in India and China: Some Critical Comparisons," *International Sociology* 2, 3 (September 1987) and V. Subramaniam, "The Indo-British Legacy in Administration: Dialectic and Dilemmas," *Indian Journal of Public Administration* 14, 2 (New Delhi).

2. R. Shama Sastry, *Kautilya's Arthasastra* (Mysore: Mysore Printing Publishing House, 1967), 7th ed.

3. The term *steel frame* was first used in 1922 by British Prime Minister Lloyd George: "I can see no period when they [Indians] can dispense with the guidance and assistance of the small numbers of the British Civil Service. They are the steel frame of the whole structure." *Parliamentary Debates* (House of Commons, 5th series, vol. 157, 1922, col. 1513).

4. The Government of India, Directorate General of Employment and Training, Ministry of Labour, *The Census of Central Government Employees, 1980*, and *India 1986: A Reference Annual* (New Delhi: Publications Division, Ministry of Information and Broadcasting, 1987) p. 225.

5. *India 1986*.

6. Article 74 of the Constitution of India.

7. The Government of India Act, 1935, Section 9(1), had fixed the maximum size of the Council of Ministers to ten, but the Indian Constitution placed no such restriction. The figures for 1947 and 1985 are drawn from the official publications, and the figure for February 1988 is from *The Hindu* (Madras), (16 February 1988).

8. Article 77(i) and Article 77(3) of the Constitution of India.

9. These figures of senior personnel in the secretariat of the government of India are taken from the official publication *India (1986) A Reference Annual* of the Ministry of Information and Broadcasting, New Delhi. The following complete list of ministries and departments as of October 1986 is also taken from *India 1986*, pp. 37–38.

1. **Ministry of Agriculture**
   (i) Department of Agriculture and Cooperation
   (ii) Department of Agricultural Research and Education
   (iii) Department of Rural Development
   (iv) Department of Fertilizers
2. **Ministry of Civil Aviation**
3. **Ministry of Commerce**
   (i) Department of Commerce
   (ii) Department of Supply
4. **Ministry of Communications**
   (i) Department of Posts
   (ii) Department of Telecommunications
5. **Ministry of Defense**
   (i) Department of Defense
   (ii) Department of Defense Production and Supplies
   (iii) Department of Defense Research and Development
6. **Ministry of Energy**
   (i) Department of Coal
   (ii) Department of Power
   (iii) Department of Nonconventional Energy Sources
7. **Ministry of Environment and Forests**
   (i) Department of Environment, Forests, and Wildlife
8. **Ministry of External Affairs**
9. **Ministry of Finance**
   (i) Department of Economic Affairs
   (ii) Department of Expenditure
   (iii) Department of Revenue
10. **Ministry of Food and Civil Supplies**
    (i) Department of Food
    (ii) Department of Civil Supplies
11. **Ministry of Health and Family Welfare**
    (i) Department of Health
    (ii) Department of Family Welfare
12. **Ministry of Home Affairs**
    (i) Department of Internal Security
    (ii) Department of States
    (iii) Department of Official Language
    (iv) Department of Home
13. **Ministry of Human Resource Development**
    (i) Department of Education
    (ii) Department of Youth Affairs and Sports
    (iii) Department of Women and Child Development
    (iv) Department of Arts
    (v) Department of Culture
14. **Ministry of Industry**
    (i) Department of Industrial Development
    (ii) Department of Company Affairs

(iii) Department of Chemicals and Petro-Chemicals
(iv) Department of Public Enterprises
15. **Ministry of Information and Broadcasting**
16. **Ministry of Labour**
17. **Ministry of Law and Justice**
    (i) Department of Legal Affairs
    (ii) Legislative Department
    (iii) Department of Justice
18. **Ministry of Parliamentary Affairs**
19. **Ministry of Personnel**
    Public Grievances and Pension
    (i) Department of Personnel and Training
    (ii) Department of Administrative Reforms and Public Grievances
    (iii) Department of Pension and Pensioners' Welfare
20. **Ministry of Petroleum and Natural Gas**
21. **Ministry of Planning**
    (i) Department of Planning
    (ii) Department of Statistics
22. **Ministry of Program Implementation**
23. **Ministry of Railways**
24. **Ministry of Science and Technology**
    (i) Department of Science and Technology
    (ii) Department of Scientific and Industrial Research
    (iii) Department of Biotechnology
25. **Ministry of Steel and Mines**
    (i) Department of Steel
    (ii) Department of Mines
26. **Ministry of Surface Transport**
27. **Ministry of Textiles**
28. **Ministry of Tourism**
29. **Ministry of Urban Development**
30. **Ministry of Water Resources**
31. **Ministry of Welfare**
32. **Department of Atomic Energy**
33. **Department of Electronics**
34. **Department of Ocean Development**
35. **Department of Space**
36. **Cabinet Secretariat**
37. **President's Secretariat**
38. **Prime Minister's Office**
39. **Planning Commission**

10. These estimates are based on inside information.

11. Committee on Public Undertakings (Seventh Lok Sabha), *Forty-ninth Report on Public Undertakings—Management and Control Systems* (New Delhi: Lok Sabha Secretariat, 1982), p. 42.

12. The use of the term *corporation* does not necessarily mean that the entity is a public corporation, created by an act of Parliament. Companies also use this term.

13. Committee on Public Undertakings (Seventh Lok Sabha), *Forty-ninth Report*, p. 43.

14. See S. R. Maheshwari, *Indian Administration* (New Delhi: Orient Longman, 1984), pp. 224–27.

15. This view has been argued by several economists. See, for example, Amartya Sen, "Carrot Sticks and Economics: Perceptions, Problems and Incentives," *Indian Economic Review* 18, 1 (New Delhi), (1983). For a more recent and sharply critical view, see Dr. R. J. Chelliah's T. T. Krishmamachari Memorial Lecture, *The Hindu* (Madras), (8 March 1988).

16. The Third Pay Commission (1973) gave the breakdown but these figures have become dated. See *Census of Central Government Employees, 1980* (New Delhi: Directorate General of Employment and Training, Ministry of Labor and Rehabilitation, 1983), p. 8. See also *India 1986*.

17. The all-India services are the Indian Administrative Service, the Indian Police Service, and the Indian Forest Service. The more important other services are the Indian Foreign Service, Indian Audit and Accounts Service, Indian Revenue Service, Indian Postal Service, Central Health Service, Central Engineering Service, Indian Economic Service, and Indian Statistical Service.

18. For a comparative critical account of the all-India services, their evolution and continuance, see V. Subramaniam, "Some Administrative Aspects of Federalism in the Third World," *International Review of Administrative Sciences*, 50, 2 (Brussels). See also S. R. Maheshwari, "The All-India Services," *Public Administration* 49, 2 (London).

19. V. Subramaniam, *Social Background of India's Administrators* (New Delhi: Publications Division, Government of India, 1971), Chapter 1.

20. The Sarkaria Commission on Center-State Relations, appointed in 1982, submitted its 4,000-page report in mid–1987. The full report had not been made public as of March 1988, but a detailed official summary with extracts was released to the Indian press on 4, 5 February 1988. The same summary was made available through the Indian High Commission, Ottawa. Hereafter it will be referred to as Summary of Sarkaria Report.

21. Union Public Service Commission, 29th report 1978–79, New Delhi, p. 131. See also Subramaniam, *Social Background of India's Administrators*, Chapter 2.

22. Subramaniam, *Social Background of India's Administrators*; see Chapter 7, for details concerning socialization of young recruits in the values of their seniors and Chapter 6 for a discussion about reservation for Scheduled Castes.

23. S. R. Maheshwari, "The Constituency Linkage of National Legislators in India," *Legislative Studies Quarterly* 3, (New Delhi, August 1976). For a comparative view on politicized civil services, see V. Subramaniam, "Politicized Administration," *International Review of Administrative Sciences*, 43, 4.

24. S. C. Verma, a former chief secretary of Madhya Pradesh and secretary to the Government of India. Verma sought premature retirement from the IAS. *The Indian Express* (18 January 1983).

25. For a more detailed discussion of the administration of States, see S. R. Maheshwari, *State Governments in India* (New Delhi: Macmillan, 1979).

26. Of these, education, originally a State subject, was made a concurrent subject by a constitutional amendment in 1976.

27. Summary of Sarkaria Report.

28. A member of the IAS becomes a district collector in the fourth or fifth year of his service, and the average stay of a district collector in a district is between one year and eighteen months.

29. The numbers of State civil services in 1980 according to official figures were as follows: Andhra Pradesh—285,576; Assam—100,660; Bihar—244,590; Gujarat—134,771; Haryana—187,427; Himachal Pradesh—N. A.; Jammu-Kashmir—N. A.; Kar-

nataka—283,614; Kerala—260,549; Madhya Pradesh—501,834; Maharashtra—338,707; Manipur—23,951; Meghalaya—20,005; Nagaland—34,815; Orissa—148,790; Punjab—259,801; Rajasthan—287,772; Sikkim—N. A.; Tamil Nadu—402,361; Tripura—26,202; Uttar Pradesh—378,865; West Bengal—313,717.

30. For a more detailed discussion of local government in India see S. R. Maheshwari, *Local Government in India* (Agra: Lakshmi Narain Agarwal, 1984), 3d. ed. See also B. S. Khanna and S. Bhatnagar, "India," Chapter 36, in Donald C. Rowat (ed.), *International Handbook of Local Government Reorganization: Contemporary Developments*, (Westport, Conn.: Greenwood Press, 1980).

31. For a sociohistorical explanation of the pro-centralizing attitude in India and postcolonial states in general, see V. Subramaniam, "Developing Countries," Chapter 47, in Rowat (ed.), *International Handbook on Local Government Reorganization*.

32. Summary of Sarkaria Report

33. The complete text of the Sarkaria Report was later submitted to both houses of Parliament. It was "adopted" without much detailed debate because it was overshadowed by several other issues such as the Indo-Sri Lanka agreement enabling India to send an Indian Peace Keeping Force to Sri Lanka; the Thakkar report which was critical about the security arrangements related to the assassination of former Prime Minister Indira Gandhi; and the bitter election campaign in the State of Tamilnadu, where the Congress party lost heavily.

But the whole issue of centralization versus decentralization was revived in a different way by the ruling Congress government at the center with a new proposal to give more powers and financial support to the local government institutions namely Panchayati Raj (village councils) and urban councils through two Constitution amendment bills passed by the lower house of Parliament, called Lok Sabha, in June 1989. The idea was mooted in March by the Congress government at the center, and the Congress party, and was strongly criticized by opposition parties as a way of weakening State governments run by non-Congress parties and as a gimmick to fight the elections in 1989. The two bills, one for Panchayati Raj and the other for urban councils provide for (1) uniform simultaneous countrywide direct elections under the supervision of the All India Election Commission every five years, (2) ensuring devolution of powers and responsibilities to these bodies by the State legislatures, and (3) the setting up of two Finance commissions for Panchayati Raj and urban councils respectively for determining grants-in-aid and assignment of taxes by the State legislature and auditing of their accounts by the Auditor General of India. The bills were passed by the overwhelming Congress majority in the Lok Sabha but could not secure the necessary two-thirds majority in the upper house called Rajya Sabha. Since then, the Congress party itself has been defeated in the general election of 1989.

It is difficult to foresee the changes in Indian public administration if the bills are passed and entrenched in the Constitution. They can lead to greater administrative centralization if the local bodies are to be helped in their daily administration by an expanded Indian Administrative Service, already controlling top administration in State governments. On the other hand, if "grass roots level democracy" as it is described by the Congress takes shape, there may arise a considerable amount of decentralization. If however the elections to these bodies are fought by the same parties at the State and All India levels, a general balance of power may take shape.

34. For an account of one of the major reform exercises, exercise, see S. R. Ma-

heshwari, *The Administrative Reform Commission* (Agra: Lakshmi Narain Agarwal, 1972).

35. For a detailed account of the ombudsman in India, see Donald C. Rowat, "The State Ombudsmen in India," *Indian Journal of Public Administration* 30, 1 (New Delhi), (January-March 1984).

36. From the late 1970s through the 1980s, the politics of States like Gujarat was befuddled by the problems arising out of the special reservation for the Scheduled Castes in government jobs and educational institutions. Upper caste groups strongly opposed it, and the resulting public violence created a law and order problem for the State ministries, leading to the imposition of presidential rule. A substantial amount of the evidence presented before the Sarkaria Commission was from pro- and antireservationist lobbies.

4

PAKISTAN

Nasir Islam

HISTORICAL INTRODUCTION: THE PERSISTING COLONIAL LEGACY

Pakistan has often been called an administrative state or a bureaucratic polity. Since independence, for almost three out of four decades, Pakistan's political system has been dominated by a coalition of civilian and military bureaucrats. They have fulfilled not only the administrative functions of rule-application, but also the political functions of rule making, interest aggregation, and interest articulation.[1] They have created a highly centralized administrative system in which almost all decisions of any policy significance are made by the officials who occupy the top echelons of the central government. Pakistan has had a federal form of government, but it has virtually functioned as a unitary regime. Part of the reason for this state of affairs is the persisting colonial legacy, and part of it may be attributed to the country's class structure and the political system.

The colonial administration in India had worked under a viceregal system in which the viceroy, the apex of power in India, was the sole agent of the British Crown. The viceroy implemented the British imperialist policies through the permanent secretaries and provincial governors who were directly responsible to him. The governors, in turn, administered their provinces through a network of secretariat officers and field representatives–divisional commissioners and collectors/deputy commissioners. An overwhelming majority of these function- aries belonged to the elite corps of civil servants—the Indian Civil Service (ICS), which came to be known as the steel frame of colonial administration in India (see Chapter 3).

The concept of the ICS originated in Thomas Babington Macaulay's renowned speech in Parliament in 1853 advocating a competitive examination to select higher civil servants.[2] The examination he and Benjamin Jowett of Balliol designed was a highly classical, generalist one. The system for entry was so designed as to permit only people with superior education to get through. As a result the exclusive, elite character of the cadre was preserved. Almost all the important positions dealing with policy and administrative issues were reserved for the ICS cadre.[3] Relatively high salaries, secure tenure, and a wide range of discretionary powers reinforced their elite character.[4] Although the natives were gradually allowed to enter the ICS, 608 (52.1 percent) out of a total of 1,157 officers were British at the time of independence.[5] According to Asaf Hussain, the natives who were accepted into the cadre were "marginal men." They were highly westernized in outlook and identified not only with the institution of the ICS, but also with the colonial political system.[6] The members of the ICS developed a paternalistic attitude toward people early in their career, when they occupied the positions of assistant collectors/commissioners and collectors/deputy commissioners.[7] Although these positions were the lowest in the hierarchy of the ICS, they conferred a great deal of discretionary powers on its membership. They had direct access to senior members of this exclusive club, occupying the highest positions in the government hierarchy. The ICS has been described as "authoritarian in tone and content."[8] They would not tolerate outside interference, particularly by the native politicians. Describing the British bureaucratic attitude toward politics, Brian Chapman maintains that the civil servants used the term *administration* for the respectable part of government and *politics* for the less respectable part. This aptly fits the ICS view of native politics and politicians. The ICS was accustomed to exercising absolute power over politicians and not taking directions from them. "True political" activity was confined to Westminster and Whitehall where politicians could give policy direction to the Indian government.[9] But in India the ICS reigned supreme within the viceregal system. Consequently, the civil servants in British India, particularly the ICS, "had no experience of working with the politician as an equal partner, let alone of accepting him as a superior."[10]

It has often been pointed out that there was an acute shortage of managerial talent when Pakistan came into existence. The ICS was considered to be the only repository of such talent, and some eighty-three Muslim ICS officers who opted to come to Pakistan were hardly enough to staff all the important policymaking positions. A group of fifty British ICS officers were recruited on contract to fill some of the most senior positions in the Pakistani administration. The argument that managerial talent was scarce rests almost exclusively on an analysis limited to the ICS-IPS (Indian Political Service) cadres.[11] There were certainly Muslim administrators and managers in the railways, postal, finance, and other specialist services of the central government as well as the provincial cadres. Instead of removing restrictions on these cadres and increasing their upward mobility, the Pakistani government chose to form the Pakistan Administrative

Service, later renamed the Civil Service of Pakistan (CSP). The CSP cadre was composed of some 157 officers: 95 former ICS officers (Muslim) who opted for Pakistan and 50 British ICS officers who were hired on contract. The rest were war service candidates. The CSP thus became the lineal descendant of the ICS-IPS tradition in Pakistan in law as well as in spirit.[12]

The Quaid-e-Azam Mohammad Ali Jinnah, chose to be the governor general of Pakistan instead of the prime minister. The adapted Government of India Act 1935 was imposed as the first Constitution, creating a highly centralized government. Three out of four provincial governors under Jinnah were British ICS officers. The chief commissioner of Baluchistan was also a British officer. The governor general (Jinnah) received advice directly from the British governors and senior secretaries, thereby undermining the position of the elected representatives. The tenor of this advice was that politicians were not allowing the government to function with its preindependence efficiency.[13]

The key positions with responsibility and authority to control the administrative system were filled with British ICS officers. The powerful Establishment Division, which had critical responsibilities for administrative reorganization, service rules, and personnel matters for the CSP, was headed by the British ICS officers from 1947 to 1961. The only exception was the one-year tenure of A. R. Khan, a member of the former ICS, in 1959. The Organization and Methods (O and M) unit within the Establishment Division was the responsibility of a British IPS officer for almost six years. Other sections of the division were also headed by British officers. The Civil Service Academy of Pakistan, the citadel of the elitist orthodoxy, was administered by Geoffrey Burgess, an ICS officer, from 1951 to 1960. It appears that most of reorganization and reform activity was also controlled by senior British officers. In addition, the most crucial policy-making positions, such as the finance secretary or agriculture secretary, were also occupied by British ICS officers for the first few years of Pakistan's existence.[14]

The highly centralized, colonial constitutional apparatus and the British ICS officers thus set the tone and tenor of Pakistani Public Administration in its formative years. The CSP which took over the control and leadership of the administration was probably "more British than the British themselves." The younger generation of the CSPs not only inherited the ICS traditions, but also internalized them through training and indoctrination.[15]

Recruitment to the Central Superior Services (CSS), including the CSP, was based on a rigorous written examination emphasizing the values of classical generalist traditions. Training in the Civil Service Academy also followed the British pattern and emphasized the generalist and elitist traditions. The academy instilled in the CSP probationers a sense of belonging to a privileged group which had a major responsibility for the future of governing Pakistan.[16] It has been pointed out that the academy promoted westernized social graces: formal dress codes, tennis, riding kits, and membership in the Gymkhana Club. The academy, in its earlier days, was lodged in a magnificent colonial building with massive grounds and gardens. This "sartorial splendor served to detach if not alienate the probationers from the larger society."[17] Maulvi Fareed Ahmed, speaking in the National Assembly of Pakistan, called the academy a "manufacturing laboratory" for producing "Anglicised officers."[18] This perception of the academy as a relic of the Raj and British elitism was widely shared by the politicians and other professionals in the late 1950s and early 1960s.

The British tradition of classical generalism was further strengthened by the preservation and continuation of the policy-administration dichotomy. The government of Pakistan remained organized into a secretariat (a group of ministries and divisions) responsible for policy formulation and attached departments charged with executing policies and providing specialist advice. Specialists were generally not allowed to hold senior policy positions, most of these being reserved for the CSP generalists. In the field, the British model remained intact in the form of the district administration under the deputy commissioner. A large majority of the latter positions were also reserved for the CSP.

The British/ICS legacy produced some brilliant officers of great integrity and dedication. They served and sustained Pakistan in very trying circumstances and chaotic conditions. In the long run, through an elitist system the CSP accumulated power, prestige, and pre-eminence. It developed vested interests. To preserve its privileged position, it often resisted administrative reform and innovation.

THE ENVIRONMENTAL CONTEXT AND PUBLIC ADMINISTRATION

The relationship between the public bureaucracy and the politicians has varied from one political regime to the other. Under the Quaid-e-Azam and his prime minister, Liaquat Ali Khan, the senior bureaucracy was composed of powerful ICS officers. These officers had a great deal of influence over the decision-making process, but the supremacy of the political leaders was beyond question. Even in the provinces, the governments of Khan Abdul Quyyum, Mumtaz Daulatana, Maulvi Tamizzuddin, and Khurro appeared to contain the influence and power of the civil servants.[19] The Muslim League—the party in power—was a relatively united political party under Jinnah and Liaquat. Its main support came from the urban middle class, commercial groups, and larger refugee populations of the urban centers who had migrated from India. Most of the landlords—the feudals—had been lying low. They had generally not supported the Pakistan movement or had given lukewarm support to the Muslim League.[20] The Muslim League had just successfully emerged from a struggle for independence. These factors had given a great deal of legitimacy to the politicians and had strengthened their hand against other contenders of power. The Muslim League politicians in important political positions were seasoned politicians with years of experience in legislative and executive positions.

After Jinnah's death and Liaquat's assassination, the Muslim League began to disintegrate and factional politics took over. Politicians failed to agree on a constitution. The Muslim League was divided into at least seven or eight political factions which formed a succession of short-lived regimes at the center. Provincial governments were in a similar state of disarray. S. J. Burki maintains that these political conditions produced a power vacuum that the bureaucracy, particularly the Civil Service of Pakistan, willingly filled.[21] Khalid B. Sayeed refers to the relatively more active role played by the civil servants. Iskandar Mirza, the fourth governor general, floated a political party to disrupt the Muslim League. Before Mirza, another governor-general had dismissed an elected prime minister of the country and later a freshly elected government in the province of East Pakistan. As Sayeed maintains: "Civil Servants who had worked in the districts and the provinces had mastered all the methods of manipulating the feudal, ethnic and political factors."[22] The bureaucracy has been generally accused of preventing the growth of democratic local self-government. During 1953–1962, an alliance was forged between the feudals and the bureaucrats. The landlords had experience working closely with the colonial bureaucracy and felt quite comfortable with the CSP—the descendants of the ICS whom the feudals fondly remembered. Pakistan was thus transformed into an administrative state or a bureaucratic polity. A weak facade of democratic institutions still existed; it lacked political legitimacy. The real power had been transferred to the senior bureaucracy.

This period witnessed a thriving and expanding bureaucracy and increased government intervention in the economy. The Pakistan Industrial Development Corporation (PIDC), under bureaucratic management, launched many new ventures in the industrial sector. According to Burki, the landlord-bureaucracy alliance used the PIDC to reduce the power of urban industrialists. The PIDC and other government credit agencies provided the technical/managerial know-how and finances to transform feudal landlords into industrial entrepreneurs.[23]

After the military takeover of 1958, the army and the bureaucracy did not develop an instant alliance. Albert Gorvine believes that the army–civil service entente came not at the beginning but during the course of the revolution.[24] Sayeed, however, believes that the martial law regime was a partnership between the civil service and the military. It is true that in the beginning this regime at least partially blamed the CSP for Pakistan's political disaster.[25] The army appointed its own officers to important civilian positions and intended to run the administration. The Ayub Cabinet was making policy decisions instead of leaving them to the secretariat staff. They appointed a Pay and Services Commission headed by Justice A. R. Cornelius, the chief justice of the Supreme Court. Thirty CSP officers were fired on charges of corruption and misconduct.

Over time, however, the army–civil service relationship improved, with two sectors becoming dependent on each other. The army had to retreat to the barracks. Gradually, the reliance of the Ayub regime on the civil bureaucracy increased. The CSP was able to convince the army leadership that a highly trained cadre of generalists was needed to coordinate the specialist programs and to preserve the unity of the country. The Ayub regime shelved the Cornelius Report and its sweeping recommendations for change. Although the central structure of the public services and secretariat organization remained intact, the Ayub regime made other additions to Pakistan's public administration, which in the long run reduced the power of the generalist cadre. The Ayub government developed elaborate planning machinery and created the Planning Commission, an organization that attracted a large number of highly qualified economists, statisticians, and technocrats. This development strengthened the technical control over the planning process and challenged the influence of the CSP. The Ayub government also established autonomous state enterprises like the Water and Power Development Authority, agricultural corporations, and industrial development corporations which were outside the jurisdiction of the traditional departments. This led to a subtle shift of power and influence away from the traditional departmental bureaucracies. The government created an economic pool of managers to staff positions in the Finance, Commerce, and Economic Affairs ministries. Forty percent of the recruitment to the economic pool was opened to the non-CSP cadres of the central government.

The mass movement which brought an end to the Ayub regime in 1969 was begun by students, urban industrial workers, and politicians. Interestingly enough, it was joined and actively supported by the professional civil servants. Doctors, engineers, and college teachers who worked for the government took to the streets in the thousands, protesting against the military–CSP oligarchy. They demanded better conditions of service and implementation of the Cornelius Commission's recommendations on administrative reorganization. These protests revealed the bitter feelings of the specialist government servants toward the elitist CSP.[26] The Yahya government gave its administration a distinct military cast. Robert Laporte, quoting an anonymous source, maintains that the distance between the army and the bureaucracy was greater under Yahya than at any other time in the history of Pakistan. Many important positions were staffed by army personnel. The onslaught of the Yahya regime and the Bangladesh secession took its toll on the Civil Service of Pakistan.[27] For more than two decades the CSP had enjoyed such power and influence that it was able to prevent all administrative reform from threatening its special status. The classical generalist tradition, the elite position of the CSP in the public service hierarchy, special privileges and promotion facilities, and the secretariat structures all remained intact until the end of the Yahya regime.

The Bhutto government brought a new constitution in 1973. The Constitution provided a parliamentary form of government with two chambers: a National Assembly with 200 seats and a Senate with 40 seats equally allocated to four provinces. The prime minister was to be elected by a majority of the National Assembly. The removal of the prime minister was quite difficult under the Constitution. Unlike the two previous constitutions adopted by the Pakistani leaders in 1956 and 1962, the 1973 Constitution did not provide any security for the civil servants. The previous documents had provided that the civil servants could only be dismissed with cause. The civil servants had recourse to the courts to defend and uphold their rights.

The Bhutto regime proposed sweeping reforms in the public service structure of Pakistan. For the first time in the history of Pakistan, a government could muster the political will to change the power structure through administrative reform. Prime Minister Bhutto's major motive was to establish political supremacy over the senior bureaucracy and to break the power monopoly of the CSP. Bhutto, as leader of the People's Party of Pakistan (PPP) had directly experienced the heavy hand of the bureaucracy in curbing the basic political freedoms of the people. Senior government officials, the chief secretaries, and the divisional commissioners had used a battery of laws to prevent Bhutto from holding protest rallies against the Ayub regime.[28] They had also used force and other dirty tricks to sabotage Bhutto's rise to power. Bhutto aptly described this period of the Ayub regime as *Naukershahi*—literally the reign of the servants.

It has been pointed out that Bhutto foresaw the discretionary powers of the CSP officials as an obstacle to the exercise of the superpowers concentrated in the office of the prime minister under the 1973 Constitution. He wanted politicians to have greater freedom to make decisions, and he wanted to make the bureaucracy accountable to the people's representatives. Senior bureaucrats had already begun to oppose Bhutto's ideological program of nationalization. Administrative reform also provided a source of patronage and placement of Bhutto loyalists in important positions.[29] One should not forget that Bhutto had come to power at the crest of a mass movement, whose major demand was to dislodge the elitist bureaucracy from its monopoly position. The professionals and specialists working within the government actively supported this demand.

Bhutto began his tenure by dismissing 1,300 civil servants,[30] including some senior CSP officials of the highest ranks. The public service structure was completely changed. The CSP lost its elite position and all the various cadres and services were merged into unified grades. The training system underwent important changes. For the first time in Pakistan's history, lateral entry to middle and senior ranks of the public service was built into the system. These were sweeping changes, particularly in the context of the history of administrative reforms in Pakistan. Since independence, the CSP had successfully been able to shelve all reforms which proposed any modification in their elite status. Burki refers to these reforms as the bending of the steel frame.[31] This was probably the first time that a civilian government had been able to establish political supremacy over the administrative organization and the bureaucracy.

The Bhutto regime was able to implement far-reaching administrative reforms with relative ease and in a very short span of time. What were the reasons for this success? First, his government had come to power through a free election with an overwhelming mandate. Second, the leader of the government enjoyed national status and was personally very popular among the masses. Third, a relatively united political party provided a legitimate power base to the leadership.

Fourth, the political leadership—particularly the central cabinet—was composed of able politicians, professionals with experience, intellect, and political clout.

Over time, the PPP lost momentum in developing and implementing new programs. Reform to change the structure of the economy and the society had originated from the urban-oriented radical left of the PPP coalition. These reforms were designed to increase income and access to public services of the poorer section of the population. At the same time, these policies discriminated against some of the most powerful urban and rural groups. The tensions that were created by these reforms eventually led to the departure of the most influential leftist leaders from the PPP.[32] By 1974, major cabinet positions were filled by center-right professionals, businesspeople, and landlords. Most of them were political unknowns. The bureaucracy thus reemerged as a powerful influence in the policy process but did not regain the same supremacy it had enjoyed during the Ayub era, particularly because of the personal, autocratic style of Prime Minister Bhutto.

Under the Zia regime, Pakistan reverted to martial law. The army bureaucracy nexus emerged as the predominant influence over public administration and public policy. The presence of the martial law administration was more overwhelming and more visible. A parallel hierarchy of military officers responsible for important civil functions exercised judicial and executive authority. All political power was concentrated in Zia as the chief martial law administrator (CMLA) and in his corp commanders who acted as zonal/provincial martial law administrators. They also controlled the civil machinery of administration as the president and the provincial governors. At the field level, every division and district had a martial law administrator of the rank of colonel/brigadier and major, respectively. This hierarchy not only made policy, but also interferred with day-to-day administration wherever and whenever they considered it appropriate. A great number of positions in state-owned enterprises and government were staffed with military personnel. The civil servants who had identified with the Bhutto regime were retired or dismissed. In some cases, the fate of an entire departmental organization was left in limbo because the new government had not decided what to do with programs and personnel closely identified with the previous regime. Scores of committees were appointed to review the conduct of the various groups of public servants. Many officials who were fired or retired prematurely by the Bhutto regime were allowed back into the civil service.

General Zia-ul Haq gradually "civilianized" and "politicized" his administration under pressure from national and international sources. The civilian bureaucracy began to assert itself and re-emerged as a powerful group. The former CSP cadre and its successor, the District Management Group, seem to have regained a great deal of power and prestige. A large number of senior policy and administrative positions are presently occupied by members of the former CSP cadre. With the elections of the National Assembly and the emergence of a civilian cabinet, a new generation of politicians gradually began to assert itself on the political scene. At least some of them are educated and socialized in the

LIBRARY OF MOUNT ST. MARY'S COLLEGE

postindependence era. They are to some extent free from the Ma-Bap (paternalistic) image of the bureaucracy. General Zia would have continued as president (with at least a five-year mandate) and the chief of army staff, with the military remaining the most powerful group in the political system. The dismissal of the cabinet in June 1988 upset the civilian army equilibrium but left the bureaucracy pretty much in power. Zia's death later that year followed by free elections and the assumption of power by Benazir Bhutto as prime minister has imposed some real limits on the power of the military-bureaucracy nexus, though they still remain the most potent force in the political system.

THE ORGANIZATIONAL STRUCTURE OF THE CENTRAL GOVERNMENT

The central government is composed of a two-tier structure: a secretariat for policy formulation and a host of attached departments or subordinate offices for policy implementation, exactly as in India. The secretariat consists of divisions and ministries. The division is the basic unit of organization in the secretariat, and it is organized as a single-purpose department. Most of the ministries are composed of one division, and six or seven ministries contain more than one division. The Ministry of Defense, for example, consists of Defense, Defense Production, and Aviation divisions.

As of 1987, the central secretariat has included forty-two divisions and numerous attached departments. In addition, there are secretariat offices for the president, the prime minister, and the National Assembly. These divisions are staffed by 2,561 senior policy-making officers (Grade 17 and above) and 12,438 clerical and other staff (Grade 16 and below).[33] In traditional public administration parlance, the attached departments are line organizations. They are usually staffed with specialists in various functional areas. The technical experts from the attached departments provide advice and information to the secretariat policy makers. But they are removed from the policy formulation area and are responsible mainly for administration.

The distinction between the secretariat and attached departments (and hence between policy and administration) is an anachronism of the colonial period. Policy making was considered a generalist function as opposed to a specialist activity. The majority of the senior positions in the secretariat were reserved for the ICS generalists. This practice continued to exist in Pakistan after Partition. The CSP and their successors—the District Management Group (DMG) and the Tribal Areas Group (TAG)—have continued to enjoy the near monopoly of senior secretariat positions, namely, deputy secretary, the joint secretary, and the secretary.

Public administration consultants hired from abroad have consistently recommended that this system be changed. Bernard Gladieux, for example, called for opening the top administrative positions to all competitors. He recommended that the secretary to government have the generalist and specialist professional qualifications.[34] The Cornelius Commission thought it not prudent to segregate the policy-making and operational functions. According to the commission, most foreign experts would like to see the integration of the secretariat with field departments. The commission recommended that the position of the secretary become chef de cabinet, a staff position of a policy specialist to advise the ministers. The heads of the operational departments should have policy-making functions, and they should be in direct contact with the ministers.[35] Almost two decades later another Reform Commission recommended that the top policy-making positions be accessible to the specialists. The reservation of such positions for generalists should be discontinued. The secretary's status should be lower than that of the executive head of an operating department.[36] These recommendations have been vehemently opposed by the generalist groups in the civil service. They have yet to be implemented. Meanwhile, the generalist orientation continues to be the dominant influence in the Pakistani Central Secretariat. The provincial secretariats have exactly the same organizational system and the same generalist bias.

The field experience gained by the DMG/TAG (and the former CSP) in the field is no doubt an asset for policy-making and coordination functions. It gives a breadth of vision and an understanding of the environment at the field level in which the policies formulated in the secretariat are eventually implemented. Over time many members of the CSP/DMG group have also acquired foreign training in economics and public administration. They are not really the literary generalists, soaked in the humanities tradition of the nineteenth-century ICS type. By far, the majority of them are eminently qualified for policy-making jobs. But reservation of positions for these generalists demoralizes the professional specialists and affects their motivation. These specialists' bitter protest at the end of the Ayub era was symptomatic of this malaise.

THE STATE ENTERPRISES

In addition to the secretariat divisions and attached departments, there is a third type of government agency: the state-owned enterprise (SOE) or autonomous body as it is called in Pakistan. State enterprises are generally attached to a supervisory ministry. The major state enterprises of an industrial nature are grouped together under the Ministry of Production. From a recent manual of the O and M Division, we compiled a list of at least seventy-seven corporations and autonomous bodies of the central government.[37] This list does not include numerous boards, councils, and institutes of research. Most of the state enterprises involved in industrial production are grouped together in a number of holding corporations. The Pakistan Automobile Corporation, for example, is composed of twelve companies. The Pakistan Industrial Development Corporation (PIDC) is a group of thirteen companies, and the Federal Chemical and Ceramic Corporation has fifteen units. The State Engineering Corporation owns twelve units.[38] There are sixty-six operating units grouped under holding companies, and they have autonomous boards of directors. These corporations operate under the overall supervision of the Ministry of Production.[39]

The earliest documentation of Pakistan's industrial policy reveals that the government's direct participation in industrial activity was to be limited to arms and ammunition, hydroelectric power, and the manufacture and operation of railways, telephone, and telegraph industries.[40] The PIDC was set up in 1950 to promote industry where the private entrepreneurs were not willing to venture—mainly in the sectors of heavy engineering, chemicals, fertilizers, and jute in former East Pakistan.[41] The motives behind the creation of public enterprises were purely pragmatic and not ideological. The business sector did not consider government activities in these sectors as hostile intervention. In fact, complementarity and healthy rivalry existed between the government enterprises and the business sector. There were many successful joint ventures between government and the private sector industrialists.[42]

Shahid Javed Burki attributes hidden political motives to the creation of state enterprises in mid–1950s. With the decline of the power of the Karachi refugee groups, the government began to give serious consideration to creating a new class of entrepreneurs belonging to the indigenous feudal classes of the Panjab and the Northwest Frontier Province. Since the feudals did not have liquid assets and technical and managerial know-how, the PIDC was used as the framework to provide these inputs.[43]

The PIDC quickly emerged as an important force in the industrial sector. By 1959, PIDC assets amounted to 16 percent of the country's industrial wealth, and its personnel represented 20 percent of total industrial employment. Toward the end of 1950s, the PIDC had become the largest industrial conglomerate in the country.[44] It has achieved remarkable success in introducing new entrepreneurs into Pakistan's industrial sector. In the late 1950s and 1960s, it created many state enterprises and successfully privatized them. However, if measured by market indicators, the performance of PIDC was not so remarkable. Its rates of profit and of return were much lower than those of the private sector firms. This had prompted economists to conclude that the reliance of Pakistani government on state enterprises for industrialization was an inefficient strategy.[45]

During the Bhutto regime, the role of the public sector assumed far greater importance than at any other period in the past. Instead of playing the role of a catalyst, public enterprises were used to acquire control of "the commanding heights of the economy." These enterprises were also to become the instrument of reducing socioeconomic disparities and to make public services more accessible to ordinary people. Consequently, in a first wave of nationalization, thirty-one large firms in basic industries—heavy engineering, automobile, petrochemicals, cement, and so on, were taken over. Later, many banks, insurance companies, and textile mills were nationalized. A third wave even took over the vegetable oil industries. The business sector became alienated from the government, and there was a large-scale flight of capital and managerial skills abroad.[46]

Since 1977, the pendulum has again swung in the opposite direction. Government began by assuring business that there would be no more takeovers of industry and began to emphasize the consolidation of SOE and slow denationalization. Rice mills, flour mills, cotton ginning factories, and vegetable oil concerns were first to be privatized because they were having managerial difficulties.[47] According to World Bank reports, in the 1980s, Pakistan has been at the forefront of developing countries that are effectively privatizing and reforming state enterprises.[48]

According to Majid Mufti, a former secretary of the Ministry of Production, in 1972 the newly nationalized companies suffered cumulative losses of Rs. 235 million. This situation was further aggravated by subsequent mismanagement. Pakistan has a long tradition of imposing bureaucratic management on public enterprises. Since the creation of the PIDC, these enterprises have been run by generalist civil servants and retired army personnel. During the Ayub regime, eighty-five civil servants occupied the most senior positions in public enterprises.[49] Initially, the Bhutto regime hired professionals to manage the public enterprises. But a paucity of managerial skills and pressures from the PPP led to a large number of patronage appointments.[50] In the 1950s and 1960s almost one-third of the directors were appointed from the elite industrial families of Pakistan. The CEOs and the financial directors came exclusively from the senior government officials.[51]

The supervisory and other ministries have a great deal of control over the public enterprises attached to them. Instead of exercising control to ensure accountability, this power has been used to interfere with the enterprise's day-to-day administration and internal decisions. The governments have failed to design appropriate organizational arrangements for the mobilization of resources and overseeing the performance of the public enterprises. Administrative procedures and structures designed to run ordinary departments, obviously unsuited to industrial and commercial enterprises, have been frequently imposed on these bodies. According to Majid Mufti, a public enterprise's investment decision has to pass through as many as seven decision points. Once the project has been approved, the financing approval often involves nine different organizations. At least four government agencies are involved in pricing decisions.[52] Evidently, this procedure leads to tremendous delays, which often leaves the final decision outcomes out of step with the economic circumstances. The delays also result in enormous cost overruns. As Jeffrey Pressman and Aaron Wildavsky concluded in their now classic implementation study, the greater the number of decision (approval) points, the lesser the chance of decision implementation.[53]

During the 1980s, the government has embarked on a reform program. Autonomous boards of directors have been appointed for each production unit, some unnecessary administrative tiers have been eliminated, and the relationship between operating units and holding companies has been redefined. The government has also initiated a program of privatization and divestiture. The companies considered totally inefficient and beyond redemption are slowly being eliminated and others denationalized.[54] These initiatives are far-reaching, and their impact will be felt in years to come.

The search for performance evaluation criteria and managerial incentives has emerged as the key issue in the management of state enterprises in developing countries. Major problems arise from the multiplicity of objectives imposed on these enterprises by the governments and politicians. The public enterprises are often expected to fulfill social objectives like the reduction of economic disparity and the accessibility of services to the poor segments of society. At the same time, these agencies are expected to perform according to the market criteria of rates of return and profitability. An effort has been made in recent years to devise performance evaluation systems that distinguish between the social and economic objectives. The *contrat de plan* originated in France is one such device being used in the French West African countries.[55]

Pakistan has developed a signalling system for its public enterprises in the manufacturing sector. The system basically aims at monitoring performance and provides incentives to management. It links bonus payments to tangible, quantifiable performance targets. The system is composed of three elements: information system, performance evaluation and bonus. Monthly data on production, costs, salaries, profits, taxes, inventories, capacity utilization, and employment are fed into a computerized information system in the Ministry of Production. The performance evaluation system is based on the concept of public profitability. Public profits are calculated by adding direct taxes, interest payments, and depreciation and by subtracting financial incomes, opportunity costs of working capital, and subsidies. Adjustments for social objectives are made. At the beginning of the year, the Ministry of Production negotiates with the company management the annual targets for each production unit, and at the end of the year it evaluates performance in terms of public profitability. The performance of the enterprises is graded into five categories from A to E. A bonus amounting to three months' salary is paid to managers of firms in category A, two months for category B, one month for category C, half a month for category D, and none for category E. All employees in managerial grades are entitled to bonuses. Actual distribution of the bonus is left to the discretion of the senior management group.[56] During the first year of implementation, eleven out of sixty-one units under the Ministry of Production received an "A" grade; five units received grade "B"; nine units grade "C"; one unit grade "D"; and fifteen units grade "E."[57] The system is limited to the industrial enterprises under the Production Ministry.

Pakistan's public sector is small in terms of its share in the country's gross national product (GNP), but it is composed of strategic industries such as steel, cement, fertilizers, chemicals, and oil and gas. In the transport sector, with the exception of road transport, other industries like railways, aviation, shipping, and ports are wholly owned and controlled by the government. According to the Economic Survey of 1984–1985, the government has invested Rs. 24 billion

($1.6 billion U.S.) in the manufacturing sector alone. Despite its contribution to industrialization, some doubts are being raised about public sector performance and efficiency.[58]

Pakistan Steel Mill was created at a cost of Rs. 24,700 million. It was expected to change the structure of the country's economy by ensuring the much-needed supply of steel and steel products. Since production began in 1980–1981, it has shown accumulated losses of Rs. 5,352 million. The Pakistan Industrial Development Corporation has also been posting losses in recent years.[59] Other corporations under the Ministry of Production which had shown pretax profits in the early 1980s are now posting declining profits. However, in line with the government's policy of rationalizing the public sector, overall employment in the public enterprise sector has begun to decline.[60]

Scores of other commercial enterprises are under the supervision of functional ministries which are still plodding along in their conventional, inefficient way. The success of the system depends largely on determining the appropriate performance targets through negotiation. Designing a social adjustment account and making a plus or minus adjustment still remains a relatively ambiguous element in the signalling system.

Public Service Structure and Personnel Management

Pakistan inherited a public service structure based on rank classification rather than position classification. Basically, the classification system of colonial administration in India remained intact until 1973. A few changes were made in the names of various cadres, and a few new services or cadres were added over time. The classification system which persisted until 1973 was both horizontal and vertical. Horizontally, the services were classified into three main categories: (1) a generalist administrative service, the Civil Service of Pakistan (CSP); (2) functional services like the Pakistan Foreign Service (PFS), the Police Service of Pakistan (PSP), and the Audit and Accounts Service (PAAS); and (3) the Specialist or Technical Services, like engineering, health, education, and scientific services. A third dimension in the classification system was the division between the All-Pakistan Services CSP and PSP and the Central Services.[61]

The members of the all-Pakistan cadres rotated between the central and provincial governments exactly as the all-India services did in India. The entrants into the CSP began their service in the field as part of the provincial administrative structures, as did the recruits of the Police Service. After acquiring a certain seniority, these officers could move freely between the central and the provincial governments, as their predecessors did under the British.

A university degree was the requisite qualification to enter Class I and Class II services (see Table 4.1). In practice, the recruits often had Master's or other postgraduate academic degrees. Class III was recruited on the basis of the lower academic or technical qualification, while Class IV imposed no such qualifications. The recruitment of Class I and Class II was done through the Public

Table 4.1
Classification of the Central Service (1947–1973)

cadres type / class	Generalist Services	Functional Services	Specialist-Technical Services
I	The Civil Service of Pakistan (CSP)	PFS, PSP, PAAS PRAS, PTS	Engineers, Scientists, Statisticians, Health Education professional
II	None	Immediate Super-visions 2nd level Super-visors Class II cadres of the above services	Assistant Engineers etc.
III	None	Office workers skilled workers	Skilled workers Technicians
IV	None	Unskilled workers	Unskilled workers

CSP-PSP = All Pakistan Services. The rest = Central Services

Service Commission. The appointing authority for the Class I services rested with the Establishment Division. Class II officers were appointed through the secretary to government, and the other two classes by much lower level officials.

The single most frequent criticism leveled against this classification system is the elitist character it has bestowed on the generalist cadre—the CSP.[62] This was achieved through restricting entry via a very rigorous competitive examination, keeping the cadre strength limited and reserving for the CSP a large number of policy positions in the secretariat and administrative positions in the line departments. In fact, the number of positions reserved for the CSP was always larger than the total strength of the cadre. The CSPs could move freely between field and headquarters, provinces and central government, and state enterprises and municipal bodies. This meant a quick promotion. Higher pay scales and perquisites attached to senior positions also conferred a special status on the CSP. The specialists/functional cadre officers often found themselves in subordinate positions to the CSP because of their limited mobility and reservation of senior positions for the generalists. This created a serious morale problem among the professional/specialist public servants.[63]

This classification scheme described above not only resembles the service structure in the United Kingdom before the Report of Lord Fulton's Enquiry Committee in 1968 with its hierarchy of four classes namely Administrative,

Executive, Clerical, and Messenger, but it also corresponds to the fourfold caste stratification in India: the Brahmins, Kshatriyas, Vaishyas, and Sudras. In fact, Prime Minister Bhutto once referred to the CSP as the Brahmins of the administrative structure.[64] After independence scores of commissions and committees had recommended the system be changed, but without any success. Bhutto's government finally reformed the classification system in 1973.

Twelve All-Pakistan and the Central Superior Services were disbanded. Horizontally, the central public services were classified into seventeen occupational groups along functional lines. The positions reserved for the CSP cadre (generalist/policy/administration) were placed in three different occupational groups. The field administration posts were classified into the new District Management Group (DMG). The policy positions in the Central Secretariat were allocated to the Secretariat Group. Lower level positions in the secretariat were grouped into an Office Management Group. A new Tribal Areas Group (TAG) was created to administer federally controlled tribal territories.

Three different accounts services were merged together into an Accounts Group. A new occupational group of Planners and Economists was created, grouping largely the positions in the Planning Commission and some other ministries. The final result of this regrouping exercise is represented in Table 4.2.

Modifications in the classification system were followed by changes in the pay structure. The government of Pakistan abolished the archaic and chaotic system of some 600 pay scales and replaced it with a Unified National Pay Scale consisting of 23 grades. The pay scales were again revised upward in 1977.[65]

The new scales were a substantial improvement in terms of equity, reducing disparities between the lowest paid employees and the highest paid officers. They also reduced the pay differentials between the specialists and the generalists. A full professor in a university has now been placed in the same grade as a secretary to the government and is entitled to same fringe benefits/nonfinancial incentives.

Charles H. Kennedy believes that these reforms achieved their main purpose and ''watered down'' the elite orientation of the service structure.[66] According to Robert Laporte, Jr., the impact of the Bhutto reforms on the capability of the public service to administer development has been negligible. The Zia government had taken steps to reverse some of the personnel changes introduced earlier.[67] Most of the people selected under the old CSP system have gone into the DMG/TAG/Secretariat groups. By seniority they still occupy the most important policy and field positions. However, the present system offers relatively more mobility to the specialists and the professionals than was the case before 1973.

THE RECRUITMENT PROCESS

Recruitment to the central public service for posts in grades 16 to 22 is done through the Federal Public Service Commission. A great majority of appointments is made at the level of grades 16 to 17, the rest being filled usually by

Table 4.2
Pre–1973 Service Cadres and Analogous Occupational Groups

Former Service Cadre	New Occupational Group
Civil Service of Pakistan (CSP) PCS (Provincial Civil Service) Secretariate Group (SG)	District Management Group (DMG) Tribal Areas Group (TAG)
Police Service of Pakistan (PSP)	Police Group
Foreign Service of Pakistan (PFS)	Foreign Affairs Group
Pakistan Audit & Accounts Service (PAAS) Pak. Military Accounts Service (PMAS)	Accounts Groups
Pak. Taxation Service (PTS)	Federal Revenues Group (Direct Taxes)
Pak. Customs and Excise Service (PLES)	Federal Revenues Group (Indirect Taxes)
Trade Service of Pakistan	Commerce Group
Information Service of Pakistan	Information Group
Pakistan Postal Service	Postal Group
Pak. Military Lands and Cantonment Service Central Secretariate Service	Cantonment Management Group Office Management Group
Pak. Railway Service	Railway Group
	Economists and Planners Group

promotion. The positions may be filled through direct recruitment (an interview by the commission) or through the written competitive examination. The positions in the groups with generalist/functional orientation are staffed by the competitive examination. The position of professors, economists, scientists, and the technical staff are generally filled through direct recruitment. A regional quota system on the basis of population is used to allocate positions to various provinces and regions. Panjab as the largest province (population-wise) receives approximately 48 percent of the positions. Ten percent of the positions are filled on a merit basis.

Traditionally, the recruits to the central superior services (and now the major occupational groups) have come from the middle and upper middle classes of Pakistani society. The academic background of the recruits selected through the competitive examination is predominantly in the social sciences and humanities. Few candidates with MBAs or MPAs tend to take the examination. Quite a large number have degrees in economics.

Women were originally allowed to enter only the Accounts and Taxation Services. It may be noted that women comprise only 3.6 percent of the employees in the central government. In the Panjab, they constitute 12 percent. Over time, women have become eligible for all services including the DMG Group. However, they continue to suffer from a relatively inhospitable environment in the public services. The government policy of transfers has had a particularly negative impact on women employees.[68] In 1970, out of 1,137 candidates who applied for the competitive examination, only eleven were women, and out of these only one was finally given a job.[69] In 1984, out of 2,074 candidates who appeared in the examination, seventy-one were women. Eighteen of these had qualified in the final examinations and received job offers.[70] However, the number of women has increased substantially in the traditionally female occupations and in some professions like medicine.

The competitive examination is a written essay-type examination and contains four required subjects: Islamiat (50 points), English (100), English Précis and Composition (50), and General Knowledge (250). Optional subjects (600) can be chosen from the social sciences, pure sciences, humanities, professional disciplines, and applied sciences. A majority of the candidates tend to choose social sciences and humanities. Candidates who qualify in the written examination go on to take the oral or the interview. After the interview, a battery of psychological tests is administered. There is no evidence as to the validity and reliability of the written tests or the interview.[71]

The present examination system does not relate the candidates' academic background to recruitment for a particular occupation. Engineers are often chosen for the Foreign Service, and people with social sciences or humanities backgrounds are chosen for the railways. People with accounting qualifications are not encouraged to join the Accounting Group. The Anwarul Haq Commission suggested that the examination system should be so devised as to make the candidate's educational background relevant to the professional requirements of the occupation.

The administrative reforms of 1973 also introduced the system of lateral entry to the central superior services. The idea behind this system was to infuse fresh blood from the private sector and other professions into the bureaucracy. Thus, it would have compensated for the bureaucratic inertia and at the same time introduced new managerial (marketing, finance) and other professional skills into the public service. In the beginning, the system of lateral entry apparently worked well, and some able people were inducted into the services. Later, the system was dominated by ministerial influence and political patronage. The Zia government vehemently criticized the system and called it a blatant attempt by the Bhutto regime to control the bureaucracy. The new government quickly abolished lateral recruitment and dismissed many officers recruited through the system.[72] This more or less amounted to throwing out the baby with the bath water. The system was certainly misused and became an instrument of patronage. Used judiciously, it could be a good vehicle to promote movement of personnel between the government and the business sector or the professions.

THE TRAINING INSTITUTIONS

A great deal of attention has been given to training in Pakistan. But Pakistan's training structures remain far from satisfactory. The Civil Service Academy, which was the main institution for the preservice training of the generalist/elitist cadre, was widely criticized in the past for producing literary generalists and arrogant civil servants.[73] The Ayub regime tried to modify the situation. The training programs at Oxford and Cambridge were discontinued in 1959. From 1964 to 1968, sixty-seven CSP officers were sent to the United States for training in public administration, economics, and community development. This trend continued during the 1970s and 1980s.

The concept of in-service training was introduced. Pakistan Administrative Staff College (PASC), the National Institutes of Public Administration (NIPAs), and the Pakistan Academy for Rural Development (PARD) were created to fill the gap in post-entry training.[74] The PASC occupies the summit of the in-service training system in Pakistan. It has been able to develop effectively, enabling linkages with the environment. During the last two decades of its existence, the principalship of the college remained in the hands of senior CSP officers. They were able to extract significant resources from the government and develop an excellent physical facility. Since most of them were steeped in the generalist tradition, they did not pay much attention to innovative training methodologies or relevant andragogical skills. Much less attention was paid to research, developing case studies on Pakistani administration, or recruiting professional trainers.

During the Bhutto regime, the principal of the college was a non-CSP officer, who became the most vehement and prolific critic of the CSP and Pakistan's traditionalist administrative structure.[75] During his tenure, the college played an active role in the reform movement of the early 1970s. The last principal, Dr. Tariq Siddiqui, was probably the ablest chief executive of the college. He belonged to the CSP cadre and thus had extensive experience in the field as well as policy positions. He also had a Ph.D. in public administration from Syracuse University. The college saw some significant changes during his tenure.

PASC provides training to senior civil servants. Those are usually executives of the rank of a joint secretary, a divisional commissioner, or heads of directorates. The potential trainees in the PASC are officers in Grade 20, due to be promoted to Grade 21. The training methodology is based on the famous syndicate method developed at Henley Staff College in the United Kingdom. The trainees are grouped into syndicates and are given a specific problem or policy issue to be resolved. They visit relevant field organizations, have group discussions, and prepare an extensive working paper on the subject. The PASC library possesses some extremely insightful materials developed by the participants. Unfortunately, these documents are not published. The training courses also feature a series of lectures from the best available people in their own fields. The Staff College has not been able to attract a highly qualified permanent staff. This is probably its major weakness.

The Academy for Administrative Training (Lahore) gives preservice training to the newly recruited Grade 17 officers, through the Combined Competitive Examination of the central government. The two NIPAs (Lahore and Karachi) are responsible for midcareer training for the middle-management-level officers (Grades 18–19). The PARD (Peshawar) is basically an institution established to impart training to the junior officers working in the rural areas.

The Anwar-ul-Haq Commission has severely criticized the in-service training arrangements in Pakistan. It has especially pointed to the lack of training facilities for professionals who enter administrative roles and to the virtual absence of training of lower-level officials. The latter group—the street-level bureaucrats—represents the most important interface between the people and the government. Their professional development is largely ignored. Despite the lip service paid by all governments, the actual allocation of resources to training is rather meagre and the training coverage is very limited. The training institutions do not have adequate autonomy. The senior officials often regard training as redundant or of little use. The training institutions have found it difficult to recruit professional trainers and retain them. Lack of adequate career prospects has been cited as the major reason for this difficulty.[76] With the exception of the PASC and the Pakistan Academy of Administrative Training (PAAT), the other institutions even find it difficult to attract suitable trainees. According to one evaluation, the majority of their participants were sent to their training courses for purposes other than improving their administrative capacity. Only sixteen out of one-hundred trainees in the sample were sent to the institution for training, preparatory to their forthcoming promotion.[77] The Anwar-ul-Haq Commission maintains that officers are seldom interested in or spared for in-service training, except when otherwise in difficulty.[78]

The commission recommended the creation of a Training Division and a National Training Council to coordinate the activities of the training institutions. But this would simply add another bureaucratic level to already overburdened institutions. What the institutions need are more autonomy, effective leadership, and qualified professional trainers, all of which would increase their legitimacy in the eyes of their clients—the organizations and individuals they serve. Pakistan should look toward the Indian Institute of Management (Ahmadabad) and the INTAN in Malaysia as models.[79]

The most fundamental problem, however, is to change the traditional approach to training. The classical training model brings participants out of their organizational environment into a classroom situation and then puts them back in the organization after training. This is a woefully inadequate approach. It does not disturb or change the basic environment of the client organization. Consequently, trainees find it very difficult to introduce into their organization, innovative techniques acquired through training. The training institutions have to take the training out to the field organizations, using a problem-solving, action-research approach. This will encourage the participation of practicing managers in training activity and expose trainers to the field experience. Recently, Pakistan's O and M Division, beefed up with new director-generals, has started experimenting with this approach.

PROMOTION PROSPECTS AND POLICIES

Government posts are grouped into two categories for the purposes of promotion: nonselection and selection posts. In the case of nonselection, the promotion is made on the basis of "seniority-cum-fitness." "Fitness" has never been operationally defined. Normally, promotion is granted to the most senior candidate unless he or she has been specifically declared unfit. Different departmental promotion committees, sometimes the same committees on different occasions, apply different yardsticks. For selection posts "merit" is considered the prime factor, seniority playing its part only when other things are equal. For positions in Grades 2–18, the promotion authority is vested in departmental committees, whereas for posts in Grades 19–21 the Central Selection Board of the federal government is the promotional authority.[80]

Since no rigorous performance evaluation system exists to determine "merit" or "fitness," seniority tends to have excessive weight. Even determination of seniority is sometimes problematic because people from various cadres have been merged into the unified grading system. The famous (or rather notorious) Annual Confidential Reports (ACRs), another legacy of the colonial past, usually form the basis for determining "merit" or "fitness." At least six different forms are used for ACRs for positions in different grades. The forms used for positions in Grade 16 and above are fairly elaborate. But it seems that the general emphasis is on subjective evaluation of the reporting officer rather than on any hard measures or performance indicators.[81]

Another significant issue that should be brought out is the differential in promotion prospects between various groups. Muneer Ahmed, a member of the Anwar-ul-Haq Commission, provides solid evidence indicating a serious gap between the promotion prospects of the specialists and the generalists. For the TAG group there exists a ratio of 2:1 for junior positions in Grades 16–18 and senior positions in Grade 20. For the DMG group the ratio is 7:1. The ratio for the same positions in the Economists and Planners Group is 9:1; for the Accountants Group 14:1; for the Agriculture Department 176:1; for the Health Group 454:1; and for the Education Department 579:1.[82] As a result, there are problems of equity, motivation, morale, and efficiency among the specialists. Clearly, the 1973 reforms have not improved the position of specialists in any significant way.

The Establishment Division is responsible for all personnel matters relating to positions falling in Grades 17 and above. Recruitment to these positions is done through the Federal Public Service Commission, which operates as a relatively autonomous organization. The commission also advises the Establishment Division and operating ministries on the creation of jobs, their classification, and promotion matters. It is also responsible for hearing the grievances of the civil servants as an appellant body for promotion and classification decisions.

PLANNING AND BUDGETING PROCESSES

The sixth Five-Year Plan, 1983–1988, provides the basic framework of targets and priorities for all sectors of the economy. The plan was formulated by the Planning and Development Division under the supervision of the National Economic Council (NEC). The NEC is headed by the prime minister and includes cabinet ministers, provincial governors, chief ministers, and provincial finance and planning ministers.[83] The NEC meets once a year to approve the Annual Development Program (ADP) which is composed of on-going and new projects. Approved projects are not automatically funded; they must receive an allocation in the Annual Expenditure Budget for eventual implementation.[84]

The Expenditure and Revenue budgets—their preparation, execution, and control—are the responsibility of the Finance Division, whereas preparation of the Development Budget (ADP) is done by the Planning and Development Division. In the provinces the corresponding departments perform the same functions. The Planning Department of the Panjab province is a well-developed organization. In the other provinces, however, until recently these departments have been rather small organizations with little real planning expertise and analytical capacity. The central Planning Division is a well-developed, elaborate organization, with adequate analytical capacity in various sectors.

The budgeting process begins in January. The ministries prepare their current expenditure estimates for the coming fiscal year. Simultaneously, estimates of revenues, including foreign aid, are prepared by the functional ministries and are consolidated by the Finance Division. The Planning Division prepares estimates of any surplus available for development programs. In the light of anticipated revenues (including foreign aid), a budget ceiling for ADP is fixed for the coming year.[85]

The funding of projects in the framework of the ADP and the Expenditure Budget is a separate process as opposed to the project selection and approval.

Therefore, all sanctioned projects prepared for inclusion in the budget of a given year are not funded that year. The funds required to finance sanctioned projects often far exceed the ceiling fixed by the Planning Division for the ADP. For example, in 1981–1982 the financial requirement for approved projects exceeded the ceiling by Rs. 1,000 million (approximately 50 million U.S. dollars). The inclusion of projects in the ADP takes a great deal of negotiation between the sponsoring or concerned ministries and the Planning Division. After these negotiations, the Planning Division formulates priorities for including the proposed projects in the ADP and presents them for the approval of the Annual Plan Coordination Committee. This committee is composed of the finance secretary, the planning secretary, the secretaries of economic ministries, provincial representatives, and the secretaries of the sponsoring ministries. Those whose projects have been excluded can use this forum as a source of appeal. The proposed ADP is presented to the NEC for final approval in June.[86]

Project identification and approval is the second stream of the planning and budgeting process. Here the focus is not on whether the money is available for a given project, but on whether a project is sound on technical and financial grounds and falls within the priorities set by the planning framework. Projects are identified and designed by the sponsoring agencies. The end product of the design process is a PC–1 (Project Completion) form, completed and submitted for the review process. The PC–1 requires information on executing agency, location, technical/engineering data, personnel requirements, and projected costs. An analysis of socioeconomic benefits and costs is also required. The decision point for administrative approval depends on the size of the project. The larger the project size (financially), the higher the approval level in the hierarchy and the higher the number of points of decision for approval. For example, a project of up to Rs. 2 million can be approved by the head of the sponsoring agency. From Rs. 2 to 5 million, projects require the concurrence of the Finance Ministry. For projects costing Rs. 5–20 million the Central Development Working party (CDWP) is the approval authority. Projects that are worth over that limit are approved by the Executive Committee of the National Council (ECNEC). These limits are revised from time to time. The CDWP is chaired by the secretary of the Planning Division, and the secretaries of concerned ministries participate as ad hoc members. The ECNEC is composed of ministers of Finance, Planning (chairman), and the Nation Building (Development) ministries.[87]

The time gap between the funding decisions and the project approval decisions is probably the weakest link in the process, probably resulting in project overruns. Over time the political priorities change, and the projects are not funded after all the work that may have gone into their preparation. There is also a tendency to design too many projects without any reference to financial discipline. Analytical capacity for project design in many sponsoring agencies and ministries is rather limited. This leads to problems in project analysis at the design level. Finally, the process is still quite centralized, and there are several approval points for technical, administrative, and financial approval. Even the central Planning Division does not have the necessary capacity to appraise projects before they are presented to the CDWP or the ECNEC.[88] A new Project Wing was set up recently in the Planning Division to strengthen the evaluation processes and the ECNEL now reviews the semiannual reports on evaluating projects.[89]

OVERALL POLICY PROCESS: SALIENT FEATURES

Policy processes may have undergone changes from time to time. The leadership style and the nature of the regime in power accounts for some of the changes in decision-making processes. From 1947 to 1958, the politicians generally allowed the senior bureaucrats to make policies. Political institutions like the Parliament and the cabinet, did exist, but they did not exercise institutionalized control over policy process. After the first few years under the Ayub regime, the Planning Commission established a framework for policy making. The government made its sectoral and project appropriations within the framework of the Five-Year Plan.[90]

Bhutto found the Perspective and the Five-Year Plans cumbersome devices. According to Burki, Bhutto was not inclined to accept the discipline imposed by PC-1 forms mentioned above. Bhutto's impatience with bureaucratic procedures also meant that the important economic decisions were taken without much participation by the bureaucrats.[91] The Government's decisions to start mega projects like the Karachi Steel Mills, the Sports Complex in Islamabad, the Lowari Pass tunnel to link Chitral with the NWFP, the Right Bank Indus Highway, and Nuclear Power Projects were all taken without any reference to PC-1 and rational benefit-cost analysis. These decisions represented Prime Minister Bhutto's grand vision of an independent Pakistan. Interestingly, the Zia regime continued some of these projects like the steel mills.

The Bhutto government came to power in Pakistan when GNP-oriented growth and medium- and long-term comprehensive planning was under attack from every quarter. Planning models had failed to grapple with the problems of increasing poverty, inequity, and social injustice. According to the chief architect of the Perspective Plans, Pakistan's Second Five-Year Plan and what Burki calls PC-1 form discipline, "Pakistan slid back from a literacy level of 18 percent in 1950, which was miserable enough to 15 percent by 1970."[92] It is no wonder that Bhutto, who was a populist leader, was so impatient with the bureaucratic procedures.

During the early days of martial law, the Zia regime was highly centralized. It inherited a system that had become highly politicized and under which the bureaucratic and rational procedures were often set aside. The country was operating without the framework of a five-year plan. Under Zia, all decision-making power was concentrated in the chief martial law administrator and his corps commanders, who were also the provincial governors as well as provincial martial law administrators. Later, a civilian cabinet was created with mostly retired military officials and civilian bureaucrats as members. It is difficult to assess their actual influence on policy formulation. We believe that until the withdrawal of the martial law, real power over major decisions rested with the president and the corps commanders. One exception to this rule was the Finance Minister Ghulam Ishaq Khan, a former bureaucrat. According to rumors in Islamabad, he wielded enormous influence in the cabinet, particularly with regard to economic decisions. He also controlled two of the traditionally most powerful bureaucratic centers of decision making: the Planning Division as well as the Finance Division. Over time, however, the Zia government's quest for legitimacy and the creation of civilian institutions encouraged the emergence of the old bureaucratic order. The sixth Five-Year Plan was formulated, and it provided the framework for setting priorities. Mahbub-ul-Haq became the minister of planning, and the PC–1 form of discipline began to reestablish itself, as we have described above in the section on the planning and budgeting process. With the election of the National Assembly in 1985 and the appointment of a civilian cabinet under a prime minister, the higher level policy formulation should have undergone some changes[93] and some stable relationship between the military and elected politicians should have emerged. But the dismissal of the cabinet in mid–1988 threw open the whole question of any enduring civilian military equilibrium. The death of President General Zia in a plane crash in November 1988 was followed by fairly peaceful and reasonably fair general elections and the revival of democracy in Pakistan, with Benazir Bhutto as prime minister. As before, senior bureaucrats in the secretariat (particularly the permanent secretaries) would normally dominate the policy process.[94] It is not clear as yet if she will follow her father's footsteps and try to debureaucratize the policy process.

The Zia regime encouraged local self-government at the district level. Zilla (district) councils have been elected in each district of Pakistan. The government, probably for the first time in Pakistan's history, provided them with a stronger tax base to raise their own revenues. The government also allocated more money for their development programs. The Zilla councils have also been involved in implementation of development programs. For example, they are responsible for selecting villages for rural electrification, determining the building sites (villages) of basic health units, and choosing villages for the construction of primary schools. The provincial governments (planning departments) formulate general guidelines and standards for such site selection, but the actual selection is made by the elected district councils. They also monitor the implementation of the provincial government projects. On the one hand, this has had a healthy effect, encouraging local participation in decisions concerning development projects. On the other hand, the implementation process has become highly politicized. Local groups are often locked into an intense political struggle to gain a basic health unit, a primary school, or an electric connection for their village. It frequently results in unnecessary delays in implementation.[95]

INTEREST GROUPS AND PUBLIC POLICY

The societal norms in Pakistan place a great deal of emphasis on primary group loyalty and solidarity. Rural Pakistan is particularly dominated by kinship, caste (Zat in Urdu), and tribal structures. In Panjab and Sind, Biradaris (literally brotherhood)—a caste-like kinship network—dominates social interaction and links the rural areas with the cities. In the NWFP and Baluchistan, the kinship patterns are reinforced by tribal organization. The predominance of these structures has inhibited the development of associational groups based on functions and cutting across the primary group loyalties.

The business groups were the first to organize themselves. Pre-Partition India had a tradition of trade and commerce organizations, but most of these organizations were located in major cities that became part of India. Whatever business group activity emerged, early in its development it passed under the control of the government. The Ayub government completed the penetration of business groups and practically governmentalized them.[96] This is particularly true of the Chambers of Commerce and their federation.

Businesspeople built personal connections on the basis of kinship and caste; where that was not possible they used gifts, favors, hospitality, and bribes. Businesspeople also employed *Sefarish* (using an influential person to put in a good word) which is a common Pakistani tradition. As industrial activities grew and the governments became more complex, the personal networks between business and government were institutionalized. The big business companies—the often-mentioned twenty-two families who controlled the industrial sector—created liaison officers in Islamabad, known as industrial embassies. These embassies were staffed with influential, well-connected people and retired army officers with lavish entertainment allowances. They were used to secure licenses and permits for spare parts and other inputs. They made sure that the company got its share of export rebates and other favors. They courted government officials for favorable solutions of specific company problems.[97]

The government, which was probably the most antibusiness in Pakistan's history, was also indirectly responsible for strengthening the organized group activity. The Bhutto regime disrupted the informal network of personal contacts developed by business and bureaucracy in the preceding regimes. A large number of senior bureaucrats were dismissed or transferred. Lateral entry introduced a new set of people in the middle and upper ranks of government. A new group of middle-class, urban leftist politicians occupied important portfolios. The antibusiness stance of the government and the policy of nationalization made the business sector realize the importance of collective action. Although the business sector remained divided, a number of collective strategies were used for the first time to influence government policy and strengthen business pressure groups.[98]

ACCOUNTABILITY IN AN ADMINISTRATIVE STATE

Accountability of the public bureaucracy has always been a problem in Pakistan. According to Justice S. Rahman, the serious and frequent interruption of the legislative process has weakened the system of administrative accountability, the legislature being the key instrument of eliciting accountability.[99] In the absence of democratic institutions, a tradition of extreme secrecy in the decision-making process, and a government-controlled media, it is very difficult to design effective mechanisms of public service accountability. All Pakistani regimes have suffered from a high degree of bureaucratic and political corruption. Generally, accountability in Pakistan is enforced on past regimes. Charges of corruption have been brought against every fallen regime in Pakistan since independence. After an initial flurry of trials, dismissals, and demotions, the new regimes have settled down to business as usual.

The traditional function of postaudit has always existed in Pakistan. The Accountant General's (AG) department has performed this function. In the absence of strong legislatures, the AG's office has also been controlled by the executive government. Their approach to control has been legal and traditional, and obviously, they have failed to do what an independent auditor general responsible to the National Parliament would do in a country like Canada. Anti-Corruption Departments—a special section of police—have also existed in all Pakistani provinces. Their own credibility may at best be questionable. In a recent conversation in Pakistan their role was given this colorful description: "they usually catch butterflies while elephants roam freely."

The Bhutto government provided that Administrative Tribunals be created to deal with some of the issues concerning accountability, but they were never established. The Anwar-ul-Haq Commission again recommended the creation of such tribunals as a way of allowing the public to vent its grievances against the bureaucracy. But as far as we know, this recommendation was not implemented. In the absence of independent or legislative mechanisms, the recourse to the courts was obvious.

With growing complaints of corruption, misconduct, irregularities, and delays under the Ayub regime, a Governor's Inspection Team was constituted for the United Province of West Pakistan. This was the highest level mechanism ever created in Pakistan to improve accountability. It consisted of two or three senior secretaries and sometimes a high-level person from other sectors. This team was directly responsible to the governor and had extensive powers and prestige. In 1970 after the dissolution of the one United Province, all four provinces created their own teams. They have continued under the Zia regime, being responsible for investigating complaints of corruption, studying law and order situations, and monitoring the implementation of development projects. These teams have exercised some limited moral restraint.

MOHTASIB, THE PAKISTANI OMBUDSMAN

The most innovative institution created so far in Pakistan to enforce accountability is the office of *Mohtasib*, an Arabic word originating from *Ihtisab* meaning accountability. Mohtasib is literally "the person who enforces accountability." The institution had existed in Islamic states in earlier periods. The role of the Mohtasib was limited to ethical censor and to enforcer of Islamic values and morals. The public service accountability in an Islamic state was enforced by a fiercely independent judiciary. The internalization of Islamic values and moral standards was probably a more important factor. The Zia government has taken the notion of accountability from Islam and combined it with the institutional underpinnings of Scandinavian ombudsman in establishing this office. President Zia appointed a senior judge of the Supreme Court, known for his integrity, to be the first Mohtasib in 1983.

According to Sardar M. Iqbal, the first Wafaqi Mohtasib (federal ombudsman), the office is functionally autonomous, has a basis in law, is external to administration, and is nonpartisan and client oriented. It is operationally independent of the legislature and the executive, and it is freely accessible and visible to the public at large.[100] Since 1983, the Mohtasib has published three voluminous annual reports about the activities of his office. (The 1985 report consists of 847 pages.) The reports indicate that the Mohtasib has examined complaints concerning both efficiency and corruption. In 1984, the secretariat received over 18,000 complaints, over 6,000 of which were carefully chosen for investigation. The annual reports have made public the names of agencies, and specify the frequency and nature of complaints against them.[101] We feel that the Mohtasib's secretariat has performed its function with reasonable effectiveness.

CONCLUSIONS

The predominance of the military-bureaucratic oligarchy is probably the most outstanding feature of the Pakistani state. After independence, a weak and undeveloped bourgeoisie was unable to establish supremacy over the colonial apparatus left by the British. As Hamza Alavi has pointed out, the state in Pakistan was not dominated by one ruling class but by at least three propertied classes. The bureaucracy assumed a mediating stance and over time acquired a relatively autonomous role.[102] In the absence of strong and sustained political leadership, the senior bureaucracy assumed the role of policy formulation as well as of policy implementation. Parliaments were either nonexistent or at best intermittent. They had practically no influence on policy formulation. The development of the interest groups was strongly influenced by a process of governmentalization.

The first few years of Prime Minister Bhutto's regime represented the only period when the politicians exercised control over the bureaucracy and initiated policies.

The power and influence of the bureaucracy have increased over time with increasing state intervention in the economy. Practically every aspect of business activity is regulated by the government. A pattern of elite accommodation has developed between big business and the policy-level bureaucracy. A similar pattern of elite accommodation has existed between the landed elite and the field administration.

During martial law regimes, the military takes over the political direction of the bureaucracy. During the initial period, martial law regimes usually keep a distance from the bureaucracy. But later a pattern of interdependence develops, and the bureaucracy emerges as a powerful force in Pakistan's military governments. Many of Pakistan's senior military officers had been trained in the pro-consulate tradition of ultimate civilian supremacy. Consequently, the military regimes have been very sensitive to the question of legitimacy. Martial law government in Pakistan has encouraged local self-government schemes and kept the civil bureaucracy intact.

The second critical feature of Pakistan's administrative system is the persistence of British colonial institutions even after four decades of independence. The secretariat system, the policy-administration dichotomy, the generalist bias, the district administration, and the land revenue system are the key examples of the colonial legacy. There has been a great deal of piecemeal reform and ad hoc innovation, but mostly there has been a proliferation and differentiation of administrative structures without much integration. Even the sweeping reforms made under the Bhutto regime have not changed the fundamental characteristics of the system.

The third important feature of Pakistan's public administration is the recent emphasis on Islamization. The military leadership of the Zia regime came from middle/lower-middle-class, orthodox, and relatively more religious families.[103] The last generation of generals, who belonged to westernized urban upper class refugee families or landed elites, has been retired. Thus, the Zia regime sought legitimacy in Islamization in addition to slow democratization. Under this regime the military became the guardian not only of Pakistan's physical borders, but also of its ideological frontiers. Pakistan, the military, and Islam have been linked inextricably. Pakistan's criminal and civil laws have been brought in line with the Islamic code of Sharia. The Islamic Ideological Council and the Islamic Court have been created to oversee policy and legislation for its Islamic orientation. A number of fiscal and monetary measures—interest-free banking, Islamic taxes like Zakat and Ushre—based on shari'ah have been introduced. On a symbolic level, the president issued directions to public officials to wear Islamic (or Pakistani) dress during office hours. The ease and rapidity with which this directive was implemented was remarkable. All Pakistani government bureaus have made arrangements for public prayers during office hours. The institution of Mohtasib has been created following the Islamic tradition. These Islamic policies are generally continued by the Benazir Bhutto regime.

It is probably too early to assess the impact of Islamization on Pakistan's administrative system. Basic structures and the decision process have not undergone any fundamental change. But to some extent, the symbolism, appearance, tone, and tenor of Pakistan's public bureaucracy, have assumed an Islamic orientation.

The elitist orientation of the Pakistani bureaucracy have persisted in spite of the 1973 reforms in the structure of the public service. Some groups (DMG/TAG/FAG) continue to enjoy a disproportionately higher degree of mobility, promotion opportunity, privilege, and power. Pakistan's elite public services have been vehemently criticized, more often for their arrogance or behavior than for their performance. We do not believe there is sufficient evidence to attribute Pakistan's lack of political development solely to the behavior of the elite public services. In fact, the elite bureaucracy deserves some credit for holding a fragmentary political system together. They were able to formulate and implement with some success six medium-term development plans. What is needed is not the complete elimination of the elite structure but an improvement in the work conditions and status of the specialists and professionals within it.

NOTES

The author is thankful to Dr. Tariq Siddiqui, Mr. S. K. Mahmood, and Mr. A. U. Khan for their advice. Many thanks to O and M Division (Islamabad) and Pakistan Administrative Staff College for providing information and data. Thanks are also extended to the Faculty of Administration, and the Graduate School, University of Ottawa, for their support without which this study would not have been possible.

1. S. C. Dube, "Bureaucracy and Nation Building in Transitional Societies," in J. L. Finkle and Richard W. Gable (eds.), *Political Development and Social Change* (New York: John Wiley, 1971), p. 328.

2. See A. C. Banerjee, *Indian Constitutional Documents (1757–1947)* (Calcutta: A. Mukherjee and Co., 1945), Vol. 1, p. 266, for the Charter Act creating the Indian Civil Service (first called the covenanted service). See *Speeches—Parliamentary and Miscellaneous by the Rt. Hon. Thomas Babington Macaulay* (London: Clarke, Beeton and Co., 1953), Vol. 2, pp. 267–73 for Macaulay's speech in Parliament advocating the creation of the ICS.

3. *Report of the Pay and Services Commission, 1959–62* (Karachi: Manager of Publication, 1969), p. 30.

4. Dube, "Bureaucracy and Nation Building in Transitional Societies," p. 326.

5. Ralph Braibanti, "Public Bureaucracy and Judiciary in Pakistan," in Joseph LaPalombra (ed.), *Bureaucracy and Political Development* (Princeton, N.J.: Princeton University Press, 1967).

6. Asaf Hussain, *Elite Politics in an Ideological State: The Case of Pakistan* (Folkstone, Kent: Dawson, 1979), p. 62.

7. Guthri Birkhead (ed.), *Administrative Problems in Pakistan* (Syracuse: Syracuse University Press, 1966), p. 11.

8. Dube, "Bureaucracy and Nation Building," p. 327.

9. *Report of the Pay and Services Commission*, p. 30.

10. Muneer Ahmad, *The Civil Servant in Pakistan* (Karachi: Oxford University Press, 1964), p. 125.

11. Braibanti, "Public Bureaucracy and Judiciary in Pakistan," p. 364.

12. Ibid., pp. 364–67.

13. See Khalid B. Sayeed, *Pakistan: The Formative Phase* (Karachi: Pakistan Publishing House, 1960), pp. 280–83 and *Politics in Pakistan* (New York: Praeger, 1980), p. 26.

14. Braibanti, "Public Bureaucracy and Judiciary in Pakistan," pp. 370–71.

15. Hussain, *Elite Politics in an Ideological State*, p. 62.

16. Henry F. Goodnow, *The Civil Service of Pakistan* (New Haven, Conn.: Yale University Press, 1964), p. 173.

17. Nazim, *Babus, Brahmins and Bureaucrats* (Lahore: People's Publishing House, 1973), p. 5.

18. National Assembly of Pakistan, *Parliamentary Debates*, 15 February 1957, pp. 344–55.

19. S. J. Burki, "Twenty Years of the Civil Service of Pakistan: A Reevaluation," *Asian Survey* 9 (April 1969), p. 446.

20. S. J. Burki, *Pakistan Under Bhutto, 1971–77* (New York: St. Martin's Press, 1980), pp. 16–21.

21. Burki, "Twenty Years of the Civil Service of Pakistan," p. 243.

22. Sayeed, *Politics in Pakistan*, p. 44.

23. Burki, *Pakistan Under Bhutto*, pp. 25–28.

24. Albert Gorvine, "The Role of the Civil Service Under the Revolutionary Government," *The Middle East Journal* 19, 3 (1965), p. 324.

25. Lt. General K. M. Sheikh's Address to the C.S.P. Probationers October 1960. Quoted in Burki, "Twenty Years of the Civil Service of Pakistan," p. 247.

26. See Muneer Ahmad, "The November Mass Movement in Pakistan," in *Aspects of Pakistan's Politics and Administration* (Lahore: South Asian Institute, 1974), pp. 34–41.

27. Robert Laporte, Jr., *Power and Privilege: Influence and Decision Making in Pakistan* (Berkeley: University of California Press, 1975), pp. 117–18.

28. Burki, *Pakistan Under Bhutto, 1971–77*, p. 100.

29. Ibid., pp. 100–103.

30. Laporte, *Power and Privilege*, pp. 118–19.

31. Burki, *Pakistan Under Bhutto, 1971–77*, p. 100.

32. Lawrence Ziring, *Pakistan: The Enigma of Political Development* (Folkstone, Kent: Dawson-Westview, 1980), p. 123.

33. Cabinet Secretariat, O and M Division, *Organization and Functions of the Federal Secretariat* (Islamabad: Printing Corporation of Pakistan, n.d.).

34. Bernard L. Galadieux, *Report of Reorganization of Pakistan Government for National Development* (Karachi: Planning Commission, 1955).

35. *Report of the Pay and Services Commission, 1959–62*, pp. 122–24.

36. Anwar-ul-Haq, *Commission on Administrative Reform: Report*, Part II, 1978–80. (Government of Pakistan), pp. 20–21.

37. *Organization and Functions of the Federal Secretariat.*

38. Ministry of Production, Government of Pakistan, State Enterprise, n.d., pp. 8, 10, 14.

39. Government of Pakistan, *Economic Survey, 1986–87* (Islamabad: Ministry of Finance, 1987), p. 68.

40. Reza H. Syed, *Role and Performance of Public Enterprises in the Economic Growth of Pakistan* (Karachi: Investment Advisory Center, 1977), pp. 24–25.

41. Government of Pakistan, *The First Five Year Plan, 1956–60*, pp. 85–87.

42. Majid Mufti, "Experience of Public Enterprises in Pakistan," *The Pakistan Times*, 23 November 1981.

43. Burki, *Pakistan Under Bhutto*, p. 25.

44. Ibid., pp. 27–28.

45. Gustav F. Papanek, *Pakistan's Development: Social Goals and Private Incentives* (Cambridge, Mass.: Harvard University Press, 1967), pp. 94–96.

46. Burki, *Pakistan Under Bhutto*, pp. 114–17.

47. Government of Pakistan, *Pakistan Economic Survey, 1984–85* (Finance Division, 1985), p. 33.

48. See Elliot Berg and Mary M. Shirly, *Divestiture in Developing Countries* (Washington, D.C.: World Bank, 1987), p. 22.

49. Burki, "Twenty Five Years of Civil Services in Pakistan: A Reevaluation," p. 254.

50. See Muzaffar Ahmad, *Public Enterprises in South Asia* (Lujubljana: International Center for Public Enterprises, 1982), p. 38.

51. Ibid.

52. Mufti, *"Experience of Public Enterprises in Pakistan,"* p. 3.

53. Jeffrey Pressman and Aaron Wildavsky, *Implementation* (Berkeley: University of California Press, 1974), pp. 99–102.

54. See *World Development Report, 1983* (Washington, D.C.: World Bank, 1983), pp. 82–83.

55. Ibid.

56. Artnaud Hartmann and Syed Ali Nawab, "Evaluating Public Manufacturing Enterprises in Pakistan," *Finance and Development* (September 1985), pp. 27–30.

57. Ibid.

58. Government of Pakistan, *Economic Survey, 1984–85* (Islamabad: Ministry of Finance, 1985), pp. 32–33.

59. Government of Pakistan, *Economic Survey, 1986–87* (Islamabad: Ministry of Finance, 1987), p. 91.

60. Ibid.

61. Muzaffar Ahmad Chaudhri, "The Organization and Composition of the Central Civil Services in Pakistan," in Inayatulla (ed.), *Bureaucracy and Development in Pakistan* (Peshawar: Pakistan Academy for Rural Development, 1970), pp. 250–58.

62. See Hussain, *Elite Politics in an Ideological State*, pp. 61–78. M. Mohabbat Khan, *Bureaucratic Self-Preservation* (Dacca: University of Dacca, 1980), pp. 118–20. Nazim, *Babus, Brahmins and Bureaucrats*.

63. Ahmad, *The Civil Servant In Pakistan*, pp. 34–38.

64. Quoted in Lawrence Ziring, "The Pakistan Bureaucracy: Administrative Reform," in *Asian Survey* 14 (December 1974), p. 1088.

65. Charles H. Kennedy, "Policy Implementation: The Case of Structural Reforms

in Administrative System of Pakistan,'' in *Journal of South Asian and Middle Eastern Studies* 4, 3, pp. 92–97.

66. Ibid., p. 99.

67. Robert Laporte, Jr., ''Administering Development,'' in S. J. Burki and R. Laporte (eds.), *Pakistan's Development Priorities* (Karachi: Oxford University Press, 1984), p. 260.

68. Anwar-ul-Haq, *Commission on Administrative Reform*, pp. 178–80.

69. Central Public Service Commission, *Annual Report* (Karachi: Printing Corporation of Pakistan, 1970), p. 79 (Table I).

70. Federal Public Service Commission, *Annual Report, 1984* (Islamabad: Printing Corporation of Pakistan, 1984), p. 142 (Table II).

71. Zafar Iqbal Qureshi, ''The Recruitment and Examination System,'' in Conference on Administrative Reforms, *Papers and Reports* (Lahore: Pakistan Administrative Staff College, 1974), p. 4.

72. Government of Pakistan, *White Paper on the Performance of the Bhutto Regime*, Vols. 1–4 (Islamabad: MPCPP, 1979). Quoted in Charles H. Kennedy, ''Prestige of Services and Bhutto's Administrative Reforms,'' *Asian Affairs* 12, 3 (1985), pp. 25–26.

73. Ralph Braibanti, ''The Higher Bureaucracy of Pakistan,'' in *Asian Bureaucratic Systems Emergent from the British Imperialist Tradition* (Durham, N.C.: Duke University Press, 1966), p. 327.

74. Burki, ''Twenty Years of Civil Service of Pakistan,'' pp. 248–49.

75. See Nazim, *Babus, Brahmins and Bureaucrats*, and numerous articles published in the local press during the 1970s and the 1980s.

76. Anwar-ul-Haq, *Commission on Administrative Reform*, pp. 131–35.

77. NIPA, *A Report on the Evaluation of Training Courses*, unpublished manuscripts, (Karachi, n.d.), p. 2.

78. Anwar-ul-Haq, *Commission on Administrative Reform*, p. 139.

79. See Kamla Chaudri, ''Strategies for Institutionalizing Public Management Education: The Indian Experience,'' in Lawrence D. Shifel et al. (eds.), *Education and Training for Public Sector Management in Developing Countries* (New York: Rockefeller Foundation, 1977), pp. 101–15. See also *World Development Report, 1983* (Washington, D.C.: World Bank, 1983), pp. 108–9.

80. Anwar-ul-Haq, *Commission on Administrative Reform*, p. 166.

81. Hafiz S. D. Jamy and M. A. Rahim, ''A Critique of Annual Confidential Reports and Criteria for Promotion,'' Working Paper No. 13, *Conference on Administrative Reforms*, pp. 2–3.

82. Dr. Muneer Ahmad, A Note Appended to the Anwar-ul-Haq Commission Report.

83. S. H. Hashmi, ''Social Development, Planning, Management and Implementation in Pakistan,'' in Chakrit N. Padungkarn (ed.), *Social Development Alternatives* (Nagoya: United Nations Centre for Regional Development, 1987), p. 81.

84. Richard W. Gable and Robert Laporte, Jr., ''Planning and Budgeting in Pakistan,'' *Public Administration and Development* 3 (1983), p. 139.

85. Ibid., p. 141.

86. Ibid., p. 142.

87. Information provided to the author by the Planning Division.

88. Information provided by the Implementation and Progress Section, Planning Division.

89. *Pakistan and the World Bank* (Washington, D.C.: World Bank, 1987), pp. 7–8.

90. Burki, *Pakistan Under Bhutto*, p. 145.

91. Ibid.

92. Mahbub-ul-Haq, *The Poverty Curtain: Choices for the Third World* (New York: Columbia University Press, 1976), p. 23.

93. S. J. Burki, *Pakistan: A Nation in the Making* (London: Oxford University Press, 1986), p. 97.

94. S. H. Hashmi, "Social Development Planning, Management and Implementation in Pakistan," in Chakrit N. Padungkarn (ed.), *Social Development Alternatives* (Ngoya: UNCRO, 1987), p. 78.

95. Information based on interviews with elected officials of five District Councils in Panjab in 1984.

96. Stanley A. Kochanek, *Interest Groups and Development: Business and Politics in Pakistan* (Karachi: Oxford University Press, 1983), pp. 123–37.

97. Ibid., pp. 266–67.

98. Ibid., pp. 185–87.

99. Justice S. Rahman, Administrative Accountability, III, *The Pakistan Times*, 2 February 1988.

100. Sardar Muhammad Iqbal, "Ombudsman-Historical Development," *Pakistan Times*, Supplement 1947–1987. *The Pakistan Times*, 1 February 1988, pp. 65–68.

101. See ibid. and Wafaqi Mohtasib's (Ombudsman) Annual Report (Islamabad: Wafaqui Mohtasib's Secretariat, 1985). See also Justice S. Rahman, "Administrative Accountability," *The Pakistan Times*, 27 January 1988.

102. See Hamza Alavi, "The State in Post Colonial Societies: Pakistan and Bangladesh," in Kathleen Gough and Hari Sharma (eds.), *Imperialism and Revolution in South Asia* (New York: Monthly Review Press, 1973).

103. Stephen P. Cohen, "Pakistan: Army, Society and Security," *Asian Affairs* 10, 2 (1983), pp. 6–9.

5

THE PHILIPPINES

Ledivina V. Cariño

The public administration system in the Philippines, like the country itself, is a creation of Western colonization. Functioning on Asian soil, it has been called a "fusion of East and West," the phrase suggesting a harmonious integration of native and alien aspects.[1] In this chapter, we will posit that the hybrid, while a distinct system, projects not harmony but many discontinuous and contradictory qualities; it is an Americanized system in an Asian setting; it has vestiges of authoritarianism while the country itself is undergoing a process of redemocratization. As such, it can be best understood through its politico-economic and historical contexts. Accordingly, we will first describe the country briefly. Next, we will trace at some length how the bureaucracy has changed through different periods of Philippine history. Finally, we will discuss the main features and dynamics of the Philippine administrative system at the end of the 1980s.

THE PHILIPPINES: AN INTRODUCTION

The Philippines is an archipelago of over 7,000 islands located south of the mainland of Asia. Its nearest neighbors are Indonesia and Malaysia with which it shares membership in the Association of Southeast Asian Nations (along with four other states). However, its closest political and economic ties are with the United States, its former colonial ruler, and hence are determined less by geography than by history and the dominance of metropolitan systems.

The Philippines extends over 300,000 square kilometers, qualifying it among the upper third of today's nations in terms of area. With almost 60 million inhabitants, it is one of the most populated countries of the world. It has a high rate of population growth, about 2.7 per annum. The size of human settlements varies widely, with Metropolitan Manila, the capital region, overcrowded with both people and high-polluting vehicles, while many remote areas remain comparatively uninhabited.

Blood and ritual kinship ties and patron-client relations involve almost all Filipinos in a network of reciprocal obligations. However, schools, the bureaucracy, and the law extol Western norms of universalism and individualism. These have differing consequences for government-people relations. Traditional values uphold authoritarianism but also humanize relations. Meanwhile, universalistic norms facilitate equitable but possibly mechanical treatment and, in a society in which certain groups have been disadvantaged over time, can be used to perpetuate such discrimination.

These value systems clash with and accommodate each other on different occasions. Some officials regularly use government positions for personal power, while others freely make available their own resources for official purposes. Either strategy, greed or unselfishness, can find a normative base in the society. So can private or civic-spirited demands on government. Which behavior will earn public approval or condemnation depends on the contingencies of the pertinent social interaction.

Filipinos are relatively homogeneous, but certain differences have great importance. For instance, the predominant faith is Roman Catholicism. However, Muslims who now comprise about 5 percent of the population used to constitute the majority in the island of Mindanao and the Sulu archipelago. They continue to predominate in what have now shrunk to a few provinces in the region. With a proud history of continuous resistance to both Spain and the United States, they have kept their own culture despite Western colonialism. But Mindanao was opened to the migration of other Filipinos and the encroachment of plantations and industrial enterprises of multinationals, wealthy Christians, and even some of their leaders. These groups crowded and marginalized the natives. The religious question has thus been joined by political and economic issues in fanning the Muslim secessionist movement.

The Muslim problem is symptomatic of other divisions among the Filipino people. Although the original question may be phrased in terms of religion, race, or occupation, it ultimately boils down to the problem of overwhelming poverty and exploitation. The majority live in dismal conditions while a small group lives in luxury and appropriates for itself the wealth of the land. To the latter belong descendants of the native, Spanish, and American colonial elites, multinational executives, and Chinese capitalists. It also includes others whose route to the top has been through the capture of political positions or their influence on government officials. This domination by a few, increasingly backed by government resources and military force, has contributed in no small way to the phenomenal growth of the New People's Army, the guerrilla arm of the local Communist party.

THE HISTORICAL CONTEXT

In discussing the evolution of the bureaucracy through the pre-Spanish era, the different colonial regimes, the period of the Republic, the authoritarian state, and the current transition toward redemocratization, we will also show its interaction with its contemporaneous political, economic, and social environment.

The Pre-Spanish Philippines

Before the Spanish conquest of 1521, the Philippines did not exist as a single entity. Rather, there were self-governing groups called *barangays*. Trade was carried on between the islands and with China, Borneo, and other neighboring areas. Where stratification between nobility, freemen, serfs, and slaves was drawn, an incipient government service could be identified, staffed largely by the ruler's relatives. In most barangays, however, land was held in common, rule was not hereditary, and the functions of politics and administration were not recognized as separate from the day-to-day activities of hunters, farmers, and fishers.

The Spanish Era

In exploiting the colony it named after king Philip II, Spain reserved previously communal lands for the king, his favorites, and the church. The people paid tribute from the produce of these lands (effectively becoming tenants) and rendered forced labor to government regularly. They became Roman Catholics, sometimes forcibly, but combined it with their animistic amulets and incantations to evolve their own folk Christianity. The priests also regrouped the people into parishes, in the process developing sedentary agriculture, including cash crops such as sugar, abaca, coconut, and other crops which, with gold and lumber products, were the Philippines' chief exports until the 1970s.

The Spanish colonial bureaucracy consisted of priests, soldiers, and officials who had bought their positions in Madrid. Most Spaniards stayed in Manila. The other areas had a governor and a contingent of feared soldiers and priests. Former native rulers undertook the rest of the administrative tasks.

Spain maintained a centralized system, running the islands through a long hierarchical chain that started with the Crown, the Overseas Ministry in Madrid, and the viceroy of Mexico to whom, half a world away, the Philippine governor-general directly reported. Another long channel relayed orders from Manila to the provinces, municipalities, and villages. Spain's laws tried to exact accountability from servants of the Crown and to minimize oppression of the natives. But few directives got to the colony on time. Even if timely, compliance with them could not be checked, since local officials and priests colluded to keep even royal investigators from the truth. Besides, with Spanish investments needing to be secured, Spain also tended to side more with the exploitative official than with the one who was more just to the "inferior" natives. So it was that under Spain, the natives were ruled by a Christian government on paper while unsuccessfully resisting and thus enduring an abusive pillaging state for almost 400 years.

The American Regime

The Americans obtained the Philippines under the Treaty of Paris of 1898 and declared that it would hold it only long enough "to teach the Filipinos the art of self-government." That statement contradicted the historical situation—that the Filipinos had thrown off the Spanish yoke in the first war of independence by an Asian colony and that they had a functioning government as of 12 June 1898—but it prevailed because of superior American arms. The United States then went on to use free public education as the other major force of domination. Proceeding to the hearts and minds of the populace, it succeeded in erasing from national memory its brutal martial law period (1898–1902).[2]

Among its first laws was the Civil Service Act of 1900 which was regarded as a condition precedent to the establishment of proper civil government.[3] That act created a bureaucracy which appeared to live up to its billing as a merit system. The few corruption scandals that surfaced were openly faced and spared neither the small fry nor their leaders, even if they were Americans.[4] On the whole, the civil service then seemed a marked contrast to those of the Spanish period and later.

This relatively idyllic situation does not signify that the American era was a golden age. It does mean that the battle was elsewhere. For one thing, the native elite had allied itself with the new gods and projected a kind of acquiescent nationalism that made the Americans confidently transfer the bureaucracy to Filipinos quite early in their colonization. But the Spanish heritage and the native culture combined to produce a Filipino style of governance. For instance, laws against patronage were followed so closely that Americans were never fully aware of their many subtle circumventions.[5]

Besides, American attention was not concentrated on the bureaucracy. The United States established a laissez-faire government that involved itself in the economy only to provide what its merchants, industrialists, and other capitalists needed. It was in these latter roles that Americans got involved. They bought mines and plantations: they got forestry and fishing concessions. They dominated foreign commerce and shared domestic trade with the Chinese. They took over public utilities and the mass media. All the apolitical bureaucracy had to do was to guard their property rights.

Spanish colonial plunder took place under the aegis of church and state. By contrast, Americans came as the bearers of free enterprise. A neutral bureaucracy served American interests better since exploitation of the colony could proceed apace while the image of a benevolent government remained untarnished.

The Japanese Interlude

During World War II, the Japanese declared the Philippines an independent state and installed a puppet government. However, Filipinos as a whole remained loyal to the United States. For those who served in the bureaucracy during this period, sabotage of the enemy became an act of high patriotism. In normal times, this would be corruption, if not treason. A civil service that allowed nationalism and personal survival to rule would not find it easy to return to the relative value-neutrality, lack of corruption, and depoliticization of the prewar era. This was the state of the administrative system when the Philippines won "flag independence" in 1946.[6] The "Third" Republic was thus formally inaugurated.[7]

The Period of the (Third) Republic

July 4, 1946, marked the "world's first negotiated and peaceful independence of a colony," further entrenching "American benevolence" in the Filipino psyche.[8] However, it was largely symbolic since the American hand would be strengthened in a new guise: as champion of technical assistance and development administration, a role it played in many new states. Although the needs of its capitalist economy are global, American relations with the Philippines differed from the others because of the following features:

1. The Philippines was (and remains) the site of American military bases, including Clark Air Force Base, the largest outside U.S. territory. Thus, the Philippines is vital to American security interests.

2. Its economy was heavily oriented to the American market. American economic interests were vouchsafed by an onerous agreement made on the very date of Philippine independence. Through it, the United States retained control of Philippine monetary policy (operative until 1954) and allowed its nationals to exploit Philippine natural resources and operate public utilities with the same rights and privileges as Filipinos (until 1994). The agreement supposedly provided for parity rights for citizens of both countries. However, it required an amendment only of the Philippine Constitution (such being a proviso for the grant of independence) and did not disturb American arrangements. Besides, reciprocity was virtually impossible since fewer Filipinos could enjoy such rights in the United States (compared to the reverse flow).

   A third provision of the agreement (later embodied in a trade act) established free trade between the two countries and their gradual elimination after eight years. This resulted in "American goods flood(ing) the domestic market to the prejudice of the local industries. . . . The disadvantages to the Philippines of tariff-free imports from the US far outweighed the benefits derived from tariff-free exports."[9]

3. Finally, one should take note of the Philippine role in America's "grand experiment." Or as a Canadian scholar has put it: "The Philippines is the only nation in which . . . American democracy [has] been so deeply transplanted that Philippine democracy continues to prosper and to mature within its own constitutional framework."[10]

Only fervent nationalists argued against the one-sided economic and security arrangements. Everyone else accepted the third factor as America's main concern in its ex-colony. Thus, its leaders eagerly sought U.S. involvement in setting the future directions of the Philippines.

The Report of the 1950 Economic Survey Mission headed by Daniel Bell set the tone for all later technical assistance programs. It embodied the philosophy that aid *is* intervention, and that social and administrative reforms were necessary for growth and political stability.[11] Accordingly it recommended a social amelioration package that was largely aimed at breaking up the Huk (local communist) rebellion that at that time boasted of being within striking distance of the capital.

In addition, the Bell Mission found a bureaucracy openly ruled by patronage, no longer bound by the need to prove to Americans the Filipino capacity for self-government. Besides, government positions were widely sought in a war-damaged economy with few opportunities for alternative employment. Corruption would further increase as the state assumed regulatory roles in the economy and bribes secured all types of licenses for unqualified or impatient business-people.

The Bell Mission recommended government-wide restructuring, the improvement of personnel, and the adoption of modern management technology. Changes along these three lines would also dominate later attempts at administrative reform. Each president, in his inaugural or first state-of-the-nation speech, would later seek congressional approval of a general reorganization.[12] Since Bell, a series of American fact-finding and aid missions has studied every facet of Philippine political, economic, and social life. Later, there would be technical assistance teams from Japan and other advanced economies or from multilaterals like the United Nations and the World Bank. Their recommendations became the bases of policy, the establishment of programs, and the creation and change of agencies.

Generally, these teams had Filipino counterparts who wanted their country to catch up with the West. Thus, many of them sought American solutions to Filipino problems. The bureaucracy therefore received massive doses of foreign aid and advice as it entered into all areas of the economy and society.[13] As a result, it became alienated from the society and technically overdeveloped relative to other political institutions, especially those which, being subject to elections, had to manifest a modicum of responsiveness to their social environment.

The bureaucracy was controlled by a president who, even under the colonial 1935 Constitution, had more authority in his domain than the U.S. president had in his. Beyond this, the political system was patterned after the American, and included checks and balances among the executive, legislative, and judicial branches. All were dominated by landlords and export crop planters (such as the sugar bloc), but the legislature, being larger, managed to have a broader representation, such as an occasional legislator from peasant or laborer stock, and some members of the nationalist bourgeosie and the fledgling middle class. Policies reflected the hold of dominant economic groups and continuing American influence. Denunciations of these issues or the performance of their advocates were championed by individual legislators, sometimes on matters of principle, at others with an eye to elections or to court other blocs. Whichever was paramount, the press freely aired and investigated their critiques and exposes of scandals.

Political parties were agglomerations of personalities and could not be differentiated by issues. They engaged in violence, vote-buying, and other electoral fraud. Although the civilian and military bureaucracies as organizations shunned partisanship, political patrons did call on their protegés to staff their electoral campaigns or private armies.

The Republic tried to move forward on many fronts. It developed economic and political ties with neighboring and socialist nations and sought acceptance by the nonaligned bloc. That was not possible since it unabashedly joined America's wars in Korea and Vietnam. Meanwhile, the economy grew rapidly and until the 1960s was performing better than most of Asia. Some economic nationalism, though insufficient, was evidenced by restrictions on foreign investments, the renegotiation of the trade relationship with the United States, and Filipinization of domestic commerce (away from the Chinese). Dependence on agriculture and the American market also decreased. However, the rich disproportionately enjoyed the benefits of growth as well as government services, both legitimate and corrupt. This gave rise to popular dissatisfaction from which insurgency, effectively squashed in the mid-1950s with American aid, would draw strength a decade later. The New Communist party of the Philippines (CPP) would be organized in 1968, and its guerrilla arm, the New People's Army, would be created a year later.

The Authoritarian Period

The Philippines maintained a liberal-democratic framework until 1972 when President Ferdinand E. Marcos declared martial law and arrogated all governmental powers unto himself. Candidly labeled "constitutional authoritarianism," the regime was effectively more authoritarian than constitutional. Indeed, the Constitution of 1973 became a most manipulable instrument for the president's dictator-like powers. With the legislature abolished, the judiciary intimidated, the mass media controlled, and political parties (except the Marcos-created New Society Movement) weakened, the presidency and the civil and military services were the only political institutions that gained strength under martial law. The suffrage exercises since 1973, the activation of a Parliament in 1978, and the cosmetic lifting of martial law in 1981 did little to change this general characterization.

Economic growth and social justice were the avowed prizes for curtailing political rights. Nevertheless, rhetoric aside, the state hardly masked its role as guarantor of elite domination. The feeble efforts at nationalism were reversed by strengthening American—or more accurately, global capitalistic—control. The Philippines became an eager client of the World Bank as it fashioned a model-dependent economy.[14] Native enterprises would not survive without subordinate licensure arrangements with the multinationals. The few local firms that flourished during this period were well connected to political officials, especially the Marcoses.

These policies did not maintain growth. Rather, the export-oriented strategy, coupled with mismanagement of the economy and the government, led to business shutdowns, overall economic crisis, and negative growth by 1984.

Social justice was not served either. The gap between the rich and the poor widened. Labor was severely restrained. Peasants found agrarian reform—the declared centerpiece of martial law programs—illusory.[15] Few tenants became landowners. Rather, many entered into unprotected new tenure arrangements or became workers in large plantations or corporate farms. Others took substandard wages in the cities or became contract workers in foreign lands. They were joined there by laborers, clerks, and even some professionals who accepted lower status jobs to escape the economic crunch.

The economic and social difficulties were accompanied by growing militarization, trampling of human rights, and extrajudicial killings.

The assassination of a major political opposition figure, Senator Benigno S. Aquino, Jr., amidst the looming economic crisis galvanized the middle class and the business community into open and widespread protests. This culminated in the People Power Revolution of February 1986 which ousted the Marcos government and catapulted the widow Corazon Aquino to the presidency.

The Transition Toward Redemocratization

Aquino presides over a government that has declared the recommitment of the Philippines to democracy. A new constitution was drafted and overwhelmingly ratified by the Filipino people within a year of her assumption to office. The legislature was reactivated and its members chosen in competitive elections within eighteen months. The third leg, local elections, took place before the second anniversary of the People Power Revolution. Other significant political events occurred in quick succession. The Supreme Court regained its old luster of independence, and the judiciary as a whole was reorganized. The mass media, unmuzzled, have flourished; there are as many as twenty dailies in Metropolitan Manila and scattered regional and local newspapers. Opposition media, particularly radio, regularly feature interviews with the deposed Marcos and his allies. Finally, successful state visits to the United States, Southeast Asia, China, and Japan, and playing host to the first ASEAN State Summit in a decade have consolidated the government's international standing.

The broadening of democratic space has had its limits, however. Although several political prisoners were released to wide acclaim upon the ouster of Marcos, many less prominent prisoners remain. Peasant and urban dissenters continue to risk imprisonment, although due process is more carefully observed.

Political stability is threatened by insurgency of the Left and the Right. The communists engage the army in pitched battles in the countryside and undertake urban terrorism in the guise of collecting blood debts for the people. Meanwhile, some members of the military, unreconciled to the return to the barracks, have attempted at least five coups, one strong enough to reach the palace courtyard and destroy the building of the armed forces headquarters. At least one key torture and assassination (of a labor leader) has also been linked to a military faction. Moreover, the massacre of peasant marchers by soldiers loyal to the new government stands as a gory symbol of its poor control over the military and its vacillation toward agrarian reform.

With assaults from both sides, the Aquino government has become centrist almost by default. Cabinet shakeups have claimed victims of both conservative or pro-military officials and human rights advocates. Aside from the desire for ideological balancing, the call of electoral politics—more than half the cabinet left to run for the legislature—rumors of corruption and factional splits have taken care of the rest. The cabinet now stands as a largely technocratic group, very few of whom were prominently identified as leaders of groups opposed to Marcos. They also come almost uniformly from the private sector, with very little government experience. Some do not even have a background in the fields they head. Except for Fidel Ramos, hero of the Revolution who was appointed in February 1988 to the defense portfolio (direct from being chief of staff of the armed forces), there are no superstars in the cabinet.

Despite marked improvement in the effectiveness of certain agencies (such as health, economic planning, and public works), there is a general impression of lack of aggressiveness and commitment to new trails toward social justice and nationalism. In addition, although the president herself is perceived to share these faults, the overwhelming affection for Cory, as she is universally fondly called, makes the people absolve her. They still focus all their hopes on her, making it nearly impossible to move the country away from the bane of personalism and centralism that has slowed its development in the past.

In many policies, the administration prefers to keep its options open. This is the declared stance in the controversy over the U.S. military bases, the agreement to which is due to expire in 1991. It also appears operative as regards agrarian reform; the comprehensive program promulgated as one of the last legislative acts of the president (on the eve of the reopening of Congress) left crucial points for its decision and therefore remains in limbo. The question of selective debt repudiation or acceptance of all Marcos-incurred loans also remains unresolved. Meanwhile, many of these funds lie unused because of poor absorptive capacity, and construction proceeding from some (such as the nuclear plant) is left to rot. Where decisions have been unequivocally made, they look like mere continuations of Marcos' policies. The commitment to the private sector as the engine for growth is a policy dating back to colonial times. The World Bank recommended the drive for privatization to Marcos, and it is only now being implemented fully, using staff papers prepared under his direction.[16]

These problems aside, the society and the economy as a whole have responded favorably. GNP is going up, although not to the extent predicted by government economists. Meanwhile, the number of people who think themselves poor has also decreased,[17] thereby reinforcing the idea that public confidence has indeed been restored by the new government.

SALIENT FEATURES OF THE ADMINISTRATIVE SYSTEM

While heavily influenced by its history, the bureaucracy is a Philippine model, not merely a poor imitation of an American one. It has also been shaped by the Filipino social structure and psychology, and the demands made on it by its domestic and foreign clients and the public at large. In this section, we will discuss its ideology, structure, and personnel, and in the next we will describe its dynamics.

The Ideological Framework

The ideological framework encompasses the system's perspective on the values, ideals, and goals that give meaning to its work. It includes development and nation building as the ultimate aims, and thus developmentalism and nationalism as important parts of its ideology. Two instrumental characteristics—technocracy and authoritarianism—like the ends, permeate the system and guide its decisions.

Developmentalism

Like other Third World nations, the Philippines has caught the fever of "developmentalism"—the desire for rapid growth within a context of political stability. Under the First Development Decade, this meant the desire for rapid economic growth, and the benefits of it were expected to trickle down to the masses eventually. Despite the increased GNP in the 1960s, welfare did not improve, particularly for those at the bottom of the pile, and the rhetoric changed to "redistribution with growth" in the annals of World Bank theorists.[18] In the Philippines, the goal itself was labeled in Marcos' five-year plan as "economic development for social justice," suggesting the primacy of social concerns over the economic. The same aim is asserted by the Aquino government which has called its plan "People-Powered Development." The term also signifies a bid for a greater role by those outside government, including commercial, industrial, and financial firms as well as the so-called cause-oriented organizations on whose support she rode to power.

The country has chosen the capitalistic model which guards the strength of the economy above the welfare of its citizens, particularly its poor majority. Thus, in conflicts between economic and social goals, the economic has nearly invariably taken priority even when the expressed policy has been in the other direction. One can glean this notion from controversies involving the displacement of peasants and tribal peoples to make way for agroindustrial investments, and in the disregard of human issues in favor of the needs of the economy.[19] One can see it even more starkly in so-called social programs which tended to cater not to the needs of the suffering majority but to the special amenities of the elite and the production of human resources for their enterprises.[20]

These projects continue undisturbed under the Aquino regime, although, to its credit, no new programs with these problems have been started. This may not reflect a greater concern for the social consequences of development as much as the lack of funding to initiate such large-scale projects.

Today the model is more openly criticized within and outside the bureaucracy. Ideological debates were sparked by the crisis of the foreign debt and World Bank pressures toward import liberalization, which have led to greater suspicion of the role of foreigners in the economy and society. However, they remain minority views since the political leadership, like its predecessors, has declared its faith in free enterprise.

Commitment to the Nation

The bureaucracy took up a special role in maintaining the Filipino nation when it became the first government instrumentality turned over to natives during the American occupation. This commitment has two facets. First is pride in being Filipino and praise for such qualities as the beauty of the land and close family ties. More directly, it involves a strong belief in the capacity of Filipinos to solve their own problems, often bolstered by the chauvinistic notion that they have superior intellect but have resources that are either inadequate or dissipated by greedy compatriots. Many cite the fact that Filipino experts serve creditably in other countries. This sense of efficacy leads to a feeling of shame in having to seek foreign advice and assistance, moving them away from the developmentalist syndrome.

This nationalism goes beyond sentimentality. It extends to a sense of public service, shown by personnel who work faithfully in their respective offices and sometimes also use their own time and resources to serve.[21] It is also not necessarily a "safe" commitment, since civil servants in close touch with the masses courted military suspicion as subversives during the authoritarian period.

Nationalism also involves some antiforeign sentiments. This characteristic was in evidence during the 1960s when President Carlos P. Garcia enunciated the Filipino First Policy and moved against Chinese businesses in favor of the native bourgeosie. The more recent outcry against American and multinational hegemony also embodies a radical critique of their global, not just Philippine, domination. As such, it would conflict with the developmentalist and technocratic elements of the bureaucracy's ideology.

Authoritarianism

Filipino culture has a strong authoritarian strain exemplified by paternal supremacy and the quick resort to violence for resolving arguments. Moreover, any bureaucracy is inherently authoritarian. Public administration has rescued the situation for democracy by positing the dominance of political leaders over the administrative system and its accountability, through them, to the people. The dictatorship cut this line of accountability, giving greater weight to capitalistic and crony demands rather than social concerns. It also engendered a reliance on military might at a very early instance, obviating the possibility of nonviolent resolution of issues dividing the government and the people.

With the reemergence of democracy, the military has been driven back to the barracks, but its penchant to maintain a political role has not been completely stilled. Meanwhile, the regime has perpetuated the authoritarian methods of its predecessor against the civil service it inherited from him. Summary dismissals, demotions, forced retirements, and political loyalty tests have cowered internal critics and silenced dissension for the most part.

Despite its distrust and repression of the bureaucracy, the new government has enthroned the ideology of popular participation. During the Marcos period, participation was a struggle of the bureaucracy against the regime but in conjunction with popular sectors. Today, participation means the increasing resort to private firms and nongovernmental as monitors of bureaucratic performance. Now, the civil service finds itself bereft of much open public support, and participation has turned inward, into organizing unions within government. Manifesting its usual ambivalence, the Aquino regime provided in the Constitution of 1987 the right of government officials and employees to form organizations, but withheld from them the right to strike.

Technocracy

Technocracy involves not only high reliance on a group of people called "technocrats"—technical experts who put rationality consideration above political concerns—but also connotes the prominence of their approach throughout the bureaucracy. Technocracy is expected to streamline the system through constant innovation, use of modern techniques, and speedy and efficacious implementation. It is manifested in the impatience with regular channels and thus the resort to other arrangements exempt from controls and resource constraints faced by the rest of the bureaucracy. Supposedly neutral with regard to ends, technocracy is an instrumental companion of developmentalism and reinforces its economistic approach. But as an important study has concluded, Philippine technocracy has also been marked by "a commitment to building a nation by locally inspired reforms for a capitalist mode economic life."[22] Moreover, its reverence for technology over politics also makes it a willing complement to authoritarianism. This approach thus absorbs and embodies many of the contradictions of the system.

Structure

The Philippines reverted to a presidential form of government under the Constitution of 1987, relegating to a historical footnote Marcos' dalliance with the semiparliamentary system patterned after the French. Like all presidents before her, Aquino decided to put her mark on the bureaucracy by reorganizing it, a process that has continued beyond the second anniversary of her inauguration. The goal of the current overhaul involves more than "trimming the fat" and "streamlining the civil service"—the catchwords of previous reorganizations. It specifically seeks to "demarcosify" the administration, and thus to cleanse this inherited institution from the stench of corruption and obsequiousness to the deposed president.[23]

Departmental Structure

Beyond the cosmetic renaming of "ministries" to "departments" and the sale of some public enterprises to the private sector, the overall structure created by Marcos' reorganization commission has not altered significantly. All agencies, including bureaus and public enterprises, are grouped into sectoral ministries. Most follow the "departmental model" under which all bureaus are staff offices and line functions are carried out by regional offices distributed throughout the country. In a few cases, there is a perceptible increase in the allocation of funds to the regions, implying greater commitment to decentralization.

On the whole, however, as of June 1987, the Aquino government has effectively installed a top-heavy structure as it increased the number of undersecretaries (Marcos' "deputy ministers") from forty-six to sixty-six, or from an average of fewer than two to almost three per department, each new appointee bringing in new staff of perhaps five persons each. Meanwhile, the percentage of assistant regional or bureau directors—the lowest management rung—has decreased from 38 to 25 percent of the career executive service.

Central Control Agencies

A prominent feature of the current structure is the enshrinement, in the Constitution of 1973 and 1987, of central agencies to ensure the democratic doctrine that a public office is a public trust. These agencies include the Civil Service Commission which is mandated to safeguard the merit system; the Commission on Audit, to ensure financial and management accountability; and the twin institutions of the ombudsman and the *Sandiganbayan*—a special administrative court—to further control the bureaucracy.[24] These bodies monitor and evaluate the performance of individuals and agencies, following the most recent trends in the personnel and auditing fields.

These were all supposed to be independent of the executive, a provision frequently breached by Marcos. Under Aquino, these agencies have not yet reestablished their distance from the president. For instance, the chairpersons of the Civil Service and Audit commissions thought nothing of attending cabinet meetings and joining the president in regional visits and campaign trips in 1986 and 1987. Nevertheless, their actions are now subject to legislative scrutiny, a factor that used to keep central agencies and regular departments on their toes before martial law, and whose vigor is gradually being reinforced under the new order.

The Unitary System and Decentralization

The Philippines functions under a unitary structure in practice, despite elected officials at four subnational levels. Local governments continue to be financially dependent on the national government and are subject to stringent controls in their exercise of delegated powers. The authoritarian government tended to reverse the decentralizing trend begun in the mid–1950s. The continued centralization under Aquino appears to be due to her inheritance of the tradition of centralism and to specific ascribed qualities. First, the love—bordering on adoration—that she inspires from the populace makes them distrust pronouncements that do not come directly from the mouth of "their" Cory. Second and ironically, the perception of her weakness and incapacity to effectively wield power makes it imperative that decisions be shown as emanating from her, thus stifling her more natural inclination to delegate power.

Decentralization may gain a foothold with the organization of regional autonomy in Mindanao and the Cordilleras. These two regions are inhabited by cultural minorities whose armed resistance convinced the center to yield them some power. Some local officials may also be able to demonstrate more independence from Manila, since the Local Government Code, even under Marcos, allowed for more autonomous governance for units able to manifest strong capacity for it. Besides, deconcentration may also result as regional officers and others at lower levels assume their powers with greater vigor and fight against the central tendency to make them little more than extra conduits in the flow of paperwork between the villages and top officials.

Personnel Resources

The civil service is one of the biggest employers of the country. It is described below in terms of representativeness, level of professionalization, and leadership. It is also very much affected by the personnel and salary changes undertaken following the Revolution.

Representativeness

Like most bureaucrats, Filipino civil servants tend to be urbanized and middle class, although most of them originate from rural areas and now have higher status than their parents. These show that government is an avenue for social mobility and may explain both its relatively low prestige (because upper class persons prefer to be in the private sector) and why many persons use membership in it for private gain.

Dominant ethnic groups like Tagalog and Cebuanos are well represented, perhaps because their regions are important centers of education and commerce. Meanwhile, an important religious minority like the Muslims have a smaller percentage than in the general population and seem to need higher qualification than other Filipinos to enter the service.[25] On the other hand, there appears to be no bias in the recruitment of women, but their proportion at higher levels is much smaller. Nevertheless, there are proportionately more female executives in the Philippines than in most other bureaucracies.[26]

Professionalization Issues

Befitting a society whose stock of educated people rivals that of many developed nations, the bureaucracy has a higher proportion of college-educated persons than other Third World states.[27] During the American period, many civil servants received their college diplomas as part-time evening students. Others are now devoting their afterwork hours to getting graduate credits, especially since graduate units in public administration (or equivalent credits in training programs) are required before promotion to higher positions. However, diplomas do not always imply competence since many colleges are profit-making firms rather than real institutions of higher learning.

The high level of professionalization has dysfunctional effects when it tends toward elitism and narrow perspectives. The first is carried over from the larger society where everyone proudly sports his or her academic degree or title (e.g., Dr., Engr., CPA), even in social gatherings. This stress on status makes the professional unwilling to understand the rationale of administrative personnel in upholding bureaucratic rules, or of other professionals in maintaining their own norms, creating a rift between two groups in the same agency.

Elite attitudes may foster the belief that no other group can handle a problem, dooming most intersectoral programs to failure. In addition, professionals may not try to see how their work can facilitate the performance of other groups. For instance, in a study of one ministry, we found an appalling lack of program awareness among professions that were supposed to assist direct providers in the delivery of a service. Rather, accountants, say, were worried only about balancing books and were immune to pleas for certifying the availability of funds for tasks that were priority to that professional group.[28] Professionalism thus appears to provide an advantage in delivering services but needs to be extended beyond its narrow confines when more than one professional group is involved in implementation.

The Career Executive Service

The highest level of the civil service is patterned after the British administrative class. Started in 1973, the Career Executive Service (CES) is supposed to constitute an elite corps of career administrators who possess competence, development orientation, and sensitivity and who can move from agency to agency according to the needs of the system. Under Marcos, the bulk of CES officers (CESOs) consisted of incumbents of positions designated as high-ranking rather than persons specifically recruited because they exemplified these special qualities. Thus, only elitism was attained, but the main rationale behind the departure from position classification was not realized.

The new government changed the complexion of CESOs as it separated 35 percent of them from the service, reassigned 16 percent, and promoted 6 percent, leaving only 43 percent untouched. Replacements and recruits to new positions almost uniformly came directly from the private sector with no prior government service. Their new orientation differed from that of the oldtimers, sometimes resulting in healthy competition and renewed developmental and nationalist commitment on both sides, and at other times resulting in a clash of personalities and distrust. Teamwork is developing in the innovative cabinet assistants' system within which selected undersecretaries and assistant secretaries lay the groundwork for cabinet decisions and their implementation.

The Changing of the Guard: Purges and New Appointments

The new government came in with some distrust of the bureaucracy, equating it with the corruption and unresponsiveness of the regime it deposed. It also had an army of followers hungry for a crack at power after twenty years of being on the outside. Furthermore, it took over a nearly bankrupt treasury, and retrenchment of the huge civil service loomed as an attractive cost-saving measure.

Article III, Section 2, of the provisional ''Freedom Constitution'' of the Revolutionary Government provided for the continuation in office of elected officials and civil servants ''until otherwise provided by proclamation or executive order or upon the appointment and qualification of their successors, if such is made within one year from February 25, 1986.''

This article provided the legal framework for removing the tenure security of career civil servants, resulting in thousands of forced resignations and retirements. The first estimates ranged up to 300,000 persons in a bureaucracy just under 1.5 million. These figures may be grossly exaggerated, since, as of June 1987, fewer than 30,000 have actually been removed.[29] Most of these have received benefits at least equal to one month's pay for every year of service, sometimes more.

The demoralization the purges caused cannot be reduced to figures because the threat of losing one's job was real to perhaps as much as half of the entire government labor force. Department secretaries demanded courtesy resignations of the top five or seven levels in their offices, affecting not only the people in those positions, but also their assistants and administrative support staff. Even if these resignations had not been accepted, the period of uncertainty could not have produced exemplary performance.

The purges were not completed in one round. After the period of courtesy resignations came agency reorganization, which resulted in persons who passed the initial screening now subject to being ''reorganized out.'' The problem was worsened by the continual growth of the bureaucracy, but new appointees were hardly better than the people they replaced.[30] Moreover, employees' organizations charged lack of good faith, unfairness, and favoritism in the reorganization process.[31] By March 1988, the overhauling process was stayed by the legislature twice as Congress attempted—unsuccessfully—to regain the prerogative of reorganization it lost under martial law.

Summary dismissals have been questioned as being without basis and violating the security of tenure of civil servants, but they have been defended as the only way to clean up the bureaucracy. Some appointments have been described as simple spoils, but they have been justified as the best means of getting persons committed to the ideals of the new order. Some changes have been criticized as vendetta against old-regime supporters who have remained professional and honest but defended as mere results of neutral reorganization and the need to restructure the bureaucracy to make it better able to fulfill its goals. Until it is completed—and the process remains very slow—one cannot really be definitive about its character and results.

The Issue of Low Pay and Equity

Apart from the purges and reorganization, the issue that has caused the most outcry in the bureaucracy is that of salaries. CESOs, classified by rank, have always been paid higher rates than the rest of the bureaucracy, the mean salary of which is hardly above the poverty line. The Aquino government widened the gap by giving pay hikes of 80 to 120 percent to CESOs, to complement the doubling of the pay of the president and other top government officials, as mandated by the new Constitution. The bulk of the civil servants received increases of 10 to 20 percent, and 35 percent if they had particularly supportive or aggressive department heads, thus aggravating their feeling of neglect and inequity. Meanwhile, military personnel, gaining from the display of force of five coup attempts, were able to wangle higher increases in base pay and merit promotions. The salary and reorganization issues of the civilian service thus continue to fester, and the bureaucracy and the political leadership still remain distrustful of each other.

DYNAMICS OF THE SYSTEM

The traditions and practices of the system show the interplay of ideology, structure, and personnel with the environment of the bureaucracy. Some technologies are traditional ways of doing things, whereas others are products of recent learning. They combine into a system that can fuse disparate elements at certain points and erupt into conflicts at others. How the system works will be illustrated in the following discussion under the sections "Financing and Implementing Development Projects," "Use and Adaptation of Western Technology," "Participatory Efforts," "A Politicized Bureaucracy," and "Organizational Learning."

Financing and Implementing Development Projects

The drive to develop the economy is funded by taxes and foreign grants and loans. Resort to external borrowing was not closely monitored, so that in 1983 the country would not meet its obligations without restructuring its foreign debt. There are other failures in implementation: many projects are delayed or not completed; some corruption takes place in their negotiation and administration; and local funds are either not available as counterpart during the project period or cannot be provided to continue it afterward. In early 1988, it was reported that the government was unable to provide counterpart funding for many millions in loans, for which it was already paying commitment fees.[32]

Use and Adaptation of Western Technology

With the host of technical assistance and training programs available to the bureaucracy, its staffs are well versed in the latest management and program technologies from the West. Some have been adopted because of pressure from their American proponents. Others are accepted because they are deemed "more rational," although personnel may later find them inapplicable for various reasons. Below are a few examples of such problems.

The American Pressure

The original position classification and pay plan of 1957 was heavily influenced by American advisers who hewed closely to the California system they were most familiar with. Despite objections from their boldest Filipino counterparts, the plan became an exercise in " 'scientism'—a valiant but vain effort at mechanical precision."[33] Yet the adaptations were not an unmixed blessing since some have produced their own inequities, having been based on political connections rather than the endeavor to realize the goal of "equal pay for equal work."

Inappropriate Assumption

Other techniques may be adopted immediately with a little training but may not be appropriate to the Philippines. For a few, it is because they require scarce machines or unwarranted quantification. For others, the problems relate to deeper issues such as their assumptions about the direction and automaticity of benefits and the effect of the outputs on the local culture and society.

Local users have their own ways of coping with the problem. For instance, they routinely use required sophisticated techniques like cost-benefit analysis or feasibility studies using assumptions relevant to Western settings. They know that favored projects will usually fare better anyway because they will spend more time on data gathering and analysis to justify them. However, few analysts actually propose modifications of the technique to take political and cui bono questions into account, even when they use them in practice. Then when the U.S. Agency for International Development comes out with "social soundness analysis" or the World Health Organization with restructured health care delivery, they have varied reactions. In the first case they contend that their own adaptations, if systematized, would have been more relevant to Philippine localities. In the second case, they see much of their own earlier recommendations in the new proposal, but realize that theirs were not accepted because they were only made by locals.[34] Sometimes the choice is for capital intensity when labor itself is in abundance. Thus, Western-style self-serve machines (e.g., duplicators) proliferate, but a person is usually hired to serve its users. Or computers may be available (often as part of a foreign loan), but the staff is not trained in their use and painstakingly makes needed calculations manually. (Sometimes this is to make sure that results do not stray too far from expectations.) Some machines may fall into disuse because a needed spare part is not available or is too expensive. In other cases, the more appropriate technology may in fact be the more labor-using kind. For instance, in rural road construction and maintenance, labor-based techniques have been found to be just as cost-effective as their equipment-based counterparts and have the added advantage of providing employment during the agricultural slack season.[35]

Toward Less Western Technology

Modifications to imported technology are now more openly pursued. Yet, although nationalism and increasing local sophistication are preferred justifications, it is also true that these techniques are undergoing drastic rethinking in their areas of origin, and their changes may be the ones being applied to the Philippines. In such cases, the changes may not be departures from developmentalism and technocracy as much as new ways of entrenching them.

Participatory Efforts

The rhetoric of the Second Development Decade elevated the people as the subject and object of development and mandated their involvement in the planning, implementation, and evaluation of government programs. In the Philippines, the ideal was loudly espoused by an authoritarian government and led to participation having two disparate manifestations. On the one hand, a government bent on control used it as a strategy to mobilize the people so that they could act as proper beneficiaries of its efforts. The creation of village brigades and other associations found a compliant public willing to do any bidding in order to receive much-needed services.

On the other hand, social animators tried to awaken communities to a sense of both popular power and rights, enjoining participation in their transformation as people and not as pawns. This second group came largely from voluntary, nongovernmental organizations. But the governmental agencies like the National Irrigation Administration (for communal irrigation systems) have also initiated and developed genuine efforts at people-involvement.[36] These were reinforced by a popular indigenous training technique called "barangay immersion" during which civil servants lived with, learned from, and worked with the masses.[37]

Participatory strategies were routinely required for practically every new government program. Sometimes, they were simply used as a herding mechanism. However, if any real sense of citizen empowerment was started, results could not be entirely under the government's control. After all, getting people involved and thus politicized is not a process that can be terminated at midstream. In fact, some analysts trace the roots of the People Power Revolution to community organizing, including change agents from within the bureaucracy.[38]

The Aquino government has taken a stronger stand in favor of participation than its predecessor. However, as before, the elite tend to be more involved in councils of government at all levels than the poor. Moreover, participation tends to be valued more when it engages people from outside the bureaucracy, but employee demands for participatory management have remained unheeded.

A Politicized Bureaucracy

From the sale of offices during the Spanish regime to the civil service examinations of the Americans, the approved sabotage of the Japanese, and the political patronage and corruption that pervaded the Third Republic and became institutionalized under the authoritarian regime, the Philippine bureaucracy now manifests different kinds of politicization and neutrality. Since no one is devoid of value, "neutrality" can only be exhibited by a person who either shares the regime's ideology or who, learning Weberian norms well, considers him- or herself bound to the goals of political masters, regardless of personal preferences. The best of the ideological example is the technocrat as portrayed by Ocampo blending in some way his developmentalist and nationalistic commitments.[39] The worst of the second group is a robot-like human who routinely complies with given rules and refuses to recognize exemptions. The bureaucracy as a whole probably falls between these extremes, generally abiding by the doctrine that it is subordinate to political leaders.

Politicization occurs when decision-makers use extrabureaucratic considerations, including deplored personalistic and partisan factors, as well as admired professional, political, and moral criteria. Corruption is a usual result of the former set. An enterprising employee may pocket government receipts, an instance of individual graft. But the more pernicious is an internal syndicate which parallels the formal organization and apportions bribes according to agreed rates. Such systemic corruption contaminates the entire agency and requires, except in rare instances, the tolerance, if not the active participation, of the agency head.

Despite purges at the beginning of martial law and under Aquino and the faithful rectitude of perhaps a majority of civil servants, corruption of both kinds has not been stemmed and continues to pollute the bureaucracy. Under Marcos, that was encouraged by negative role models at the top who not only enriched themselves in office, but also spewed out policies that manifestly favored special persons or groups, thus showing that corruption is a problem not only of the bureaucracy, but of the political leadership as well.[40]

On the other hand, Aquino is widely seen as a moral leader, untainted by corruption. However, she appears to lack the strength to go after the rumored crooks in her government, resorting only to the Marcosian copout demand to "provide the documents." With corrupt leaders being both shrewd and legalistic, and lower level personnel having found willing patrons to shield them from investigations, corruption in the Philippines is unlikely to diminish voluntarily.

Other kinds of politicized behavior were encouraged in an authoritarian regime which strove to appear legitimate. There was the partisan use of employees for election campaigns and manipulation of election results, and the intimidation of those who joined opposition rallies.[41] There was also the use of the staff's expertise to provide statistics or interpretations more favorable to the regime in power, even against the technical criteria in which they were so well trained.[42]

Electioneering and circulation of false data appear to have been largely swept away. However, the gap between rhetoric and practice continues. Like the previous government, the current regime constantly harps on compassion and the priority of the poor but allows the bureaucracy to formulate and implement rules against that spirit.[43]

Organizational Learning

Filipino bureaucrats learned from Spain that they should keep meticulous records and cover every decision with all applicable legal provisions. Yet strict adherence to rules is only part of the picture. Why exceptions are not reflected in the recorded organizational memory can probably be traced to personalism which is manifested in two ways here. First is personalism with a touch of authoritarianism as subordinates take the cue from the boss and tend to follow his or her lead, whatever the rules say. Thus, despite training in records management and management information systems, organizational records reflect the current sense of what is important, according to one's reading of the desire of the present leadership.

Second is personalism in terms of reliance on what individual employees decide to remember. A system memory is not developed because records are viewed as personal property, collected to advance one's analysis and interest or to protect oneself from future problems, following the legacy of those investigated by Madrid. Civil servants may thus avoid being held responsible for a possibly controversial action by not putting its records on file. They also try to keep important documents themselves, rather than surrender them to the central records unit.

To be sure, some divergence is fueled by corruption or bias. Sometimes, however, a flexible approach may be occasioned by more accurate reading of public needs. It may serve as a counterpoint to rigid directives that ignore special needs at local levels. Since such departures from precedents are not recorded, lessons that may be learned from both mistakes and innovations are not clarified and analyzed to become part of any new criteria for making decisions. This problem gains importance when issues at hand are not mere exercises in logic but have direct effects on people's lives. This may also explain why there are many instances of responsive public service, but the entire bureaucracy can be characterized as technocratic and dehumanized.

CONCLUDING REMARKS

Existing within a nation still in crisis, the administrative system manifests rather than resolves the contradictions of Philippine society. Two years after the People Power Revolution, it is clear that a change of government alone will not bring the country to nirvana. A few changes have been evident. Although some are clearly toward more responsiveness and national commitment, others tend to reinforce the Marcosian qualities decried in the bureaucracy of the previous incarnation.

Each major feature meets counterpoints which, though weaker, are echoed in some other social fractions. These minor themes together can create a radically different system from the current one. For instance, the developmentalist, authoritarian syndrome is countered by participatory, decentralized strategies that can move an alienated bureaucracy into a more responsive system. Such a development would be helped by the fact that the redemocratization process is still fragile and the government must thus be perceived as trying to reach out to all sectors. Thus, it has to provide outlets for nationalistic pressures, perhaps by supporting the indigenization of imported technology, sometimes by listening to local experts. It must appear to give in to some popular demands that can be used by its politicized personnel as bases for their own actions. It must from time to time listen to its own personnel, as even the grudging salary increases and the postponement of reorganization manifest that attempt at reconciliation. When government is criticized as too distant and uncaring, it can delegate power to the local areas and create offices closer to the grassroots. Or, alternatively, it can use a ploy of centralism and summon village residents to the special regional visits where they can see and speak with Cory Aquino herself.

While guaranteeing elite domination and providing ever more incentives to private firms, the state must also fight insurgency. Thus it must take steps to pacify the poor by providing basic services, restoring labor's right to strike and increasing the minimum wage, even if only by the minimum amount.

These counterpoints are not simply proposed reforms but are supported by formal mandates and are in effect in pockets of the bureaucracy. However, it cannot be predicted that they will succeed in overhauling the system because they are not the only themes identifiable in the civil service. Politicization does not always signify nationalistic commitments; it may presage more corruption and greater partisanship. Professionalization may lead to more responsiveness, but it also opens up the system to elitism. Participatory councils can mean more control by the people, or more effective authority over them. On the other hand, more technology may not dehumanize but may give a concerned professional more time for caring service. In other words, the seeds toward a bureaucracy that can provide more effective servants of the people or more efficient masters over them have both been sown. The bureaucracy alone cannot choose which direction will win out. Its fate cannot be independent of the conflicting forces struggling in the Philippine society in which it is embedded.

NOTES

I am grateful to my colleagues, Ma. Concepcion P. Alfiler and Luz G. Tancangco, for comments on an earlier draft.

1. See Ferrel Heady, "The Philippines: A Fusion of East and West," *Philippine Journal of Public Administration,* 1 (Manila), (January 1957), pp. 27–45.

2. Leon Wolff, *Little Brown Brother: America's Bid for Empire Which Cost 250,000 Lives* (New York: Doubleday and Co., 1960).

3. The Schurman Commission, April 9, 1899, cited in Jose N. Endriga, "The Influence of American Bureaucratic Institutions in the Philippines," paper read before the Seminar on Bureaucratic Theory, Bureaucratic Practice: Public Administration in the Philippines and America, held at the University of the Philippines at Los Baños, Laguna (9–13 October 1978), pp. 3–4.

4. Jose N. Endriga, "Historical Notes or Graft and Corruption in the Philippines," *Philippine Journal of Public Administration,* 23 (Manila, July-October 1979), pp. 241–54.

5. Onofre D. Corpuz, *The Philippines* (Englewood Cliffs, N.J.: Prentice-Hall, 1965, Philippine edition, 1970), pp. 83–85.

6. "Flag independence" is the term applied to the nominal withdrawal of sovereignty of the colonial power despite continuing exercise of its domination over a new state. For the Philippines, it recalls the stirring symbol of the hauling down of the American flag and the unfurling of the Philippine flag on 4 July 1946. The term comes from Renato Constantino and Letizia R. Constantino, *The Philippines: The Continuing Past* (Quezon City: Foundation for Nationalist Studies, 1978).

7. During Marcos' time, it became fashionable to designate different "Republics" by an ordinal number. The First Republic refers to the government established by the Revolution of 1896; the Second, the Japanese puppet republic, 1942–1945; the Third, the Republic established following flag independence until the imposition of martial law, 1946–1972. Marcos wanted his nominal lifting of martial law to be recognized as the "Fourth Philippine Republic." Since that was still effectively a dictatorship, the people generally used the term with derision, although the reference to the previous three stuck. The current government is understandably reluctant to take over that name, but also has not decided how it should be referred to.

8. Ramon M. Osmeña, "Osmeña's Legacy: Integrity and Nationalism," *Bulletin Today* (9 September 1985), p. 7.

9. Benito Legarda, Jr., and Roberto Y. Garcia, "Economic Collaboration: The Trading Relationship," in Frank Golay (ed.), *Philippine American Relations* (Manila, Bombay, and New York: Solidaridad Publishing House, 1966), p. 134.

10. David Wurfel, "Problems of Decolonization," in Golay, *Philippine American Relations,* p. 150.

11. Ibid, pp. 156–57.

12. Jose V. Abueva (ed.), *Perspectives in Government Reorganization* (Manila: University of the Philippines, College of Public Administration, 1969), pp. 6–7.

13. This faith has since been shaken by their failures and frustrations in implementing the programs, their heightened awareness of the objective conditions in the country and the global economy, and faltering of Pax Americana. For a discussion of the failure and ensuing end of the American century, see Robert B. Stauffer, "The American Devel-

opment Model: Hidden Agenda for the Third World," *Philippine Journal of Public Administration*, 21 (Manila April 1977), pp. 123–40.

14. Walden Bello, David Kinley, and Elaine Elinson, *Development Debacle: The World Bank in the Philippines* (San Francisco: Institute for Food and Development Policy, 1982).

15. Ma. Aurora Carbonell-Catilo, "Agrarian Reform Policies: Their Social Justice Content and Consequences on Rural Development," *Philippine Journal of Public Administration* 25 (Manila, April 1981), pp. 172–91.

16. Romeo B. Ocampo, "Privatization, Public Choice and Public Administration," paper delivered during the Third National Conference on Public Administration, 28–30 September 1987, Manila.

17. Mahar Mangahas, "Economic Welfare Has Recovered from 1983–85 Debacle: Survey," *Manila Chronicle*, 23 February 1988, pp. 1, 15.

18. Hollis Chenery, *Redistribution with Growth* (London: Oxford University Press, 1974).

19. See, for instance, Bello et al., *Development Debacle*; Ledivina V. Cariño, "Some Problems in the Pursuit of Social Development in the Philippines," *Philippine Journal of Public Administration*, 22 (Manila),(April 1978), pp. 140–54; Ernest Feder, *Perverse Development* (Quezon City, Philippines: Foundation for Nationalist Studies, 1983); Institute for Food and Development Studies, *The Banana Industry in the Philippines* (San Francisco, 1977).

20. See, for instance, P. S. Manalang, "Issues in Philippine Education," *Philippine Sociological Review* 25 (Quezon City, January-April 1977), pp. 63–68 and Linda K. Richter, "Priorities in National Development: A Comparative Analysis of Philippine Policy Implementation under Martial Law," *Philippine Journal of Public Administration* 24 (Manila, January 1980), pp. 1–25.

21. I have personally witnessed such performances, some bordering on the heroic, among health personnel, extension workers, and local officials, among others. These are partially written up in "Why Some Medical Personnel Do Not Leave: Correlates of Migration Intentions," *Philippine Journal of Public Administration* 24 (Manila, July 1980), pp. 249–83; "A Functional Analysis of the Ministry of Health," report submitted to the Ministry and the World Bank (with Ma. Conception P. Alfiler, and Rebecca P. Albano) (Manila: College of Public Administration, University of the Philippines, 1980), pp. 101–10; and "Agricultural Extension Workers: Problems of Organization and of the Profession" (with Obdulia P. Sison), paper presented in the First Agricultural Policy Conference (14–16 April 1975) (Los Baños, Laguna, Philippines: Center for Policy and Development Studies, 1975), pp. 16–18.

22. Romeo B. Ocampo, "Technocrats and Planning: Sketch and Exploration," *Philippine Journal of Public Administration* 15 (Manila, January 1971), pp. 1–62.

23. Presidential Commission on Government Reorganization, *Report on Principles and Policy Proposals, Book I* (Manila, 1986).

24. Under the Constitution of 1973, a *Tanodbayan* (literally, watchdog for the people) was given the functions of the ombudsman. Under the Constitution of 1987, the Tanodbayan becomes only a special prosecutor for administrative offenses and is overshadowed by the ombudsman who has both proactive, initiatory, and investigative powers.

25. Virginia Maglangit, "The Muslim Filipinos in the Government Service: Their Problems and Their Participation" (Ph.D. diss., submitted to the Centro Escolar University, 1975).

26. Proserpina D. Tapales, "Women in the Philippine Bureaucracy" (Ph.D. diss., submitted to Northern Illinois University, 1984).

27. The Philippine percentage as of 1977 is fifteenth in the world and about twice the proportion of college-educated people in other middle-income countries. The World Bank, *World Development Report, 1980* (New York: Oxford University Press, 1981), pp. 178–79.

28. Cariño, Alfiler, and Albano, "A Functional Analysis of the Ministry of Health." The Ministry has since retrained its personnel to develop and show this program awareness. Unfortunately, the problem is not unique to this office.

29. Author's estimates, based on a staff study by Dolores Gaffud of ninety-two public enterprises and twenty-three departments, figures provided by the Senate Committee on Civil Service and Government Reorganization as submitted by the Department of Budget and Management, and data of the Committee on Review of Executive Order No. 17.

30. Emanuel V. Soriano. "Upgrading the Civil Service System," paper delivered at the Colloquium on Public Management sponsored by the Development Academy of the Philippines and the University of the Philippines College of Public Administration, 4 August 1986.

31. See Confederation for Unity, Recognition and Advancement of Government Employees (COURAGE), Letter Circular for a Week-Long Protest dated 15 February 1987. See also Summary of Position Papers submitted to the Chairman during Public Hearings on Government Reorganization conducted by the Committee on Civil Service and Government Reorganization on 9 February 1988 and 22 February 1988, Office of the Chairman, Senate Committee on Civil Service and Government Reorganization (Manila, 1988).

32. Amando Doronila, "Unspent Aid Poses Problems for Government," *Manila Chronicle*, 16 January 1988, pp. 1, 9.

33. Abelardo G. Samonte, "WAPCO: A Case Study of Administrative Reform in the Philippines," in Hahn-Been Lee and Abelardo G. Samonte (eds.), *Administrative Reforms in Asia* (Manila: Eastern Regional Organization for Public Administration, 1970), pp. 1–71.

34. The CPA Research Team, "Methodological Aspects of Adaptations of Public Administration for Endogenous Development in the Socio-Cultural Contexts of Southeast Asian Regions" (Manila: Eastern Regional Organization for Public Administration, 1983), pp. 1–40.

35. International Labour Organization, World Employment Programme, *A Study of Labour Based/Equipment Supported Road Construction in the Philippines*, report prepared for the Ministry of Local Government, Republic of the Philippines, Regional Office for Asia and the Pacific, Bangkok and the ILO Office in Manila, August 1983.

36. Frances F. Korten, "Stimulating Community Participation: Obstacles and Options at Agency, Community and Societal Levels," *Rural Development Participation Review* (Spring 1981), pp. 1–6, and Jeanne Frances Illo and Ma. Elena Chiong-Javier, *Organizing Farmers for Irrigation Management: The Buhi-Lalo Experience* (Naga City: Research and Service Center, Ateneo de Naga, 1983), pp. 1–323.

37. Ledivina V. Cariño and Emma B. Viñeza (eds.), *The Indang Experience: Lessons from the First Barrio Immersion of the Career Executive Service Development Program* (Makati, Philippines: Development Academy of the Philippines, 1980), pp. 1–199, and "The Special Issue on the Barangay (Village) Immersion," *Philippine Journal of Public Administration* 24 (Manila, October 1980), pp. 323–92.

38. Emanuel V. Soriano, Patricia B. Licuanan, and Ledivina V. Cariño, *Understanding*

People Power: A Collection of Papers Presented at a DAP Symposium on People Power (Manila, 1986).

39. Ocampo, "Technocrats and Planning."

40. "The Special Issue on Graft and Corruption," *Philippine Journal of Public Administration* 23 (Manila, July-October 1979), pp. 221–406, and Victoria A. Bautista, "Public Interest Perspective: A Neglected Dimension in the Study of Corruption," *Philippine Sociological Review* 31 (Quezon City, July-December 1983), pp. 45–54.

41. Raul P. de Guzman and Luzviminda G. Tancangco, *An Assessment of the May 1984 Batasang Pambansa Elections* (Manila: University of the Philippines, College of Public Administration, 1986). See also R. P. de Guzman and L. G. Tancangco, *An Assessment of the February 1986 Special Presidential Elections: A Study of Political Change Through People Power* (Manila: University of the Philippines, College of Public Administration, 1986).

42. For instance, the use of legislated minimum wages instead of actual income received to describe the labor situation, the liberalizing of the meaning of "employment" to include fewer hours of work and backyard gardens, the inclusion of foreign debts among the country's export receipts (which allowed it to incur obligations beyond its ability to pay), among many other similar distortions. These are regularly unmasked in such publications as *Ibon Facts and Figures*, Manila, 1978 to date.

43. This is well analyzed in Roman Dubsky, "Development and Technocratic Thought in the Philippines" (DPA diss., submitted to the University of the Philippines, 1981).

PART II

THE MIDDLE EAST AND NORTH AFRICA

6

EGYPT

E. H. Valsan

HISTORICAL BACKGROUND

Egypt has inherited a system of administration whose changes over the ages reflect the country's long and turbulent history. Many expressions we use in management studies today—pyramidal form, for instance—point to the standing monuments which were built during the dawn of history through organization and mass mobilization. From the Pharaonic times to the modern days of revolution and development, Egypt has nurtured and sustained a centralized system of bureaucracy that has borne the brunt of its public administration.

In modern times, three major events have had considerable impact on the administration inherited by the "Free Officers" (a group of army officers who took the lead in 1952 in freeing Egypt from the monarchy and launching the revolution) who came to power in 1952: (1) the French invasion under Napoleon; (2) the rule of Turkish Viceroy Mohamed Aly; and (3) the British occupation of Egypt.

The French invasion in 1798 opened the door of European influence. The cultural impact of the three-year rule of Napoleon was everlasting.

The rule of Mohamed Aly (1805–1849) introduced major reforms that lay down the foundations of economic and administrative modernization mainly with the help of French and other foreign advisers. He too followed a highly centralized system of administration which was prevalent in Egypt and France, but he also introduced a system of civil service training. Whereas personal loyalty to the ruler was emphasized, the functions of the civil servants were directed largely toward the development and modernization of Egypt.

The British occupation took place in the wake of the extravagance of Mohamed Aly's successors and continued for seventy years despite vigorous opposition from nationalistic Egyptians. During this period, the British occupied higher levels of civil service. For example, in 1921 only forty-five Egyptians against forty-seven British got a monthly salary above 70 Egyptian pounds.[1]

In spite of British predominance and the earlier claims of Lord Cromer and others that they would clean up the administration, the British did not leave a major imprint on Egyptian administration as they did in India. This was probably because they were only occupying Egypt and not really ruling over it.

INTRODUCTION OF THE MERIT SYSTEM

In 1951 the government of Egypt invited a British expert to study its system of administration and to make recommendations. The report of A. P. Sinker (chairman, British Civil Service Commission) became an important document in the history of Egyptian public administration because, on its recommendation, a Civil Service Commission was established in October 1951.[2] For the first time the principle of merit as the basis for recruitment was made a rule, and the Civil Service Commission was authorized to regulate personnel administration in the government. However, before the government could effectively utilize the Civil Service Commission, the monarchy was overthrown and a new revolutionary regime took over in July 1952.

The recent history of Egyptian administration has reflected a mixture of the traditional influences of centralization and patrimonial influences in running a modernizing merit-oriented bureaucracy. In many ways, the concepts of overlapping and formalism suggested by Fred W. Riggs in his prismatic model find examples in Egyptian public administration.[3]

Social Setting

Religion plays an important part in both the personal and official life of Egyptian citizens. The majority community of Muslims and the minority of Coptic Christians are basically religious. Because Islam is a religion with a clear guide on socioeconomic and political behavior, its values are also reflected in the administrative system. Islam encourages social welfare; hence, the state is regarded as the proper and rightful initiator of social change and development. It is a religion that includes a social, political, legal, and cultural system.[4] Commonly used social expressions like "Incha Allah" (God willing) and "Al Hamdulillah" (thanks to God) reflect the hope and satisfaction with which citizens accept matters, including the political and administrative.

The Family

Another social institution with tremendous impact on the conduct of government is the family, which includes not just the husband, wife, and children, but a network of close relatives as well. An individual is supposed to share his or her success with the family: "With the patterns of sharing and solidarity, it is possible to understand why public officials in Egypt are made to feel that it is less of a crime to take money from public funds than to fail to find jobs for their relatives."[5]

Another value that emanates from the family is the subservience to authority typically vested in the father. The absolute authority of the father is sanctioned by the Koran.[6] Such respect and obedience make subordinates grow up with similar attitudes to their superiors in the office and government. Consequently, all decisions are expected from above, and "bureaucrats tend to do what their superiors want them to do, regardless of what they themselves think or what they do."[7]

The Economic Setting

The economic setting of Egypt has gone through different phases since 1952. The egalitarian ideological orientations of the leadership influenced the nationalization of several enterprises which began with the Suez Canal in 1956 and climaxed in 1961. The socialist approach in the beginning drove away national capitalists and brought much of business and industry into the government fold. As the country was involved in four wars during the same period, these undertakings lacked resources and the economy was shattered, particularly after the war of 1967.

After the October war of 1973, when Egypt regained self-confidence by crossing the Suez Canal, President Anwar Sadat initiated unprecedented changes in government policies. A policy of liberalization called the Open Door Policy was started in 1974. With the policy of peace initiated later and with more international investment coming in, the country was able to launch a new era of development. With the help of the U.S. Agency for International Development (USAID), the World Bank, and other international agencies, many economic activities were undertaken. The second Five-Year Plan, 1982–1986 gave the private sector an investment allocation of 23.3 percent.[8]

At the same time, the statistics on labor distribution show that employment offered by the public and government sectors put together is only 24.8 percent, leaving two-thirds of the labor force in the private sector.[9] The major economic problems are inflation, balance-of-payment deficits, as well as foreign debts. A population increase of about 1.3 million a year adds to the burden on the state but the family planning effort has not succeeded in controlling it, despite huge sums of international assistance received for more than two decades. The Five-Year Plan document attributes some of the problems to the overburdened infrastructure[10] and others to organizational and managerial constraints.[11]

The second Five-Year Plan, with an overall direction and coordinated policy, has helped to some extent in pursuing government activities, though several problems in implementing the plan remain. Whereas the major sources of income for the government are the Suez Canal, overseas remittances from Egyptian expatriates, oil, and tourism, all these have suffered recently owing to the recession and the decline in the price of oil. Tourism has suffered not only because of the decline in Arab tourists but also because of the tensions in the area and international terrorism.

Egypt is a large semiagricultural country. Fifty percent of its population participate in farming and related activities; about 30 percent in industries; and the remaining 20 percent in service. At the same time, the urban population in 1986 was estimated to be 47.7 percent.[12] The per capita income in 1985 was 700 U.S. dollars. More than half of the adult population is illiterate, among whom women are worse off.

EDUCATION AND PUBLIC SERVICE

Whereas Mohamed Aly initiated the policy of making education and training essential for public employment, Lord Cromer made the school certificate a requirement for a job in the civil service.[13] This linkage between education policy and efficiency in civil service continued until further developments took place after the Revolution. The decision in 1962 to make education free at all levels— primary, secondary, and university—contributed to the increase in the number of educated people. By 1964 the government issued a decree on the obligation of the Egyptian civil service and public sector to offer employment to all graduates of universities as well as of higher and technical institutes.[14] As a result of this policy, the Ministry of Labor was assigned a major role in the recruitment of personnel. Currently, the Ministry of Manpower and Vocational Training is responsible for recruiting and placing all college graduates and returning servicemen into public service and vocational training.

As the number of college and higher institute graduates increased through the years, the ministry was obliged to send their names to various other ministries, government agencies, and public sector companies, all of which subsequently suffered from "overstaffing." However, overstaffing does not mean that adequate types of employees are available. On the contrary, it indicates a maldistribution of personnel with very little consideration for matching qualifications with job requirements.[15]

THE CONSTITUTIONAL STRUCTURE AND FUNCTIONING

The present Constitution of 1971 prepared under President Sadat replaced the earlier one passed under President Gamal Abdel Nasser after the Revolution. It was further amended in 1981 and 1983. The president is the head of the state and continues to be the most important political and administrative figure in the country. He assumes executive power and in conjunction with the government lays down the general policy of the state and supervises its implementation. He is first nominated by the People's Assembly and is then endorsed by the public through a plebiscite.

The president may appoint one or more vice presidents. At times in its history Egypt has had two vice presidents. However, president Hosni Mubarak, who was the vice president under Sadat, has not yet appointed a vice president, even though his second term of office began in October 1987.

THE PRIME MINISTER AND THE CABINET

The president appoints the prime minister, his deputies, and the ministers who constitute the cabinet. Sadat served as his own prime minister more than once. Even when there is a prime minister heading the government, the role of the president vis-à-vis the cabinet has been predominant. He presides over the meetings of the cabinet if he chooses to attend. Sadat had five deputy prime ministers when he assumed the role of prime minister in 1980.

The prime minister is first among the equal ministers. Normally, the ministers enjoy considerable autonomy and power within their ministries. The personality and persuasiveness of the prime minister can sometimes influence the decisions of the individual ministers. Although the president plays an important role in the selection of ministers, a few among them are selected according to the wishes of the prime minister. In short, the president shares the executive authority with the cabinet.

With the increase in developmental activities and general concerns undertaken by the revolutionary government, the number of ministries also increased. Whereas in 1952 there were only fifteen ministries, by 1975 there were thirty-six.[16] At present there are thirty-two ministries in the Council of Ministers. In Egypt, the ministers of state are also considered members of the cabinet. They are normally in charge of certain specific activities within a ministry without having the responsibility of line supervision. Thus, one finds a minister of state in foreign affairs, and a minister in charge of local administration works closer with the minister of interior. Local administration was a part of the ministry of interior, and hence this arrangement arose. Quite often, the minister of state for local administration has been a former minister of interior or a former governor who worked under the minister of interior.

THE LEGISLATURE: THE PEOPLE'S ASSEMBLY (Majlis Al Sha'ab)

The People's Assembly exercises the legislative authority and approves the general policy of the state, the general plan of economic and social development, and the general budget. With the introduction of the multiparty system and the amendment of the Constitution in 1983, a kind of proportional representational system was created. Political parties are required to gain a minimum of 8 percent of the votes polled in order to be represented in the People's Assembly. Thus, in the elections held in May 1984, three parties which got less than 8 percent of the vote did not get any seat, though together they had obtained nearly 12 percent of the total votes polled. Because of the constitutional controversy surrounding this issue, a new amendment was introduced in 1987 providing for the election of forty-eight members as individual candidates besides 400 seats allocated for party-based contest. Provision for the nomination of ten members by the president was retained. Accordingly, the old Assembly was dissolved, and new elections were held in April 1987. The number of seats gained by the respective parties and independents in the present National Assembly is given in the accompanying table.

Party	Party seats	Individual seats	Nominated
National Democratic Party	311	41*	9
New Wafd Party	32		
Alliance of Labor, Liberal & Muslim Brotherhood Parties)	57	1**	
Independents		6	1
Total	400	48	10
Total Membership : 458			

* NDP supported   ** Liberal supported.

It is clear from the table that although the new amendment was meant to solve the anomaly of smaller parties not getting adequate representation (allowing their members to contest as individuals), in reality, forty-one NDP-supported candidates won those seats. Even among the nominated members, nine belong to NDP. However, the minimum requirement of 8 percent prompted three minority parties (Labor, Liberal, and Muslim Brotherhood) to form an alliance that helped them get fifty-eight seats constituting the main opposition group in the Parliament. It pushed the New Wafd party to a third position: the New Wafd party which was the main opposition party with fifty-nine seats in the previous People's Assembly, now won only thirty-two seats. Smaller parties which contested on their own did not get any seat.

The Constitution specifies that one-half of the elected members must be workers and farmers. Political parties are supposed to follow this provision.

THE SHURA COUNCIL (Majlis al Shura)

The Shura Council was created in 1980 as an advisory body with an amendment to the 1971 Constitution. Two-thirds of its members (140) are elected, and the rest (70) are appointed by the president for six years. Half of the membership is renewed every three years. The council transmits its advice to the president and the People's Assembly. Its advice is sought mainly on:

1. Proposals for constitutional amendments
2. Laws complementing the Constitution
3. Socioeconomic development projects within the framework of the general plan
4 All agreements involving sovereignty
5. Laws presented by the president
6. Subjects referred to by the president on external and internal policy

THE PARTY SYSTEM

Whereas a multiparty system has come into existence after a long spell of single Vanguard party rule of the Arab Socialist Union, the figures mentioned earlier indicate that the vast majority of parliamentarians belong to the ruling National Democratic party. This does not mean that there is an ideological preference in favor of the NDP. Its main attraction is that it is the ruling party. The New Wafd party has made many contributions to parliamentary debates and alternate thinking, but the resources which the NDP command are enormous.

Although the Socialist Labor party and the National Progressive Unionist party can be considered leftist parties, the Liberal Socialist party advocates freedom of private enterprises and the expansion of the Open Door Policy. The National Democratic party, on the other hand, having inherited power, accommodates different viewpoints of left, right, and center as well as many individuals to whom being close to power is more important than having a rigid ideological commitment.

INTEREST GROUPS

The constitutional provision that one-half of the elected representatives in the People's Assembly and the Shura Council must come from the workers and the farmers gives these two categories considerable importance. Quite often, however, educated and well-placed individuals usurp these positions posing "dual identity."[17]

For most other professions, the syndicates are the vehicles to carry their message and press their demands. The lawyers, the engineers, the doctors, and teachers have organized themselves into powerful syndicates.[18] The Syndicate of Commerce Graduates is an important body; the elections to the offices of this organization are therefore fought with great personal rivalry. The economic open door policy has activated the Chamber of Commerce as well as bodies like the U.S.–Egypt Business Council which try to influence both the United States and the Egyptian governments.

THE GENERAL STRUCTURE OF MINISTRIES

Each of the thirty-two ministries of Egypt has its own internal hierarchy with several departments and public authorities working under one or two ministers.

The number of people employed varies from 5,144 in the Ministry of Foreign Affairs to 502,960 in the Ministry of Interior.[19] The levels in each ministry are also unique. Most ministers now have deputy ministers who are the senior most bureaucrats from the ministry itself.

The under secretary formerly used to be the principal civil servant under the minister. With the expansion of government activities and the increase in the number of employees, however, Parkinson's Law influenced the creation of several under secretaries in each ministry. Later, one of them was designated the first under secretary. Today there are ministries with more than one first under secretary; the one with the greatest seniority becomes the deputy minister. Below the under secretary is the general director, and below him are the three grades for graduate employees.

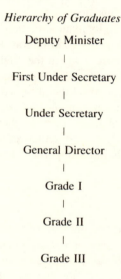

Hierarchy of Graduates

Deputy Minister

|

First Under Secretary

|

Under Secretary

|

General Director

|

Grade I

|

Grade II

|

Grade III

NONDEPARTMENTAL AGENCIES

Besides the departments under the ministries, three major central agencies perform important administrative tasks: (1) the Central Agency for Public Mobilization and Statistics; (2) the Central Agency for Organization and Administration; and (3) the Central Audit Organization. Each agency is constituted differently and hence will be discussed separately.

Central Agency for Public Mobilization and Statistics (CAPMAS)

CAPMAS collects information and conducts research. Those wishing to do serious research in the country need permission from CAPMAS. Its public mobilization role, which was considered important during the days of revolution and wars, has diminished. At the same time, its research work, and its national and international collaboration, particularly in demographic and economic aspects, have expanded recently. CAPMAS, the main source of official information and data on Egypt is headed by a chairman selected from the army.

Another important source of information on Egypt is the National Specialized Council. These Councils are involved in conducting specialized studies on different aspects of Egypt for the year 2000 A.D., and they suggest policy recommendations. This is purely an advisory body, however, headed by a former deputy prime minister and a minister of culture.

Central Agency for Organization and Administration (CAOA)

This agency was created in 1964 as a replacement for the Civil Service Agency, emphasizing its role in administrative reforms besides strengthening the civil service. In 1977, the government gave management development due recognition and spelled out the agency's role in it. The main objectives of the agency are: (1) to develop personnel administration; (2) to assure justice and equality in employment; and (3) to secure efficiency and productivity in fulfillment of the responsibilities of ministries, departments, local administration, and public corporations.[20]

The organization and management units (OMUs) of the agency are established in each ministry, department, and governorate. A senior official of the agency heads the CMU in each governorate. These units carry out the following functions:

1. Job classification

2. Work simplification and work methods

3. Training

4. Personnel planning

5. Management audit

6. Personnel information

Although originally started under the direct supervision of the prime minister, later it was placed under the Ministry of Treasury and more recently under the Ministry of Management Development. The chairman of the agency enjoys ministerial rank.

Whereas the agency was created more than two decades ago in order to solve some of the bureaucratic problems of administration, today it has itself grown into a bureaucracy reflecting many of the problems it was supposed to solve elsewhere.[21]

Central Audit Organization (CAO)

This agency, created in 1964, has grown more automomous in function and responsibility. It audits all public sector units and national development plan expenditures, and is responsible for the performance evaluation of governmental ministries and public sector enterprises. It has an independent budget passed by the People's Assembly. The chairman of the Central Audit Organization has ministerial status and similar prerogatives vis-à-via his staff as does the chairman of the Central Agency for Organization and Administration. In 1975 it was attached as an independent institution to the People's Assembly. It audits any administrative authority on behalf of the Assembly.[22]

BUDGETARY PROCESSES AND FINANCIAL CONTROL

The Ministry of finance is primarily responsible for preparation of the budgets. The process of budgeting begins in September every year with the Finance Ministry preparing an estimate of anticipated revenue for the next fiscal year, 1 July–30 June. The budgeting procedures to be followed by ministries, gover- norates, and lower level local units are developed and sent to them. The Ministry of Planning sends its specific forms for preparing investment projects for the next year. By the middle of February, all governorates as well as ministries will have sent their studied proposal regarding wages and salaries as well as capital investment projects. During March and April the Finance Ministry discusses and negotiates the submitted estimates with the concerned ministries and governor- ates. During May and June the draft budget is submitted to the People's Assem- bly, which discusses them and approves, specifying necessary changes. Once it is approved, the draft becomes the state budget.

PERSONNEL ADMINISTRATION

As mentioned earlier, the major functions of personnel administration are carried out by the Central Agency for Organization and Administration and the Ministry of Manpower and Vocational Training. The recruitment function is performed through the Ministry of Manpower which allocates eligible graduates to various ministries. However, some ministries like the Foreign Affairs and Defense Ministry have their own methods of selection. The Ministry of Foreign Affairs conducts a written and oral competitive examination of its own, and those who are selected are sent to the Diplomatic Institute for training.

Once the candidates are appointed in a particular ministry or enterprise, there is very little horizontal mobility. The ministries become particularly jealous of their jurisdiction, and the Central Agency for Organization and Administration vis-à-vis the ministries becomes more of a staff agency that give assistance and advice than a control agency.

PROMOTION

Despite various efforts to introduce merit as the main criterion for promotion, seniority seems to play a crucial role in promotion. The exception is found mostly in the armed forces which have their own rules and procedures.

TRAINING

The first effort to train civil servants after the 1952 Revolution was made by establishing the Institute of Public Administration in 1954 which mainly trained middle-level managers in government. Later, the National Institute of Management Development was created to train senior executives in business administration in the public sector. The Institute of Nation Planning (1962) and the Institute of Local Administration (1968) were also created to train civil servants in their respective areas. Later, the Institute of Public Administration and the Institute of Local Administration were merged with the National Institute of Management Development, which is now called the Sadat Academy of Administrative Sciences.

Training has assumed considerable importance in the socioeconomic and industrial development projects supported by USAID. Through the General Organization for Industrialization, the Ministry of Agriculture, the Ministry of Local Administration, and many other ministries and governorates, USAID has distributed and sponsored a variety of training programs.

In spite of what has been done in the area of civil service training, there is general dissatisfaction within government circles over the achievements of major training institutes. Consequently, the minister of state for management development has recently taken the initiative to create the Center for Administrative and Managerial Development (CAMD) with the support of USAID. Its goals are ambitious and funds are already allocated. It plans to emphasize policy studies, banking, the public sector, management, vocational training, and self-development. One of the proposals of the Ministry of Management Development is to have a national training policy. Given enough reflection on past experiences, such a policy can be of great use to the government. However, it is worthwhile to recall that Egyptian scholars and administrators had recommended such a policy as early as in 1957:[23]

1. The training policy should be coordinated with educational policy and personnel policy.
2. Ample funds should be allotted in establishments and organizations to meet the expenses necessary for training programs.
3. A Central National Board should be established for planning, direction, coordination, and followup (of training).

Execution, however, should be done on a decentralized basis.

Experience since 1959 suggests that coordination, direction, and followup have not been effective in training. Moreover, there has been a total lack of leadership in this field. Little effort has been made to link training with research and to make it relevant to day-to-day administration.[24]

UNIONS AND STRIKES

The Arab Socialist Union (ASU) had its cells in all major departments, and bureaucrats other than those of the armed forces and police were active in them. Although they were essentially meant for mobilization purposes, those who were active could use the ASU as a vehicle to convey their complaints. Today, whereas bureaucrats belong to various syndicates mentioned earlier, active unionization is not there. Strikes are forbidden and put down with force. The riots by the conscripts of the constabulary forces in February 1986 were quelled with the help of the army.

THE SOCIAL BACKGROUND OF THE CIVIL SERVICE

There is no recent statistical study on the social background of the higher civil service. Morroe Berger's study (*Bureaucracy and Society in Modern Egypt*, Princeton, N.J.: Princeton University Press, 1957, Chapter 2) of a sample of 242 people found that the bureaucracy is dominated by sons of civil servants (38.8 percent) and other urban middle-class groups (21.5 percent). Since the 1952 Revolution, the opening of the educational system to all social classes and the government's undertaking to offer employment to all graduates have brought large numbers of men and women of the middle and lower classes into the civil service. Those who joined the service at lower levels in the 1960s are now senior directors and under secretaries.

Before the Revolution, a civil service position was considered prestigious, and members of elite families occupied important positions. Closeness to the royal family and to prominent citizens was a help in obtaining such positions. Today, because seniority is the main criterion for promotion to higher echelons, candidates have to go through various levels before reaching the top. Remuneration is negligible compared to what is available to those who work for private business and multinationals. As a result, the quality of graduates who enter government service is steadily declining. This factor will affect the quality of higher level employees who hold responsible positions and help in policy formulation and implementation. At the same time, the fact that many of them obtained free education at secondary and university levels and rose in the hierarchy step by step has added to the democratic character of the civil service. Those who have worked hard and improved through commitment and training are definitely contributing to the stability of the state. Comparatively better opportunities available in the foreign service and the armed forces have kept their prestige high, so that one comes across middle and higher class graduates trying to enter these services. An interesting recent development is that many stay in government despite poor salaries, while at the same time working privately in another job or business for the sake of maintaining a better social life.

ADMINISTRATIVE LAW

According to Article 172 of the Constitution: "The State Council shall be an independent judicial organization which has the competence of decisions in administrative disputes and disciplinary cases."[25]

The Constitution also provides for the socialist public prosecutor who

shall be responsible for taking the procedure which secures the people's rights, the safety of the society and its political system, the preservation of the socialist achievements and commitment to the social behaviour. The law shall define his other competences. He shall be subject to the control of the People's Assembly in accordance to what is prescribed by law.[26]

Recently, most cases involving bureaucratic or political corruption have been referred to the Socialist public prosecutor.

PUBLIC ENTERPRISE IN EGYPT

Public enterprise in Egypt has been an instrument of the state's economic policies from the very beginning. It has undergone vicissitudes of state support and negligence from time to time according to the climate of national political developments. However, the public sector continues to be the mainstay of economic policy and planning in the country, despite recent efforts to encourage private initiative and investment. Neither Sadat's Open Door Policy nor the competition from multinationals has prompted the authorities to undermine the importance of public enterprise in official declarations of policy. In the latest five-year plan, the private sector is given a greater share in investment than ever before (23.3 percent), but the plan emphasizes the role of the public sector and the need to strengthen it. President Mubarak has more than once stated the role of the public sector in increasing productivity. In his major speech to the national Parliament after assuming office as president, Mubarak cited the public sector as one of the major policy areas which would be tackled by his administration. In his recent May Day speech, the president declared that efforts are being made to further consolidate and develop it. He added: "We will do everything to update management in various units of public sector, replace old machines with new ones; more funds will be poured into them."[27]

To understand the new momentum attempted in the operation of the public sector, it is essential to have a picture of the development of the system as it is today, along with an analysis of the major problems that have challenged their operations.

Egypt was an "early starter" in industrialization under government auspices when in the early 1880s Mohamed Aly launched textile and food processing enterprises along with metal workshops and foundries for the army. Though not in the modern sense of public enterprise, these ventures were essentially state-run and meant for the self-reliance of the nation in military and other essential sectors. Later, however, the free market idea came with external forces that dominated and exploited commercial and industrial enterprise in Egypt for another century. Private enterprise became the prime force concentrating itself in agriculture and the export of its products, and it dominated the scene in the import of industrial products from abroad. Foreign collaboration and domination continued until the beginning of a new resurgence of commercial and industrial patriotism under the leadership of Talat Harb who started the Misr Group of industries and banks which had become a force in the private sector by 1940.

The industrialization drive continued through private enterprise even after the 1952 Revolution, although the government began to invest in heavy industries like steel for the sake of speedy industrialization of the country. It was not until 1956 that the private sector initiative was reduced, owing to several national and international developments. The Suez War was the beginning of a series of sequestrations and nationalizations which reached a climax during 1960 when the Misr Group was nationalized and in 1961 when a major nationalization thrust was launched bringing under state ownership most of the large and medium enterprises. By 1963, private ownership was limited to agriculture, urban real estate, and small business. Whereas the landlords, national capitalists, and foreign companies lost much, the ordinary citizen was provided with cheaper consumer goods and reduced rates of services, and employment opportunities were enhanced. A parallel reform of free education at all levels, which was followed by the promise of employment to all graduates, had their impact on the public sector which was required to absorb more hands regardless of productivity or demand for them. By now public enterprise had became an important element of state policy from political, economic, and social points of view.

Some important organizational innovations were introduced in order to control the expanded numbers of enterprises. By 1966, about thirty-six general organizations were established along sectoral criteria in all industries and services. They were given a wide range of authority and responsibility over more than 350 enterprises which in turn were brought under several ministers who were directly concerned with enterprise. The minister presided over the board of directors of those companies, thus making the minister of industry responsible for about 160 enterprises. Pharmaceuticals were under the minister of health, whereas building materials were under the minister of housing. Although there was considerable enthusiasm and a sense of direction in the beginning for making these experiments succeed, the very size of the operations and the political and economic crises that followed deteriorated the conditions of the enterprises. In the next section we list some of the problems that have cropped up in the implementation of the state policy surveyed so far.[28]

Problems of State Enterprises

In a study, Samir Youssef lists a number of forces that hinder the performance of public enterprises.[29] These forces have to do with the defective practices related to input factors, operating systems, human components, internal organization, financing, and government control, and each item is elaborated further:

1. *Input factors*
   Purchasing process
   (Non) Availability of materials

2. *Inadequacies in the operating system*
   Facilities
   Maintenance
   Transport

3. *Human component*
   Inadequate incentives
   Alienation
   Emigration
   Deficient evaluation system
   Shortage of skills
   Shortage of second-level managers
   Inadequate training
   Overstaffing
   Maldistribution of labor

4. *Internal organization*
   Inadequate information system
   Poor communications
   Centralization of authorities
   Inadequate planning and poor supervision
   Deficient structure
   Inadequate followup
   Deficient cashing system
   Deficient work schedules
   Inadequate performance measures

5. *Financial Problems*
   Liquidity problems
   Slow process of debt collection
   Slow execution of projects

6. *Government Control*
   Excessive interference
   Inadequate support
   Inappropriate rules
   Inadequate government planning
   Inadequate financing

Materials supply problems
Multiple controls

Of the above, from the point of view of policy and implementation, the relationship with the government is of great importance. Dr. Samir Youssef deals with this problem, giving particular attention to what is called interference. He refers extensively to a dissertation by Ibrahim Abdel Gabr[30] and cites several forms of government interference in the affairs of public enterprises.

1. *Presence of inspectors to scrutinize company activities* from ministries or government agencies concerned to check on product quality and specialization. For instance, the Central Agency for Auditing checks on financial matters whereas the Central Agency for Organization and Administration checks on labor laws and agency instructions. The inspectors as well as the managers of the enterprises become preoccupied with rules and regulations, which in turn have made the enterprises more bureaucratic. Flexibility and initiative are lost at the enterprise level.

2. *A flow of instructions* from the ministries and government agencies reach the companies continuously. They are full of clarifications, regulations, limitations of time or quality, and foreign currency restrictions. While instructions do not carry the force of law, they are usually taken seriously by enterprise management. However, the degree of conformity in their application can vary, depending on the persuasiveness of the company director in presenting his case to the ministry officials.[31]

3. *Impositions of requirements* such as the need to get the approval of export are made only after the ministry concerned has studied the prices.

4. *Government laws and by-laws* (which are frequently introduced and amended) are applied.

5. *Prior authorization* is needed from the Ministry of Industry and the General Organization for Industrialization for yearly plans of the enterprises and for purchasing capital goods beyond 750,000 pounds.

6. *The Ministry of Industries* makes decisions regarding selling and pricing for exchanged items with representatives of the concerned companies.

7. *Allocation of essential items* like soap, oil, fertilizers, sugar, and vital machines is generally a prerogative of the government. Their production, volume, pricing, and system of allocation are often made by the concerned ministry or by national committees formed for that purpose.

8. *Financial decisions* like the one on increasing the enterprise capital can be taken only at a meeting presided over by the minister.

9. *Distribution of profits* is governed by legal statutes.

10. *Labor laws* insist on a uniform wage structure for all public enterprises.

11. *Terms of transactions* as in exports or sale to other enterprises are determined by the government.

According to Samir Youssef, the result of the various types of control or interference mentioned is that the enterprise manager becomes an enforcer of rules and regulations—like a government bureaucrat.[32] Most of their decisions are of a routine character. The fact that the budget of the public sector company is an integral part of the state budget makes them become totally dependent on the government for annual allocations.

POST–1967 PERIOD

Whereas most of the problems mentioned above continue, some of them were aggravated by the financial and social compulsions that followed the war of 1967. The country was under stringent financial conditions, and the much needed repairs, replacements, and reinvestments for the public sector had to be postponed. The social obligations prevailed on the decision to continue the employment policy and subsidies. At the same time, the public sector became the sole producer in the industrial sector, and despite all the constraints, it was able to maintain the overall production level. This was no small achievement. For that reason even after the general policies were changed, the public sector was not abandoned. Hence, in his joint address to the People's Assembly and the Shura Council President Mubarak suggested that public decisions "boost and strengthen the public sector which is the backbone of industrial production and the basic source of financing the development process."[33]

Actually, public discussion on the public sector began earlier along with Sadat's Open Door Policy which was introduced after the successful experiences of the 1973 war when an attempt was made to probe into Egyptian potentialities in the internal front as well. In what was known as the October Paper,[34] Sadat emphasized the need to liberalize the society in economic and political matters. This also followed the trade relations, and the gradual shift of emphasis from the Eastern Bloc to the Western and particularly American side began. A massive drive was initiated to attract Arab and foreign investments in Egypt, and the trade barriers gave way to a multinational thrust into the Egyptian market which until now was a closed arena monopolized by its own public sector companies or those imported through public sector export–import companies. This restatement of policy and the onslaught of the international thrust through trade, as well as massive aid which came largely from the United States, has had great impact on the public sector. On the positive side, they were able to import much needed spare parts and other essential items for their production. On the other hand, the new policy was not that clear, and in many areas they had to face stiff competition from the imported goods that were preferred by the people who could afford them.

Because it was felt that under the new strategy there should be certain structural changes in the organization of the public sector, Law 111 was introduced in 1975 to replace the General Organizations Law 32 of 1966, with the specific purpose of giving the public sector more autonomy. The new law abolished the general organizations and attempted to create sectoral boards instead to integrate the activities of each productive sector industry. Each board had about thirty-two members, including representatives from the Ministry of Finance, Planning, and Economy. This was too large a number to be effective. According to Samir Youssef, the board's responsibilities are not defined clearly, most of them do not meet often enough, and the minister of industry presides over five of them.[35] Companies were supposed to have been given discretion in the areas of employment, wage payment, and pricing. However, except in a few cases, like areas of banking, contracting and the Railway Authority to some extent, the industrial firms as such did not introduce these reforms.

CONTINUING PROBLEMS

In spite of the legislative and economic reforms introduced after the announcement of the Open Door Policy, several of the problems continue to plague the public enterprises. World Bank experts like Khalid Ikram have elaborated some of those problem mentioned earlier in this chapter and have suggested radical reforms.[36] For instance, underutilization of capacity is a chronic ailment of Egyptian industry. Inadequate supervision, lack of incentives, ineffective management and negligence on the part of labor have also been blamed.[37] Again, investment planning was responsible for costly errors when scarce resources were devoted to projects that were either ill-conceived (wrong scale, wrong technology, faulty linkages) or ill-suited to the conditions of the country.[38]

Another complicated area is that of pricing products of the public sector. Complaints relate to lack of adequate administrative resources, such as personnel, information, and the ability to monitor and verify. Khalid Ikram recommends a transition period during which policy interference with the market mechanism would be restricted to a few measures and controls for distributional objectives.[39]

Employment policy continues to be as costly from the point of view of the firms that are forced to accept excess labor. Little can be done without disturbing the status quo and the sociopolitical equilibrium. World Bank experts and others have recommended gradual changes in the area, but tremendous skill in economic management and sociopolitical manipulation are required. Khalid Ikram summarized the need as follows:

Management of public sector industries must be given more responsibility over marketing decisions and greater freedom over pricing decisions. Management should also be allowed to raise wages of some employees beyond the limits now imposed and to reduce excess staff. Responsibilities for investment need to be defined. Management must be given responsibility and incentives for proper maintenance.[40]

In the context of the above recommendations, President Mubarak's May Day statement quoted earlier gives new hope for public enterprises in Egypt. It

suggests a certain awareness on the part of the highest echelons in the government, of the problems as well as the need for rapid solutions in the area of the
public sector. This realization is reflected in the following statement in the Five-
Year Plan:

Managerial and organizational factors remained a constraint on increasing production and
productivity in both public and private sectors. Moreover, the legal and institutional
framework—although have been subject to reform during the same period—has been
inadequate to meet development needs. The plan aims at strengthening this reform trend,
in order to improve productivity as performance is the foundation for development and
progress.[41]

PROSPECTS

Whereas the new Five-Year Plan and the new Mubarak government have
shown keen interest and concern for the success of public sector operations, it
is too early to predict the total elimination of the causes for their continuing
problems. President Mubarak has recently made surprise visits to several public
sector companies and looked into their operations. This gesture itself is a good
beginning.

Another recent development is the emergence of the armed forces as a new
type of "public sector" activist in the country. This is the result of the environment of peace which has rendered many army personnel relatively underemployed. The army, with its long experience of construction and combat management, finds itself able to render support to civilian projects. The dynamic
leadership of the Egyptian army has therefore come forward to participate in the
construction of factories, bakeries, and other enterprises. For instance, Major
General Mohsen Sedki, project assistant to the minister of defense, announced
in February 1983 that they would soon begin construction of cement factories
in Cairo, Beni Suef, and North Sinai with a total capacity of 2.2 million tons
yearly.[42] The major general added that twenty-four semiautomatic bakeries with
a daily combined turnout of 750,000 loaves of bread were also being started.
In addition, the army was planning to establish a village for fishermen. It is also
not uncommon to see the streets of different parts of Cairo being dug by soldiers
from the army who are helping to construct a better telecommunication system.

With the emergence of the armed forces in public sector activities, existing
public sector enterprises must meet a new challenge. The government as well
as those enterprises now have an opportunity to reconsider some of the rules,
regulations, and practices that have been rendering the public sector fruitless in
many fields. Questions relating to pricing, subsidies, autonomy, employment,
and other crucial issues of the public sector are being reexamined. If such inquiry
and diagnosis are followed by determined action based on sound ideological and
pragmatic approaches, without doubt the Egyptian public sector will have many
new heights to conquer.

LOCAL ADMINISTRATION

Egypt is divided into twenty-six governorates headed by governors appointed by the president. They enjoy ministerial rank, "presidential power," protocol, and privileges. The governorates are further divided into districts known as *markas*. Each markas has further been divided into town council and village council areas. Whereas town councils are constituted at the head quarters of the markas, several villages are included in the village council area. At present, at each level, village council, markas, and governorate, there are two councils. The popular council is elected by the people and headed by a chairman and an executive council is composed of the principal civil servants of the particular level. The governor heads the governorate executive council.

Many efforts have been made to decentralize government activities in view of the development activities undertaken after the Revolution.[43] The first effort was Law No. 124 of 1960 which was amended in 1971 and again in 1981. At present, there is a supreme council of local government under the chairmanship of the prime minister.

An important development in the field of local administration is the flow of specific funds from the USAID to the governorates under USAID's decentralization support program. A total of 455.2 million U.S. dollars and 125,000 Egyptian pounds was allocated to the decentralization sector between 1981 and 1986. It must be noted that these funds are meant for local infrastructural projects and are spent mostly by the local level bureaucracy who are part of the national bureaucracy. Popular participation in taking decisions regarding their selection for projects is more on paper than in reality. Even in the urban districts of Cairo, decisions are made by the USAID technical assistance contractor and accepted by the local bureaucrat. This may lead to strengthening local administration, but not the capacity for local self-government.

In the name of decentralization, a new element of centralization has emerged— one of depending on decisions made not only by the central government in Cairo, but also by those in USAID headquarters in Washington, D.C., whose decisions are guidelines for the technical assistance bureaucracy.[44] Nevertheless, the massive aid given to local development program created some awareness among local beneficiaries regarding their problems and potentials.

Features of Policy Making: Major responsibility for policy making lies with the president. Often the personality and ideological orientation of the president have influenced the initiation of policy. The president's advisers play a crucial role in this matter. The cabinet has specialized groups for various subjects especially for discussing economic policy.

The Five-Year Plan has become a basis for most of the policy discussions. Recently, a policy planning group has been set up with senior ministers as members. The role of the People's Assembly is not yet clear except as the approver of all the overall policies. The committees of the Assembly as well as the Shura Council have begun to play a significant advisory role in this respect.

One of the major problems in policy planning has been the lack of coordination among various ministries. In addition, lack of personnel with policy-planning perspective among the higher level bureaucrats has been a problem for the government. A recent suggested solution has been to train a certain number of graduates in policy making by sending them to the United States (mainly to Harvard University) on condition that they come back and serve different ministries as advisers to the ministers. The USAID has apparently agreed to support such training abroad and at the Center for Administrative and Managerial Development.

AN OVERVIEW

Several issues persistently emerge in connection with Egyptian administration. A recent study done by the Central Agency for Organization and Administration has found imbalances in the distribution of employees, showing shortages in educational services and development administration, especially in rural areas with surpluses in the ministries of agriculture and health, and in clerical jobs. The absence of real human resources planning is a continuing problem.

Much has been written about bureaucratic corruption in Egypt, some of which has been attributed to the Open Door Policy and controlled commercialism.[45] The Free Officers who launched the Revolution of 1952 and the successive Presidents Nasser, Sadat, and Mubarak have dealt with this problem in speeches, declarations, and policy statements in the parliament. Whereas much talk has taken place on this topic, very little action seems to have been taken even against individuals, and cases are given a lot of publicity for a while. One reason is that it is very difficult to distinguish between bureaucratic corruption and political corruption in Egypt. Here it is difficult to say where bureaucracy ends and politics begins. Both are so intertwined that most of the ministers are bureaucratic by training and background if we also include the military among the bureaucrats.

The president remains the center of politics as long as he is in power, and it is difficult to assess if anybody else has a political constituency. Nor do the press and the media indicate that anyone has. Once ministers or speakers are appointed, one reads about them, watches them on television, and follows their travels and activities. Once they are out of power, no one knows what happened to them. In many instances it may also be because they are promoted as ministers from the bureaucracy and lack political experience or background.

The introduction of multiparty democracy is likely to change the situation. At present, however, the ruling party seems to have inherited the mantle of the former Arab Socialist Union. The president is the chairman of the National Democratic party and the general secretary is a minister appointed by him, as are all other office bearers. Although the ministers enjoy considerable political power within their own ministries, they join the ruling party regardless of their earlier political affiliation or lack of it. Some ministers are treated as government or party bureaucrats and are not sure when they are likely to fall from grace.

This uncertainty about continuance in power is one of the reasons for allegations of political corruption. One has to amass as much wealth and influence as possible while remaining in power. The Open Door Policy has opened the doors of corruption and embezzlement to many. It is unfair, however, to those who are honest and dedicated, and thereby sacrifice a great deal of energy, time, and wealth in agreeing to become a minister with negligible salary, to make a generalization that all ministers are corrupt. Many would not accept the position because of the sacrifices called for, including that of reputation. This is all the more because they are likely to be treated as politically appointed bureaucrats.

Administrative reform is a topic that has engaged the attention of Egyptian government for more than three decades. Several studies, seminars, and conferences conducted by the government have emphasized the importance of improving the techniques, reorganizing the structures, modernizing the technology, and improving human behavior in the organization.

The foremost study was the famous Gulick and Pollock report. The report was excellent from the point of view of POSDCORB* activities, for which Gulick and Urwick are famous, but development administration in Egypt needed to add to POSDCORB the need to be aware of the importance of the five ''i'' s: information, inspiration, innovation, introjection, and integration.[46]

Samir Farid, after a thorough review of administrative reform efforts in the 1960s and 1970s, came to a similar conclusion:

The Egyptian reformers' approach has been a structural one which emphasized the formal institutions, structures, procedures and processes, and as a result, has failed to tackle the real issues involved. Political, sociocultural, and economic factors which are no less important than the organizational structure of bureaucracy have never been addressed by successive administrative reform activities.[47]

Another observation made about successful experiments in administration in Egypt, such as the Suez Canal after nationalization and the High Dam, is that such operations gave the trusted men chosen to run them a freedom and flexibility not permitted in the regular administrative institutions.[48]

In one sense, the creation of CAMD with USAID assistance is also said to be following the same method, giving its management and employees higher salaries and greater freedom of operation. The question is, what impact will these exceptional freedom of operation and higher conditions of service given to selected agencies have on the regular administrative apparatus. A recent article describes the apparatus:

The bureaucracy is well established and its inertia continues. While the advisor or minister realized full well the need for change, those responsible for administering it, the middle

---

*Planning, Organization, Staffing Direction, Coordination, Reporting and Budgeting, POSDCORB is a mnemonic for all these management activities.

level bureaucrats, have a vested interest in maintaining the status quo. They have established their kingdoms and do not wish to surrender them.[49]

Observers of Egyptian administration have noticed that one of the unique features of the Egyptian cabinet and managerial class is the presence of highly educated individuals trained in technology or management. Thus, a class of technocrats and managers have been responsible for the achievements, as well as for the failures. But however much the managerial class may have done to improve their specific areas, there seems to have been a lack of a comprehensive approach to study the problems. During the days of wars when people lived from day to day, security considerations may have made piecemeal approaches necessary. Today, with an expanded bureaucracy and an exploding population, there is the need for a comprehensive approach to public administration in the country.[50] The time has come to make a similar study as was done by Gulick and Pollock in 1962, with greater emphasis on the dynamics of Egyptian administration. Egypt was one of the pioneers in the Third World to start an Institute of Public Administration (1954); it gained considerable reputation in its early days but was merged with the Sadat Academy. The spirit of public administration which was kindled three decades ago needs to be re-lighted. Ancient Egypt was the cradle of world bureaucracy. Today it is a crucible of the bureaucratic dilemmas of development.

NOTES

The author acknowledges with gratitude the help rendered by many, particularly by Inaam B. Hassanein, in writing this chapter.

1. Samir Farid, "Administrative Reforms in Developing Countries: The Case of Egypt 1952–1978" (Ph.D. thesis, Department of Politics of the University of Wales, University College, Cardiff, 1983), p. 28.

2. E. H. Valsan, "Challenges to Development Administration," *Middle East Management Review* 1 (Cairo, 1976), p. 85; Samir Farid, "Administrative Reform," p. 30; see also A. P. Sinker, *Report on Personnel Questions of the Egyptian Civil Service* (Cairo: Ministry of Finance, Government Press, 1951).

3. See Fred W. Riggs, *Administration in Developing Countries: The Theory of Prismatic Society* (Boston: Houghton Mifflin, 1964).

4. Farid, "Administrative Reforms," pp. 171, 172.

5. Ibid., p. 280.

6. Ibid., p. 281.

7. Ibid., p. 282.

8. Ministry of Planning, Arab Republic of Egypt, *The Detailed Frame of the Five Year Plan for Economic and Social Development 1982–83—1986–87*, Part I (Cairo, 1982), p. 63.

9. Ibid., p. 112.

10. Ibid., p. 15.

11. Ibid., p. 17.

12. World Bank, *World Development Report, 1985* (New York: Oxford University Press, 1985), p. 214. An earlier and useful World Bank publication with valuable data and insights is Khalid Ikram, *Egypt: Economic Management in a Period of Transition* (Baltimore: Johns Hopkins University Press, 1980).

13. See John Waterbury, *The Egypt of Nasser and Sadat: The Political Economy of Two Regimes* (Princeton, N.J.: Princeton University Press, 1983), p. 234; Samir Farid, "Administrative Reforms," p. 285.

14. Waterbury, *The Egypt of Nasser and Sadat*, p. 234.

15. At a conference by the Central Agency for Organization and Administration in 1965, this was listed as the number one problem of personnel (cited by Valsan, "Challenges to Development Administration," p. 85).

16. A chart of the gradual increase of ministries is given in Samir Farid, "Administrative Reforms," p. 250.

17. Nazih Ayubi, *Bureaucracy and Politics in Contemporary Egypt* (London: Ithaca Press, 1980), p. 447.

18. Waterbury, *The Egypt of Nasser and Sadat*, pp. 342–46. Clement Henry Moore analyzes the role of the engineers in his book, *Images of Development: Egyptian Engineers in Search of Industry* (Cambridge, Mass.: MIT Press, 1980).

19. Source: Central Agency for Organization and Administration (CAOA).

20. From a pamphlet of the CAOA.

21. Two articles by this author refer to the agency's role and performance in the 1960s and 1970s; see Valsan, "Challenges to Development Administration," pp. 79–93 and "An Essay on Egyptian Experience in Development Administration," *Journal of the Social Sciences* 4, 3 (Kuwait, October 1979), pp. 1–14.

22. An analysis of the role and functions of the CAO is available in Amr Abbas Helmy, "Management of Training in State Audit Organizations: A Case Study of Central Audit Organization of Egypt" (unpublished MPA thesis, Cairo, American University in Cairo, 1986).

23. *Public Administration: Report of the Seminar on Comparative Studies* (Cairo: Dar Al Maaref, 1959), p. 156. The seminar was supported by the Institute of Public Administration and the Congress for Cultural Freedom.

24. The need to link training, research, and practice was emphasized in Valsan, "An Essay on Egyptian Experience," p. 13.

25. Ministry of Information, State Information Service, *The Constitution of the Arab Republic of Egypt* (Cairo, September 1971), p. 61.

26. Ibid., Article 179, pp. 63–64.

27. *Cairo Press Review*, The Middle East News Agency, Cairo, 2 May 1983, p. 7.

28. For more details and assessments of the period mentioned, see Robert Mabro and Samir Radwan, *The Industrialization of Egypt, 1939–1973* (Oxford: Clarendon Press, 1976) and Ikram, *Egypt*.

29. Samir Mohamed Youssef, *System of Management in Egyptian Public Enterprise*, (Cairo: American University of Cairo Press, 1983), p. 43.

30. Ibrahim Abdel Gabr, "Participation in the Decision-making Process in the Egyptian Public Sector" (M.A. thesis, College of Commerce, Tanta University, Tanta, 1979), quoted by Samir Youssef, *System of Management*, pp. 55–59.

31. Youssef, *System of Management*, p. 57.

32. Ibid., p. 63.

33. *An Address by President Mubarak*, 8 November 1981, ARE, State Information Service, Cairo, p. 9.

34. President Anwar El-Sadat, *The October Working Paper* (Cairo: Arab Republic of Egypt, Ministry of Information, May 1974).

35. Youssef, *System of Management*, pp. 91–92.

36. Ikram, *Egypt*.

37. Ibid., p. 258.

38. Ibid., p. 259.

39. Ibid.

40. Ibid., p. 270.

41. Arab Republic of Egypt, Ministry of Planning, *The Detailed Frame of the Five Year Plan for Economic and Social Development—1982–83—1986–87, Part 1. Principal Components* (Cairo: December 1982), p. 41.

42. *Egyptian Gazette*, Cairo, 20 February 1983, p. 1.

43. Joseph Marino, "Decentralization and Public Participation in Urban Egypt" (MPA thesis, Cairo, American University of Cairo, 1986), p. 81; see also Margaret Suzanne Plum, "Decentralization as Public Policy: The Government of Egypt/US Agency for International Development Experience in Egypt" (MPA thesis, Cairo, American University of Cairo, 1985), for more understanding of the origin of the project.

44. Joseph Marino, "Decentralization and Public Participation in Urban Egypt," pp. 143–44.

45. See Nazih Ayubi, "From State Socialism to Controlled Commercialism: The Emergence of Egypt's Open Door Policy," *Journal of Commonwealth and Comparative Politics* 20, 3 (November 1982), pp. 264–85; Ayubi, *Bureaucracy and Politics*; Waterbury, *The Egypt of Nasser and Sadat*, and Raymond W. Baker, *Egypt under Nasser and Sadat* (Cambridge, Mass.: Harvard University Press, 1978).

46. Valsan, "Challenges to Development Administration."

47. Farid, "Administrative Reforms," summary page.

48. This writer and Nazih Ayubi have written separately on this subject. See Valsan, *An Essay on Egyptian Experience*, and Ayubi, *Bureaucracy and Politics*, pp. 273–79.

49. G. H. Horn, "Egypt's Economy: Dealing with the Debt," *Business in Egypt*, A Special Supplement Prepared by *Cairo Today* (Cairo, Fall 1986), p. 10.

50. Mohga A. Badran, *Co-ordination in Multiactor Programmes: An Empirical Investigation of Factors Affecting Co-ordination Among Organizations at the Local Level in Egyptian Family Planning Program* (Stockholm: Department of Business Administration, University of Stockholm, 1984).

7

IRAN

Ali Farazmand

INTRODUCTION

Iran (Persia) is a large country with a long history. It is five times the size of Great Britain, with an estimated population of 40 million (in 1986), 60 percent of whom live in urban areas. The original inhabitants were Aryans who still form the majority of the population, but after several centuries of imperial expansion and invasion by Arabs, Turks, and Mongols, the population became multiethnic. About 98 percent of the population is Muslim, and 90 percent are Shi'i adherents.

Public administration in Iran dates back as far as the fourth millennium B.C.[1] A little later, the Achaemenid Empire, the first "world state," developed an indigenous administrative system with a highly centralized bureaucracy that lasted from the sixth to fourth centuries B.C. It was further developed under the Persians' second world state, the Sassanian Empire (220–641 A.D.), which became the model state for the Muslim Arabs who established the Caliphate Empire during the seventh and later centuries. Consequently, the Persian administrators and their Sassanian bureaucracy took over the Islamic Empire for several centuries, making the Abbasid Caliphate a Persianized bureaucratic empire. The centralized developed state of the Safavids further revived and strengthened the administrative system of Iran during the sixteenth and seventeenth centuries when massive public works were performed.

The Persians' reputation as effective administrators has been acknowledged and documented by many historians, as well as social and political scientists.[2] When Aristotle was still discussing the problems of the Greek city-state, the Persians were successfully administering the greatest empire the world had then known, but the system lagged behind that of the West during the eighteenth and nineteenth centuries. The feudal, despotic system of the Qajar Dynasty prevented the development of a modern efficient administration. The weak Iranian monarchy was exposed to Czarist Russian and British demands for concessions and capitulations. The constitutional revolution of 1905–1911 established a parliamentary system, and in 1920 Reza Shah captured the throne, establishing a new Pahlavi dynasty. During the Second World War, the Allies forced him to abdicate in favor of his son. From 1941 to 1953, the new Shah ruled more or less as a constitutional monarch, but after the crucial challenge to his rule by the nationalists under Dr. Mossadegh and the Shah's return after a successful military coup in 1953, his rule became absolute and dictatorial with the help of his notorious secret police, the SAVAK. He was overthrown by the 1978–1979 Revolution led by Ayatollah Khomeini, and an Islamic Republic was established.

The administrative system of Iran under the present Islamic Republic, as well as earlier under the Shah, is based on the traditional Sassanian administrative system, together with the adoption of Western management concepts and practices. This traditional system rested on the concept of a world state under the Achaemenid Empire, with different races and religions under the imperial umbrella held together by a tightly and hierarchically organized bureaucracy. Its crucial feature was the territorial division of the state into manageable provinces, each of which was under a satrap or governor appointed by the king and totally responsible to him. He was assisted by a general in command of the army, a chief minister, and a state attorney—each independent and reporting directly to the king in the capital. The king's authority was further reinforced by an official Inspector sent every year to the provinces to report on its administration and by a system of royal roads with postal stations for effective communication. Taxation was based on regular surveys of land, past yields, and tolls from the Suez Canal and city gates; a regular system of gold and silver coinage was maintained. A system of publicly proclaimed laws and a system of royal courts made the realm more controllable by the king. In short, it was a highly centralized bureaucratic system that survived different dynasties. The Selucids took it over as such, and the Sassanian Empire adopted and adapted it with a few additions. The central administration was more elaborately organized into several departments or divans such as secretary of state (*Dapirān Mahist*), joint commander in chief (*Iran Sipahpāt*) agriculture (*Vastryosan Satar*), and commerce (*Hutokhshpat*). The satrapy system remained, but the designation was changed to *Marzpan* or *Ostandar*. Urbanization grew, and the name Iranshahr was adopted for the empire. With Zoroastrianism as the state religion, the high priest became an important state functionary, and society as a whole became hierarchically structured. More importantly, the educated bureaucrats or scribes were legally recognized as a high caste, and the Sassanian bureaucracy became the most powerful next to the army.

After the Islamic conquest of the seventh century, the Abbasid caliphate took over the system wholesale, adding even greater pomp and ceremony to the royal courts. The Safavid Empire of Iran continued the same system, reforming the bureaucracy by introducing merit-based recruitment. The bureaucracy declined under the feudalistic system of the Qajar Dynasty but came into its own gradually under the Pahlavis after 1920, with the addition of Western management concepts and practices. The administrative system under the Islamic Republic is in many ways a continuation of the earlier systems.

THE GENERAL STRUCTURE OF ADMINISTRATION

The structure of territorial or provincial administration has retained the Sassanian heritage, despite the major political change from a despotic monarchy to an Islamic republic. Even the names and titles of the Sassanian state remain. Although a few of Iran's provinces (Gilan, Azarbayejan, and Kordestan) experienced a republican system of administration autonomous from the central government during 1918–1922 and in the 1940s, the centralized structure of Iranian government has continued under governorships.

The country is divided into twenty-two provinces (*Ostans*) and a few general governorships (*Farmandari-e-Koll*). The provinces are headed by governor-generals (*Ostandaran*), and the governorships are headed by governors (*Farmandaran-e-Koll*). Every province is divided into several large counties (*Shahrestans*), headed by governors (*Farmandaran*). Moreover, each Shahrestan is divided into districts (*Bakhsha*), administered by lieutenant-governors (*Bakhshdaran*). Each district is further divided into subdistricts (*Dehistans*) under administrators (*Dehdaran*); each subdistrict is divided into villages (*Deh-ha*), headed by village headmen (*Dehbanan*). The Safavid title, *Kadkhoda,* was used for the village headman until the administrative reforms of the 1960s and 1970s; the title is still used informally in many parts of the country. The general trend in the 1960s and 1970s had been to recruit young college graduates in public administration for the position of Bakhshdar. They administered the districts and then moved upward if they remained loyal to the regime.[3]

Prior to the 1962 land reforms and subsequent rural bureaucratization, the administrative structure was shaped and controlled mainly by the feudal landlords and Khans (tribal leaders) who, in turn, appointed the Kadkhodayan in the villages to handle political, administrative, and judicial affairs. The Kadkhodayan were very powerful, responsible to both the landlords and the local governor. In addition, Reza Shah's bureaucratic reform of the 1920s armed the local feudal power structure with the Gendarmerie which strengthened the power of the local aristocracy.[4] The municipalities are headed by mayors (*Shahrdaran*).

All provincial governor-generals and country governors are appointed by the minister of interior with the approval of the prime minister, the president, and, in more important provinces, the National Consultative Assembly (NCA Majlis). Prior to the Revolution, all of these appointments including the Bakhsdaran, were made, with the approval of the Shah. The Ostandaran, however, were appointed by the Shah with the recommendation of the minister of the interior.[5]

The Presidency

Before the Revolution of 1978–1979, the highest executive in the government was the Shah, who appointed and dismissed the ministers and the prime minister. Under the Constitution of the Islamic Republic, the president is the highest executive power holder and must be elected to a four-year term by direct vote of the people. The president is responsible for implementing constitutional laws and coordinating relationships among the three branches of power. He has policy and administrative roles and is accountable to both the NCA (Majlis) and the leader (Faghih).[6] Although the first president of the republic, Bani Sadr, was elected as an independent office seeker, the recent presidents, including Ali Khamenehie, have been from the dominant Islamic Republic party (IRP). All laws passed by the Majlis must be signed by the president for implementation, and he is responsible before the people.[7]

The president presents the annual and five-year development plans, budgets, and legislative bills to the NCA, and signs all treaties, contracts, and agreements with other governments. Moreover, all laws and decrees, after being approved by the cabinet, must be accepted by the president before implementation. Should the president be absent or ill, a temporary council carries out his duties. This council consists of the prime minister and the heads of the NCA and the Supreme Court. In case of death, resignation, dismissal, or absence of more than two months, the council is responsible for carrying out the election of a new president within the next fifty days.[8]

The office of the president is becoming more institutionalized as its staff increases in response to the growing demands and complaints of the populace against the resurrection of the bureaucracy.

The Cabinet and the Prime Minister

According to the law, the Council of Ministers, that is, the cabinet, is formed by the prime minister who heads the council. The prime minister appoints and dismisses the ministers with the approval of the president and the NCA. The prime minister is responsible to the president and the NCA and may stay in office as long as the NCA vote of confidence is secured. He is appointed by the president and is approved by the NCA. All members of the cabinet are individually responsible to the NCA. The cabinet meets upon the president's demand and in his presence or under his chairmanship.

The cabinet must approve decrees and legislative proposals (bills) before they are submitted to the NCA for action.[9] If a bill is rejected by the cabinet, it may be sent back to the related minister for change or revision. At times when a minister's bill is rejected, the prime minister will form a special committee to make inquiries and a recommendation, or to prepare a separate bill.

Resolving litigation related to government and the public is subject to cabinet approval and, in the case of foreign involvement, to the approval of the NCA as well. The prime minister is the chief executive, and his decision-making powers, along with his cabinet, are far greater than they were under the Pahlavi system. The prime minister and the cabinet had no actual power under the Shah as he made most of the decisions himself; cabinet meetings were a matter of formality.[10] The actual power and executive actions of the prime minister and the president are dependent on, among other factors, the political power sources with which they are affiliated. For example, the former president, Bani Sadr, was powerless vis-à-vis his prime minister, Rajai, who had the political support of the Islamic Republic Party (IRP).[11] In short, while the Pahlavi prime minister and his cabinet were nominal institutions, they are powerful in the executive sense under the Islamic Republic. However, it must be noted that their major limitation is the supreme authority of the leader (Ayatollah Khomeini) or Leadership Council under the Constitution.[12] The prime minister supervises the work of the ministries, agencies, special institutions, and public enterprises described below.

Organizational Structure of the Executive (Bureaucracy)
Ministries and Agencies

The ministries have a broad scope and large organizations in the bureaucracy. The main organizations of the executive ministries are as follows:

Interior

Agriculture and Rural Development, composed of the several former Ministries of Agriculture, Natural Resources, Rural Cooperative, and Land Reform which merged in the 1970s to form the Ministry of Agriculture and Rural Development (MARD).

Economy and Finance

Education

Sciences and Higher Education

Energy (water and power)

Foreign Affairs

Culture and Arts

Health and Social Welfare

Housing and Urban Development

Heavy Industry and Mines

Information and Tourism

Justice

Labor and Social Affairs

P.T.T. (post, telegraph, and telephone)

Roads and Transportation

Defense

Oil (formerly the National Iranian Oil Co.)

Commerce, Plan and Budget

The prerevolutionary Ministry of Court has been abolished, but several new ministries have been added to the list since the recent NCA legislation. The Revolutionary Guards Organization, a militia paramilitary organization, is now the Ministry of Revolutionary Guards (*Sepah-e-Pasdaran*); the Reconstruction Crusades (*Jihad-e-Sazandagi*) is now the Ministry of Reconstruction Crusades. In addition, the previous Ministry of Information, which officially supervised the Shah's secret police organization, SAVAK (abolished during the Revolution), is again an entity.[13]

Other ministries are joining the list. During and after the Revolution, thousands of mass organizations sprang up from the people. With their antibureaucratic characteristics, these organizations established numerous development projects throughout the country and have played a remarkable role in the country's defense since the Iraqi invasion. The recent administrative policy of bringing them under the centralized bureaucracy of the executive branch by giving them the title of "ministry" has become a controversial issue in the NCA, creating resentment among the members of these organizations.[14]

The agencies are not as large as the ministries, and they have a limited scope and mission. Some of the important agencies are the Iran Statistical Center; the Industrial Development and Renovation Organization (DRO); the Companies Registration Office; the Office for Aliens' Affairs and Residence; the Institute of Standards and Industrial Research of Iran (ISIRI); the Small Industries Organization; the Price Regulation Center; the Fertilizer Distribution Company; the Public Warehouses Company; the Iran Customs Department; the Export Promotion Center of Iran; the International Trade Fairs and Exhibition Corporation; the Housing Organization; the Mostazafan Foundation (formerly Pahlavi Foundation); the Islamic Inspectorate Organization (formerly Imperial Inspector); the Social Security Organization; The Sound and Sight of the Islamic Republic (formerly National Iranian Radio and TV—NIRT); and State Organizations for Administrative and Employment Affairs (SDAEA). In addition to these agencies, a number of independent agencies were established during and after the Revolution including, the War Refugee Organization, the Administrative Justice Court, the Office of Imam, and the National Bureau of Investigation (NBI).[15]

PUBLIC ENTERPRISES

Public enterprises are state organizations or corporations that operate as businesses and earn revenues and profits. The Mostazafan Foundation alone supervises more than 400 enterprises for which complete information is not available. It is the second largest employer in the country after the government. Some of the important enterprises are the National Iranian Steel Corporation; Mobarekeh Steel Mills (formerly Aryamehr); the National Iranian Copper Industries Company; the Persian Gulf Shipbuilding Company; the National Pharmaceutical Company; the Iranian State Railways Organization; the National Insurance Company; Banks; Ports and Shipping Organization; the Telecommunication Company of Iran; P.T.T. (post, telegraph, and telephone); the Tehran Regional Electric Company; the Tehran Regional Water Organization; the Khuzestan Water and Power Authority; the Tehran Bus Company; the Gilan Regional Power and Water Authority; the Isfahan Regional Electric Authority; the Khurasan Regional Electric Company; the Foreign Transaction Company; the Meat Organization; the Iran Farsh Corporation (Iran Carpet Company); the Iran Tobacco Company; the Haft Tappeh Cane Sugar Agro-Industrial Company; the Moghan Agro-Industrial and Cattle-Breeding Company; Southern and Northern Fisheries Companies; and the Fertilizer Distribution Company. A large number of these state-operated companies and enterprises were taken over by the state from the large private owners including the royal family who fled the country during the Revolution. They are now managed by the Mostazafan Foundation.[16]

BUREAUCRATIC ELITE

The bureaucratic elite occupies key formal positions in the administrative apparatus of society, where it exercises great power, possesses special privileges, and enjoys high prestige, status, and income.[17] Among the elite are influential officials whose decisions affect society, and whose concerns and actions reach beyond their administrative functions. They are the higher civil servants whose positions are political and administrative in nature.

Before the Revolution, the Iranian bureaucratic elite was an integral part of the political and economic elite. Under the Islamic Republic, the bureaucratic-administrative elites are drawn from the religious, economic, and political groups (both religious and secular). In 1970, according to James Bill and Carl Leiden, the civil bureaucracy was headed by an elite whose "number fluctuated between 450–500 persons."[18] This elite included only the highly strategic elites of the bureaucracy.

An identification of the strategic bureaucratic elites at national and provincial-local levels is useful. This can be done through an analysis of the internal organizational hierarchy of the ministries and agencies.[19]

A ministry's bureaucratic elites from the national down to the district-village levels can be seen in the organizational chart of a ministry (MARD) (see Figure 7.1). The bureaucratic elites include the minister (*Vazir*); deputy ministers (e.g., in political, parliamentary, administrative, financial, legal, social, research, and international affairs); agency heads (*Modiran-e-Amel*) and their deputies; special secretaries of the ministers; high inspectors; and director-generals (*Modiran-e-Koll*), whose number can be as high as functional specialization in a variety of fields allows for further structural differentiation of the bureaucracy. Perhaps the most powerful Modiran-e-Koll is the one who directs the Department of Ad-

Figure 7.1
Organization Chart for the Ministry of Agriculture and Rural Development (MARD) 1970s—
Bureaucratic Elite Orientation

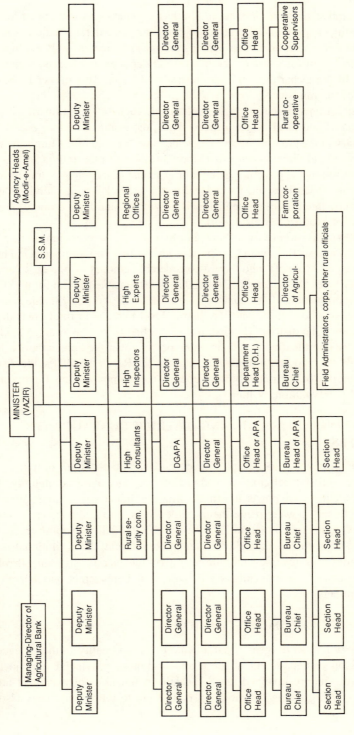

Note: This figure illustrates only the basic formal organizational structure of the Ministry, with an elite orientation and may not exact; it is not comprehensive. It shows elite positions.
Source: A. Farazmand, "Bureaucratic Politics Under the Shah: Development or System Maintenance," Ph.D. diss. (Syracuse University, 1982), p. 113.

ministrative Affairs, since he or she has a tremendous amount of influence on recruitment, promotion, discipline, compensation, determination, and the like. In addition, this officer plays perhaps the most political, as well as administrative, role in the ministry. He or she has several deputies to manage specialized functions of the Department of Administrative Affairs. This officer is the eyes and ears of the minister.[20]

Since Iran's bureaucracy is centralized, each of the ministries has its own provincial and local-district offices. Thus, the central director-general heads the ministry in the province where he or she plays the role of the minister. However, all functional director-generals (Modiran-e-Koll) in the provinces are generally supervised by the governor-general or Ostandar (the ancient Satrap or Marzpan). The functional departments under director-generals are also divided within the hierarchy into offices at the national, provincial, and local (county) levels under an office head (Raies-e-Edareh).

The subdivision of the offices into bureaus is also common; in turn, they are divided into sections with an official as an administrator or manager. The bureaus are headed by chiefs who have a considerable amount of power.[21] Again, at the county level, the governor (Farmandar) is responsible general for the supervision and coordination of the functional offices of the county (Shahrestan). Further subdivisions of offices into the district-level bureaus in rural areas depends on the size of the districts (Bakhsh-ha) where the district governors (Bakhshdaran) exercise coordinating and supervising powers over the bureau chiefs. But in the case of more powerful ministries, like the MARD in the 1970s, the district-rural bureaucrats of the ministry may operate autonomously—a situation that dominated prerevolutionary Iran.[22]

PROVINCIAL, LOCAL, AND DISTRICT BUREAUCRATIC ELITES

The provincial, local, and district bureaucratic elites are formed by the economic, political, religious, and administrative elites of the community. The rural-district elites were powerful officers whose political and administrative roles and discretionary powers made them "little kings," to quote James Fesler, during prerevolutionary rural Iran. They were the "stability maximizers" and maintained the regime in the field.[23] After the Revolution, the institutionalized Islamic Societies took over several administrative-managerial and political roles in the bureaucracy. Their members are both rural bureaucrats and Islamic system-maintainers.

PERSONNEL ADMINISTRATION

Every ministry, agency, public enterprise, and entity in the bureaucracy has a personnel department at all levels—national, provincial, and local. These departments are involved in all specialized functions of personnel administration—from granting vacations to recruitment to retirement. They also perform training and indoctrination functions and play the role of watchdog and disciplinarian. Although the provincial and local administrative personnel have been recruited from the local communities, their appointments have to be officially made by the center. After the Revolution, changes may have taken place—especially in the case of independent revolutionary organizations, but no major alteration was seen until 1984.[24] Recent changes have again favored centralization.

Personnel Policies

Since the 1920s, the prevalent expectation among the public has been that the public sector should be the principal provider of jobs for the people. The Pahlavi government, taking advantage of this perception, used public employment as a chief means of keeping discontented youth, especially the university graduates, off the street. As a result, the bureaucracy grew dramatically during the 1950s and through the 1970s, without consideration for the rational need for created positions. Consequently, according to many studies, perhaps more than one-third of the bureaucracy's personnel were superfluous, and the administrative system was overstaffed while it was also understaffed in terms of qualified personnel.

The basic premise of the personnel policy was to keep all existing personnel since they were deemed necessary. (The booming oil revenues of the 1970s heavily promoted this policy.) In addition, justifications were frequently made to hire new personnel who were not needed.[25] Since the Revolution, the policy has been twofold but contradictory: on the one hand, there has been the hiring and promotion of war veterans, loyalists, and religious believers to the Islamic government; on the other, there has existed a general policy of freeze on personnel employment in the bureaucracy. This contradictory policy has served the system-maintainers while discouraging the rest. This situation seems to have changed recently, and hiring has been resumed in select industrial, educational, and service sectors.

CIVIL SERVICE LAW IN IRAN

The first modern civil service law in Iran was adopted from Belgium and introduced in 1922. The system was rudimentary, with few basic rules for personnel management, and provided for nine levels: four clerical and five supervisory. The law called for a number of merit-based functions to be performed but did not make any distinction between blue-collar and white-collar workers, or between clerical and administrative employees. Until 1966, when the new law was introduced, the 1922 law remained on paper only: merit principles were violated in hiring, promotion, compensation, and the like.[26]

The United States and the United Nations introduced reforms in the 1950s and 1960s, resulting in several changes. The most important of these changes was the Position Classification Plan (PCP) and the 1966 Comprehensive State Employment Law covering almost 300,000 public employees. According to one of the reformers, Frank Sherwood, the PCP was rigid, inflexible, and control-oriented for keeping people busy: "we built roads nowhere just to keep people busy and to have some legitimacy in paying them."[27]

The PCP divided government positions into twelve groups with fifteen steps in each group; this classification is still in operation. The 1966 law also called for consistency, coordination, a merit system, and remuneration on the basis of equal pay for equal work. For the first time, the law established a central personnel agency, the State Organization for Administration and Employment Affairs (SOAEA). By 1978, more than 700,000 public employees were covered by the PCP and supervised by the SOAEA. Despite the new provisions, most of the ministries and agencies continued to hire and practice their own personnel administrative principles. Thus, fragmentation in the personnel management system continued. However, one major change took place when the SOAEA took over the civil service retirement plan.

Since the Revolution, civil service has undergone several structural and procedural changes, but the trend is more or less a throwback to the past system. In addition to the initial formation of the committee system, participatory decision making in the bureaucracy, and heavy purges (more than 25 percent) in the civil service, some other structural changes have taken place. One of the major laws passed in the legislature affects full-time female civil servants. According to the new law, full-time women employees are to be made part-time—although it is on a voluntary basis. The law may affect more than 320,000 female employees. The labor law has also become controversial, especially its Article 33 which gives the employer an absolute right to fire workers without reason or due process. The labor movement has strongly resisted this move, and so far its fate is uncertain. As of early 1988, the labor law was still being debated. Still another important change in the civil service is the return to the personnel merit system and the trend of rebureaucratization of all public-created organizations, concurrent with the attempts to make some public corporations private.[28]

Until World War II, a person holding any level of formal European-oriented education was allowed to hold administrative positions in the bureaucracy. Later, a high school diploma became the major criterion for administrative-supervisory jobs. During the 1960s and 1970s, college degrees became one of the most important criteria for recruitment in public administration positions. However, technical and job-related qualifications were not very important. Thus, the bureaucracy absorbed university and other high school graduates regardless of the administration's needs.[29] Nevertheless, as Bill correctly states, the new bureaucracy in Iran became "more professional." Thus, the bureaucracy in Iran provided an excellent channel for aspirants to enter and move up in the political system.[30]

RECRUITMENT CRITERIA AND METHODS

Evidence shows that the following criteria have determined recruitment in Iran: political loyalty, personal connections, family ties and class background, educational degree, and expertise. In addition, the Pahlavi administration used political cooptation to recruit members from possible opposition groups or the intelligentsia.[31]

During the 1970s, the SOAEA formulated a personnel policy of recruitment for all ministries which required all applicants to take nationally administered employment tests. The ministries and agencies would then select applicants with acceptable scores, a test similar to the United States PACE tests for civil servants. However, many limitations and exceptions made this policy inoperative. Another method of recruitment was first the selection of personnel from politically and personally favored groups. Cooptation was a common method.

Most, if not all, of the strategic personnel were selected from the dominant party and politically loyal individuals, with a careful security clearance of SAVAK. Since the Revolution, key personnel have been recruited from among the fundamentalist religious individuals (*Maktabi*), believers in Islam and its government, and politically loyal to the regime. Thus, religious and political criteria outweigh other standards.

FINANCIAL CONTROL OF ADMINISTRATION

The Budget

Until the 1960s, the line-item budget was the main budgeting system used in the government, with some program budgeting. During the 1960s, the Planning, Programming, and Budgeting System (PPBS) was introduced in the Planning and Budget Organization (PBO), and agencies had to prepare their budgets accordingly. But the PPBS failed owing to lack of political support, analytical expertise, and coordination among the agencies. Since the 1970s, program budgeting has been the main budgetary system, with a line-item budgeting approach for control purposes. The present budgeting system is a continuation of the last, combined with a modification on the basis of Islamic principles.[32]

The ever expanding public sector in Iran has been heavily dependent on oil revenues as a major source of financing since the 1960s. The central government has always played a dominant role in the mobilization and allocation of resources. Until the Revolution, the government budget has shown a major feature on the revenue side: oil and gas revenues share the largest part—from 50 percent in 1971–1972 to 84.9 percent in 1974–1975.

On the expenditure side, military, general government, and capital expenditure shares are the largest parts of the budget. Since 1941, Iran has had budget deficits almost every year, which were made up of domestic and foreign borrowings.[33] According to Islamic administration officials, no foreign borrowing has been made since the Revolution. Domestic borrowing and printing money by the Central Bank have been used to cover the deficits that are increasing dramatically, primarily because of rising defense expenditures to finance the war with Iraq.

The nonoil government revenues consist of direct and indirect taxes. Indirect taxation has traditionally been the backbone of government revenues in Iran. Direct taxes include individual and corporate taxes; public expenditures consist of capital and current expenditures. Although capital or development expenditures have increased substantially over the last two decades, current expenditures have always been significantly higher than capital expenditures, with defense taking the largest share (40 percent).[34] Since the Revolution, the general fiscal policy of the government has been to hold down administrative costs. In addition, the Islamic government's first long-term plan—the Five-Year Plan—calls for a huge amount of capital expenditures for social, economic, and industrial developments. The role of the Plan and Budget Organization (now a Ministry) which controls the operation of administrative organizations, the bureaucracy, can therefore be significant.

Plan and Budget Ministry (PB)

The most important institution with financial control over the administration is the Plan and Budget (PB) Ministry. Established in 1949 to implement the first long-term development plan, the PB was responsible for preparing development plans until the 1960s. Since 1949, the PB has formulated six development plans; the last one, under the Islamic Republic, began in 1983. Until the 1960s, the state budget and the development budget were separate, and no budgetary regulations were observed.[35]

Since the late 1960s, the PB has had major financial control over the administration but has been frustrated by a sea of bureaucratic inertia, corruption, and incompetence in the administrative system. Presently, the PB is an executive arm of the president through which the chief executive exercises a substantial amount of control. After the budget appropriation and approval by the NCA, the budget execution process becomes a major instrument of control for the president and the PBO. Before the Revolution, the PB did not have much influence since the Shah had his own mechanisms of control over the bureaucracy. The situation is different now because power is relatively diffuse, and multiple sources of influence and power make it possible to have some control over the bureaucracy if effectively applied.[36] Financial control is supplemented by the legislative, executive, judicial, and leadership controls of the administration.

OTHER FORMS OF CONTROL OVER THE ADMINISTRATION

Legislative Control

In addition to the PB, the NCA (Majlis) plays a dominant role in checking and controlling the administration and its bureaucracy. The NCA's control is exercised through legislation, power over the Council of Ministers (cabinet), budget authorization and appropriation, and audit and investigation in the administration's activities. Not only must the appointment of cabinet members, including the prime minister, be approved, but they may also be questioned individually and collectively by the NCA.

In addition, all administrative programs and institutions have to be authorized and appropriated by the Authorization and Appropriation Committees. Hearings may be held before the various committees of the legislature, and sunset actions of the NCA may affect the administration's program. The NCA also conducts the auditing of administrative operations, and its Investigative Committee has considerable influence on the legislature.[37] In order to deal with the bureaucracy's expertise, the NCA is becoming increasingly bureaucratized itself as the number of technical experts is increasing. Whereas the Pahlavi Parliament was a rubber stamp of the Shah, the new NCA is a powerful institution of control over the executive branch.

Executive Control

Executive control over the administration is exercised by the president who is the chief executive. Control mechanisms include appointing the prime minister, approving or disapproving the cabinet members, assigning all political appointees and high-ranking officials of the administration, signing or vetoing the legislated budget, issuing presidential orders and decrees affecting the administration, and approving or disapproving all foreign contracts concluded by the prime minister and the cabinet.

With regard to the budget, the president has the power of impoundment and recision, but he must report to the NCA concerning his verdict on recisions. In addition, the president exercises major control over the preparation and submission of plans and budget to the NCA. It is interesting that the Executive Office of the Presidency (EOP) is also becoming bureaucratized as its staff increases rapidly. Under the former president, Bani Sadr, the office was extremely large and acted independently of the rest of the government.[38]

Judicial Control

The High Council of the Judiciary (HCJ) is the highest judicial office with broad functions, including reorganizing the Ministry of Justice; preparing judiciary bills; and hiring, appointing, dismissing, and other administrative affairs. The HCJ consists of five members: the head of the Supreme Court, the attorney-general, and three religious and secular judges, chosen by the judges of the country. The council members serve for five years, subject to extension.

The Religious Judges

Since the Revolution, the religious judges have had an enormous amount of control over the administration and its bureaucracy in districts and provinces throughout the country. In addition to resolving disputes, they have taken up many administrative functions in the bureaucracy. But since the recent activation of the old Ministry of Justice, and the trend toward rebureaucratization of the country, the religious judges have refrained from administrative functions. Instead, the Administrative Justice Courts are becoming more powerful institutions in resolving citizen–bureaucracy conflicts.

The Ministry of Justice (MJ)

This institution has responsibility for all problems involving the legislative, executive, and judiciary powers. The minister is selected by the prime minister from the suggested candidates of the HCJ.[39] In the bureaucracy–public relationship, the MJ has often supported the bureaucracy in the past. The present situation seems to follow the old pattern as complaints against the MJ are pouring into the HCJ, EOP, and other justice agencies.

The Supreme Court

The Supreme Court is another powerful body that has judicial control over the administration. Its main duty is the supervision of correct law enforcement. The Supreme Judges, most of whom are religious jurists (*Mujtahids*), serve for five years. They must be appointed by the Leadership Council.

The Court of Administrative Justice (CAJ)

This judicial body was created after the Revolution, when a lot of personnel misconduct occurred and many employees were illegally fired without due process. Borrowed from the French system, the CAJ handles "complaints, criticisms, and objections of the people concerning state public officials, units, regulations, and administration of their rights." It also protects the individual rights of state employees through due process, and operates under the supervision of the High Judicial Council. More than 100,000 cases poured into the court in the one year following its formation.[40] The CAJ is supported by an investigative organization.

The General National Investigative Organization (GNIO)

This body has been created to supervise judicial affairs related to the administrative system's legal procedures; it is supervised by the High Judicial Council. The GNIO resembles the Soviet Union's system of procurators.[41]

The Islamic Inspectorate Organization (IIO)

The IIO has a long history in the Iranian administrative system. The Achaemenid and Sassanian administrations were subject to this mode of control; the shah established its modern institutional version in 1957. The Imperial Inspectorate Organization, recruited from the upper class of the military and bureaucratic origins, had an absolute right to make an on-the-spot inspection of any administrative and military organization at any level and at any location in the country. It was abolished after the Revolution but was reestablished in recent years under the name of Islamic Inspectorate Organization (IIO). As an arm of the leadership, the IIO can exercise effective control over administration and its bureaucracy.[42]

The Office of Imam

Formed during the Revolution, the Office of Imam Khomeini (simply Imam) has been the highest form of appeal for anyone (primarily the oppressed people Mostazafin), in the country. The initial arbitrating role of the office is not, in a sense, institutionalized, since it routinely acts on cases and demands quick responses from the administrative agencies regarding allegations or accusations of abuse of power. The shadow of the office over organizational actions is a powerful reminder of control.

THE LEADERSHIP AND LEADERSHIP COUNCIL

In addition to the above controlling mechanisms, the leader (of the Revolution and country) has the supreme power over any branch of the government. This supreme power is granted by the Constitution. The all-powerful leader until recently, Ayatollah Khomeini, for example, could dismiss the president as he did in the case of Bani Sadr. Thus, the leader's control over the administration should be taken seriously by officials, although the leader rarely interferes in the operations of the government.

The Leadership Council has been established by law in order to function as a collective leadership in the leader's absence or in the event of the leader's illness. Membership is determined by law and the Assembly of Experts (*Majlis-e-Khobregan*), composed of knowledgeable ulama. Thus, the leadership role can also be considered another form of check and control over the administration. It is widely used as a reference for administrative decisions as well as controlling the territorial councils and Islamic societies throughout the country.[43]

TERRITORIAL COUNCILS AND ISLAMIC SOCIETIES

In addition to the national legislative control of the administration, there are councils at provincial, county, and district levels. Their main function is legislative but they do not make laws. Rather, they oversee the performance of the administration and approve, or disapprove, the decisions of the executive officials.

The Islamic councils are formed in every village, town, township, administrative unit, factory, and office throughout the country. They replaced their counterpart, the secular council, in every location as they became dominant. The Islamic societies are affiliated with the religious community and the local functionaries of the IRP. Their main functions are to enforce religious and political rules, and to oversee the management of the administration. But their oversight role has been confusing since they have interfered in the administration of public affairs. One must not underestimate the strength of these societies, since they are supported by powerful religious leaders, including Ayatollah Khomeini. In the villages, for example, they are the supreme authorities.[44]

DISTRICT/FIELD ADMINISTRATION

Until the 1950s and 1960s, local field administration had historically enjoyed relative autonomy, despite the attempts of the central government to bring it under control. In addition, popular attitudes toward field administration have traditionally been negative, especially since the establishment of the rural police (Gendarmerie) by Reza Shah during the 1920s. It was a corrupt, oppressive instrument of the feudal landlords (tribal khans) who actually controlled the local government and assured their own rural self-administration in Iran until the 1960s.[45]

Since the 1960s, rural Iran has come under the firm control of the state. Under the Pahlavi regime, the concept of district self-administration was lost because of the rapid development of capitalism under the direct and active supervision of the state which bureaucratized the rural areas. Although, in theory the field administration of rural Iran was under the control of the Interior Ministry, in actuality, rural-district areas were administered by the powerful, ever expanding bureaucracy of the Ministry of Agriculture and Rural Development. Figure 7.2 illustrates the power and influence of MARD in Iran's bureaucratized rural areas before the Revolution.

During the 1970s, as the number of bureaucratic officials increased, the popular attitude toward the local-district administration and the regime became more and more negative, as massive displacement, proletarianization, widening gaps between rich and poor, town and country, and migration to cities increased. The negative attitudes qualitatively changed to antagonism during the 1970s as the bureaucratic officials in the villages pressed for system maintenance. These antagonistic attitudes led to active rural participation in the Revolution of 1978–1979.[46]

After the Revolution, democratic collective self-administration prevailed in the districts for a few years as the bureaucracy was replaced by independent popular organizations. These organizations included various cooperative systems—from single-purpose to multiple-purpose entities, village and district councils, and

Figure 7.2
Rural Administration after the Land Reform

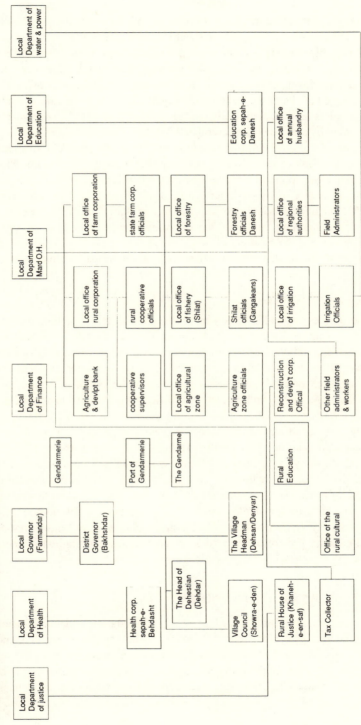

Source: A. Farazmand, "Bureaucratic Politics Under the Shah: Development or System Maintenance," Ph.D. diss. (Syracuse University, 1982), p. 203

other organs of self-administration. Class conflicts intensified as a result of the field administration's control of popular forces. These conflicts and tensions often resulted in bloodshed, as incidents in Turkamansahra, Fars, Mazandran, and Gilan have shown where the landlords and khans reclaimed lands under Bani Sadr's presidency. Nevertheless, as time passed, these field organizations were gradually replaced by the officially organized institutions of administration and control, such as the Islamic Societies, village councils, and the district administration, accompanied by the rest of the centralized functional bureaucracies.[47]

As the process of Islamization continues, the role of the religious leaders and their institutions in rural Iran is becoming increasingly important. Studies are needed to assess popular attitudes toward the new field administration. However, the phenomenon of massive rural migration to major cities as a result of the state's land policy (which has supported some large landlords returning to the field and reclaiming land) may be interpreted as an indication of some dissatisfaction among the rural populace.[48] The phenomenon of bureaucratization can be better understood when it is analyzed in the political context.

THE BUREAUCRACY AND BUREAUCRATIC POLITICS

The politics of bureaucracy can be analyzed in terms of bureaucratism—the exercise of power by bureaucrats—and in terms of the use of bureaucracy as an instrument of power for system (regime) maintenance and rule making in societies. Elsewhere it is argued, in detail, that the bureaucracy is an instrument of power and that the phenomenon of bureaucratization is a political process aimed at maintaining and enhancing political regimes and furthering their economic interests.[49] This section discusses the issue of bureaucratization in Iran, followed by a number of interrelated issues. The Marxist theory of state views bureaucracy as an instrument of the ruling class, whereas the non-Marxists take a pluralistic view of bureaucracy. While acknowledging that bureaucracy can be an instrument of power for the rulers and masters, it maintains that bureaucracy is a public service institution for all strata of society and is not a class instrument.[50] As an instrument of power and as a self-perpetuating and autonomous institution, the bureaucracy can also be instrumental in social system transformation and in development. The following issues are analyzed in the context of bureaucratic politics in Iran before and after the Revolution.

BUREAUCRATIZATION IN IRAN

As mentioned before, rural Iran was predominantly under the social system of feudalism, with more than 70 percent of the population residing there. The central government had little control over the self-administered rural areas, despite the existence of the rural police, which actually was an arm of the feudal landlords. Since the 1960s the social system of rural Iran has changed into capitalism with the development of the extended administration of the central government. The process of bureaucratization of rural Iran, as well as other areas of society, began with the partial implementation of the land reforms and other reforms in the 1960s.[51]

Conditions for rural bureaucratization were set through the replacement of the feudal landlords' local administrative management by the ever expanding, competing, rival bureaucracies of the central administration.

The process of bureaucratization in rural areas began with the implementation of nine out of the twelve points of the "White Revolution." A large number of bureaucratic institutions of the central administration, mainly in the Ministry of Agriculture, were created in rural areas. The land reform set the conditions for establishing a huge number of state-run cooperatives which were bureaucratically planned, organized, managed, and controlled by the central administration of MARD. The cooperatives were, in effect, bureaucratic organizations in villages where officials were appointed and paid by the state; the peasants had no say in decisions or in control of their management. The cooperative officials were the regime's rule enforcers and system-maintainers rather than the farmer's helpers.[52]

If rural bureaucratization was started by the cooperatives, it was completed by the establishment of a huge network of farm corporations during the 1960s and 1970s. The main role of farm corporations was to promote the development of capitalism in rural Iran. It was mainly dependent capitalism since the internal national economic capacity was weakened, or destroyed, and the dependence on the multinational corporations increased. As a result of the state's policy of establishing corporations—the Shah ordered their creation everywhere and he wanted the policy enforced—the implementation of agricultural zones, massive rural displacement, and administrative and political control mechanisms went into effect for the purpose of capitalist development and system maintenance.[53]

These bureaucratically organized and managed corporations completed the process of rural bureaucratization since they covered areas not controlled by cooperatives in replacing the landlords. By the mid–1970s, the number of coops was reduced, and they were consolidated for further state control. In addition to the cooperatives, farm corporations, and zones, a number of other bureaucratic networks were created as a result of the nationalization of forests, waterways, and so on.[54]

The political role of regime maintenance, the economic role of capitalist development, and the administrative role of managing both political and economic affairs were the major functions of the administrative system in bureaucratized Iran during the 1960s and 1970s. After the Revolution, the bureaucratic machine underwent a major debureaucratizational process, as a massive number of popular revolutionary organizations sprang up and took over many administrative functions in the country. But, as mentioned before, the revival of the old bureaucracy and its further rebureaucratization, started in recent years, is continuing.[55]

POLITICIZATION OF THE BUREAUCRACY

Under the Pahlavi regime, the bureaucracy was controlled through a number of internal and external mechanisms, one being the politicization of the administrative system. Politicization of the bureaucracy takes place through political socialization, indoctrination, and subjugation. The practical methods of politicization of bureaucracy in Iran can be divided into three categories for examination: political parties, Shah-worshipping (Shah-parasti), and SAVAK.[56]

During the 1960s and 1970s, the dominant Iran-Novin and Rastakhiz parties were extensively involved in the politicization of the bureaucracy throughout the country. Especially during the mid–1970s, all Iranians were forced to join the single Rastakhiz party; all public employees were ordered to sign membership books placed in offices. Those who did not join were considered un-Iranian, according to the Shah, and "should not have any expectations." Moreover, "promotion, security, contacts" depended on party membership.[57] Politicization of the bureaucracy after the Revolution was a natural phenomenon, but relative democracy prevailed for a few years. In recent years, however, the government's efforts to further politicize the administrative system through ideological indoctrination have shifted the emphasis to Islamization of the bureaucracy. Patronage and ideological criteria are dominant factors in personnel decisions and in administration; the IRP is playing a major role.

Under the Pahlavi regime, those individuals who worshipped the Shah were called Shah-parasts. They were mainly from the upper and privileged classes, which benefited from the regime in power, and were rewarded for their open support. They were mainly identified as the strategic bureaucratic elite, and their role was to promote monarchy, the Shah, and his policies in the bureaucracy. They were extremely loyal to the Shah. For example, in the late 1960s, the then Prime Minister Amir Abbas Hoveyda publicly said: "I am a slave of the Shah."[58] In short, their role was to promote the regime's control over the bureaucracy. The postrevolutionary Hezbollahis (followers of the party of God), and the followers of the Line of Iman, and the Maktabis (followers of the doctrinal school of Islam) are probably the best examples of worshippers of God, devotion to His representative, Hidden Imam, and loyalty to the Imam (Khomeini). The daily prayers of religious people in almost every office building is one such practice.

The role of SAVAK is self-explanatory; its deadly reputation is known to the world. Briefly stated, SAVAK also played a major role in the political socialization of the bureaucracy through direct and indirect methods. Although this institution of control was abolished during the Revolution, debates on whether a new security institution, SAVAMA, should be established continue in the government.[59]

THE BUREAUCRACY, DEVELOPMENT, AND SYSTEM MAINTENANCE

The role of the bureaucracy as an instrument of power was effective in maintaining the Pahlavi regime for several decades, but it failed to contribute to the economic and social development of Iran. Suffice it to say that, by a number of economic and social standards, the bureaucracy's role in development was a failure. In brief, on the basis of the following standards of labor market structuring, home market expansion, surplus generation and agricultural products, the bureaucracy performed very poorly. The national economy became almost totally dependent on the international capital and multinational corporations for agricultural and industrial products. Many view this development as a negative one, with a loss of national economic independence.[60]

NATIONALIZATION OF THE ECONOMY

The bureaucracy performed well when it helped transform the social system of feudalism in rural Iran to the capitalist system of economic and social relations. This change was effected through the partial implementation of the phased land reform and the subsequent institutional and socioeconomic policies of the state during the 1960s and 1970s.

The issue of nationalizing different areas of the economy of Iran has always been the subject of a major political as well as economic and administrative controversy. The nationalization of the Anglo-Iranian Oil Company by Dr. Mohammad Mossadegh during 1951–1953 created strong political opposition from the British-backed segment of the economic bourgeoisie and feudal landlords in the Parliament. Internationally, the United States and its allies joined Great Britain in boycotting Iranian oil in order to paralyze the Mossadegh administration. The impact paid off, along with the successful military coup of 1953, resulting in the overthrow of Mossadegh's administration. Consequently, oil came under the control of the U.S.–dominated International Oil Consortium in the 1950s, and the National Iranian Oil Company was created.[61]

During the 1960s, the Pahlavi regime nationalized a number of waterways, forest lands, and the like. Although the move can be considered a step forward to public ownership, it should be emphasized that private capitalism was not weakened under Pahlavi. On the contrary, the highly bureaucratized system of the state under the Shah actively promoted the development of capitalism. In addition, since "oil revenues [were] paid directly to the state, it had become the dominant force in the economy while its aim remained the promotion of capitalist development."[62]

BUREAUCRATIC CORRUPTION

No administrative system, whether modern or transitional, is free from corruption. In the case of Iran, according to many studies by scholars such as Bill, Zonis, and Cottam, corruption was encouraged, and became pervasive in the political system before the Revolution. For example, as Bill states, "The rich, complex traditions of corruption in Iran are generally distinguishable from the more simple bribery found in Sudan."[63]

Bureaucratic corruption was so institutionalized that people were faced with it throughout their lives, from an extra payment for a birth certificate to one for a death certificate. Sporadic reforms were never taken seriously and thus were ineffective. As the studies indicate, the reasons for corruption and the flourishing tendency of its patterns in Iranian bureaucracy can be found in the nature of the political system and in the demands of the bureaucratic system. According to Feneydoon Hoveyda, "Corruption ran wild in the heart of the royal family."[64]

Social and political representation was sought by unrepresented individuals through the "back door." There are widespread reports on Iranian bureaucratic corruption before the Revolution. In brief, several U.S. Congressional hearings in 1973, clearly indicate the pervasiveness of corruption in the Iranian bureau-cracy which had functional implications for the regime in power. The booming oil revenues of the 1970s resulted in larger public expenditures, increasing the scope of bureaucratic corruption in Iran.[65]

Bureaucratic corruption in Iran can be classified under four general categories: contracts, purchases, internal payoffs, and external payoffs. As a significant source of income for the strategic bureaucratic elite, contracts were in two forms: private and public. For the strategic elite who played the three roles of politician, bureaucrat, and business functionary, contracts (domestic and international) had great payoffs. This was encouraged by the royal family, as Hoveyda notes: "The Shah's brothers and sisters charged exorbitant commissions on contracts by acting as go-betweens." Purchase of materials and technologies in the bureaucracy was yet another source of income in the form of kickbacks.[66] Internal and external payoffs in the form of bribery, nepotism, and returns for favors were common.

Bureaucratic corruption under Pahlavis served system maintenance in several ways. It perpetuated the system, and it served as a political lubricant and an effective alternative to violence and use of force. Moreover, it served the system with "an overall flexibility and fluidity," and as a cooptive instrument for the Shah against the counterelite.[67]

SUMMING UP

Public administration has existed in Iran for more than 4,000 years. The well-established, efficient administrative system of the ancient Achaemenid world state was highly organized, with a centralized bureaucracy. The administrative system of Persia was further developed and advanced both technically and in-tellectually during the second world state of the Sassanian Empire.

The highly developed Sassanian administrative system and its bureaucracy have since been adopted by Iran and many Middle Eastern countries. Although Islamic Arabs invaded Iran during the seventh century, the Sassanian system became the model state for Arabs. The Abbasid Caliphate became a Persianized bureaucratic empire. Intellectual as well as technical contributions to public administration continued by Persians throughout the later centuries, especially under the centralized Safavid Empire (1501–1737).

The administrative system of Iran, however, lagged behind the West during the eighteenth and nineteenth centuries. While Europe was rapidly coming out of the age of feudalism and was transformed into a capitalist system of economy, conducive to the development of a rational administrative system, despotic rule and traditionalism in Iran prevented its administrative system from developing. The administrative reforms of the 1920s reestablished a centralized bureaucracy with some features of modern management. Yet, its main provision of civil service law remained on paper only until the 1960s, as the traditional system of management remained in operation with pervasive corruption encouraged by the Pahlavi regime.

In the 1950s and 1960s, the U.S.- and U.N.-led administrative reforms in Iran had several structural and procedural impacts on Iran's administrative system. The most important impact of the civil service reform was the bureaucratic reorganization of the old system, which was characterized by rigidity, inflexibility, and control orientation for system maintenance.

The socioeconomic reforms of the 1960s led to the intentional bureaucratization of Iranian society, with a high degree of bureaucratism and pervasive corruption, both of which were functional to the political system. The booming oil revenues of the 1970s strengthened the corrupt bureaucratic machinery of the state with a mission to maintain the Pahlavi regime and to further its economic interests. Although the political role of the bureaucracy was effective in terms of system maintenance until 1978, its administrative mission in the social system, to change the rural feudal system into capitalism, had greater success. However, the bureaucracy's role as a tool for developing Iran has been a major failure, as several socioeconomic standards clearly indicate.

Public administration as it is practiced in Iran today, despite the establishment of the Islamic Republic and a change in the political system, is predominantly an indigenous system of administration, with the main features of the Sassanian administration as a bureaucratic model. Many of these features can also be observed in other Middle Eastern countries. The present administrative system is a combination of the ancient administrative model—particularly in administrative distribution of power—with the modern concept of organization and management theory adopted from the West, and as well as Islamic principles.

AFTERWORD

This chapter was written before the death of Ayatollah Khomeini. Therefore, it does not reflect the changes that have been taking place in the Iranian political system.

NOTES

1. This brief historical account of Iranian administration is summarized from standard works such as Richard Frye, *Iran* (New York: Henry Holt, 1953); E. Burke Inlow,

Shahansha: A Study of Monarchy (Delhi: Motilal Banarsidas, 1979), and S. N. Eisenstadt, *The Political Systems of Empires* (New York: Free Press, 1963).

2. For information on the Persian influence on the Arabs and the West, see Frye, *Heritage of Persia* (London: Weidenfeld, 1962), Chapter 7; Frye, *The Golden Age of Persia* (New York: Harper and Row, 1975), Chapter 8. Also see P. Sharan, *Government and Politics of Persia* (New Delhi; Metropolitan Publishers, 1983), and R. Ghirshman, *Iran: From the Earliest Times to the Islamic Conquest* (Baltimore: Penguin Books, 1954).

3. For further information, see Ali Frazamand, "Bureaucratic Politics" (Ph.D. Dissertation, Syracuse University), Chapter 5; Farazmand, *The State, Bureaucracy, and Revolution in Modern Iran: Agrarian Reforms and Regime Politics* (New York: Praeger, 1989), Chapters 3, 5; Government of Iran, Ministry of Information, *Basic Facts About Iran* (Tehran: MQI, 1974).

4. See Farazmand, "Bureaucratic Politics"; Ann Lambton, *Landlord and Peasant in Persia* (London: Clarendon Press, 1953), p. 335; Nikki Keddie, "The Iranian Village Before and After Land Reform," in Eric J. Hoogland, *Land and Revolution in Iran, 1960–1980* (Austin: University of Texas Press, 1982).

5. Ibid.

6. *The Constitution of the Islamic Republic of Iran.*

7. Sharan, *Government and Politics of Persia*, Chapter 7.

8. Ibid.

9. *The Constitution of the Islamic Republic of Iran*, Chapter 9.

10. See Farazmand, "Bureaucratic Politics," Chapters 2 and 6; *The State, Bureaucracy and Revolution in Modern Iran*, Chapters 2 and 3. Leonard Binder, *Iran, Political Development in a Changing Society* (Los Angeles: University of California Press, 1962), pp. 96–127; Sharan, *Government and Politics of Persia*, Chapter 7.

11. Bani Sadr was eventually dismissed in 1981 by Ayatollah Khomeini who, as the leader, had the power to do so, according to the Islamic Republic Constitution. However, he rarely used this power provision. Bani Sadr was dismissed because he challenged the government and joined the political opposition organizations. After dismissal he fled to Paris in 1981. See Sepehr Zabih, *Iran Since the Revolution* (Baltimore: Johns Hopkins University Press, 1989), pp. 133–35.

12. *The Constitution of the Islamic Republic of Iran*, Chapter 8.

13. See Ali Farazmand, "The Impacts of the Revolution," *International Journal of Public Administration* (IJPA) 10, 4, pp. 337–65.

14. For more information, see Farazmand, "The Impacts of the Revolution," and "Bureaucracy, Development, and Regime Politics," *IJPA* 12, 1 (1989), pp. 79–111. Also, for a listing of the ministries, agencies, and public enterprises, see Business International, *Operating in Iran: An Economy Coming of Age* (New York: Business International, 1978), pp. 143–48.

15. Farazmand, "The Impacts of the Revolution"; "Bureaucracy, Development, and Regime Politics"; *Daily Ettalaat*, 29/11/1363 (1 February 1984).

16. Ibid.

17. Frederick Mosher, *Democracy and the Public Service* (New York: Oxford University Press, 1968), p. 19; James Bill, *The Politics of Iran* (Columbus, Ohio; Charles E. Merrill Press, 1972). Wright C. Mills, *The Power Elite of Iran* (Princeton, N.J.: Princeton University Press, 1971). For more discussion on this subject, see Farazmand, "Bureaucratic Politics," Chapter 3, and *The State, Bureaucracy and Revolution*, Chapter 3.

18. James Bill and Carl Leiden, *The Middle East: Politics and Power* (Boston: Allyn and Bacon, 1974), p. 26.

19. Farazmand, "Bureaucratic Politics," *Daily Ettalaat*, 1 February 1984.

20. Farazmand, "Bureaucratic Politics," Chapter 3.

21. Ibid.

22. Ibid.

23. See James Fesler, "The Political Role of Field Administration," in Ferrell Heady and Sybil L. Stokes (eds.), *Papers in Comparative Public Administration* (Ann Arbor, Mich., 1962), pp. 118–20.

24. Farazmand, "Bureaucratic Politics," Chapter 4.

25. Ibid., Chapters 4 and 6; Norman Jacobs, *The Sociology of Development: Iran as a Case Study* (New York: Praeger, 1963), p. 33; Bill, *Politics of Iran*; "Economy of Iran," *Iran Almanac and Book of Facts* (Tehran: Echoprint, 1977), p. 115.

26. For details, see Farazmand, "Bureaucratic Politics." Also see Parviz Keghobadi, "The Evolution of Iran's Civil Service System," *Symposium on Management Training in Public Administration* (Lahore, Pakistan: CENTO-U.N. Library, 1964), pp. 92–95; Iraj Ayman, Prime Minister's Office, "An Iranian Approach to Executive Development," *Symposium on Management Training in Public Administration*, p. 172; Iraj Valipour, "Departmental and Agency Training Programs in Iran," *Symposium on Management Training in Public Administration*; and Hooshang Kuklan, "Civil Service Reform in Iran: Myth and Reality," *International Review of Administrative Sciences* 43 (1977), pp. 345–51.

27. Frank Sherwood, "Learning from the Iranian Experience," *Public Administration Review* 40 (1980), pp. 413–21, 415.

28. For further details, see Farazmand, "The Impacts of the Revolution."

29. See Farazmand, "Bureaucratic Politics," Chapter 4. Also see Ayman, "An Iranian Approach," p. 171.

30. Bill and Leiden, *The Middle East*, p. 188.

31. See Farazmand, "Bureaucratic Politics"; Ayman, "An Iranian Approach"; Amin Banani, *The Modernization of Iran* (Stanford, Calif.: Stanford University Press, 1961); Bill and Leiden, *The Middle East*; Keyghobadi, "Evolution"; Marvin Zonis, *The Political Elite of Iran* (Princeton, N.J.: Princeton University Press, 1971); Valipour, "Departmental and Agency Training." About 98 percent of the officials interviewed by the author (N–47) confirmed the criteria listed in the text. Also, as a former public personnel administrator, the author's personal experiences and observations support the list.

32. The Budget 2535 (1977–1978): A Summary. Government of Iran, Plan and Budget Organization (Tehran, 1977), *The First Five-Year Development Plan of the Islamic Republic*. The Government of Islamic Republic of Iran, Plan and Budget Organization (Tehran, 1983).

33. Jahangir Amuzegar, *Iran: An Economic Profile* (Washington, D.C.: Middle East Institute, 1977), pp. 189–99; Cherye Benard and Zalmay Khalilzad, "*The Government of God*"—*Iran's Islamic Republic* (New York: Columbia University Press, 1984).

34. *Echo of Iran*, Iran Almanac, pp. 435–62. Amuzegar, *Iran* (New York: Praeger, 1963), pp. 189–99.

35. Donald Wilber, *Contemporary Iran* (New York: Praeger, 1963), pp. 173–80.

36. *The First Five-Year Development Plan*.

37. Sharan, *Government and Politics of Persia*.

38. Ibid., Chapter 7.

39. Ibid., Chapter 7.

40. Ibid., p. 145; Farazmand, "The Impacts of the Revolution," and *The State, Bureaucracy, and Revolution in Modern Iran*, Chapter 8.

41. Ibid.

42. Farazmand, "Bureaucratic Politics," pp. 235–36; Jacobs, *The Sociology of Development*, p. 49; Binder, *Iran*, p. 130; Marvin Zonis, "Iran," in Taro Ismael (ed.), *Comparative Politics in the Middle East* (Homewood, Ill.: Dorsey Press, 1970), pp. 66–67.

43. Sharan, *Government and Politics of Persia*; Personal observations of the author in Iran, Metropolitan, 1983.

44. Ibid.

45. For details, see Farazmand, "Bureaucratic Politics," Chapter 5; *The State, Bureaucracy, and Revolution in Modern Iran*, Chapters 4, 5, and 6; Keddie, "The Iranian Village Before and After Land Reform"; Helmut, "Land Reform and Agribusiness in Iran," *MERIP Reports* 3, 43 (December 1975); Halliday, *Iran*; Hooglund, *Land and Revolution in Iran*.

46. Ibid.; also see Eric Hooglund, "Rural Participation in the Revolution," *MERIP REPORTS*, No. 87; *Middle East Research and Information Project*, Inc., May 1980; and *Land and Revolution in Iran*.

47. Ibid. See also Farazmand, "The Impacts of the Revolution," and "Bureaucracy, Development, and Regime Politics."

48. Ibid. Also see "Political Attitudes in an Iranian Village" by an anonymous author, *Iranian Studies* 17, 4 (Autumn 1984), pp. 543–66.

49. For details on bureaucratic politics, see Farazmand, "Bureaucratic Politics," Chapters 6, 7 and "The Impacts of the Revolution"; Fred Riggs, "Bureaucratic Politics in Comparative Perspectives," *Journal of Public Administration* 1 (1969–1970), pp. 5–39.

50. See, for example, Marx and Engels, *Collected Works* (London, 1975); Vladimir Illich Lenin, *State and Revolution* (New York: International Publishers, 1971); Victor Thompson, *Without Sympathy and Enthusiasm; The Problems of Administrative Compassion* (University: University of Alabama Press, 1975); Ferrel Heady, *Public Administration: A Comparative Perspective*, 3rd ed. (Englewood Cliffs, N.J.: Prentice-Hall, 1987); Max Weber, From *Max Weber: Essays in Sociology*, trans. and ed. H. H. Gerth and C. Wright Mills (New York: Oxford University Press, 1946).

51. For details, see Farazmand, "Bureaucratic Politics"; *The State, Bureaucracy and Revolution*; Keddie, "The Iranian Village"; Halliday, *Iran*, Chapter 3; Helmut, "Land Reform"; Bill, *The Politics of Iran*; also see Farazmand, "Bureaucracy, Bureaucratization and Maintenance: The Case of Iran Before and After the Revolution," unpublished paper presented at the Annual Conference of the American Society for Public Administration in Boston, 1987.

52. Ibid.

53. Also see USAID: Kenneth Platt, "Land Reform in Iran" (Spring Review, County paper) (Washington, D.C., 1970), SR/LR/c–18, p. 80.

54. Ibid.

55. Ibid.

56. R. Dawson, K. Prewitt, and K. Dawson, *Political Socialization* (Boston: Little, Brown & Co., 1977), Chapter 4; Farazmand, "Bureaucratic Politics," Chapter 6, pp. 222–28.

57. Farazmand, ''Bureaucratic Politics,'' p. 224. The Shah's speech of 2 March 1975, quoted in Halliday, *Iran*, pp. 47–48.

58. Farazmand, ''Bureaucratic Politics,'' pp. 225–28.

59. Ibid., pp. 228.

60. Halliday, *Iran*; Bizhan Jazani, *Capitalism and Revolution in Iran* (London: Zed Press, 1980); Ali-Reza Nobari (ed.), *Iran Erupts: Independence News and Analysis of the Iranian National Movement* (Stanford, Calif.: Iran-American Documentation Group, Stanford University, 1978); Farazmand, ''Bureaucracy, Development, and Regime Politics.''

61. See references related to the political history of Iran.

62. Halliday, *Iran*, p. 41.

63. Bill and Leiden, *The Middle East*, pp. 179–80; Bill, *The Politics of Iran*, p. 110; Zonis, *The Political Elite of Iran*.

64. Feneydoon Hoveyda, *The Fall of the Shah* (London: Weidenfeld and Nicolson, 1980), p. 63. Hoveyda is the brother of the Shah's prime minister who served for about fifteen years during the 1960s and 1970s.

65. Ibid.; U.S. Congress, ''New Perspectives on the Persian Gulf,'' pp. 91, 142–43 (Participants: Marvin Zonis, 23 July 1973; Richard Cottam, 24 July 1973).

66. Hoveyda, *The Fall of the Shah*, p. 63.

67. Ibid.; Bill and Leiden, *The Middle East*, p. 180.

8

SAUDI ARABIA

Ayman Al-Yassini

HISTORICAL INTRODUCTION

Over two decades, from its proclamation as a unified kingdom in 1932 until 1953, Saudi Arabia survived without any elaborate administrative institutions. During this period King Ibn Saud ruled personally and informally. He administered the country as a gigantic personal household, prohibiting the concentration of power at any point in the system. The expansion of the oil-extracting industry in the 1950s and the subsequent increase in government revenues, however, brought about an increasing complexity in governmental institutions and the expansion of government jurisdiction over a large number of societal areas. The death of Ibn Saud in 1953 was not followed by the disintegration of the state he had founded. Instead, the Saudi state survived its founder's death, and Ibn Saud's successors (Saud, 1953–1964; Faisal, 1964–1975; Khalid, 1975–1982; Fahd, 1982 until the present) have continued to establish modern administrative structures to enhance governmental performance that complement the traditional base of the regime's legitimacy. Indeed, the development of complex and modern administrative institutions has enabled Saudi rulers to control society and maintain their traditional rule.

The creation of complex administrative institutions has led to two fundamental changes affecting the traditional relationship between religion and state in the Saudi Kingdom. First, it has increased role differentiation between the religious and political spheres. Second, it has routinized state control of a broad range of areas that were formerly dominated by religion and the religious establishment. Subsequent to this routinization, the *ulama* (religious leaders) lost many of their traditional functions and became a pressure group limited to exerting influence over the government's activities and policies but never acting as an autonomous center of power. To understand the position and role of the ulama in the newly founded structures, it is necessary to outline the evolution and characteristics of the country's administrative system.

ENVIRONMENTAL FACTORS AFFECTING THE ADMINISTRATIVE TRANSFORMATION OF THE POLITY

The 1932 declaration of Saudi Arabia as a unified kingdom did not in reality affect the traditional administrative structures that had existed in the country. Indeed, the transition from fragmented regional governments to a centralized administrative structure took place only two decades later. Although centralized and modern administrative structures had existed in the Hejaz, other parts of the Saudi domain were administered in the traditional manner. Some administrative structures were created in the 1930s in Hasa and Najd, but they were generally limited in scope and ad hoc in nature.

Because of the diversity of administrative structures in the country, the extent of role differentiation between the religious and political spheres and the degree of the extension of government jurisdiction over areas that were traditionally controlled by religion and the religious establishment varied from one region to another. In Najd, functional differentiation between the religious and political domains was minimal. This region was hardly subjected to external influences prior to the 1930s and consequently preserved its cultural homogeneity. It was ruled by Ibn Saud through Crown Prince Saud, who acted as an administrative governor and as the personal representative of the king. A number of local *umara* (rulers) acted as the king's representatives in their areas. Assisting the umara in day-to-day activities was a corps of ulama, who acted as judges and imams of mosques, as well as some financial administrators and police officers. With the exception of the ulama who were responsible to their superiors in Riyadh, all other administrators were accountable to the amir, who was accountable to the governor, who in turn was accountable to the king.

In contrast to Najd, Hejaz was influenced by foreign administrative systems, especially those of Egypt and Turkey. A number of administrative structures existed prior to the Saudi conquest of the region. For instance, Mecca had several departments such as health, municipal affairs, water supplies, and the judiciary, all coordinated by the City Council under the direct control of the Sherifi ruler. These structures remained intact following the Saudi takeover but fell under the direct control of Faisal, the governor of Hejaz.

The difference in the administrative background between the Hejaz and Najd regions would not have been of great significance had it not been for differences in the educational systems of the two regions that subsequently determined, enforced, and perpetuated certain patterns in the newly founded administrative structures. Although Hejaz had a number of secular schools at the turn of the century, it was not until 1983 that secular elementary education was introduced into Najd. Moreover, whereas the ulama were influential in shaping the educational system in Najd and consequently maintained the religious orientation of the curriculum, the Hejazi educational system was more secular and was oriented toward satisfying the needs of a differentiated and complex administration.

The immediate outcome of the differences in the educational system between the two regions was the control by Hejazis of key administrative positions that required secular education. Moreover, whereas Najdis saw in religious education a vehicle for social mobility, many Hejazis attended secular schools and were in a better position to meet the demands of the newly structured institutions.[1] With the centralization of administration in the 1950s, however, and following the increase in the number of Najdis who attained secular education, Najdi representation in the country's administration witnessed a shift in favor of this region.

THE OIL ECONOMY AS A DETERMINANT OF ADMINISTRATIVE CHANGE

The development of an oil economy affected not only the creation of complex administrative structures, but also the overall orientation of the political system. Prior to his death in 1953, Ibn Saud witnessed the drastic increase in his country's wealth—from $200,000 prior to World War I to $10 million in the interwar period; $60 million in 1948; $160 million in 1952; and $250 million in 1953.[2]

The emphasis on oil revenues, as a factor affecting government services as opposed to the development of new social classes in Saudi Arabia, has been dictated by the nature both of the Saudi society and of the oil industry itself. Three factors have minimized the impact of the oil industry.[3] The first is the background of the Saudi society. The oil industry penetrated a society that had no industrial tradition. Legislative and institutional mechanisms have been developed in recent years in order to regulate industrial activities to satisfy existing needs and demands. A second factor has to do with the nature of the industry. According to T. W. Schultz, this industry is not particularly effective in transmitting new knowledge to other sectors or in training workers who acquire skills that serve them well when they do other kinds of work.[4] The techniques of production in mining and oil tend to be specific and do not lend themselves to useful application in other sectors. Accordingly, as far as the needs of other industries are concerned, few of the mining and oil techniques are useful to them, and few workers are trained in mining and oil from which others can recruit their skilled labor force.

In addition, the oil industry is a one-sided developer given that it does not require a drastic expansion of the transport and power systems. It uses its own facilities and requires little in the way of public services.[5] A final factor is the remote location of the industry, which limits its impact on the society.

Despite the minimal effects of the industry, the mighty spending power that resulted from oil revenues shocked the stationary economy of the country.[6] Oil revenues became the most significant single source of the state's revenues. In 1932, Saudi government revenues reached 12 million riyals, 60 percent of which came from the hajj (pilgrimage). By the year Ibn Saud died, state revenues were 757 million Saudi riyals, 90 percent of which were drawn from oil.[7]

The major problem associated with the tremendous increase in wealth was the fact that until 1959 no distinction existed between the finances of the state and those of the royal family. True to Max Weber's ideal type of patrimonial rule, Ibn Saud and his successor, King Saud, considered the country's wealth to be their own. Even in the first budget ever to be introduced in Saudi Arabia in 1958–1959, the royal household was assigned 17 percent of the budget, to be spent at the discretion of the king. An additional 19 percent was entered under the category of "other expenditures," to be decided by the king as well.

Instead of spending this wealth on development projects, Ibn Saud singled out for special favors and privileges his forty-two sons, his five brothers and their descendants, and the large clans of the Jiluwi, Sudayri, and Al Shaykh, all of whom were related to the royal family. Wahhabi puritanism, which integrated the tribal society and legitimated Ibn Saud's conquests and rule, proved to be incompatible with extreme affluence. As H. St. John Philby describes it:

One by one, at first furtively and later more brazenly, the inhibitions of the old Wahhabi regime went by the board. In the name of military efficiency, the once forbidden charms of music were openly paraded on the palace square. . . . The forbidden cinema reared its ogling screens in scores of princely palaces and wealthy mansions to flaunt the less respectable products of Hollywood before audiences which would have blushed or shuddered at the sight but ten or fifteen years ago.[8]

Whereas Ibn Saud was able to maintain his patrimonial rule through his charismatic personality and the disbursement of financial favors, King Saud failed miserably when he attempted to emulate this pattern of authority. Saud lacked both the charisma and the ability of his father to persuade men and recognize pressing needs. Despite colossal oil revenues, few improvements were made in the living conditions of Saudis; the country's economy became handicapped by serious inflationary pressures. A weak leader with extravagant habits, Saud was unable to arrest the social and moral disintegration of Saudi society, nor was he skillful enough to meet the external socialist challenge posed by Nasser.

In an attempt to avoid increased popular dissatisfaction with Saudi rule, the royal family and ulama leaders transferred the executive function to Crown Prince Faisal in 1958. Although Saud recovered these powers in 1960, Faisal continued to be the decision maker in the polity. It was not until 1964 that Saud was deposed and Faisal was proclaimed king by the royal family and leading ulama.[9]

Under Faisal, the erosion of Saudi political legitimacy was controlled, and the system bequeathed to King Khalid in 1975 proved to be capable of adapting to change and confronting external political challenges. Faisal reasserted the traditional legitimacy that is the sine qua non of patrimonial rule and developed a complete bureaucratic structure parallel to, but interlocked with and subordinate to, the royal family, so as to enhance the system's capabilities and performance.

The structural changes that occurred in the Saudi political system took place after the discovery of oil in the kingdom, following the Saudi rulers' realization of the need for political change. The resultant change, however, must not be seen as a conscious desire to radically transform the society. Rather, it was more in the nature of an adjustment response of patrimonial rule intended to preserve the regime's basic values and characteristics in a changing environment.

ROLE DIFFERENTIATION AND INSTITUTIONAL COMPLEXITY

The presence of differentiated and complex administrative structures enhances the capability of the political system to manipulate its environment. As the political system confronts a wide range of areas that require state intervention, the pressures to develop complex administrative institutions become tremendous. If the political elite desires to maintain its position in society, it must develop these institutions.

Prior to the 1950s, when Ibn Saud realized the need to develop modern administrative institutions, political life in the kingdom revolved around the king, through whom both the executive and legislative powers were exercised. He surrounded himself with advisers who enjoyed his personal trust. The advisers "never demanded, seldom suggested, and only advised when advice was actively sought" by the king.[10]

Following the conquest of Hejaz in 1926 and the subsequent unification of the kingdom in 1932, Ibn Saud needed a more effective administrative structure to meet the ever increasing economic and social needs generated by oil revenues. While preserving the patrimonial character of his authority, Ibn Saud laid the structural foundation for more differentiated and complex bureaucratic institutions. Although all legislative and executive powers are concentrated in the person of the king, who is the chief-of-state, the prime minister, the commander-in-chief of the armed forces, and the imam of the community, the king's orders, decrees, and policies are channeled downward and implemented by the Council of Ministers.[11]

The present Council of Ministers was preceded by ad hoc committees and administrative institutions. Following the conquest of Mecca in 1924, the Domestic Council of Mecca was created and included in its membership twenty-five deputies representing different interest groups in the city, including the ulama. This council was headed by Ibn Saud's son, Prince Faisal, and its activities included the following: review of the city's judicial system, issuance of regulations concerning pilgrimage and awaqf (religious foundation and trust) supervision of religious education, issuance of commercial laws, and establishment of a judicial committee to settle disputes according to Islamic and tribal laws.[12]

Following the annexation of Jeddah in 1925, the Domestic Council was replaced by the Instructive Committee. This committee, too, was headed by Prince Faisal. It included three members appointed by Ibn Saud and eight elected in a secret ballot by representatives of the major interest groups in the Hejaz, including the ulama. Ibn Saud authorized the committee to assist Prince Faisal in administering the region. Two years later, Ibn Saud established the Committee of Investigation and Reform to review the government's organizational structure.[13] This committee recommended the unification of the country's administrative regions as well as the creation of a national advisory council to represent regional interests. These recommendations were implemented by the establishment of an Advisory Council with eight members appointed by the king, four of whom were appointed after consultation with community leaders, including the ulama. To broaden national representation, the eight members were drawn from the Hejaz and Najd regions. Ibn Saud empowered the Advisory Council to formulate socioeconomic policies, supervise the expenditures of government departments and agencies, and act as a legislative body.[14]

Despite the Advisory Council's formal powers, its decisions were subject to approval by the king. Its jurisdiction and activities were further weakened by two developments. First, a Council of Deputies was created in 1930 to assist Faisal in the administration of the Hejaz region; second, a Council of Ministers was established in 1953 to act as Ibn Saud's cabinet.

The Council of Deputies was established in recognition of the relatively advanced administrative background of the Hejaz. It served as a central agency for coordinating activities among branches of government organizations in the Hejaz region and the Advisory Council, as well as other national agencies. As a result of the expansion of government operations throughout the country, the Council of Deputies acquired legislative and executive powers that were derived from the king. As a result of the creation of the Council of Ministers in 1953 and the subsequent centralization of administration in the country, the Council of Deputies was dismantled and the Council of Ministers became the sole national decision-making agency.

THE COUNCIL OF MINISTERS

The Council of Ministers was created by Ibn Saud in 1953 to act as a central agency for all existing and future departments and agencies. Its membership was made up of existing ministers and was headed by Ibn Saud. The royal decree establishing the council dealt with five areas: (1) organization of the council; (2) jurisdiction of the council; (3) procedures of the council; (4) jurisdiction of the president of the council; and (5) divisions of the council, that is, the cabinet.[15] Accordingly, the council is headed by the king and, in his absence, by the crown prince. It consists of the king's ministers, advisers, and all those whose attendance at the council is desired by the king. Its jurisdiction is outlined in Article 7 of the royal decree, which states that "state policy within the country and abroad shall be under the surveillance of the Council of Ministers."[16] All council decisions "shall not come into effect until they have been sanctioned by His Majesty the King."[17]

The structure and functions of the council were modified by a royal decree on 12 May 1958, which redefined and clarified the council's jurisdictions and created the post of deputy prime minister. The decree stipulated that members of the council were responsible to the prime minister (i.e., the crown prince), who was responsible to the king. Moreover, the prime minister had the right to appeal to the king for the dismissal of any member of the council. The relative weakness of the king's powers as expressed in the 1958 royal order came into existence as a result of the royal family's dismay with King Saud's rule. It was not surprising, therefore, that after Faisal's assumption of power in 1964 the king again assumed the position of prime minister.

The fusion of all powers in the person of the king in 1964 reestablished the supremacy of the monarch and defined the role of the council as the only manager of the country's socioeconomic, administrative, and political affairs. It is the effective arm of the king, and, subject to the king's approval, it has the exclusive jurisdiction to pass laws, initiate policies, and oversee their implementation.

The council's policies and decisions are implemented by a complex bureaucratic structure that has evolved throughout the years from a small number of disjointed departments and ministries to the present system, which exhibits phenomenal centralization. This structure is divided into three components: (1) ministries; (2) independent departments and bureaus; and (3) public agencies.[18]

Until 1951, only three ministries existed—the Ministry of Foreign Affairs (established in 1930), the Ministry of Finance (1932), and the Ministry of Defense (1946). The structure and activities of these ministries were rudimentary. The Ministry of Finance, for example, was administered by Ibn Saud's treasurer, Shaykh Abd Allah alSulayman, whose main function was to meet Ibn Saud's personal needs and demands. But its structure and activities today bear no resemblance to those of its predecessor. The ministry has become the most complex and influential of all governmental institutions. It is staffed by highly qualified personnel whose activities and decisions have a direct bearing on all other departments and ministries.[19]

During the period 1951 to 1954, the ministries of Interior, Education, Agriculture, Communication, Commerce and Industry, and Health were established. Between 1960 and 1962, the ministries of Petroleum and Mineral Resources; Labor and Social Affairs; Pilgrimage and Awqaf; Information; and Justice were created. Finally, in 1975, six additional ministries, as well as three ministers of state without portfolio, were established, thus bringing the total number to twenty. Among the ministries created in 1975 were Public Works and Housing; Industry and Power; Telegraph, Post, and Telephone; Planning; Higher Education; and Municipal and Rural Affairs.

Independent departments and bureaus exist in the state administration. These include the General Personnel Bureau, the Central Planning Commission, the Grievance Board, the General Department of Intelligence, the Advisory Council,

the National Guard, and the Committees for Commanding the Good and Forbidding Evil.[20] These departments and bureaus enjoy relative autonomy, for they
report directly to the prime minister (i.e. the king), but general personnel rules
and procedures apply to these organizations as if they were ministries.

Finally, to avoid general governmental rules and procedures, which may hinder
the activities of certain agencies, the Council of Ministers created public agencies
in the 1960s. These include the railroad system, the Institution of Petroleum and
Minerals, Saudi Arabian Airlines, the Institute of Public Administration, King
Saud University, the Petroleum and Minerals College, the Institution of Social
Security, the Center for Research and Economic Development, the Saudi Arabian
Monetary Agency, the Agricultural Bank, and the Red Crescent. Though formally attached to a ministry, each agency is governed by an executive board
which, in several cases, is headed by a minister and includes the membership
of deputy ministers as well as the director general of the agency itself.[21]

THE BUREAUCRATIZATION OF THE ULAMA

The expansion in government administrative structures was accompanied by
increased jurisdiction of these structures over a large number of societal areas,
including those formerly regulated by religion and the religious establishment.
For example, the jurisdiction and activities of the Domestic Council profoundly
affected the position of the ulama in two ways. First, although the ulama were
represented in the council, their representation was limited to two members, thus
minimizing their presence and influence. Second, the council's jurisdiction affected areas that formerly came under the exclusive control of the ulama, such
as the administration of awqaf, religious schools, and education. The extent of
the ulama's participation in the newly founded structures was influenced by the
needs and orientation of the political sphere. The ulama were given prominence
when religious legitimation was needed, and they assumed a secondary position
when their stance contradicted that of the ruler or when other sources of legitimacy were invoked. As the process of territorial shaping neared completion,
the ulama lost whatever limited autonomy they had enjoyed. They became paid
civil servants whose status, income, and general activities were governed by
state regulations and objectives.

The incorporation of the ulama into the state administration routinized the use
of religion and the religious establishment as a source of legitimacy. The ulama's
role in society and their activities in the administrative structure were channeled
through the following fields and agencies: the Committees for Commanding the
Good and Forbidding Evil; the Directorate of Religious Research, Ifta', Da'wa,
and Guidance; religious education; the Ministry of Justice; preaching and guidance of Islam at home and abroad; supervision of girls' education; supervision
of mosques and awqaf; notaries public; and finally, spreading Islam and consolidating Saudi international prestige through the activities of Muslim organizations, such as the World Muslim League and the World Assembly of Muslim

Youth. The following description of the general activities of three of these agencies, as well as of the role of the ulama in the present judicial system, will enable us to assess their role and position in the country's administrative system.

The Committees for Commanding the Good and Forbidding Evil

The need to establish effective structures of political authority became more imperative as the process of territorial expansion advanced. Ibn Saud realized the necessity of developing an administrative system that would meet the peculiar needs of Wahhabism as well as accommodate his political objectives. Consequently, his position vis-à-vis the religious establishment was modified to meet emerging needs. Thus, the Committees for Commanding the Good and Forbidding Evil, initially established to enforce Wahhabi principles, were incorporated into the state machinery. Moreover, whenever Wahhabi principles conflicted with Ibn Saud's political needs, Ibn Saud prevailed. The conclusion of agreements with the British, the elimination of the Ikhwan Brothers (a religious order), the introduction of secular education, and the influx of non-Muslims into the kingdom to develop the oil industry are instances in which Ibn Saud's objectives of development prevailed.

The initial impulse for founding the Committees for Commanding the Good and Forbidding Evil is attributed to Shaykh Abd al-Asis Ibn Abd al-Latif Al Shaykh, who, in 1903, enforced the observance of Wahhabi principles in Riyadh.[22] As the Saudi state expanded throughout Najd and the Hasa, Ibn Saud institutionalized the Shaykh's activities by formally establishing committees with similar functions. The committees were empowered to arrest, bring to trial, and imprison those found guilty of offending Wahhabi teachings.

A number of posts were opened for the enforcers in Riyadh and other Saudi cities and towns. A police officer and director were installed at each post. The director was responsible to the committees' director general, a position usually held by a member of Al Shaykh. All key matters pertinent to the committees were decided by the committees' director general, who in turn received instructions from the king. Despite the existence of an organizational network, the exact duties of enforcers remained undefined, and the promotion and dismissal policies were never specified. It was not until the 1960s that the general regulations governing the Saudi civil service were extended to the committees.

In enforcing Wahhabi principles and establishing control over society, the activities of the mutawi'a (religious and morality enforcers) often covered a wide range of areas. They policed market areas to prevent mingling between men and women and ensured that no individual violated public morality; that merchants and traders did not defraud the consumer; that no places of entertainment were established; that no musical instruments were manufactured or sold, that men did not wear silk or gold, and that members of the community attended public prayers. They also enforced the prohibitions against smoking and alcohol, and made certain that men followed the Sunna in lengthening their beards and shaving off their moustaches.

The restrictions enforced by the mutawi'a were in compliance with Wahhabi principles. The application of these principles enabled Ibn Saud to control all the activities of his citizens and to consolidate his rule. It was therefore not surprising that Ibn Saud extended the mutawi's system to the Hejaz region in the late 1920s. Ibn Saud delegated the task of forming this network in the Hejaz to Chief Qadi Abd Allah al-Bulayhid, who in turn asked Shaykh Abd Allah al-Shaybi to organize committee posts throughout the region. To justify the extension of the committees to the Hejaz, Abd Allah al-Bulayhid asked Shaykh Muhammad Bahjat al-Bitar, a leading Meccan theologian, to compose writings explaining the principle of commanding the good and forbidding evil and the duties of the mutawi'a.[23] Although Shaykh Abd Allah al-Shaybi headed the committees in the Hejaz, ultimate responsibility for the direction and policies of the committees rested with Prince Faisal, governor of the region. In turn, Faisal was accountable to his father, Ibn Saud.

Whereas Ibn Saud was interested in the mutawi'a as a mechanism of social control, some mutawi'a viewed themselves as guardians of the Wahhabi principles and as existing beyond the control of the ruler. In their diligent attempt to enforce Wahhabi principles, the mutawi'a opposed some of Ibn Saud's policies. To curb the mutawi'a, Ibn Saud issued a royal decree in 1930 incorporating the Committees for Commanding the Good and Forbidding Evil into the Directorate General of the police force. He stripped the mutawi'a of the power of arrest, which they had hitherto enjoyed, and restricted their function to reporting violations to the police. In case of a dispute between the committees' director general and the director general of the police force, the decree provided for the king to act as arbitrator.

The 1930 decree established the modality that defined both the position of the mutawi'a within the Saudi administrative structure and the nature of their activities. Although the committees are collectively considered to form an independent bureau and its director general, Shaykh Abd al-Aziz Ibn Allah Ibn Hassan Al Shaykh, was assigned ministerial status in 1976, their role was relegated to a status subservient to that of the state bureaucracy. As the country's administrative structure became more complex, the mutawi'a were restricted to enforcing public attendance at prayers. Today, the ministries of Commerce, Interior, Health, Finance and National Economy, Agriculture, and Justice, as well as the municipalities, perform the many duties that were traditionally undertaken by the enforcers. A considerable number of the committee members are now aged and illiterate and lack the basic education expected of religious enforcers. The general decline in the caliber of the mutawi'a may be attributed to the lack of specific policies governing recruitment, promotion, and dismissal. Mutawi'a recruits are not required to pass entrance exams or possess any academic training. Entrance eligibility is confined to "good religious and social behavior," promotion is determined by seniority, and dismissal is rare.

The committees provided Ibn Saud with the mechanism to consolidate his authority. As Ibn Saud's authority became well entrenched in the region, and as the process of creating a modern administrative structure succeeded, the mutawi'a institution was no longer needed. Instead of eliminating the mutawi'a, a measure that might antagonize the ulama, Ibn Saud incorporated this institution into the civil service and stripped it of effective power.

THE DIRECTORATE OF RELIGIOUS RESEARCH, IFTA', DA'WA, AND GUIDANCE

Like the Committees of Commanding the Good and Forbidding Evil, the Directorate of Religious Research, Ifta', Da'wa, and Guidance is an independent state department that accounts directly to the king in his capacity as prime minister.[24] It publishes religious books propagating Wahhabi views and principles and distributes them upon request. It also sponsors research projects on Islam and Wahhabism, organizes seminars for training preachers, and sends preachers on foreign assignments. The symbolic consequence of the publication and distribution of religious texts is the projection of Saudi rule as the propagator of Islam, as well as the reaffirmation of its identification with Wahhabism.

In addition to its publication and distribution of religious texts, the directorate issues fatwas (religious proclamations) on questions submitted to it by the king, government agencies, and the public at large. Its activities and members are directed by the king. Royal Decree 1/137, issued in 1971, specified that members of the Higher Council of the Ifta' be appointed by the king. Their function, the decree noted, is "to express opinion based on the shari'ah regarding matters submitted to them by the wali al-amr, i.e., the King, to recommend policy on religious matters to guide the wali al-amr; and to issue fatwas to guide Muslims in the areas of aqida, ibadat, and mu'amalat."[25] The same decree named fifteen leading ulama to the directorate.[26] Interestingly, of the fifteen members of the directorate only one is from Al Shaykh. The minimal representation of Al Shaykh in this vital religious body could be viewed as a continuation of Ibn Saud's policy of not allowing any one group to wield more power than the royal family. Indeed, the representation and influence of Al Shaykh in religious activities have declined since the 1940s. Although members of Al Shaykh are presently ministers of Higher Education, Justice, and Agriculture and Water, the major religious positions of the director general of Religious Research, Ifta', Da'wa, and Guidance, the president of the Muslim League, as well as the more junior positions in religious or religiously inspired institutions are no longer held by Al Shaykh. Moreover, although traditional career pattern of Al Shaykh has focused on the religious profession, some Al Shaykh members are increasingly receiving secular education and holding secular positions. A survey of thirty-three names of Al Shaykh students registered at Riyadh University in 1979–1980 showed that only thirteen were registered in religious studies, whereas the remaining twenty were pursuing secular studies ranging from business administration to dentistry.[27]

WORLD ASSEMBLY OF MUSLIM YOUTH

Although the activities of the Directorate of Religious Research, Ifta', Da'wa, and Guidance are mostly confined to Saudi Arabia, other agencies have been established by the Saudi government to spread Islam and enhance its prestige among world Muslims. Although Wahhabism is the Saudi point of reference at home, Islamic solidarity is projected as a prime consideration affecting Saudi foreign policy. In a 1979 memorandum submitted by al-Ma'had al-Islami in Riyadh to the Islamic Secretariat for the Celebration of the Fourteenth Hijirah Century, Islamic solidarity is defined as the mobilization of the intellectual, material, and spiritual resources of the ummah (Muslim community) in pursuit of commonly and clearly defined socioeconomic and cultural goals. "Islamic solidarity can be pursued in a framework that involves total acceptance of the requirements that arise from total commitment to Islam; the creation of, and commitment to, new institutions . . . which undertake specialized functions for the ummah as a whole across national, ethnic, linguistic, and other boundaries that now divide the Islamic community."[28]

To achieve Islamic solidarity, a number of permanent agencies and organizations were established. An important but little known government organization whose activities attempt to assert Saudi leadership among Muslim states is the World Assembly of Muslim Youth (WAMY). Headquartered in Riyadh, WAMY was established in December 1972 following a meeting of the representatives of world Muslim youth organizations, which was sponsored by the Saudi Ministry of Education. The objectives of WAMY are to

serve the ideology of Islam through the propagation of tawhid; to strengthen the sense of pride in Islam among Muslim youth and to arm them with rational bases and full confidence in the supremacy of the Islamic system over all other systems; and to help them practice Islamic teachings in all their activities; to support Muslim youth and student organizations all over the world and to help them implement their plans and programs whenever possible; to guide and help Muslim youth to set up professional organizations; to take a leading part in the existing professional organizations and to help them perform their Islamic role in building the Islamic nation and to confront the existing challenge.[29]

The Saudi government finances WAMY's activities, which include the construction of mosques and religious schools abroad, the sponsorship of preachers, visits to Muslim communities abroad, the hosting of annual conferences for representatives of Muslim youth organizations, and the publication and distribution of religious texts.[30] Consistent with the government's two-pronged policy of affirming the religious character of the state while not allowing the ulama to direct or judge the state's activities, WAMY's policy and activities are planned and administered by secular-educated Saudis. For example, the secretary holds a Ph.D. in international relations from the University of Pennsylvania, and almost all the organization's personnel have a secular education.[31] In addition, a survey of the books published and/or distributed by WAMY reveals the use of religion to be an instrument of legitimation. Although most of these books are introductory texts on Islam, some deal with specialized subjects such as Jihad, the Islamic economic order, and the Islamic legal system. The most prominent of these books are the writings of Sayid Qutub, Abul A'la Maududi, Muhammad Qutub, and Abd al-Qadir Awda.[32] They carry a message that is consistent with the Saudi ideological interpretation of Islam: "Islam is the best system to be found on this earth. . . . [It] is the only means to regain honour, leadership and social justice."[33]

THE ULAMA AND THE JUDICIAL SYSTEM

The interpretation of the shari'ah principles has traditionally been the ulama's exclusive domain. The importance of this function is dictated by the fact that the shari'ah regulates all human activities. As outlined in the Quran and the Sunna, and elaborated by the ulama through ijma' (consensus) and quyas (analogy), the shari'ah is a comprehensive code of God's commands and recommendations laid down for human guidance. The principles of the shari'ah cover all areas of human activity and conduct: How and what to eat, when to wash, what to wear, how and when to pray and fast—these and similar matters are treated on the same basis and with just as much meticulous concern as matters more strictly legal, such as marriage and divorce, or commercial transactions, or crime. Governing the whole range of the individual's relations with God and society, and in the absence of any organized Muslim church hierarchy, the shari'ah is incomparably the central institution of Islam.[34]

When Ibn Saud extended his rule over the Hejaz region, and prior to the unification of the Saudi judicial system in 1927, three distinct systems of law existed. The first was that of the Hejaz, with an Ottoman orientation in which the Hanafi and Shafi'i interpretations were predominant. The second was the system of Najd, whereby each governor, assisted by a qadi (judge), solved disputes submitted to him or referred them to the qadi.[35] The rigid Hanbali tradition prevailed in this region. The third judicial system was the tribal law, under which conflicting parties referred disputes to the head of the tribe, whose decisions were based on traditions and customs.[36]

Whereas Ibn Saud's initial desire was to maintain Ottoman laws in the Hejaz, the Ikhwan considered these laws antithetical to the shari'ah and demanded their abolition. To counter the Ikhwan's demands, Ibn Saud solicited the opinion of his ulama, hoping for a more tolerant and temperate attitude. However, on 11 February 1927, the ulama issued a fatwa that supported the Ikhwan's position by noting, "and as to the laws, if there be any of them [Ottoman laws] in the Hejaz, it will be immediately abolished and nothing except the pure shari'ah will be applied."[37]

Neither the fatwa nor the demands of the Ikhwan were able to influence Ibn Saud's decision to maintain Ottoman secular laws. Indeed, Ibn Saud was in no mood to allow the ulama to control his political objective of initiating change in his realm. Consequently, a royal order sanctioning the existing laws of the Hejaz was issued four months after the proclamation of the fatwa. Instructing Prince Faisal, governor of the region, the order noted that "the legal rulings of Ottoman law should remain in effect. We have not repealed them nor have we issued laws replacing them. . . . We accept your suggestion concerning the maintenance of these laws."[38]

In addition to the retention of Ottoman laws in the Hejaz region, the Saudi legal system of the period was not confined to the Hanbali school. As early as August 1927, Ibn Saud instructed his judges in the Hejaz "as to what school of law [the court] should apply, it is not restricted to any particular school. Rather, the court decides according to what appears to it applicable from any of the schools and there is no difference between one school or another."[39] The same theme was reiterated two years following the unification of the country, when Ibn Saud noted that "we are not bound by one school of law to the exclusion of another. Whenever strong evidence is lacking, we adopt the opinion of Imam Ahmad Ibn Hanbal."[40]

In the early period of the creation of the Saudi state, Ibn Saud maintained the Ottoman laws that prevailed in the Hejaz region and instructed his ulama not to restrict themselves to the Hanbali school. In doing so, Ibn Saud demonstrated his willingness to depart from the rigid Wahhabi interpretation of the shari'ah in order to accommodate changing circumstances and needs.

MODIFICATION OF THE JUDICIARY AND THE LOSS OF ULAMA CONTROL

The increase in state jurisdiction and in the complexity of its administrative structures affected all areas of governmental activities, including the judiciary. Although the country's judicial system was simple and lacked differentiation, and although the ulama dominated all judicial activities, the system became highly complex by the 1950s. The ulama's role was confined to the interpretation of the civil and criminal aspects of the shari'ah law.

The transformation of the legal system from simple to complex and the ulama's loss of their traditional position in the legal system were attained gradually. The impetus of this change was initiated in 1927 when Ibn Saud issued a decree urging his citizens to bring their complaints to him personally. "Any one who may have a grievance against whoever may be . . . and then hides it, he will be sinning only against himself."[41] The decree noted further that grievances could be relayed to the ruler through a "box of complaints" positioned at the door of the government buildings in Mecca and Riyadh and that the keys to the two boxes were kept by the king himself.[42]

Whereas the box system may have been effective in 1927, changes were needed in 1932. A royal order issued in that year noted that there were four ways in which citizens could express their grievances or bring complaints against individuals or government agencies.[43]

The organizational restructuring of the judicial system took place a year later when a royal decree was issued classifying the court system into three levels: Summary Courts, Shari'ah Courts, and the Commission on Judicial Supervision.[44] These courts were confined to Mecca, Jeddah, and Medina. Affairs in Najd continued to be administered by a single judge who dealt with all cases.

The jurisdiction of Summary Courts covered cases involving misdemeanors and discretionary and statutory punishments. The Shari'ah Courts had jurisdiction over all cases that were not included in the jurisdiction of Summary Courts. The Commission on Judicial Supervision consisted of a chairman, a deputy chairman, and three members, all chosen by the king from among the ulama. In addition to supervising and inspecting the courts, this commission had the function of judicial review through the power of confirming or reversing judgments of the Shari'ah Courts. It also had the power of giving legal opinions concerning matters not included in the jurisdiction of the Shari'ah Courts.[45]

This early classification and jurisdictional delimitation of legal institutions in the Saudi kingdom may be considered the organizational outline of the present system. Although amendments to the first royal decree creating the judiciary were made, the structural characteristics have remained the same. For example, while initially Ibn Saud instructed his ulama not to restrict themselves to the Hanbali interpretation of the shari'ah, once the unification of the country was accomplished and Ibn Saud's authority became well entrenched, the ulama were instructed that legal decisions should be based on the Hanbalite schools "because of the easy accessibility of its books and its authors' obligation to cite the legal evidence supporting their views." Concurrently, Ibn Saud informed his ulama to draw on the other orthodox schools only in those cases in which the application of the Hanbalite opinion would cause strain and incompatibility with public interest. The invocation of public interest is significant because it gave both the ruler and the judiciary broad scope in interpreting the shari'ah.[46]

The judiciary's adherence to the Hanbalite school was reaffirmed in a royal decree stating that what was cited in Hanbalite texts should be applied by the courts. Cases that require legal reasoning and are not covered in Hanbalite texts should be referred either to the greater Shari'ah Court or to the Commission on Judicial Supervision.[47] To routinize the adoption of Hanbali interpretation, the judiciary adopted six Hanbalite texts.[48]

Detailed regulations governing the judiciary were issued in 1938. These affected the classification of judges and increased the complexity of the court system. The final restructuring of the judicial system took place in 1962 when Faisal proclaimed his Ten Point Reform Program, which included, among other things, the creation of a Ministry of Justice. The implementation of this program took place in 1970 when the Grand Mufti died. A royal decree was issued creating a Ministry of Justice and a Supreme Judicial Council.[49] Accordingly, the minister of justice replaced the Grand Mufti.

THE DECLINE OF THE ROLE OF THE ULAMA IN THE JUDICIARY

The discovery of oil and the resultant expansion of government services and jurisdiction proved too cumbersome for the Shari'ah Courts to handle. Although Ibn Saud dealt in person with many of the cases involving the interaction with foreigners, by the 1930s he was unable to deal with all situations. The Shari'ah Courts were able to deal with civil and penal matters, but he became helpless in confronting the many conflicts that resulted from the development of an oil economy. Consequently, Ibn Saud delegated judicial authority to committees, commissions, boards, councils, and tribunals, but these were originally of an ad hoc nature and distinct from the judicial system. In recent years, many of the these structures have acquired a permanent status and now constitute part of the judiciary. Some of these organs, such as the Grievance Board, the Commission on the Settlement of Commercial Disputes, and the Central Committee on Cases of Adulteration, were subsequently incorporated into the judicial system. The personnel responsible for the activities of these organs are secularly educated individuals with little background in the shari'ah law. These activities dominate the judicial system and have displaced some of the ulama's judicial role.

The Grievance Board, for example, was established in 1955 through a royal decree. The king enjoys tremendous power over the activities of the board. Not only are the chairman and vice chairman of the board appointed by the king through a royal decree, but also the decisions of the chairman are subject to the king's ratification. In cases of a dispute between a minister or head of a department and decisions made by the board, the matter must be referred to the king. In cases where no regulations exist concerning a certain situation, the matter can be settled only by order of the king. Moreover, every six months the chairman of the board must submit to the king a comprehensive report of the board's activity.

The board's jurisdiction includes grievances by citizens against state departments or agencies. It also has the jurisdiction to follow up its investigation of government officials and to adjudicate on disputes pertaining to salaries, retirement, pensions, and decisions of administrative disciplinary councils. In addition, the board receives applications for the execution of foreign judgments and has a representative in tribunals or commissions dealing with bribery offenses, disciplinary actions of military personnel, and violation of the Arab League's policy concerning the boycott of Israel.

The Grievance Board is perhaps the most important of the supplementary organs with judicial functions. This is due in part to its wide jurisdiction and its permanent character. Although not so designated, the board is in fact a tribunal. The central position it occupies in the judicial system is an outcome of the expansion of state jurisdiction and activities and of the inability of the Shari'ah

Courts to deal with all issues in so complex a society. The ulama's representation on the board is limited to two shari'ah consultants.

In sum, the discovery of oil in the 1930s and the resultant expansion in government activities and jurisdiction necessitated the regulation of these activities through formal rules. It required the creation of institutions to arbitrate the interpretation and application of these rules. The promulgation of laws and the creation of modern administrative and judicial institutions stripped the ulama of their role as the only guardian and interpreter of the most sacred of all Islamic institutions—the shari'ah. Instead of enjoying an exclusive monopoly over the interpretation of the shari'ah, the ulama now share this role with secularly educated individuals.

As a result of the loss of many of their roles, and resulting from the introduction of laws not present in, or derived from, the shari'ah, the ulama found themselves incapable of exercising their judicial role. A most telling statement expressing the ulama's situation was made in 1967 by the chief judge, who informed members of the Shari'ah Courts thus:

we have been informed that some judges have the habit of returning certain cases to the Labour and other offices under the pretext that they fall under the jurisdiction of these authorities. It is recognized that the shari'ah is completely equipped to solve disputes, and to end litigations as well as to clarify every issue. The submission of cases to those authorities implies recognition of the man-made laws and of the regulations repugnant to the provisions of the shari'ah. It also makes the courts appear incapable. . . . You must look into all cases you receive and make your decisions according to the sublime shari'ah. . . . Whenever you have difficulty in doing so, write to us about it.[50]

CONCLUSION

The development of an oil economy in Saudi Arabia ushered in a period of increased government activities that necessitated the expansion of state jurisdiction over areas formerly dominated by the religious establishment. It led to the creation of a complex administrative structure to implement these policies. In turn, the expansion of jurisdiction and the corresponding increase in role differentiation between the religious and political spheres resulted in the bureaucratization of the ulama. Indeed, the ulama in the current Saudi state are dependent on the state for their survival. They are paid civil servants whose activities are determined by the needs of the political sphere. Ulama leaders are appointed by the king, and ulama activities are regulated by state laws.

Following the introduction of secular laws to regulate the many state activities, the role of the ulama became confined to the interpretation of the civil and criminal aspects of the shari'ah, whereas commercial, labor, and international laws, to name only three, are formulated and interpreted by secularly educated individuals. The state took over religion for the purpose of restructuring to bring its beliefs and institutions into conformity with national objectives. The activities of WAMY and the Directorate of Research, Ifta', Da'wa, and Guidance are geared toward presenting Wahhabi principles that coincide with state objectives and toward projecting the Saudi rulers as the protectors and propagators of Islam. In effect, the political sphere enhanced its legitimacy through the rationalization of policies in religious terms. The emergence and increased role of individuals in the system with a secular education reflects the overall position of the political sphere in relation to the ulama: While religion remains an important source of legitimation, the ulama's traditional role in evaluating government policy and activities has been reduced significantly.

NOTES

This chapter is reprinted by permission of Westview Press from *Religion and State in the Kingdom of Saudi Arabia* by Ayman Al-Yassini. © Westview Press, Boulder, Colo., 1985.

1. For instance, in 1930 more than 70 percent of the students attending Dar al-Tawhid, a religious institution in Ta'if concerned with the teaching of the principles of Wahhabism as well as other Islamic sciences, were from Najd. The students received monthly stipends from the government, and upon graduation they were assigned administrative and religious positions.

2. *The Impact of Petroleum on the Economy of Saudi Arabia* (Riyadh: Ministry of Information, 1979), p. 4.

3. Kamal S. Sayegh, *Oil and Arab Regional Development* (New York: Praeger Publishers, 1968), pp. 81–82. The first concession to exploit Saudi oil was granted in 1933 to the Standard Oil Company of California, which in 1936 had sold a half-interest to the Texas Company and with which it was jointly renamed in 1944 the Arabian American Oil Company (ARAMCO). Four years later, the shareholdings in ARAMCO were redistributed among Standard of California (30 percent), Texas (30 percent), Standard of New Jersey (30 percent), and Socony Mobil (10 percent). In 1949 another concession was granted to the Pacific Western Oil Corporation (J. Paul Getty, 100 percent), covering all of Saudi Arabia's half-interest in the Saudi-Kuwait Neutral Zone. In 1950, the agreement with the ARAMCO group was revised, increasing the Saudi shares to 50 percent of the total profits. In 1957, Saudi Arabia granted a third concession to a Japanese company covering the offshore area of Saudi half-interest in the Neutral Zone, with Saudi Arabia receiving 56 percent of total profits, including those derived from refining, transportation, and marketing operations.

4. T. W. Schultz, "Economic Prospects of Primary Product," cited in Sayegh, *Oil and Arab Regional Development*, p. 82.

5. Ibid.

6. For a study of the economic impact of the oil industry on Saudi society, see Fayez Bader, "Developmental Planning in Saudi Arabia: A Multi-Dimensional Study" (Ph.D. diss., University of Southern California, 1968).

7. Four and a half Saudi riyals are equal to one U.S. dollar. For information on state revenues, see *Annual Report 1978* (Riyadh: Saudi Arabian Monetary Agency, 1979).

8. H. St. John Philby, *Saudi Arabia* (Beirut: Librairie du Liban, 1968), p. xiii.

9. The text of the fatwa deposing King Saud is found in Hafiz Wahbah, *Arabian Days* (London: Arthur Barker, 1964), pp. 176–80.

10. James A. Bill and Carl Leiden, *Politics in the Middle East* (Boston: Little, Brown, 1979), p. 155. Most of Ibn Saud's advisers were non-Saudis. Among them we can note Dr. Abd Allah Damluji from Iraq; Shaykh Yussef Yassin, Khalid Hakim, Dr. Mahmoud Hamdi Hamoudah, Dr. Midhat Shaykh al-Ard, Dr. Rashad Far'oun, and Khair al-Din al-Zirkli from Syria; Shaykh Fouad Hamzah from Lebanon; Shaykh Hakiz Wahbah from Egypt; and Khalid Kirkam from Libya.

11. There is also the Royal Court, which is divided into six administrative divisions: General Administration, Personnel, Translation, Press, Office of Bedouin Affairs, and Political Affairs. The Royal Court's activities, however, are limited to advising the king.

12. Mohammad Sadek, *Tatawur al-Nizam al-Siyassi wa al-Idari fi al-Mamlaka al-Arabiya al-Saudiya* (Riyadh: Ma'had al-Idara al-Ama, 1965), p. 28.

13. Ibid., p. 34.

14. Ibid., p. 36. See the royal decree ordering the establishment of the committee in Umm al-Qura (official gazette of Saudi Arabia and publisher of government documents), no. 186 (12 July 1928).

15. See "Constitution of the Council of Ministers and Constitution of the Division of the Council of Ministers," Umm al-Qura, no. 1508 (March 1954).

16. Ibid., p. 7.

17. Ibid.

18. Ibrahim Muhammad al-Awaji, "Bureaucracy and Society in Saudi Arabia" (Ph.D. diss., University of Virginia, 1971), p. 127. For a study of the procedures and activities of the Saudi bureaucracy, see also Mohammad A. Tawil, "The Procedures and Instruments of Administrative Development in Saudi Arabia" (Ph.D. diss., University of Pittsburgh, 1970).

19. For the Ministry of Finance and National Economy's organizational chart, see Fouad al-Farsy, *Saudi Arabia: A Case Study in Development* (London: Stacey International, 1978), p. 119.

20. Ibrahim al-Awaji, "Bureaucracy and Society," p. 128. For a study of the structure and function of these departments as well as those of the general public personnel administration, see Sulayman al-Mazyed, "The Structure and Function of Public Personnel Administration in Saudi Arabia" (Ph.D. diss., Claremont Men's College, Claremont, Calif., 1972).

21. al-Awaji, "Bureaucracy and Society."

22. Information on the Committees for Commanding the Good and Forbidding Evil was gathered through two interviews with the deputy director of the committees in Riyadh, 11–12 March 1980.

23. Shaykh al-Bitar's text was based on the writings of Taki al-Din Ahmad Ibn Taymiya, especially the work entitled *al-Hisba fi al-Islam* (Beirut: Dar al-Katib al-Arabi, n.d.).

24. Information on the directorate is compiled from an interview with the directorate's assistant director in Riyadh, 10 October 1979.

25. *Majmu'at al-Maraisim al-Malakiya* (Riyadh: Government Printing Office, 1980), p. 81.

26. The present Higher Council of the Ifta' is composed of the following: Muhdar

Afifi, Abd al-Razaq Afifi, Muhammad Amin al-Shanqiti, Abd Allah al-Khayat, Abd Allah Ibn Hamid, Abd al-Aziz Ibn Saleh, Abd al-Majid Hassan, Muhammad al-Harkan, Abd Allah al-Ghadyan, Muhammad Ibn Jubayr, Abd Allah Ibn Mani', Salih Ibn Luhaydan, Sulayman Ibn Ubaid, Ibrahim Ibn Muhammad Al Shaykh, and Rashid Ibn Hanyn.

27. Information was gathered from the Student Affairs Bureau at Riyadh University in 1979 and 1980.

28. al-Ma'had al-Islami, *Memorandum Submitted to the Islamic Secretariat for the Celebration of the Fourteenth Hijirah Century* (Riyadh: Islamic Institute, 1979), p. 8.

29. Information on WAMY was gathered in Riyadh in 1979.

30. The 1977 conference, for example, was held in Kuala Lumpur and was attended by Muslim youth organizations from Afghanistan, Australia, Bangladesh, Fiji, Hong Kong, India, Indonesia, Japan, Malaysia, Pakistan, Singapore, Sri Lanka, South Korea, and Turkey.

31. For the director's views of the Islamic concept of International Relations, see Abd al-Hamid Abu Sulayman, "The Islamic Theory of International Relations: Its Relevance, Past and Present" (Ph.D. diss., University of Pennsylvania, 1973).

32. A representative sample of the books includes Muhammad Qutab, *Shubuhat Hawl al-Islam* (al-Itihad al-Islami: n.p., n.d.); Abd al-Qadir Awda, *al-Islam wa Awda'una al-Qanuniya* (Damascus: Holy Koran Publishing House, 1977); and Sayid Qutub, *al-Mustakbal li hadha al-Din* (Damascus: Holy Koran Publishing House, 1978).

33. Qutub, *Shubuhat*, p. xi.

34. Richard H. Nolte, "The Rule of Law in the Arab Middle East," *Muslim World* 48 (October 1958), pp. 295–96.

35. Subhi al-Mahmasani, *al-Awda' al-Tashri'iya wa al-Qada'iha fi al-Bilad al-Arabiya* (Beirut: Dar al-Ilm li al-Malayin, 1965), pp. 443–64.

36. Ibid.

37. The Arabic text of the fatwa is found in Hafiz Wahba, *Jazirat al-Arab* (Cairo: n.p., n.d.), pp. 319–21.

38. *Majmu'at al-Nuzum fi Qism al-Qada' al-Shar'i* (Mecca: Umn al-Qura, 1938), p. 8.

39. *Umm al-Qura* (5 August 1927).

40. *Umm al-Qura* (24 March 1934).

41. *Umm al-Qura* (7 June 1926).

42. Ibid.

43. The order noted the following: first, that citizens can mail their complaints to the Royal Court; second, that grievances can be brought directly to the Royal Court; third, that the complainant may request an audience with the king for an oral presentation of his grievance; and fourth, that a complainant can wait and present his grievance to the king outside the royal palace.

44. *Majmu'at al-Nazum*, pp. 9–12.

45. Soliman Solaim, "Constitutional and Judicial Organization in Saudi Arabia" (Ph.D. diss., Johns Hopkins University, 1970), p. 94.

46. Ibid.

47. Ibid., p. 132.

48. The texts are as follows: Musa al-Hijawi, *al-Igna'*; Mansur al-Hanbali al-Buhuti, *Kashf al-Qina' an Matn al-Igna'*; al-Futuhi, *Muntaha al-Iradat*; Mansur al-Buhuti, *Sharh*

Muntaha al-Iradat; Shams al-Din al-Qudamah, *al-Mughni*; and Abd al-Rahman Ibn Qadamah, *al-Sharh al-Kabir*.

49. See Sa'dun al-Jasir, *al-Shari'ah fi al-Mamlaka al-Arabiya al-Saudiya* (Riyadh: Ma'had al-Da'wa al-Islami, 1973).

50. Quoted in Abd al-Karim al-Karim al-Huqayl, *Alagat al-Muwatin bi al-Dawa'ir al-Shari'iya* (Beirut: Dar al-Ma'arif, 1967), pp. 189–90.

9

TURKEY

Metin Heper

INTRODUCTION

The Third World includes a majority of Afro-Asian countries freed from colonial rule in the second half of this century, Latin American states liberated from Spain and Portugal in the nineteenth century, and a few countries that were never under Western colonial rule. Turkey is perhaps the only state that shrank from the Ottoman Empire, including much of Eastern Europe, into a nation-state after the First World War.[1] The empire built up its own administrative system—taken partly from the Byzantine Empire it took over, partly from Islamic ideas of governance, and partly from its own Turkish tribal inheritance. Ultimately, imperial administration was based on the two pillars common to all empires of occupation: (1) division of the empire into territorial units, with a local all-purpose representative/or governor for each unit or province who was totally accountable to the Sultan-emperor, and (2) centralization of all power in this representative's hands with a personally controlled army and trusty advisers. This system finally fell into the same trap of all decadent empires governing hostile populations—a continuing tug-of-war between the center and the periphery—in all its Christian domains in Eastern Europe as well as in Arab territories. Much as in the case of the decadent Mughal Empire, this situation gave the central and local bureaucracies the self-image and responsibility as guardians of the realm.

At the same, time, throughout the third quarter of the nineteenth century, the Christian provinces were liberating themselves with or without help from Czarist Russia. The Ottoman Empire fell into a process of rapid decline earning the nickname "the sick man of Europe." The governing elite resorted to a selective process of "modernization," borrowing European technology and some administrative techniques in an attempt to bolster a non-European traditional, centralized despotic polity. The technology was essentially military and communication technology whereas the administrative system was the French Napoleonic one. It was chosen partly because of the Turks' admiration for it and partly because of its compatibility with the French desire for effective centralization. When Turkey was finally deprived of its last Christian East European possessions in 1911–1912 and defeated as an ally of the German Empire in the First World War, Kemal Ataturk established Turkey as a nation-state without European or Arab territorial encumbrances. But the Turkish Republic nevertheless inherited the dual problems of center versus periphery on the one hand and the peculiar incompatibilities of selective instrumental modernization without the complementary changes in society and polity as in Europe on the other. As a result, the Turkish administrative-legal structure or organization resembled that of a European unitary state, in particular France. At the same time the Turkish bureaucracy tried to retain the self-image, power, and privilege of guardianship of the realm, thus generating a conflict between its latent and manifest roles. The following account of Turkey's public administration is therefore divided into two sections: the first dealing with the bare formal structure for administrative organization, and the second dealing with the role of the bureaucracy.

ADMINISTRATIVE ORGANIZATION IN TURKEY

The main administrative organizations in Turkey are the central administration, which is also called the general administration, and local and functionally autonomous units, which are under the tutelage of the central administration. The government, appointed by the president of the Republic and acting with the confidence of the Parliament, is at the head of the general administrative organization, and has supervision over the local and functionally autonomous units. This arrangement demonstrates that, not unlike France, Turkey is a unitary state.

The central administration is divided into central departments and provincial and regional branches. Each of the ministries is headed by a minister who is a member of the Council of Ministers. His top assistant is an administrative official called an adviser (*mustesar*).

The country is administratively divided into provinces (*ii*), which are divided into subprovinces (*ilce*), which are in turn divided into districts (*bucak*). Each of these divisions is headed by an official who is the local representative of the government and has authority over all the other civilian branches of the central departments in that division, including the police.

The head of a province is the governor (*vali*), who is appointed by the Council of Ministers. The head of a subprovince is the subgovernor (*kaymakam*), who is appointed by a joint decree signed by the president of the Republic, the prime minister, and the minister of interior. The head of a district is the director (*mudur*) appointed by the minister of the interior (at the disposal of the governor). The administration of the provinces is based on the principle of the deconcentration of the authority of central administration. In effect, this leads to the enlargement of the power of the governor.

There are three main local autonomous units: the province as a unit of local government; the municipal administration of the towns (municipalities, or *belediyeler*); and the village administration (*koy idaresi*). Each type is organized under a separate law which enumerates its tasks, consisting mainly of local services. In addition, the head of the village administration is entrusted with a few central governmental tasks. This is also the case with mayors of a municipality, but only to a very limited degree.

All three types of local administration possess legal personality, and have budgets and the authority to tax. They are all under the democratic control of the citizens. This control is greater in the villages and towns and moderate in the provinces. The citizens in the villages and towns directly elect both the head official and decision-making councils. In the provinces they elect only the councils.

The head official of the village is the headman (*muhtar*), and the head of the town is the mayor (*belediye baskani*). In the provinces the equivalent function is discharged by the governor, who is the local head of the central administration. Thus, the governor is both an agent of the central government and the head of the local government at the provincial level.

Local elections for the provinces and towns involve the competition of the political parties; for councils, elections are based on proportional representation. Until recently, the election campaigns have tended to revolve around national issues. During recent years local problems have begun to have a greater impact. Village elections are based on the majority system and on the official exclusion of political parties, although they exert indirect influence.

The degree of tutelage (*idari vesayet*) over local government is defined by the governing laws which mostly entrust it to the heads of the provincial administration. The scope of this tutelage was increased by the 1982 Constitution, a handiwork of the military that ruled the country from 1980 to 1983.

In general, the local governments in Turkey have always suffered from an inadequacy of funds. Until 1981, they received certain percentages from specific revenues; otherwise, they have depended on grants from the central government. In 1981, they started to receive 5 percent of all the revenues generated within their boundaries. More recently, this figure was raised to 10 percent. The central government has gradually begun to provide larger revenues for the local government. To what extent it will be adequate remains to be seen.

Quarters of a town within a municipality also constitute local administrative units (*mahalle idaresi*). They are the town equivalent of village administrations, having similar administrators elected by the citizens of the quarters. They have fewer functions, however, mostly limited to the issuance of a number of official documents.

The main functionally autonomous units, all of which have legal standing, are the universities, some research and social institutions, and most public enterprises. The degree of their autonomy varies. Some of them do not possess much financial autonomy, with their budgets and accounts subject to parliamentary and administrative control similar to that of the central administration. The universities are the best example of this category. After the 1980 military intervention (which gave way to civilian government again in 1983), the administrative autonomy of the universities was also somewhat curtailed. Many other autonomous agencies, particularly public enterprises in the economic and social field, enjoy a rather broad degree of financial autonomy.

There are three main types of public enterprises in Turkey—affiliated enterprises, mixed companies, and autonomous agencies. Most public utility enterprises owned by the municipalities are affiliated enterprises. This is due partly to the lack of a general legal authority to create autonomous public units, but mostly to the fact that it is not worthwhile for the small municipalities to have complicated legal structures or separate organizations. The result is partly met by legal rules that permit appropriation to such enterprises of working capital exempt from public financial procedures and subject their transactions to private law.

Most mixed companies are of two kinds. Some are established under the Commercial Code, and these would have private shareholders. Others are established by an ad hoc bill, giving the government more control than provided by the Commercial Code. An example is the Central Bank of Turkey.

Public Enterprises

The main type of autonomous public agencies are state economic enterprises owned by the central government. The municipal enterprises of certain larger cities such as Istanbul and Ankara also fall into this category.

A range of economic undertakings are entrusted to a central agency called a State Economic Enterprise. These central agencies create and run such undertakings by subordinate autonomous "establishments" under their financial and administrative control. Thus, the task of the central agency is similar to that of a holding company. Sometimes the principal subordinate autonomous units are given the status of a central agency.

In addition to the usual ministerial control, these enterprises are subject to the control of a specialized body called the High Board of Supervision, which reports on their balance sheets. The Parliament approves the accounts and performance of the enterprises upon the report of a standing parliamentary committee.

The public enterprises started in the early 1930s were based on a degree of planning. In 1947, a comprehensive development plan was adopted, having been prepared with the help of the relevant agencies without any permanent central planning organization. Between 1950 and 1960 planning was neglected. A permanent planning office attached to the prime minister's office was set up in 1960 with the task of preparing national economic plans and supervising their implementation. Since 1980, greater emphasis has been placed on market forces. Accordingly, the office now has less influence than it had earlier.

Although public enterprises are now a common feature of public administration all over the world and a prominent feature of Third World administration, in Turkey they have their own special history, which may be summarized briefly as follows.

While the founders of the new Turkish Republic (established in 1923) placed an emphasis on the private sector, during the 1920s the Turkish economy did not evince a satisfactory level of growth, let alone development.[2] In particular during this period, no breakthrough could be achieved concerning industrialization. The economic stagnation of the 1920s was due to a number of factors: (1) The Treaty of Lausanne that the young Republic had to sign in the wake of the Turkish War of Independence (1919–1922) brought restrictions on raising custom levies and imposing quotas on imports. The indigenous industry could not be protected; the state was deprived of a critical source of income. (2) During the Ottoman period, economic activities were monopolized by minority groups. By the early 1920s many members of these groups had emigrated. The Muslim-Turkish bourgeoisie which the Ottoman statesmen aspired to nurture during the early decades of the twentieth century was not yet ready to take over. It lacked not only capital, but also technological know-how. There was a lack of experience and, therefore, of organization. (3) The world economic crisis of the late 1920s further exacerbated the situation.

From 1930 on, Turkey began to search for a new economic strategy. This search for a different approach led to the adoption of the policy of statism. The new policy comprised (1) an industrialization strategy of import substitution with protective foreign exchange and trade policies, (2) the founding of state economic enterprises (SEE) which were to play a pioneering role in industrialization efforts, and (3) the financial policy of transferring resources from agriculture to industry through taxation and pricing policies.

The SEEs founded from 1933 on played a critical role in the Turkish economy. They were instrumental in increasing the volume of investment and the creation of new jobs. It must be added, however, that even during this initial stage the SEEs were not valued in and of themselves. The State Economic Enterprises Act of 1938 unequivocally stipulated that their establishment was no more than a stop-gap measure. They were not to monopolize the economy. They were designed to fill a vacuum, and, therefore they were to invest in areas, that is, manufacturing goods, where the private sector was weak. Their role in the economy was to be temporary; they were to wither away as soon as the private sector could take over. (This particular approach to the matter of the SEEs was bound to be significant for later views on the issue of privatization.)

The SEEs did in fact play a significant role in the development of the private sector. For one thing, the SEEs did not monopolize all economic activities. The private sector played a critical role in providing raw materials for, and in the marketing of, manufactured goods. At the same time, the SEEs provided the private sector with inexpensive intermediary goods and services, for the goods and services of the SEEs were underpriced. The SEEs were also training grounds for the future managers of the private sector.

In the long run, however, the noneconomic pricing policy coupled with other characteristics of the SEEs was to make them a heavy burden on the economy. Their dysfunctional role was to become all the more problematic because soon the initial rationale, that is, their role as a stop-gap measure, was to be forgotten. They turned out to be a convenient weapon in the hands of the "intellectual-bureaucratic elite" in their struggle with the rising entrepreneurial middle class. After 1950, despite the fact that the incumbent political party, the Demokrat party, was supposed to be the representative among others of the entrepreneurial groups in question, the number of SEEs did not decrease but rather increased. This turned out to be the case because the Demokrats quickly discovered that the SEEs were indispensable for the machine politics they introduced to Turkish politics.

From their very inception and later, then, the SEEs (1) operated in a non-competitive economic environment and (2) outright political considerations governed their mode of operation. Not only were they free from competition in the internal markets, but they were also isolated from the international markets. Sensitive to the unfavorable consequences of the gradual incorporation of the Ottoman economy to the European markets from the 1930s on, the Turkish statesmen of the single-party years (1923–1945) pursued autarkic economic policies. In the process, the SEEs were financed with low-interest rate funds. Their amortization policies, too, were rather unrealistic. Thus, their financial losses were greater than was generally assumed. There was also a lack of a profit motive in the absence of the danger of insolvency. These factors did not help develop expertise. The directors of the SEE were changed at a bewildering pace. A report prepared in 1982 by the Association of Turkish Industrialists and Businessmen summarized the ills of these enterprises under numerous familiar headings:

- In terms of the initial rationale behind their establishment, their organizational structures are anachronistic.

- Intraorganization coordination is less than satisfactory; they lack a well-functioning system of communications.

- They do not formulate long-range policies and targets; the goals designated are not realistic.

- Appointments to executive positions are overly politicized.

- Their managers can exercise limited initiative in matters of investment, finance, pricing, salaries and wages, and personnel.

- There is no effective system of supervision.

- Investment decisions are not based on reliable feasibility studies and projects; they are made with a view to political cost-benefit analyses.

- The realization of investments takes too long a time, turns out to be very costly, and is carried out with obsolete technology.

- The projects are started despite lack of sufficient resources.

- Modern personnel principles and practices such as planning of the workforce, determination of salaries and wages with a view to evaluation of work, recruitment on the bases of objective criteria, and the like, are given short shrift.

- The SEEs' own capital is insufficient in terms of the scope and volume of their activities.

- They do not have standard accounting and budgeting systems by means of which their activities can be monitored.

- They operate at very low levels of capacity. Their productivity is also low, and they are always in the red.

- They do not have modern systems of purchasing and control.

- They cannot carry out effective quality control.

- They remain indifferent to technological developments and modern management techniques.

- Research and development activities are either less than satisfactory or totally absent.

- Marketing of their products in both internal and external markets is rather deficient; the distribution of their products is very costly.[3]

The economic cost of the SEEs with their characteristics enumerated above can be better appreciated if the scope of their place in the economy is also taken into account. Toward the end of the period under consideration, that is, toward the late 1970s, the SEEs were responsible for one-third of the total investment and production in the economy. (In passing, it must be pointed out that in the late 1960s they accounted for only one-sixth of the total investment.) Of the one-third of the total investment made by the SEEs in 1979, 44 percent was in manufacturing goods. As the SEEs could not themselves finance their investments, in 1979, for instance, 9.1 percent of the GNP had to be set aside for this very purpose. The result of this state of affairs was demand inflation.

It was at this critical juncture of Turkish economic development that, along with other economies, the Turkish economy, too, was hit by the world oil crisis, the worst impact of which was felt in Turkey after 1977. The Turkish economy had no effective defense mechanisms against this new development, and the woes of the Turkish economy increased by leaps and bounds.

It was against this background that, in 1980, the then Justice party government effected a radical policy change. On the whole, the governments under the military regime that followed (1980–1983) adopted intact the changes introduced by the Justice party government. When the Motherland party government came to power in the wake of the transition to multiparty politics and the 1983 general elections, the new policies were further elaborated and pursued with even greater vigor.

The long-term objective of the new policy package was to decrease the state's role and intervention in the economy to a minimum, to place greater emphasis on the market mechanism, and to ensure that prices reflected the relative scarcity of goods and services. This meant that the state was going to be engaged in price controls only as a last resort; the state would not provide subventions; the state would set realistic foreign exchange and interest rates, pursue a tight monetary policy, and balance the budget. The strategy of import substitution was abandoned and was supplanted by a strategy of promoting exports on the basis of comparative advantage. Special incentives were provided for export-oriented private sector enterprises.

As part of the general objective of decreasing the state's role in the economy, the state's funds were not to be channeled primarily into infrastructure investments. The private sector was to play a greater role in manufacturing industry. In the short run, the goal was to prevent the SEEs from siphoning off from the economy the savings needed to promote manufacturing and export-oriented activities. It was figured that this could be achieved if the SEEs no longer pursued a policy of underpricing their goods and services. The SEEs had to be self-financing and no longer dependent on public funds. To fulfill this objective, the SEEs were granted greater leeway in determining the prices of the goods and services they produced.

This new policy quickly bore fruit. The SEEs raised the prices of their goods and services, and in 1985 they registered a profit of 1,274 billion liras.[4] Their expected profits for 1986 were 1,322 billion liras,[5] and their targeted profits for 1987 were 1,985 billion liras.[6] Put differently, their profits in 1985 increased by 390 percent;[7] they were expected to increase 50 percent in 1986[8] and 35 percent in 1987.[9] As such, in 1985 their level of profit was higher than that of the private sector—55 percent versus 40 percent.[10] Still, that very year, 1,215 billion liras had to be transferred to the SEEs from the Treasury.[11]

This outcome can be traced to the fact that the SEEs had chosen the easy way out—making profits by exorbitant price increases rather than by increasing their efficiency. It was estimated that in early 1986 the manufacture of 1 kilogram of sugar cost the relevant SEE TL67.5; its selling price was TL235. Abroad, the same amount of sugar sold for a little over TL100. Similarly, in Turkey, one kilowatt of electricity was produced at a cost of TL13.5 and sold for TL29.7 to domestic users and TL68.7 to industrial users.[12] In some SEEs, profits per worker increased by 5,998 and even 8,641 percent. These very high levels of profit could only be explained by arbitrary price increases in areas where the SEEs had a monopoly. This policy led to cost inflation.

Furthermore, the SEEs' level of exports remained below that of the private sector, particularly where manufactured goods were concerned. In 1985, they were responsible for only 16.3 percent of all investment in the manufacturing industry. In any event, with their low level of efficiency the SEEs could not be competitive in international markets.

It was obvious that, in order to prevent the waste of resources and thus modernize the economy as a whole, new measures were necessary. This point was soon brought home not only by the representatives of the private sector but also by those close to the government. Privatization was now on the agenda. The Association of Turkish Industrialists and Businessmen demanded that, except in areas of strategic importance and social welfare, the state should no longer interfere in economic life. The SEEs should not monopolize certain economic sectors. They should compete with other enterprises within the rules of the market. This could not be achieved unless they were shielded against political interference. Such autonomy could be obtained only through privatization, that is, the transfer of their management to the people and the private sector. Similarly, a report on the SEEs by the High Board of Supervision affiliated to the Prime Ministry not only repeated the then well-known ills of the SEEs, but also emphasized their inefficiency and their obsolete modes of operation. These developments were capped by the government's adoption of the policy of privatization for the SEEs.

Since then, the government on its own initiative has sold quite a few plants, but not as many as they planned. The State Planning Organization then selected the Morgan Guaranty Bank of the United States to work out a strategy for sales and privatization, which they did on the basis of a detailed survey. The Morgan Team's report was endorsed by the High Board of Coordination in 1987, and the privatization strategy is being actively implemented. One may add that Turkey is one of the very few Third World countries that is attempting to privatize a sizable chunk of its public enterprises.

THE BUREAUCRACY, LATENT AND PATENT ROLES

The Turkish bureaucratic elite, which chose for themselves the latent social role of guardians of the state, conceived it as their function to maintain a moderate transcendentalist state in Turkey. After the successful transition to multiparty politics in the 1940s, the Turkish political process has on the whole consistently moved toward a polyarchal competitive regime.[13] To this day, however, in Turkey the effective functioning of popular representative institutions and the broad dispersion of political power across government branches and across different sociopolitical strata have been problematic. This is due to the fact that the basic cleavage in the Ottoman-Turkish polity has been that between the center and the periphery.[14]

In the Ottoman polity, no distinctive socioeconomic class emerged to challenge the center, which was in general represented by the Sultan and the military, civil, and religious bureaucracies. At different periods, different groups at the center acted as the locus of the state. From the mid-nineteenth century on, the civil and the military bureaucratic elite acted as the agents of the state. During this century, what looked like representative councils were conceived by the state elite as no more than means for effective levying of taxes. The local notables who were asked to participate in those councils hardly resembled the intransigent members of the French *parlements*. Some were even confused about what was going on.[15]

The political approach of the center remained the same, despite some changes in the periphery. It was regulation from above. The center never doubted its ability to implement the legal measures it took. During the earlier centuries when the realm was not challenged from outside, the state could easily draw resources from civil society and maintain its supremacy in the polity. Later, when this proved increasingly difficult, the center resorted to borrowing from abroad. Mercantilism and related developments in the West remained alien to the Ottoman scene.[16]

The Turkish Republic inherited this particular mode of statecraft. The intellectual-bureaucratic elite in Republican Turkey, not unlike the German "liberals" of the second part of the nineteenth century, has always cherished a juridical concept of state, placing greater faith in the rule of law than in the rule of Parliament. This elite adopted a prescribed value system expressed in principles such as secularism, nationalism, populism, and etatism. They presumed themselves to have the sole truth in politics, and they did not believe politics to be a matter of trial and error.[17] Serif Mardin noted this predilection when he referred to the Turkish state as having a bureaucracy "which for centuries has been entrusted with the application of the values embodied in its political culture."[18]

Thus, in contrast to the basic patterns of social transformation in Western Europe, the evolution of Ottoman-Turkish polity fits an induced rather than an organic model of change. Organic development in the West begins with (1) a change in economic activities leading first to (2) the emergence of a new force in society, the entrepreneurial middle class, and then, through the incorporation of this new interest grouping with the rulers to (3) the establishment of the centralized political authority and a royal bureaucracy. Later, the entrepreneurial middle class extends its power further, and constitutional government reaches its maturity. In the process the major instruments of government are rendered responsive to "civil society."

In the induced change pattern, the initial impetus does not come from the entrepreneurial middle class. Induced change evinces in order of sequence (1) an outside stimulus, usually in the form of threat to national integrity and/or independence, (2) the emergence of a leader, or leaders, who seek to elevate their nation to a position of power, (3) the creation of new or modernized instruments of governmental power, that is civil and military bureaucracies, (4) economic change, planned and in part executed by the central government, and (5) the emergence of an entrepreneurial middle class followed by a variety of further expressions of collective economic interest, and the growing political influence of these economic groups.[19]

The induced pattern of change lacks the "internal consistency" of the organic one. In organic change, the different sectors and institutions of society interact and affect each other; as a consequence, change in one sector does not remain isolated. Each sector or institution monitors and, in turn, is influenced by changes in other sectors and institutions. That the development of a capitalist economy, a liberal-constitutional political system, the general secularization of culture, and the emergence of secondary types of interpersonal relationship in Western Europe took place in an interrelated fashion is a case in point.

As already noted, the induced change lacks such internal consistency. The change induced within the system is necessarily partial. The new "institutions" copied from outside may long remain unintegrated with the rest of the system. The induced pattern of change usually manifests a strategy of borrowing the end products of another so as to bring about selected aspects of the foreign system.

Because of this particular pattern of social change, that is induced pattern of change;[20] emphasis on control and regulation on the part of the state elites, most of whom have been bureaucrats; absence of efforts by this elite to shore up its position in the society by mobilizing certain strata or social classes, thus entering into an organic relationship with them,[21] and finally, a successful inculcation to the bureaucrats of values derived from such an experience,[22] there emerged a latent versus manifest role conflict on the part of the Turkish bureaucrats.

One may perhaps conclude that there is no close relationship between the Turkish civil servants "modern" attitudes and the tasks they carry out. The Turkish "revolution" seems to have led to an administrative modernization in an abstract sense, i.e. holding modernistic attitudes for their own sake, and did not bring about an adequate level of functional specialization.[23]

Growth of the Bureaucracy

In Turkey, the number of civil servants has increased faster than that of the general population.[24] The rate of increase accelerated in recent decades. From the 1930s to the present, while the general population increased about three times, the administrative population increased about ten times. From 1938 to 1963, the administrative population increased by 233 percent. The corresponding percentages for 1976, 1977–1978, and 1979 are 614,771, and 1,000 percent, respectively. It is, therefore, hardly possible to explain the growth in the size of the bureaucracy in terms of increase in general population.

Could the increase in the size of bureaucracy in turn be explained in terms of expansion of the services provided? The response to this query cannot be in the affirmative. The share of the personnel expenditures in the general public expenditures has been consistently increasing. Whereas this share was 70.4 percent in 1963, it was 74.2 percent in 1967 and 77.5 percent in 1972. The increase of personnel at the upper echelons of the bureaucracy is greater than that in the lower ones. If there were no intervening variables and the size of the bureaucracy increased basically because of increases in the services provided, the rate of increase at the upper echelons would not have been greater than that in the lower ones. Even in the state economic enterprises, the number of regular civil servants and the technicians taken together has been more than keeping pace with the increase in the number of workers.

Thus, expansion in the size of the bureaucracy cannot be explained in terms of "natural tendencies." Impetus for this expansion came largely from the bureaucracy itself. In the Turkish bureaucracy there is a rather rigid conception of career service. Consequently, an effort has been made to promote as many civil servants as possible to the upper grades. In order to do so, a number of superfluous positions have been established in the upper grades. For instance, between the directors and assistant directors, the position of chief assistant director was created. The bureaucratic elite tenaciously held on to governmental jobs at the highest levels. In this context it is significant that the lower grades are filled with civil servants born in rural areas.[25] The traditional center-periphery conflict in the Ottoman-Turkish society is replayed within the bureaucratic ranks, too. When faced with lack of adequate administrative slots in urban areas, efforts have been made to transfer such slots from the rural areas.

Impetus for the increase in the size of the bureaucracy also came from the political elite. After each of the four changes of government between 1973 and 1980, basically because of distortion of policy and passive resistance on the part of the bureaucratic elite, each political party (and sometimes each minister within the same political party) tried to bring in a new team of civil servants, usually from the ranks of the respective political party organizations. Since the bureaucratic elite in Turkey has tenure that cannot be easily tampered with, additions were made to the ranks without laying off the old hands, who were only relieved of line duties.

Accountability and Patrimonialism

Bureaucratic accountability has at least three dimensions:

1. Accountability of the bureaucracy as a whole to its outside environment, that is, to political authority and to beneficiaries.
2. Accountability of individual organizational units, that is, project units, divisions/sections in ministries to higher echelons of the bureaucracy.
3. Accountability of individuals for their performance.

The Turkish Republic inherited patrimonialism from the Ottomans. Mardin has summarized its Republican version under four headings: "barriers to the legitimation of an autonomous civil society, unwillingness of the bureaucratic elite to assume the role of carrying out popular demands, the rigidity of the prebendial system, and the complex web of derivations—in the Paretian sense—that enter into the cultural ideology of Turkish intellectuals."[26] Mardin's account of patrimonialism in the Turkish policy refers to Type 1 bureaucratic accountability, or (political) responsiveness of the bureaucracy. The tradition in question is operationalization of the latent role tradition which we attribute to the bureaucratic elite. This tradition precludes responsiveness on the part of the bureaucratic elite.

In 1969, I posed the following statement to thirty-six civil servants who had occupied the highest grades in the Turkish public bureaucracy during 1945–1960:

"People with strange and wild opinions should not be allowed a public platform from which to preach." Thirty of them did not disagree, and only one strongly disagreed. Out of the thirty-six former higher civil servants, thirty-four agreed with the following idea: "What Turkey needs more than anything else is experienced and informed people significantly contributing to public policy making." None of this group agreed with the following suggestion: "In order to alleviate some of the tensions and bottlenecks in Turkish political life it might perhaps be wise in political debates to compromise on some tenets of Atatürkism like secularism, nationalism and étatism."[27] In 1974, among 510 civil servants in eight central ministries, mean scores (on a Likert scale ranging from 1 to 5, with higher scores indicating a higher ranking on each scale) were 1.48 for "tolerance for democratic way of life," 3.58 for "elitism," and 3.53 for "social responsibility."[28] In 1978, among all the civil servants in the central organizations of three ministries, only 16.4 percent disagreed with the statement that civil servants as compared to other citizens are better judges of the country's interests.[29]

The tradition of patrimonialism in question has had its impact in Turkey on the Type 2 and Type 3 bureaucratic accountability, or bureaucratic responsibility, too. The emphasis of Turkish civil servants on precedents can be attributed to their efforts to maintain their autonomy vis-à-vis the politicians, and does not indicate legal rationalism. The antecedents of this practice go back to the second part of the nineteenth century when the then bureaucratic elite emphasized rules in order to decrease the Sultan's discretion.[30]

The Republican administration is designed formally as "a legal-rational bureaucracy." Viewed solely from a legal perspective, one may conclude that the dominant ethos of the bureaucracy should be formal rationality. In fact, at each level of Turkish government rules are perceived either as a means of regulating the behavior of subordinates so as to render them completely loyal or, conversely, as a means of circumventing supervision and direction from above.[31]

The duties of subordinates are determined on an ad hoc basis. As the whole administration revolves around the persons of the senior civil servants, "bureaucratizing" would be unthinkable; this process would wrest from the senior administrators the opportunity to be arbitrary. Thus, in the Turkish public bureaucracy, (1) what should be the same job turns out to be different from one ministry to another; (2) the same is true concerning the title of the jobs; (3) there is little standardization concerning appointments and promotions; and (4) the nature and effectiveness of supervision show great variation from one ministry to another.[32] Despite classification efforts since the 1950s and 1960s to this day, not much has changed in this regard.[33]

Prestige

If the present analysis concerning the latent social roles of the Turkish bureaucratic elite has any validity, it may be expected that the prestige of the

Turkish civil service, and therefore its ability to attract and retain qualified personnel, would be high only when the bureaucracy had political clout. Only then would the Turkish bureaucratic elite be able to fulfill its self-appointed mission of acting as guardian of the state. Turkish politics has no tradition of French *grand corps*—"a self-conscious, cohesive, almost evangelical and prestigious group, the prestige of which is based upon their expertise and professionalism."[34]

Since the mid-nineteenth century, the civil bureaucracy alternated with the military in Turkey as a significant member of the polity. Its political fortunes dwindled from the last decades of the nineteenth century. From the end of the nineteenth century to the 1930s, there seems to have been a trend toward recruitment from less privileged families and regions.[35] From the 1930s on, however, the civil bureaucracy came to play a significant role in Turkish politics. Thus, in 1955 it was found that more than 71 percent of the students at the School of Political Science, Ankara University, which has traditionally provided the bulk of Turkish civil servants, came from the relatively better off regions.[36]

With the coming to power of the Democratic party in 1950, the political power of the civil bureaucracy began to decrease. First to go down was their income. For a while, however, the bureaucrats held their ground against politicization of their ranks. For instance, as late as the period 1965 to 1971, the Council of State (the Turkish version of the French *Conseil d'État*) rendered null and void a total of 1,400 governmental decrees concerning appointments of civil servants. The government respected all of these rulings except forty of them, in the latter cases, however, the civil servants were paid indemnity.[37]

During the 1970s, Turkish politics experienced ideological polarization and political fragmentation. Civil servants were not spared the effects of this profound change. Particularly during the post–1973 period, turnover in the civil bureaucracy reached very high levels. Whereas in the 1962–1974 period the average number of years that a director general of a state economic enterprise kept his office was 3.5 years, for the 1974–1980 period the corresponding figure was 1.7 years. From 1 December 1979 to 1 May 1980, 1,223 high-ranking civil servants were removed from their posts and 1,367 appointed.[38] Reshuffling involved all ranks.

Under these circumstances, the bureaucrats inevitably became insecure in their posts. A recent study has shown that among those civil servants who joined the civil service recently the percentage of those who said they preferred civil service because it was safe dropped significantly compared to those who had joined before 1970 (35.1 percent versus 47.3 percent).[39]

From the perspective of the latent versus manifest role identities of the Turkish bureaucrats, a finding in this context by Leslie Roos and Noralou Roos is also significant. Their panel study of 1949–1956 graduates of the School of Political Science showed that these civil servants were relatively more dissatisfied in 1965 than in 1956 as far as "political factors," their pay, security, and autonomy were concerned. However, their satisfaction level had not dropped with regard to the "opportunity to increase knowledge" dimension of "self-realization."[40] This is not an unexpected finding; the latent role identity of the Turkish civil bureaucrats lacked a dimension of expertise and professionalism for the reasons already cited.

Civil servants consider social prestige to be the most significant factor making their jobs interesting. However, they seem to think that a job is prestigious not when it is infused with norms of professionalism and expertise, but when it provides opportunities to exercise political and/or organizational authority and influence.[41]

Omer Bozkurt found that the top servants gave a much more favorable evaluation of the service than those at lower echelons, and that their chief satisfaction came from their exercise of authority. Bozkurt also found that those at the lower echelons, particularly street-level bureaucrats, were also less critical, as they, too, had ample opportunity to exercise authority, mostly over the citizens who could not deal effectively with these petty bureaucrats.[42]

Development Between 1980 and 1983

In the eyes of the post–1980 military, the bureaucratic intelligentsia did not enjoy high esteem.[43] On the very day the military took over, General Kenan Evren asserted that, among others, those in the civil bureaucratic ranks had long subscribed to "reactionary ideas" and "perverted ideologies." Later (in public addresses in Konya and Adana on 15 and 16 January 1981), he warned that civil servants should loyally serve the new regime and should not attempt to take their cues from the leaders of the existing political parties. This point was also implied in the government program set up by the military regime, which was presented on 27 September 1980.

Initially, the military chose to take action only against those civil servants who had committed administrative acts falling under the class of "punishable offense." During the first week of the regime, only "extremist" governors and mayors were replaced by more moderate officials or by retired officers. Steps were also taken to reduce factionalism among the police. Later, the number of civil servants who in some fashion came to be affected by the measures taken by the military reached staggering proportions. Between 12 September 1980 and 12 September 1981, a total of 18,000 civil servants were either taken into custody, or formally arrested, or convicted.

At first, the military regime experimented working with the existing civil bureaucrats—at least with those who were not subject to some kind of legal proceedings. Toward the end of 1981, however, there were signs that large-scale purges were in prospect. Some previous appointments were viewed as having been influenced politically—by both left and right.

The next step was to retire as many civil servants as possible. Civil servants were offered certain inducements to take voluntary retirement; some who did not wish to leave, were forced to do so by unilateral action. Paralleling these developments was the abrogation of as many as seventy-one general directorates in various administrative agencies, except the Ministry of Defense. By special governmental decree, many higher civil servants were also relieved of their duties.

The military also took action against the Council of State and the universities. An appeal could no longer be made to the Council of State against decrees signed by three ministers or more. The 1961 Constitution had placed each administrative action within the jurisdiction of the Council, to which civil servants could appeal when decisions affected them. In an administrative law system where no absolute discretion is granted to the government, and where every executive action needs to be carefully justified on legally recognized grounds, the council could be, and was, used by the civil servants as a bulwark against the politicians, particularly in those cases where the politicians had tried to transfer civil servants to other posts.

The military chose to impose constraints not only on the general jurisdiction of the council, but also on its internal autonomy: the president was empowered to appoint all the important members of the council. This measure against the council seems to have been motivated by the concern that in the past the council, too, had been unduly politicized.

The military's attempt to contain the civil bureaucracy is, of course, a reaction to the civil bureaucracy's polarization during the earlier two decades around hard ideologies of a leftist and, to a lesser extent, a rightist variety, though this basic intention was not clearly spelled out despite General Evren's early accusation.

During the early months of 1982, the civilian government established by the military regime asked for powers to streamline the civil bureaucracy by governmental decree in order to render it functional for developmental efforts. As already noted, the government had submitted its program to the National Security Council on 27 September 1980. In that program, too, the civil bureaucracy was mentioned as constituting an obstacle to economic development.

Thus, the military's treatment of the civil bureaucracy was informed by two parallel attitudes. On the one hand, the ideological stance of the civil bureaucrats was considered to be a vitally important matter. Therefore, first priority was given to the issue of polarization. The military went so far as to establish a High Board of Supervision affiliated to the Office of the Presidency; its sole function was to act as a watchdog in this issue. Moreover, the inculcation of Ataturkist thought (as the military interpreted it), which this matter represented, led to the overhauling of the whole system of education, a matter already noted. These attitudes and the measures that sprang from them reflected the transcendentalist aspect of the new regime. It aimed at close hierarchical control of the civil bureaucracy.

Political Versus Bureaucratic Elites: Post–1983 Developments

With the transition to multiparty politics in the mid–1950s, there emerged a clash between the bureaucratic elites and the political elites. The political elites could not get the upper hand during the first two decades of this conflict. The 1961 Constitution had stacked the bureaucratic elites against the political elites. Among other things, the newly created Constitutional Court along with the Council of State provided the mechanisms through which the bureaucratic elites could stand up to the political elites. This state of affairs began to change particularly during the 1970s.

One novelty was the unbridled politicization of the bureaucracy. Particularly during the period of coalition governments that started in 1973 and lasted until the 1980 military intervention, the party supporters began to be appointed to the bureaucratic ranks in great numbers. In the process, some radical fringe parties that could obtain a niche in the coalition governments tried to colonize the ministries under their jurisdiction with their militant members.

During the period in question, the general quality of the civil service, also deteriorated. The increased rate of inflation during the 1970s made the lot of the civil servants even more worse than it already was. The civil service could no longer attract qualified personnel.

The measures taken to deal with these maladies during the interregnum (1980–1983) have already been noted. One aim was to remove the twin ills of polarization and fragmentation within the bureaucracy. The second was to transfer the bureaucracy into a legal-rational one. It was hoped that the bureaucracy would be made subservient to the political authority and that it would function efficiently and effectively.

The post–1983 Motherland Government came to power at this juncture. This government, under Prime Minister Turgut Ozal, attempted to launch Turkey's ''liberal revolution.''[44] Among other things, Turgut Ozal has attempted to realize Turkey's takeoff toward a self-sustained growth. Such an ambitious project necessitated a thorough streamlining as well as a restructuring of the bureaucracy.

The bureaucracy had to be a prop for, and not an obstacle, to the economic leap forward in question. The Ozal government tried to simplify bureaucratic procedures. Through some mergers, the total number of agencies was also decreased.

Along with streamlining the bureaucracy, the Ozal government also attempted to restructure it. As the new strategy of development placed greater emphasis on the market forces, the bureaucracy, that is, its upper reaches, had to be taken out of the decision-making process. The steps taken in this direction went as far as sidestepping such critical ministries as Finance and Foreign Affairs. Although the Ministry of Finance was practically limited to collecting revenues, the responsibility for critical allocation of funds and expenditures was transferred to a newly created Undersecretariat of Treasure and Foreign Trade, affiliated to the Prime Ministry. The Ozal government also created several special funds outside the supervision of the Court of Accounts. In the domain of foreign affairs, some critical functions were transferred to newly established ministries of state or were carried out singlehandedly by the prime minister himself.

The new economic policy also necessitated installing technocrats in critical decision-making units or centers. One did come across the emergence of a new type of managerial elite in civil bureaucracy in the earlier decades.[45] The Ozal government, however, could not trust the old hands in the civil service. Consequently, it brought in its own team of so-called young princes to the helm of critical agencies and state-run banks. In doing so, at times, the age-old usages of the bureaucracy were given short shrift.

For his part, the prime minister assembled a close circle of advisers. Some of them came from the members of the Ozal family—so much so that people began talking about the ''Ozal Dynasty.'' It was claimed that these advisers were very influential vis-à-vis appointments to some critical posts as well as some vital decisions. Their influence was bound to increase as Ozal has tended to work with a small circle of advisers, and not with greater bodies. In the process, even the Council of Ministers was sometimes relegated to a secondary place.[46]

If the Ozal government had been less than successful in its fight against red-tape, it had been quite ''successful'' in removing the bureaucratic elite from effective centers of power. The civil bureaucracy is no longer able to pursue ''negative policies.'' In the present conflict between ''the old Ottoman bureaucracy and the American *école*,'' as this encounter is sometimes referred to in Turkey, the ''young princes'' have had the upper hand.

When we sum up the changes of the post–Second World War years, we see that for a long time the Turkish bureaucracy resisted all reform efforts to divest it of its guardian role and self-image. In 1953, attempts began to be made to depoliticize and bureaucratize or professionalize them through academic instruction and training—with the establishment of an Institute of Public Administration in 1953 and with research projects and courses. These failed mainly because they left untouched the social composition of the service and its sociopolitical environment. On the other hand, army rule with its ruthless arrests and dismissals, struck the bureaucracy dumb, but very soon it reverted to its old role, as the army needed the bureaucracy for day-to-day governance. The latest civilian efforts under the Ozal regime seem to be succeeding in making bureaucracy a pliable instrument partly by changing its composition and environment. Only time can tell whether the change will last.

NOTES

1. The brief introduction on the transformation of the shrinking Ottoman Empire into the Turkish Republic is based on Suna Kili, *Kemalism* (Istanbul: Robert College, 1969) and the allied references: Philip Paneth, *Turkey, Decadence and Rebirth* (London: Richard Madley, 1943), and Bernard Lewis, *The Emergence of Modern Turkey* (London: Oxford University Press, 1961).

2. Unless otherwise indicated, the following account of the Turkish economy as background to the privatization policies of the 1980s at places draws heavily on Orhan Morgil, ''Kamu Iktisadi Tesebbuslerinin Ozellestirilmesi'' [Privatization of State Economic Enterprises], *Yeni Forum* (1 March 1985); Hasan Deniz Kurdu, ''Kit'lerin Ozel-

lestirilmesi'' [Privatization of State Economic Enterprises], *Dunya* (18 September 1986); Adnan Gulerman, ''KIT Karlari ve Satilmalari'' [Profits of State Economic Enterprises and their Sale], *Turkiye Iktisat Gazetesi* (11 November 1986); Mehmet Hamedi, ''Ozellestirime Projesine Bir Sans Taninmali'' [Need to Give the Benefit of Doubt to the Privatization Project], *Dunya* (9 April 1986); Turk Sanayicileri ve is Adamlari Dernegi, *KIT Raporu* [Report on State Economic Enterprises] (Istanbul: TUSIAD, 1982); and Turk Sanayicileri ve is Adamlari Dernegi, *Ozellestirme: KIT'lerin Halka Satisinda Basari Kosullari* [Privatization: Preconditions for Success in the Sale of State Economic Enterprises to the People], (Istanbul: TUSIAD, 1986).

3. *KIT Raporu*, passim.

4. *Dunya*, 18 October 1985.

5. Ibid., 22 November 1985.

6. Ibid., 8 February 1986.

7. Ibid., 18 October 1985.

8. Ibid., 22 November 1985.

9. Ibid., 8 February 1986.

10. Ibid., 9 October 1985.

11. *Ozellestirme: KIT'lerin Halka Satisinda Basari Kosullari*, p. 9.

12. Tevfik Gungor, ''Kamu Tekellerinin Yuksek Fiyatiyla KIT'ler Nasil Kar Eder, Devlet Nasil Vergi Toplar, Enflasyon Nasil Hizlanir?'' [How Do the SEEs Make Profits Through High Prices, How Does the State Tax People, and How is Inflation Exacerbated?], *Dunya*, 21 January 1986.

13. For a particularly sympathetic evaluation of Turkish politics from this perspective, see Walter F. Weiker, *The Modernization of Turkey: From Ataturk to the Present Day* (New York: Holmes and Meier, 1981). See also Metin Heper, ''The State, the Military and Democracy in Turkey,'' *The Jerusalem Journal of International Relations* 9 (1987), pp. 52–64.

14. Serif Mardin, ''Center-Periphery Relations: A Key to Turkish Politics?'' *Daedalus* 102 (1973), pp. 169–90.

15. See Metin Heper, ''Center-Periphery in the Ottoman Empire: With Special Reference to the Nineteenth Century,'' *International Political Science Review* (1980), pp. 81–105.

16. See, in general, Serif Mardin, ''Power, Civil Society and Culture in the Ottoman Empire,'' *Comparative Studies in Society and History* 11 (1969), pp. 258–81.

17. These points are elaborated in Metin Heper, ''Recent Instability in Turkish Politics: End of a Monocentrist Polity?'' *International Journal of Turkish Studies* 1 (1979–1980), pp. 102–13.

18. Serif Mardin, ''Opposition and Control in Turkey,'' *Government and Opposition* 1 (1966), p. 375. The problem this particular political heritage posed for recent attempts at decentralization are discussed in three separate volumes edited by Metin Heper: *Dilemmas of Decentralization: Municipal Government in Turkey* (Bonn: Friedrich-Ebert-Stiftung, 1986); *Democracy and Local Government: Istanbul in the 1980s* (Walkington, England: Eothen Press, 1987); and *Local Government in Turkey, Governing Greater Istanbul* (London: Routledge, 1989).

19. Karl Polanyi, *The Great Transformation: The Political and Economic Origins of Our Times* (Boston: Beacon Press, 1968).

20. See, *inter alia*, Lewis, *The Emergence of Modern Turkey*.

21. This point is developed in Metin Heper and A. Umit Berkman, *Development*

Administration in Turkey: Conceptual Theory and Methodology (Istanbul: Bogazici University Publications, 1980).

22. Metin Heper and Ersin Kalaycioglu, "Organizational Socialization as Reality-Testing: The Case of the Turkish Higher Civil Servants," *International Journal of Political Education* 6 (1983), pp. 175–98.

23. Metin Heper, "A Methodological Note on Bureaucratic Modernization: Prevalent Attitudes of the Turkish Civil Servants," *International Review of Modern Sociology* 11 (1982), pp. 75–103.

24. Unless otherwise indicated, my account of bureaucratic growth in Turkey draws heavily on Sait Guran, *Memurlar Hukukunda Kayirma ve Liyakat Sistemleri* (Istanbul: Fakultet Matbaasi, 1980), Chapter 1.

25. Omer Bozkurt, *Memurlar: Turkiye'de Kamu Burokrasisinin Sosyolojik Gorunumu* (Ankara: Turkiye ve Orta Dogu Amme Idaresi Enstitusu Yayini, 1980), pp. 47–51, 61, 197, 203.

26. Mardin, "Power, Civil Society and Culture in the Ottoman Empire," p. 279.

27. Reported in Metin Heper, "Political Modernization as Reflected in Bureaucratic Change: The Turkish Bureaucracy and a Historical Bureaucratic Empire Tradition," *International Journal of Middle East Studies* 7 (1976), pp. 516–17.

28. Reported in Metin Heper, "Negative Bureaucratic Politics in a Modernizing Context: The Turkish Case," *Journal of South Asian and Middle Eastern Studies* 1 (1977), p. 76.

29. Reported in Bozkurt, *Memurlar: Turkiye'de Kamu Burokrasisinin Sosyolojik Gorunumu*, p. 130.

30. Roderic H. Davison, *Reform in the Ottoman Empire, 1856–1976* (Princeton, N.J.: Princeton University Press, 1963).

31. Frederick T. Bent, "Turkish Bureaucracy as an Agent of Change," *Journal of Comparative Administration* 1 (1969), pp. 58–59.

32. Maurice Chailloux-Dantel, "Turkiye'de Devlet Personel Teskilati Hakkinda Bir Arastirma," in T. C. Basbakanlik Devlet Personel Dairesi (ed.), *Hukumete Sunulan Yabanci Uzman Raporlari* (Ankara: T. C. Basbakanlik Devlet Personel Dairesi Yayini, 1963), pp. 117–18.

33. Nabi Dincer and Turan Ersoy, *Merkezi Hukumet Teskilati Arastirma Projesi (Mehtap) Tavsiyelerinin Uygulanma Durumunu Degerlendirme Arastirmasi* (Ankara: Turkiye ve Orta Dogu Amme Idaresi Enstitusu, 1974), p. 358.

34. Oguz Onaran, *Yonetici Sinifin Egitimi: Belcika, Fransa, Ingiltere ve Turkiye'de* (Ankara: Turkiye ve Orta Dogu Amme Idaresi Enstitusu Yayini, 1976), pp. 21–32. On the French case, see Ezra N. Suleiman, *Politics, Power and Bureaucracy in France: The Administrative Elite* (Princeton, N.J.: Princeton University Press, 1974).

35. Leslie L. Roos, Jr., and Noralou P. Roos, "Changing Patterns of Turkish Public Administration," *Middle Eastern Studies* 5 (1986), pp. 28–36.

36. Fahir Armaoglu and Gutherie Birkhead, *Siyasal Bilgiler Fakultesi 1946–1955 Mezunlar Hakkinda Bir Arastirma* (Ankara: Turkiye ve Orta Dogu Amme Idaresi Enstitusu Yayini, 1956), pp. 6–7.

37. Cahit Tutum, *Turkiye'de Memur Guvenligi* (Ankara: Turkiye ve Orta Dogu Amme Idaresi Enstitusu, 1972), p. 98.

38. Bulent Ardanic and Turgay Ergun, "Siyasal Nitelikli Yuksek Yonetici Atamalari," *Amme Idaresi Dergisi* 13 (1980), p. 11.

39. Bozkurt, *Memurlar: Turkiye'de Kamu Burokrasisinin Sosyolojik Gorunumu*, p. 108.

40. Leslie L. Roos, Jr., and Noralou P. Roos, *Managers of Modernization: Organizations and Elite in Turkey (1950–1969)* (Cambridge, Mass.: Harvard University Press, 1971), p. 123.

41. Yucel Ertekin, *Orgut Iklimi* (Ankara: Turkiye ve Orta Dogu Amme Idaresi Enstitusu Yayini, 1978), pp. 72–73.

42. Bozkurt, *Memurlar: Turkiye'de Kamu Burokrasininin Sosyolojik Gorunumu*, p. 123.

43. This account is taken from Metin Heper, *The State Tradition in Turkey* (Walkington, England: Eothen Press, 1985).

44. Dankwart A. Rustow, "Turkey's Liberal Revolution," *Middle East Review* 17 (1985), pp. 5–11.

45. Ahmet Evin, "Changing Patterns of Cleavages Before and After 1980," in Metin Heper and Ahmet Evin (eds.), *State, Democracy and the Military: Turkey in the 1980s* (Berlin and New York: Walter de Gruyter, 1988), pp. 201–13.

46. For an elaboration of the post–1983 developments regarding the bureaucracy, see Metin Heper, "Some Notes on the Post–1983 Bureaucracy in Turkey," *Governance: An International Journal of Policy and Administration*, 1989.

PART III

SUB-SAHARAN AFRICA

10

GHANA

E. Gyimah-Boadi
and Donald Rothchild

The systems, the structures and social arrangements of the huge and parasitic
Public Services which has been so unwieldy but which continues to service
the existing neo-colonial arrangements must be dismantled, pruned or abolished if we are to make any headway in our national struggle during this
phase of the Revolution.

Preamble to policy guidelines of the
Provisional National Defence Council
(May 1982), p. 4.

Although Ghana's public service was greatly enlarged in scope, personnel, and
functions in colonial and postcolonial times, this expansion has not been accompanied by an improved capacity to provide effective administration. The statement noted at the outset of this chapter which was issued by Ghana's most recent
postcolonial government, captures some of this feeling of deep disappointment
over the past performance of the public service and the related desire to reorganize
its activities. The statement also highlights some of the themes that have recurred
across regimes since the country attained independence in 1957.

This chapter attempts to analyze the relations between Ghana's public service
and the various regimes it has been called on to service in postindependence
times. In examining these relations, it seeks to shed light on the problems arising
from this interaction and the efforts at reform. We do so by placing the public
service in its historical, economic, and sociopolitical context, seeking thereby
to underscore the linkages between administration, government, and society. As
used here, Ghana's public service includes not only the civil service as traditionally constituted, but also the judiciary service, the armed forces, and police,
the regional, district, and local administrative services, and the personnel of the

state economic institutions, that is, the marketing boards, the parastatals (state corporations engaged in commercial activities), the regional development corporations and other supporting institutions (see Table 10.1).[1]

THE COLONIAL LEGACY

A discussion of public administration in Ghana must begin by focusing on the colonial bureaucracy, the basis for much of the present system. The colonial administrative system, largely patterned after the British civil service, featured a governor-general, a secretariat (headed by the colonial secretary), and various technical departments. Roughly speaking, the service included six grades: administrative and professional, technical, executive, artisan and clerical, and subordinate. Entry into the various grades corresponded with the candidate's level of education and training. The Colonial Office (in London) recruited people into senior-level positions, usually through the local efforts of the Crown agents. The secretariat handled matters of recruitment at the junior level, comprising the junior executive, clerical, semiskilled, and unskilled grades.

In theory, Africans with the necessary training and experience could be appointed to the relevant positions. In practice, however, those appointed to senior posts were invariably recruited from Britain and the older Commonwealth countries of Canada, Australia, New Zealand, and South Africa. Positions in the administrative, managerial, supervisory, professional, and senior technical grades therefore became known as European posts.[2]

FIELD ADMINISTRATION IN THE COLONIAL PERIOD

The English tradition of centralized government with limited deconcentration was also preserved in matters of field administration. The Colony of the Gold Coast was divided into regions (sometimes referred to as provinces), and then further into districts. The regions were headed by chief provincial commissioners who reported directly to the governor-general in Accra. The districts were headed by district commissioners, who reported directly to the chief provincial commissioners. The chief provincial commissioners were assigned the responsibility for collecting taxes, maintaining law and order, advising and guiding the native administrations (through the chiefs), and exercising a vague supervisory authority over the activities of the various technical departments in the field. However, the district commissioner constituted the linchpin of colonial authority in the rural areas. Just as the governor-general represented the Crown in the colony, the district officer represented the government in the field. He controlled and regulated all aspects of labor, commerce, land tenure, and judicial matters.[3]

As Britain's colonial officials introduced a system of indirect rule in the Gold Coast, the native authorities (i.e., the traditional chiefs) were authorized by law

Table 10.1
The Public Service

Civil Service	Other Public Services
Central ministries and other government departments (e.g., Health, Education, Finance, and Economic Planning)	Armed forces
	Police service
	Judicial service
	Ghana education services
Support services (e.g., Ghana Supply Commission)	Support/control units such as Judicial Council, Armed Forces Directorate
Control units (e.g., the Auditor and Accountant Generals' departments)	State marketing boards
	Public corporations
	Parastatals
	Universities
	Research institutes
Regional administration (including regional units of civil service agencies, support and control units)	Regional units of police, judiciary, Ghana education services
	Regional development corporations
	Regional branches of public corporations
	Parastatals
District administration (including district units of civil service)	District units of police, judiciary, Ghana education services
Local administration (including Local Council, Town/Village Development Committee)	

to discharge the functions of local government—albeit under the supervision and ultimate control of the district officers. These district officials often exercised considerable autonomous powers in their rural areas, although they were assisted by branches of the technical departments, presided over by district department heads domiciled locally.

STAGNATION IN THE COLONIAL PUBLIC ADMINISTRATIVE SYSTEM

The colonial administrative system had been successful in consolidating British rule, pacifying conquered areas, maintaining law and order, and promoting the development of commercial, mining, and, to some extent, agricultural activities. Over time, however, it grew less capable of achieving its developmental goals, displaying an increasing tendency toward immobility in the interwar years. During this time, the Colonial Department of Agriculture was caught unawares by the outbreak of the swollen shoot disease that spread panic throughout the cocoa industry, the country's main foreign exchange earner. In the wake of this epidemic, the department did not provide a ready facility for diagnosing or prescribing a remedy.[4] Similarly, the Department of Commerce proved unable to mediate the dispute over cocoa prices between the country's many small farmers and the large purchasing firms, leading to the so-called cocoa holdups of the 1930s. Moreover, the native administrative system became increasingly unacceptable to the majority of the population living in the rural areas. The chiefs, on whom this system of administration relied, had themselves become sources of disruption. They extorted monies from the populace, accumulating land by fair or foul means and becoming the cause of intense political struggles.[5] The weakening of the native administration system is also explained by the activities of the educated elite, who vehemently opposed this system on the grounds that its members (and not the chiefs) were the ones who possessed the necessary qualifications and training for local and central administrative roles. Within the public service itself, frustrations became evident among the educated and experienced African bureaucrats over their lack of advancement opportunities.

These problems of public administration mounted during the late colonial period, adding fuel to the general anticolonial sentiment that prevailed from this time to the country's formal independence on 6 March 1957. As for the system of colonial administration itself, it was apparent that that system had had a most difficult time adapting to the social, political, and economic changes occurring in the country in the post–World War II period. The colonial officials, especially those assigned to the rural areas, found themselves pressed by social forces over which they exercised only limited control and to which they could respond with ad hoc improvisation only.[6] Thus, the handling of the swollen shoot disease was inept, as was the response to the dramatic shooting of ex-servicemen in 1948.[7] Viewed in terms of this inability to manage postwar traumas and instability, termination of imperial rule represented a failure on the part of the administrative service to cope with the pressures emanating from the environment.

PUBLIC ADMINISTRATION IN POSTCOLONIAL GHANA

With the advent of independence, the new government led by Dr. Kwame Nkrumah inaugurated some predictable changes in the administration of Ghana's public service. The service was given a new orientation to emphasize its role as an arm of the government (i.e., as an agency for implementing government policy rather than being tantamount in the public mind with the government itself). The old technical departments were divided up into ministries and placed under politically appointed ministers. Moreover, responsibility for recruiting civil servants was transferred from the Colonial Office to a constitutionally mandated Public Services Commission. Nevertheless, the basic structures and procedures of the colonial public service were largely maintained intact. Such British civil service traditions as anonymity, political neutrality, impartiality, and security of tenure were guaranteed in the Independence Constitution as well as in the General Orders and regulations introduced after the transfer of power to African hands.[8]

In the postcolonial period, however, certain inherited structures and administrative procedures did give rise to political and organizational problems. The colonial public service had not been given adequate preparation for the contingencies that were to arise following independence. A major difficulty arose from the fact that the colonial public service was part of the government, and its senior officers were involved in policy formulation as well as implementation. As noted above, this changed with independence, as the service was designated an arm of the government and expected to implement government policies faithfully. Nevertheless, the tensions resulting from this change in the role of the administrative arm were evident in the late 1950s when one of the authors visited Ghana and are reflected in Nkrumah's declaration that he would see to it that there were no "civil masters" as under colonial rule "but servants . . . carrying out the policy decided by the cabinet."[9] The colonial origins of the public service rendered it somewhat suspect in the eyes of nationalist politicians, and the methods and procedures it relied on were liable to public misinterpretation as tantamount to sabotage. Senior officers were regarded with suspicion, their loyalty to the new African-run regime being questioned by members of the new political elite and the Convention People's Party stalwarts. Referring to this problem of loyalty, Nkrumah spoke as follows:

to all those civil servants who feel that they cannot with a clear conscience give loyal service to the government, my advice is that they should resign from the service at once. It is our intention to tighten up the regulations and to wipe out the disloyal elements in the civil service, even if by doing so we suffer some temporary dislocations of service.[10]

Clearly, this tension between the senior administrative service and the political leadership was complicated by a civil service structure that appeared racist in its composition, the senior positions being largely in European hands. To many members of the Ghanaian public, it appeared that some European officers were simply unwilling to take orders from their African superiors.[11]

Conflicts between the government and the senior administrative service also reflected class and generational issues. The senior public servants were by and large older and better educated than their political counterparts. Consequently, they tended to be on a higher social ranking than those who had just entered the top positions of government. However, the new men of power were determined to deal effectively with any competition from among the bureaucrats in favor of the new officeholders.[12] Although this represented a not surprising response to interelite competition, it had the deleterious effect of heightening public service attitudes of cynicism and noncooperation at a critical time in the development of the country's political system.

Perhaps the most serious problem that the Ghanaian public service faced immediately after independence was the proper response to the public's call for rapid economic and social development. In the past, the colonial bureaucracy had been structured to service the limited needs of British authorities for extraction of revenues and for maintenance of law and order. As such, its methods were largely oriented toward routines and toward compliance with well-established procedures. However, with the coming of independence, the activities of government were greatly expanded, in part because of the requirement of statehood and in part in response to the demands of the citizenry for new resources and opportunities. Programs to develop the economic and social infrastructure were initiated, with the public service being expected to provide the administrative support for such programs. Inveighing against the public service's alleged lack of commitment to the new activities sponsored by the state, Nkrumah spoke as follows:

It amazes me that up to the present, many civil servants do not realise that we are living in a revolutionary era. This Ghana which has lost so much time serving colonial authorities, cannot afford to be tied down to archaic snail-pace methods of work which obstruct expeditious progress. . . . Civil servants therefore must develop a new sense of mission and urgency, to enable them to eliminate all tendencies towards red-tapism, bureaucracy and waste. Civil Servants must use their initiative to make the Civil Service an effective instrument in the rapid development of Ghana.[13]

In Nkrumah's eyes, the postcolonial situation required a reorientation of the colonially established bureaucracy, in terms of both its functions and values. He insisted on the bureaucracy's commitment to the goals of his administration, not a spirit of detachment and rationality characteristic of the older order. This call for transformed attitudes and practices has not been met, however. As the next section indicates, the demand by Nkrumah and successor regimes for reform and adaptation met with a resistance that could not be anticipated during the heady moments of the decolonization process.

POSTCOLONIAL PROBLEMS AND ADAPTATIONS

The public service underwent major changes soon after power was transferred to a nationalist regime. The Nkrumah regime's goals of increased capacity on the part of the service to implement its development program of strengthened cabinet control over the various institutions of the state led inevitably to efforts to reorganize the inherited administrative service. Hence, the Nkrumah regime created new ministries and departments to undertake such functions as foreign affairs and defense, activities that had not been needed or not been run autonomously by authorities in the former Gold Coast. Other ministries or departments were enlarged in order to be able to cope with the new programs initiated by the Convention People's party and its government. For example, the departments of Social Welfare and Community Development and Education were greatly expanded, and the various armed forces and the prisons services were expanded. In the cases of the armed forces and prisons, this increase in size and capacity is partly explained by the government's determination to consolidate the regime's rule, and in particular to put down evidence of armed resistance in such areas as Ashanti and Togoland.[14]

To overcome the perceived problems of civil service inflexibility, lack of dynamism, and political unreliability, the Nkrumah government created several new agencies and placed them directly under the prime minister's (and subsequently, the president's) authority. These agencies included the State Planning Commission, the Ghana Education Trust, the Ghana Academy of Sciences, the Medical Research Council, and the Publicity Secretariat. In other cases, existing agencies were removed from civil service authority as normally practiced and placed under direct presidential control. Such agencies were expected to operate without the encumbrances of civil service procedures and regulations, for the new regime held these to blame for the alleged inertia and lack of initiative they considered to be manifest in the Ghanaian public service.

Typical of these unorthodox agencies was the Ghana Education Trust which was formed in 1957 to spur elementary education. At its beginning, it was given a grant of £2 million, the funds being allocated even before the National Assembly could meet and agree on this expenditure item. In addition, the Trust's procedure for awarding contracts diverged noticeably from standard civil service practices. It adopted a system of "negotiated contracts" which allowed for the selection of contractors prior to agreement on prices. The Trust neither advertised bidding in a public manner nor submitted the final contracts to the Central Tenders Board, presumably in order to circumvent the "laborious procedures of formal tender, excessive documentation and bureaucracy."[15]

Perhaps the most significant change in the Nkrumah effort to reorganize the public service was its decision to increase the number of public corporations and other quasi-governmental agencies (or parastatals). Such bodies were publicly owned and manned, yet expected to operate on a commercially profitable basis. Although the colonial administrations had made use of such statutory corporations for commercial purposes in the past (in particular, the State Cocoa Marketing Board and its subsidiary, the Cocoa Purchasing Company and the Agricultural Development Corporation), their experience with such enterprises was minimal compared to that of the postcolonial regime.[16] By the end of 1965, sixty public corporations had been established in Ghana to provide a wide range of services. Notable among these were the Water and Sewerage Corporation, the State Insurance Corporation, the State Shipping Corporation, the United Ghana Farmers Council, the State Transport Corporation, and the Omnibus Services Authority. Other public corporations engaging directly in productive ventures were the State Pharmaceutical Corporation, the State Distilleries, the State Electronics Corporation, the State Fishing Corporation, and the State Farms Corporation. If capitalist entrepreneurs appeared to be slackening in their investments in independent and socialist-inclined Ghana, the Nkrumah regime was making up for this loss by heavy state investments in both production and distribution. The result clearly was a vast expansion in the size of the bureaucracy and the scope of its responsibilities.[17]

Although the government, in its haste to get on with the development process, saw little alternative to an expanded public corporate role, it was not keen to entrust this additional responsibility to the old-line civil service. As noted above, it regarded the civil service as routine-minded, conservative, and lacking in the necessary commitment. Hence, it sought to restrict this civil service role to its traditional pursuits and to allow the public corporations a large measure of autonomy in managing their day-to-day tasks. Initially, both the government and the National Assembly exercised a limited kind of supervisory control over the actions of the public corporations. However, with the decline in the functions and powers of the National Assembly in the 1960s, the president and his ministers assumed the main responsibility for watching over the activities of these public agencies.

A key element in the process of postcolonial reforms and adaptations was the Nkrumah administration's felt need to strengthen its political control over the public service. Because the new government regarded a European-dominated service to be somewhat insulated from its control, it moved rapidly after taking office to introduce measures of Africanization. Colonial regimes from the time of Governor Jordon Guggisberg had made some cautious moves toward Africanizing the civil service in the 1920s. The Watson Commission enquiring into the 1948 riots mentioned earlier, took note of those previous measures toward Africanization and declared that, "The Commission have recognised that it is the settled policy of the Gold Coast Government to encourage to the maximum possible extent the entry of Africans into the higher branches of the public service."[18] Yet for all their efforts, the upper echelons of the service remained firmly in the hands of European officials at the time Nkrumah came to office. Indeed, at independence, all permanent secretaries, regional commissioners, and the heads of the army, police, and prisons services were in European hands.[19]

Naturally, the nationalist regime found such a situation to be untenable. Its spokesmen considered the loyalty of some European officers suspect[20] and, in line with their promise to Africanize the public service after independence, progressively appointed Africans to sensitive posts in the bureaucracy. Between 1958 and 1960, the ratio of expatriate to African officers in the administrative class changed from parity to four-to-one in favor of the Africans. After 1961, this process of Africanization was further accelerated, for a series of government decisions terminated the appointment of overseas officers holding top service posts.

Nevertheless, a substantially Africanized public service was not necessarily the equivalent of a responsive and reform-minded one. A change in recruitment and promotion policies was not in fact accompanied by a significant transformation in attitudes toward work and civil service privilege. The new civil servants perceived the decolonizing process essentially as an opportunity to advance themselves personally. They wanted the benefits of office to be preserved and regarded any tampering with their perquisites of office to represent a kind of "reverse racism" which demanded sacrifices of them not previously sought from their European counterparts. In conceding to this demand for continuity in salaries and perquisites, the new government placed an enormous burden on the new state. Not only did it have fewer resources at its disposal for development purposes, but it was helping to establish a new mandarin class which was conservative in its political outlook and likely therefore to resist the egalitarian measures which the Convention People's party (CPP) and its leaders had promised the nation.

Under these circumstances, it was not surprising that the CPP resorted to direct actions intended to promote political responsiveness in the service. It created special departments and agencies outside the regular public service and placed them directly under the President's Office. It is noteworthy that most of these agencies (for example, the Presidential Guard and the Farmers' Council) ran parallel to the regular public service (i.e., the Ministries of Defense and Agriculture). In fact, this presidential sector of the public sector grew to encompass virtually all areas of public administration—from such central control agencies as the Auditor General's Department, the Civil Service Commission, the State Enterprises Commission, and the Establishment Secretariat to such politically important agencies within the regular civil service as the Budget Division of the Ministry of Finance and the Chieftaincy Secretariat of the Ministry of Local Government.

The 1960 Constitution and other basic laws of the republican era generally strengthened the regime's (and particularly the president's) control over the public service. The general public rarely questioned the president's ultimate power to appoint, promote, and discipline the civil service. Indicative of this new political control, the government renamed the Public Services Commission the Civil Service Commission. This new commission ceased to be an independent executive body with original jurisdiction over all branches and departments. Rather, its responsibilities were reduced to cover the civil service (and not the public service as before), and its role in appointments, promotions, and discipline was regarded as merely advisory. In addition, it became commonplace for the president and his ministers to issue directives that countermanded department policies and transferred (and in some cases, dismissed) recalcitrant senior officers from their posts.

The CPP regime also made use of ideological education to bring civil servants in line with its goals and purposes. The president and his close circle of advisers constantly exhorted public servants to conform to the party ideology, variously described as socialism, Nkrumahism, or consciencism.[21] Seminars were held for public servants and others at the Kwame Nkrumah Ideological Institute at Winneba for the express purpose of inculcating this worldview.

The government's capacity for control was increased not only at the center but in field administration as well. Under the Independence Constitution, the heads of the regional and district administrations were the senior career public servants who had been placed in charge of the field branches of the departments. The new CPP regime now replaced them with political appointees. It justified this move in terms of the impelling need to infuse the party's dynamism into the regional and district administrations. The regime was also determined to counteract the regionalist tendencies that it viewed as emerging from a partially autonomous field administration. Consequently, the new authorities at the center weakened the autonomous authority of the regional and district commissioners (as well as their administrative units), transforming these officers from subnational authorities to representatives of the CPP government in the rural areas. At the local level, a situation of countervailing power was promoted. The Town/Village Development Committees and their politically appointed chairmen now competed with local urban municipal councils and their civil servant heads for control. In this way, the regime hoped to diffuse regionalist tendencies and thereby to enhance its control over the society.

THE GROWTH OF ADMINISTRATIVE MALAISE

The regime's administrative reforms and adaptation did not lead to the improvements in civil service capabilities and efficiency that its spokespersons anticipated. Instead, red-tape, maladministration, and administrative corruption became readily apparent, causing heavy losses among the parastatals, grave budgetary deficits, and a loss of public purpose generally. Expressing his alarm over this deteriorating situation, Nkrumah, in one of his famous "Dawn Broadcasts," stated that, "I am aware that the evil of patronage finds a good deal of place in our society." Not only did he declare himself determined to "uproot" this evil, but he also went on to warn against civil service red-tape and lack of a sense of urgency.[22]

Rather than being "functional" in the sense of speeding up economic development by cutting down bureaucratic red-tape, as many political scientists have contended, commission after commission has documented the high costs of civil service corruption in terms of wasted fiscal resources, squandered service credibility, and lost public morale. Because corruption "undermines the dependability of government organizations it reduces government's capacity to respond to and control its environment."[23] Thus, a 1964 commission on irregularities and malpractices in the issuance of import licenses found that senior officers in the Ministry of Trade manipulated the issuance of licenses in such a way as to benefit their contacts and themselves and at great cost to the country.[24] Other evidence on administrative wrongdoing included a Commission of Inquiry into the Cocoa Purchasing Company, trade malpractices, and the operations of public institutions. The result was a crisis of confidence in the government and the bureaucracy which served it, damaging its capacity to rule in a fair and effective manner.

Although the sources of corruption and other administrative problems are many and complex, it is quite clear that some of the difficulties are attributable to the regime's efforts to overhaul the colonial structure of the bureaucracy as rapidly as feasible. The swift nature of the bureaucracy's expansion and Africanization put a severe strain on the country's meager administrative resources, particularly its fiscal and personnel resources. If Ghana possessed a relatively ample supply of bureaucratic talent at the time of independence (augmented by the expansion of university opportunities and the output of the newly established Ghana Institute of Management and Public Administration), this supply was quickly outstripped by the demands of the Nkrumah regime for structural transformation. Shortages of senior technical and management-level personnel placed severe limitations on the government's efforts to bring about social change. Tony Killick, analyzing the problems encountered by the parastatal enterprises, shows how personnel shortages affected public sector performance. He writes:

Nowhere did shortages of qualified personnel have a more critical impact than in the agencies responsible for the selection, creation and overall management of state manufacturing enterprises. In the fifties responsibility rested with the IDC but, although it was set up in 1951, it was not until 1953 that its first projects officer was appointed and he did not remain long in office. Throughout its history, the IDC was under great pressure to process a large number of potential state projects and was inadequately staffed to do the job. Precisely the same could be said of the Ministry of Industries. . . . The INDUSTRIAL STATISTICS shows there to have been a total of 53 manufacturing enterprises wholly or partly owned by the state in 1966, most of which had been created during the early sixties, but during most of these years there were fewer than twenty senior officers in the Ministry to plan and oversee this expansion as well as undertaking all the other responsibilities of the Ministry.[25]

Clearly, the combination of rapid expansion and Africanization in a situation of personnel shortages made inevitable the recruitment and promotion of less qualified people. The resulting loss in administrative effectiveness was the longer term consequence of this process.

When taken together, then, rapid expansion of bureaucratic tasks and personnel and overlapping and competing lines of authority created what Elliot Berg has so aptly described as an "administrative jungle," in which coordination was virtually nonexistent and duplication of activities commonplace.[26] The example of agricultural development is particularly illuminating in this respect. This broad field of responsibility was parceled out among the Ministry of Agriculture, the State Farms Corporation, the United Ghana Farmers Council, the agricultural wing of the Workers Brigade, and twenty-five other agencies. Like any other state corporation, moreover, control and supervision of the State Farms Corporation was divided among the President's Office, the responsible minister, the Ministry of Industries, the State Enterprises Secretariat, and the Board of Directors of the corporation. Such blurred lines of authority and duplication caused administrative controls to weaken and, in some instances, to break down entirely. Thus, the exercise of financial control by the Ministry of Finance and its Auditor General's Department was gravely complicated by the unorthodox structure of the civil service and the freedom of some agencies from civil service regulations and procedures. The President's Office made large disbursements from its Contingency Fund which could not be given a proper audit by the Auditor General's Office. Clearly, the fragmentation of administrative authority gravely undermined the process of financial accountability.

The diffusion of administrative responsibility led to mismanagement and corruption, and the attempt to subordinate the civil service to the CPP's political leadership created a feeling of insecurity, cynicism, and apathy on the part of many senior civil servants. Some of the ablest of these, including A. L. Adu and R. A. Gardiner, left the service at this time to take up positions with the United Nations or the Organization of African Unity, or other international organizations. Others, meanwhile, stayed at their posts in Ghana but became increasingly circumspect and inward-looking. This group of bureaucrats found a measure of security by complying in a strict manner with administrative procedures and general orders. It is noteworthy that a majority of these "survivors" were holdovers from the colonial service and, in some cases at least, had little hope of alternative employment in other countries.[27]

Finally, if the administrative service was fragmented by the Nkrumah reforms, it was at the same time overcentralized. To be sure, there was nothing new about the drive to centralize the public administrative structure in Ghana. Public administration had in fact been highly centralized during colonial times. However, the Independence Constitution, in an effort to safeguard ethnic and political minorities against an overweening political center, attempted to introduce a measure of decentralized authority by devolving a limited measure of autonomy to the regional assemblies.[28] However, soon after independence the CPP regime dismantled these provisions on devolution. This action was largely explained by Nkrumah's sense of urgency about consolidating political power and establishing an "energetic" executive at the center. The regional assemblies were quickly legislated out of existence, enabling the government to replace career public servants with political appointees at the regional and district levels. The early 1960s witnessed a further effort at centralization, for the Republican Constitution placed a number of additional governmental agencies (and their senior personnel) under the direct authority of the president.[29] Many analysts attribute the administrative ineffectiveness that became apparent during this period in large part to this determined drive to centralize the decision-making apparatus. These critics note, among other things, the tendency to make key decisions in Accra, far from the project being reviewed; to concentrate personnel at Accra, leaving the rural areas short of trained and experienced personnel; and to stifle local initiative by requiring that key decisions be referred to Accra.[30]

POST-NKRUMAH REFORMS

Following the 1966 military coup that toppled the Nkrumah government, the successor regimes were no less committed to civil service reform. In fact, some of the National Liberation Council's (NLC) first initiatives were intended to boost civil service morale and to make the service a more efficient instrument of administration. The NLC raised civil service salaries in an effort to bring new talent into the service and to remove salary inequities in the different parts of the bureaucracy.[31] It reintroduced the Public Services Commission, reintegrating former members into this body in an effort to provide continuity.[32] Clearly, something of a consensus had developed in the post-Nkrumah period over the importance of such a commission as a morale booster and as a guarantor of the service's integrity. This value agreement was reflected in part in successive constitutions (Chapter 18 of the 1969 and Chapter 12 of the 1979 Constitution), each of which provided for the establishment of an independent Public Services Commission.

The various post-Nkrumah regimes also showed an inclination to depoliticize the public service, especially with respect to the field administration. Thus, the NLC replaced the politically appointed district commissioners of the previous regime with district administrators (designated district chief executives) who were career civil servants. The NLC replaced the regional commissioners with career civil servants, then known as regional secretaries. It is important to note, however, that this change did not hold up for long. After a brief interlude, the NLC fell back on the practice of making noncareer appointments to the previously designated post of regional commissioner. Hence, it selected military and police officers for this post, and subsequent regimes continued in a similar vein, appointing politically trusted people to take on the duties of regional commissioner.

Without doubt, decentralization was to prove the most significant aspect in the post-Nkrumah reorganization plans. A broad-based agreement, in principle at least, emerged during this period on decentralization as the best and most efficient means of administrative organization in a resource-constrained situation such as Ghana's. Thus, three commissions of inquiry set up by the NLC regime to examine the public service, local government, and the Constitution all fundamentally concurred on the need for effective decentralization of state functions.[33] These recommendations were later included in the 1969 Constitution, which, in turn, provided the basis for the enabling legislation—in particular, the Local Administration Act, 1971, and its 1972 and 1974 amendments. As envisaged in this legislation, the district authorities were regarded as the linchpins of a decentralized field administration system.

The 1969 Constitution made the District Councils responsible for the administration of their areas.[34] These councils, which had responsibility for both the existing local government units and the district branches of the departments at the political center, were expected to provide all government services for their area, save for matters relating to national security and technology. The District Councils received general assistance from the Town/Village Development Committees, and, above the District Council, regional authorities played a coordinating and supervising role. Moreover, regional development corporations were created to complement this decentralized development scheme. These corporations were established to conduct businesses of an industrial, commercial, and agricultural nature along "sound commercial lines" (i.e., the criterion of profitability).[35] Although the purpose of this legislation was to set up effective commercial and business organizations at the regional level, these bodies, acting alone or in collaboration with private persons, all too often succumbed to the problems of maladministration and ineffectiveness.

In general, it seems fair to conclude that the desire for reform did not always match the capacity to put such changes into effect. The precipitous economic decline, especially the runaway inflation of the 1970s, negated the periodic salary adjustments, leaving those on fixed salaries in relatively difficult circumstances. As a consequence, many public servants resorted to a wide range of private entrepreneurial activities, seeking to supplement their meager incomes through their initiatives on the side. All too often, their worsening situations and the pressure of their kinspeople for the "benefits of modernity" made some of the less committed in their ranks susceptible to corrupt practices. What became known locally as "Kalabule," the diversion of state-distributed goods to private purposes, embezzlement, fraud, skimming, and theft, became commonplace among public servants (as well as the society in which they carried on their affairs).[36] Their preferred access to state-distributed and highly subsidized goods in the late 1970s was a distinct advantage in itself, and it gave them a power that could be used to personal benefit if particular individuals were so inclined that way.

Implementation of the decentralization program was halfhearted at best. The proposals of the mid–1960s were not put into effect until 1974, and, even then, they amounted to little more than a limited form of deconcentration. The district authorities were not provided with any authority over decision making or with the necessary financial support for effective performance. For example, the central government retained a virtual monopoly over taxation, leaving local government units dependent on a combination of grants from the political center and whatever monies they could extract from local levies.[37] In addition the field administrative units (the regional and district authorities) continued to operate without an effective local base; their personnel consisted of appointed government employees who had not established a local mandate for themselves through some kind of election process. Moreover, the regional commissioners and the district chief executives lacked effective control over the local government officers under their jurisdiction, largely because the officers looked primarily to their central headquarters in Accra for an authoritative statement of position on critical issues.[38]

If the weak implementation of the decentralization proposals represented "sins of omission," the failure of reforms in other areas of the administrative process could be considered "sins of commission." Statist inclinations, which receded somewhat under the NLC, returned in full force under General I. K. Acheampong's National Redemption Council/Supreme Military Council (NRC/SMC) regime in the 1970s. The central government was immersed in various aspects of the production and distribution processes. Government intervention in the distributive process gave certain public officials broad opportunities for misuse of their positions. For example, the 1979 auditor-general's report noted extensive embezzlement on the part of a number of Ghana National Trading Corporation officials during the Acheampong period.[39]

If post-Nkrumah public service reforms appeared to make some limited progress, it was not reflected in the importance and prestige enjoyed by that service at this time. Various and diverse factors account for the persistence of such high status. First, the public service continued to expand in terms of size and functions. After a brief period of limited growth under the NLC (with its emphasis on the virtues of private sector activity), a rapid process of public service expansion resumed. This enlargement was especially evident during the Acheampong years, when statist intention in the economic sphere resumed in full force. As noted above, the Acheampong regime took a majority of shares in a number of foreign-owned companies. In addition, through such agencies as the Food Distribution Corporation, the State Farms Corporation, and various consumer cooperatives, it returned to state procurement and distribution of both consumer and capital goods. Such a process was bound to result in an increased role for the public service, whose total personnel expanded at an annual rate of 19 percent between the years 1975 and 1979.[40]

Second, the prevailing instability of the regimes of the 1970s and 1980s tended, albeit indirectly, to make the public service seem an institution of continuity, thereby enhancing the prestige of its members. By comparison with the politicians, public service institutions and personnel were increasingly regarded as representing the permanent, ongoing element in state-organized activities in the post–1966 period. Indeed, the various military and civilian regimes ruled in close collaboration with their civil service advisers, and, not surprisingly, these senior cadres gained additional influence from this association, being viewed as "experts." It is noteworthy, for example, that the NLC Administrative Committee was composed solely of civil servants and that the Economic Advisory Committee included E. N. Omaboe, the chief government statistician, and six other high-ranking civil servants from important ministries. Policy functions formerly dealt with by CPP ministers now became the responsibility of principal secretaries and other heads of departments. In the early phase of NLC rule, the government asked the most senior officers in the regional and district administrations to serve as the regional and district commissioners. On the whole, then, senior civil servants have gained in status and power under the military regimes, serving on various ad hoc committees, commissions of inquiry, and the boards of public corporations. During this time, a number of super-civil servants can be said to have emerged: E. N. Omaboe, A. L. Adu, and Justice Nii Amaa Ollenu under the NLC regime, and Robert Gardiner, E. K. Buckman, and Anane Benefo under the NRC/SMC regime.

This increased public service responsibility and enhanced prestige were not without cost. Although the public held high expectations as for civil service performance in a period of reforms, the bureaucrats' actual ability to perform remained substantially unchanged, if not diminished. Faced with the perennial constraints of centralization, inadequate skilled personnel, limited financial resources, and an environment conducive of corruption, the post-Nkrumah public servant was unable to take advantage of this involvement in the decision-making process to establish a more effective and responsive posture. By the late 1970s, evidence of economic and social decline was apparent. Agricultural and industrial production had fallen off sharply, and the quality of life indicators were moving in a negative direction. The result was widespread disaffection with and alienation from the government and public institutions, including the parastatals, the state marketing boards, and the ministries. In the eyes of the general public, the entire civil service, and especially its senior officers, were to be identified with an inefficient governmental apparatus and its declining social and economic infrastructure. This was not in fact an accurate perception in many instances, as public service officers were sometimes the victims of the general economic and social malaise gripping the entire country. But accurate or not, such a perception and its accompanying antibureaucratic sentiment became an important element in the general populist sentiment brought to the fore by Flight Lieutenant Jerry John Rawlings and the regime he helped to father on 31 December 1981.

THE RAWLINGS "REVOLUTION" AND PUBLIC SERVICE

By the end of the SMC's rule, public service was in considerable disarray. It had lost much of its capacity to administer development and to organize and operate state services. Its institutions had suffered a decline in legitimacy, especially as some of its senior officials had gravely compromised their positions. Bureaucrats routinely ignored normal accounting procedures; controls seemed ineffective; and corruption and other forms of malfeasance seemed widespread. It was a period of considerable demoralization, both within the public service and among the public at large.

The brief Rawlings interregnum of June 1979 gave a foretaste of the intended populist reforms in store for the country. Immediately after taking power, the Armed Forces Revolutionary Council (AFRC) began an overhaul of the public service, purging officers deemed corrupt or unsympathetic with its objectives. A number of senior civil servants or high ranking officials in the parastatal organizations were abruptly dismissed from office or forced to retire. The AFRC abolished the posts of principal secretary and supervising senior secretary, the two highest positions in the civil service as previously constituted, and "dissolved" the Cocoa Marketing Board in its entirety. Public officials suspected of serious wrongdoing were criminally indicted and then placed on trial in the "revolutionary" courts set up by the AFRC. As might be expected, the sentences meted out by these courts were severe indeed. Such heavy-handed measures, depicted by some as a purge, had two clear objectives: to rid the civil service of those officials who had collaborated improperly with the Acheampong regime, and to reestablish, forcefully, the notion of the public accountability of state officials.[41]

The impetus toward reform given by the AFRC program was not, however, sustained by Dr. Hilla Limann's constitutionally elected regime of September 1979. Under his People's National party (PNP) regime, state bureaucratic institutions continued to decline in terms of capabilities and to lose legitimacy in the eyes of the general public.[42] Moreover, the "housekeeping" operations undertaken by Rawlings and his AFRC had precipitated a drop in civil service morale as well as a weakening in the chain of command among its various agencies. Limann's PNP government, unable to get the stalled economy back on track, could not long survive in this weakened state, and consequently fell from power with the first push from a determined "military" opposition.

RAWLINGS' POPULIST REFORMS

The Provisional National Defence Council (PNDC) was the ruling body established following the coup of 31 December 1981. It consisted of three military and three civilian members under the leadership of Flight Lieutenant Rawlings. Upon assuming power, Rawlings appointed sixteen secretaries, accountable to the PNDC, to run the ministries. The PNDC's views on Ghana's public service ran the gamut from conventional perceptions of it as inefficient and overly centralized to radical perceptions of it as representing and perpetuating structural linkages with an inequitable world capitalist order. These populist and radical outlooks converge, however, in looking on the current ineffectiveness of the civil service as arising from the continuing "colonial mentality" of the senior officers, who remain elitist and prone to a misuse of office for private purposes.[43] Consequently, the members of both schools have placed the reform of the public service very high on the PNDC agenda. As an early PNDC policy statement put the matter: "Any revolutionary transformation, in order to be truly effective, must aim at a complete and radical change of . . . the existing social, political and economic structures . . . within the government machinery."[44] The PNDC also declared that the various ministries and parastatal bodies would be examined to determine whether they had been responsible for furthering foreign interests in the country. Where these public institutions had failed to promote the national interest, the PNDC promised to restructure them as necessary.[45] From the very outset, then, the public service was given a clear signal that a major overhaul was impending.

As part of its promised reform effort, the PNDC soon resumed the purges of the civil service started earlier under the AFRC. It established committees of inquiry and investigative boards to probe the operations of public agencies and the conduct of their officials. Following the institution of extralegal courts and tribunals to try public servants suspected of corruption and other offenses, interdictions, suspensions, dismissals, and forced retirements became commonplace. For example, in November 1982 the government announced that it had dismissed twenty senior public officials for corruption and misuse of public office, including six managers of the Ghana Industrial Holding Corporation (GIHOC), nine Health Ministry officials, and five senior staff of the Ghanaian Enterprises Development Commission.[46] Some of the sentences meted out by the extralegal courts resulted in very severe punishments for politician and civil servant alike. Thus, public tribunals have sentenced a number of public officials to be executed by firing squads. In November 1985, for example, it was reported that the Brong-Ahafo Regional Public Tribunal condemned a district purchasing officer to death for conspiring to commit an offense and doing an act with intent to sabotage the economy.[47]

In an effort to institutionalize a greater role for the public in watching over the activities of civil servants and in participating in affairs of state, the PNDC created a number of new populist organizations known as Peoples' Defense Committees (PDCS) and Workers' Defense Committees (WDCs). These organizations were composed largely of junior staff, senior officers being excluded for the most part. These organizations worked in close liaison with the army and police in enforcing PNDC laws and decrees and helped the government to implement its policies on rent and price controls. They also kept a close watch over the activities of the senior civil servants, reporting instances of abuse of office and disloyalty to the new regime. Moreover, they went beyond this watchdog role to changes in personnel, structures, and procedures regarded as desirable. Indeed, during the early days of the "Revolution," the junior staff can be said to have assumed critical administrative and supervisory powers in a number of public agencies. For instance, the workers in the partly state-owned Ghana Textile Printing Company seized the company. They ordered the expatriate manager to return home and declared the assets and accounts of the company to be held in the name of the "people." On the orders of their respective WDC/PDCs, the country's three universities were closed down, and at the National Commission for Democracy (formerly, the Electoral Commission), the PDC/WDC declared the chairman "banned" from office. It was also reported that the Central WDC in Accra had announced the suspension of the General Orders that had governed civil service procedures from the days of colonial rule. Such initiatives were reported in the mass media as examples of heroic deeds carried out by the workers in the name of the Revolution. Thus, Ebo Tawiah, a PNDC member, reportedly declared that the actions of the Ghana Textile Workers were "clear example[s] of the historic vigilance of the working class to protect themselves and the national interest."[48]

In addition to these populist reforms, the PNDC also attempted to institute structural reforms. It appointed a seven-member committee for the express purpose of restructuring the top positions in the civil service, an exercise it described as "liberating the monopolistic advising mechanism at the top."[49] Moreover, the managements of various public boards and corporations were dismissed, and interim management committees were appointed in their place. The PNDC also undertook a program of redeployment and retraining, laying off redundant workers and retraining them for other positions. Under this program, the Cocoa Marketing Board was expected to redeploy some 27,500 employees over a five-year period to help restore the country's once-leading position as a marketer of cocoa and cocoa products on the world scene. The regime charged the National Mobilization Committee with responsibility for coordinating the retraining and absorption of redeployed workers into agricultural activities in the rural area.[50]

Probably the most significant effort at structural reform has been the regime's decentralization initiative. In 1982, the PNDC's Policy Guidelines noted an intention to decentralize the country's public services and their staffs. Viewing decentralization as complementing its wider efforts at promoting democratization and efficiency, the new regime announced a comprehensive and systematic eleven-point program in late 1982 for putting decentralization into effect. Similar in many respects to the plans for decentralization put forward by the Acheampong regime, the PNDC proposed that the District Councils be the basic units of field administration. However, the PNDC scheme went on from there to call for a strengthening of grassroots involvement through an increased role for the local Ward and Village Development Committees and PDC's. Between December 1982 and January 1983, the first phase of the program set out in the Policy Guidelines was carried out. The government launched an intensive program to educate the general public as to the merits of the plan and the modalities of its implementation, and it moved ahead on schedule to appoint PNDC district secretaries. In addition, the Ministry of Local Government, charged by Rawlings with the main responsibility for implementing the decentralization plan, submitted its policy guidelines for the formulation of central, regional, and district decentralization on schedule. In making its provisional estimates for the last quarter of the 1982 fiscal year, the PNDC showed its commitment to the program by providing the funds to speed up the decentralization initiative.[51]

The Rawlings reforms of the civil service have not been without their problems. The combined AFRC-PNDC purges have had a demoralizing effect on the public service, especially its senior officers. The strident rhetoric of these regimes against the Ghanaian middle-class establishment and their encouragement of militancy on the part of workers and junior staff officers spread considerable alarm among the administrative and managerial classes. Rightly or wrongly, some of these senior public officials have perceived themselves as targets of the Rawlings' "Revolution." They have responded by voluntarily resigning from public service and, in some cases, leaving the country. Others have stayed on, performing their duties in an apathetic and lethargic manner. Populism has thus displayed its own productivity-inhibiting tendencies. Militant workers have been known to lock out management, to overturn long-standing agency policies, and to disrupt the previously accepted line of command in their various organizations.

As the implications of such behavior became apparent to those in power, the PNDC came to feel that it had little choice but to rein in what were euphemistically described as "revolutionary excesses." In 1984, the PNDC transformed the PDCs and WDCs into Committees for the Defense of the Revolution, narrowing their functions as far as possible to the mobilization of public support for the regime's developmental objectives.[52] The government also tried to appease the middle-class establishment by altering earlier practices on appointments, allocations, control of the judicial process, and jurisdictions of the people's and worker's councils and by stressing the importance of productivity over what it now described as "populist nonsense."[53] In brief, PNDC populist rhetoric was now joined with a new sense of pragmatism.

It is also important to note that the Rawlings regime's various economic reforms and austerity measures (e.g., wage controls, removal of subsidies, and so forth) have worked a decided hardship on the civil service, with its dependence on fixed incomes. This, in turn, has led to considerable restlessness and alienation among the junior civil servants, whose continued political support is indispensable to the PNDC. Among the senior-level civil servants, hard times have also become evident. Some of them have found it difficult to maintain their middle-class lifestyles, falling into a category described as "the respectable poor."[54] The civil service has displayed signs of demoralization and resentment over what seems to it to be inadequate rewards for meritorious service. The net effect has been a decline in administrative effectiveness and, exacerbating this problem, a loss of key personnel, as managerial and administrative talent has continued to depart from the bureaucracy for opportunities elsewhere.

At the same time that it has become apparent that populist reforms and economic rationalization have complicated the task of running a public service in Ghana, it is also important to note that the PNDC's structural reforms have yet to materialize in any significant fashion. The redeployment exercise has encountered public misgivings, especially among the trade unionists.[55] In addition, early hopes of a smooth implementation of the decentralization plan dimmed, as Rawlings and others felt it necessary to warn the public against expecting any kind of parallel structures of government to emerge in Ghana during his administration.[56]

Although the PNDC moved cautiously to implement the politically difficult stages of the decentralization plan (in particular, the redeployment of personnel from the central ministries to the local units and the devolution of administrative autonomy and fiscal responsibility), indications as to the government's wishes became evident in 1987.[57] In order to facilitate domestic resource mobilization at the local level, the PNDC administration stated its intention to create district assemblies after the District Council elections. These assemblies would be the highest political authority in each district for the purposes of socioeconomic planning and financial management.[58] Described as "an important step in the PNDC's program of evolving national political authority through [a] democratic process," the document outlining the government's plan regarding these bodies stated that "such political and administrative authorities will make and implement decisions and engage in activities required to meet the needs of the people in the areas under their jurisdiction in economic, cultural, educational and recreational services." In assigning the district assemblies a broad array of tasks involving the development of agriculture, industry, transport, construction, and so forth, the government statement was careful to note that these activities would "be performed within the framework of policies determined by the national political authority without prejudice to the initiative, imagination and creativity of the people in the local authority area."[59] The PNDC administration was taking no chances of creating a parallel system of government.

As envisaged by the PNDC statement, 110 administrative districts are to be set up throughout the country. Each district will have its own assembly, composed of a district secretary (who presides over the meetings of the assembly's Executive Committee), two-thirds of the members directly elected by the public, and one-third, consisting of the traditional authorities or others, appointed by the central government after consultations with various local interests. The district assemblies are to prepare budgets for approval by the central government; they are also to have deliberative, legislative, and executive functions, "subject to the general guidance and direction of the Central Government as to national policy," over a wide variety of socioeconomic programs and responsibilities.[60]

Not only must the National Commission for Democracy work out the relationship between the district assemblies and the national political institutions to be created in the future, but the Rawlings regime must act to inspire public interest and involvement in the new administrative bodies. Thus far, considerable public apathy (described locally as a "culture of silence") seems in evidence. In part to create more public support for the regime and its institutions, Rawlings announced plans to hold elections in 1988 for the district assemblies, and registration assistants reportedly were lodged at key vantage points waiting to enroll qualified persons as voters. When an embarrassingly small number of eligible persons came forward to participate, the registration assistants went from door to door enrolling potential voters.[61] The difficulties of mobilizing public participation from the top downward had become evident. As one correspondent noted: "The absence of enthusiasm in the voter registration exercise shows that the PNDC has not, in nearly six years, succeeded in tuning the minds of Ghanaians to its new political democracy which is devoid of 'political party politics.' "[62]

If the Rawlings regime has sought to appease the middle class's concern over declines in productivity, the alienation of key administrators, and the exodus of senior public servants from government employment, it has had to pay dearly for this effort. Its belated concessions to the middle class have provoked considerable anger from its original working-class and leftist supporters, who now complain about the loss of "revolutionary gains" and the consolidation of the "forces of reaction."[63] Nevertheless, some short-term improvements in civil service morale and efficiency surfaced by the end of the second year of a somewhat chastened Rawlings administration. The signs are varied and include the Cocoa Board's and GIHOC's return to profitability, improvements in a number of state services (in particular, public transportation), restraints in monetary expansion, and a reduction in budgetary deficits.[64] Real gross domestic product (GDP) grew by 5.1 percent in 1985, and this rate improved modestly to 5.3 percent in 1986.[65]

The problems besetting the Ghanaian administrative system are far from resolved, however. The relations between the PNDC regime and the public service, especially its senior officials, remain tenuous. The limited measures of reconciliation continue to be counterbalanced by publicly stated criticisms and suspicions. Much as before, government spokespersons persist in describing the service and its officers as neo-colonial, parasitic, and even subversive. They also express frustration over what they allege is the service's lack of responsiveness to political direction and point to what they regard as a low implementation capacity.[66] Some government spokespersons have explained the slow implementation of the decentralization scheme on civil service bad faith, noting what they describe as the "characteristic intrigues" of public servants in Ghana.[67] In addition, corruption among public officials remains endemic despite all the exposures and prosecutions of the early years of the "Revolution."[68]

Yet despite these suspicions and recriminations on both sides of the civil service-PNDC dialogue, the Rawlings government did make some moves toward reconciliation in the 1987–1988 period. In an effort to improve the interface between the senior civil service and the political authorities, as well as to attract high-level managerial talent into the service, in February 1988 the government announced plans to reorganize the civil service. Henceforth a chief director would be appointed in each ministry to serve as the link between the political authorities and the bureaucracy. This chief director would be a noncareer officer appointed by the head of state in consultation with the Public Services Administration, and that person would be given a renewable four-year appointment. In addition, steps were announced to pare down the size of the civil service. Under a program of redeployment, the PNDC announced plans to lay off redundant public employees and to redirect them into employment outside of the government sector. Under this program, a total of 45,000 people are to be discharged from the civil service and the Ghana Education Service between 1987 and 1989. The Rawlings administration established a Redeployment Management Committee and charged it with responsibility for discharging, compensating, restraining, and resettling those affected by the exercise. A similar exercise is also to take effect in the Cocoa Board (formerly the Cocoa Marketing Board) where 27,000 workers are to be discharged over a five-year period. Because of the serious implications of this program, the PNDC appears to be moving ahead cautiously in implementing it.

CONCLUSION: TOWARD A NEW BALANCE

The picture of the Ghanaian public service emerging from this analysis brings into focus a number of prominent features: colonial origins; a greatly expanded size and scope in the postcolonial period; a tendency to concentrate administrative and supervisory activities at the political center; an eroding legitimacy in the eyes of the general public; and an inability to alter norms of behavior or to perform in an efficient manner. To be sure, the public service carried on with an inadequate and rapidly deteriorating administrative structure, but its incapacity to meet Rawlings' performance expectations involved more than fiscal weakness, inadequate secretarial support, or a deteriorating telephone or transportation system. In Rawlings' view, this limp performance can also be explained by something broader, what he described as a lack of commitment to the objectives of his "Revolution."

The persistence of such problems in the face of repeated reform efforts requires the observer to look for broader, multicausal explanations of the difficulties at hand. Clearly, part of the explanation for these difficulties can be traced to the apparent fragility or "softness" of the Ghanaian state and to its dependent and underdeveloped economy. As is the case in many similarly situated African polities, state structures are overdeveloped in terms of the resources that can be extracted from society. If politicians can agree on public policies, they are unable, for want of fiscal resources and trained personnel, to implement these programs and to monitor the results. The state's bureaucracy is large but programmatically ineffective, costly but relatively unproductive, fully extended but unable to control. It bears considerable responsibility for creating the scarcity that limits public choice.[69] The postcolonial states emphasized the development of bureaucratic (public service, military, and police) institutions at the expense of other state structures, such as legislatures, judiciaries, and constitutions. These structures were viewed as impeding their consolidation of power and their promotion of rapid economic development. But the state expanded bureaucratic institutions at a time when financial and other resources were severely strained, thus creating administrative loads that were in excess of its capacity.

Chronic shortages in skilled and experienced personnel persisted throughout independence times. Yet these strains became more noticeable in the 1980s as the "brain drain" siphoned off scarce talent and as the gains of past administrative training programs seemed to disappear. Although reliable data on the magnitude of the brain drain are difficult to come by, signs of an extensive exodus of talent are at hand. In 1982, for example, there were reports of 14,000 trained teachers leaving the Ghana Education Service, approximately 3,000 of whom were university graduates. Moreover, another report indicates that 1,218 Ghanaian doctors and nurses were practicing in one of the nineteen states of Nigeria.[70] Clearly, Ghana had become a major aid giver. Its schools and universities had educated many trained and experienced professionals who were now using their skills to the advantage of other countries.

The emphasis on the development of bureaucratic institutions was accompanied by the emergence of well-defined interests within the bureaucratic apparatus. The corporate interests of the public servants (which may be defined to include the capacity to influence policy making and implementation, as well as to achieve satisfaction for their own psychic and material needs) were well served by the state's extensive involvement in all aspects of allocating public values. From their strategic positions within the administrative apparatus, public servants have been at a unique vantage point from which to advance their purposes. They have opposed and frustrated the implementation of reforms (i.e., decentralization, redeployment, and greater service accountability) which seemingly threatened their short-run corporate interests. On the other hand, they have pressed for such self-serving reforms as improvements in salaries and fringe benefits, the equalization of public and private sector incomes, and security of tenure.[71]

Ghanaian regimes, for their part, have considered it imperative to bring the public service under their full political control and to use the service to achieve their purposes. However, the effort to curb the autonomy of the public service has left the service demoralized and has weakened its public image and effectiveness. Like other state institutions in an environment of scarcity, the public service lacks an ability to achieve its tasks, contributing to a loss of public esteem and legitimacy. To be sure, this decline in legitimacy can be traced in part to other factors such as the colonial origins of the service and recurrent instances of corruption and misuse of office. Nevertheless, the perceived link between lackluster performance and low levels of credibility in the eyes of the public has rendered the bureaucracy vulnerable to assaults from political authorities and promoted the politicization of the service.

Administrative performance is also hampered by the weak internalization of bureaucratic values on the part of a number of bureaucrats. As Robert Price maintains, the "exogenously introduced bureaucratic organizations and their constituent positions have been institutionalized in their status but not in their role aspects."[72] Selective institutionalization (or internalization) of bureaucratic values has often meant that an ethic of self (or familial or solidarity group) service has developed over an "ethic of the public service."[73] The absence or weakness of formal regulations and codes of conduct combines with bureaucratic amoralism to promote the corruption, nepotism, and other abuses of office that have become so widespread in Ghanaian civil service history.

Pertinent questions may also be raised about the appropriateness of the Western organizational structures and infrastructure inherited from colonialism. Ghana's environment is marked by scarcity, uncertainty, and pluralism. Its society requires a public service capable of managing change and development under complex conditions.[74] Such an environmental context raises legitimate doubts as to whether the Weberian bureaucratic model can be adapted in a meaningful way to its circumstances.[75] Seen from this perspective, successive administrative reforms in postcolonial times have failed to come to grips with some of the fundamental issues of a modern public service in Ghanaian circumstances: how to create an effective public service under soft state circumstances, how to establish a fit between bureaucratic loads and the service's capacity to achieve its tasks, how to avoid overcentralization while exerting sufficient control over field agencies and service personnel, and how to legitimate the public service and protect its integrity. Clearly, the public service must be reshaped and re-organized to achieve the desired goals of efficiency, responsiveness, and integrity. Yet, it is also apparent that politically inspired reforms that undermine the civil service's morale and sense of self-worth will prove counterproductive. What is needed is a sustained restructuring effort which will combine the zeal for populist transformation with a careful regard for those civil service values and procedures indispensable to system goals. In brief, a new balance must be struck between populist commitment and utilitarian continuity in order to assure the development of a civil service that can manage Ghana's development effectively and efficiently.

NOTES

1. For an earlier description of the composition of the Ghanaian public service after independence, see Victor C. Ferkiss, "The Role of the Public Services in Nigeria and Ghana," in F. Heady and S. Stokes (eds.), *Papers in Comparative Administration* (Ann Arbor: University of Michigan Press, 1962), pp. 173–206.

2. On this matter, see A. L. Adu, *The Civil Service in Commonwealth Africa* (London: Allen and Unwin, 1969).

3. On the comparison with the functions of a French "prefect," see David Apter, *The Gold Coast in Transition* (Princeton, N.J.: Princeton University Press, 1955), p. 13.

4. For a discussion of the swollen shoot disease and the government's handling of it, see Dennis Austin, *Politics in Ghana 1946–60* (London: Oxford University Press, 1970), pp. 49–102.

5. See K. A. Busia, *The Position of the Chief in the Modern Political System of Ashanti: A Study of the Influence of Contemporary Social Changes on Ashanti Political Institutions* (London: Oxford University Press, 1951), p. 209.

6. See Bruce Berman, "Structure and Process in the Bureaucratic States of Colonial Africa," *Development and Change* 15, 2 (April 1984), pp. 161–202.

7. See Austin, *Politics in Ghana*, pp. 73–74. On 28 February 1948, some 2,000 ex-servicemen marched on Christianborg Castle in Accra to present a petition to the governor. At the castle crossroads, their way was blocked by a police unit; in the growing disorder, a police officer seized a rifle and opened fire killing two servicemen and wounding several others. This action set off a series of riots in Accra and other parts of the country.

8. See *The Ghana (Constitution) Order-in-Council*, No. 51277 (1957).

9. Kwame Nkrumah, *I Speak of Freedom* (London: Heinemann Press, 1961), p. 27.

10. Ibid., pp. 172–73.

11. See Kenneth Younger, *The Public Service in the New States* (London: Oxford University Press, 1960), pp. 72–75.

12. On the growth of multiple and competing hierarchies in Nkrumah's Ghana, see Richard Crook, "Bureaucracy and Politics in Ghana: A Comparative Perspective," in P. Lyon and J. Manor (eds.), *Transfer and Transformation: Political Institutions in the New Commonwealth* (Leicester: Leicester University Press, 1983), p. 195.

13. Quoted in *Evening News* (Accra), 8 April 1961.

14. On fears of secessionist outcomes—that is, the splitup of "the country into mutually antagonistic fragments"—see Donald Rothchild, "On the Application of the Westminster Model to Ghana," *Centennial Review* 4, 4 (Fall 1960), p. 467.

15. The Trust's success in building thirty-one secondary schools by the end of 1960 was widely credited to its nonbureaucratic approach. See Ben Amonoo, *Ghana: The Politics of Institutional Dualism* (London: Allen and Unwin, 1981), p. 37.

16. See D. K. Greenstreet, "Public Corporations in Ghana," *The African Review* 3, 1 (1973), pp. 21–22.

17. On Nkrumah's alleged preference for public over private sector activities, see Tony Killick, *Development Economics in Action* (London: Heinemann Educational Books, 1978), pp. 36–38.

18. His Majesty's Colonial Office, *Statement by His Majesty's Government on the Report of the Commission of Enquiry into Disturbances in the Gold Coast 1948*, Colonial No. 232 (London: H.M.S.O., 1948), p. 10.

19. Amonoo, *Ghana*, pp. 26–27; and *Report of the Select Committee on Africanisation of the Public Service* (Accra: Government Printer, 1950), passim.

20. For a statement of an expatriate officer's ambivalence to the Nkrumah regime and its style of governance, see Major General H. T. Alexander, *African Tightrope* (London: Pall Mall Press, 1965), pp. 99, 108.

21. See Kwame Nkrumah, *Consciencism: Philosophy and Ideology for De-Colonization* (New York: Monthly Review Press, 1970), Chapter 4.

22. See *Evening News*, 8 April 1961.

23. Robert M. Price, *Society and Bureaucracy in Contemporary Ghana* (Berkeley: University of California Press, 1975), p. 145.

24. Ghana, *Report of Commission of Enquiry into Alleged Irregularities and Malpractices in Connection with the Issue of Import Licenses* (Accra: Ministry of Information and Broadcasting, 1964), pp. 12–13.

25. Killick, *Development Economics in Action*, p. 240.

26. Elliot Berg, "Structural Transformation Versus Gradualism: Recent Economic Development in Ghana and the Ivory Coast," in Philip Foster and Aristide R. Zolberg (eds.), *Ghana and the Ivory Coast* (Chicago: University of Chicago Press, 1971), p. 211.

27. Amonoo, *Ghana*, p. 54.

28. The provisions on devolution and the fate of the regional assemblies is discussed in Rothchild, "On the Application," pp. 476–82.

29. For further details on Nkrumah's efforts to centralize the administrative system, see Henry Bretton, *The Rise and Fall of Kwame Nkrumah* (New York: Praeger, 1967), and Naomi Chazan, *An Anatomy of Ghanaian Politics* (Boulder, Colo.: Westview Press, 1983), p. 65.

30. On the effects of overcentralization, see S. A. Nkrumah, "Atrophisation of Rural Ghana" (Ph.D. diss., New York University, 1979), Chapter 2.

31. *Report of the Commission on the Structure and Remuneration of the Public Services in Ghana* (Mills Odoi Commission) (Accra: Ghana Publishing Corp., 1967).

32. NLC Decree No. 112.

33. See *Mills Odoi Commission Report*; also see the *Report of the Commission of Enquiry into Electoral and Local Government Reform* (Siriboe Commission) (Accra: Government Printer, 1968); and *Proposals of the Constitution Commission for a Constitution for Ghana* (Akuffo-Addo Commission) (Accra: Ghana Publishing Corp., 1968).

34. Chapter 16, Article 158.

35. See Donald Rothchild, "Military Regime Performance: An Appraisal of the Ghana Experience, 1972–78," *Comparative Politics* 12, 4 (July 1980), pp. 469–70.

36. For details, see *Republic of Ghana, Third Interim Report of the Commission of Inquiry into Bribery and Corruption* (Accra: Ghana Publishing Corp., 1972), especially pp. 14–25.

37. On this subject, see Nkrumah, "Atrophisation," especially pp. 48–76, and Kweku Folson, "Mobilising and Managing Financial and Physical Resources under Decentralisation Schemes," a paper read at the United Nations Interregional Seminar on Decentralisation for Development, Khartoum, mimeo (September 1981), pp. 14–18.

38. Nkrumah, "Atrophisation" pp. 48–76.

39. Mike Oquaye, *Politics in Ghana 1972–1979* (Accra: Tornado Publications, 1980), p. 148.

40. Coralie Bryant and Louise White, *Managing Development in the Third World* (Boulder, Colo.: Westview Press, 1982), p. 31.

41. In carrying out this purge of the civil service, the AFRC was aided considerably by several commissions of inquiry set up by General Akuffo's SMC II regime in 1978. On this and other details of the AFRC "housekeeping" measures, see Emmanuel Hansen and Paul Collins, "The Army, the State and the Rawlings Revolution in Ghana," *African Affairs* 79, 314 (January 1980), pp. 3–24.

42. Donald Rothchild and E. Gyimah-Boadi, "Ghana's Return to Civilian Rule," *Africa Today* 28, 1 (1981), pp. 5–6, and Jon Kraus, "The Political Economy of Conflict in Ghana," *Africa Report* 25, 2 (March/April 1980), pp. 9–16.

43. See, for example, *Preamble to the Policy Guidelines of the Provisional National Defence Council* (Accra: Ghana Information Services, 1982), p. 5.

44. Ibid., pp. 4–5.

45. Ibid., p. 5.

46. *West Africa*, 22 November 1982, p. 3054. For further details, see E. Gyimah-Boadi and Donald Rothchild, "Rawlings, Populism and the Civil Liberties Tradition in Ghana," *Issue* 12, 3/4 (Fall/Winter 1982), pp. 64–69.

47. *West Africa*, 18 October 1982, p. 2742.

48. Ibid., 29 November 1982, p. 3111.

49. Ibid., 12 July 1982, p. 1841.

50. Ibid., 24/31 December 1984, pp. 2656–57.

51. *Ghana News* 11, 11 (November/December 1982). Since then, the government has appointed interim management committees to administer the regional and district councils.

52. Jon Kraus, "Ghana's Shift from Radical Populism," *Current History* 86, 520 (May 1987), p. 207.

53. This topic is discussed at length in Donald Rothchild and E. Gyimah-Boadi, "Ghana's Economic Decline and Development Strategies" in John Ravenhill (ed.), *Africa in Economic Crisis* (London: Macmillan, 1986), pp. 274–75.

54. For a discussion of the privations of Ghana's middle class under Rawlings, see "The Respectable Poor," *West Africa*, 25 July 1983, pp. 1710–11.

55. On this subject, see Rothchild and Gyimah-Boadi, "Ghana's Economic Decline," pp. 275–76. For a PNDC statement on the need for redeployment, see Republic of Ghana, *National Programme for Economic Development* (Accra: Ghana Publishing Corp., 1987), p. 17.

56. *West Africa*, 12 September 1983, p. 2103.

57. Interview with PNDC Chairman J. J. Rawlings, *Africa Report* 31, 6 (November-December 1986), p. 7.

58. *National Programme for Economic Development*, p. 22.

59. Republic of Ghana, *District Political Authority and Modalities for District Level Elections* (Accra: Ghana Publishing Corp., 1987), pp. 1–2.

60. Ibid., p. 3.

61. For comments on apathy and the elections, see *West Africa*, 30 November 1987, pp. 2339–40, 2367.

62. Nana Fredua-Agyeman, "Ghana: Shake the Fence," *West Africa*, 30 November 1987, p. 2339.

63. For statements by concerned organizations and individuals on these issues, see *West Africa*, 1 January 1985, p. 291.

64. Ghana Commercial Bank, *Quarterly Economic Review* 16, 1 (1983), p. 2; *West Africa*, 17 June 1984, pp. 1213–14; Mike Ocloo, "GIHOC Surges Ahead," *The Post* (Accra, April 1987), pp. 1, 14; and *Ghana News* 16, 2 (March-April 1987), pp. 6–8.

65. *Statement by Dr. Kwasi Botchwey . . . in Accra on February 20, 1987 on the State of the National Economy and the 1987 Budget* (Accra: Department of Information and Services, 1987), p. 1.

66. On allegations of civil service sabotage, see *West Africa*, 20 September 1982, p. 2462. Regarding lack of responsiveness to political direction, see the statement by Dr. Kwasi Botchwey, the PNDC secretary for finance and economic planning, in *West Africa*, 19 September 1983, p. 2205.

67. *People's Daily Graphic* (Accra), 14 March 1983, p. 1, and 17 April 1983, p. 1.

68. For a report on recent trials and executions of officials involved in bank frauds and embezzlement, see *West Africa*, 15 July 1985, pp. 1414–15.

69. On the concept of the "soft state," see Gunnar Myrdal, *The Asian Drama*, Vol. 2 (New York: Pantheon Books, 1968), pp. 895–96; for an application of this concept under African circumstances, see Donald Rothchild and Michael Foley, "Implications of Scarcity for Governance in Africa," *International Political Science Review* 4, 1 (1983), pp. 311–26.

70. *West Africa*, 6 September 1982, p. 2319, and Akin Adebayo, "Brain Drain Within ECOWAS Region," *ISSUE* 14 (1985), pp. 37–38.

71. For an excellent review of the administrative reforms in postcolonial Anglophone states, see Bernard Schaffer, "Administrative Legacies and Links in the Post-Colonial State: Preparation, Training and Administrative Reform," *Development and Change* 9, 2 (April 1978), pp. 175–200.

72. Price, *Society and Bureaucracy*, pp. 37–38.

73. On ethics in Africa's public life, see Peter Ekeh, "Colonialism and the Two Publics in Africa," *Comparative Studies in History and Society* 17, 1 (1975), pp. 91–112. Also see Goran Hyden, *No Shortcuts to Progress* (Berkeley: University of California Press, 1983), Chapter 2.

74. See the articles by J. R. Morris and W. J. Siffin in J. E. Black, J. S. Coleman, and L. Stiffel (eds.), *Education and Training for Public Sector Management in Developing Countries* (New York: Rockefeller Foundation, 1977). Also see Naomi Caiden and Aaron Wildavsky, *Planning and Budgeting in Poor Countries* (New York: John Wiley, 1974).

75. In Rawlings' words: "We are building our own system. . . . To do this, we may borrow from the experiences of others, those that will be suitable. But let it be clearly understood that we are cutting out our path, we are hammering out our own solutions." *The Process of Consolidation*, Vol. 3, *Selected Speeches and interviews of Flt.-Lt. Jerry John Rawlings, January 1, 1984–December 31, 1984* (Accra: Ghana Publishing Corp., 1985), p. 67.

11

NIGERIA

Ladipo Adamolekun
and Victor Ayeni

INTRODUCTION

Public administration as practiced in Nigeria can be defined as the administration of the public service which by the country's 1979 Constitution covers "the service of the Federation (or state) in any capacity in respect of the Government." This broad definition covers diverse activities and institutions such as the civil service, local government authorities, public enterprises, educational institutions, the armed forces, the police, the judiciary, and staff of the legislature. This broad conception of the scope of public administration is not peculiar to Nigeria, as it is found in many other Third World countries. However, the public administration system in Nigeria has some distinguishing features that are traceable to the peculiarities of the country's socioeconomic and political environments. The history, structure, and operation of Nigerian public administration sharply exhibit features that arise from the combined impact of a federal and populous society, the legacy of British colonialism, the persistence of political instability, an unreliable economic dependence on petroleum wealth, and the problems of technological underdevelopment.

The Federal Republic of Nigeria, with its constituent nineteen state-units, occupies a land area of over 356,669 square miles or 923,773 square kilometers within the tropical region. Latest estimates put the population at about 90 million which is increasing at a growth rate of about 2.5 percent. Over half of this population, which is generally put in the range of 60 to 70 percent, is said to be illiterate and resident in rural areas. The remaining 30 percent or so live in urban centers scattered around the country. Nigeria is a land of great diversity in both peoples and cultures. There are over 200 ethnic groups, each of which has its own customs, traditions, and language. These diversities are reinforced by the location of the major ethnic groups within distinct geographical regions and the preponderance of two rival religions: Islam in the north and Christianity in the south. These features provide the rationale for Nigeria's adoption of a federal system. At the same time, they have greatly complicated the political and administrative evolution of the Nigerian state.

In this chapter, we will examine the evolution of the Nigerian public administration system within its socioeconomic and political contexts. The discussion will be limited to the civil service, local government authorities, and public enterprises. We will exclude from detailed examination educational institutions, the armed forces, the police, the judiciary, and the defunct legislature (since the military coup of December 1983) which have some distinctive characteristics that separate them from the other services.

HISTORICAL BACKGROUND

The subsistence economy of the precolonial era was significantly transformed under colonial rule into a dependent extension of the worldwide capitalist economic system of the British rulers. The emphasis was on the production and export of tropical raw materials (notably cocoa, cotton, groundnuts, and palm oil) within Nigeria and on the importation of manufactured goods and a limited range of luxury items into Nigeria from Britain. This economic structure was maintained after independence with minor modifications until the advent of huge revenues from petroleum in the 1970s made possible giant strides in the provision of infrastructures and the expansion of activities in the industrial, manufacturing, and trading sectors. At about the same time, a conscious effort was made to increase the share of indigenous entrepreneurs in economic activities (the indigenization decrees of the 1970s), and it was formally asserted that the Nigerian state would control the "commanding heights" of the economy. A notable consequence of the economic policies of the 1970s was a huge increase in the scope of public sector organizations, especially the category that is commonly referred to as public enterprises or parastatals.

Toward the end of the 1970s, it was clear that the "easy" money from petroleum had led to a neglect of the agricultural sector. From a position of near sufficiency in food production before the oil boom, the country had become heavily dependent on food imports. To worsen matters, the international oil market became unstable, and the heavy reliance on oil revenue for between 75 and 90 percent of total foreign exchange earnings meant that the country's economic position became precarious. Since 1982, the economy has become depressed, and the efforts aimed at revamping it have had serious consequences for the public administration system. References will be made to these consequences in the appropriate sections of this chapter.

With regard to the political context of the Nigerian public administration system, the starting point is the manner in which the precolonial patterns of governance in the different parts of the country were forced to accommodate a "standard" colonial system called "Indirect Rule." This meant rule by the officers of the colonial administration through the intermediary of Nigerian tra-ditional leaders. In all cases, there was no question about the ultimate authority of the colonial officers. However, the pattern of "Anglo-African" partnership varied in different parts of the country. The pattern in the northern parts of the country was regarded as the "model," whereas varying degrees of difficulty were experienced in the southern parts. When the decolonization process eventually set in after the Second World War, the colonial administration officers agreed on the transplantation into Nigeria of British-style parliamentary government commonly referred to as the Westminster model.

At independence in 1960, it was widely accepted that the government and administration of Nigeria would follow the Westminster-Whitehall arrangement in Britain. For various reasons, the experiment collapsed in January 1966, and it was succeeded by a military government that remained in power (with four different heads of state) until September 1979. After the return of civilian rule in October 1979, a presidential system of government was adopted as a better alternative to the parliamentary system of government.[1] In practice, the expectations placed in the new system were not fulfilled, and civilian rule collapsed once again after only fifty-one months. The country had passed through four and half years of army rule by mid–1988 after the military came a second time.

To complete our examination of the political context of Nigerian public administration, it is important to mention the major political crises that have marked the twenty-five years under review. The most explosive crisis was the thirty-month civil war between 1967 and 1970. The other crisis situations were the census controversies of 1962–1963, the electoral conflicts of 1964–1965, the coups d'etat of 1966 (bis), 1975, and 1983 and the assassination of a head of state in 1976. The actual changes of government (each time without respect for the established rules), together with the political crises, highlighted above, add up to a very unstable political landscape within which the public administration system has had to evolve since independence. Before examining the salient features of the emerging postindependence public administration system in some detail, it will be useful to highlight the key features of the administrative arrangements transplanted into the country during the decolonization process.

ADMINISTRATIVE STRUCTURE

As already mentioned, the objective of both the Nigerian nationalist leaders and the British colonial administration officers was to transplant the Whitehall-Westminster politico-administrative arrangements into Nigeria in the 1950s. The key features of the administrative arrangements were as follows. First, the idea of a career civil service was adopted, and public service commissions were established (and guaranteed in the country's 1954 Constitution)[2] to manage and protect the service. It was expected that, as was the case in Britain, recruitment would be through open competition and the progress of each officer would be determined on the basis of performance and seniority. In other words, the civil service was to function on the basis of the merit principle.

A second important feature of the career civil service was that its members (especially those in the senior posts) were expected to observe the norms of anonymity, impartiality, and political neutrality. This requirement would enable them to serve successive teams of political leaders with loyalty. It was also expected that, as in Britain, Nigerian ministers would bear total responsibility for the conduct of government business (the doctrine of ministerial responsibility). Although the civil servants were to assist in policy formulation and to execute settled policies, they were to be named neither for praise nor for blame; praise and blame were to be reserved for the ministers in all circumstances.

Next, the actual structure of the machinery of government was organized along the same lines as the British government administration. Thus, there were ministries and departments of government which were placed directly under ministers. To accomplish this arrangement, it was necessary to reorganize the departments of the colonial administration secretariat which were headed by British officers. The report on which this exercise was based at the federal level was given the following revealing title: *Integration of Departments with Ministries with Special Reference to United Kingdom.*[3] The hierarchical (class) structure of the civil service and the grading of the officers were also established along lines similar to those that existed at the time in the United Kingdom.[4]

Furthermore, the aspects of government business that were organized outside the central machinery of government were entrusted to two British-inspired institutions: local governments and public or statutory corporations. Although Nigeria had a system of local governance prior to the 1950s, the new local governments were conceived as instruments for promoting local democracy and ensuring the effective administration of local affairs. The public corporations were formally constituted outside the ministries and departments under ministers with a view to allow them to function with some degree of autonomy.

A final feature of the Nigerian public administration system of the 1950s was its federal structure. Both the nationalist leaders and the British colonial rulers agreed that the peculiarities of the Nigerian milieu (some of which have been summarized above) called for a federal administration. It is possible that in preparing Nigeria's 1954 federal Constitution, the authors were inspired by the decision taken some years earlier to establish two former British colonies in Asia, India, and Pakistan as federations. From 1954 onward, the Nigerian federal administration system consisted of one central or federal government and three regional governments. The subsequent increase in the number of regional/state governments will be discussed later in this chapter.

Having highlighted the key features of the Nigerian public administration of the 1950s which were largely British-inspired, we will mention that the single most important activity that dominated the attention of government leaders at both the federal and regional levels was how to ensure that Nigerian officers took effective control of the administrative institutions. Specifically, the task before the governments was the replacement of serving British officers by Nigerians and the recruitment of trained Nigerians to posts in the emerging civil services of the federal and regional governments. This exercise was called the Nigerianization of the civil services. Notwithstanding the divergent interpretations given to the Nigerianization policy (notably the regional slants and the significant variations in respect of speed among the governments), the management of the four civil services was largely in the hands of Nigerians at independence in 1960. Thus, for example, all the holders of the topmost posts in the Western Nigerian civil service (called permanent secretaries) were Nigerians. Similarly, although there were only 172 Nigerians out of a total of 2,207 senior officers of the central government in 1948, the number of Nigerians had risen to 2,308 (out of a total of 4,057) in 1960.[5] Predictably, the implementation of the Nigerianization policy continued during the immediate postindependence years.

MAIN FEATURES OF ADMINISTRATION SINCE INDEPENDENCE

The Political Regimes

Attention has already been drawn to the great instability that has characterized the Nigerian political landscape since independence. One obvious question is the extent to which the changes in regime type have affected the emerging public administration system. A comparison of the current broad features of Nigerian public administration with the features of what existed in the 1950s (as summarized above) leads to the conclusion that there has been more continuity than change. The federal administration system was called into question only once, under military rule in 1966. But the unitary system that was adopted in its place had not become operational when the federal system was restored in the same year. Otherwise, all the regime types have accepted the idea of a career civil service together with a constitutional Public/Civil Service Commission to manage and protect it. The modifications introduced by both civilian and military governments in respect of the principles of permanency of tenure and merit have not yet amounted to a repudiation of both principles.

It is only in respect of the feature of administration at the meeting point between the political doctrine of ministerial responsibility and the administrative norms of anonymity, impartiality, and political neutrality that each of the three regime types has had its distinct impact. What emerged as the relationship between politics and administration under presidential government (1979–1983) was different in some significant respects from what had existed earlier under parliamentary government (1960–1966). The different military leadership teams (1966–1979; 1984–present) have failed to articulate new political or administrative doctrines and have been content with random modifications of what they inherited from the civilian governments—with the marginal exception of the

Babangida reforms discussed later. The result has been the evidence of both similarities and differences in the pattern of relationship between politics and administration under military rule on the one hand and under civilian governments on the other. This subject will be examined in some detail later in this chapter.

In many respects, then, changes in regime type have not had significant consequences for the country's public administration system.[6] It is possible that the quick succession of regimes and governments—seven heads of state in twenty-five years and three regime types—has prevented each regime or government from having a meaningful impact. This point is crucial. It is further underlined by the fact that none of the rulers has had a strong commitment to a distinct Nigerian-centered political ideological orientation. Instead, there has been a remarkable consistency in the efforts made to tinker with the administrative principles and practices inherited from the British. In examining the various aspects of the postindependence public administration system in the subsequent sections of this part, attention will be drawn to the continued impact of the British administrative legacy as well as to any innovations in respect of both administrative principles and practices.

The Executive

Structure and Organization: Federal and State

At both the federal and state levels, the central feature of governmental administration is the ministerial organization whose structure and functioning have remained largely unchanged since they were first constituted in the 1950s. Of course, the number of ministries has changed over the years, but the hierarchical organization and the division of work within each ministry have broadly remained unchanged. However, some important changes have taken place in the structure of the executive of each regime type. The structure of the presidential executive differed in some important respects from what existed under parliamentary government, and the structure of the military executive has certain characteristics that were unknown under the civilian governments.

Under parliamentary government, the prime minister, as head of the federal government, was responsible for the coordination of government work. The secretary to the government was the prime minister's key collaborator in carrying out this function. In addition to his role as the head of the government secretariat, the secretary to the government also served as the head (de facto) of the federal civil service whose members staffed the individual ministries headed by ministers. This structural arrangement was replicated at the regional level, and the coordinating role of the premiers (title of regional heads of government) was emphasized as at the federal level. Each of the regional governments had the additional advantage of a de jure head of the civil service who was formally charged with responsibility for providing leadership for the regional civil service under the overall direction of the premier.

The major change introduced under the presidential government consisted of the emphasis on an executive office of the president which was intended to serve as the nerve-center, the power house, of the federal government in a manner that was different from the coordinating role of the prime minister. Thus, a vice president and a number of special advisers assisted the president. The executive office of the president was headed by a secretary to the federal government who coordinated the work of government. The head of the federal civil service provided leadership for the career civil servants who, as was the case under parliamentary government, staffed the individual ministries headed by ministers. At the state level,* there was an executive office of the governor headed by a secretary to the government, as well as a deputy governor and a number of special advisers to assist the governor.

After the early months of uncertainty about the appropriate pattern of governmental structure (compounded by profound political problems), the structure of military executive that emerged from mid–1967 onward was similar to what existed under parliamentary government in most respects, with only one major difference. To assist the head of government (who was also the head of state)[†] in the coordination of government work at the federal level, there was a secretary to the federal military government who was also the de jure head of the civil service. As was the case under parliamentary government, the civil servants conducted government business within the individual ministries which were headed by selected political heads called commissioners. The major innovation was the existence of a supreme military council (SMC) consisting of the top-ranking military officers, the most senior police officer, and the military governors of the constituent states of the federation. The only civilian member was the attorney general of the federation. The SMC served as the national executive cum legislative body and as the institutional mechanism for coordinating the activities of the federal and state governments. (The federal executive council consisting of the political heads of ministries and presided over by the head of state, exercised executive power at a level lower than that of the SMC.)

The important point to note in the post–1967 arrangement was the quasi-unitary executive cum legislative body that ruled the country. All the military governors had their own state executive council with the same administrative support inherited from the civilians, but there was no question about the supremacy of the SMC. The new military leadership team that took over power in 1975 further accentuated the unitary power structure by excluding state military governors from the SMC. A new body called the National Council of States (NCS) was created comprising all members of the new SMC (old membership

---

*The three regions of 1954 were increased to four in 1963, and all four were restructured into twelve states in 1967. The number of states was increased to nineteen in 1976 and twenty-one in 1985.

[†] This arrangement was different from that which existed under parliamentary government when the head of state was distinct form the head of government.

excluding the state military governors) and the state military governors. The NCS served as the forum for monitoring and coordinating the activities of the federal and state governments. This post–1975 arrangement was adopted by the incumbent military leadership team that assumed power in 1983. Some of the changes introduced after 1985 are examined later in this chapter.

Another innovation of the 1975 military leadership was the emergence of a certain dualism in the structure of the military executive. While maintaining a secretary to the federal military government whose functions were defined, as was the case under the post–1967 arrangements, a small group of political technocrats, consisting partly of career civil servants and partly of outsiders, worked directly with the head of state and his immediate lieutenant, the chief of staff, supreme headquarters. The functions of this politico-technocratic body overlapped significantly with those of the secretary to the government, especially with regard to channeling policy advice. The incumbent military leadership had pushed this dualism further. Instead of the politico-technocratic body of the 1975–1979 period, the immediate collaborators of the head of state and his chief of staff are now organized within two directorates, staffed predominantly by senior military officers. The functions of these directorates (directorates of federal and state administration) suggest that the coordinating role of the cabinet office headed by the secretary to the federal military government has been significantly reduced. This new orientation, which is yet to become firmly and fully established, is likely to produce a new pattern of relationship between senior military officers and senior civil servants. We will discuss these changes later in the chapter.

Ministries

At the level of the individual ministry, the overall head who is at the apex of the hierarchical organization is the minister or commissioner. Until January 1988, the head of the permanent group of officials who assisted him (that is, the career civil servants) was known as the permanent secretary but is now called the director-general (DG). This official is usually assisted by a deputy known as the secretary for finance and administration (SFA). In large ministries (at the federal level), the DG has two or more deputies who are designated as secretaries for distinct groups of activities. Below the DG and the deputies are senior administrative officers, known variously as principal secretaries, under secretaries, principal assistant secretaries, senior assistant secretaries, and assistant secretaries; they head or work within the divisions, subdivisions, and sections of each ministry. In ministries with substantial technical services (works, agriculture, health, education, etc.), most divisions and their subunits are concerned exclusively with aspects of the technical services of the ministry. Such units are headed by professional officers with such titles as assistant directors, directors, and director-general. The senior officers in every ministry are assisted by a large number of intermediate and junior officers. The higher hierarchical structure has remained the same over the years, but the structure of the top has undergone changes again after 1985, which we discuss later in the chapter.

With regard to the number of ministries and the allocation of functions, successive federal and regional/state governments have been influenced more by the political factor than by the standard criteria in the literature on the allocation of functions among ministries: the functional principle, the process principle, the clientale principle, and the area principle.[7] Successive military governments, including the incumbent one, have favored a small number of ministries at both the federal and state levels. However, the actual allocation of functions has not followed any systematic attachment to one or a combination of the criteria mentioned above. Each state government is limited to the following nine ministries: Agriculture and Natural Resources; Information, Social Development, Youth, Sports, and Culture; Local Government; Commerce and Industry; Finance and Economic Planning; Justice; Education; Works and Housing; and Health. At the federal level there are nineteen ministries: Agriculture; Water Resources and Rural Development; Commerce and Industries; Communications; Defense; Education, Science, and Technology; Employment; Labor and Productivity; External Affairs; Federal Capital Territory; Finance; Health; Information, Social Development, Youth, Sports, and Culture; Internal Affairs, Mines, Power, and Steel; National Planning; Justice; Petroleum and Energy; Transport and Aviation; and Works and Housing.

Nonministerial Organizations

Outside the ministries there are a number of nonministerial organizations that do not come directly under ministers and commissioners. Five broad types can be distinguished:[8]

1. Autonomous governmental agencies. They are established by government but are independent of it in their mode of operation. Some of them are enshrined in the Constitution and may therefore also be referred to as constitutional bodies. The Civil Service Commission, the Public Complaints Commission, universities, and research institutes fall into this subdivision of nonministerial organizations.

2. Advisory governmental bodies. They are expected to provide information and advice or to serve as a forum for consultation with interested individuals and groups, or a combination of both. Some of them are provided for by the Constitution. Examples are the State Council of Chiefs, the Advisory Council on the Prerogative of Mercy and the National Advisory Council on Education.

3. Administrative Tribunals. They are bodies with quasi-judicial functions and are commonly established to adjudicate in matters affecting individual rights and entitlement in the areas of employment, welfare provisions, and rented accommodation.

4. Quasi-ministerial agencies. They are bodies that would normally have formed part of one government ministry or the other but are given a separate identity usually for reasons of administrative convenience. Rural development agencies are common examples.

5. Public enterprises. This is the widest of all as it encompasses a large number and
   varieties of what are generally referred to as public corporations, state-owned companies, and mixed companies. Public enterprises are public organizations that have
   specifically emerged as a result of government acting in the capacity of an entrepreneur.
   We will therefore say more about them shortly.

Field Administration

A final dimension of the organization of governmental administration is provided by their external services or field organization outside the federal or state
headquarters.[9] Every federal ministry has a field organization that covers the
entire territorial area of the federation while the field organization of state ministries covers the territorial area of each state. Between 1975 and 1979, the
federal military government embarked on the establishment of a federal secretariat in each state to serve as the focal point for coordinating the activities of
federal ministries and other agencies. Although the successor governments have
maintained this plan, the secretariats are yet to be completed in several states.
Under the presidential government, a politician was designated as presidential
liaison officer in each state, and he was expected to serve as the head of the
federal secretariat. These political officers were resented by the governors of
states that were under the control of a political party different from that of the
president. They disappeared from the politico-administrative landscape at the
return of the military in December 1983.

There is a real sense in which the problems of field administration in respect
of the federal and state governments touch directly on what is commonly called
intergovernmental relations. At the federal level, the central question is the
relationship between the federal and state governments, while at the state level
the question is the relationship between state and local governments. Although
Nigeria has exhibited an increasing concern with this subject in recent years,
there is as yet no systematic approach to it. Since the early 1970s, each state
government has maintained a liaison office in the federal capital to monitor and
follow up the activities of federal ministries that are of interest to the state
governments. Furthermore, intergovernmental conferences are held at fairly regular intervals to discuss matters of interest to the federal and state governments.[10]

Personnel Administration

Four features can be identified as salient to public personnel administration
in Nigeria. First, since 1975 the quasi-totality of the personnel has been administered under a unified grading and salary structure. This followed government's
acceptance of the recommendation of the Public Service Review Commission

set up in 1974.* The commission's recommendation was aimed at simplifying and reordering the existing chaotic policies and practices on grading and salary administration. The unified system has a seventeen-level salary structure that applies to all public sector organizations except the universities, for which a separate salary structure was established in 1980.[11]

Second, the general principle on which appointment is made is that of merit, which means ability and competence. However, because the country operates a federal system of government, considerable attention is paid to the principle of representativeness. Section 14 of the 1979 Constitution expressly provides that this principle should be taken into account in respect of appointments to public service posts at all levels of government. However, what has become known as the "Federal Character" debate shows that the constitutional provision is rather vague. One obvious solution is the adoption of guidelines on how to achieve a harmonious marriage of the principles of merit and representativeness.[12]

Third is the principle of job security. This applies in varying degrees to all public services except the public enterprises. To ensure that this principle and that of merit and the practice that flow from them are maintained, a special independent and impartial body exists for the civil service, the local government service, and the teaching service. Introduction of such a body in respect of public corporations and parastatals was tried and subsequently abandoned in the early 1970s. The most important of these bodies is the Civil Service Commission (CSC), of which there is one for each of the governments. The CSC dates back to the colonial period. Its independence in guaranteed by the Constitution. The CSC has responsibility for recruitment, promotion, and discipline. It can delegate its powers to senior civil servants, *not* to political heads of ministries. Usually, the powers of recruitment, promotion, and discipline delegated to senior civil servants are contained in a document called *Civil Service Rules.*

Notwithstanding the elaborate provisions on job security for civil servants in the *Civil Service Rules*, successive governments since 1975 (both military and civilian) have taken measures that undermine the principle of job security.[13] First, the military government that took over power in 1975 embarked on a "purge" of public servants that involved several thousand civil servants. The purge was a rough and ready justice that ignored the established rules and procedures in retiring, terminating, or dismissing public servants on such grounds as "declining productivity," "old age," "divided loyalty," and so on. Unfortunately, there was a repeat performance in 1984 under the incumbent military government. In addition, the government embarked on a large-scale retrenchment of civil servants with a view to reducing the size of government personnel. During the civilian interlude between the two military governments, the civilian politicians introduced varying doses of partisan politicization which also under-

---

*The Public Service Review Commission is also commonly referred to as the Udoji Commission, after its chairman, Chief J. Udoji. Henceforth, the two terms will be used interchangeably in this chapter.

mined the principle of job security. In sum, then, the principle of job security is under serious threat in the country.

The fourth and final key feature of the Nigerian public personnel system is the use of commissions in dealing with most issues in the personnel field. This is a British heritage that has been maintained. A good illustration of this practice is the fact that collective bargaining and employers-employees consultations have played little direct role in the initiation of personnel reform measures, especially those relating to salary reviews. In a general manner, it is correct to say that industrial relations in the public sector organizations are relatively under-developed.

Finance

With regard to public financial management in Nigeria, three major issue-areas can be identified: the legal and constitutional framework, the budgetary process, and financial accountability. The 1979 Constitution as amended by the military contains fairly comprehensive provisions on financial management. It recognizes the head of state at the federal level, or the governor at the state level, as ultimately accountable for the management of government financial resources. There are also provisions relating to the Consolidated Revenue Fund (General Fund) and the Contingencies Fund. The responsibility to direct or conduct investigations concerning public funds is now vested in the Supreme Military Council and the State Executive Council, which under the defunct civilian government was vested in the National Assembly or the State Assembly. In addition to these constitutional provisions, there is various legislation such as the Finance (Control and Management) Act, 1958, and the Audit Act, 1958, as well as financial regulations or instructions and periodic circulars or circular letters issued by the Ministries of Finance.

The fiscal year in Nigeria begins in January and ends in December. (Until 1980 it ran from April to March.) Therefore, the process of making the budget usually begins as early as the first quarter of each calendar year. With the abolition of the office of the director of budget by the military, responsibility for preparing the budget has been placed squarely on the Ministry of Finance. The ministry coordinates the demands and estimates of other government ministries and de-partments, and collates and submits them to various interdepartmental bodies and the Executive Council until a final submission is made to the Supreme Military Council (or the State Executive Council) for approval. The Ministry of Finance, in conjunction with the Ministry of National Planning, is responsible for overall supervision of the implementation of the approved budget.[14]

One final comment that may be made about the budgetary process in Nigeria relates to the use of appropriate techniques. The management style in Nigeria is generally old-fashioned, inefficient, and not oriented to ensuring adequate accountability. This situation has been perpetuated by the failure to institution-

alize various modern management techniques such as the planning, programming, and budgeting system (PPBS).[15]

The final area that needs to be examined is that of financial accountability.
Three major methods are used to ensure financial accountability. One is the
appointment of an independent official charged with responsibility for auditing
government accounts; this officer is known as the auditor general at the federal
level and the director of audit at the state level. This official, however, does not
audit the accounts of public enterprises; this is done by hired private accounting
firms. As in most other countries, the office of the auditor general is guaranteed
in the Constitution, and he enjoys independence in the performance of his work.
A second method is a Public Accounts Committee (PAC) which is an organ of
the legislative body. Although the legislatures have been abolished, a few state
governments have established PACs which will have to report to the State Executive Councils. The PACs examine the reports of the auditor general or directors of audit. Lastly, there are internal checks and balances through the
ministries of finance and the various instructions and circulars released periodically.

Notwithstanding the existence of these methods of control, the available evidence suggests that financial accountability is unsatisfactory. It appears that the
methods have to be strengthened and more effective financial management techniques have to be introduced.

Local Government Administration

The objectives of the "modern" local governments established in the country
in the 1950s remained unchanged for almost eighteen years after independence.
On the whole, the two southern regions which emphasized democratic local self-
government with the stress on citizen participation continued with the same broad
orientation during the immediate postindependence years. Similarly, the postindependence government of the northern region continued to attach greater importance to the socioeconomic mission of local governments than to the objective
of citizen participation. This continuity in policy orientation was largely due to
the fact that the political leadership teams who "collected" powers from the
British rulers in the 1950s remained in power in the immediate postindependence
years.

Regardless of whether or not the emphasis was on citizen participation or
socioeconomic development, all the regional political leadership teams paid great
attention to the role of local governments as instruments of controlling the mass
of the population—the so-called law and order function of the colonial era. It
was in respect of this critically important role of local governments that each
regional government sought ways of maintaining effective control over the local
governments either through the ruling political party or the manipulation of
traditional rulers.

The first ten years of military rule (1966–1976) witnessed efforts by military politicians to reorient and/or strengthen the local governments. In the former southern regions, attention was focused on "efficiency," and efforts were made to achieve this goal through either the council-manager system or through decentralized services of the state governments at the local levels. The latter arrangement, which was called "divisional" administration, was a form of deconcentration. In northern Nigeria, the newly established states (from 1967 onward) adopted the pursuit of local democracy as a goal, and steps were taken to ensure the involvement of the representatives of the people (chosen not elected) in the management of local affairs.[16]

In broad terms, the successive postindependence governments (civilian and military) tried as best they could to cope with two basic problems. First, there was confusion over what ideological position official policies should take in regard to the involvement of the masses in the management of local affairs. A critical dimension to this problem is the question about the exact role of traditional rulers in local administration. The second problem, which relates to the first, is the uncertainty of the different governments about what kind of organizational framework should be established at the local level. Should there be elective participatory institutions, or should the state ministries and departments be extended to govern the local areas? The nationwide reform of the country's local government system, which was initiated in 1976 by the federal government, sought to tackle these problems.

What distinguished the 1976 local government reform from all previous reform exercises in the country was the formal and unequivocal recognition of local government as constituting a distinct level of government with defined boundaries, clearly stated functions, and provisions for ensuring adequate human and financial resources. Clear guidelines were provided on these issues and on other matters connected with the organization and functioning of the local governments.[17] The overall objective of the reform was to constitute local governments into the third tier of government, after the federal and state tiers. The 1979 presidential Constitution maintained the essential features of the local government system established in 1976, especially with regard to functions and finance. It was also specifically stated in section 7 of the Constitution that "the system of local government by democratically elected local government councils is under this Constitution guaranteed."

In practice, the military government that introduced the 1976 reform tried hard to implement it. There is evidence that the local governments recorded some significant achievements. In practically every state, the local governments successfully formulated and implemented economic and social development projects that contributed to the improvement of the standard of living of citizens in their respective areas. In most cases efforts were concentrated on markets, motor parks, roads, bridges, culverts, classrooms, dams, wells, dispensaries, and maternity centers. Furthermore, the local governments were intimately involved in the democratic process, which eventually culminated in the return to civilian rule in October 1979. Thus, the local government elections held in December

1976 were the first electoral exercise in the country in thirteen years, and the election of the majority of members of the constituent assembly which completed the work on the making of the 1979 Constitution was conducted within the local governments.[18]

Notwithstanding these successes, some problems persisted regarding structure, finance, personnel, corruption, and intergovernmental relations. Almost without exception, the civilian governments that assumed power in 1979 showed special interest in the structural problem, and the common solution that they all adopted was to increase the number of local governments. Within the fifty-one-month existence of these governments, the number of local governments rose from 301 to over 800. This proliferation of local governments was not accompanied by any effort to solve the other problems mentioned above. Indeed, the problems of finance and personnel became accentuated. Above all, the idea of "democratically elected" local governments was abandoned.

When the incumbent military government which came to power in December 1983 announced a return to the 301 local governments in existence by September 1979, it was generally assumed that the 1976 reform package was being restored. Although this interpretation was eventually confirmed, the new military government proceeded to establish a committee to review local government administration in the country. The twenty-man Dasuki Committee (after the name of its chairman, Alhaji Ibrahim Dasuki) was inaugurated in May 1984, and it submitted its report in September 1984.[19]

The big question that still remains unanswered is the linkage between local governments and rural development. This question was somewhat muddled between 1976 and 1979 when both the federal and state governments established separate institutions to undertake the qualitative transformation of the rural areas, especially in the field of agriculture. Two of these institutions were the river basin development authorities and agricultural development projects. Although the river basin development authorities are financed by the federal government, the agricultural projects are jointly financed by the federal and state governments and the World Bank. In almost every case, these rural development programs were poorly coordinated, and the essential linkage to the local governments was weak. The new regime of General Ibrahim Babangida from August 1985 has devoted more money and attention to rural development as part of its restructuring of the economy but has linked it weakly with local government, as we note later. This new experiment is worth watching.

MAJOR ISSUES

Socioeconomic Development

Over the years public service in Nigeria, like that in other Third World states, has assumed the managerial role of promoting and directing the process of socioeconomic development. This role has had significant consequences for public administration. In this section, we will direct our attention to how Nigerian public administration seeks to meet the challenges of managing changes. Emphasis will be placed on two issues: central planning, and the administration of development plans and public enterprises.

Planning of the public sector's development expenditures started in Nigeria in 1945 under colonial rule with a ten-year plan (1946–1956). The plan was revised halfway for the period 1951 to 1955. Another economic program was drawn up for the period 1955 to 1960 and subsequently extended to 1962. The first postindependence (or National Development Plan) was launched in June 1962 for the period 1962–1968. Although this plan was due for completion on 31 March 1968, the political crisis of 1966–1967 and the subsequent civil war made it impossible for the country to embark on the preparation of another plan until the end of the war in January 1970. During this interim period, the various governments used annual capital budgets as the main instrument of effective allocation and utilization of the country's resources. The Second National Development Plan, 1970–1974, was launched in 1970. This was followed by the Third National Development Plan, 1975–1980. At the time it was launched, this plan was reputed to be the most ambitious development program ever launched in the whole of sub-Saharan Africa. The plan for 1980–1985, launched under the civilian-presidential regime, envisages a total capital investment program of about 82 billion naira. (At the time of writing in mid–1988, 1N = 1.3 U.S. dollars.) This far exceeds the 30 billion originally envisaged in the preceding plan which, owing to inflationary pressures, rose to about 53 billion at the end of the plan period.

Although serious efforts to organize the planning machinery in Nigeria began after the attainment of independence in 1960, the key features of the present machinery were not established until the early 1970s. The 1979 Constitution established the idea of a planned economy as a constitutional obligation. One dominant feature of the planning machinery is the principle of federal supremacy. The federal government is expected to provide the overall direction and leadership in the planning process from the formulation stage through implementation and review and evaluation.

Federal supremacy in the planning process is underlined by the fact that the 1979 Constitution specifically requires the National Economic Council presided over by the vice president to "advise the President concerning economic affairs of the Federation, and in particular on measures necessary for the co-ordination of the economic planning efforts or the economic programmes of the various Governments of the Federation."[20] The two key governmental agencies involved in the national plan are the ministries of Finance and National Planning. Policy inputs come from the various ministries and departments of the Ministry of National Planning. Here policy alternatives are examined and evaluated and then translated into programs within the financial parameters set by the Ministry of Finance. They key agency in the Ministry of National Planning is the National Planning Office, which is divided into four directorates, each headed by a director who is responsible to the director-general of the ministry as the permanent secretary is now called. Besides the National Planning Office, there are two other important organs of the Ministry of National Planning; the National Manpower Board (NMB) and the Federal Office of Statistics (FOS). The functions of the NMB consist of determining personnel needs and formulating programs for personnel development. The FOS is the national agency responsible for collecting social and economic data throughout the federation.

In addition to these institutions, a number of interdepartmental and intergovernmental agencies and bodies participate in plan formulation. The most notable among them are the Joint Planning Board (JPB) and the Conference of Ministers and Commissioners for National and Economic Planning. The JPB consists of the leading planning officers of the federal and state governments. Judging by past experiences, the JPB meets periodically, usually in advance of the conferences of commissioners of economic planning. It serves as a clearinghouse and coordinating organ for policy proposals emanating from the states.

The institutional framework for planning at the state level differs from that described above in one major respect. The policy inputs that come to each state Ministry of Economic Development also include inputs from local authorities which are channeled through the Ministry of Local Government or the equivalent institution. The position is clearly recognized in the Constitution where it is stated that:

It shall be the duty of a local government council within the State to participate in economic planning and development of [its] area . . . and to this end an economic planning board shall be established by a Law enacted by the House of Assembly of the state.[21]

The on-going preparation of the Fifth National Development Plan (1986–1990) shows the extent to which the major problems of planning, which were first noted in the 1960s, have persisted.[22] The problem areas in the planning process can be broadly grouped into administrative and policy problems. Among the administrative problems are the ineffectiveness of the existing agencies and bodies; shortages of qualified personnel especially in the scientific and technical fields; the lack of reliable census figures; and the absence of effective coordination within and outside government. With regard to coordination, the praiseworthy goal of ensuring grassroots participation in the planning process has remained a statement of intention in almost every state. For example, none of the state houses of assembly established a planning board as prescribed in the 1979 Constitution between 1979 and 1983. At the national level, the debate over the relative merit of a high-powered National Planning Commission *a l'indienne* and a Ministry of National Planning as the key national institution to coordinate the national plan has persisted for about two decades without a definite decision being taken. The president of the Nigerian Economic Society provided a new perspective on this problem in May 1985 when he argued the case for transferring the national budget from the Ministry of Finance to the Ministry of National Planning as a means of ensuring coordination between planning and budgeting.[23]

The fundamental policy problem in Nigeria's planning experience is the absence of a clear national ideology which incorporates explicit developmental goals and objectives. The authors of the Fourth National Plan admitted this problem in the following terms:

It is time we raised the fundamental question: what kind of society are we evolving: Is it our aim to "close the gap" between our society and the Western [European] society accepting the latter, by implication, as our model? What, indeed, is development.[24]

An effort was made to spell out the country's economic and social objectives in the 1979 Constitution, but the provisions, especially those on a mixed economy system, are characterized by considerable vagueness. The current military government continues the vagueness in articulating a national ideology of development which means that the problem will remain unresolved for several more years.[25]

Notwithstanding the important limitations on the effectiveness of planned development in the Nigerian milieu, it must also be mentioned that the successive plans have produced some concrete results. Thus, for example, it has been asserted that the First Plan made distinct and important contributions to the effective allocation of resources and to economic growth. The Second and Third Plans witnessed the indigenization measures which assigned the "commanding heights" of the national economy to the state and increased the proportion of economic activities controlled by indigenous entrepreneurs in comparison to their foreign counterparts. The benefits to the mass of the population were in the form of programs and projects in the social and economic sectors. In addition to the tremendous development of the oil sector, giant strides were made in the fields of transportation, manufacturing, and industrialization. The major strategy used for accomplishing these developmental activities was the direct involvement of the state in entrepreneurial activities covering such diverse fields as finance, manufacturing, industry, banking, and mining. These state-owned enterprises are discussed below.

Public Enterprises

The term *public enterprises* or *state-owned enterprises* is used to comprehend all statutory corporations, authorities, boards, and limited-liability companies in which the government has full or majority interests. Together these number over 500 throughout the country. Public enterprises may be grouped into three main categories: public utilities, financial institutions, and commercial and industrial companies.[26] The public utilities are infrastructural organizations and are of vital importance to the national economy. They provide such services as water, electricity, transport, ports, posts, and telecommunication and broadcasting. The financial institutions comprise mainly banks and insurance houses. The commercial and industrial enterprises provide a wide range of goods and services covering such activities as agriculture, meat processing, production of drinks, mining, textile manufacture, transportation, and operation of garages and hotels.

Like most administrative institutions in Nigeria, the establishment of public enterprises was British-inspired, and the earliest of them were established by the British colonial administrators. The nationalist leaders who progressively took over the governance of Nigeria in the 1950s established several more public enterprises. But the great expansion in the number of these enterprises occurred in the 1970s when it was officially declared that the "commanding heights" of the Nigerian economy should be controlled by the state. The huge increase in oil revenues enabled the federal government to establish many new enterprises. The state governments (which had numbered nineteen by 1976 in contrast to only four regions ten years earlier) established their own enterprises, ranging from a minimum of about fifteen (Niger State) to over eighty (Bendel State) in 1983.

The policy option that asserts the desirability of state control of the commanding heights of the economy is a formal rejection of the two available alternatives of foreign control (exploitation) and control by indigenous entrepreneurs (serious inequality). The policy option is therefore a commitment to economic nationalism and the promotion of social equity through the goods and services that the enterprises will make available for the entire population.[27] The economic and social objectives that are spelled out in the 1979 Constitution broadly support this policy orientation. Unfortunately, the vagueness of the term *mixed economy* used to sum up the country's economic philosophy in the 1979 Constitution has led to the emergence of a group of opinion leaders who would like to see an important reduction in the number and scope of public enterprises in the country. The defunct civilian regime began to pay some attention to this "privatization" school following the submission of the Onasode Report in 1981. The incumbent military regime accepts the idea that some sort of privatization would be of help in the effort to revamp the nation's economy. But available studies of the operations of Nigerian public enterprises show clearly that the philosophical and management problems are being confused.[28] Although the management problems that have been diagnosed in detail by a succession of committees and commissions persist largely because of failure to take appropriate remedial steps[29] (the political will has been lacking), the philosophical bogey of "privatization equals efficient management" is being canvassed. The danger posed by the willingness of the incumbent government to privatize is that the foreign exploitation and social inequality that were officially exposed in the 1970s will grow unchecked with obvious negative consequences for the society. They will have to take an unequivocal position in respect to overall philosophical orientation without dodging the critical questions of foreign domination and social equity. They will also have to exercise the political will that is essential for implementing the relevant recommendations that could help to ensure improved performance of public enterprises, privatization, or otherwise.

PUBLIC ACCOUNTABILITY

As already mentioned above, the Westminster-Whitehall model was transplanted into Nigeria in the 1950s and maintained at independence. As part of this transplantation exercise, the British arrangements for enforcing accountability in governmental administration were adopted in Nigeria. Central to the British conception of accountability is the doctrine of ministerial responsibility. According to this doctrine, the members of the cabinet who constitute the executive arm of government are individually and collectively responsible to Parliament for the conduct of government business. Because of this doctrine, the permanent group of officers, called civil servants, who assist the ministers (members of the cabinet) are expected to observe the norms of anonymity, impartiality, and political neutrality. These civil servants assist the ministers in the formulation of policies and perform the critically important duty of executing these policies, but the responsibility for every activity belongs to the ministers who take the credit for the good things done and accept the blame for all the mistakes.

Existing studies of the British public administration system emphasize the central position occupied by the elected assembly (Parliament) in the enforcement of accountability. The package of accountability measures at the disposal of Parliament (referred to collectively as methods of parliamentary control) include parliamentary debates and motions, question time, letters to ministers, parliamentary committees, and the parliamentary commissioner for administration. These control devices were created as the parliamentary system of government evolved in Britain. The last among them, the parliamentary commissioner for administration, was created only in 1967. In addition to the respective roles of Parliament and the Executive, the judiciary and public opinion (through the role of the mass media) are also regarded as instruments for enforcing accountability in Britain. Finally, internal arrangements within the governmental bureaucracy are intended to assist in the enforcement of accountability. These arrangements include the rules and regulations that govern the conduct of officials, the hierarchical relationships within the ministries, and the measures aimed at enforcing financial control.

This British conception of accountability together with attendant institutional arrangements was adopted by the Nigerian government leaders in the 1950s and maintained after independence in 1960. Although Parliament was suspended after the first military coup of January 1966 and remained so throughout the thirteen years of military rule, the inherited conception of accountability was not redefined. The only important change that occurred during the period with regard to the enforcement of public accountability was the creation of two specialized instruments for enforcing accountability: a Nigerian version of the Scandinavian-inspired ombudsman system in the form of a network of public complaints commissions (PCC); and a Corrupt Practices Investigation Bureau, established in 1975 and 1976, respectively. The two instruments were subsequently enshrined in the 1979 Constitution, and the anticorruption bureau was transformed into a Code of Conduct for Public Officials. While restoring the important role assigned to the legislative body (called National Assembly at the federal level and the House of Assembly at the state level), the 1979 Constitution strengthened the role of the political executives (the president at the federal level and the governors in the states) who were given wide powers of control over the civil service, including the power to appoint special advisers. The Constitution maintained the role of the judiciary as an instrument for enforcing accountability, and for the first time in the country's history, the mass media were formally enjoined to ensure that the governments were accountable to the governed.[30]

Political Control: On the whole, the civilian political leaders paid very little attention to the enforcement of accountability measures. The idea of a *public mandate* which underpins democratic responsiveness under both the parliamentary and presidential systems of government (Britain and the United States, respectively) was not respected by the political actors. Those who became the governors under both systems of government were essentially concerned about how best to ensure their permanence in office; they concentrated most of their energy and attention on self-preservation and self-enrichment. Some services were rendered to the society at large, but the governors were unwilling to be assessed by the public through free and fair elections and every ruling group was intolerant of organized opposition. In these circumstances, neither the British-style parliamentary methods of control nor the accountability measures associated with the U.S.-inspired presidential system of government were effective in the Nigerian milieu. Specifically, the Question Time in Parliament and the Public Accounts Committee, which are effective in Britain because of the important role played by a loyal opposition, could not achieve similar results in Nigeria where the idea of a loyal opposition was practically considered anathema. Under the presidential system of government, the investigative powers of the legislators were either unutilized or misutilized because, rather than use these powers to enforce accountability and responsiveness, the legislators were more interested in obtaining favors from the political executives.

The legislative paraphernalia for enforcing accountability have not been maintained by successive military governments. However, practically every military leadership team in Nigeria has formally committed itself to the enforcement of accountability in the conduct of government business. The commitment was largely at the level of rhetoric until the Mohammed/Obasanjo regime introduced the Public Complaints Commission (PCC) and Corrupt Practices Investigation Bureau (CPIB) in 1975 and 1976, respectively (see above). According to the regime's leaders, these new instruments were created because the existing measures for enforcing accountability were inadequate.

The Judiciary: With regard to the judiciary, the constraints on judicial remedies that exist in Britain have been maintained in Nigeria, and some statutory re-strictions that have been lifted in Britain (e.g., the doctrine of sovereign im-munity) are still maintained in Nigeria. Two additional limitations to the usefulness of the judiciary as a way of enforcing accountability which are totally endogenous are the tendency of some law officials (judges as well as magistrates) to get involved in partisan politics and the persistent attempts of successive political leadership teams (both civilian and military) to erode the independence of the judiciary. For example, the incumbent military government, like its pred-ecessors, has placed certain of its enactments beyond the scope of judicial review.

The Press: Although the mass media have always been recognized as having a role to play in ensuring that governments are accountable to the governed, this role was not given constitutional sanction until the 1979 presidential Constitution. In Chapter II of the Constitution, "Fundamental Objectives and Directive Prin-ciples of State Policy," it is stated that: "The press, radio, television and other agencies of the mass media shall at all times be free to . . . uphold the respon-sibility and accountability of the Government to the people."[31] The record of the mass media in upholding the accountability of government to the people since independence has been a mixture of praiseworthy efforts and achievements and numerous acts of omission and commission.

On the positive side, they have generally supported the governed at critical periods when the governors became insensitive or repressive, or both, and such support was crucial to the change of governments in 1966, 1975, and 1983. The press, in particular, supported the pressures that led to the adoption of the Public Complaints Commission (1975) and a Code of Conduct for Public Officers (1979). On the negative side, each agency of the mass media has tended to support the owner (an entrepreneur, a political party, the federal or state gov-ernment) and this idea of supporting the owner, "right or wrong," has under-mined the mass media's role as an instrument for enforcing accountability.

Another limitation on the usefulness of the mass media in matters of account-ability is the relative underdevelopment of journalism as a profession in the country. A sizeable proportion of practicing journalists are not sufficiently ed-ucated and trained to be able to undertake the careful, systematic research that is required in order to meaningfully probe into the conduct of government busi-ness. Finally, the journalists have been constrained by laws and decrees enacted by successive civilian and military governments ostensibly in the interest of ensuring a responsible press. In reality, the laws and decrees have the effect of "gagging" the press and protecting public officials. General Buhari's military government passed a press decree with the revealing title, Public Officers (Pro-tection Against False Accusation), Decree No. 4 of 1984. According to a high court judge, "statements about public officers which bring them into disrepute or ridicule do constitute an offence punishable under Decree No. 4 as it now stands."[32] Fortunately, General Babangida's military government canceled that decree in 1985 as part of its package of liberalization.

Internal Methods of Control: The internal methods of control which are expected to keep administrators accountable to the public include the rules and regulations, including ethical standards of behavior, which every administrator is expected to observe. These rules and regulations are spelled out in a handbook called *Civil Service Rules*. It was probably in acknowledgment of the inadequacy of the self-administered code of conduct described in the *Civil Service Rules* that a constitutionally imposed code of conduct was introduced in 1979. A special group of rules and regulations relate specifically to financial administration, and these are in the form of instructions and circulars issued by the Ministry of Finance. The objective is to ensure the honesty of the officials and regularity in financial practice. All these rules and regulations are expected to be observed within the hierarchical organization of each ministry or department of government, with emphasis on superior-subordinate relationships such that the work of a subordinate is supposed to be supervised by one or more superiors.

Existing studies of accountability measures in Nigerian public administration point up the inadequacies of both the external and internal methods.[33] Neither the civilian political leaders nor the military rulers have taken seriously the task of being responsive and accountable to the public. The only possible exception was the military leadership of 1975–1979, which created the Public Complaints Commission (PCC) and enshrined a code of conduct for public officials in the 1979 Constitution. Although the PCC has recorded some achievements with regard to securing redress for the grievances of some citizens against acts of omission and commission by the governments, civilian politicians neglected the code of conduct between 1979 and 1983. Although the code is being enforced by the incumbent military government, the idea of asking public officials to declare their assets in secret seriously limits its effectiveness as a check on abuse of office for self-enrichment by public officers.

The Problem of Corruption: The most notable consequence of the general ineffectiveness of accountability measures in Nigerian public administration is the scope of abuse of office by both political and administrative fuctionaries for self-enrichment. These are commonly referred to as corrupt practices, and they take the forms of embezzlement, bribery, fraud, or straightforward theft. This problem of corruption has grown unabated since independence, in spite of the declared intentions of successive governments to check it. Indeed, it is generally agreed that the period of presidential government between 1979 and 1983 marked "the golden age of corruption," with corrupt practices assuming staggering proportions. Huge sums of money were embezzled and stolen in numerous organizations and by different categories of officers, including ministers, career administrators (senior and junior), and functionaries of parastatals. In one single parastatal, two senior officials embezzled about 20 million naira ($22 million in U.S. dollars at the 1983 conversion rate) within twelve months. (At the rate of 1.3 it is $26 million.)

The sources of corrupt practices include the regularity with which political leaders collude with career officials to enrich themselves for a variety of selfish reasons (economic security, to facilitate acquisition of more political power and enhanced social status) and the political leaders' illegal channeling of public funds to party accounts (under civilian rule). These corrupt practices are facilitated by a system of government contracts that introduce private (national and foreign) contractors as willing partners in collusion resulting in what are commonly called "kickbacks." The absence of a strong commitment to professional ethical standards on the part of the public functionaries, together with the absence of business ethics on the part of the private sector entrepreneurs, has produced a climate in which corrupt practices have been allowed to flourish. Although the incumbent military government has demonstrated the will to expose and punish persons guilty of corrupt practices, it has not yet tackled the fundamental issues of rethinking the system of government contracts, setting limits to individual wealth, and imposing clearly articulated professional ethical standards for public functionaries.[34]

GENERAL BABANGIDA'S REFORMS

In August 1985, General Buhari, along with his immediate lieutenant and a handful of other top government officials, were removed from office in a palace coup. The succeeding administration of General I. B. Babangida accused its predecessor of gross abuse of human rights and of being overly stubborn and insensitive to popular feelings.[35] Babangida's immediate efforts were directed at redeeming this image. Besides this motivation, two additional influences have affected the overall orientation of the present administration. These are Nigeria's World Bank-inspired economic recovery program and the plan to return to civilian rule in 1992.

The overall problem of political instability continues, but at the same time, significant areas of continuity remain in the Nigerian federal administration system. Indeed, it is on these continuities that the Babangida administration has tried to establish its far-reaching effort to reform and evolve an enduring public administration system. The reform initiative has three major thrusts.

First, on the assumption of power a few structural changes were introduced. The Supreme Military Council was renamed the Armed Forces Ruling Council, with a larger and wider membership of about thirty military men. The head of state also assumed the title of president with powers akin to the 1979 Constitution's version of the executive president. As a result, the Office of the President has expanded considerably. The president's immediate lieutenant, the chief of general staff as he is now called, has in turn lost much of his previous executive powers. Finally, the number of federal ministries has been increased, even though the former Ministry of Finance and National Planning now forms a single Ministry of Finance and Economic Development. At the same time, a separate National Planning Commission was established in the Office of the President in May 1988.

All these initial changes were coupled with a grand design to project the administration as populist and participatory. The controversial Decree 4 of 1984 was abrogated, and at least two major public policy items—namely, the question of the acceptance of an International Monetary Fund loan and the political transition program—were subjected to public debate before the government's final decisions were announced. However, the administration has significantly reneged on this posture. For example, various high-handed actions against labor have taken place, including the dissolution of the National Labor Congress.

The second level of developments centers around the administration's economic recovery program, the Structural Adjustment Program (SAP). This program seeks to institute a self-reliant, productive, and liberalized economy through such component strategies as a privatization policy and establishment of a foreign exchange market.[36]

The dramatic effects of these economic policies on the public administration system can be seen in the vigorous attempts to cut back on the size and range of activities performed by the public service. The government has pursued this objective in four main ways: retrenchment of public officials; rationalization of departments and agencies; commercialization of government services; and transfer of the government's equity holding to private individuals and groups. So far, not many concrete efforts have been made in regard to the equity transfer. But it is estimated that the public sector will have been divested of an average of 30 to 50 percent of the existing public enterprises by the time the entire economic recovery program is implemented. By then, it should also be possible to realize an annual rate of return of about 10 percent as against the present 1.39 percent from investments in these enterprises.

In spite of adverse social consequences such as a phenomenal upsurge in the population of unemployed Nigerians, these policies have significantly influenced the administrative system into being more cost-conscious and free-market-oriented. The Babangida administration has obviously been thrilled by this fact. Hence, we find a manifest desire to entrench all the regime's other activities in this basic philosophy. The administration's local government and rural development efforts illustrate this attitude.

Rural development has two main importances for the regime. On the one hand, it wants to consolidate the gains of the economic recovery and ensure that the mass of the rural people benefit fully from the results. On the other hand, it evidences the administration's determination to establish a firm grassroots base for the coming Third Republic. Already, democratically elected local councils have been reconstituted throughout the federation. According to the transition arrangements, these councils will provide basic training and exposure to a new breed of politicians expected to assume power after 1992. The present administration has been more responsive than most of its predecessors to local and rural development.[37]

The pivot of the administration's rural program is the Directorate of Food, Roads, and Rural Infrastructure (DFRRI), which is based in the Office of the

President and has branches throughout the federation. In the last two years alone, the Directorate has spent about 1 billion naira in trying to revamp the rural economies through construction of more access roads and provision of essential infrastructural facilities. The Directorate's activities also include research into rural problems and extension services. However, questions have been raised about the extent to which the concrete achievements correspond with the huge sums already expended. This situation has fueled speculations about corruption and waste. The centralization of the Directorate's operation in Lagos, arguably in contradiction to the spirit enunciated above, has given added support to this apprehension.

Third and finally, the Babangida regime's transition arrangement toward civilian rule in 1992 is itself an elaborate, multifaceted program affecting practically every sector of society.[38] First has come the creation of two additional states—Katsina and Akwa Ibom. Second is the decision to readapt the executive presidential system toward a more open politicized American model. This reform has radically transformed the civil service system from its erstwhile British orientation.[39] As of January 1988, a permanent secretary, now called the director-general, has become an entirely political officer whose tenure is tied to that of the regime that appoints him. He is also no longer the accounting officer as the minister has now been so empowered. Indeed, the minister is now appropriately the chief executive of the ministry with powers to appoint, discipline, and promote. He has therefore taken over a good part of the previous functions of the Civil Service Commission which now serves more as an appellate and supervisory body. This reordering in public personnel management is coupled with a redefinition of the federal character provision in the Constitution. Federal character will now be applicable only at the point of entry to the service, namely, grade levels 07–10, with the Civil Service Commission being empowered to handle such recruitments.

The other aspects of the reform exercise include the professionalization and reorganization of ministries. Every civil servant becomes an expert in the working of a ministry and will be expected to serve his entire career there. Each ministry has in turn been reorganized into a maximum of eight definite functional areas. In addition, the Office of the Auditor-General has been considerably strengthened to cope with the enormous accountability implications of this reform. An Audit Alarm Committee, which enables the auditor-general to alert the president of any prepayment audit queries, has also been created.

Mindful of the limitations of structural changes alone, the regime has launched a nationwide program of social mobilization and reorientation of values, attitudes, and behavior. This is commonly known as MAMSER (Mass Mobilization for Social and Economic Reconstruction).[40] It developed from previous programs such as the War Against Indiscipline (WAI). MAMSER is expected to influence the ethics of public service as well as to inculcate a sense of discipline and responsibility in the citizenry at large. Like DFRRI, the Directorate of MAMSER is based in the Office of the President and has already spent substantial funds. As expected, it has been subjected to severe criticisms for its inability to make appreciable social impacts, or even define its mission in concrete terms.

The Babangida regime is certain to go down in history as one that has introduced the most radical structural changes into Nigerian public administration since independence, in response to pressing domestic and international economic realities. To the extent that these realities will hold for some time, Babangida's changes represent pointers to the future of public administration in Nigeria. But the reforms rest on certain fundamental assumptions, especially an expectation of viable and competent political leadership. The ultimate success of the reform will depend largely on who becomes president at the federal level and governor at the state level. Even if one were to ignore the disappointments of the past, there is little assurance, especially in the light of Babangida's occasional prevarications about the activities of past politicians, that a set of responsible leaders will emerge in 1992. Similarly, the administrative reforms, founded on the success of the regime's economic liberalization program may also fail, as indeed several critics have contended. This may lead to a reappearance of what the reforms are trying to prevent, namely, a situation in which the administrative system is not properly reconciled with the realization of the long-term goals of the larger society. Time alone will tell whether radicalist administrative reforms can produce significant results without a basic commitment to overall societal change.

CONCLUSION

Because of the numerous problems of Nigerian public administration since independence, some readers may consider it a good example of Third World public administration systems that some Western scholars describe as obstacles to development. Such a conclusion will be grossly inaccurate. Real achievements can be credited to the Nigerian public service system in general and the civil service has successfully maintained the continuity of the machinery of government, in spite of all the changes in regime type and the high degree of political instability as evidenced by five successful coups d'etat, the frequent political violence, and a thirty-month-long civil war.

Second, the civil service system constituted the key instrument for restructuring the federation from three units to four, twelve, nineteen, and twenty-one units in 1963, 1967, 1976, and 1985, respectively. It is widely agreed that this restructuring contributed immensely to the relative stability of the country's federal administrative system.

Third, the development activities carried out in the social and economic sectors under the country's four national development plans were made possible in large measure by the framework of order, the policy guidelines, and the regulatory functions of the civil services. The fact that the public sector held the major share of the four plans (67 percent, 62 percent, 81 percent, and 86 percent of the first, second, third, and fourth plans, respectively) underscores the significant role played by the civil services in respect of socioeconomic development. The current proposals for privatization may reduce this share but not to such a significant extent. Again, the stimulatory and catalytic role of public enterprises will remain.

The basic source of strength of Nigerian administration lies in the high quality of its personnel, who are the products of sound schooling and the university system. In spite of disparities in educational opportunities between the north and south, similar standards of achievement are expected and are also enforced in education as well as in the civil service. Regardless of regional background, civil servants have practiced much cooperation and mutual understanding.

The weakness of the Nigerian public administration system revolves around its political and ideological foundations. What exists is a veritable confusion that can be traced to the prevailing confusion with regard to political doctrines and institutions. The declared objectives of "a free and democratic society" and "a just and egalitarian society," together with a commitment to the "rule of law," suggest that Nigeria will operate as a kind of Western liberal democratic state, which the 1979 Constitution confirmed as its broad goal. The failure to operate successfully the British- and U.S.-inspired parliamentary and presidential systems of government in 1960–1966 and 1979–1983, respectively, reveal the incongruence between proclaimed political orientations and the realities of political behavior. This incongruence has, of course, spilled over into administrative doctrines and institutions. Until this problem is solved within the political sphere, the negative consequences will continue to affect administrative behavior and performance. Perhaps the only immediately viable reform strategy that can be launched with a view to improving administrative performance is the establishment of some permanent machinery for ongoing administrative reform which will formulate appropriate reform measures (e.g., with regard to structure, training) and monitor their faithful implementation on a continuing basis. The cumulative effects may be more long lasting than those possible with quick and radical changes, producing their own backlash.

NOTES

1. See Federal Republic of Nigeria, *The Constitution of the Federal Republic of Nigeria, 1979* (Lagos: Federal Ministry of Information, 1979).

2. This Constitution established Nigeria as a federal administration system with one central and three regional governments. Each government had its own Public Service Commission.

3. This report was published as *The Integration of Departments with Ministries* (Lagos: Government Printer, 1959).

4. See Federal Government of Nigeria, *Report of the Commission on the Public Services of the Governments in the Federation of Nigeria* (Lagos: Government Printer, 1955).

5. See G. O. Olusanya, *The Evolution of the Nigerian Civil Service, 1901–1960, The Problems of Nigerianization* (Lagos: University of Lagos Press, 1975).

6. For a detailed discussion of this point, see Ladipo Adamolekun, *Politics and Administration in Nigeria* (London: Hutchinson, forthcoming), especially Chapters 1 and 7. A. O. Sanda, O. Ojo, and V. Ayeni (eds.), *The Impact of Military Rule on Nigeria's Administration* (Ile-Ife: Faculty of Administration, University of Ife, 1986), and V. Ayeni and K. Soremekun (eds.), *Nigeria's Second Republic* (Lagos: Daily Times Publications, 1988).

7. For more details, see Ladipo Adamolekun, *Public Administration, A Nigerian and Comparative Perspective* (London: Longman, 1983), pp. 31–33.

8. Ibid.

9. On the evolution of field administration in Nigerian public administration, see D. J. Murray, "Nigerian Field Administration: A Comparative Analysis," in D. J. Murray (ed.), *Studies in Nigerian Administration* (London: Hutchinson, 1978).

10. The intergovernmental relations perspective on Nigerian public administration is discussed in Adamolekun, *Public Administration*, Chapter 7. Also see D. Olowu (ed.), *The Nigerian Federal System* (Ibadan: Evans, 1988).

11. See Federal Republic of Nigeria, *Report of the Presidential Commission on Salary and Conditions of Service of University Staff* (Lagos: National Assembly Press, 1981).

12. For a detailed discussion of the issues involved in the "Federal character" debate, see A. Gboyega, "The Federal Character or the Attempt to Create Representative Bureaucracies in Nigeria," *International Review of Administrative Sciences* 50, 1 (1984), pp. 17–24, and A. H. M. Kirk-Greene, "Ethnic Engineering and the Federal Character of Nigeria: Boon of Contentment or Bone of Contention?," *Ethnic and Racial Studies* 6 (1983), pp. 457–76.

13. The threat to the principle of job security is real as it was more or less institutionalized by the Civil Service Commissions and other Statutory Bodies, etc. (Removal of Certain Persons from Office), Decree of 1984, which has the effect of denying an officer removed from office recourse to the law courts. See also M. J. Balogun, "Security of Tenure in Nigerian Public Administration: A Brief History and Recent Developments," *International Review of Administrative Sciences* 4 (1976).

14. The operation of the budgetary process is discussed in some detail in A. O. Phillips, "Government Budgetary Decision-Making in Nigeria: A Review of Two Decades' Experience," in L. Adamolekun (ed.), *Nigerian Public Administration, 1960–1980: Perspectives and Prospects* (Ibadan: Heinemann, 1985).

15. See, for example, P. Morellos, "Practical Concepts of Development Programming for Underdeveloped Economies," *Quarterly Journal of Administration* (Ife), 13, 1 (October 1978).

16. For an overview of these experiments, see L. Adamolekun and L. Rowland (eds.), *The New Local Government System* (Ibadan: Heinemann, 1979). On the drive for local democracy in the northern states, see, for example, Ladipo Adamolekun, "The Theory and Practice of Local Government Reform in the Benue-Plateau States of Nigeria," *Journal of Administration Overseas* (London), 16, 1 (1977), pp. 30–42. Also see G. Orewa and J. Adewunmi, *Local Government in Nigeria: The Changing Scene* (Benin: Ethiope Publishing Co., 1983).

17. The reference document on this subject is Federal Republic of Nigeria, *Guidelines for Local Government Reform* (Kaduna: Government Printer, 1976).

18. For a detailed study of the 1976 reform and its implementation up to 1978, see

Adamolekun and Rowland, *The New Local Government System* and the chapters by A. E. Gboyega and O. Oyediran, and A. Y. Aliyu in K. Panter-Brick (ed.), *Soldiers and Oil: The Political Transformation of Nigeria* (London: Frank Cass, 1978).

19. See Federal Republic of Nigeria, *Local Government—Report by the Committee on the Review of Local Government Administration in Nigeria*, Lagos, September 1984, mimeo.

20. Third Schedule, Part I, F.

21. Section 7(3).

22. For a competent overview of the Nigerian Planning Experience in the 1960s, see W. Stolpher, *Planning Without Facts, Lessons in Resource Allocation from Nigeria's Development* (Cambridge, Mass.: Harvard University Press, 1966).

23. See C. Chikolu, "Development Planning: Lessons of Experience," Presidential Address to the Nigerian Economic Society, May 1985. For a negative reaction, see *Daily Sketch* (Ibadan), Editorial, 18 May 1985.

24. Cited in Adamolekun, *Public Administration*, p. 170.

25. The incumbent regime's lack of interest in a formal statement on the ideological orientation of the society was reaffirmed by the chief of staff, Supreme Headquarters (the number 2 strong man of the regime) at the Opening Session of the Annual Conference of the Nigerian Political Science Association held in Ilorin in May 1985.

26. For competing categorization schemes of Nigerian public enterprises, see Adamolekun, *Public Administration*, pp. 43–46; M. J. Balogun, *Public Administration in Nigeria, A Developmental Approach* (London: Macmillan, 1983), pp. 197–205; and Federal Republic of Nigeria, *Report of the Presidential Commission on Parastatals* (Lagos: Federal Government Press, 1981), pp. 35–38.

27. An articulate theoretical discussion of the justification of public enterprises in Nigeria is O. Aboyade, "Nigerian Public Enterprises as an Organisational Dilemma," in Nigerian Economic Society, *Public Enterprises in Nigeria*, Proceedings of the 1973 Annual Conference (Ibadan: University of Ibadan Press, 1975).

28. See, for example, the report of plans to privatize certain state-owned agricultural enterprises in *West Africa* (London), 28 January 1985; for an assessment see L. Adamolekun and O. M. Laleye, "Privatisation and State-Control of the Nigerian Economy," *Nigerian Journal of Policy and Strategy* 1, 1 (October 1986).

29. These reports include Federal Government, Sessional Paper Number 7 of 1964; *The Policy of the Federal Military Government on Statutory Corporations and State-Owned Companies*, 1968; and the *Report of the Presidential Commission on Parastatals*, 1981. See also O. M. Laleye, "The Role of Public Enterprises in the Development of Nigeria" (Ph.D. thesis, University of Ife, 1986), for a general assessment of the operation of public enterprises in Nigeria.

30. For further discussion of the British-oriented methods of control in Nigeria, see L. Adamolekun, "Accountability and Control Measures in Public Bureaucracies—A Comparative Analysis of Anglophone and Francophone Africa," *International Review of Administrative Sciences* 40, 4 (1974), and L. Adamolekun, "Parliament and the Executive in Nigeria: The Federal Government Experience, 1952–1965," in C. Baker and M. J. Balogun (eds.), *Ife Essays in Administration* (Ile-Ife: University of Ife Press, 1975). Also see L. Adamolekun and E. L. Osunkunle, *Nigeria's Ombudsman System: Five Years of the Public Complaints Commission* (Ibadan: Heinemann, 1982); V. Ayeni, "The Public Complaints Commission and Nigerian Bureaucracy" (Ph.D. thesis, University of Ife, Ile-Ife, 1984), B. O. Iluyomade and B. U. Eka, *Cases and Materials on*

Administrative Law in Nigeria (Ile-Ife: University of Ife Press, 1980). V. Ayeni, "Nigeria's Bureaucratised Ombudsman System," *Public Administration and Development* 7, 3. (1987), and V. Ayeni and D. Olowu, "Public Service Accountability in Nigeria," in J. G. Jabbra (ed.), *Public Service Accountability: A Comparative Perspective* (West Hartford, Conn.: Kumarian Press, 1988).

31. Section 21.

32. *The Guardian* (Lagos), 30 July 1984.

33. See references in note 30 above.

34. For some suggestions on how the various dimensions of corrupt practices can be tackled, see D. Olowu, "The Nature of Bureaucratic Corruption in Nigeria," *International Review of Administrative Sciences* 49, 3 (1983); M. U. Ekpo (ed.), *Bureaucratic Corruption in Sub-Saharan Africa: Toward a Search for Causes and Consequences* (Washington, D.C.: University Press of America, 1979); O. P. Dwivedi, *Public Service Ethics* (Brussels: International Institute of Administrative Sciences, June 1978); F. Odekunle (ed.), *Nigeria: Corruption in Development* (Ibadan: Ibadan University Press, 1986).

35. See Special Edition on "20 years of Military Rule," *Newswatch* (Lagos), 20 January 1986, and T. Momoh, "Nigeria: Yesterday, Today and Tomorrow," *The African Guardian*, 9 May 1988, pp. 11–15.

36. See Nigerian Economic Society, *Structural Adjustment Programme and the Nigerian Economy*, Proceedings of 29th Annual Conference, Obafemi Awolowo University, Ile-Ife, May 1988.

37. For an overview, see Special Issue on "The Challenge of Rural Development in Nigeria," *Quarterly Journal of Administration* 20, 3 and 4, (April/July 1986). Also see L. Adamolekun, "The Idea of Local Government as a Third Tier Government Revisited," *Quarterly Journal of Administration* 18, 3 and 4 (April/July 1984), pp. 113–38.

38. See Federal Republic of Nigeria, *Government Views and Comments on the Findings and Recommendations of the Political Bureau* (Lagos: Federal Government Printer, 1987), and Address by Major General I. B. Babangida to the Nation on Political Programme for the Country, Lagos, Federal Government Press, 1987.

39. For a general assessment of the state of the civil service at the time of the reform, see C. Dike, *The Nigerian Civil Service* (Owerri: Alfa Publishing Co., 1985). For details on the reform, see Federal Republic of Nigeria, *Presidential Task Force on the Implementation of the Civil Service Reforms—Main Report and Summary of Recommendations* (Lagos: Federal Government Printer, 1988). Also see *Government Views on Political Bureau*, and Federal Republic of Nigeria, *Dotun Philips Report—The Nigerian Civil Service in the Mid '80's and Beyond* (Lagos, mimeo, 1988) which provide the background to the reforms. Refer, too, to *Newswatch* (Lagos), 25 January 1988; and 25 April 1988 for some insights into the politics of the reform.

40. See Directorate of Social Mobilisation Decree Number 34 of 1987.

12

ZAMBIA

Chibwe Chibaye
and J. M. Bwalya

INTRODUCTION

Although politics and administration may be analytically distinguishable aspects of certain relationships found in any government, they are never separate in the sense that one act or role is exclusively administrative and another exclusively political. In Zambia public administration is enmeshed in politics,[1] and more formally so than in most Third World countries.

Zambia has a long history of the process or activity of administering public affairs. This chapter, however, does not intend to discuss all facets of public administration. Rather, it seeks to examine the historical development of the civil service in Zambia. In discussing the civil service,[2] some of the features that have remained resilient will be identified. At the same time, we will review some of the attempts to make the public service accountable to the people.

HISTORICAL DEVELOPMENT

Prior to the intrusion and entrenchment of colonial rule in Northern Rhodesia, the societies existent then were governed by a number of territorial chiefs. Although some differences may have existed in the organization and management of the many different tribes, a number of generalizations can be made about the political and administrative arrangements. Authority in these societies was based on descent and, on certain occasions, on military power. The chiefs exercised and combined legislative, executive, judicial, as well as ritual functions. The existent hierarchies ensured that power was held by different lineages but only of one single royal clan. This was partly because power and prerogatives were concentrated in the original lineage group. In this respect, the appointment of administrative officers, army leaders, and chiefs' advisers was based on kinship and descent.

In precolonial Zambia, recruitment, promotion, and rewards were a privilege of those born in the "right" lineage groups. Persons were designated a stratum in the hierarchy by their birth. The training of personnel was done within the family as well as the social "group." Through the family and the social "groups," obedience to authority was imparted to the younger generation. On the other hand, "public servants" were aware that they did not owe loyalty to the citizens at large, but rather their positions depended on pleasing their superiors. In this instance, public servants could overlook meeting the citizens' demands as long as their actions were in line with the chief's interests.

These arrangements were disrupted by the coming of colonialism. Zambia, prior to the attainment of its political independence on 24 October 1964, was a British colony. Thus, the form of public administration introduced by Britain was geared to the attainment, consolidation, and maintenance of British colonial policies. As the primary objective of British colonialism in Northern Rhodesia was to pacify the country to allow for continued uninhibited exploitation of the country's raw materials, the early personnel recruited to administer the country were military men. These military men were employees of the British South Africa Company (BSAC) which had a monopoly over Northern Rhodesia's mineral exploitation.[3] In addition to providing a suitable climate for mineral exploitation, these administrators had to find cheap labor for the companies. This they did by directing, ordering, and forcing the indigenous population to pay poll and hut taxes. This aspect of the colonial policy increased the responsibilities and duties of the administration.

This type of administration was operating according to the dictates of the BSAC. The local people had relatively no influence over it. The colonial administration which was introduced and later consolidated in Northern Rhodesia attempted to incorporate the existing traditional government structure. This was done by the introduction of indirect rule.

The colonial administration was very decentralized, and effective control was in the hands of the district commissioner and his small staff. The district commissioner and his staff had extensive operational responsibilities and performed a wide range of legislative, administrative and judicial tasks. The district commissioner was "king" in his district. The official policy of indirect rule led to the establishment of native authorities. Some local chiefs, who accepted British rule, were appointed to serve on the native authorities in advisory capacities. These chiefs were also to explain the meaning and importance of administrative regulations to local villagers. The rationale behind indirect rule was for the colonial administration to gain legitimacy as it ruled through local leaders. At the same time, the colonial administration could exert pressure on local chiefs to ensure compliance with the wishes of the administration. In addition, it was cheaper to administer the area through chiefs than it would have been through direct rule.

In 1924, the British South Africa Company, arguing that the costs of administering Northern Rhodesia outweighed the benefits, surrendered the responsibility to the British Colonial Office. This transfer of power did not alter the structure and functions of the civil servants. The political and economic setup was tightly controlled, operating strictly to the general imperial policy, and hence promoting Britain's interests. In this perspective, the man on the spot was given more powers to ensure that the metropolitan country acquired the benefits. The local population had no influence on the administration. Instead, the district commissioner and his staff combined many functions; they were policemen, judges, and tax collectors as well as bureaucrats.[4]

The major change instituted in the administration of the country after 1924 was the intrusion of the public school and landed aristocratic ethic. Thus, although some of the military administrators remained, the Colonial Office recruited some "oxbridge" personnel. The personnel, like their predecessors, believed that the success of the system lay in their efficiency, patriotism, and self-sacrifice. To this end, they still encouraged indirect rule.

It must be noted that the colonial administration, like the BSAC administration, was concerned principally with maintaining law and order. Its financial administration was restricted to the accounting of revenue and the balancing of the budget. Revenues in the form of customs and export duty were used primarily for raising funds to meet recruitment expenditure. The government's major policy was to create a climate in which private enterprise would flourish. Thus, capital expenditure was directed at constructing office, residential, and other social infrastructures to help the administrators realize their objectives.

It is for these reasons that the civil service was a monopoly of generalists. Furthermore, generalists came to the fore because agricultural and development policies were not prominent, and the agricultural policies only came into existence when poll and hut taxes were introduced. However, this policy was altered when the Department of Agriculture was established.[5] This department concentrated on extension work and on encouraging better animal husbandry by peasant farmers.

Other aspects of agriculture were left unattended. It should be noted that the generalists dominated the public service posts because the government did not see itself as responsible primarily for the provision of social services. The government had established a few "local education authority" schools and hospitals. The bulk of schools and hospitals however, were funded and managed by missionaries.[6] Staff development was initially only for whites; only after World War II did changes begin. Prior to and shortly after World War II, Africans held no commanding positions in the civil service because they were considered uneducated. Their role was to be office orderlies and to perform menial jobs. This situation was enhanced by the fact that the Colonial Office was responsible for recruitment. The territorial secretariat began to offer posts to a few Africans after World War II only as a means of pacifying the few Africans who were becoming articulate. Furthermore, the recruitment was aimed at thwarting criticism from some liberal-minded persons in United Kingdom. In essence, the administrative, executive, and the few professional and technical posts remained mainly a privilege for the whites.[7]

Not surprisingly, then, when Zambia attained independence in 1964, the departure of the colonial civil servants created a vacuum. Since all the senior, middle, and responsible posts were filled by non-Zambians, the departure of these foreigners meant loss of skills and expertise. Most of the Zambians did not possess the qualifications, let alone the experience, required to run the administration. Indeed, even those white public servants who chose to remain could not easily begin to take orders from the former "trouble makers."

Despite the foregoing, Zambia and Britain entered into a pact in which Britain would pay in London part of the salaries for those expatriate civil servants who preferred to work for the new United National Independence party (UNIP) government.[8] This arrangement entailed that some of the colonial public administration ethics such as political neutrality, professionalism, and the middle-class ethic remained intact. The fact that the civil servants had remained "running the show" without much control by the colonial or local secretariat meant that the Zambian civil servants were being initiated into those practices. Thus, the new UNIP government saw its task as principally that of changing the inherited pattern of administration.

Zambia's problems on the eve of independence, apart from inheriting a civil service concerned primarily with maintaining law and order, centered on the existence of ministries that had been created in the 1950s out of a loose amalgam of departments that had yet to be fully integrated into the ministries. The organization of most of the ministries was seldom based on rational principles. Interministerial coordination was lax, if not absent. These problems were further compounded by structural disruptions that had become necessary in January 1964 when the former federal government departments were handed over to the Northern Rhodesia government.[9] This adjustment called for extensive reorganization, in addition to the amalgamation of hitherto racially segregated ministries and departments such as African Education and European Education.

TOWARD A ZAMBIAN CIVIL SERVICE

Politicization of the Civil Service

Zambia's attainment of political independence called for a drastic transformation of the civil service. The new government had its own philosophy and ideology. Whereas the British colonial administration had little interest in the development of the socioeconomic infrastructure, the UNIP government made social services one of its priorities. The policies advocated during the nationalist era, as well as the central features of the philosophy of Zambian humanism introduced in 1967, called for rapid development and provision of social services to the people.[10]

The policies of the UNIP government required an administrative cadre that would promote these ideas. This cadre had to be nationally oriented and not colonially oriented. These policies, therefore, called for rapid Zambianization of the civil service. The process of Zambianization entailed the opening of posts to qualified Zambians who would replace foreign personnel.

The public service had to be reorganized incrementally because few Zambians had the expertise, let alone the time, to overhaul the machinery of government. The government's major task was to entrench its legitimacy—a problem that was more pressing than reshaping government ministries and that was a prerequisite for the implementation of the economic development programs. In doing so, radical changes were avoided, if only to prevent disruption. Thus, most of the former colonial officers tended to look to Britain for guidelines. In addition, the problems of recruiting Zambian personnel continued. Although the lower civil service ranks were Zambianized and the senior levels were slowly being adequately staffed, the middle and technical levels remained largely dominated by foreigners. This problem could only be solved with adequate training. The Zambian government, apart from training Zambians in various areas abroad, also continued to train civil servants at the National Institute of Public Administration, which was opened in 1963 as the center for civil service training. The provision of this training went a long way in ameliorating staff problems in the public service. However, although the government was becoming the largest employer, some of the ably trained personnel opted to join private companies that were better paying than the public service. In addition, the size of the National Institute of Public Administration could not permit it to rapidly train and retrain civil servants.

In order to provide for mass-based programs, the UNIP government further called for people's active involvement and participation in the process of policy initiation, formulation, and implementation. This policy of participatory democracy also entailed a departure from the organizational structures that had been championing British imperial policies. In addition, the new government moved from being passive observers to active participants in the economic organization, production, and distribution. This government policy of determining the economic destiny of the country led to the enlargement of government departments and ministries. It also led to the creation of public corporations known as parastatals. This measure entailed the expansion of the public service. It further meant drawing up a new form of communication, coordination, and control. These changes were to be an on-going process. The composition, size, structure, and hierarchy of the Zambian civil service is continuously under review and in a state of flux, so that an accepted and Zambian-oriented civil service can be established.

The foregoing ideas and measures reflect the incremental policy process that exists in Zambia. This process has usually been associated with an adoption of no-choice policies. For instance, while the new UNIP government wanted to make sure that major policy decisions were made by the Zambians in Lusaka, where a closer watch could be kept on decision making, the inherited structure and the concept of participatory democracy entailed a continuation of some form of decentralized system. For the new government, although decision making would be highly improved if the local people were involved in the initiation and formulation of policies, it was important to ensure that the loci of power in Lusaka be identified. Furthermore, the dominance of Lusaka lay in the fact that the new policies would be subverted by administrators if the local people were not trained in their rights and roles. It is thus not surprising that a desire arose to maintain a balance of power between the central government and local government, even though the central government had a dominant role to play.

Zambia, like many other countries, has a career civil service whose administrative heads of departments or ministries are appointed by the president. The president as chief executive in Zambia holds a powerful office. The Constitution has assured the executive overriding control in a system that blends a presidential system with a parliamentary form of government. The president's powers in relation to the public service are partly exercised through the cabinet office which falls under the prime minister's office. It is also under the prime minister's office where the permanent secretary responsible for provincial administration is found. But despite these arrangements, it is the president who is the chief administrator and is responsible for the general conduct of government affairs as well as for implementing some specific policies. Furthermore, the president is not bound to follow the advice of any other person. In terms of the public service, the president has power over its structure and personnel. This is reflected in the fact that the president is empowered to create and abolish offices in the state, subject only to constitutional provisions. The president may also declare by statutory instrument that any office he has established does not form part of the public service. In addition, the president has full powers of appointment and dismissal without reference to the Public Service Commission.[11]

These powers vested in the president have contributed to the demise of civil service neutrality. Civil servants in Zambia may stand for party posts and parliamentary elections. Furthermore, former politicians may be and have been appointed to civil service posts. Apart from Zambia being a de jure one-party system, President Kaunda ably justified this politicization of the civil service:

The principle behind politicisation of the Civil Service within the confines of their disciplines must be regarded as a very important development. Just as in the case of the armed forces and other services we are discussing, a humanist leader does not want anybody to follow a certain line of action like a machine—a robot in fact.

Civil Servants are required to implement decisions which are taken by the Party that believes and works for the establishment of a humanist society. How do we expect civil servants to follow humanist principles if we exclude them from politics? Unless they are helped to understand and appreciate why the Party works for the establishment of a humanist society, they are bound to follow different lines of action due mainly to ignorance rather than sabotage.[12]

The implication of this statement is that civil servants implement policies of the single party and that in order to effectively implement these policies, they must be members of the party. Civil service neutrality has no room in such a single-party country, because civil servants will all along have to implement policies of the same party. Moreover, the effective and efficient realization of goals, policies, and programs requires that politics and administration be in equilibrium.

The Public Service Commission, which advises the president on the appointment of permanent secretaries and which is charged with the responsibility of appointing professional, technical, executive, and related civil servants, is also appointed by the president. The Public Service Commission is responsible for appointment, confirmation, promotion, and discipline of the civil servants on the basis of a clear delegation of authority by the Constitution, with its extent and purpose made explicit. The president may also direct the commission to refer certain questions of appointment, dismissal, or discipline to him.[13]

The guiding principles of the Public Service Commission are merit, ability, and competence. In addition, the Public Service Commission relies on legal guidelines in its work as defined in the public service regulations, general orders, and financial regulations.[14] But here, too, being a party member is important for civil servants. This is partly because the party constitution provides that leading posts in the party and its government be occupied by party members.[15] In this respect, party membership is an added advantage for all those seeking public office. Those civil servants already in the system risk being transferred, frustrated, or dismissed if their activities are proved to be inimical to party policies and programs.

The tenure of civil servants was secured by the establishment of the Civil Servants Union of Zambia in 1976. This union, which involves personnel in the civil service, was established when the General Orders were altered. Classified daily employees of the civil service, however, are represented by the National Union of Public Service Workers, and not by the Civil Servants Union of Zambia. The permament secretaries and other departmental heads are not represented by any of the two unions as these are classified as part of management. The decision to unionize the civil service is in line with the philosophy that all workers in the republic should have a union to represent their interests. The argument of the public nature of the civil service has been discarded because, although the government may be seen as the "invisible employer," there are persons in the public service who make policies and determine conditions of service. The contact point of all these unions has become the cabinet office, specifically the Personnel Division.

The politicization of the civil service is further premised on another factor. The basic means of control in the service is hierarchical, which means that authority flows downward through the organization, with each level responsible to the level above. In this instance, one method of controlling the civil service lies in controlling the administrative head of department or ministry. Thus, the party is able to control a department or ministry more effectively if the permament secretary is sympathetic and in agreement with the goals and objectives of the party and its government. To do so, this officer must belong to the party. If a permanent secretary has to retain the confidence of the party, he must not only act professionally but also be politically adept and loyal.

The politicization of the public service has made the service more responsive to the demands of the party and the people. Nevertheless, the civil service is still basically middle-class-oriented. This orientation has come as a result of the inherited colonial practices that have been passed to each new generation of public administrators. Even though public service training has been localized, the products still retain a middle-class tag. This may be explained in part by examining the colleges and institutions to which public institution lecturers go. This middle-class orientation has affected the organization of the civil service and can in part explain the dominance in Zambia of urban interests vis-à-vis rural interests, in the manner in which government services are rendered.

Civil service in Zambia is organized as a bureaucracy. This bureaucratic structure may be seen in ministries and departments that perform specific and related functions. Furthermore, the bureaucratic form in Zambia is emphasized by insistence on roles played by offices and not the incumbent. Indeed, the chains of command and coordination are reflected in the organizational structures of ministries. Each ministry is under a separate minister who is responsible for the actions of both departments and officials, but leaves most administrative issues to the permanent staff (civil servants). The permanent secretary as the administrative head of the department controls the activities of the ministry and coordinates the ministry's activities with other ministries. He is appointed by the president and holds office at the pleasure of the appointing authority. His other major function is to advise the cabinet on issues relating to his ministry.

The number of ministries has tended to grow and vary with the times. Thus, in 1964, there were sixteen ministries, including the offices of the president and the vice president; in 1965, the number increased to seventeen and in 1970 to twenty-four when eight ministers were appointed to head provinces. In 1984, there were twenty-five ministers in the cabinet, including the president, secretary general of the party, and the prime minister.[16] The Office of the Prime Minister, where the Cabinet Office and the Personnel Division fall, plays a dominant role in the public service system of Zambia (1) because the prime minister is head of government administration and is responsible for day-to-day government operations; and (2) because the prime minister as head of government business answers questions in the National Assembly on civil service operations. Thus, the Office of the Prime Minister is the important link in government operations, for it is this office that supervises provincial and local government operations.

CIVIL SERVICE TRAINING

Of all the British African colonies, Zambia was probably the most neglected in matters of education and had the smallest number of qualified Zambians for taking over administration at the time of independence. We have already noted how this situation necessitated several interim arrangements with the British government in retaining colonial officers and in recruiting qualified specialists and generalist officers from other Third World countries in Asia, Africa, and the West Indies. Simultaneously, the National Institute of Public Administration was set up to train Zambians in the lower rungs to take over more responsible positions.

All of Africa customarily relies on training as the magic wand for accelerating Africanization, and in Zambia there had arisen a tendency toward disorganized proliferation. Thus, by the mid–1970s several training agencies and courses had been established, but coordination was lacking. The University of Zambia was producing graduates with a major in public administration, and there were problems with their training at the National Institute of Public Administration, which to that point had been geared to training nongraduates with barely school-leaving qualifications. The International Labor Office and the British Institute of Management were also invited to advise on training. The Mindolo Ecumenical Foundation ran a number of short-term courses to fulfill some immediate needs. Later, various ministerial departments organized in-service training, and the United National Independence party, after the declaration of the one-party state in 1972, began to organize some training courses as it was deeply involved in the governing process.

By 1978, this confused medley demanded some coordination. The government of Zambia embarked on a process of centralizing and coordinating civil service training with the help of the Overseas Development Administration, London.[17] This action led to the establishment of a Directorate of Manpower Development and Training (DMDT) to coordinate the various dispersed training efforts. A review in 1981 showed considerable progress, and in 1982 all permanent secretaries and several senior officers were invited to comment on the implementation process. The comments were positive, and a full-time cadre of personnel development officers was launched. A further review in 1984 revealed that, while some duplication and lack of coordination remained, the situation was mostly under control. The exercise did not seriously try to cover the parastatals or public enterprises, but Zambia is not unique in this regard as few Third World countries have coordinated the training for the ministerial and nonministerial sector.

PUBLIC ENTERPRISES

Zambia's economy is dominated by public enterprises known as parastatals locally which represent a world apart from the mainstream of public administration. Partly for reasons of preserving their autonomy of operation, their policies and practices of recruitment, training, and compensation are almost totally outside the purview of civil service regulations. A further practical reason in the case of Zambia with its severe personnel shortages is to allow the parastatals freedom to offer tempting salaries and working conditions to foreign experts, as well as to lure first-rate Zambian civil servants and managers away from their jobs. The salary differentials between parastatals and ministerial departments have been a sore point, and many efforts have been made to close the salary gap.

The same reasons have operated in most African countries, regardless of professed ideology to promote state-owned enterprises—namely, the dearth of private capital and entrepreneurship and economic nationalism. In Zambia, the reasons are much stronger. First, there was practically no Zambian private businessperson of any stature at the time of independence, and compared to Kenya or Nigeria, no great effort was made in Zambia to create a local commercial bourgeoisie partly owing to the influence of the national philosophy of humanism. Second, the visible control of the country's most valuable mineral resource, copper, by foreign corporations provided a compelling reason for economic nationalism. But the nationalization of copper mines, a policy adopted in 1970, has been costly in terms of compensation, entailing foreign borrowing and difficulty in retaining expatriate officers.

The size of the parastatal sector as a whole was again awesome in terms of capacity to control it administratively and technologically. When the parastatals were bunched together into three large controlling corporations, Indeco (for the industrials), Mindeco (for the mining sector), and Findeco (for the financial sector), President Kaunda himself remarked that they were like three parallel governments. A parliamentary committee in 1978 reported on the problems of parastatals—namely, lack of control, inefficiency, lack of technical personnel, and political interference. The problems are similar all over Africa, including, in addition, dictation by the International Monetary Fund and foreign banks, but they are a little more acute in Zambia, exacerbated by the additional problems of a frontline state.

PROVINCIAL AND LOCAL ADMINISTRATION

The Zambia Independence Act (1964), enacted by the British Parliament, paved the way for Zambia's independence and was repealed by the Zambian Parliament in 1972. The Zambian Parliament thereafter established Zambia as a de jure one-party system. The Zambian Independence Act (1964) and the 1972 Constitution had created a unitary state with almost all powers vested in the central government. However, Chapter 480 of the laws of Zambia, as well as inherited administrative arrangements, provided for local government.

The inherited administrative structures did not augur well for efficient and effective administration. Furthermore, the inherited colonial structures could not be used to attain the goals of modern Zambia.[18] The administrative structure and organization tended to promote delays in that local government officials were given the power to implement policy, but not to make policy. In this case, local government officials had to refer all policy issues to the center. As a result, the center was overburdened and could not respond to requests quickly. In addition, the decisions from the center tended to overlook existing political, social, economic, and cultural realities as the professionals making the decisions were far removed from the area being affected by their decisions. This system tended to thwart development efforts. Indeed, since the funds for development were being released quarterly, the Lusaka-based civil servants could hold on to the funds and thereby defeat the local initiatives.

The Zambian government began to examine the inherited systems in order to make them meet the aspirations of the new nation. But these aspirations could not be realized as the existence of numerous government departments, municipal, rural, and township councils, as well as party organs at the district level, tended to promote duplication of work, delays, and inaction. For instance, the municipal councils were responsible for certain tasks such as road maintenance, health, and sanitation in their respective jurisdictions. At the same time, the central government departments were also responsible for the same facilities within the areas that fell outside municipal jurisdiction. But at times the boundaries were obscure, leading to certain areas lagging behind.

The Zambian government, aware of these problems, has been attempting to find ways and means of making local administration effective, including Zambianizing all local administration posts. Among the measures has been the posting of certain officers from the central ministry to the field. These officers are assigned specific functions and given the necessary authority to discharge these functions. However, the central ministry retains the power to make policy.

The idea of transforming local government has been tackled from another angle. The Zambian government has been making structural and organizational changes. The move toward transferring power to the people began with the enactment of the Local Government Act in 1965 which allowed the people to exercise power over their destinies through their elected representatives. But the exercise of this power was limited because the local authorities (municipal, city, and rural councils) were subject to strict control by the minister responsible for local government. Furthermore, the local authorities had to refer certain policy questions to the central government. In addition, the local authorities depended for their financing on the central government.

As a result of these shortcomings, the president appointed a cabinet minister to head each of the then eight provinces. (There are now nine provinces in Zambia.) The president also appointed a district governor to head each of the fifty-three districts. These measures were aimed at providing each local area with a political head who would sit on the policy-making body. The national convention of 1967 proposed a thorough consideration of decentralization. The administrative committee appointed in 1968 worked out certain proposals for decentralizing certain ministries, and it was from these recommendations that the post of provincial cabinet minister developed in 1969. Each provincial cabinet minister was given an adequate budget to help in the realization of the projects identified in his province. The district governor was in turn to be a personal representative of the president in each district and was to coordinate party and government responsibilities.

This system faced some problems. The district governors faced opposition from some civil servants and mayors who felt that their status in the districts had been undermined. Furthermore, the district civil servants were still answerable to their respective departmental heads. The governors' biggest hurdle was their lack of legal powers; their position was weakened as they had to operate within already existing machinery.

The provincial cabinet ministers had jurisdiction over their respective provinces. However, civil servants within the province were still answerable to their parent ministries. For instance, the provincial minister had jurisdiction over the teachers resident within his province, yet the minister of education was also principally responsible for all the teachers in the country. The result was that civil servants in provinces could not be sufficiently responsive to provincial directives, and this hindered decentralization.

These problems led to the appointment of the Simmance Commission in 1971 which reviewed the entire process of decentralization. The Simmance report made strong recommendations on the issue of transferring power to the people.[19]

In 1972, a working committee to review and evaluate the operability of the Simmance Report was appointed. A number of measures were accepted, as they tended to reflect the views enshrined in humanism in Zambia and a guide to its implementation, Part II. In June 1973, the party, through its National Council, approved new measures on decentralization. These measures were followed by the appointment of members of the Central Committee to head provinces. These incremental changes in the process of transferring power to the people and changing the structure of local government culminated in the passage of Local Administration Act No. 15 of 1980.

The logic behind the new system of decentralization may be summed up in the reasons behind the rejection of a centralized form of administration. These reasons include the following:

1. Decisions made at the center for local areas usually became inapplicable and irrelevant at the area of their application as they tended to overlook existing political, economic, social, and cultural realities.

2. Accountability became difficult as the implementers were not involved in the actual policy-formulating process.

3. Knowledge was seen not as a monopoly of a few technocrats but was spread throughout society.

Owing to these problems and resulting from earlier experiences, Zambia's local administration Act No. 15 of 1980 has attempted

1. To reduce duplication of work. This has been done by amalgamating the three former existing organs of administration at the local level. Thus, the municipal councils, the

government departments, and the party are unified and work in harmony. This is advantageous in that the loci of power in each district is clearly identified.

2. To provide staff in all areas. While the three organs existed, the distribution of personnel was problematic in that many of the trained persons preferred to work in urban areas. With decentralization, all the civil servants are appointed by the Public Service Commission. As a result, all district councils have been allocated some qualified personnel.

3. To encourage local participation and accountability. Since the elected ward chairmen are the councillors, local people feel they are partaking in decision making. They therefore put their viewpoints across. In return, the civil servants also implement decisions as they are the advisers of the policy makers, and the decisions made at the local level indicate their personal observations and experiences. Civil servants know they will be held accountable for any shortcomings. They do not have to pass the blame to somebody else.

4. To cut down on red-tape. In those areas where the councils have been given jurisdiction, the decisions are made promptly. Information to and from the people is not delayed or grossly distorted.

Decentralization has brought a change in the structure of government. It has also promoted effective participation of the people, thus promoting the feeling that the local people are not only in control of their destiny, but are benefiting from the objectives of the party.

There are problems regarding decentralization, however. First, since the powers of the district councils are delegated to them by the central government through Parliament, these powers may be revoked or reversed by the Parliament. Second, some civil servants may and do take advantage of the ignorance of some councillors to push their views to the fore. Third, in certain districts, some specialist posts are still vacant. Fourth, the major source of funds for these councils is still the central government. Although councils may raise funds from levies, charges, fees, productive investments, and loans, grants from the central government are the major source of the council's finances. Thus, if the central government decided to limit or withhold its grants, the district councils would grind to a halt. Fifth, the central government still retains the powers of confirming, amending, and revoking district council by-laws and other policy matters.

In essence, therefore, decentralization has taken power to the people of Zambia. However, there are more steps to be undertaken to ensure that the system works to the advantage of the majority of the citizens. This is because civil servants, though politicized, may still stifle the wishes of the people. Civil servants by their training and experience still play a dominant role in the policy-making process.

The working of the integrated system has produced mixed results. A recent review starts with the revealing title "Mission Impossible: Integrating Central and Local Administration in Zambia" (G. F. Lungu in *Planning and Administration*, 13, 1, 1986). The basic difficulties of persuading the branch offices of national functional departments from Lusaka to take orders willingly from a district council have not been solved. The basic conflict between local needs and national priorities can never be completely resolved at the local level. Some anomalies continue, as, for example, mining townships under the new classification of "specified residential areas." More recently, another critic (Carole Rakodi, "The Local State and Urban Local Government in Zambia," *Public Administration and Development* 8, 1 [January-March 1988]) has pointed out that, in spite of the elaborate machinery for coordinating the political and bureaucratic wings at the district level, there is little provision for direct consultation with the public. In Rakodi's view, the district councils are oriented to solve or tone down conflicts between party, government, and bureaucracy. They "have essentially a political watchdog function, intended to integrate administration and party matters at provincial and district level, to mobilize residents and workers in Party and public organizations and to ensure that contradictions do not occur between Party policy and government plans and program implementation."

DOMINANCE OF CIVIL SERVICE IN POLICY FORMULATION

The National Assembly and the president constitute the Parliament in Zambia. The Constitution of Zambia (1972) provides that Parliament is the supreme legislative body in the country. This supremacy is reflected in the fact that one Parliament cannot bind its successors: each Parliament enacts, amends, and revokes laws as it sees fit; each Parliament approves or rejects government estimates and expenditure as it sees fit.

In the process of enacting, amending and revoking laws, civil servants play a dominant role because it is the civil servants who draft the bills and who implement the laws. This point gains prominence when it is noted that Zambian parliamentarians do not employ personal advisers. It is the civil servants who are a source of technical information needed by parliamentarians for legislation.

The influence of civil servants stems from their training, expertise, and long service. Indeed, even the way in which ministers are appointed enables civil servants to gain power. In appointing ministers the president consults the secretary general and prime minister. In this process, consideration is made of the following factors: geographical origins of potential ministers; social and political cleavage; and career patterns of the persons to be appointed.

The cabinet, which plays a dominant role, in addition to the Central Committee, must be consciously designed to be representative of the country's major cleavages. Hence, ministers are not necessarily specialists in matters pertaining to their departments or ministries. Furthermore, some departments or ministries require a longer time for a minister to understand not only the minute details but also the intricacies, intrigues, and politics that underline them. As a result, ministers rely on civil servants. Furthermore, civil servants stay relatively longer in the departments and ministries in comparison to ministers. Thus, civil servants may not only ursurp the ministers' powers, but also develop multiple ways of ensuring that ministers comply with their interpretation of laws and take their advice. This is done because civil servants rely on their expert training, the functional specialization of work, and an attitude set on habitual mastery of methodically integrated functions. In addition, civil servants have time and access to most information. They may decide to pass it on to the ministers or restrict it to themselves.

Civil servants have come to dominate the policy process because ministers have numerous tasks to tackle. There are problems from within ministries and departments, demands from the press, from individuals, from cabinet, from the electorate, from interest groups, as well as from the Parliament. Ministers therefore have to depend on civil servants to summarize various viewpoints. Furthermore, even when the question of who should see the minister comes up, it is the civil servants who decide who should meet the minister, when, and for how long. If a minister shows that he wants to undercut the civil servants' authority, he may find the civil servants working without enthusiasm.

These viewpoints are based on the fact that civil servants see themselves as part of the political elite. This is not surprising inasmuch as civil service jobs provide the incumbents with influence over public policy. This influence arises from the monopolistic planning and professional consensus that is inherent in the civil service.

The foregoing does not mean that civil servants have it all their way. Ministers and other politicians are aware of the dangers inherent in leaving the civil service uncontrolled. Thus, we have the logic behind the politicization of the civil service, and hence the many attempts to make civil servants accountable to the people for their decisions, actions, omissions, and commissions.

ACCOUNTABILITY AND THE ZAMBIAN CIVIL SERVICE

As argued above, ever since the introduction of the civil service in Zambia, attempts have been made to make civil servants accountable for their actions, decisions, and commissions. The rationale behind the need for civil service accountability is that public administration is a matter for public concern. Public administration utilizes public revenue and makes decisions affecting every aspect of an individual's life. This aspect of public administration makes it desirable for the public to have a say in the public service that will affect them. This is important because public servants do not have a direct mandate from the public. Public servants derive their strength from the fact that they are specialists employed by the government not only to advise, but also to implement decisions. Thus, the first form of control is from Parliament, especially in the budgetary process.

The money spent by civil servants is approved by the legislature. No money can be raised or expended without the sanction of Parliament. The budgets are passed and tabled in the National Assembly prior to the beginning of each financial year. Even when money has been spent, an audit of financial operations is conducted to ensure that the money has been spent on items for which it was approved and that there has been no embezzlement or misappropriation. Even so, it is imperative to observe that budgetary control has many weaknesses. Although the budget is supposed to provide self-control and discipline to civil servants, it is the public servants who draw up the budget, and they may include items that are of no immediate concern. Furthermore, some members of parliament may not be in a position to understand the logic behind the budgets. In addition to the foregoing, after the passage of the budget in the National Assembly, members of Parliament have relatively little control over the money. The responsibility remains with the civil servants.

Review of how public money is spent is the task of the Public Accounts Committee of Parliament and the auditor general. The function of the auditor general is to examine government spending and overspending. The limitation is that the auditor general examines government expenditure after the money has been spent. After his investigations, the auditor general reports to Parliament on what went wrong. This does not enable the auditor general to effectively control public expenditure. The Public Accounts Committee is plagued by this same handicap. These two organs are not the day-to-day supervisor of government financial management. The problems of control continue to exist because in the final analysis it is the civil servants who are supposed to implement the recommendations of the auditor general as well as the Public Accounts Committee on improved financial management. Even the recommendations of the auditor general and the Public Accounts Committee do not go into details about government inability to control its expenses. This is partly because Parliament and the auditor general encounter problems in getting facts and information from civil servants.[20]

Many civil servants overspend because, if at the end of a particular financial year a department or ministry has not spent its allocation the Ministry of Finance may decide that the money was not needed. In such a case, the Finance Ministry gets the remaining amount and reduces the budget for the following year. This reduction in budget may lead to reduction in the number of personnel in the department, and eventually to the ministry's loss of prestige and importance. Spending ministries, therefore, see overspending as a way of retaining and improving both the status and prestige of a department or ministry.

Parliament's inability to control the civil service stems from the technical specialization of civil servants; the civil servants' accessibility to information which members of Parliament lack; and the fact that many citizens do not know where to complain vis-à-vis civil service acts.

The judiciary can be used to control civil servants because the courts have to ensure that civil servants do not act ultra-vires and that civil servants apply the principles of natural justice in the management of public affairs. Thus, any person who feels injured by an administrative act, omission, or commission may apply for redress to the appropriate organ of the judiciary. In this perspective, the judiciary ensures that people's rights are not trampled on and that the rule of law remains the guiding light for administrators.

Judicial redress, however, still remains ex post facto in that individuals typically seek it only after having been disadvantaged. Nevertheless, the judiciary may be conceptualized as a salient means of controlling administrators by establishing guidelines for subsequent administrative conduct through a series of court decisions.

Although courts have powers to review almost any administrative act except in those areas where Parliament has specifically excluded judicial review, an individual does not ordinarily resort to the courts for remedy until he or she has exhausted all available administrative remedies. Furthermore, courts take a long time to resolve complaints. In addition, courts are expensive, a problem exacerbated by the fact that courts are managed by specialists who may not comprehend some administrative issues. At any rate, courts are not an effective way of controlling public administration, because many people have an inherent fear and distrust of courts. Hence, they do not go to court for remedy.

These problems have made the party and its government look for other strategies to help control the civil service. Thus, the Zambian Constitution provides for the existence of the Commission for Investigations (ombudsman). This commission is composed of a chairman who is known as the investigator-general and three other persons appointed by the president. The chairman of the commission is supposed to be a person qualified to be a high court judge, whereas the other members should be persons with administrative experience.

The commission is empowered to investigate public officers. Article 7 of the Commission for Investigations Act of 1974 provides the commission with

jurisdiction to inquire into the conduct of any person to whom its Article applies in the exercise of his office or authority or abuse thereof, whenever so directed by the President and may unless the President so directs, inquire into such conduct in any case in which it considers that an allegation of misconduct or abuse of office or authority by such person ought to be investigated.

The rationale behind the creation of the commission is that some cases cannot be dealt with by courts of law because of their nature or because courts have been expressly exempted from arbitrating in such cases by the legislature. Furthermore, the commission is not expensive: complainants do not have to pay fees for their cases to be investigated. In addition, the commission allows the complainants to state their cases in their own words. It does not operate like a court of law. Aggrieved persons do not have to go with attorneys as of right. The commission also does not take as long as courts of law take to determine or settle problems.

Because of these advantages many people have complained to the commission about administrative abuse of power. Indeed, the creation of the commission has provided citizens with a mechanism for controlling the public service. With the establishment of the commission, public servants have tended to be careful in dealing with administrative issues.

The commission may initiate its own investigations or institute investigations when directed by the president or upon receiving complaints from individuals. However, the commission does not investigate cases that are sub-judice or matters that may be resolved in a court of law or through other administrative channels. At the same time, the commission may refuse to investigate cases that are frivolous, vexatious, or made in bad faith. The commission may, but is not required to, give reasons for rejecting to investigate a case. The commission may discontinue investigations before they are completed if it considers them futile.

When the investigations are completed, the commission forwards its opinion to the president, who may then accept, alter, or reject its opinion or advice. At the end of the year, the commission reports its activities to Parliament.

This avenue of redressing administrative abuse of power is not without problems. The fact that the commission is not mandated to give reasons for rejecting or discontinuing investigations, as well as the fact that the findings and decisions of the commission are not final, point to some weaknesses in the commission. These provisions provide a base on which the commission may be manipulated. The same applies to the process of presidential assent.

Although the presidential confirmation and endorsement of the commission's findings gives the commission more clout, the arrangement may be seen as curtailing the commission's powers. This is because some of the commission's recommendations may be rejected. The commission staffing is inadequate when viewed against the number of cases reported to it. Hence, cases take longer to be investigated. It should also be mentioned that most of the cases going to the commission are complaints by public officers themselves against treatment by their superiors. The commission has, therefore, benefited public officers more than it has done ordinary citizens, especially the silent majority in the rural areas.

Despite these limitations, the commission has been able to help control the public service. This is because its existence acts as a warning to public servants who may want to flout public service ethics.

CONCLUSION

The Zambian public service has retained some characteristics of the colonial era. However, historical episodes, traumas, failures, and successes have had an impact on the size, composition, and structure of this system. The philosophy and ideology of Zambian humanism, the attempts by the party and its government to provide social services to the people, state control over the economy as well as the party's roles in national development, have all contributed to these changes. These changes have included, first, the growth in the size of the public service. There are currently more public servants than there were at the time of independence. Second, the public servants are mainly Zambians who are trained (locally and abroad), and they advise the authoritative policy makers. In this case, the public servants still play a dominant role in policy formulation and implementation. The Zambian civil service has also seen the transfer of power from the center to local organs like district councils. While institutions such as native authorities existed in colonial days, the form of recent decentralization has involved the ordinary people in the management of their own affairs.

What this means is simply that the public service has grown powerful and affects almost every aspect of an individual's life. This has necessitated the review of the mechanism for controlling the public service. To the methods that existed prior to independence, the Zambian Constitution has added new methods such as politicization of the public service and fiscal superintendence. These measures, in addition to parliamentary control, and the Commission for Investigations may have their own weaknesses. However, when operating at maximum efficiency, and when taken together, they provide strong bulwarks against improprieties by the civil service. Apart from the foregoing, it must be noted that civil servants by their training, process of recruitment, as well as their professional ethics, do pay heed to the sentiments of the people. They know and appreciate the fact that they live in a community and that the community expects them to display Zambian values. What has initiated this process has been the politicization of the Zambian public service and the knowledge that the party expects public servants to deliver the goods to the people of Zambia.

NOTES

1. The term *public administration* is beset by definitional problems; see D. Waldo, *The Study of Public Administration* (Garden City, N.Y.: Doubleday, 1955), p. 3; H. Stein, *Public Administration and Policy Development* (New York: Harcourt, Brace, 1952), p. x; W. Wilson, "The Study of Administration," *Political Science Quarterly* 2 (1987), pp. 197–222.

2. The terms *public servant* and *civil servant* are used interchangeably here to refer to nonelected officials who work in and for the Public Service Commission.

3. L. H. Gann, *The Birth of a Plural Society: Northern Rhodesia, 1894–1914* (Manchester: Manchester University Press, 1958), pp. 44–59.

4. Ibid., pp. 60–114.

5. Ibid., pp. 136–50.

6. John M. Mwanakatwe, *The Growth of Education in Zambia since Independence* (Lusaka: Oxford University Press, 1971), pp. 14.

7. Ibid., pp. 36–43.

8. British-aided Conditions of Service Act Cap 409 of the Laws of Zambia.

9. Between 1953 and 1963, Northern Rhodesia was part of the Federation of Rhodesia and Nyasaland, which was opposed by the Nationalists in Northern Rhodesia, Southern Rhodesia, and Nyasaland. The federation was dismantled when the Nationalists came to power in Nyasaland and later in Northern Rhodesia.

10. K. D. Kaunda, *Humanism in Zambia, Part I* (Lusaka: Zambia Information Services, 1967).

11. Republic of Zambia, "Constitution of the Republic of Zambia," Article 48–62.

12. K. D. Kaunda, *Humanism in Zambia, Part II* (Lusaka: Zambia Information Services, 1973), p. 30.

13. Republic of Zambia, *The Constitution of Zambia—Public Service Commission* (Delegation directions).

14. Decisions as to what roles and functions should be performed by the public servants are the concern of the cabinet office, which is responsible for day-to-day administration of government. This is despite the fact that certain functions have to be performed by ministries as a result of their jurisdiction.

15. *The Constitution of the United National Independence Party*, Article 3. In addition, the establishment of party committees at all places of work, as directed by the secretary of the party in 1976, has entailed that the party, through these committees, ensures that all institutions are operative in conformity with party aims and objectives.

16. Jan Pettman, *Zambia: Security and Conflict* (Sussex: Julian Friedman, 1974), p. 247

17. For a detailed account of the reorganization of civil service training, see C. L. Carmichael, "Improving the Organization and Management of Civil Service Training in Zambia," *Public Administration and Development* 6, 2 (1986).

18. For a discussion of the steps taken to decentralize the administration, see C., Chibaye, "The Role of Zambian Public Servants in the Efforts to Decentralise the Administrative System"; Aapam, *Public Policy in Africa* (Addis Ababa: Artistic Printers, 1982).

19. Republic of Zambia, *Decentralised Government: Proposals for Integrated Local Government Administration* (Lusaka: Government Printers, 1976).

20. In his 1979 Annual Report, the auditor general referred to an instance in which a team of auditors on an audit tour of a district were denied access to the account books maintained by a department.

Appendix I
Colonial Administrative System

COLONIAL SECRETARY (LONDON)

- Responsible for all colonial policies and administartion in British colonies and territories.

GOVERNOR (Based in Lusaka)

- Responsible for supervising and coordination of colonial policies in Northern Rhodesia (Now, Zambia)

- Answerable to colonial office.

- Commander-in-chief of Armed Forces as major policy was pacify Northern Rhodesians and ensure unihibited exploitation of country's resources.

- Latter responsible for coordination of economic, agricultural and social development.

- Controlled territorial colonial secretariat.

PROVINCIAL COMMISSIONER

- Responsible for supervision and coordination of all District Commissioners within their provinces.

- Answerable to Governor.

DISTRICT COMMISSIONER

- Responsible for peace, welfare and good order in his District;

- Supervised and coordinated the functions and activites of all local departments including the police and treasury.

- Ensured that British policies were carried on within District.

- Created and appointed African Chiefs through whom he rules (even in those areas where none existed before).

Appendix II
Provincial and Local Government Administration (Prior to 1980)

CABINET OFFICE (Under Prime Minister)

SECRETARY TO THE CABINET

LUSAKA BASED PERMANENT SECRETARIES

Administrative head of department and Ministry

PROVINCIAL PERMANENT SECRETARIES

Administrative head of province

Assisted by Under-Secretary and Assistant Secretary just like at Central Ministry.

PROVINCIAL HEADS OF DEPARTMENTS SUCH AS HEALTH, AGRICULTURE, LOCAL GOVERNMENT, ETC.

The Officers are responsible to both Permanent Secretary at Provincial Headquarters as well as Permanent Secretary at Ministry Headquarters.

DISTRICT GOVERNOR

Political head of District and Personal representative of the President.

DISTRICT SECRETARY

Administrative Head of District assisted by various District heads such as Health, Agriculture, etc.

PARTY'S REGIONAL SECRETARY

responsible for Party Organisation assisted by Women Regional and Youth Regional Secretaries.

LOCAL AUTHORITY

CITY, MUNICIPAL, RURAL COUNCILS

Constituted of elected councillors

MAYOR (TOWNS) CHAIRMAN (RURAL COUNCIL)

TOWN CLERK (RURAL COUNCIL SECRETARY)

Assisted by various specialists in such fields as health, community, roads, water and to implement Council decisions in conformity with Cap. 480 of the Laws of Zambia.

Appendix III
Post–1980 Local Administration

DISTRICT COUNCIL

CHAIRMAN (District Governor)
COUNCILLORS - Elected
- Representatives of Mass Organisations, Unions, etc.

DISTRICT EXECUTIVE SECRETARY

POLITICAL SECRETARY	ADMINISTRATIVE SECRETARY	FINANCIAL SECRETARY	DEVELOPMENT SECRETARY	COMMERCIAL AND INDUSTRIAL	SOCIAL SECRETARY	SECURITY SECRETARY	LEGAL SECRETARY

Functions responsible for:

Publicity Information Public Relations Party Organ. Ward/Branch/	Administration methods and organisation Census Staff matters Records, etc.	Budget accounting revenue personal levy Insurance etc.	Planning Public works mechanical services Traffic Fire Services Cooperatives, etc.	Commerce/Trade Parastatal bodies Price control Liquor undertaking taking, etc.	Community social welfare public educ. housing Youth and Sport	All security work	All legal matters

The Council is empowered to make policies for the District in conformity with Party and Government aims and objectives. The Secretariate headed by the District Executive Secretary is to provide the administrative, professional and technica assistance to the Council.

Appendix IV
Structure of Lusaka-Based Ministries

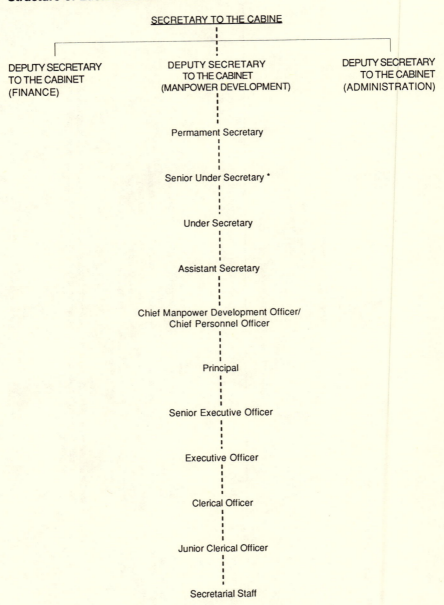

SECRETARY TO THE CABINE

DEPUTY SECRETARY
TO THE CABINET
(FINANCE)

DEPUTY SECRETARY
TO THE CABINET
(MANPOWER DEVELOPMENT)

DEPUTY SECRETARY
TO THE CABINET
(ADMINISTRATION)

Permament Secretary

Senior Under Secretary *

Under Secretary

Assistant Secretary

Chief Manpower Development Officer/
Chief Personnel Officer

Principal

Senior Executive Officer

Executive Officer

Clerical Officer

Junior Clerical Officer

Secretarial Staff

* This post exists only in certain Ministries such as
Finance and Cabinet.

Appendix V
Structure of Policy Making in Zambia

General Conference of the Party

—Meets once every five years but may meet for extraordinary session.

—Members include all members of National Council plus 600 delegates from each of the nine provinces.

—Highest policy-making institution of the land.

—Elects president and members of Central Committee.

National Council

—Meets at least twice every year.

—Members include all members of Central Committee, members of Parliament, provincial political secretaries, district governors, representatives of trade unions, mass organizations, defense forces, and accredited institutions.

—Second highest policy-making body.

—Receives reports from provincial councils (provincial council receives reports from districts, which in turn receives information from wards, branches).

Central Committee

—Consists of president, 20 elected persons, 3 persons appointed by the president and prime minister as ex-officio. One of the 23 MCCs is appointed secretary general of the party.

—Divided into 10 subcommittees which coordinate and supervise ministries.

—Advised by Research Bureau and other technocrats attached to subcommittees.

—Meets regularly at least once a month.

—Since August 1988, the Central Committee consists of the president, prime minister as ex-officio, and 66 members of whom 46 are elected and 20 appointed by the president.

Cabinet

—Consists of president, secretary-general (ex-officio), prime minister, and ministers.

—Advises president on policy making and implementation, runs missions and departments.

—Assisted by the civil servants in advising president and managing ministries.

—Meets regularly, i.e., once a month.

Parliament

—Consists of the president and the National Assembly.

—National Assembly consists of 125 elected MPs plus up to 10 nominated by president plus 1 Speaker chosen by the elected and nominated MPs from outside their numbers.

—Makes, amends, and revokes laws.

—Approves or rejects government estimates and expenditures.

—Must meet regularly but at least once every year.

PART IV

THE WEST INDIES AND LATIN AMERICA

13

THE ENGLISH-SPEAKING CARIBBEAN

Gladstone Mills

INTRODUCTION

This chapter focuses on the public administration systems of the Commonwealth Caribbean—a region most of which falls within the Caribbean Sea but part of which is also contiguous to that sea, with a spillover into the Atlantic.[1] The region is bounded by North, Central, and South America, straddling a distance of 2,500 miles of sea; at its northern boundary lie the polymerous Bahamas, a hundred miles from Florida; at the western, Belize, and to the southeast, Trinidad and Tobago, and Guyana in South America. The region consists of a group of current and former British colonies in this area: a number of small islands (the former British West Indies plus the Bahamas), and two large mainland countries in Central and South America.

The location of these small states, at the doorstep of the United States of America, has obvious and significant implications and consequences for them in geopolitical, economic, and cultural terms. This proximity imposed constraints on the shaping of their international relations policies in the political, economic, and especially trade dimensions. Moreover, the peoples of the region are over-exposed via easy physical access and the communications media to a dominant culture and life-style and to material goods and services that are far beyond the capacity of the slender resource base of Caribbean economies. The U.S. invasion of Grenada in October 1983 and President Reagan's Caribbean Basin Initiative (CBI) are conspicuous manifestations—albeit of entirely different aspects—of the influence and impact of the United States.

Most of the constituent countries were units (or groupings) within the old British Empire—some for more than three centuries—and they have emerged since the 1960s as independent nation-states or internally self-governed countries within the British Commonwealth. In addition to geographical location, they share other common features: similarities in historical background in terms of their long experience of colonial rule (with Great Britain as the primary and most recent imperial power), the common bond of slavery and the plantation system, and similarities in political and constitutional evolution.

They also vary considerably in size (area and population), ethnic composition, resource endowment, and in economic, political, and administrative development. At one end of the continuum is Jamaica, which by far has the largest population (2.3 million or 40 percent of the region's total) with Trinidad-Tobago: 1.1 million. At the other end are the microterritories of the British Virgin Islands, the Cayman, Turks, and Caicos Islands and Montserrat—still British colonies—with populations between 8,000 and 12,000.

The size, topographical features, and population distribution of some units and the dispersed geographical spread of others have produced a variety of decentralized political and administrative arrangements ranging from the old local government systems of Belize, Jamaica, and Trinidad, to the deconcentrated institution of the "family island" commissioners in the Bahama islands, the district commissioners of Belize, and the regional councils of Guyana. Moreover, attempts to devise political and administrative systems for the governance of multi-island states such as St. Kitts-Nevis-Anguilla, Trinidad-Tobago, and Antigua-Barbuda have not succeeded in suppressing the periphery's feeling of being neglected by the metropole—the "capital island": hence, the movements for secession in Anguilla, Nevis, Tobago, and Barbuda. The formal constitutional spectrum of the region also represents a melange ranging from independent states, through internally self-governing territories to Crown colonies.

The differences among the constituent countries are reflected in physical terms: in varying scales of government operations, in the range and size of public agencies, the feasibility of creating specialized ministries and departments and of hiring specialist personnel. But, more fundamentally, the differences appear in the styles of political behavior and the nature of political activities. Despite the differences, their overriding similarities remain evident and pertinent: the countries of the region are small-scale, developing colonial, and ex-colonial states set within plantation societies.

THE ENVIRONMENT OF PUBLIC ADMINISTRATION

The Social-Cultural Context

Two historical features—namely, centuries of slavery and the plantation system, and colonial rule—have dominated the Caribbean's social and cultural life.[2] They have had continuing consequences, leaving deep psychological and social imprints that have persisted a century and a half after emancipation and into the age of independence.

The peoples of the region represent a racial amalgam: their forbearers, immigrants, some voluntary and others forced, originated from Africa, Asia, Europe, and the Middle East.

European (mainly British) cultures and institutions transplanted by the sugar plantation proprietors and managers and reinforced later by colonial officials, were imposed on the detribalized groups of Africans who had been transported to the region as slaves—unwilling migrants. These people—the ancestors of the present preponderant black majority—were stripped of their cultural heritage. Thus, unlike Africa and Asia where traditional cultures and long-established indigenous social and political institutions predated the appearance of the colonizing powers and/or the modernizing process, in the Caribbean the European cultures and institutions encountered no strong, competing indigenous social and political organizations.[3]

British institutions, then, are deeply embedded in Caribbean societies following their long exposure, especially in states such as Barbados, the Bahamas, and Jamaica, with an unbroken history of more than three centuries of the British nexus. For instance, the heritage includes (1) the Westminster-Whitehall system of government and public administration based partly on the essential elements of a formally recognized opposition in a multiple party milieu and (2) the triad of interrelated concepts concerning the civil service—the notions of anonymity, neutrality, and impartiality—also set within that same context. Yet, the Westminster-Whitehall and other transplanted institutions that are part of this legacy tend to behave quite differently in the Caribbean environment than the parent institutions. The parent institutions were nurtured and developed in an environment in which tradition and convention played (and still play) very important roles.[4]

Often, too, there is a long time-lag between changes (or the recognition that such changes have occurred) in the original British institutions and modifications in their corresponding Caribbean derivatives. Thus, certain illusions about the working of institutions, which have been largely dispelled in the United Kingdom within the last few decades, continue to survive in the Caribbean.

Although, as indicated earlier, persons of African ancestry represent a preponderant majority of the Caribbean population, in two states, Guyana and Trinidad-Tobago, the presence of significant proportions of people of Indian origin (52 percent and 40 percent, respectively) has an impact on sociocultural, economic, and political life in these countries. This impact is demonstrated in the leadership, composition, and character of the main political parties. Even more conspicuously in Guyana, overt racial conflict, a dominant feature of the early 1960s, erupted violently, with strong political ingredients, the effects of which spilled over into the public administration arena. The participation of British Guiana's civil service[5] in the long general strike of 1963 reflected not only opposition of a conservative bureaucracy to the ideology and policies of a newly elected Marxist government, but also the reactions of a civil service consisting primarily of black and ''near white'' senior personnel to a government led by an (East) Indian Premier, Dr. Cheddi Jagan, given the racial context of

British Guiana. Within a year, following the overthrow of Dr. Jagan's government, the International Commission of Jurists, at the request of Guyanese Indians, investigated their allegations of racial discrimination in recruitment to and promotion within the public service. In the event, the commission decided that the allegations were unfounded.[6]

Slavery, the plantation system, and colonial rule all generated and perpetuated ideas that emphasized the distinction between the dominant and the dominated: those who were born to rule and those who were born to be ruled. These systems have left a heritage in the social and class structure and relations and in attitudes and behavior patterns that have important consequences for the administrative processes.

Social stratifications with its complex pattern of class, color, and shades of complexion—a hierarchical structure of expatriate whites, "creole" whites, browns, and blacks—was reflected in the microcosmic mirror of the colonial civil service hierarchy.[7] Black West Indians were not to be found in the higher administrative echelons of the service and rarely in the elite Colonial Secretariat which stood at the apex of the administrative system. They were relegated to subordinate positions, constituting the lumpen mass of clerks at the bottom of the ladder.

The few who attained relatively senior positions as professional officers—doctors, lawyers, engineers—represented a sample of the rare ones who won the annual Jamaica or Rhodes Scholarship for study overseas or whose parents could afford them this facility. Throughout the region, with the possible exception of Barbados, an undemocratic education system restricted secondary education (by limitations in the number of school places and cost) to a fraction of 1 percent of the secondary school-age population. There was no local university.[8]

The establishment of the University College of the West Indies (now University of the West Indies [UWI]), in 1948 and the movement toward democratization of secondary education in the larger states beginning in the mid–1950s, have opened up many career opportunities for a much wider section of Caribbean communities. The highest management, administrative, and professional positions in the civil services are now open to West Indians, regardless of racial origin, and a very high percentage of such positions are now held by graduates of the UWI.

This contrasts sharply with the conditions obtaining at the introduction of ministerial systems during the 1950s, when most of the new permanent secretaries and especially those in the small Leeward and Windward Islands were clerical officers who had moved up to these positions through the passing of time and without higher education or special training. This condition was one of the causes of conflict in the relations between professional and administrative officers at the time.[9]

Caribbean societies display certain characteristics that appear to be endemic and are present in their public administration systems and the modus operandi of these systems. These are nonparticipative decision-making reflected in excessive centralization and reluctance to delegate, authoritarian-submissive attitudes, remoteness of the governors from the governed, and a deeply ingrained dependence syndrome.

Excessive centralization is best illustrated in the relations between central governments and local government authorities, in the processes of national planning—an exercise in "development from above"—and in the attitudes and processes of central agencies, for example, the ministries of Finance, Establishments Departments, and Public Service Commissions vis-à-vis line ministries and departments. As a consequence of some of these behavior patterns, a premium is placed on overcautiousness, decision making becomes timid, and attributes such as creativity, innovativeness, and dynamism, which are essential for development administrators, are stultified and frustrated.[10]

The Economic Environment

A number of features of the economic environment play critical roles in the shaping of Caribbean public policy agendas. They are small, open, developing economies with a high ratio of foreign trade to gross domestic product and dependence on the export of primary products in agriculture, minerals, and tourism—all of which are vulnerable to changes in conditions in the international marketplace.[11]

During the late 1960s, policies of localization and nationalization reduced the dominance of foreign ownership in financial institutions, in mineral exploitation, and in sugar plantations and processing. During the 1970s, the process of nationalization of industrial and commercial undertakings accelerated especially in Guyana, Jamaica, and Trinidad and Tobago. The trend toward public ownership and enlargement of the scope of public enterprise during this period was partly a reflection of socialist ideological motives, at least in Guyana and Jamaica.[12]

But even in Trinidad-Tobago, without the underpinning of socialist ideology, the "increasing level of economic nationalism led to a growing mood of the people that they should own and control their economies to a greater extent than now exists."[13] Hence, the Guyana and Trinidad governments, respectively, decided to "win economic independence as a means of consolidating political independence"[14] and to "accelerate the transfer of foreign-owned firms to local hands."[15] In Jamaica, however, the general election of October 1980 brought to power a new government with a policy of divestment/privatization aimed at reversing the public enterprise trend of the previous regime.[16] So far, this has included the sale to the public of shares in the highly successful government-owned bank and cement company, a number of hotels, and plans for partial divestment of electronic media.

As for resource endowment, Trinidad-Tobago, by far the wealthiest of the group (GNP per head: U.S. $5,670), enjoyed the benefit of an oil revenue boom until the end of the 1970s, but since 1982 has entered a period of fiscal and foreign exchange deficits. The Bahamas now leads in terms of GNP (U.S. $7,100) per head, while Guyana and Jamaica, earning significant revenues and foreign exchange from bauxite exploitation for two decades, have since the mid–1970s been experiencing considerable balance-of-payment problems with the decline of the aluminum market, and a continuing fall in gross domestic product. As a result, Jamaica has had to resort to the International Monetary Fund for assistance, a development that has intensified financial, social, and economic problems. The societies, particularly the Jamaican, are bedevilled by problems of highly skewed income distribution patterns and chronically high unemployment. All these factors have created considerable social tensions and increased pressures on governments.

Beginning in the 1950s and concurrently with political and constitutional development, governments throughout the region have moved increasingly toward the assumption of a developmental role. For decades economic development policies have been based primarily on import substitution and on the Puerto Rican-inspired notion of industrialization by invitation[17]—the encouragement of private, and particularly foreign, investment in manufacturing industry and tourism, by special concessionary fiscal, tariff, and other incentives. But the modest impact of these policies, coupled with the continuing crisis in its foreign exchange reserves, has led the new Jamaican government to introduce a revised policy oriented toward export promotion.

Governments have succumbed to pressures from transnational and other investors from overseas to provide monopoly franchises for manufacturing industry, compounded in some cases by the guarantee of specific rates of profit and package concessions to land developers. The investor commanding superior technical resources, relevant information, and experience in bargaining frequently emerges from negotiations with the governments of these small states with terms entirely advantageous to the individual investor but detrimental to local community interests.

The Political-Constitutional Framework

Constitutional Development: The most conspicuous characteristic of West Indian constitutional change has been its gradual evolutionary and peaceful nature. Constitutional development of the territories followed a pattern that became institutionalized throughout the former British Empire: the movement toward representative and then responsible government, passing through stages from Crown colony status, through embryonic ministerial systems, to the development of full cabinet systems and of internal self-government, and ultimately, the attainment of independence.

In the former African and Asian parts of the empire, the freedom struggle was based on continuous public agitation and led ultimately to independence. But in the West Indian colonies, constitutional changes were peacefully impelled, with the exception of the riots over poor social and economic conditions during the period 1936–1938, which led to new constitutions. The pace of real political change was slow even though universal adult suffrage was introduced in 1944, and Jamaica already had an advanced British Colonial constitution for some years.[18] As a result of this tardy, peaceful constitutional development, Jamaica became independent fifteen years after India and five years after Ghana.

It should be noted, too, that three states, Guyana, Trinidad-Tobago, and Dominica, have republican constitutions (within the British Commonwealth), though the roles and powers of the respective presidents differ. At one end, the president of the Co-operative Republic of Guyana wields strong executive powers, while at the other, the president of Dominica performs primarily ceremonial functions, assuming a role similar to that of a governor-general, with the head of state in Trinidad-Tobago falling somewhere in between.

Although public opinion has generally been apathetic, ill informed, and inarticulate, facilitating the emergence and dominance of charismatic and messianic political leaders, two countries, Trinidad and Jamaica, have experienced significant improvements in levels of political consciousness and awareness, primarily resulting from efforts toward political education by political parties.

The first of these efforts occurred in Trinidad during the mid–1950s with the emergence of the People's National Movement (PNM) and the late Dr. Eric Williams' "University of Woodford Square," though it was to a large extent a middle-class educational experience. In Jamaica, over the past decade, a process of political education has contributed to the development of an electorate that has become more politically conscious and aware of both political and social issues than ever before in that country's history.[19]

Political Parties: The riots of the 1930s also led to the development of a trade union movement and in most cases, at a later date, to the beginnings of a formally structured political party system. Indeed, in a number of states, notably Jamaica, Antigua, Barbados, and St. Kitts-Nevis, a close interlocking emerged between the main parties and trade unions—stemming from the circumstances that gave birth to the two sets of institutions—with both sharing the same leadership. This nexus has played a dominant role in economic and political life in those states during the past four decades.

With few exceptions, and these have occurred only relatively recently, real ideological differences between the major parties in any one state have been minimal. Parties have tended to follow personalities "held together by the charisma of the party bossman" rather than by ideology.[20] Regardless of their designation ("Labor," "National," etc.) and platform rhetoric, most of the major parties have been of a liberal-democratic genre. However, British Guiana represented an early aberration from this pattern, with the Marxist People's Progressive Party (PPP) coming to power as early as 1953. More recently, the events in Grenada (the coup that toppled the Gairy government in 1979 followed by the four-year rule of the People's Revolutionary government of Maurice Bishop) have also represented a departure from customary liberal-democratic and Westminster-Whitehall models.

In Jamaica, despite its socialist manifesto ever since its founding in 1938, the policies of the People's National party (PNP) during the 1950s and early 1960s scarcely differed from those of the rival Jamaica Labor party (JLP) when actually in office. But the position has changed dramatically since 1975 when, almost three years after returning to office, the PNP declared its philosophy of "democratic socialism." Between then and the end of 1980, this new orientation, reflected in a number of policy thrusts, raised controversial public administration issues that will be considered later in this chapter.

Elections within the region during the past five years have shown an ideological shift toward the center and right of center. The Co-operative Republic of Guyana's People's National Congress (PNC), in power continuously since 1964, is the sole remaining socialist government in the region. (Interestingly, the opposition party is also left-wing—Dr. Jagan's Marxist PPP.) Also in Guyana, two departures from the regional norm are evidenced in the declaration of the "paramountcy of the party" and the graduation of a number of civil service technocrats to the position of ministers holding the portfolios of finance, planning, and agriculture.

A contrast is evident between those states, for example, Jamaica and Barbados, where two strong parties compete for power and where party rivalry is intense, and others that are virtually one-party states de facto, having weak opposition parties. For example, in Trinidad and Tobago, the late Dr. Eric Williams' PNM held office continuously from 1956 until its landslide defeat in December 1986, whereas in Belize George Price's People's United party (PUP) was continuously in power for thirty years until December 1984.

Jamaica represents the prime example of a two-party system, with the major parties alternating in office in a regular process during the more than forty years since party government was introduced. No party has had more than two consecutive terms, and no third party has ever won a seat in Parliament; nor has an independent candidate won since the election of 1949. Indeed, "the entrenchment of the two-party system with its accompanying feature of intense party competition has culminated, especially during the past decade, in a condition of deep-seated cleavage and political polarization of the society."[21]

These differences among the states have significant implications in a number of public administration areas. Among other problems, they raise issues concerning civil service neutrality, and the relations between central governments on the one hand, and local government authorities and public enterprise organizations on the other.

Relations Between Ministers and Administrators: The transfer of power to locally elected political heads brought in its train friction and conflict between ministers and senior civil servants, partly because of differing social and educational backgrounds, and partly because of difficulties experienced by the older members of the bureaucracy in adjusting to a new subordinate status and role. These problems have lessened in states where there has been a relatively long experience of the ministerial system and where ministers and senior civil servants share similar social and educational backgrounds.

But in the Leeward and Windward Islands with small, highly personalized communities, "political sympathies and loyalties are generally widely known, civil servants are overexposed in the political arena and conflict and tension between politicians and civil servants are intensified."[22]

In Trinidad and Tobago, a different phenomenon has been evident, especially during the latter part of the 1970s when a number of "super" permanent secretaries, including the permanent secretary to the prime minister (and head of the civil service), were suspended on the allegation that "a small and ambitious technocratic elite" was conspiring to arrogate authority for governing the country from the elected representatives. In the event, the allegations were never really substantiated. These incidents reflected, to a great extent, the personalist rule of the late prime minister, Dr. Williams.[23]

Interest Groups: During the colonial period, the dominant economic interests— sugar plantation and other landed proprietors and managers, and commodity importers and distributors—wielded considerable influence. Later, their influence was strengthened through collective representation via chambers of commerce (some more than one hundred years old), specialized commodity associations representing, for example, sugar and bananas, and more recently through the formation of manufacturers' associations.

The political party–trade union link and the dominant position held by unions in the political and economic arenas in some states have been noted. Generally and for the most part, these are blanket unions, though specific industrial unions, for example, the Oil Workers Trade Union in Trinidad and Tobago also play important roles.

In his typology of interest groups in Jamaica, Edwin Jones[24] has classified their stratification profile as follows

Strong client stratum: the plantocracy and large farmers, commercial and industrial businesspeople, senior bureaucrats, technical advisers.

Middle stratum: lawyers and teachers, unionized workers, the church (especially the established wing).

Weak stratum: small peasants, small farmers, small businesspersons, unorganized workers, consumers.

Jones has observed that a number of institutional arrangements tend to "conspire" to the disadvantage of the weaker groups; these include "differential access to the centers of power," with representatives of the strong client stratum incorporated into the decision-making structures and the overrepresentation of this latter stratum on statutory boards, agricultural policy-making structures, and the boards of public enterprise organizations. Jones points further to government sponsorship and cooptation of certain groups, especially in agriculture, and to the "colonization" of other groups, for example, the trade unions, by political parties.

An interesting feature emerged during the 1950s and 1960s as a consequence of industrialization by governments' incentive and import-substitution policies, accompanied by the pressure brought by new local manufacturers for protective measures. This was the conflict between the new manufacturers' associations and the long-established chambers of commerce, which had deeply vested interests in import-distribution activities. Such conflicts have significant implications for the prices and quality of consumer goods—important considerations in relatively poor societies, where, in addition to their low income levels, consumers who tend to be less effectively organized than large producers and importers, are at a disadvantage even in those states where consumer associations have developed. Some governments have attempted to strengthen consumer interests by establishing Bureaus of Standards and Consumer Protection Divisions in Ministries of Industry and Commerce.[25]

THE STRUCTURE OF ADMINISTRATION

Central Administration

The introduction of ministerial systems, beginning in the more advanced states in the early 1950s, was followed by a process of integration—the fusion of ministries with departments falling under their portfolio with the objectives of facilitating more effective policy, financial and personnel control, more efficient communications, and economies from rationalization.

The implementation of the integration process has been relatively easy in the larger states that have specialized ministries with responsibilities for one or two related subjects. But in the very small states, the scarcity of skilled personnel and financial resources and the small size of the clientele to be served impose constraints on the creation of highly specialized public agencies, thus resulting in the development of multisubject ministries—each covering a wide range of unrelated subjects and departments. Hence, difficulties are involved in integrating such ministries with their portfolio departments.

Following the arrangement generally obtaining in ministerial forms of government of British parentage, the permanent secretary serves as top manager of his ministry and technical advice is expected to be channeled from professional and technical personnel through him, to the minister. Moreover, although those attaining permanent secretary positions increasingly tend to be university graduates, for the most part (with a few exceptions) they are not qualified in the subject matter area of their ministry's portfolio. Emphasis is placed, rather, on their management and administrative rather than technical skills. In the more advanced states, recognition is now being given to the need to allow the chief technical adviser equal access to the minister, a requirement facilitated by the formation of a policy/management group in some ministries.

Until the 1960s, the grading and classification of posts in the civil service were imprecise. Posts were traditionally grouped into broad amorphous classes, for example, administrative, executive, clerical without a clear definition of the duties of each class. Consequently, positions that involved differing types and levels of functions and responsibilities were often placed in the same grades and groupings. This situation still obtains in most of the smaller states.

In Trinidad-Tobago, Jamaica, and Barbados, comprehensive reclassification exercises undertaken during the 1960s and 1970s have produced more rational systems based on functions, level of responsibilities, and qualifications required for the post. In Jamaica, however, the system is currently being reviewed. At present, the structure includes the following groups, among others, each containing a number of grade levels:

Executive Management (all permanent secretaries and the auditor-general)

Senior Management (including directors of divisions)

Program Management and Administration

Financial Administration, Accounts, and Audit

Natural, Physical, and Social Sciences

Medical, Veterinary Medicine, and Dentistry*

Judicial and Legal*

Education

Electronic Data Processing Systems Administration

Applied Sciences

Clerical

Secretarial

(*Includes subgroups)

Local Government

As indicated earlier, local government systems have existed in some of the larger states for centuries. Indeed, in Jamaica the system was introduced shortly after the English conquest in 1655 and was patterned on the sixteenth-century Elizabethan parochial model of vestry and justices. The beginnings of the local government system of Trinidad reflected that island's history of alternating Spanish and French occupation until the early nineteenth century. Hence, the present Port of Spain City Council had its origins in the Spanish Cabildo, an ecclesiastical and municipal council. Later, the administration of the counties developed out of a system of wardenship, as a replica of the French Prefecture.[26] Belize reflects its Latin America environment and population mixture of Spanish, Mayan, Carib and Mestizo, and British origins. Thus, the Spanish cabildo and alcalde (mayor) function side by side with district town boards and village councils.[27]

In the Caribbean, local government authorities are almost totally dependent on central government for resources. With the exception of Guyana, not only are they given relatively minor statutory functions, but central governments have been most reluctant to devolve authority on them. They have virtually become departments of government. Despite repeated statements by political leaders emphasizing the virtues and value of preserving and strengthening local government in the interest of democratic values, and numerous reports of commissions and committees[28] recommending a greater degree of autonomy to the authorities, the movement has, in fact, been in the opposite direction: a trend toward creeping centralization and the transfer of full control over areas to central or newly created statutory bodies, for example, poor relief, water supplies, and public cleansing, sections of which were hitherto in the domain of local authorities.[29] Furthermore, in Jamaica the municipal authority, Kingston and St. Andrew Corporation (KSAC), which for more than sixty years has been responsible for the capital city (Kingston) and its environs, was dissolved in October 1984, and its authority and functions distributed among a number of ministries.[30]

The trend is perhaps inevitable, given the size of countries such as Jamaica and increasingly severe economic and financial resource constraints. Such conditions strengthen the arguments of those who contend that the cost of maintaining a local government system is too high in relation to its contribution to preserving the democratic ideal and process.

Regionalism in Guyana

In Guyana, an exception to the general pattern, the old system of local government has been fundamentally restructured via the new Constitution of the Co-operative Republic and the Local Democratic Organizations Act, both of 1980. The country has now been divided into regions and subregions, and six sectors, each with its own council and each charged with specific functions, have been created. The objective is "to create self-reliant, productive and prosperous communities of people . . . and to ensure 'power to the people' in the political process, exercised through institutions."[31] These six sectors are: Region, Subregion, District, Community, Neighborhood, and People's Cooperative Unit. Thus far, only the regional councils have been established.

The councils are elected by residents of the region and have responsibility for "ensuring the efficient management and development of their areas and especially for organizing popular co-operation in respect of political, social, economic and cultural life."[32] The areas are intended to be both planning and development regions, with the councils providing for the maximum participation of the people.

In addition, a National Congress of Local Democratic Organizations is elected by and from members of the local democratic organs; its responsibility is to represent the interests of local government in Guyana. The Constitution views "the establishment of the organs of local democratic power as an integral part of the political organization of the state."[33]

Concurrently with the restructuring of the local government system, a number of key central government agencies, for example, the Treasury, have been decentralized and a formal relationship established between their field branches and the regional councils. The field public officers are required to report through the regional executive officers. The system is supervised by a Ministry of Regional Development.

Other Community-Based Institutions

A significant development of the late 1970s was the evolution of community councils designed to "encourage a co-ordinated approach to the development of the community, to provide a link between national and local government programmes and the local community, and encourage social, cultural, educational and economic activities." Furthermore, the councils were seen as "people-based" organizations performing omnibus mobilizational, functional ("activity-oriented") and representational roles. They served as a forum for developing consensus opinion and as a vehicle for channeling community efforts in productive ways.[34]

Unfortunately, many local government councillors viewed the councils as competitive institutions. Indeed, some saw them as a threat, whereas the public viewed them as partisan political institutions. As a result, their effectiveness has been limited.

Nondepartmental Agencies

Constituting an integral component of the institutional structure of the public sector is a complex of nondepartmental agencies which in the larger states, notably Jamaica, assume significant proportions. Indeed, a committee appointed by the government of Jamaica to examine and review the operations of statutory bodies commented on the proliferation of such bodies. More than 200 existed in 1975.[35]

Statutory bodies are found in a wide variety of areas including finance, commerce, and commodity marketing (bananas, cocoa, coffee, nutmeg), cultural activities, and social services. A U.N. team reporting on public administration in Jamaica (1965)[36] classified the then existing complex of statutory authorities as follows: Advisory; Appellate; Regulatory; Commercial and/or Executive. Included in the last category are the commercial and industrial type, operating as public enterprises in the form of statutory or public corporations in fields such as development financing, agricultural development and marketing, mineral exploitation and processing, transportation, broadcasting, and tourism.

In addition, the state company form of parastatal enterprise set up under the umbrella of the company law is being increasingly adopted, particularly in the areas of public utilities, manufacturing industry, and state trading. Associated with the development of public enterprise has been the creation of monitoring and controlling institutions such as the Guyana State Corporation, an umbrella-type holding corporation that also serves as the supervisor of other corporations and as the authority controlling the appointment and emoluments of top officers in these organizations; and the less elaborate Advisory and Monitoring Unit within the Ministry of Public Utilities, Jamaica.

The proliferation of nondepartmental agencies has been an issue of concern for more than a decade. We will return to this subject in the section, Important Issues. The appointment of special advisers will also be discussed in that section.

Special Structures and Units

Paradoxically, in spite of the strong recommendation made by the Committee on Statutory Bodies in Jamaica (1975) against the creation of new bodies of this type, nondepartmental agencies have recently been established in four important areas: two by the conversion of government departments and two assuming functions originally performed by existing ministries.

It has long been recognized that one of the principal constraints to public sector development in the Caribbean reflects deficiencies in project analysis, management, and implementation. Attempts have been made to remedy this weakness in Jamaica by the establishment of a small Project Monitoring and Review Unit in the Ministry of Finance. This unit has more recently been hived off as a state company, the Project Analysis and Monitoring Company (PAMCO). In addition to its assumptions of these functions, PAMCO contributes to project management training for the public sector.[37]

A Revenue Board (staffed by former civil servants) now advises the minister of finance on all matters concerning taxation and the achievement of an equitable and effective system of taxation, including improvement of the assessment and collection of revenue. In effect, the board has assumed functions hitherto falling within the purview of the Taxation Section of the Ministry of Finance. As a result, conflicts have arisen in the relations between members of the board and the minister's civil service advisers.

In 1984, the Department of Statistics and the National Planning Agency were transformed by special statutes into the Institute of Statistics and the Planning Institute, respectively, thus removing both of these institutions from the category of departmental agencies. The rationale for the change was evidently to facilitate greater flexibility and freedom especially in the level of emoluments and in recruitment and promotion of personnel. These are important factors in these fields of skills scarcity.

Emphasis should also be placed on the creation of a complex of new nondepartmental agencies in Jamaica designed to implement the government's policy on attracting investments and on increasing exports in the context of severe unemployment and foreign exchange problems.

Hence, in addition to the long-established Industrial Development Corporation[38] (1952) which concentrates on encouraging the development of manufacturing industry via the provision of factory space and other incentives, more recent institutions include:

Jamaica National Investment Promotion: exclusively a promotional and not an operations agency, focusing primarily on agriculture, agrobusiness, and tourism construction.

National Investment Bank of Jamaica Ltd.: a state company directly involved in investment (including joint ventures) and the divestment of specific public enterprises.

Jamaica National Export Corporation: an export promotion agency.

All these institutions are public corporations or state companies with boards comprising a mix of government and private sector personnel.

Before the creation of these organizations, the former democratic socialist PNP government, in the face of strong criticism and opposition from private sector interest associations and the opposition party, had established a State Trading Corporation (STC) in 1977 "to take over control of all imports deemed essential for national development and in the public interest."[39] Four years earlier, the government had created a wholly owned state company, Jamaica Nutrition Holdings Ltd. (JNH), designed to serve as a centralized agency for the bulk importation of nutrient-rich foods in order to stabilize the prices of such mass-consumed foods.[40]

The subsequently established STC, which now embraced JNH Ltd. as a subsidiary, was created, in the words of a ministry paper, "as part of the Government's policy of ensuring 'social control' of the economy."[41]

Interestingly, despite the divestment policy of the new JLP government, not only has the corporation remained in existence (as a highly successful institution), but also its bulk importation operations (food, drugs, lumber) have not been reduced. The only changes since the general elections of 1980 have been in terms of form. Specifically, there is a state company in place of a statutory corporation and a new name, the Jamaica Commodity Trading Company. Indeed, the managing director, a well-known active supporter of the former governing party, has been retained. All this has happened in spite of the very strong statements made by the then JLP opposition spokesman on industry and commerce (now minister in charge of these subjects). He is reported to have described the STC initially as "a blood sucking vampire . . . an economic vampire [which] has the potential to grind production and employment to a halt."[42]

Though not a new institution, the Urban Development Corporation (UDC), a statutory body established in Jamaica in 1968 and St. Lucia (1971), deserves mention as an interesting innovation. The rationale for creating the Jamaican UDC stemmed from awareness of the problems of urban growth and the need to create new and viable centers in rural areas in order to ease the pressure from existing centers, and to improve the urban fabric in metropolitan regions. Thus, the UDC is envisaged as an instrument designed to perform the role of "developer in the public interest," bringing together the authority and resources of the government and the expertise and dynamism of the private sector.

Among the functions of the UDC are the acquisition, management, and disposal of land; construction of roads and buildings; and provision of parks, gardens, and other public amenities. The UDC is an implementing body which complements the Town Planning Department and the Town Planning Authority, bodies that share responsibilities for land use planning and control.[43] Like the public enterprise organizations described earlier, the UDC's board consists of public and private sector personnel.

Gradual awareness of the relevance and importance of the role of science and technology and their implications for developing countries has led to the formation, in the more advanced states of the region, of Ministries of Science and Technology, or embryonic divisions of other ministries, to assume responsibilities for these interrelated subjects.

One additional innovation is the introduction in Jamaica of a position of contractor general by legislation enacted in 1983 (Law 15 of 1983). This follows allegations made persistently over a long period about corruption and partisan political discrimination in the award of government contracts and licenses. It fulfills an electioneering promise of the JLP.

The contractor general is to be appointed by the governor general after consultation with the prime minister and the leader of the opposition, with functions of monitoring the grant, issue, and revocation of licenses; and the award and implementation of government contracts so as to ensure that contracts are awarded impartially and on merit. The first contractor general was appointed on 1 October 1986.

Regional Organizations

In addition to central and local government structures, the states and territories, following the demise of the Federation of the West Indies (1958–1962), have developed a number of regional and subregional institutions in an effort to strengthen bonds of regionalism and further the integration movement. The most significant of these are the Caribbean Common Market (CARICOM) with an emphasis on economic and trade matters, governed by a Council of Ministers and served by a secretariat; the Caribbean Development Bank (CDB); and the recently formed Organization of Eastern Caribbean States (OECS) comprising the less developed countries (LDCs).

FINANCIAL ADMINISTRATION AND CONTROL

Generally, financial administration and control institutions, mechanisms, and processes in Commonwealth Caribbean states follow the British model of a dominant central controlling agency—the Ministry of Finance (or Treasury), the Consolidated Fund, an Accountant (or Paymaster) General's Department, and Auditor or Comptroller and Auditor General. The auditor-general is responsible to Parliament rather than to a minister. The budgeting systems of almost all the states are based on the old traditional line-item approach, although strong criticisms have for decades been made against this system in terms of its inadequacy in facilitating identification of the output expected and the performance (results) of items of expenditure. Jamaica is currently in the process of introducing performance budgeting as an integral element in its program of financial management reform.

A Public Accounts Committee (PAC) of Parliament (normally under the chairmanship of an opposition member) examines the accounts flowing from appropriation grants by Parliament, other accounts representing expenditures approved under legislative acts and the auditor general's report on these accounts. The PAC checks whether funds have been expended as appropriated, and exposes any waste, inefficiency, or irregularities in the disbursement of funds, summoning, if necessary, any accounting officers to explain and justify items of expenditure.

The permanent secretary (in some cases, a head of department) is designated the accounting officer. He, not the minister, is held responsible to the PAC, and therefore to Parliament, for the proper control of expenditures appropriated for the activities of the ministry and departments falling within its portfolio.

Commission of Public Accountability

During the past decade the auditor general of Jamaica in his annual report has repeatedly commented in trenchant terms on the delay in completion and submission of accounts by some agencies, the inefficiencies in financial administration, and the waste of public funds. (Both in Jamaica and Trinidad/Tobago strong criticisms have been made about the failure of public enterprise organizations to submit their annual accounts and in these countries state companies and public corporations represent a considerable investment of public funds.) As a consequence of these strictures, and following the findings of a management audit carried out on the Ministry of Finance in Jamaica, modern techniques are to be introduced and a new institution created as part of a comprehensive program of administrative reforms to upgrade management in the public sector and to improve accountability.

These reforms include the introduction of a performance budgeting system, the development of a corps of Finance Officers, and extension of the scope of decentralization of financial authority to line ministries and departments. In addition, a Commission of Public Accountability was established in 1985 whose responsibilities embrace the total public sector, that is, central and local government agencies, public enterprises, and other statutory authorities. The commission's functions include monitoring the preparation, auditing, and submission of audited financial statements and audit reports; the appointment of auditors, and financial breaches, irregularities and weaknesses; ensuring that such irregularities, etc., are investigated, following up the reports of the PAC and ensuring that its recommendations are implemented. To complete the complex of Jamaican financial controlling institutions, a post of controller general has been created in 1987 to see that public monies are spent in accordance with the wishes of Parliament and the law and that public revenue is properly brought to account.

In Trinidad the state enterprises are monitored by a special Public Enterprises Accounts Committee of Parliament.

PERSONNEL ADMINISTRATION

Personnel administration throughout the region is based on the pattern inherited from the British parent. This system is characterized by a dichotomy between the "establishment" and personnel functions and the assignment of these sets of functions to two separate agencies. Thus, the establishment functions concerning the determination of organizational structure, position-classification and grading of posts, staff complements, salaries and conditions of service, training policy and programs, and superannuation arrangements are placed under the responsibility of a minister—in most cases the minister of finance or the prime minister—because of the policy issues and financial implications involved. In two states, Guyana and Jamaica, the establishment responsibilities have been transferred from the Ministry of Finance to specially created public service ministries[44] which have also been assigned administrative reform and management service functions. The management service functions reflect a more positive, initiating approach than the traditional organization and methods (O & M) function.

Responsibility for the personnel function, in terms of the career of the individual officer (his recruitment, appointment, transfer, promotion, development, exercise of disciplinary proceedings) is assigned to an independent, impartial, and nonpolitical body, the Public Service or Civil Service Commission (PSC/CSC). In the performance of its role, the PSC is expected to emphasize protection of the individual civil servant's career and the integrity of the service as a whole against the incidence of nepotism and favoritism and especially against political favoritism or discrimination.[45]

Generally, the commission consists of a small group of persons, functioning on a part-time basis, appointed by the head of state on the recommendation of the prime minister. In some states, the appointment is made after consultation with the leader of the opposition. In Jamaica and Guyana, the Civil Service Staff Association has the constitutional right to submit a panel of names from which one or two members, respectively, are selected. Unlike the United Kingdom Commission, Caribbean constitutions expressly forbid serving public officers to sit as members. In the independent monarchical states, although the constitutions stipulate that the governor general shall make appointments, and so forth, on the advice of the PSC, this language expresses one of the tenets of the Westminster-Whitehall model of monarchical government. In fact, the PSC holds full executive powers and is entrenched in the constitutions.

Other commissions have jurisdiction over personnel in services such as the police, judiciary, teaching, local government, and statutory authorities.

Recruitment and Appointments

At the lowest clerical levels, the qualification for entry into the civil service is generally a prescribed minimum number of subjects at the Ordinary Level Cambridge examinations or the Caribbean equivalent. In addition, some states prescribe a civil service examination and interview. At higher levels, for example, the administrative grades, entry is based either on possession of a university degree (direct entry) or on promotion from the executive grades. Only in a few states are vacancies generally advertised.

In cases where skills are in scarce supply, for example, accounting, actuarial science, engineering, and medicine, overseas advertisement is undertaken (especially in the United Kingdom and North America). The government's overseas missions (Foreign Service) are used as points of contact, and from time to time recruiting teams travel to these countries.

In Jamaica special arrangements are made for the development of corps of personnel managers and financial managers.

Promotion and Career Advancement

The policy and criteria on which promotion is based have long been a highly sensitive and controversial issue throughout the region. While lip-service is paid to the development of a merit service, career advancement tends generally to be based on length of service and seniority,[46] partly because of inertia, and partly because this basis requires less elaborate means for evaluation. "Promotion by merit requires more discriminating criteria than seniority or paper qualifications."[47]

In 1975, Jamaica's PSC, in association with the Ministry of the Public Service, decided that, in the future, career advancement would be based on merit. The commission elaborated on this decision by explaining that the criteria would include "performance, qualifications, work-experience and general suitability for the higher post." Unfortunately, the new system has foundered on the problem of designing an effective mechanism for performance evaluation in place of the traditional confidential report that has for a long time been strongly criticized in all the states as being ineffectual. An important constraint lies in the absence of consistency and uniformity in the standards of assessment among the reporting officers and the significant element of subjectivity involved in a process that cannot by its nature be as objective as the seniority method. Hopefully, efforts directed toward improvement of the reporting form and better training for reporting officers will in time remedy these defects.

Despite these difficulties, two improvements over the old system have been in place since 1975. One is the appointment of small promotions boards or committees in a number of ministries and departments, consisting of representatives from both the management and "staff" levels. The other is the requirement that the person whose performance is being assessed should see and sign the evaluation, with a right of appeal. The assessment is intended to serve the purpose not only of assisting in determining the staff member's suitability for promotion, but also of identifying areas of need for development and weaknesses so that efforts might be made to correct them.

In Jamaica attempts have been made to introduce a system of examinations for promotions within the management/administrative grades, but these have been resisted by the Staff Association.

Training

Training for civil servants began during the 1940s, but it took the form mainly of overseas training and involved a relatively small number of officers from the larger territories. Since then, there have been significant developments in both local and regional training facilities. All the larger and more developed states have established active government training units and management development centers, while most of the less developed have a training officer located in the establishment or personnel department.

Much of the stimulus to training has been given by the University of the West Indies (UWI), which in 1960 introduced a Diploma in Public Administration for serving public officials in the region and simultaneously established a post of director of training in public administration within a new Department of Government. Since then, the UWI has added to its curriculum, certificate, and degree programs in management studies. The University of Guyana also includes in its offerings a bachelor's degree in public management and a diploma in public administration.[48]

Other regional facilities include the Caribbean Center for Development Administration (CARICAD), which was set up in 1979 to improve management capability and to further organization development, particularly within the public sector;[49] and the CDB which regularly conducts a project management course.

The Jamaican government has a highly developed complex of public sector training institutions which consists of

The Administrative Staff College conducting general management and project management training.

The Finance and Accounts College of Training, providing training in the field of public financial management.

The Center for Supervisory Training.

The Language Training Center.

Some of the local and regional governmental institutions work closely with the UWI.

Discipline

A code of conduct for public officers and rules prescribing disciplinary policy and procedures are contained in staff orders and public service regulations, respectively. Both are made in accordance with constitutional provisions.

The staff orders expressly prohibit public officers from engaging in private work for payment or in trade or any form of commercial undertaking; and from writing to the press or engaging in public broadcasting activities without permission of the appropriate authority. Furthermore, they are forbidden from participating actively on behalf of any political party or candidate in national or local elections.

In the conduct of disciplinary proceedings certain procedures are observed, including ensuring that the accused are fully provided with information about the charges against them, are given facilities for questioning persons who have given evidence against them and have the opportunity to defend themselves.

A distinction is drawn between major offenses, in respect of which charges may be laid against an officer "with a view to dismissal" and lesser offenses. In relation to dismissal charges, the proceedings assume a very formal form. The officer appears before a tribunal—often presided over by a retired judge—appointed by the Public Service Commission (after advice is obtained from the government's law officers), and the accused is permitted to be represented by a lawyer or by one of his colleagues. The constitutions make provision for the right of appeal. Although it is recognized that disciplinary cases should be dealt with expeditiously, there is often too great a backlog of such cases involving, in some instances, officers remaining on suspension for unduly long periods.

Both the personnel and establishment sets of functions are highly centralized. A modicum of authority is delegated to line agencies in respect of appointments and the exercise of disciplinary functions in respect of certain categories of staff at very low levels of the services.

CONTROL OVER ADMINISTRATION

With institutions whose foundations are embedded in the Westminster cabinet-parliamentary system, checks and controls over the administration in Commonwealth Caribbean states rest primarily in the legislature and in the judicial process.

Legislature

Despite the theory of the executive's responsibility to Parliament and, consequently, parliamentary control over the executive, the exercise of control by the legislature tends to be ineffectual. Cabinet dictatorship (and personalist rule) assume an even stronger role than in the United Kingdom, and back-bencher revolts or less overt dissidence are unlikely to occur.

Sittings of the lower House are dominated by government business, and the impact of the opposition and of private members generally tends to be minimal. Nor does Question Time represent an effective instrument of control. Stephen Yorke has illustrated the extent to which ministers have ignored questions asked in the Jamaica House of Representatives, often delaying answers for inordinately long periods, or allowing questions to lapse with the prorogation of Parliament or merely declining to reply.[50] Lloyd Barnett contends that the system of Question Time has been stymied in Jamaica because the necessary conditions for ensuring its effectiveness have not been established.[51]

Perhaps the most effectual instrument rests in the operation of the Public Accounts Committee which tends to be very active, under the chairmanship of an opposition "shadow minister." However, as already noted in the section on Financial Administration and Control, the effectiveness of this mechanism has been vitiated in some states, especially in Jamaica, by failure to follow up the findings of the committee. In this country too, as in Trinidad-Tobago, there has long been laxity in the submission of annual reports and accounts by public enterprise organizations. Efforts are currently being made to remedy these shortcomings.

In Jamaica, the major opposition party's boycotting of the General Elections of December 1983 has resulted in the phenomenon of a one-party House of Representatives. This development intensifies the ineffectiveness of Parliament and particularly the PAC, as checking and controlling bodies. The prime minister has attempted to meet this problem partially by the appointment to the Senate of a number of independent persons who are not supporters of the governing party. Most of these senators have been vocal in criticisms, but the upper house has very limited powers.

Judicial Review

With their heritage of the British common law and legal tradition, British Caribbean countries have no complex of administrative tribunals where decisions can be made in a judicial manner, as are found in France and other continental European countries. However, a body of case law has grown up, which provides avenues for judicial review of administrative action via the ordinary courts. Such avenues include recourse to the doctrine of *ultra vires* and use of writs of *certiorari* and *prohibition*, together with provisions for appeal in certain statutes in relation to the exercise of discretionary power by the executive.

The Public

Recourse to the courts is normally expensive and slow. With a limited legal aid system, the ordinary, relatively poor citizen may be unable to seek redress through the judicial process. Moreover, despite the appearance of close contact between the governors and the citizenry in the age of self-government and independence, the mass of less educated and poorer citizens regards the state bureaucracy as a remote entity.

The office of ombudsman was instituted partly because of these shortcomings—"to deal with citizens' grievances against maladministration, especially in these 'grey areas' for which there are no legal rights and which political sanctions fail to redress."[52]

Unlike their British counterparts, Caribbean ministers do not as a rule resign, nor are they dismissed for neglect, inefficiency, or acts of misfeasance or malfeasance which fall short of criminal behavior. It is unusual for sanctions to be imposed for such derelictions, and the electorate rarely exercises its ultimate sanction at the polls. Unfortunately, with few exceptions, for example, Jamaica, public opinion tends to be too tolerant, ill informed, and apathetic.[53]

The Ombudsman

The office of ombudsman has been instituted in four states: Guyana, Jamaica, and Trinidad-Tobago, and Barbados. The first of these, established in Guyana, within the provisions of the Independence Constitution of 1966, resulted partly from the visit in 1965 of the International Commission of Jurists which had been invited to "investigate and make recommendations in regard to certain problems concerning racial balance in the public services." The commission recommended the creation of an office of ombudsman to investigate maladministration, defined broadly to include racial discrimination. In fact, H. Lutchman observes that the Guyana government made much of the fact in public declarations that "Guyana was the first country in the Western Hemisphere to provide for such an office and was the first anywhere to provide for it in the National Constitution."[54]

Trinidad's office is also set up under constitutional provisions, while the Jamaican ombudsman derives powers from an act of Parliament. Interestingly, following a chorus of complaints by consumers concerning inefficiencies in the Jamaican complex of public utilities (operated by state companies), a second office of ombudsman has been created to deal specifically with grievances in the area of public utilities.[55]

Although the principal Jamaican ombudsman has succeeded in securing redress of significant hardship in a few individual cases, generally the ombudsman in the Caribbean has not been effective. Indeed, in Guyana the office appears to be in limbo at present. The effectiveness of the office depends to a great extent on the cooperation of the state bureaucracy and the opportunities and facilities provided by the executive to enable it to function freely.

In a few states Citizens Complaints Units have been established within the Police Department. These are staffed by senior police officers who investigate allegations made against the police.

FEATURES OF POLICY MAKING

Certain features of the public administration environment influence the shaping of public policy agendas and help determine policy outcomes in the Caribbean region. The salient features may be summarized in terms of the British heritage of the Westminster-Whitehall model of government, the continuing influence of the plantation and colonial systems, the syndrome of dependence, the dominance of liberal-democratic and conservative political parties led by charismatic politicians, and economies that are mainly mixed, and heavily dependent on external trade and exports of primary products—agriculture, minerals, and tourism—and are generally foreign oriented.

External Influences

The close proximity of the Caribbean countries to a superpower, the United States, influences the economic, trade, and political aspects of foreign policy. Moreover, as small and relatively poor states, they tend to be inordinately dependent on bilateral and international donor agencies that directly or indirectly influence the shaping of their domestic social and economic policies. This is particularly so in respect of those states, notably Jamaica, which, because of balance-of-payment crises, are heavily dependent on assistance from the International Monetary Fund and must accordingly submit to stringent policy conditions imposed by the Fund which have involved, among other things, the cutting back of social programs. Moreover, these conditions have resulted in the laying off of more than 5,000 civil servants in Jamaica in order "to reduce the top-heavy ratio of the Jamaican Civil Service to the general population as an integral part of the present Economic Adjustment Programme of the Government . . . much of it based on IMF agreements."[56]

The welcoming societies of these small Caribbean countries are particularly vulnerable to the intrusion of and domination by large transnational corporations and other overseas investors.

Package-deal proposals with demands for immediate decisions are presented to governments by businessmen supported by teams of consultants. A flood of private sector activities inundates the basic government functions, placing a considerable burden on senior administrative and technical public sector staff. As a result of the tendency for governments to respond indiscriminately to private sector pressures, planning and execution of public development programmes and projects lag far behind normal requirements.[57]

Reference has already been made to the disadvantageous bargaining position in which governments find themselves when negotiating such agreements.[58]

Interest Groups

Edwin Jones contends that the decision-making machinery of governments is dominated by elite economic interests. The less favored worker-peasant stratum and mass public find great difficulty in gaining access and influencing traditional patterns of decision making. In his view, the machinery of government has been operated "to harmonise and conciliate existing dominant interests and where possible, to exclude other interests."[59]

In addition, Carl Stone suggests that agricultural policy options and outputs have reflected "a clear collaboration between the large planters, the urban middle class party leaders, and bureaucrat-technocrats," and a "strategy of elite consensus." In his view, although large planters have been incorporated preponderantly into, and play leading advisory roles on, statutory boards administering agricultural policy, significant inputs from farming organizations and the small peasantry in particular have been excluded.[60]

Another relevant feature of the public policy matrix is the degree to which "dominant private sector interests (both local and international, with the two often interlinked) in agriculture, manufacturing industry, mining and commerce, are supported and their influence and control bolstered by linkages with and representation in government decision-making institutions including cabinets and statutory boards."[61]

Among the more direct manifestations of this phenomenon is the negotiation of monopoly franchises and other special concessionary agreements entered into by governments with local companies or transnational corporations. In many of these cases local legal and other representatives of the applicant companies simultaneously hold important public offices. Of significance too, is the network of multiple directorships circulating among a few persons—both in private sector firms and on public statutory boards.[62]

During the 1970s, beginnings were made toward broadening representation on public enterprise boards by introducing an element of worker participation, but since then, there has been minimal progress in this direction.

Technical Expertise

As regards the role of expertise, problems arise from time to time from the technical expert's sense of grievance that his or her advice has been ignored or subordinated to other inputs. The difficulty stems in certain cases from the resentment which the chief technical adviser in a ministry feels to the application of procedures that require technical advice to be channeled to the minister via a lay administrator, the permanent secretary.

In other cases, technical experts expect their opinions and findings to take precedence over all others—including the views and decisions of the appropriate minister and the cabinet—in the determination of public policy. Cases illustrating this conflict of opinion among parties have occurred primarily in the area of physical planning where strong interests exert pressure on administrators and politicians in relation to "development" and decisions that are considered disadvantageous to the environment emerge in the face of strong advice to the contrary from town and country planning and ecology experts.

One dimension deserving comment is the inordinate respect accorded, on the contrary, to technical advice given by consultants from overseas. It needs to be stated, too, that precedence continues to play an important role in policy making. From experience gained in a survey of Jamaica's senior civil servants in 1972–1973, G.E. Mills and Paul Robertson noted their marginal reading levels. They speculated that "the ideas of civil servants come out of the folklore of the service itself—some of this handed down by word of mouth, some contained in well-worn files." They discovered that the "definitive" work on agriculture which informed successive governments until the 1960s was the product of an English agricultural expert in a report written in 1945.[63]

Public Policy Institutions

In addition to the traditional policy institutions of the cabinet, ministries, and departments, and their administrative and technical advisory personnel, there are, of course, other policy-making and policy-influencing institutions. These include the complex of statutory and other nondepartmental agencies already mentioned, as well as central planning organizations which are to be found in the larger states. These latter agencies are responsible for the formulation of medium and long-range plans. In addition, they provide individual ministers and the cabinet with day-to-day advice on social and economic matters.

Moreover, in a few states, the central planning agencies are interconnected with small sectoral planning units, most frequently in health, agriculture, and education. From time to time attempts have been made to develop planning advisory institutions that embrace representation beyond the confines of the public sector. For instance, the Trinidad-Tobago National Economic Planning Commission set up recently to advise on the formulation of government policy includes representatives from the private sector, trade unions, the public sector, and a few individuals appointed in their own right, with the prime minister as chairman. Such bodies have tended to be ineffectual, serving symbolic rather than functional roles.

For almost a decade, a National Advisory Council, similarly composed but under the chairmanship of a UWI professor, was actively engaged in advising the prime minister and cabinet on a wide range of policy issues, including rural development, measures to reduce unemployment, national ownership, and control over the country's resources, cultural development, and improvement of the public administration system. So active was this body, coupled with the chairman's easy access to the prime minister, that other agencies resented its powers and influence. It appeared, too, that the council assumed functions in areas that were long considered the domain of certain traditional central line agencies. Shortly after the death of Prime Minister Dr. Eric Williams, the council was abolished.

Consistent with British practice and continuing the colonial tradition, the commission of inquiry has become a standard mechanism and source for public policy on specific individual issues. However, the reports of these commissions are often shelved. What is more interesting is the view expressed by Edwin Jones that commissions have been deliberately deployed as a device to "distract the attention of the public from certain matters not favourable to the dominant strata, . . . to convey the impression that something worthwhile is in progress when in actual fact national problems are being by-passed, . . . and to postpone action or to kill issues which might be unfavourable to elites."[64] Jones is therefore convinced that commissions primarily serve symbolic purposes.

A new source of policy advice which was employed to a significant extent by the PNP government of Michael Manley (1972–1980) was the institution of the special adviser. Addressing the Civil Service Staff Association in an effort to allay the anxieties of senior members of the service who felt insecure because of the introduction of such advisers, the prime minister explained the *raison d'être* for the institution, as a means of drawing on "the huge reservoir of ideas and thinking which Government should not cut themselves away from . . . as pipelines into opinions and views . . . they are no threat to you."[65]

Jones and Mills have commented on the possible dysfunctional effects of the increasing use of such advisers "in diminishing the importance of permanent secretaries or other public officials and introducing conflict with the executive authority and responsibility of the permanent secretary."[66]

Despite the formally expressed rationale in terms of extending the range of policy sources and options available to the government, there is no doubt that the primary purpose of the special adviser is to provide the political directorate with the services of a group of persons who bring strong political commitment to, and support for, the governing party's ideology and goals. As former United Kingdom Prime Minister Harold Wilson put it: "For policies without politics are of no more use than politics without policies."[67]

To some extent, the increasing tendency to resort to the use of institutions such as statutory boards and special advisers reflects an evasion of the real problem, namely the need to examine *de novo*, the traditional departmental structure and the composition, attitudes and processes of the civil service. Perhaps the objectives sought [by the political directorate] . . . could be attained by fundamental restructuring and re-orientation of the established administrative machinery and the civil service.[68]

IMPORTANT ISSUES

Alternatives to a Depoliticized Civil Service

Some of the most significant topical issues concerning public administration in the region may be inferred from the foregoing. The use of special advisers by the PNP government in Jamaica during the 1970s became a controversial issue in the context of questioning the relevance of the inherited Westminster-Whitehall notion of a depoliticized civil service for the needs of a small developing society. The controversy became intensified following the declaration by the governing party, of its ideology of "democratic socialism." Doubts began to be expressed as to whether the traditional civil service, conditioned in an ethos of neutrality, could be relied on for support in moving along a noncapitalist path of development. Similar considerations have obtained in Guyana in respect of that government's ideology of "cooperative socialism."

It is appropriate to quote from statements made by political leaders of these countries, namely former Prime Minister Michael Manley of Jamaica and Labour Minister (now deputy prime minister) Hamilton Green of Guyana:

The very word "neutral" connotes the idea of the car whose gear is in neutral, that is "cautious to commit." It is a negative concept and third world countries cannot survive the neutrality of their citizens. If a third world country is to have a hope of survival, the first challenge is not that of this loftiness of neutrality, but the earthly ground based reality of commitment. . . . But, the problem is, how to be committed without ever crossing the line of your professional integrity as a civil servant. (Manley)[69]

Caribbean civil servants must become involved in politics to do an efficient job . . . this does not mean they should become political party activists but rather their actions must be motivated by the ideological objective of the Government. Colonialists left a myth that public servants should be apolitical and should not be involved in politics. This was a bit dishonest because it was only during the transition to independence that the civil servant was removed from the political scene. (Green)[70]

Hence, there was a resort to alternative or supplemental mechanisms, for example, special advisers and the increasing use of extradepartmental agencies. Moreover, concern was heightened when the PNP government created a party "Accreditation Committee" to screen and clear candidates for appointments to boards and committees so as to ensure that appointees satisfied ideological criteria. This stimulated a public debate about the comparative merits of commitment and competence as selection criteria.[71]

Proliferation of Extradepartmental Agencies

The proliferation of statutory bodies and other nondepartmental agencies has induced concern partly because their growth involves bypassing the normal administrative machinery and the civil service, and partly because it increases fragmentation and poses problems for national planning and administrative coordination. In addition, the practice of paying much higher emoluments to staff not only causes resentment among civil servants, but also creates dysfunctional competition for skills that are in short supply in these states.

In Jamaica, attempts are being made to bring these bodies into a rationalized arrangement of public sector organizations in which all agencies would fit within the same general system of position—classification, grading, and compensation. Furthermore, the complex of nondepartmental agencies is currently being examined to identify those institutions that may conveniently be abolished and those that may be absorbed into appropriate ministries and departments.

Ethics and the Issue of Corruption

A subject of considerable concern to some observers is the significant increase in the incidence of unethical conduct and political and bureaucratic corruption. In certain societies of the region, public service corruption was negligible until the 1970s, but since then, the practice has become so prevalent that members of the public have begun to take corruption for granted.

The increasing level of unethical behavior is perhaps due partly to the conditions in those countries where, because of economic circumstances, public goods, services and employment are in very scarce supply in the face of considerable demands and pressures. Some officials, faced with inflationary conditions and inadequate incomes, ignore staff regulations that restrict their involvement in extraofficial income-earning activities. In addition, the extended range of the state's involvement in the society and economy has resulted in its exercise of a much wider regulatory role. Both sets of phenomena have resulted in a proliferation of bureaucratic controls. They have extended the scope and opportunities for public officials to peddle scarce benefits for commissions, or to dispense discriminatory treatment in favor of friends, political supporters, relatives, or special interests.

In the highly competitive two-party context of Jamaica, charges and countercharges abound, leveled by one side or the other (depending on which party happens to be in power at the time) alleging victimization in the distribution of the scarce spoils of victory at the polls; and the denial of government contracts, housing, and nonestablished public sector jobs to nonsupporters of the governing party.

As indicated earlier, problems are aggravated when "political executives perform simultaneously, the dual roles of cabinet ministers and businessmen."[72] From time to time, following public exposures and scandals, commissions of inquiry have been appointed. Some have been given occasionally general terms of reference to investigate alleged corrupt practices; and others have been asked to investigate specific cases.[73] All these activities have flowered in an environment in which increasing emphasis is being placed on the acquisition of material goods, while other values expressed in less tangible terms tend to be sacrificed.

Although codes of conduct and integrity legislation have been introduced,[74] these instruments are not effectively enforced and are more honored in the breach than in the observance. More fundamental measures are required, and these should be based essentially in the prerequisite of an effective system of public accountability. Associated with this requirement and as an essential element is the need to reduce the degree of privatization of information and of secrecy in the governmental systems. This is a characteristic of systems of British parentage. Thus, greater freedom and communication of information—more "open government"—are required if the accountability of public officials is to be effectively enforced.

Electoral Administration[75]

The electoral system, including the conduct of personnel in the system, has been a controversial subject in a number of states, especially Guyana and Jamaica. Criticisms and strictures have perennially been expressed in election postmortems—usually by the losers—focusing on charges of impersonation, multiple voting, the deliberate omission of qualified persons from the electoral lists, the padding of the lists, and the stuffing of ballot boxes.

In Jamaica these problems have intensified with the entrenchment of the two-party system and the political polarization of the society. Following protracted discussions between government and opposition and agreement on fundamental issues, a Special Joint Bipartisan Committee on Constitutional and Electoral Reform was appointed by Parliament. As an outcome of its deliberations, a new statutory institution, the Electoral Advisory Committee, was created which, with the director of elections, has taken over from the government of the day, authority and responsibility for the electoral system. These responsibilities include assumption of control over the appointment of all election officials, the enumeration-registration processes, and the conduct of general and local elections.

The committee consists of a unique blend of political and independent appointees: four members nominated equally by the prime minister and the leader of the opposition, and three independent members of whom one is chairman—all appointed by the governor-general. However, the statute provides for the selection of the independent members by majority decision of the political nominees. An interesting device, rendered necessary by the polarization and deep distrust within the society, is the statutory stipulation. This device is used in the event of the failure of the political nominees to agree within fourteen days of their own appointment, vesting in the governor-general the right to make the appointments of independent members after consultation with the prime minister and the leader of the opposition. In fact, the governor-general found it necessary to exercise this right when the appointments were made initially.

The committee was appointed in October 1979 (with the author of this chapter as chairman)[76] and has implemented a number of reforms and safeguards in the enumeration-registration and polling procedures. It is intended to entrench the committee within the Constitution, adding control over the determination of constituency boundaries to its responsibilities, as part of the bipartisan program of constitutional and electoral reform. In Guyana, the government has continuously resisted representations and pressures for electoral reform from opposition parties and external groups.

Administrative Reform

These considerations lead inevitably to the subject of administrative reform. Since 1984, task forces in Jamaica and Trinidad-Tobago have been actively engaged in advising the respective governments on reorganization of the public services in these states and measures to improve their efficiency and effectiveness. The establishment of these task forces follows much expressed dissatisfaction by the public and among sections of the services themselves over inefficiencies and deficiencies, especially with respect to the public financial and personnel management systems. In addition, in the case of Jamaica, certain international donor and technical assistance agencies have indicated that inefficiencies in specific areas of the public administration system have vitiated the effectiveness of aid.

The Trinidad-Tobago Public Service Review Task Force consists of representatives from the civil service, public enterprise organizations, significant private sector companies, and the University of the West Indies.

The Jamaican Project, funded by the World Bank, is supported by a number of local, regional and international consultants. The ultimate objective is to promote improved performance by central and line agencies, particularly those critical to the structural adjustment process and to economic development in general. In addition to World Bank assistance, the region is a beneficiary of substantial financial and technical support toward improvement of public administration systems in the constituent states from bilateral and multilateral agencies including the Canadian International Development Agency (CIDA), the United States Agency for International Development (USAID), British Aid, the European Economic Community, and the United Nations Development Program (UNDP).

The attainment of the objective of the Jamaican project requires that line agencies be structured to operate around the concept of program management. Unlike the current system, program managers in these agencies are to be given authority and control over the human and financial resources allocated to the program. They will therefore be held accountable for the attainment of specific objectives and their performance measured against the yardstick of specific output criteria. Accordingly, the project consists of three distinct but interrelated components:

Human resource management
Financial resource management
Line agency restructuring

The human resource component involves rationalizing the roles and functions of the central personnel management agencies, namely Ministry of the Public Service and the Public Service Commission. Both have become primarily policy-making and standard-setting agencies and the PSC also assumes reviewing and appellate functions. A considerable degree of decentralization of personnel management and financial management authority to line agencies is proposed.

The progress which has been made on this reform project and the success so far in sensitizing personnel of the central and line agencies augur well for the success of the project. Administrative restructuring is urgently needed in all states of the region. Others could benefit from the Jamaican experience.

NOTES

1. The terms *English-Speaking Caribbean* and *Commonwealth Caribbean* are used interchangeably in this chapter.

2. Parts of this section are taken from G.E. Mills, "The Environment of Commonwealth Caribbean Bureaucracies," *International Review of Administrative Sciences*, 39, 1 (1973), pp. 14–24. See also G.E. Mills, "Public Administration in the Commonwealth Caribbean: Evolution, Conflicts and Challenges," *Social and Economic Studies (SES)*, University of the West Indies (UWI), 19, 1 (March 1970), pp. 5–25.

3. Mills, "Public Administrating."

4. G.E. Mills, "Public Administration and Change in a Small Developing Country: Jamaica," *Public Administration and International Development* 4, Ecole Nationale d'Administration Publique, University of Quebec, 1979, pp. 697–726. Note that similar comments are relevant in respect of another inherited institution, viz., cricket.

5. For comments on the strike (said to have been the longest general strike up to that time in the history of the Commonwealth), see B.A.N. Collins, "The Civil Service of British Guiana in the General Strike of 1963," *Caribbean Quarterly* 10, 2 (June 1964), pp. 3–15.

6. *Racial Problems in the Public Service: Report of the British Guiana Commission of Inquiry*, (Geneva: International Commission of Jurists, 1965).

7. G.E. Mills, "The Environment of Commonwealth Caribbean Bureaucracies."

8. See G.E. Mills, "Education and Training for the Public Services in the West Indies," *Journal of Administration Overseas* 5, 3 (July 1966), pp. 155–66.

9. G.E. Mills, "The Relative Roles of the Technician and the Administrator in the Public Service," *Report of Conference on Organization and Administration of Health Services in the Caribbean* (Washington D.C.: PAHO, 1963), pp. 155–84.

10. G.E. Mills, "The Environment of Commonwealth Caribbean Bureaucracies."

11. See W.G. Demas, *The Economics of Development with Special Reference to the Caribbean* (Montreal: McGill University Press, 1965).

12. G.E. Mills, "The Administration of Public Enterprise: Jamaica and Trinidad-Tobago," *SES* 30, 1 (March 1981), pp. 45–74.

13. Paul Chen Young, *Report on Private Investment in the Caribbean* (Kingston: Atlas Publishing Co., 1973).

14. Prime Minister L. Burnham, "Guyana's Bauxite," Broadcast to the Nation, 28 November 1970, published in *The Daily Chronicle*.

15. Government of Trinidad and Tobago, White Paper on *Public Participation in Industrial and Commercial Activities* (Port of Spain: Government Printer, 1972). See also "Perspectives for the New Society," *The Nation*, Port of Spain, 25 August 1972; and Trinidad and Tobago, *Third Five Year Plan 1969–73* (Government Printer, 1970).

16. See the JLP Election Manifesto of 1980 and Ministry Paper Nos. 9 and 18 of 1981.

17. An expression coined by Lloyd Best of the UWI.

18. Martin Wight, *The Development of the Legislative Council: 1606–1945* (London: Faber and Faber, 1946).

19. Carl Stone, "Public Opinion and the 1980 Elections in Jamaica," *Caribbean Quarterly* 27, 1 (March 1981), pp. 1–19.

20. Urias Forbes, "The West Indies Associated States," *SES* 19, 1 (March 1970), pp. 57–88.

21. G.E. Mills, "Electoral Reform in Jamaica," *The Parliamentarian* 62, 2 (April 1981), pp. 97–104.

22. G.E. Mills, "The Environment of Commonwealth Caribbean Bureaucracies."

23. Selwyn Ryan, "The Prime Minister and New Technocratic Elite," *Sunday Guardian*, 12 October 1975. See also G.E. Mills, "Conflict Between Ministers and Civil Servants," *Sunday Gleaner*, 3 April 1977.

24. E.S. Jones, "Interest Group–Bureaucracy Interaction and Public Policy in Jamaica," *Journal of Social and Behavioural Sciences* 20, 4 (Fall 1974), pp. 5–19; see also "Pressure Group Politics in the West Indies" (Ph.D. thesis, Manchester University, 1970).

25. G.E. Mills, "The Environment of Commonwealth Caribbean Bureaucracies."

26. From *Report of the Trinidad-Tobago Constitutional Commission*, 1974.

27. See C.H. Grant, "Rural Local Government in Guyana and British Honduras," *SES* 16, 1 (March 1967), pp. 57–76.

28. Reports of Commissions/Committees on Local Government Reform in Jamaica: L.C. Hill (1943), Meyer Brownstone, UNTAB (1963), Association of Local Government Authorities (1968), M. Rodrigues (1970), and G.E. Mills (1974); in Trinidad-Tobago: J. Imrie (1957) and M. Sinanan (1965). See also Paul G. Singh, *Local Democracy in the Commonwealth Caribbean* (Longman Caribbean, 1972), and G.E. Mills, "Local Government in a Small Developing State: Jamaica," *Journal of Administration Overseas* 18, 3 (July 1979), pp. 180–92.

29. See Government of Jamaica, Ministry Paper Nos. 65 and 10 presented to the House of Representatives 1984 and 1985, respectively. A state company, Metropolitan Parks and Markets (MPM) was formed in 1985 and assumed responsibility for public cleansing in the Kingston corporate area.

30. The KSAC was revised in 1986, but like the Parish Councils, shorn of most of its powers.

31. Local Democratic Organs Act, 1980.

32. Constitution of Co-operative Republic of Guyana, 1980.

33. Ibid.

34. Government of Jamaica, Green Paper No. 1, October 1978.

35. See *Report of Statutory Boards Committee* (Barrett), 1975.

36. United Nations, *Public Administration in Jamaica*, TAO/JAM 6 (New York, April 1965).

37. The Caribbean Development Bank (CDB) also provides training in project management.

38. Industrial development corporations have been established in most of the states since the 1950s.

39. Hon. R.D. Williams, Minister of Industry and Commerce, reported in the *Daily Gleaner*, 11 December 1977.

40. See Edwin Jones and G.E. Mills, "Institutional Innovation and Change in the Commonwealth Caribbean," *SES* 25, 4 (December 1976), pp. 323–46.

41. Government of Jamaica, Ministry Paper No. 10, May 1978.

42. Statement of Mr. Douglas Vaz, reported in the *Daily Gleaner*, 30 November 1977.

43. See brochures published by the Urban Development Corporation.

44. See Government of Jamaica, Ministry Paper No. 21, 17 April 1973.

45. See B.A.N. Collins, "Some Notes on Public Service Commissions in the Commonwealth Caribbean," *SES* 16, 1 (March 1967), pp. 1–16. See also G.E. Mills, "Government and the Public Service Commission," *Sunday Gleaner*, 6 March 1977.

46. From time to time, allegations have been made in several states that career advance is based primarily on political influence.

47. United Nations, *Public Administration in Jamaica*.

48. See G.E. Mills and M. Kubr, *Identification of Priority Needs for Management Development in the English-Speaking Caribbean* (Report of CARICAD MISSION), December 1979, and Jamal Khan, *Public Management: The Eastern Caribbean Experience*, Caribbean Studies (The Hague, 1982).

49. Ibid.

50. Stephen Yorke, "Parliamentary Control of the Executive in a Small Developing Country, Jamaica, 1962–1970" (unpublished M.Sc. Government thesis, UWI, 1972). See also Vishnu Ramlogan, "Parliamentary Control of Public Finances in Trinidad/Tobago" (mimeo), April 1981.

51. L.G. Barnett, *Constitutional Law of Jamaica* (London: Oxford University Press, 1977.)

52. Stephen Nancoo, "Administrative Theory and Bureaucratic Control: A Study of the Ombudsman Idea in Trinidad/Tobago," *International Journal of Public Administration* 23, 2 (April-June 1977), pp. 242–54.

53. G.E. Mills, "Public Administration and Change: Jamaica."

54. H. Lutchman, "The Office of the Ombudsman in Guyana," *Caribbean Studies* 13, 1 (April 1973).

55. Ina Barrett, "The Ombudsman in Jamaica," *SES* 34, 1 (March 1985), pp. 59–75.

56. Hon. E. Anderson, Minister of the Public Service in JAMPRESS Release reported in the *Daily Gleaner*, 18 October 1984. According to Anderson, the ratio of the Jamaican civil service to the total population is currently 1:53.

57. G.E. Mills, "The Environment of Commonwealth Caribbean Bureaucracies."

58. See the section "The Economic Environment."

59. Edwin Jones, "Some Notes on Decision-Making and Change in Caribbean Administrative System," *SES* 23, 2 (June 1974), pp. 292–310.

60. Carl Stone, "The Political Aspects of Post-war Agricultural Policies in Jamaica," *SES* 23, 2 (June 1974), pp. 145–75.

61. G.E. Mills, "Public Policy and Private Enterprise in the Commonwealth Caribbean," *SES* 23, 2 (June 1974), 216–41.

62. Ibid.

63. G.E. Mills, and Paul D. Robertson, "The Attitudes and Behaviour of the Senior Civil Service in Jamaica," *SES* 23, 2 (June 1974), pp. 311–43.

64. E.S. Jones, "The Political Uses of Commissions of Enquiry," *SES* 27, 3 (September 1978), pp. 284–312.

65. Hon. M. Manley, Address to the Jamaica Civil Service Association, 19 April 1972.

66. Jones and Mills, "Institutional Innovation and Change." See also Mills, "Public Administration and Change."

67. "Political Advisers," Paper presented to Commonwealth Heads of Government Meeting in Jamaica, 1975 (published in Harold Wilson, *The Governance of Britain*).

68. Mills, "The Administration of Public Enterprise."

69. Reported in the *Jamaica Civil Service Magazine* (July 1972).

70. Reported in the *Daily News*, 28 July 1977.

71. See Mills, "Public Administration and Change."

72. Mills, "The Environment of Commonwealth Caribbean Bureaucracies."

73. Examples are Reports: *on the Commission of Enquiry into the Operation of Casinos in Freeport and in Nassau* (London: HMSO, 1967); on *Control of Public Expenditure during 1961 in Grenada* (St. George's, 1961); on *The Awards of Contracts and Grant of Work Permits and Licenses, Jamaica* (DaCosta Report), (Kingston, 1973); *Corruption in Barbados* (Duffus), 1978. See also W. Richard Jacobs, "Patterns of Political Corruption in Caribbean Society," *Occasional Papers* (ISER: UWI, December 1978), pp. 49–91.

74. For instance, in Jamaica: The Parliament (Integrity of Members Act, Law 26 of 1973) requires the declaration of assets by members of Parliament. Note also the recent statutory provision for the appointment of a contractor-general.

75. See Mills, "Electoral Reform in Jamaica."

76. Coincidentally, two of the original political appointees to the committee, the general secretaries of the PNP and JLP, respectively, are graduates of the Department of Government, UWI, of which the chairman was head.

14

LATIN AMERICA: THE SOUTHERN CONE

Jorge Nef

It is difficult to understand the special position of government bureaucracies and their relation to society in Latin American countries without examining the historical development of that area from the late nineteenth century down to the present day. This is even more necessary in the case of the southern cone countries, namely, Argentina, Chile, and Uruguay, as they consciously created an administrative state by a process of premature popular mobilization, participation, and welfarism. Hence, we start our study with a detailed sociohistorical analysis of the origins and the chequered evolution of the administrative state in the three southern cone countries, in particular the rise of the middle class that accompanied it. After a discussion of administrative structures and practices, we will reinterpret the triangular relationship of bureaucracy, military, and society in the context of economic stagnation—in the light of some standard approaches to socioeconomic and administrative evolution. The structuring of this chapter in this order is dictated largely by the special characteristics of the subject matter.

HISTORICAL BACKGROUND: THE RISE OF THE ADMINISTRATIVE STATE[1]

The Export Economy: Class Conflicts and the Consolidation of the Oligarchical State

The socioeconomic structure of the southern cone has reflected a historically established pattern of early colonial and neo-colonial insertion in the international division of labor. This structural-historical condition, begun under Spanish colonial rule, was modernized throughout the nineteenth century, presided over by

British capital and technology. Since the First World War and as a direct result of it, a rapid process of dependency substitution from a British to an American "center" took place. The structure of dependence that had been consolidated in the mid–1880s (Argentina with beef and wheat; Uruguay with wool, meat, and hides; and Chile with nitrate and later copper) remained unaltered. A "modern" urban, transportation, and administrative infrastructure was laid down to facilitate the undisturbed export of primary commodities. This transition from rural-based patrimonialism[2] to a commercial-urban, liberal-aristocratic society laid the foundations of a modern bureaucratic state.

The "development policies" pursued, as well as the administrative machinery in the region, reflected the configuration of the sociopolitical alliances in control of the state. The expansion and consolidation of the export economy enhanced the power of the commercial and export factions of an urban *comprador* bourgeoisie, linked to foreign capital. These factions became the hub of the grand alliance. Unlike Europe, no significant discontinuity obtained between the capitalist (*comprador*) classes and the landed gentry. The gentry could accommodate their interests in an expanding export base. By the turn of the century, all three countries possessed large, complex, and, by the standards of the time, fairly professional bureaucracies. These administrative systems also played a decisive role in a development model based on laissez-faire liberalism and external financing. They provided the necessary stability and continuity of "order" and "governance" required for the reproductibility of private capital. The state, however, especially its uppermost echelons, was not "autonomous" from the upper socioeconomic strata of society. In fact, "gentlemen politics" meant a direct elitist management of Parliament, the chief executive, the bench, as well as the commanding heights of the civil and military services.

With the consolidation of the export economy and the exigencies of labor-intensive nonagricultural activities such as dockworks, slaughterhouses, transportation, mining, and processing, a rapid process of proletarianization of the subordinate classes began.[3] In Chile it resulted mostly in rural to urban migration facilitated by the War of the Pacific (1879–1884), the expansion of nitrate fields, and demand for coal. This process brought about a sort of "instant proletariat" with rural roots and subject to the new and alienating characteristics of industrial capitalism. The traditional latency of class conflicts gave way to a new militancy. In Argentina and Uruguay, while internal migration was important, the bulk of the "modern" labor force was foreign. In either case, alienation, extreme exploitation, and the influence of European socialism and anarchism created a highly politicized and unionized social force objectively and subjectively in opposition to the ruling elites.

Class conflicts increased in scope and intensity. The era between the 1890s and the First World War was one of extreme, open, *manifest* class warfare. *La cuestion social* (demands for labor legislation, medical services, insurance, and safety and an improvement in overall working conditions, including the political participation of the nonelites class) became a central political issue.

The oligarchical republics were characterized by restricted political participation—limited to those with property qualifications. Yet, the growth of the state, and the professionalization of the repressive forces to control unrest as well as the expansion of liberal professions, had created a new social phenomenon: a "middle stratum" of sorts. This constituted an amalgam of downwardly mobile aristocrats, upwardly mobile immigrants, and a few upwardly mobile members of the lower classes. Unlike its European counterpart, this "petite bourgeoisie" was not a small capitalist class but rather a state and clerical class of white-collar *empleados*.[4] From its very origins, this sector was an ideological appendage of the elites: a product of behavioral and educational models (the lycee, the university, and the military academy) set up by the upper classes, whose prime directive was to protect and maintain the status quo.

Electoral reforms (such as the 1912 Saenz Pena Law in Argentina), the further expansion of free secondary and postsecondary education, the establishment of "merit" civil service, as well as the creation of white-collar social security funds, played an important role in changing the nature of a middle stratum into a middle class. These classes were ideologically bourgeois from the beginning but lacked a capitalist base. The access to public service through elite patronage and later the control of the state became the major source of their political and social sustenance.

The Crisis of the Export Economy: Institutionalized Class Conflicts and the Rise of the Mesocratic State

Between World War I and the Great Depression, the upper-middle-class alliance increasingly gave room for a pattern of middle-class political control. This period initiated by the governments of Hipolito Yrigoyen in Argentina (1916–1922), Jose Batlle y Ordonez in Uruguay (1904–1915), and Arturo Alessandri in Chile (1920–1925) ushered in a third stage in the pattern of class relations: the institutionalization of the class conflict into political and collective bargaining procedures. The welfare state was born.[5]

The process of accelerated bureaucratization was thus closely related to both the institutionalization of the class conflict and the ascent of the middle sectors. This, in turn, enhanced the relative autonomy of the state—and the state classes—from the direct control of the aristocracy. Politically, middle-class ascendancy broadened political participation through an expansion of the electoral franchise as well as legislation that legitimated union activity, though not necessarily encouraged it. The new system of labor relations expressed itself in labor codes and in mechanisms for tripartite bargaining. It also implied the establishment of social security (Cajas de Prevision), medical services (servicios del seguro social), and pension funds for workers, which in all three countries preceded similar developments in North America and even Western Europe.

The welfare state, besides its obvious role in conflict management, resulted in an expansion of white-collar employment, reinforcing the political strength of the middle sectors. But this welfare state had built-in constraints and severe weaknesses such as the increased fragility of the export economy to provide the basis for the new sociopolitical arrangements without undergoing profound social changes. The difference between the patterns of conflict management in the southern cone and those that emerged as a result of the institutionalization of class conflicts in Europe, North America, and Australia is largely related to the incongruity between a political formula of power sharing and a dependent non-producing and underdeveloped economic structure. The latter was unable to provide steady support to the commitments of widened participation and the welfare state.

Depression, Import Substitution, and Populism: The Entrepreneurial State

The sudden decline of exports resulting from the Depression broke the precarious system of accommodation between the upper and middle classes. It also shattered the system of labor relations which maintained mass-elites balances within manageable bounds—the institutionalized class conflict. In all three cases, fiscal crisis and politico-institutional crises went hand in hand. Political demobilization entailed a period of right-wing reaction, which began in Argentina with the military coup of 1931. It was primarily aimed at reducing the scope of political competitiveness created by the reformist but white-collar Radical party. In Chile and Uruguay, the post-Depression shock exhibited similar structural characteristics but was of relatively shorter duration. It mutated sooner into less restrictive forms, such as the second governments of Alessandri with conservative backing (1932–1938) in Chile and the dictatorial administrations of President Rafael Terra and General Alfredo Baldomir in Uruguay. After the initial disarray, the government response in all three cases was to utilize and expand the existing state apparatus as a mechanism to bring about economic recovery and reactivation. This seemingly "socialist" strategy was a pragmatic response to the crisis of exports and imports produced by the collapse of the world markets. It aimed at a model of accelerated and internally based development: import substitution industrialization (ISI).[6]

In the early stages, these policies were undertaken by conservative administrations. But increasingly labor pressures brought to power a new political project with a strong populist[7] flavor. This was particularly the case with Chile's Popular Front (1938–1941) and with Peron's populist-corporatist experiment (1946–1955) in Argentina. Import substitution meant a dramatic horizontal and vertical expansion of the administrative state. Structurally, it took the form of a proliferation and expansion of the role of existing parastatals. These functionally decentralized entities managed the most varied sectors of the economy: energy, (State Oil Deposits [YPE] in Argentina, which had been created by Yrigoyen in 1922, the National Corporation of Fuels, Alcohol and Cement [ANCAP] in Uruguay, created in 1928, and in the late 1940s the National Petroleum Enterprise

[ENAP] in Chile), steel mills, transportation, airlines, finance, sectoral planning (the Development Corporation [CORFO] in Chile), communication, and the like. Import substitution with populism consolidated a new political alliance: a coalition of state-protected manufacturers, blue-collar workers, and, most important, the state classes, which provided hegemonic leadership. This de facto Keynesianism set the basis for a national development strategy that relied heavily on the state, but also included sectors of the popular classes as support groups. The expansion of state interventionism helped to consolidate the relative power of the middle classes and to expand the relative autonomy of the state through a new network of corporate transactions between business, labor and the bureaucracy.

On the whole, however, import substitution did not radically alter the external dependency of the economies or the rigid class configuration of the societies. In fact, with a dramatic reactivation of demands for Latin American raw materials following the war, industrialization, short of deficit financing, became heavily dependent on export expansion, not on taxing the rich. For as long as there was demand for copper, meat, wool, or wheat, the governments' ambitious programs could be carried out. Thus, they could keep pace to accommodate the internal demands for white-collar employment, social welfare, and finance capital by domestic industrialists.

The End of Import Substitution: Stalemate, Repression, and the Rise of Bureaucratic Authoritarianism

When economic capabilities shrank shortly after the Korean War, a protracted fiscal crisis set in. Its consequences would be increased social and political polarization, stalemate, and hyperinflation. This resulted in a crisis of hegemony. In the context of this crisis of the bureaucratic populist state of the 1940s, the stage had been set for the bureaucratic authoritarian state of the 1970s.

By the 1960s when the export crises had brought import substitution to an end, the three countries exhibited a large and all-encompassing interventionist, welfarist (and costly) administrative state. The overall policy framework was distinctively neo-Keynesian but the severe underfinancing (fiscal crises) as well as mounting social tensions and unfulfilled expectations made this bureaucracy highly immobilistic. In a sense, bureaucratic deadlock was both cause and effect of the politics of social stalemate. The middle-class-controlled state had become increasingly incapable of building enduring alliances to maintain social and political integration. Instead, a protracted period of class confrontation, fought through the price and wage mechanism, set in. The public sector without appropriate resources, while performing in the short run a system-maintenance function (buying time), exacerbated social and political frustrations. This process culminated with the Uruguayan and Chilean coups of 1973. These military interventions resulted in a profound militarization of the state and the civil society.

The military, representing a distinct fraction of the middle class, introduced a new type of bureaucratic politics, the politics of antipolitics.

Although the national security doctrine that inspired this strategy of extreme demobilization of the lower strata was based on the Brazilian experience of some ten years earlier (1964), the main concern of the new civilian and military alliances in Chile, Argentina, and Uruguay, and their external constituencies was security—lower class containment and demobilization—rather than development.[8] Likewise, in spite of rhetorical nationalism, the military pursued a conscious, aggressive policy of denationalization of the economy, as well as the state.

"Redemocratization": The Management of Bankruptcy

The paradox with national security was that by the early 1980s, repression had become extremely expensive to sustain. It had been an unqualified economic failure and had also created as circumstances that made insurrectional alternatives very likely occurrences. Finally, under heavy public opinion pressure, the American government began to pursue a political strategy that would make revolutionary upheavals such as those of Central America less likely. This new research for stability, beyond the authoritarian overtones of the Rockefeller Report[9] of 1969, was outlined in the Linowitz Report of 1975.[10] The Linowitz Report was an expression of a broader trilateralist project for the "return to democracy" and more recently, debt management through the creation of "restricted democracies."

DEVELOPMENT ADMINISTRATION AND THE ADMINISTRATION OF UNDERDEVELOPMENT IN THE SOUTHERN CONE

The Context of Policy Choices: Stalemate and Repression

Characteristic in the history and structure of these three societies is a relatively weak and unstable pattern of economic growth linked to basic single-commodity production, combined with a rapid process of social mobilization and an incomplete and dependent process of industrialization. The consequence has been an increased tension between both expectations and capabilities, as well as between elites and masses. In this context, the devaluation of elite ideology, resulting from a growing mobilization of the subordinate strata, has weakened constitutional procedure and brought about full-fledged crises of political authority. The correlation of forces, however, has not been favorable to a revolutionary breakthrough. With consensus ruled out as an objective possibility, the political style of conflict management in all three countries has oscillated between stalemate and repression.[11] Formal political pluralism has at times coexisted with a highly inflationary form of social and political deadlock. Thus, the bureaucratized and highly elaborate administrative systems, besides their limited goal attainment value, have become arenas and mechanisms to fight a bitter and protracted social conflict.

Since the 1970s, the administrative state (and the white-collar bureaucracies of middle-class functionaries allied to the military and the obligarchy) has played a central role in the politics of demobilization. A considerable part (in both personnel and budget) of the state bureaucracies is made up of the national security establishment. Both S. M. Lipset's observation about the "fascisization" of the middle classes under stress[12] and Jose Nun's thesis of the "middle-class military coup"[13] seem sustained when examining the political patterns of these three countries.

The predatory nature of accumulation for the sake of a small domestic elite and its transnational associates, in the absence of sustained growth, makes legitimation a limited possibility. It also explains the prevalence of a fragmented, polarized, and alienated political culture.[14] Instead, accumulation has been facilitated by extreme exclusion and state terrorism.[15] The apparent irrationality of the Argentinean, Uruguayan, and Chilean "regimes of exception" that emerged in the 1970s are at close scrutiny rational techniques to maintain accumulation and elite political control. In this context, it is hardly surprising that national "development" is almost an impossibility despite rhetoric to the contrary. The objective role of the state under such conditions is not to develop their countries or to provide a modicum of sovereignty. On the contrary, its central role is to maintain and reproduce the status quo: the dependent, elitist, and underdeveloped nature of their respective societies.

Alliances, Brokerage, and Political Mediators: Support and Opposition[16]

The highly fragmented pattern of cultural orientation referred to earlier has been further polarized by the continuation of repressive socioeconomic policies after the return of civilian rule. In fact, one characteristic of the post-"redemocratization" era in Argentina and Uruguay is the persistence of sociopolitical deadlock. The liberal centrist governments that have emerged there—President Raul Alfonsin's Radical party and President Julio Maria Sanguinetti's Colorado rule—are not significant departures from the mold of weak centrist dominance of the political scene prior to military intervention, nor are their socioeconomic agendas too different from the monetarist policies of the recent past.

The 1983 presidential election in Argentina weakened the internally fragmented and polarized Peronista movement and questioned its effectiveness as a voice for organized labor. However, on the whole, both the policy options and the room for maneuverability of the radicals are extremely narrow. The real power brokers remain the powerful agroexporting interests (the Agricultural Society), the industrialists (the Argentinian Industrial Corporation [UIA]), and the bankers confronting the much beleaguered, yet still significant, CGT (Central

Labor Confederation), under Peronist control. The balancer continues to be, as usual, the military establishment. Despite drastic setbacks after the Falklands fiasco and the human rights trails as a consequence of their "dirty war," the armed bureaucrats are by and large still unscathed and capable of intervening as they have done in the past. The passage of the legislation to condone acts of brutality committed by the security forces under orders from their superiors (Ley de Punto Final) weakened the government's ability to prosecute. Moreover, military resistance, culminating in various aborted uprisings in 1987 and 1988, has had the effect of enshrining a de facto as well as de jure, extraterritoriality of the military.

The governing middle-class Radical party enjoys, for the moment, the unstable and eroding support of business, whereas business acts as a lightning rod against precipitous military intervention. The implementation of a series of austerity measures along IMF recipes, known as Plan Austral,[17] while receiving at first general public endorsement, contained a package of policies that were ultimately geared to curb labor demands. For all intents and purposes, the plan collapsed in the second half of 1987, amidst a record inflation of over 200 percent.[18] Labor, on the other hand, retains a great deal of veto power by mobilizing its large constituency. The highly bureaucratized union movements hold, as in the past, the key to destabilizing the government.

None of these symptoms augurs well for the formulation, let alone the implementation, of an assertive policy of economic development based on national consensus. The Plan Austral is designed for survival, not for expansion. It is mostly geared to managing the overwhelming burden of the country's foreign debt as well as a rapid privatization of the state sector. In fact, debt management which is second only to the prevention of another military coup is the government's central policy priority (as in most of the region's "new" democracies). Under this arrangement, a centrist civilian government acts as a receiver regime to satisfy foreign creditors. It has extremely limited political agendas and it operates largely by exclusion of significant popular demands. Moreover, those regimes are superintended by a thoroughly transnationalized military establishment waiting in the wings to correct political deviations.

This general characterization also describes the present correlation of forces in Uruguay. Unlike Argentina, the military establishment there did not have to contend with a Falklands-like embarrassment other than widespread popular opposition. The repressive apparatus retreated to their barracks in an orderly fashion and still remains the decisive, yet nonostensible, arbiter of Uruguayan politics and a voracious consumer of meager budgetary resources—41 percent of total state expenditures in 1984.[19] As in Argentina, the business–labor polarization dominates the political scene, albeit in a relatively less catastrophic way.[20] The present centrist government, as in the Argentine case, has pushed a series of "emergency" economic measures, IMF style, which are geared ultimately to further eroding the position of blue-collar workers.

The present alliance structure in Chile is even more complicated.[21] Unlike the other two cases, the military dictatorship, though beleaguered and discredited, remains in the saddle, vis-à-vis a weakened, divided, and "legally" nonexisting opposition. Moreover, the Chilean economy fared relatively better than the economies of Argentina and Uruguay for the 1987–1988 period.[22]

The regime is based on two sociopolitical components which make up the power bloc. On the one hand, there is the military and security apparatus with close ties to the U.S. military establishment. It is a large and cohesive bureaucracy comprising all three services (with army dominance), the militarized national police (Carabineros) and the intelligence services (the National Information Central [CNI], formerly the National Intelligence Directorate [DINA]). In the vertical military tradition all power lies at the top, but the lower echelons directly partake in the structure of privileges and " extraterritorialities" (immunities) provided by the "state of emergency." In an objective sense, the military and, more specifically, the officer corps have been the most privileged sector of Chilean society over the last decade. They are bonded not only by the aforementioned verticality of command, " anticommunism," and a caste-like culture, but also by the fear of losing their exorbitant privileges through retribution.

The other component of the power bloc is the business community. Until 1982, it was a rather cohesive group unified by a hatred of the socializing policies of the deposed Unida Popular (UP) government and the mirage of an "economic miracle" advocated by the group of U.S. trained economists known as the Chicago Boys.[23] With the economic collapse of 1982, the neo-liberal economic project that gave content to the military regime lost part of its hegemonic appeal and gave room to hardline economic "nationalists" within the military (duros). However, the business elite retained the commanding heights of the economy and society through powerful organizations such as the umbrella-like National Confederation of Production and Commerce. The short-lived removal from center stage made the foreign-linked economic clans increasingly critical of military rule. However, the 1987–1988 economic recovery made possible a patching up of tactical differences. By 1988, the Chicago Boys had reentered the hegemonic faction, though without the preeminence of the previous decade. At present, two dominant discourses articulate Chile's dominant class alliance: (1) national security—the struggle against "subversion, terrorism and communism," and (2) neo-liberalism. The ideological base of public policy remains what former DINA Chief General Manuel Contreas called "the management of silence" mitigated by middle-class consumerism.

Across from the political arena, there stands a fragmented and immobilized opposition. Old rivalries, diverse class bases, divergences over tactics, and, most important, an inability to incorporate the grassroots makes the opposition, despite its size, an extremely weak conglomerate. Part of the old right-wing parties, mildly disaffected with the dictatorship, is calling for a return to democracy— a sort of Pinochetismo without Pinochet. The centrist Christian Democratic party, thoroughly purged of its left-wing elements, comprises the bulk of middle-class opposition. While rejecting the enforcement side of the present regime, it does not necessarily offer a substantive critique of the neo-liberal policy of accumulation. It also seeks to exclude the Marxist left from any negotiation to "bring back democracy."

The moderate left, a small and equally isolated nucleus of intellectuals, attempts to act, rather unsuccessfully, as a bridge among contending factions. Finally, there is the Popular Democratic Movement (MDP), comprised mainly of the communists, a section of the socialists, and "leftist hardliners" following a line of relentless opposition to the dictatorship. The MDP, unlike the rest of the opposition, has not rejected outright armed struggle and maintains tenuous linkages with the country's main guerrilla organization, the Manuel Rodriguez Patriotic Front (FPMR).

The movement, unlike the other forces, also possesses an underground functional connection with a myriad of grassroots organizations in shantytowns, factories, student groups, and unions. Only the centrist Christian Democrats maintain some degree of baseline coordination with a segment of the labor movement—a pale ghost of the once powerful left-leaning CUT (Central Workers Organization) which was forcefully disbanded after the 1973 coup.[24]

The weakness of the opposition has been compounded by internal squabbles and increased U.S. pressures for "redemocratization." Both the official State Department and the U.S. business community policy has been to push for an end to the dictatorship, following the lines of similar "pacification" approaches in the Philippines, Haiti, and South Africa. The greatest recipients of such U.S. political support have been the Christian Democrats. The price tag entails a complete marginalization of the Marxist left from any political negotiation or meaningful participation in the future. This means the exclusion of a political broker which represents between one-fourth and one-third of the population— chiefly the bulk of the labor movement. It also entails maintaining the institutional changes imposed by the military—such as the 1980 Constitution enshrining authoritarian capitalism—and the untouchability of the military and security apparatus. However, even this mild policy of normalization, much in line with the views of the Trilateral Commission, is resisted by the military establishments in both Chile and the United States.

Public Policies: Demobilization, Denationalization, and Transnationalization

The aforementioned alliance structure is essential to an understanding of the policy constraints that obtain in all three countries. The greatest limitations are present in the Chilean case. In the other two, however, not only are the options extremely limited, but also policy paralysis appears to predominate. In Chile the number one priority of the regime remains the management of national security. Second is the management of the debt. Development, other than debt management through "debt equity swaps" (which have received enthusiastic reviews by Western economic interests)[25] is an almost irrelevant aspect. In Argentina and Uruguay, management of the debt takes preeminence, with national security as a sort of insurance policy; more "developmental" policies fall by the wayside.

In this sense, especially in the present situation, system maintenance has clearly displaced the attainment of development goals in all three countries, let alone any pretense of progressive social reform. In Chile, this system-maintenance function relies more heavily on manifest repression and on the conscious fragmentation of the potential opposition. In Argentina and Uruguay, with "restricted" civilian democratic regimes, the maintenance of the system relies more heavily on persuasion enforced by the fear of a return to military rule. This situation stands in sharp contrast to the more aggressive and developmental role played by the public sector in these countries during the heyday of import substitution, as well as the induced reformism of the Alliance for Progress. Normalization constitutes a mask for the continuation of the status quo forged during the decade of military repression. Despite differences in style, the main public policy thrust in all three is centered on growing privatization, denationalization, and the shrinkage of the welfare state.

State and Bureaucracy

Constitutional Framework: Shadow and Substance

All three countries have followed a constitutional structure based on the U.S. model of separation of powers. The prolonged periods of "states of exception," however, have made a mockery of the real constitutional practices. Greater correspondence between formality and reality existed in both Chile and Uruguay until the early 1970s, whereas Argentina's liberal constitution (promulgated in 1853) has remained a facade with little substance, other than the maintenance of an elite-dominated socioeconomic order. Since the 1930s, de facto government in Argentina has been more the rule than the exception. In Uruguay, the 1918 Constitution and its subsequent modifications (1942, 1951) remained in effect until 1966–1967.[26] Legal and de facto changes provided a heavily centralized executive replacing the old "Collegial" system. In Chile, the 1925 Constitution, except for very short intervals, constituted the basic government power map. The 1973 military coup crushed this long constitutional tradition. The Pinochet regime suspended the Constitution and ruled by decree through a series of "institutional" acts. More than "fighting subversion," the main thrust of the dictatorship in the years to follow was to rid the country of all its "democratic" trappings, establishing instead a protofascist, pyramidal, socioeconomic order—authoritarian capitalism. In 1980, in an ostensibly rigged plebiscite, the regime's new corporatist constitution, which legalized dictatorial practices, was "legitimated."

The present constitutional structures of Uruguay and Argentina provide a presidential system with executive predominance and an independent judiciary. This tradition of an independent judiciary could even be observable during the "emergency." Because of its very circumscribed role as well as its upper class biases, the judiciary has played a very marginal role in the preservation of civil rights. Far from being a bastion of citizen's defense against arbitrary abuses of the state, the stand taken by these judicial bodies, with a few honorable exceptions, has been one of subservience, if not willing quiescence and even complicity regarding human rights violations.

Legislatures: Checks, Balances, and Deadlocks

Parliamentary controls on the executive are weak and intermittent. In Chile, which enjoyed the most established tradition of parliamentary checks and balances, Parliament is, at present, nonexistent. Its function has been abrogated by the junta (the navy, air force, and police chiefs) which provide a sort of collective leadership to the president and junta head.

In both Uruguay and Argentina, the bicameral parliaments are the weaker partners of the executive. Internally, they are deadlocked and lack the ability to oversee, let alone check on, the actions of the president. The president has a great deal of power, including the ability to co-legislate. But neither the president's nor Parliament's power can be exercised to curb the extraterritorial power of the security forces. In fact, the formal political structures are weak vis-à-vis the military and powerful sectors of the civil society.

Argentina's Congress is made up of both a Senate and a Chamber of Deputies. Half of the Senate's forty-six members are elected every three years. In the 1986 congressional election, its composition was as follows:[27]

Justice party (Peronists)	21 seats
Radical Civic Union (UCR)	18 seats
Minor parties	7 seats

The House of Deputies has 257 seats, half of which are up for reelection every two years. The 1985 election gave a majority to President Alfonsin's Radicals with 130 seats. Second came the opposition Justice party with 103. The Intransigent Radicals received six seats, the balance was made up by a small rightist party (the Centrist Democratic Union) with six seats and various regional parties fifteen seats).[28] This picture was reversed in the 1987 election in which the Radicals received severe "punishment" for their austerity programs. The Radicals went down to 116 seats while the Peronists controlled 110 seats, the difference going to minor parties which also increased their share. In percentages of vote, the comparative picture looks as follows.[29]

	1983	1985	1987
UCR	49	43	37
Peronists	40	24	41
Others	11	23	22

The 1984 elections in Uruguay gave a majority to the Colorado (liberal party): thirteen out of thirty seats in the Senate and forty-one out of ninety-nine in the House.

The second largest plurality went to the more conservative Blanco party: eleven seats in the Senate and thirty-five in the House.[30] The left-wing Broad Front received six and twenty-one seats, respectively. This configuration is deceiving, however, for Uruguay's party system is essentially factional. Both Colorados and Blancos have right- and left-wing, factions which makes for a good deal of internal deadlock. Moreover, in 1985 the military regime refused to accept candidates from both parties (as well as from the Broad Front) whom they perceived as "subversives." Thus, the transition occurred with very limited choices. The officers also imposed an agreement (Institutional Act No. 19) with the civilian multiparty coalition in order to give immunity to officers who had violated human rights during the emergency. They also imposed the continuation of a military-controlled National Security Council to advise the executive with a de facto veto power on the government.[31]

The Weakening of Local Governments

As far as territorial decentralization is concerned, Argentina is one of three remaining Latin American states to be formally organized as a federal republic with twenty-two provinces and one federal district (Buenos Aires). This arrangement has been severely curtailed by the continuous practice of federal intervention. Provincial legislatures have often been dismissed and governorships have frequently been in the hands of military appointees. This situation has weakened provincial autonomy and reduced local effectiveness. The same is true of municipal governments which, like their provincial counterparts, play a relatively marginal role vis-à-vis the chief executive. Thus, within this three-tier system of government, only the central government is of any great political significance.

Uruguay, on the other hand, is a unitary state with a long tradition of local, departmental autonomy. Since the early days of the republic,[32] a strong local and autonomous administration was established. As in Chile, this tradition was interrupted by the 1973 coup. Elected councils and majors were replaced by military appointees in all nineteen departments, thus producing a long hiatus in local administration.

Chile's tradition of municipal autonomy in an otherwise centralized, unitary state was also one of strong independence. Arturo Valenzuela has argued that the municipality was a central piece in the bargaining networks of Chilean democracy.[33] The military in one of its first acts, abolished these democratic channels. Instead, it made the municipalities the last link in a vertical administrative chain controlled through the Ministry of Interior.[34] All municipalities (over 300 of them) were staffed with governmental appointees—mostly right-wing politicians and military officers. These were made dependent on departmental governors (largely military officers appointed by provincial intendents). Several departments were grouped into provincial and, subsequently, into regional intendencies; these were also occupied by military men. Intendents report directly to the Ministry of Interior. Since the mid–1970s the country's twenty-five traditional provinces have been regrouped into thirteen administrative regions which represent the executive and coordinate all kinds of deconcentrated public services.

The Administrative Machinery: The Presidency and the Bureaucracy

The Executive and the Bureaucracy in Uruguay. The present executive structure in Uruguay consists of one president elected for a five-year term, assisted by a cabinet and various advisory bodies. For several decades, Uruguay had a unique type of dual executive: the Colegiado. It operated in two different forms—first, between 1918 and 1933 and second, between 1952 and 1967. The earlier model, established in the 1918 Constitution drafted by President Batlle, comprised an elected president and a bipartisan nine-member Council of Administration. The president controlled the ministries of Interior, Defense, and Foreign Relations, and the council the remaining six cabinet posts.[35] The 1952 Constitution abolished the chief executive and vested all power in a nine-member elected National Council with a minimum number of seats given to the opposition.[36] This experiment was terminated in the 1967 Constitution which designed a more conventional presidential system with a twelve-member cabinet. In mid–1987, these ministries were (1) Interior; (2) Foreign Relations; (3) Defense; (4) Economy and Finance; (5) Public Health; (6) Agriculture and Fisheries; (6) Labor and Social Welfare; (7) Industry and Energy; (8) Transport and Public Works; (9) Education, Culture, and Justice; (10) Tourism; (11) the secretary of the presidency; and (12) the Directorate of Planning and Budgeting.[37]

The 1966–1967 reforms also included the creation of a Social Security Bank to coordinate the chaotic administration of the multitude of autonomous retirement and social security funds. Likewise, a Central Bank was belatedly established to articulate monetary and fiscal policy, and an Office of Planning and Budget with ministerial rank was created in an attempt to bolster the "developmentalist" image of the new government.[38] In addition, provisions to depoliticize and increase executive control over the autonomous agencies were instituted. One of the main agencies established during these reforms was the "Accounts Tribunal, whose senior members are elected by the legislature for five-year terms. . . . [It] is responsible for checking on expenditures and the collection of revenues, investigating prices charged by public corporations, and reporting fiscal irregularities on all levels of government to the legislature."[39]

Under the ministries, there lies a vast and complex bureaucratic machinery that covers roughly one-third of the country's labor force. Some of these functionaries (nearly 300,000 in total) work in the centralized services, but most are employed in the vast network of state enterprises and autonomous entities.

In 1968, Eduardo Galeano observed that:

an . . . irrational swelling of the entire bureaucratic machinery has taken place; the public officers serve to absorb a substantial portion of unemployment [unemployed] labour force from the cities and the countryside. Thus, to the 350 thousand retired workers must be added, in a sense, a considerable number of the 230 thousand government employees. A large, though difficult to estimate, percentage of the latter constitutes a parasitic bureaucracy that is only nominally included in the economically *active population*.[40]

This tradition of big government has deep historical roots, dating back to Batlle's reforms. By 1915, a state insurance bank, a state mortgage bank, and a state electric facilities corporation had been created to ensure economic independence and national prosperity. Thus, the government participated directly in the provision of low-cost fire insurance, social security retirement, housing loans, and low-cost utility services. The government pattern of involvement in economic activity continued after Batlle's death. In 1928, the government established the Frigorifico Nacional (FRIGONAL), Uruguay's largest meatpacking corporation. In addition, through a series of entes (parastatals), it controlled 53 percent of all wool and over 30 percent of all beef exports. In 1944, government activity extended to airlines (PLUNA) and in 1949, to railroads. In 1947, Congress created AMDET, the National Transport Administration. As Marvin Aliski observed in 1974: "The largest importer in Uruguay is the Government Corporation Administracion Nacional de Combustibles, Alcohol y Portland (AN-CAP). ANCAP has a monopoly of importing and refining crude oil. . . . In addition, numerous boards and commissions regulate rents, control prices and oversee tourist facilities."[41]

Oscar Oszlak, in his diagnosis of the Uruguayan public administration, has noted that this hypertrophic growth of the bureaucracy took on clearly dysfunctional characteristics[42] after the 1950s. Bureaucratic effectiveness decreased as resources shrank dramatically. Meanwhile, the whole network of corporate arrangements, which maintained the political balance, was thrown into disarray. This catastrophic equilibrium ultimately led to a breakdown of the state, including the Tupamaro insurgency and the imposition of military rule. Despite the imposition of authoritarian capitalism with its claim to market economic principles and less government intervention, the basic parasitic nature of the bureaucracy remained intact. If anything, the military apparatus grew by leaps and bounds, becoming Uruguay's most entrenched, corrupt, and costly bureaucracy.

Historically, autonomous government agencies have often attempted to influence government policy by direct pressure on their members. Among these the most powerful have been "the cement, alcohol and petroleum corporation (AN-CAP), the state railroad system (AFE), the electrical and telephone corporation (UTE), state banks, like the Bank of the Republic and the Mortgage Bank of Uruguay, and state planning agencies like the Commission of Investment and Economic Development (CIDE) and the National Institute of Economic Housing (INVE)."[43] This influence of specific institutional interests and pressure groups such as the Camara de Industrias and the Union de Exportacion has been facilitated as deadlock has increased at the level of governmental policy making. Decentralized agencies, with their independent boards of directors, have also facilitated corporate arrangements where clienteles and powerful "lobbies" affect public policy. With the exception of the 1973–1985 dictatorial period, the interests of the public bureaucracy and the civil service in general have been reflected in government policies. Public service unions have been equally influential, and since the aforementioned proscription, they have once again become active. The Confederacion de Organizaciones de Funcionarios (COFE) represents the employees of the central government, whereas the Mesa Sindical Coordinadora (Coordinating Union Roundtable, MSC) represents the parastatals (especially the ANACAP federation of workers). Both (COFE and MSC) maintain a loose affiliation with the Plenario Intersindical de Trabajadores—Confederacion Nacional de Trabajadores (PIT-CNT).

The Executive and the Bureaucracy in Argentina. In Argentina, in both law and practice, the center of the political system is the chief executive. In some instances, however, the president has been a virtual prisoner of the armed forces, as was the case with Presidents Arturo Illia and José Mayía Guido in the 1960s or with General Levingston in the 1970s. Centrality does not necessarily imply the incumbency of a strong president. In fact, one main characteristic of the large and bureaucratized Argentinean state is its weakness and disorganization. The existence of the so-called *factores de poder,* deadlocked outside both the government and the party structure, make the Argentinean state a case of institutional power vacuum.

The 1853 Constitution calls for a president (for a six-year term) assisted by a presidentially appointed cabinet. Both the president and the vice president are chosen by an electoral college, the vice president through proportional representation. The cabinet, which has existed formally for more than a century, is fairly small. It encompasses eight ministries: (1) Defense; (2) Economy; (3) Education and Justice; (4) Foreign Affairs; (5) Interior; (6) Labor and Social Security; (7) Public Health and Social Action; and (8) Public Works and Services.[44] The ministerial structure is quite traditional, reflecting a more limited state role than that of Uruguay and Chile. Some ministries are subdivided into secretariats. For instance, the Ministry of Finance has six secretariats: Agriculture and Livestock, Commerce, Finance, Marine Resources, Mineral Resources, and Regional Development. The Ministry of Education and Justice has two secretariats (Justice and Culture); Labor and Social Security has two (Labor and Social Security); Public Health and Social Action four (Sports, Social Promotion, Human and Family Development, and Housing and Urban Environment); and the Ministry of Public Works and Services four (Water Resources, Communications, Energy, and Transportation).

The president is also directly assisted by a staff of five secretariats: the General Secretariat (Services), a Secretariat of Public Administration (currently charged with administrative reform), a Secretariat of Planning, a Secretariat of Public Information, and a civilian-controlled Secretariat of State Intelligence.[45] Beneath these secretariats, as well as those under the command of cabinet ministers, are numerous undersecretariats. Generally, the centralized services and operating units (Direcciones Generales) are under the jurisdiction of undersecretariats. Argentina also possesses a vast and complex network of functionally decentralized agencies. Despite efforts at privatization, these "continue to play a key role in Argentina's economy where they account for approximately 50% of the nation's GDP and about one third of the external debt."[46] These include the two largest Argentinean corporations, YPF (State Petroleum Deposits), and ENTEL (National Telecommunications Enterprise), as well the State National Gas Company (sixth in size), National Sanitation Works, Argentinean Railroads, Argentinean Airlines, and Water and Electricity,[47] all under the umbrella of the Ministry of Public Works. In turn, the Ministry of Public Health and Social Action has a number of parastatals under its nominal control: the National Institute of Social Works, the National Mortgage Bank, the National Institute of Social Services for Retired Persons and Pensioners, and the National Welfare Lottery.

In addition, at the provincial level, there are twenty-four publicly owned provincial banks and five municipal banks. There are seven autonomous regulatory bodies: the National Investment Council, the National Economic Council, the National Forestry Commission, the National Meat Board, the National Grain Board, the Superintendency of Insurance, and the Central Bank. As in the American system, independent regulatory agencies are widely controlled by the business associations; they are supposed to regulate agencies such as the Argentinean Rural Society (SRA), the Agroexporters of Cereals Association, and the Argentinean Industrial Union. The same is the case with regards to the linkage between Argentina's powerful financial interests grouped in the Bankers' Association (ADEBA), the Superintendency of Insurance, and the Central Bank. Private interest groups also partake in some state-sponsored development organizations such as the Argentinean Petroleum Institute, the Institute for Socioeconomic Development (IDES), and the National Institute of Economic Planning.

A 1985 study by the right-wing business think-tank FIEL (Fundacion de Instituciones Economicas Latinoamericanas) indicated that 59.5 percent of the GDP was generated by public spending. "Two components of spending have been increasing constantly since 1960: outlays on state enterprises and social security. Of the 305 state enterprises, YPF and the seven utility monopolies absorb 69.5 percent of the spending in that sector."[48] The same study also indicated that social security absorbed 3.4 percent of GDP, that nearly one-half of all state spending went into salaries, and that the state sector as a whole employed more than 2 million people (18.4 percent of the economically active population). If pensioners were added to the figures, the total number of individuals under the state sector would increase to 5.4 million, or 27.4 percent of the population over eighteen years of age.[49]

Despite its size (about 10 to 18 percent of the labor force, depending on the counting) and its fairly high technical competence, the Argentinean civil service has been characterized by a very limited role in policy making. For one, the Argentinean bureaucracy has remained weak, disorganized, and dominated by a political spoils system. In relation to the other two southern cone countries, the Argentinean bureaucracy has been on the whole a peripheral component of an otherwise weak state. Until recently, the dynamism and penetration of both the Uruguayan and the Chilean civil services at crucial facets of national life has been largely absent in the Argentinean case. There have been a few noteworthy exceptions. One has been YPF, the State Petroleum Deposits, created by Yrigoyen in 1922 with a fiercely nationalistic mandate to formulate a national petroleum policy and to develop, process, and market hydrocarbons. The second case was the short-lived experience with the Instituto Argentino de Promocion de Intercambio (IAPI). This state monopoly was created during the Peron era for the export of farm produce. Its profits financed most of the regime's social security and import-substitution industrialization programs.[50]

In both cases, as has been the situation in most of the country's bureaucratic agencies, the developmental results have been quite marginal. This was mostly due to external pressures from industrial and agricultural groups, inadequate staffing, governmental insecurity, military intervention, and inefficient planning.[51]

As Louis Ascher has observed, Argentinean bureaucrats and technocrats have lacked the authority, stability, and prestige to produce policy continuity or to carry out a national project.[52] They have been "subjected to political pressures without being able to balance them."[53] Nor has the bureaucracy been capable of managing conflict. This creates a sort of vicious cycle. The arena for negotiations moves further and further away from the institutional mechanisms of the state into the Hobbesian reality of "power politics"—the factores de poder. Military intervention, attempting to manage social conflict by force in the last fifty years, has paradoxically weakened the Argentinean state and dramatically limited both its goal attainment and system-maintenance capabilities. The administration of Dr. Raul Alfonsin has attempted to break this pattern of protracted administrative malaise. Administrative experts from the Secretariat of Public Administration have recognized the need for profound administrative rationalization. This has led to a number of bold initiatives. Paradoxically, however, owing to the extreme constraints on policy formulation and implementation discussed earlier, these initiatives have been concentrated on formal measures of administrative reorganization and reform.

The reorganization of the state apparatus constitutes one of the "four pillars" of the government program. The other three are constitutional reform leading to a semiparliamentary system, the physical and economic development of Patagonia (including the moving of the federal capital to Viedma) and the attempt to make democracy more social and participatory, especially in labor relations. The terms of reference regarding administrative reform are to make the state "leaner and more energetic."[54] For instance, in the area of food security, a National Food Program (PAN) has been set in motion.

. . . as a top priority . . . by the government . . . [it] has been one of the most effective and successful in meeting its objectives. With extreme efficiency, PAN reaches over 1,400,000 families throughout the country (17% of its population) and does so with a much smaller amount of resources than was originally allocated to it. It has achieved many objectives relating to social organization and community development in addition to its direct goals. Its management has made extensive use of innovative models of inter-institutional co-operation in order to optimize the available resources within the public apparatus itself.[55]

Another area of reorganization has been in the realm of public enterprises. In 1987, a Directorate of Public Enterprises (DEP) was created in the form of a holding company with a broad mandate. It is able to regulate measures to cut red tape, set salaries for all the entities under its jurisdiction, as well as to set policies and tariffs. The stated aim is to establish public companies that provide "efficient public services and non-bureaucratic offices."[56] Especially targeted have been enterprises such as National Railways, sanitation (OSN), electricity (SEGBA), telecommunications (ENTEL), maritime transportation (ELMA) and the gigantic hydrocarbon complex, YPF.

YPF is to be divided into four operational units dealing with oil exploration and exploitation, processing, marketing, and transport. The goals of the reor-ganization are both to reduce the U.S. $173 million deficit (1986 figures), as well as to establish closer linkages with the private sector. In the case of National Railways, with its 100,000 employees, its U.S. $72 million deficit, and its 59 percent personnel expenditures above company revenue, the reorganization has aimed at improving fiscal controls and attaining some degree of privatization. A similar approach has been taken in the cases of OSN and SEGBA which serve Buenos Aires. In the case of the shipping lines, ELMA, 25 percent of the operation has already been privatized,[57] whereas the entirety of ENTEL has been decentralized and slated for privatization. Equally singled out for privatization is the large conglomerate of firms comprising the military-industrial complex.

In addition, the reform of the public sector contemplates the voluntary retire-ment of over 15,000 employees, the start of a vigorous program of deregulation, and a curbing of spending by state concerns.[58] All these liberalizing trends constitute a move toward a less interventionist and less nationalistic policy and state apparatus. This is partly in response to intense pressure from business concerns (such as the aforementioned think-tank FIEL) as well as from the IMF.[59]

It is against this kind of Radical party policy that the electorate rebelled in September 1987 with a drop in the polls from 43 percent to 37 percent. For all their dramatics, these austerity measures failed to slow down the economic crisis. Not only did inflation grow by 200 percent, but also business bankruptcies reached a record number of 1,308 in 1987, an 80 percent growth over the previous year.[60] This has compounded a debt service burden that poses a most severe growth constraint, thus reducing even further government maneuverability.

Dictatorship and Bureaucracy in Chile. Chile's contemporary institutional arrangement is not only "presidentialist" and heavily centralized, but also an unabashedly personal dictatorship. All power is exercised by the captain general (a title derived from early colonial times), General Pinochet, who is advised by a junta of four members which exercises "legislative power." There are also numerous other advisory boards.

the most significant body is the Presidential Staff . . . , which acted to coordinate the work between the various ministries. . . . The Presidential Advisory Committee was formed in 1981, in large part from what had been the advisory committee of the Military junta. . . . [It] performs much of the technical work of . . . legislation. . . . The Casa Militar consists of a small number of military officers who arrange the president's work schedule and accompany him at official functions.

There was also a now inoperative advisory Council of State (a board of appointed notables) as well as a Presidential Advisory Committee and a presidential staff. The Controller General's Office (once an independent agency), as well as the judiciary, are subordinated to the executive in a de facto advisory capacity. Administratively, perhaps the most important organs are the National Security Council, the Planning Office, and a seventeen-member cabinet made of presidentially appointed ministers.

Since May, 1986, the cabinet positions have included the ministries of: (1) Interior; (2) Foreign Relations; (3) Economics, Development, and Reconstruction; (4) Finance; (5) Education; (6) Defense; (7) Public Works; (8) Agriculture; (9) National Patrimony; (10) Labor and Social Security; (11) Health; (12) Mines; (13) Housing and Urbanization; (14) Justice; and (15) Transport and Communications.[61] In addition to these ministries, the secretary-general of government and the Planning Office with ministerial rank should be added. All ministries, except for those of Foreign Relations, Planning, and Defense have ministerial regional offices, one for each of the thirteen regions into which the country is administratively divided. In general, as far as the centralized administration is concerned, the ministries are subdivided in undersecretariats. There are a total of twenty-four undersecretariats. These, in turn, control over sixty centralized services (General Directorates, or Direcciones Generales) whose functions range the whole gamut of administrative activities. The largest number of agencies, however, obtains in the decentralized area. In addition to the 300 or so municipalities, which in theory are autonomous, but in actuality are territorial dependencies of the Ministry of Interior subordinated to the agents of the Servicio de Administracion Interior del Estado such as intendents and governors, there are nearly 100 functionally decentralized entities. These range from regulatory and control bodies such as the General Comptroller's Office and the Central Bank through the complex social security system with some twelve social security funds, through CORFO, the Development Corporation, to the State Mining Enterprise (SONAMI), the National Petroleum Enterprise (ENAP), the National Electric Company (ENDESA), and the gigantic Copper Corporation (CODELCO).[62]

As indicated earlier, state involvement in economic and social development has a long tradition in Chile, dating back to the 1930s. Chilean development policies, from the Popular Front (1939–1941) onward, have followed a distinct Keynesian state-interventionist mold.[63] This policy framework can be traced back to the creation of Chile's model Development Corporation. "From its foundation on, CORFO played a crucial role in the growth of the Chilean economy through its promotion of mining, agriculture, industry and commerce. It was under its aegis that heavy industry, including the great steel mill at Huachipato was established in the 1940s and 1950s."[64]

Although the proportion of the labor force employed by the public sector is about that of Argentina (over 13 percent—albeit certainly much smaller than that of Uruguay) the bureaucracy has played a central role in Chilean politics. In 1981, out of the fifty most important business, eleven establishments were state-owned. These included six of the top ten corporations: copper production, oil, smelters, steel mills, railways and electricity, which ranked, respectively first, second, fourth, fifth, sixth, and eighth in both volume of sales and personnel.[65] James Petras has seen the role of Chilean bureaucracy in the 1960s as one of "anchor of the Chilean system, moderating the effects of frequent changes in government ministries."[66] Unlike Argentina, where a civil service based on spoils and a weak political technocracy failed to develop a national project, Chile's "technobureaucracy"—a "national productivity bureaucracy" in Warren Ilchman's terms[67]—was a crucial political player with expanding responsibilities.[68]

Since the 1973 coup, the military has considerably reduced the size and scope of government, both to implement a U.S. policy of limited government and to reduce fiscal burdens. In a five-year period.

between 1974 and 1979, public expenditures fell almost 18% in real terms—public employment was reduced by fully 20% between 1973 and 1980 at the cost of some 100,000 jobs, mostly in autonomous agencies and state corporations. The Development Corporation (CORFO) was reduced most dramatically—449 of nearly 500 firms held in 1973 had been returned to the private sector by 1977, and its former staff of 6,000 had been reduced to 800. A notable exception to this trend to reduce government was in the armed forces, whose numbers increased from 60,000 in 1973 to 92,000 by 1981 and whose budget expanded significantly.[69]

The tendency has been to reduce the importance of civilian *tecnicos* and public servants and to replace the key positions with military personnel. Although the earlier trend of having an almost all-military cabinet has been reversed, an examination of the commanding heights of most crucial government agencies indicates that practically all of them are in military hands.[70] These include, CORFO itself, Chilectra, the phone company (CTC), the National Coal Company, ENAMI (mining), and Chile's largest corporation, the Copper Corporation (CODELCO) with over 30,000 employees, over $1.5 billion annual sales, and net assets of about half a billion dollars. This military penetration of the state also applies to the science and technology and educational areas. The National

Energy Commission, the Chilean Nuclear Energy Commission, and, until 1987, the rectorships of practically all the Chilean universities were headed by military appointees. Thus, although the orientation of public policy has changed dramatically from development and welfare to demobilization, denationalization, and social control, the state by its sheer weight is still an important component in the national economy. It still plays a larger role than in any other Latin American country,[71] with the exception of Cuba. Military hardliners linked to the U.S. military are less prone to pursue a policy of Friedmanian neo-liberalism than their softliner counterparts and business allies in Chile and the United States. Their outright fascist views (albeit of a dependent strain) go well with a notion of "big government," as long as "national security" concerns are given priority and its operations remain authoritarian. In this sense, the militarization of the bureaucracy is both a concession to the "duros" (hardliners) and a payoff to maintain military support.

The corporate representation which obtains in the councils of the autonomous agencies lends itself to a good deal of penetration by the dominant business groups as well: the National Society of Agriculture (SNA), the National Society for Industrial Promotion (SOFOFA), the Chamber of Construction, the National Society of Mining (SONAMI), the Chamber of Commerce, and the Bankers' Associations. However, this arrangement is neither fully corporatist nor a drastic departure from the past, except for the elimination of labor representation.

The hub of the present administrative structure of Chile is the relationship between the president, the National Security Council, the Ministry of Interior (which controls the CNI, the secret police) and the Ministry of Defense.[72] Planning, budgeting, administrative reform, as well as the functions exercised by the once powerful and independent Office of the Comptroller General take a back seat. In the absence of real accountability and responsible external controls on the executive and on the military clique, much of the technicalities, legalisms, and procedural rationality which decorate the language of Chilean bureaucracy mean very little. Without a real role to play in economic development, curtailed in its traditional mediating function, the present Chilean civil service and the civilian technocracy are a feeble remnant of their past. As in Argentina and later in Uruguay, the replacement of civilian by military "conflict managers" has greatly reduced the scope for compromise and maneuver. This, in turn, makes both development and democratization an even more unattainable possibility.

CONCLUSIONS: THE CRISIS OF BUREAUCRACY AND THE CRISIS OF THE STATE

The preceding historical and structural analysis of the relationship between bureaucratization and development in the southern cone suggests a number of general traits and trends which can be grouped under two major headings. The first refers to a diagnostic characterization of the crisis of the state sector in these countries. The second is an attempt to go beyond the crude interpretation of the diagnosis of the crisis and look ahead in a sort of interpretative prognosis. Needless to say, these conclusions are by force tentative oversimplifications of an extremely complex and unfolding process.

Characteristics of Bureaucratization and Underdevelopment in the Southern Cone

The emergence and evolution of the administrative state in the three countries studied have been directly related to major socioeconomic crises. The specific characteristics of bureaucratization have responded to concrete patterns of mass-elite relations, levels of economic surplus versus social mobilization, as well as to the degree of vulnerability of the state and society to external factors. Thus, it is not possible to say a priori that bureaucratization has been a precondition, a consequence, or an obstacle to development in all the countries at any time. It is possible, however, to construct a series of a posteriori generalizations that can shed some light on this complex relationship. The sequential model outlined below attempts to synthesize such a relationship. It concentrates basically on the linkages between the pattern of social antagonism, the development policies, and the type of state and bureaucratic ensemble through which such policies are implemented. One aspect that needs to be stressed here is the strong linkage between Latin America's middle sectors and the white-collar bureaucracy. In all three countries, the aforementioned identity is an historical constant with specific structural variations within the countries.

*The Incorporation of the Middle Sectors and the Emergence of a
Legal Rational Bureaucracy (1910–1930)*

The middle strata entered the political game of the three countries between the turn of the century and the 1920s under the sponsorship of elite sectors to prevent a political explosion. This corresponded to what Petras has referred to as the "insurgent" period[73] of middle-class mobilization. Social reforms a la Batlle, Yrigoyen, or Alessandri had the effect of institutionalizing class antagonism, arbitrated by a legal-bureaucratic order sorting out social demands from its own ranks as well as those coming from the nascent proletariat. Abundant resources from the still growing export economy (the period of *crecimiento hacia afuera*) allowed demands to be satisfied through an expansion of welfare program without threatening the basic structure of the property of the traditional classes. This bureaucratic arrangement, like its North American and European counterparts, was then a consequence of the process of capitalist development.

*The Transition of the Middle Sectors and the Formation of a
"Rational Productivity Bureaucracy" (1930–1950)*

The world Depression which shattered the pattern of outward-oriented development brought about a crisis of the early welfare state. The middle-class controlled states and the state classes sought a transitional strategy of accommodation with both selectively incorporated sectors of labor and the industrial bourgeoisie to pursue a reformist policy of Keynesian economic reactivation. This constituted what Petras has called the "transitional" period[74] of the middle classes in which nationalist populism was the response to the export-import crisis. This policy brought about a new type of managerial or entrepreneurial state: a "rational productivity bureaucracy" with a direct involvement in economic development. In Chile and Uruguay, direct management was the dominant pattern, whereas Argentina relied more on indirect measures: protectionism, promotion, and financing of business activity. At any rate, the greatest beneficiaries of this new institutional arrangement—as with the "welfare state"—were the middle sectors themselves, especially the upper echelons of the technobureaucracy. This, in turn, made it possible for state-sponsored new industrialists and senior civil servants to enter the circles of the traditional aristocracy. As in the rest of the West, *etatisme* and broadened political participation had become a condition for further development.

The Stabilization of the Middle Sectors and the Politics of Immobilism (1950–1960)

With the exhaustion of import substitution as well as the forging of an alliance between the upper middle classes and the traditional aristocracy, the administrative state became increasingly incapable of arbitrating social antagonisms. Lower class mobilization, accompanied by growing expectations and a decline of economic surplus, brought about a long period of institutionalized, yet extremely polarized, class conflict. This growing polarization brought about an acute fractionalization of the white-collar workers which led to insecurity and radicalization. In the midst of hyperinflation, authoritarian ideologies from the center emerged (though the most vulnerable sectors on occasion moved left as in Uruguay and to a lesser extent in Chile). The paralysis of the state as well as the bureaucracy opened the gates for direct social confrontations in which the security bureaucracy increasingly replaced the lawyers, managers, and *tecnicos* of the old system. Likewise, a growing transnationalization of the economy and the national security apparatus gave internal political struggles a Cold War coloration. Attempts at administrative nationalization—planning, budgeting, O & M, central personnel systems, and the like, carried out by external inducement under the Alliance for Progress—had no real developmental effects. In fact, they further enhanced such features of a "mock" bureaucracy as formalism, rigidity, and a tendency toward immobilism. Worse, the new transnationalized technobureaucracy became even more alienated from "politics."

The "Repressive Rationality Bureaucracy" (1970–1980)

Toward the end of the 1960s and early 1970s, these conditions resulted in a crisis of "governability" exacerbated by the frankly antidevelopmentalist and authoritarian doctrines toward the region sponsored by the American official, business, and military establishments.

It is no accident that, by 1977, fifteen out of all twenty Latin American countries were under military rule. The coups of 1973 in Chile and Uruguay and 1976 in Argentina were institutional interventions, with the entire military bureaucracy abolishing "politics" and declaring war on the civil society. In so doing, they displaced the bulk of the middle strata and the middle-class parties, as well as their labor "adversaries" from center stage. This substitution of a "repressive rationality bureaucracy" for the traditional bureaucratic bargaining of previous eras (both "legal" and "productive") also meant an increase in official repression. This repression was unleashed by a new kind of "terrorist state" whose central function had become the "authoritative allocation of violence" rather than responding to societal needs. It also meant the introduction in the political arena of probably the most incompetent, disingenuous, and brutal conflict managers the area had seen since the end of the "barbarian *caudillos*" of the early 1800s. The objective consequences of this intervention were not to eradicate any of the problems *ex ante* but to compound them. Growing corruption, gross human rights abuses, extreme transnationalization of both the state and the economy, not to mention an unmanageable foreign debt, were the legacies of a clearly antidevelopmentalist bureaucratic authoritarian state.

The Systemic Paralysis of the "New Democracies": The Receiver State

The civilian regimes that have emerged in Argentina and Uruguay are not only fragile economically, but also weak politically and administratively. The long experience of military rule has severely weakened the administrative base of the state. This both perpetuates the presence of the military as conflict managers and makes political compromise impossible. The task of the state, under a streamlined and weak middle class, centrist alliance, cannot conceivably be one of development but of survival. The intent is to prevent further internal deterioration until foreign creditors have collected their debts. (Images of the "stabilizing" effects of the U.S. dollar diplomacy in the early 1900s in Central America come to mind.) It may well be an *après moi le déluge* situation in which weak civilian governments will have to resort to military repression to contain "excessive" labor demands, leading to yet another cycle of praetorianism.[75] It is essentially a no-win situation. The economies are bankrupt, the living standards of the majorities have been purposely and forcefully eroded for over a decade, and democratic illusions have faded away. Worse, no single sector within the state can provide legitimate and effective leadership. The parties, the bureaucracy, and the military as well as the whole of the state are discredited; the popular movement is fragmented and just recovering from the trauma of years of extreme repression.

Despite apparent regime differences, one striking similarity of the three administrative systems studied here is the present underlying metapolicy framework. As a consequence of the process of demobilization and authoritarian "liberalization" of the economy, the earlier Keynesian direction of the state has taken a drastic turn. Instead, a neo-conservative orientation, much in line with Reaganomics and Thatcherism, constitutes the matrix of public policy formulation and implementation, euphemistically called "structural adjustment." This administrative and public policy counterrevolution is most noticeable in Chile. To a varying degree, however, the restricted civilian democracies in Argentina and Uruguay pursue a similar course. The current trends of privatization, deregulation, reorganization of labor relations, denationalization and a shrinking of the welfare state have to be seen in this light. On a national scale, such trends represent a global redirection in the pattern of north-south relations: the reinsertion of the Latin American economies in the international division of labor.

Looking Ahead "Through a Glass Darkly"

The above overview suggests that the present crisis of the state in the southern cone countries, besides the obvious effects of transnationalization, stems from two possible sources within the domestic societies. One is internal to the state: the fracturing of the bureaucratic system of "civil" conflict management and its replacement by "expert" violence. Here we are confronted with the tendency of violence to reproduce and expand itself both as a tool of politics and as a culture. Bernard Fall, an expert on insurgency, reminded us that "when a government is being subverted it is not being outfought. It is being outadministered."[76] The case of outadministration in the southern cone is not, at least not yet, that of Vietnam, Cuba, or Nicaragua where an insurgent force presents an alternative set of rules and organizations. Outadministration has been largely self-inflicted by sectors within the state, particularly by the national security bureaucracy. As mentioned earlier, this has created a power vacuum that no present domestic institutional actor has been able to fill, expect, of course, for the external U.S. military and business constituencies.

The second source of the crisis is external to the state but not to the Latin American countries themselves: the growing alienation affecting most sectors of the civil society. While a discussion of the first source of the crisis was presented from the position of a "morphostatic" consideration—the maintenance of the present social order—the second source is distinctively "morphogenic." It relates to the circumstances and possibilities of radical systemic change. Most of the countries' populations experience the power vacuum and the increasing meaninglessness of, and alienation from, the state. Times and circumstances permitting, this may lead to a new crisis of governability: a full-fledged crisis of domination. It is possible to argue that the process of decomposition that affected the middle strata and rendered the administrative state inoperative may well affect the very heart of the power structure, that is, the military establishment. Signs of this organizational malaise have been seen in prerevolutionary situations (Cuba, Nicaragua) as well as in transitional periods (Portugal, Greece). The Argentinean and Uruguayan armed bureaucrats are far from cohesive and are marred by internal paralysis. (The Falklands episode is interesting here.)

But there is more to these internal developments than meets the eye. As the state has become incompetent to arbitrate conflict, to master development, and even to provide its essential services, grassroots spontaneous organizations have proliferated. During the years of the repression, myriads of human rights groups (e.g. the Mothers of Plaza de Mayo, committees for the *desaparecidos*), social services, soup kitchens, and self-help, educational, and productive associations have emerged. These are not "resistance" groups in the traditional sense of guerrilla forces but rather survival shelters whose functions have continued well after the end of the emergency. What is most important, however, is that these are not "pressure groups" in the usual sense either. They are all guided by a productive rationality (Malvinas); they render a service and create a product or even a commodity. They are also generally democratic and participatory, face-to-face, nonbureaucratic organizations. We are talking about both *grupos de base* (base groups) and more "elite" alternatives such as scientific and technological *centros independientes* (independent centers). As a result of necessity, they have become naturally integrated in horizontal networks and information grids with the capacity to elude repression and minimize the effects of infiltration.

The present situation in Chile, despite the continuity of the dictatorship, offers an example of these "subterranean tendencies" at work. A 1986 Oxfam release indicated that they are made by

thousands of ordinary people who, despite the growing reign of terror, are taking their lives into their own hands and creating change. They are students, housewives, and labour leaders as well as a wide range of political parties. . . . (They) are working in their communities to build the foundations of a new democracy. Small but successful local initiatives—health clinics, peasant cooperatives, youth leadership training, shantytown organizations—are meeting people's urgent everyday needs.[77]

These developments are also taking place in most other Latin American countries. They constitute a new type of popular movement at the margin, and potentially against, existing state institutions—a redefinition of *public* administration, development, *and* democracy. As Maurice Zeitlin states:

"social structures" are partially contingent historical products, actively created and re-created by real men and women involved in determinate social relations that were themselves produced historically, by prior human activity. . . . Classes, and the societies they constitute, *form themselves* in the struggles not only between them but also within them, among their contending segments, shaping and being shaped by the already existing class relations and their underlying forms of production.[78]

SOME COMPARATIVE REFLECTIONS

It is clear that Latin America did not replicate the European pattern of relations between economic development, bureaucratization, and the nature of the state.

It is equally clear that there is no single pattern of development in world history. One can identify at least the following three patterns.

In the Western industrial world, the record seems to indicate that bureaucratization first followed a process of spontaneous development that began with the first industrial and bourgeois revolutions and continued throughout the phase of imperialist expansion. Since the Depression, however, it appears that the Western administrative state has become a functional necessity to *prevent* economic recession and to facilitate expansion. In this case, bureaucratization has not only accompanied development, but has also been an intervening variable in the overall process of democratization of the bourgeois-liberal state.

Barrington Moore has observed another route to capitalist development, and thus a different causal linkage between development and bureaucratization. This is the "fascist" pattern of belated industrialization, as in Germany, Italy, and Japan where a strong aristocratic, autocratic, and interventionist state created, through rapid and efficient bureaucratization, the conditions for capital accumulation.[79] This constituted a form of nationalist capitalism[80] where bureaucratization preceded the "development" of the civil society and the economy. In Moore's theory, each pattern is inextricably connected to a constellation of social alliances (and opposition) which gives substance and meaning to the development project. Such a constellation is manifested in a type of state. The Western pattern with bourgeois hegemony crystallized in the liberal-democratic state. The fascist pattern with a dominant "modernizing" elite expressed itself in a corporatist-authoritarian arrangement,[81] which, in the long run, created the conditions for postwar liberal democracy.

Guillermo O'Donnell, observing the experience of the southern cone—including that of Brazil—offers a variant of this second road of induced capitalist development which leads to a radical reformulation of Moore's theories. This may be called the third pattern. It also relates to a different type of state, one that does not necessarily lead to development but rather to the reproduction of underdevelopment. In O'Donnell's view, the experience of these societies indicates a peculiar situation of the "deepening" of capitalism "far removed from the archetypic situations of 'underdevelopment' which nevertheless does not follow the patterns of growth and distribution of the central economies."[82] Taking Helio Jaguaribe's characterization of "national-capitalism" to task, O'Donnell suggests that the context of bureaucratic interventionism in the more "advanced" Latin American countries is different from both Moore's characterization of fascism and that of the Anglo-Saxon and overall Western experience. He links these differences to a much later tempo in the process of industrialization.

First, in the Latin American cases discussed here "the demands of the popular sectors for political participation emerged much earlier [than in the German, Italian and Japanese cases], and the composition of the dominant classes is not the same."[83] Second, the case of the southern cone (and that of the relatively more advanced countries in the region) is one in which foreign capital has played a decisive role. This situation affects the technological capacity of these economies, and their ability to create capital goods and even to generate much needed currency. As a result, those countries find it impossible to complete a self-sustained cycle of capital accumulation and mass consumption in their own markets. Instead, their economies appear to be marred by slow growth and instability resulting from external dependency on one basic commodity. Since the level of social mobilization far exceeds the economy's capacity to satisfy demands, tensions between elites and masses tend to be extensive.[84] A further complicating factor is the dependent nature of both the economy and the state. The political result is a chronic crisis of legitimacy—what Jose Nun has called a crisis of hegemony[85]—in which violence and instability are ubiquitous. The working of consensual liberal-democratic modalities of conflict management becomes virtually impossible. The outcome is a kind of "constipated corporatism" as a form of intermediation between state and society. O'Donnell characterizes this pathological form as the combination of two intimately related processes:

The first comprises changes in the economy, mainly directed towards a high degree of vertical integration and property concentration in industry and the productive structure in general, basically benefitting large organizations both public and private, national and foreign. . . .

The second process . . . [is] . . . the "expansion" of a new type of state, the bureaucratic authoritarian. This state is more (1) comprehensive, in the range of activities it controls or directly manages; (2) dynamic, in its rates of growth compared to those of society as a whole; (3) penetrating through its subordination of various "private" areas of civil society; (4) repressive, in the extension and efficacy of the coercion it applies; (5) bureaucratic in the formalization and differentiation of its own structures; and (6) technocratic in the growing weight of teams of *tecnicos*, expert in the application of "efficientist" techniques of formal rationality. Furthermore, the bureaucratic-authoritarian state is closely linked to international capital, although this relationship is subject to tensions.[86]

The type of administrative (both managerial and organizational) style under bureaucratic authoritarianism is far removed from Frederick Riggs' "sala model."[87] It is distinctively "modern" in form and substance. It constitutes a blend of punishment-centered and "mock" bureaucracies[88] in the context of a highly polarized, though deadlocked, polity and society. This administrative arrangement, a most salient feature of the state of *advanced underdevelopment*, is not capable of breaking the centrifugal cycle of capital generation. Far from it, its "efficiency" gravitates against the possibilities of popular movements and self-sustained, autonomous, and need-oriented development.

NOTES

1. A systematic and succinct historical sketch of Latin American socioeconomic history is contained in E. Bradford Burns, "The Continuity of the National Period," in Jan Black (ed.), *Latin America: Its Problems and Its Promise* (Boulder, Colo.: Westview Press, 1984), pp. 61–80.

2. For a discussion of the "patrimonial state," see Jacques Sylberberg, "Etat-cor-poratisme-populisme, contribution à une sociologie politique de l'Amérique latine," *Etudes internationales* 7, 2 (June 1976), pp. 223–25.

3. I have elaborated on the subject in my "Crise politique et transnationalisation de l'état en Amérique latine: une interprétation théorique," *Etudes internationales* 17, 2 (June 1986), pp. 284–98.

4. Ibid.

5. See Marvin Alisky, "Uruguay," in Helen Delpar (ed.), *Encyclopedia of Latin America* (New York: McGraw-Hill, 1974), p. 606.

6. See William Glade, *The Latin American Economies: A Study of Their Institutional Evolution* (New York: Van Nostrand Reinhold, 1969), pp. 402–82. See also Elso Furtado, *Economic Development of Latin America-Historical Background and Contemporary Problems*, 2d ed. (London: Cambridge University Press, 1970), pp. 107–17.

7. A very coherent study of Latin American populism is provided by D. L. Raby, "Populism: A Marxist Analysis," *McGill Studies in International Development* 32, passim.

8. The argument has been presented by Philip O'Brien and Paul Cammack, in *Generals in Retreat: The Crisis of Military Rule in Latin America* (Manchester: Manchester University Press, 1985), passim.

9. Nelson Rockefeller, *The Rockefeller Report of a United States Presidential Mission to the Western Hemisphere* (Chicago: Quadrangle Press, 1969), passim.

10. Sol Linowitz (Chairman, Commission of the United States–Latin American Relations), *The Americans in a Changing World* (New York: Quadrangle Press, 1975), passim.

11. J. Nef, "Stalemate and Repression in the Southern Cone: An Interpretive Synopsis," *New Scholar* 8 (1983), pp. 373–81.

12. Seymour Martin Lipset, *Political Man, The Social Basis of Politics* (Garden City, N.Y.: Doubleday, 1963), pp. 127–29.

13. Jose Nun, "A Latin American Phenomenon: The Middle Class Military Coup," in James Petras and Maurice Zeitlin (eds.), *Latin America: Reform or Revolution? A Reader* (Greenwich, Conn.: Fawcett, 1968), pp. 145–85.

14. See Gabriel Almond and Sidney Verba, *The Civic Culture* (Princeton, N.J.: Princeton University Press, 1963), pp. 82–86.

15. A definition is contained in Marcio Moreira Alves, "Urban Guerrillas and the Terrorist State," in Jon Rosembaum (ed.), *Contemporary Brazil: Issues in Economic and Political Development* (New York: Praeger, 1972), p. 51.

16. For a detailed characterization of political movements and alliances in these countries, see Ciaran O Maolain (ed.), *Latin American Political Movements* (Harlow: Longman Group Ltd., 1987), pp. 2–13, 40–57, 242–53.

17. Cf. Anibal Mayo, "Opiniones: E Plan Sourrouille," *Realidad Economica* (Buenos Aires: 2d bimonthly, 1985), p. 5. For the effects of the Plan, see *Facts on File* 42, 2393, 3 October 1986: pp. 731–32.

18. *Latin American Weekly Report (LAWR)*, 24 December 1987, p. 4.

19. See *Keesing's Contemporary Archives—Record of World Events* 32, 6 (1986), p. 34420.

20. Ibid. The growth of the GDP for 1987 was calculated as 4 percent below the 6.2 percent growth of 1986 while inflation went down from 70 percent in 1986 to 60 percent in 1987. There has also been a slow and slight upward trend in wages.

21. For a description of Chile's political alliances under dictatorial rule circa 1985, see Arthur S. Banks (ed.), *Political Handbook of the World 1984–1985* (Binghampton: Centre for Social Analysis, 1985), pp. 96–98.

22. Ibid. GDP growth of over 5 percent with investment gaining. Inflation is over 20 percent whereas real wages are very depressed. (Minimum wage is under $38 U.S. per month.)

23. For a discussion of the economic team, see " 'The Chicago Boys' in Chile: Economic Freedom's Awful Toll," *The Nation*, 28 August 1976, pp. 138, 142.

24. A description of union configuration and activity in Chile (circa 1985–1986) can be found in Banks, *Political Handbook*.

25. *LAWR*, 2 July 1987, and 7 May 1987, p. 9, where the so-called Baker Formula is explained.

26. Banks, *Political Handbook*, p. 608; also Richard McDonald, "Uruguay," in Jack Hopkins (ed.), *Latin America and Caribbean Contemporary Record* 3, 1983–1984 (New York: Holmes and Meier, 1985), pp. 459, 461.

27. Ibid., pp. 27–28.

28. Ibid.

29. *LAWR*, 17 September 1987, p. 2.

30. Ibid., pp. 609–10.

31. Ibid., p. 608.

32. Oscar Oszlak, Projecto de Capacitacion del Servicio Civil—Uruguay, *Diagnostico de la Administracion Publica Uruguaya* (San Jose: ICAP, 1975), pp. 25–27.

33. See Arturo Valenzuela, *Political Brokers in Chile: Local Government in a Centralized Polity* (Durham, N.C.: Duke University Press, 1977), pp. 155–230.

34. Chile, Contraloria General de la Republica, *Organigrama del Gobierno de Chile* (Organizational Chart), July 1986.

35. For information on the Colegiado in Uruguay, see Diego Abente, "Uruguay and Paraguay," in Black, *Latin America*, pp. 454–55; see also Marvin Alisky "Uruguay," in Delpar, *Encyclopedia of Latin America*.

36. See *Keesing's Contemporary Archives* 32, 6 (1986), p. 34419.

37. *LAWR*, 4 June 1987, p. 6.

38. Martin Weinstein, *Uruguay, The Politics of Failure* (Westport, Conn.: Greenwood Press, 1975), p. 116.

39. Marvin Alisky, *Uruguay: A Contemporary Survey* (New York: Praeger, 1969), pp. 51–52.

40. Eduardo Galeano, "Uruguay: Promise and Betrayal," in James Petras and Maurice Zeitlin (eds.), *Latin America: Reform or Revolution? A Reader* (Greenwich, Conn.: Fawcett, 1968), p. 456.

41. Alisky, in Delpar (ed.), *Encyclopedia* of *Latin America*, p. 60.

42. Oszlak, *Diagnostico de la Administracion*, p. 22.

43. *Uruguay: Election Factbook* (Washington, D.C.: ICSPS, 1966), p. 29.

44. Cf. *Lambert's Worldwide Government Directory Fall/Winter 1984* (Washington, D.C.: Lambert Publications, 1984), pp. 33–38.

45. Ibid.

46. Jack Child, "Argentina," in Hopkins, *Latin America*, p. 284.

47. Besides *Lambert's*, a listing of decentralized agencies in Argentina can be found in *Statistical Abstract of Latin America* (Los Angeles: Center of Latin America Studies, 1984), vol. 24, p. 677.

48. *LAWR*, 13 August 1987, p. 2.

49. Ibid.

50. Torcuato di Tella, "Stalemate and Coexistence in Argentina," in James Petras and Maurice Zeitlin (eds.), *Latin America: Performer Revolution? A Reader* (Greenwich, Conn.: Fawcett, 1968), p. 258.

51. Ibid.

52. Louis Ascher, "Planners, Politics and Technology in Argentina and Chile," (Ph.D. thesis, Yale University Department of Political Science, 1975), pp. 141–42.

53. Ibid., p. 144.

54. *LAWR*, 13 August 1987, p. 2.

55. See Bernardo Kliksberg, "New Technological Frontiers of Management in Latin America," *CEPAL Review*, no. 31, U.N. Economic Commission for Latin America and the Caribbean, April 1987, pp. 181–82 n. 9.

56. *LAWR*, 13 August 1987, p. 2.

57. *LAWR*, 7 May 1987.

58. *LAWR*, 30 July 1987, p. 1.

59. Ibid.

60. *LAWR*, 18 January 1988, p. 12.

61. U.S. Department of the Army, *Chile, A Country Study*, 2d ed. (Washington, D.C.: U.S. Department of the Army, 1982), pp. 152–60.

62. Contraloria, *"Organigrama."*

63. Barbara Stallings, *Class Conflict and Economic Development in Chile, 1958–1973* (Stanford Calif.: Stanford University Press, 1978), pp. 234–35.

64. Harold Blackemore, "Chile," in Delpar (ed.), *Encyclopedia of Latin America*, p. 72.

65. *Statistical Abstract*, p. 681.

66. James Petras, *Politics and Social Forces in Chilean Development* (Berkeley: University of California Press, 1969), p. 288.

67. See Warren Ilchman, "Productivity, Administrative Reform and Antipolitics: Dilemmas for Developing Countries," in Ralph Brailbanti (ed.), *Political and Administrative Development* (Durham, N.C.: Duke University Press, 1969), pp. 472–526.

68. Ascher, "Planners, Politics and Technology," pp. 142–60.

69. U.S. Department of the Army, *Chile*, pp. 150–51.

70. For a list of key parastatals under military control (circa 1984–1985), see Banks, *Political Handbook*, pp. 97–98.

71. U.S. AID, Office of Foreign Disaster Assistance, *Chile: A Country Profile* (Washington, D.C.: AID, 1978), p. 2.

72. See U.S. Department of the Army, *Chile*, pp. 152–53.

73. Petras, *Politics and Social Forces* pp. 135–36.

74. Ibid.

75. I have argued about this cycle of praetorianism in "Violence and Ideology in Latin American Politics: An Overview," in Marcel Daneau (ed.), *Violence et conflits en Amérique latine* (Quebec: Centre québécois de relations internationales, 1985), pp. 5–34.

76. See Bernard Fall, "The Theory and Practice of Insurgency and Counterinsurgency," in M. Smith and C. Johns (eds.), *American Defence Policy*, 2d ed. (Baltimore: Johns Hopkins University Press, 1965), quoted in O. P. Dwivedi and J. Nef, "Crises and Continuities in Development Theory and Administration: First and Third World Perspectives," in *Public Administration and Development* 2 (1982), pp. 59–77.

77. Cf. Paul Malby, Andean Regional Coordinator of OXFAM, flier, "September 1986," p. 1.

78. Maurice Zeitlin, *The Civil Wars in Chile (or Bourgeois Revolutions That Never Were)* (Princeton N.J.: Princeton University Press, 1984), pp. 235–36.

79. Barrington Moore, *Social Origins of Dictatorship and Democracy: Lord and Peasant in the Making of the Modern World* (Beacon: Beacon Press, 1966), pp. 433–52.

80. Helio Jaguaribe, *Economic and Political Development: A Theoretical Approach and a Brazilian Case Study* (Cambridge, Mass.: Harvard University Press, 1968), pp. 57–58.

81. Moore, *Social Origins of Dictatorship and Democracy*.

82. Guillermo O'Donnell, "Corporatism and the Question of the State," in James Malloy (ed.), *Authoritarianism and Corporatism in Latin America* (Pittsburgh: Pittsburgh University Press, 1977), pp. 41–87.

83. Ibid., p. 55.

84. J. Nef, "Stalemate and Repression in the Southern Cone," pp. 371–86.

85. Jose Nun, "A Latin American Phenomenon," pp. 145–85.

86. O'Donnell, "Corporatism," p. 54.

87. See Frederick Riggs, *Administrative Reform and Political Responses* (Beverly Hills, Calif.: Sage Publications, 1970), pp. 567–606.

88. See Alvin Gouldner, *Patterns of Industrial Bureaucracy* (Glencoe, Ill.: Free Press, 1954), pp. 216–18.

15

CONCLUSION

V. Subramaniam

We have surveyed in some detail the structures and processes of public administration in a representative sample of Third World countries. Our survey reveals several important common features in administration, in spite of differences in size, population, geographical location, race, or religion. We will attempt to explain such common features by relating them to each other or to common sociohistorical causes. In doing so, we will focus primarily on the empirical evidence presented, exploring and working inductively toward a tentative theory and bypassing comprehensive macro-theoretical presuppositions.[1]

Briefly, there are five common features in the public administration systems of Third World countries. (1) The government's coordinating power is concentrated at the district level (with a manageable area and population) and is in the hands of a single regional overlord variously called the collector, commissioner, or prefect, while elected local bodies are weak or subordinate. (2) In the case of postcolonial states, the colonial administrative structures continue with minor changes, and in general, there is considerable centralization of administrative power. (3) The dominant position of state-owned enterprises is probably the most common visible feature in all the countries surveyed, and in Africa in particular, state intervention is visible in all social action. (4) The higher bureaucracy in these countries is drawn from a small urban professional middle class and is clearly unrepresentative of the population. (5) The civil service is also politicized in the Third World, but the degree of politicization varies from country to country.

THE DISTRICT OVERLORD

In all early bureaucratic kingdoms and empires, administration was firmly based on the division of the country into smaller territorial units and was headed by a royal representative or governor with full delegated royal powers. We have already noted how Third World countries such as India, Iran, Egypt, and Turkey had developed this type of administrative system on their own many centuries before modern bureaucracy took shape in Europe in France and Prussia.[2] India and Iran in particular developed a tentacular imperial bureaucracy with rules, regulations, records, and clear allotment of duties, based on division of labor. The principles of public administration were recorded in several manuals, the most advanced and widely known of these being the Indian classic, *Kautilya's Arthasastra*.[3] In spite of discontinuities, this important element of the traditional administrative system survived, namely the division of the kingdom into manageable territorial units called Nadu, Kottam, or Zila in India, Shahrestan and Baksha in Iran, or Vilayat in Turkey. Each unit was governed by an all-purpose administrative overlord appointed by, and responsible to, the king or emperor. This system satisfied the sociopsychological needs of those times for the subject to present their various grievances to a single authority who was an alter-ego of the monarch. In those periods of slow communication, it also fulfilled the organizational needs of the king to have a single person answerable to him in each territorial unit.[4] This "synthetic" administrative system or protobureaucracy survived for centuries, for after each disruption by invasion or civil war it could be resurrected without much difficulty.

The adaptation and entrenchment of this system in several Third World countries was due mainly to British and French colonialism. The East India Company, after wresting the Diwani of Bengal (right of revenue collection) from the Mughal emperor, Shah Alam, in 1765, and after a brief and inglorious predatory period, resuscitated the decaying Mughal institution of district revenue officer into an all-purpose administrator under the title of district collector. He was later entrusted with coordinating public works and education, and even supervising the work of elected local bodies. Every British viceroy and every royal commission sang the praises of this institution as the ultimate glory of British rule in India.[5]

By 1855 the British administrators in India modernized this protobureaucratic, age-old Indian institution by creating the unique Indian Civil Service to man the district. Members of the civil service were recruited by competitive examination given to honors graduates from Oxford and Cambridge universities. Thus, a protobureaucratic institution of patrimonial origins was anchored firmly to modern education and then entrenched as a powerful instrument of imperial-colonial administration.[6] As a next step, the British "exported" this tried and tested Indo-British institution to all other parts of their empire under slightly different names—to Sri Lanka as "agent," to Malaya as "collector-magistrate" and to Africa as "commissioner" or "resident."

The French had created a similar institution—the all-purpose administrator of the *departement* (equivalent to the district)—during the period of absolute monarchy under Louis XIV. The purpose was to forge national unification and to liquidate the vestiges of feudalism, much as the Indian or Iranian emperors used their district overlords but with more modern means.[7] Here again, the protobureaucratic institution was modernized and entrenched by Napoleon Bonaparte as the prefect of the department. When France became a colonial power in Africa and Indochina in the nineteenth century, this institution was replicated under a different name, that is, *commandant de cercle* in accordance with the French colonial policy of assimilation which dictated treating colonies exactly as part of France as *La France d'Outre-mer* for administrative purposes.[8]

In summary, the all-purpose administrative overlord in territorial administration, which is a special administrative feature of postcolonial countries of the Third World, requires no complicated theoretical explanation. The British, who did not have any such institution at home, discovered it in India as a continuing instrument of monarchical rule, adapted and modernized it and spread it throughout their possessions in Africa and Asia. The French, who had shaped it at home under absolute monarchy and partly modernized it under Napoleon, simply replicated it in their colonies as an obligation under their policy of assimilation. In noncolonial Third World countries like Iran and Turkey, it was a natural protobureaucratic development that continued into the modern period with modifications.

The continuation of the institution in postcolonial public administration is based on the faith that it can serve as a most efficient instrument of regional and rural economic development with or without the collaboration of elected local representatives. Indeed, as we have noted in the earlier chapters, all postcolonial regimes in South Asia or Africa have tried in several ways to marry centralized direction through the district overlord with some local representative institution like a *zila parishad* in India or district development committees in Africa.

THE REPLICATION OF METROPOLITAN INSTITUTIONS

Along with the persistence of the colonial structures of field administration, the second most common feature of public administration in postcolonial countries has been the replication of the metropolitan institutions and processes. The central administration of postcolonial Third World countries is, in general, copied from the former metropole—from London's Whitehall in the case of former British colonies or Quai d'Orsay of Paris in the case of former French colonies—by the local nationalist politicians who took over from the colonial rulers. The replication of the metropole's pattern of central administration, along with the general persistence of the colonial pattern of district administration, is often the subject of much self-accusation. Advocates of *development* administration complain that it is nonfunctional; Western critics, both liberal and left wing (e.g., Rene Dumont, or Frantz Fanon) scorn it, and some Afro-Asian statesmen blame it on themselves.[9] But it persists with only minor modifications.

The most obvious reason for its persistence is the smooth transfer of power from the colonial rulers to the local nationalist leaders in all the colonies. The nationalist movement in the British colonies was based on agitation and propaganda and was generally nonviolent, taking over from the British with a peaceful celebration. In India, although the partition of the country that accompanied independence was violent and traumatic, the administrative transfer itself was smooth to the point of anticlimax, as all the administrative cadres (except for a few positions at the top) were already Indianized. India's independence was followed by a smooth transfer of power to African nationalist leaders in the African colonies. These colonies retained as well as recruited administrators and professionals from Britain and other Commonwealth countries, thus re-creating the British pattern of central administration. In short, there was no immediate provocation for administrative change, and there was every favorable condition for administrative continuity.

The transfer of power in the French colonies (except Indochina) ensured even greater continuity. The French colonial policy of assimilation had encouraged educated Africans to merge into the French culture, society, and administration, so that there was no strong nationalist movement.[10] During the Second World War, African nationalists and soldiers helped De Gaulle, and thereafter the French African elites were fully involved in the French political process in Paris as members of Parliament and even as ministers in the cabinet. Ultimately, when the French union was dissolved and the African colonies became independent in 1960, their socioeconomic, cultural, and political Gallicization was far too deep for them to give up French institutions and French professional assistance. Moreover, France had already replicated its administrative structures and practices in Africa during the colonial rule, and these were automatically carried on by the Francophone African elite.

The smooth transfer of power was the obvious reason, but the more basic reason for the smooth transfer itself was the nature of the nationalist elites who engineered the transfer and the continuity. They were all drawn from a new educated middle class, generated by the colonial confrontation. We will discuss this class a little later for a deeper understanding of Third World public administration.

In the earlier chapters we have noted the general tendency to establish strong centralized administrations, weakening elected local bodies if necessary or using them instrumentally. The first reason for this trend is sociohistorical. Colonial rule was centralized and authoritarian, and the nationalists who struggled against it built up fairly centralized parties and continued this pattern into the postindependence period.[11] Second, the nationalist leaders, faced with divisive tribal, caste, religious, and linguistic loyalties after independence, resorted to administrative centralization as one way of controlling them. Third, their commitment to quick economic development also led them to centralize economic planning and public enterprises as suitable instruments.

PUBLIC ENTERPRISE AND THE INTERVENTIONIST POSTCOLONIAL STATE

All the authors in this book have discussed the large part played by state-owned public enterprises in their respective countries and their economic and administrative problems. The reasons for this process may be apparently different, but the results are quite similar. Thus, in 1971 Bangladesh nationalized all enterprises owned by Pakistanis after it became free; Turkey, left economically weak by the profligate Ottomans, unable to secure aid from Europe, and deserted by entrepreneurial ethnic minorities, started several public enterprises in the 1920s to fill an economic vacuum; India deliberately launched its public enterprises for planned economic growth as an established policy of the ruling Congress party; and most African governments launched state-run enterprises as the only way to achieve economic development, as they had no large supply of private capital.[12] Indeed, public enterprises are entrenched and justified in African states with opposing ideologies—as Kenya and Tanzania are, for opposite reasons. Criticisms about their poor performance have become louder in almost all Third World countries, but very few have launched an active process of privatization in spite of loud threats about it.[13]

Public enterprises are not unique to the Third World, nor are frequent criticisms peculiar to the Third World.[14] In fact, state-run enterprises occupy a substantial portion of the economies of almost all First World democracies except that of the United States. This proliferation of public enterprises in First World countries came about for reasons not too different from those that apply to the Third World. It is often more meaningful to classify public enterprise systems of different countries on the basis of the original reasons for their establishment and the nature of the national economy. In new colonies of settlement like Canada, Australia, and New Zealand, the state had to provide the rail and road transport infrastructure, as well as other facilities for human settlement, primary industry, and commerce, through direct public enterprise as in Australia or through subsidization of, and collaboration with, private enterprise as in Canada.[15] Second, a country like Germany after unification in 1870 was anxious to catch up with industrialized Britain by sponsoring public enterprise or subsidizing private enterprise. Third, ideology drives some states to take over sectors of private industry; the British Labour government and the Labour governments in Australia and New Zealand nationalized several private industries for socialist reasons, and the French government took over factories owned by Nazi collaborators for socialist as well as patriotic reasons.

In the case of most Third World countries, all the above reasons seem to converge. Underdeveloped and eager to develop like Anglo-Saxon colonies in the last century, they use public enterprise to lay the infrastructure of industry and economy. Anxious to catch up with the more advanced states, as nineteenth-century Germany was, they depend on public enterprise to narrow the gap, and socialist and nationalist ideology again meet and merge to nationalize local resource industries owned by foreign capitalists. In the case of India, the provision of infrastructure and the need to catch up with industrialized nations dominate public enterprise. Iran's or Nigeria's nationalization of oil, or Zambia's nationalization of copper mining, combine patriotic and economic reasons. In most cases, it is impossible to distinguish clearly the various motivations and justifications that combine to establish public enterprises. What is clear is that they are not very different from the impelling reasons in the case of First World countries in different periods of their history.

The convergence of all such reasons in a short period after independence has produced a larger and more visible public sector and an impression of its dominance. At the same time, many Third World countries, particularly in Africa, lack a good supply of the necessary instruments for success, namely, capital, skilled personnel, and knowhow, which places them at the mercy of foreign sources.[16] This predicament is the result of sociohistorical causes. Most First World countries, through their industrialization in the nineteenth century, had already generated private capital, technical know-how, and management capacity. The public sector developed in a second wave of development by emigration in the colonies, or by imitation and nationalization in Europe, to supplement the private sector, using the already developed resources of entrepreneurial and technical know-how and management ability.[17] Third World countries under colonial rule could not generate these to the same measure even as they developed an educated middle class, which ultimately took over the reins of government from the colonial rulers. By its historical antecedents, the class was inclined to use the state and the bureaucracy as instruments of development by creating a public sector, but without enough technical, entrepreneurial, capital, and managerial resources. The size and use of the public sector are pretty much the same in the First and Third Worlds, but they differ substantially in regard to the availability of the inputs needed for success.

Added to this hegemonic image of public enterprise is the obvious part played by the state in other spheres such as culture, sports, media, and communications, thus becoming much more visible in Africa in particular. The self-sufficient, internally well-adjusted, tribally organized societies of Africa were first disrupted by slave trade in the eighteenth century and again by the creation of colonies that disregarded natural and tribal territorial divisions in the nineteenth century, and were finally and formally declared independent sovereign states by the 1960s. The nationalist leaders of Africa were committed by their conviction, people's expectations, and the very spirit of the times to integrate each state into a modern nation and to generate rapid socioeconomic development. There was not much private African capital, the old tribal organization had been disrupted, and new *Gesellschaft* organizations—like trade unions and thrift societies—were too young and had weak roots. Not surprisingly, African leaders commandeered the one legitimized instrument they had, the state or, more precisely, the government, for all purposes, social, cultural, economic, or political. To give the state emotional content, the one-party system (Le Parti Unique) was devised as the suitable inspirational medium.[18] The penetration of the one-party state into all sociocultural activity and the management of all law and order and all economic activity by the departments and agencies of the state has created the picture of the omnipresent state and has led to some theorizing about the overdeveloped state. In Asian countries the state is less omnipresent but still very visible. Still, in recent times the theory has been extended to cover all developing countries or the Third World.

This substratum of fact has been exaggerated into a theory by a concatenation of circumstances in academic inquiry. Neo-Marxists, intrigued by the persistence of the capitalist state in the West in good health late into the twentieth century, had started discussing "the relative autonomy of the state" away from class rivalries.[19] This resuscitation of the state in Western neo-Marxist discourse corresponded with the widening use of the state and the party in Africa for all purposes, inviting considerable left-wing interest in theorizing about the state in Africa. Dependencists in Dar-es-Salaam, Tanzania, had not yet taken a definite position on the "relative autonomy" question, but Issa Shivji's categorization of the Tanzanian state bureaucracy as a class in itself and for itself stirred up controversy—first about the class status of bureaucracy and then about the overall role of the state itself.[20] At about the same time, other researchers at the Sussex Institute of Development Studies were looking at the state in Pakistan, Bangladesh, and Southeast Asia. There followed an exchange of views on the state and bureaucracy, giving rise to some theorizing about the "overdeveloped state" in the Third World and the "bureaucratic bourgeoisie."

It is significant, however, that few participants in this debate took note of very similar developments in the First World characterized by Western political scientists as "overload" or "ungovernability." Briefly, the demands on the state, by industry and trade unions, the unemployed and the deprived, producers and consumers, and all sorts of such rival groups, have grown so large that the state cannot cope with them, even with all the policy tools and resources at its command. The situation is euphemistically termed "overload" by some and bluntly called "ungovernability" by others. Different political scientists have proposed contrary solutions.[21] Some tell the state to give up trying to integrate demands and recommend delegating it, whereas others advise the state to impose solutions, and still others discuss the *fait accompli* as an "etatized society."[22] Thus, the intervention of the state in most human collective activity is common to the First and Third Worlds. What is not common is the capacity of the state to meet the demands of this situation. First World states have built up some capacity over a century to meet the gradually increasing demands. Now they confess more honestly the limits of this capacity, whereas several Third World countries have felt obliged to develop and use in a short time the single instrument of the state to integrate all demands in the economy, society, and polity. In this context, the term *overdeveloped state* is misleading. It would be more appropriate to describe the state in Africa as overambitious regarding ends and underdeveloped regarding means.

UNREPRESENTATIVE BUREAUCRACY: CAUSES AND CONSEQUENCES

All the authors in this book have noted the generally superior attitude of the bureaucrats toward the citizenry. Some have discussed briefly how the higher bureaucrats are drawn from a rather small socioeconomically advantaged section of the country's population, with some suggestion that this social background and superior attitude may be interrelated. The available research on Asian and African countries generally confirms the facts about narrow social origins, though they are not as plentiful and detailed as for First World countries.[23]

Among Asian countries, detailed social background studies are available for India, the Philippines, and Turkey and for Egypt included as part of the Middle East. In the case of India, we have noted that until the late 1960s, over 80 percent of the coveted Indian Administrative Service was drawn from the urban middle class, which then constituted about 10 percent of the workforce. They were mostly from six major universities out of over eighty in India, substantially from the Brahmin and the higher non-Brahmin castes, and in terms of regions and states, mostly from the coastal states and languages. We may also note that the regions and languages and the Brahmin caste, which were overrepresented, formed a disproportionate share of the middle class. The universities overrepresented also drew their alumni disproportionately from the middle class.[24] In other words, the middle-class origin itself is reflected in the overrepresentation of certain castes, regions, and universities. But the 1970s and 1980s witnessed some broadening of the socioeconomic as well as the caste and regional base of recruitment, partly through the reserved quotas allocated to the Scheduled Castes and Scheduled Tribes (who are also socioeconomically handicapped) and partly through the greater attraction of professional and managerial careers in private enterprise for the young men and women from the higher socioeconomic strata. The less coveted central services have generally drawn their recruits from a broader social base. At the same time, the degree of overrepresentation of the urban middle class has decreased essentially because the class itself has grown proportionately larger, accounting for about a fifth of India's population.[25]

The picture is broadly the same one of urban middle-class dominance for the Philippines, Turkey, and Egypt. Studies of the Philippine administrators' social background highlight the large share of those drawn from middle-class homes in the civil service; C. H. Dodd's study of Turkish civil servants presents a similar picture.[26] Morroe Berger's study of the Egyptian bureaucracy in the 1950s pointed to the advantaged social background of higher bureaucrats, and E. H. Valsan also refers to such a popular impression.[27] The civil service in Egypt absorbs a good number of university graduates whose education was probably funded by their middle-class families. Detailed as well as impressionistic studies generally confirm a degree of middle-class dominance of the civil services in all these countries.

Few direct social background studies of higher bureaucrats have been done in Africa, but there are more such studies of school and university students, providing some indication of the social origins of higher bureaucrats. Studies in the late 1960s indicate that about 34 percent of Zambian bureaucrats were drawn from white-collar and urban commercial lower middle-class homes; 42 percent had similar origins in Tanzania and 56 percent in Senegal.[28] The lower middle-class representation in Zambia indicates a newly independent country which had little opportunity to develop a middle class during colonial days. Consequently, the urban middle class itself is too small, and the expanding bureaucracy has opened up opportunities for offspring from a wider social base. Ghana and Senegal had a much longer time to develop, as a result of which an entrenched middle class has come to dominate the civil services.

More research material is available on the social origins of secondary school students, showing the dominance of urban middle-class offspring in the secondary school population: 52 percent in Senegal, 50.6 percent in Ghana, 45 percent in Southern Nigeria, and 43 percent in Zambia's final year university students. Since the civil service recruits are drawn from this population, we can presume that this middle-class dominance will carry over at the level of the higher bureaucracy. Indeed, Philip Foster, after an exhaustive survey of all the research material on access to education in Africa, concludes that (1) class and family exercise an enormous influence on educational success by proxy through upbringing; (2) these advantages are likely to be retained and entrenched inasmuch as the cost of broadening educational opportunity any further is beyond the means of any African government, and (3) education is the passport to the civil services and the professions and thus to upward mobility.[29]

The dominance of the higher civil services by recruits drawn from the middle class is not peculiar to Third World countries. It is almost a universal phenomenon, and it is statistically better documented for First World democracies.[30] This dominance flows from the same causes, namely, the substantial educational and motivational advantages conferred by middle-class upbringing on their children very early in life. These advantages are actually augmented as they go through the standardized schooling and university educational systems all over the world. In other words, the middle-class's dominance of the bureaucracy and its causes are the same in the First and Third Worlds. Its consequences are more disruptive in the Third World, however.

The common causes are now fairly well established. Research literature in Western countries on the educational and motivational advantages of the middle-class family shows that in spite of marginal differences, middle-class children cultivate a high degree of verbal ability and a capacity for deferred gratification and rational manipulation of the environment.[31] They thereby have a great advantage at school over working-class children. The nature of the schooling system itself increases these advantages at various stages of selection, so that there is already a substantial overrepresentation of the middle class at the secondary school-leaving level. This effect is accentuated at the university graduation level. As recruitment to the higher civil services and the professions is based on a university degree in almost all countries, this cumulative middle-class overrepresentation is reflected in the composition of the higher civil service and professions, with minor variations from one Western country to another. The same cumulative advantage based on education and upbringing is still being maintained in several Eastern Bloc countries such as Hungary or Czechoslovakia.[32] Even though there are far fewer and less detailed studies of social stratification, educational sociology, and elite social backgrounds in Afro-Asian countries, enough is known to indicate that the same process of cumulative advantage works in favor of an emerging or expanding middle class, regardless of the efforts of some statesmen to control it.[33]

We have noted that the secondary school population overrepresents the middle class in Africa and that this overrepresentation is further accentuated at the university stage. This situation automatically carries over to the higher civil service in established educational and employment systems, with an equilibrium between the civil service and education as in Ghana or India. In countries like Zambia which may experience a sudden expansion of the civil service, a period of apparent equal opportunity takes place for the lower rungs of society, but this opening is closed up as soon as social and educational stratification builds up. In summary, middle-class overrepresentation in higher civil service occurs pretty much to the same extent in First and Third World countries for the same reasons, but unfortunately it does greater damage in the Third World in at least three different ways.

In the first place, a wider gulf emerges between the administrators and the masses of the people, which the authors in this book describe as the characteristic insensitivity and bossiness of the bureaucrats vis-à-vis the citizen. It is actually a distorted symbol of the mutual misunderstanding between the dominant middle class and the masses in the specific context of class evolution in colonial and postcolonial societies.

The modern class structure evolved in Western Europe along with the growth of commerce, industry, and the professions in the eighteenth and nineteenth centuries. The modern civil service was also drawn mainly from the middle class and was quite accustomed to dominating the masses, as described by Karl Marx, Alexis de Tocqueville, and novelists such as Nikolai Gogol.[34] Even recently, left-wing proponents of representative bureaucracy have been critical of the insensitivities of the higher bureaucracy in Britain, France, and Germany.[35] But in general, the gap in mutual understanding has narrowed greatly over a century and a half, for several reasons. The middle and working classes form part of the same *Gesellschaft* society in their negotiating stances. Keynesian economics and the welfare state have diluted earlier antagonisms, and democratic administrative safeguards have toned down others.

In the colonial period of the Third World, a local middle class took shape and fulfilled mediatory functions. It partook of the characteristics of Western *Gesellschaft* and Afro-Asian *Gemeinschaft*, and the local civil servants were drawn mostly from this class. As time passed, this class and the civil servants drawn from it became more *Gesellschaft* and more alienated from the rural masses. But after independence the ruling politicians wanted to retain the structure of district administration (which colonial rulers had devised for limited purposes for a *Gemeinschaft* society) for its rapid economic development through a civil service recruited mainly from the urban middle classes. This incongruity makes relations at the interface between the administrator and the rural masses difficult, if not hostile.

A second reason why middle-class overrepresentation is damaging to the Third World is that in most Afro-Asian countries this overrepresentation is seen not in class terms as in Europe and America, but in terms of *Gemeinschaft* groups such as tribe, caste, or religion, leading to political demands for compensatory action. Thus, in Nigeria, the coastal Christian Ibo and Yoruba tribes and in India, the coastal resident groups of Bengal, Bombay, and Madras and Brahmin and upper caste non-Brahmins, are overrepresented in the civil services and professions, mainly because these tribes, areas, and castes came into contact with British naval colonialism or Christian missionary activity at an early date.[36] They rapidly transformed themselves into an educated middle class and retained the advantages of the middle-class family much as in the West. But with the coming of independence, adult franchise, and mass democracy, the other underrepresented tribes, castes, and regions interpreted this situation as the unfair dominance by the others and demanded compensatory represenation, regardless of examination requirements.

The process started in India almost simultaneously with the rise of the nationalist movement in the 1880s, with Muslim organizations demanding guaranteed proportionate representation in the civil services well before they demanded separate electorates and a separate state.[37] In South India again the organized non-Brahmin movement fought for it and entrenched the Communal Government Order in 1926 guaranteeing proportionate representation for non-Brahmin groups.[38] It became a bigger issue after independence than before. The Constitution of India provided for reserved quotas in civil service recruitment for only Scheduled Castes (known earlier as untouchables and later called Harijans by Mahatma Gandhi) and Scheduled Tribes in order to make up for their deprivations, isolation, and backwardness over the centuries. These were fixed and confirmed by legislation as 12½ percent and 5 percent, respectively, of the vacancies to be filled in the Indian Administrative Service (IAS) and other services.[39] In the 1950s and 1960s, there were not enough qualified candidates to fill the reserved quota, even as the central government was beginning to provide special educational facilities to coach the candidates for the competition. But by the 1970s the quotas began to fill up rapidly, partly owing to the continuous pressure of the commissioner for Scheduled Castes and Scheduled Tribes who urged positive action on the government and Parliament of India.

Simultaneously with this development, the Scheduled Castes and other "backward" castes began to mobilize politically and to demand more reservations in state civil services and in educational institutions, particularly medical colleges, from the mid–1970s onward. This demand was met with stiff resistance from the upper castes in several States of India. The politics of the State of Gujarat in particular has been dominated by violent clashes between the proponents and opponents of this reservation. At an all-India level too, special reservation for "backward" castes and classes became a major political issue before the high-powered Sarkaria Commission.[40]

The demands in Nigeria for proportionate representation of the different tribes in the federal civil service have a similar origin in colonial history, with the Southern Christian Yorubas and Ibos gaining a head start in Western education over the Northern Muslim Hausa and Fulani, and thereby dominating the civil services. Again the demands for more representation from the more populous and politically strong north were accommodated in the constitutional provision that the civil service should represent the federal character of Nigeria. Actual accommodation was negotiated informally during the civilian regime without legislation. Counterparts to these demands in the West are the demands from racial and cultural minorities and women. Remedies are sought through varieties of "affirmative action," but they do not affect the body politic to the same extent as they do in the Third World.

POLITICIZED CIVIL SERVICES

The third consequence of the middle-class dominance of bureaucracy in the Third World is the increasing politicization of administration, particularly in Africa and to a lesser extent in Asia. The phenomenon has been documented and analyzed in some detail by several scholars, including this writer.[41] Briefly, most English-speaking African states adopted the British doctrine of the political neutrality of the civil service at the time of their independence but gave it up quickly in two or three stages, along with the establishment of the one-party state. The district administrator became a political party official advised by civil servants; the top administrators or permanent secretaries of departments were coopted as members of the ruling party's central committee; and the administrative and party hierarchies were intertwined at various levels into competition and cooperation. In Francophone Africa, politicization was more open. From the Third Republic onward, France did not profess the same degree of civil service neutrality as Britain; its colonial administration, which included quite a number of Africans, had no such tradition either, and the Gaullist Republic of the 1960s provided a model of legitimized civil service involvement in policy and politics. Thus, Francophone Africa politicized administration as a matter of course.

By comparison with Africa, there is less overt politicization of administration in India but more in Bangladesh and Pakistan. The Congress Party willingly accepted the British ideal of civil service neutrality at the time of independence under the plebiscital leadership of Jawaharlal Nehru and Vallabbhai Patel.[42] Under Indira Gandhi, there was more talk of a " committed civil service" from 1966 to 1977 mainly for the top echelons, but Janata party rule from 1977 to 1979 reversed it under Morarji Desai as prime minister. Later, Indira Gandhi (1980–1984) and Rajiv Gandhi kept to the overall principle of neutrality. Actual political interference in the civil service is more at the level of state administration. In general, however, it is mostly in the shape of informal pressure and inducements and is kept within bounds by a general acknowledgment of the doctrine of neutrality.

Several reasons may be cited for the difference in the degree and content of politicization of administration in Third World countries. At one extreme in military regimes, the embargo on political activity imposes some political obligations on the bureaucracy that cooperates with the army chiefs. At a minimum, the one-party state demands civil service loyalty to the party's ideology, if not active support. But over and above such specific reasons the general determinant factor of the degree of politicization is the size and maturity of the middle class. In the case of India, the educated middle class took shape from the literary nonfeudal castes by the 1840s and grew rapidly, gradually filling up the civil services and professions and leading the nationalist movement. Under Gandhiji's leadership beginning in the 1920s, it widened mass political consciousness and participation substantially. Well before freedom at midnight on 14 August 1947, it had filled up the civil services and all the professions with a substantial reservoir for further recruitment and expansion.

By contrast, the educated middle class in Africa took shape late and grew very slowly, mainly as a result of British and French colonial policy.[43] The late-born nationalist movement did not create such wide and deep mass consciousness as in India, and the class was too small to fill all the expanding administrative needs at the time of independence. As a result, the civil service was commandeered along with the ruling party into the basic political activity of mobilization for development. The very small size of the educated middle class also encouraged and legitimized the frequent migration of talent from politics to administration and vice versa. But in India, there was no pressing need for civil service initiative in mobilization, already achieved under Gandhian leadership. The large size of the middle class and its professional ethic of guarding professional independence, along with its numerical clout, seemed to work in favor of civil service neutrality to some extent.

This discussion of some common features of Third World public administration is not meant to downplay the common features of public administration in all the three worlds or to ignore the specific features of each Third World country or of regional clusters in the Third World. Thus, Latin American countries have their pattern of collusion between the military and the bureaucracy, which is partly replicated in the military regimes of Nigeria or Pakistan. The successor states of the Indian subcontinent, India, Pakistan, and Bangladesh, have preserved the same elitist civil service system, and the Muslim states of the Middle East have come to terms with Islamic practices and institutions. But over and above all such ideological or regional resemblances or differences, we have identified and discussed five common features of Third World public administration. These features are largely based on an educated middle class, its colonial or paracolonial origins, its size, maturity, and its relation to the wider traditional

Gemeinschaft society. We need a deeper sociohistorical understanding of this class to explore the problems and possibilities of Third World societies.

NOTES

1. My general search for specific sociohistorical factors that explain the features of administration in both the First and Third World is illustrated in detail in V. Subramaniam, *Transplanted Indo-British Administration* (New Delhi: Ashish Publishing House, 1977).

2. See the earlier chapters on India and Iran. See also V. Subramaniam, "Status and Function of Intellectuals in State and Society in India and China: Some Critical Comparisons," *International Sociology* 2, 3 (September 1987).

3. R. Shama Sastry, *Kautilya's Arthasastra* (Mysore: Mysore Printing Publishing House, 1967), 7th ed.

4. For a further elaboration of this explanation of the historical origins of the district overlord, see V. Subramaniam, "The Indo-British Legacy in Administration: Its Dialectic and Dilemmas," *Indian Journal of Public Administration* 14, 2.

5. E.g., Ramsay Macdonald, *The Government of India* (London, 1920), pp. 95–98. See also *Report of the Indian Statutory Commission* (Simon Commission), Cnd. 3569, Vol. 1, para 307 and paras 315–22.

6. For details about modernizing the recruitment of the district administrator, see Subramaniam, "The Indo-British Legacy in Administration," and V. Subramaniam, "Graduates in the Public Services: A Comparative Study of Attitudes," *Public Administration* (Winter 1957).

7. For the history of the administrative evolution of France, see Herman Finer, *Theory and Practice of Government* 2, Chapter 29 (London: Methuen, 1946), 2d ed.; Brian Chapman, *The Prefects of Provincial France* (London: Allen and Unwin, 1955); Ernest Barker, *The Development of Public Services in Europe* (Hamden, Conn.: Archon Books, 1966); John Armstrong, *The European Administrative Elite* (Princeton, N.J.: Princeton University Press, 1973); and Martin Albrow, *Bureaucracy* (London: Pall Mall Press, 1970). But I am solely responsible for the sociohistorical reinterpretation of their material.

8. There are several classical works on French colonial policy. The following two address it more directly from opposite viewpoints. Hubert Deschamps, *Methodes et Doctrines Coloniales de la France* (Paris: Armand Colin, 1953) is a sympathetic account by a pro-consul; Jean-Suret Canale, *L'Afrique Noire: L'ere Coloniale 1900–1945* (Paris: Editions Sociales, 1964) is a critical account by a left-wing academic.

9. For criticisms of the colonial legacy of law and order administration from the viewpoint of the Development Administration School, see George F. Gant, *Development Administration: Concepts, Goals, Methods* (Madison: University of Wisconsin Press, 1979), Chapter 1, pp. 18–22. These criticisms are mostly implied. For left-wing criticisms, see Rene Dumont, *False Start in Africa*, Sphere paperbacks (1967) and Frantz Fanon, *The Wretched of the Earth* (London: McGibbon and Kee, 1965).

10. For a detailed account of the way power was transferred to African leaders in French colonial Africa, see Edward Mortimer, *France and the Africans 1944–1960: A Political History* (London: Faber and Faber, 1969).

11. This argument about how centralized colonial rule generated centralized nationalist movements to confront it is developed in more detail in V. Subramaniam, "Some Administrative aspects of Federalism in the Third World," *International Review of Admin-*

istrative Sciences 50, 2. See also V. Subramaniam, "Developing Countries," in Donald C. Rowat (ed.), *International Handbook on Local Government Reorganization* (Westport, Conn.: Greenwood Press, 1980).

12. For a detailed account of the ideology and practical reasons for public enterprises in India, see Baldev Nayar, "State Entrepreneurship in the Nehru Era: Ideology Versus Necessity," in *Issues in Public Sector Analysis* (Calgary: Shastri Indo-Canadian Institute, 1986). Re public enterprises in Africa, see Robert J. Berg and Jennifer Seymour Whitaker (eds.), *Strategies for African Development* (Berkeley: University of California Press, 1986), Chapters 3 and 16.

13. See chapter on Turkey by Metin Heper. Several other countries have discussed privatization (e.g., Zimbabwe, Nigeria, and Ghana) but have not pursued it seriously.

14. Canada is a prime example of a First World country in which criticism of the public sector has dominated all discussion of public administration from 1976 onward. For a brief summary with references, see Robert F. Adie and Paul G. Thomas, *Canadian Public Administration: Problematical Perspectives* (Scarborough: Prentice-Hall, Canada, 1987), Chapter 10.

15. There is considerable detailed material on the crucial role of government investment in various economic histories of Australia. Dr. Butlin's (Australian National University) estimates put it at over 50 percent of the total capital investment at some stage. See N. G. Butlin, *Investment in Australian Economic Development* (London: Cambridge University Press, 1964), Part C., "The Public Sector," in particular.

16. This is particularly so in the case of countries like Zambia in the 1970s, when there was practically no large-scale private business or industry except retailing. All the state enterprises called parastatals were grouped under three major holding corporations: Mindeco for all copper mining companies; Findeco for all financial institutions; and Indeco for all industrial enterprises.

17. The development of the public sector in the First World came soon after the evolution of capitalism to a stage where management and technology were clearly differentiated from capital. Hence, governments in Australia and Canada could use the first two separately from capital and control them all. Countries in Africa lacking all three were "hostages to fortune" in developing public enterprises too fast.

18. The supremacy of the party is usually acknowledged as a doctrine in all one-party states in Africa. In Francophone Africa, "the Party" is venerated with a capital P and glorified with slogans such as "Le Parti avant tout." The late Sekou Toure of Guinea went furthest in his sacralization of the party when he told an audience that it was their father and mother.

19. Ralph Miliband's *The State in Capitalist Society* (London: Weidenfeld and Nicolson, 1969) and Nicos Poulantzaas, *Les classes sociales dans le capitalisme Aujourd'hui* (Paris: Editions de seuil, 1974) and his *L'Eglise et l'état* were among the seminal works that started neo-Marxist discussions of the state. All of them derived inspiration from Marx's *The 18th Brumaire of Louis Napoleon* (New York: International Publishers, 1963), which discusses the possibility that the state will dominate in a fluid situation when the bourgeoisie is not strong enough and the proletariat too weak.

The implications of this debate for other areas of neo-Marxist thinking are explored in V. Subramaniam, "Western Marxist Approaches to Management and Organization Theory," *Indian Journal of Public Administration* 28, 4 (October, December 1982).

20. Issa Shivji, *The Silent Class Struggle* (Dar-es-Salaam: Tanzania Publishing House, 1973).

21. A good number of representative articles discussing "overload" and "ungovernability" are found in the *Journal of Comparative Politics* in 1976–1977. For a presentation of several viewpoints, see Richard Rose (ed.), *Challenge to Governance: Studies in Overload Politics* (London, 1985). See also Ghita Ionescu (ed.), *Between Sovereignty and Integration* (London: Croom Helm, 1974).

22. Theodore Lowi has advocated the imposition of solutions by the state itself in his *The End of Liberalism* (New York: W.W. Norton, 1979), 2d ed., whereas Ghita Ionescu recommends the opposite solution of involving syndicates and pressure groups in policy making. Symon Chodak's *Etatized Society* (Berkeley: University of California Press, 1988), discusses the whole phenomenon of increasing state involvement as a widespread one.

23. Re the overrepresentation of the urban middle class in the civil services in general, see V. Subramaniam, "Representative Bureaucracy: A Reassessment," *American Political Science Review* 59, 4 (December 1967) and Peta Sheriff, "Unrepresentative Bureaucracy," *Sociology* 8, 3.

24. V. Subramaniam, *Social Background of India's Administrators* (New Delhi: Publication Division, 1971). See Chapter 8, "A Middle Class Monopoly: So What" for the general argument.

25. The size of the fast growing Indian middle class has been recently estimated as about 150 million, about 20 percent of India's 750 million total.

26. C. H. Dodd, "The Social and Educational Background of Turkish Officials," *Middle Eastern Studies* (London), 1.

27. Morroe Berger, *Bureaucracy and Society in Modern Egypt* (Princeton, N.J.: Princeton University Press, 1957), p. 45, for father's occupations; 38.8 percent are sons of civil servants, and an overwhelming 60.4 percent belong to the urban middle class. See also Chapter 7 "Egypt" by E. H. Valsan in this volume.

28. The figures for Zambia are drawn from uncompleted work at the University of Zambia, 1968–1974; for Tanzania, see Raymond Hopkins, "Political Roles in a New State" (Ph.D. diss., Yale University, New Haven 1968). For Senegal, see Fatou Sow, "Fonctionnariat et mobilite sociale dans les Administrations Centrales Senegalaises," *Annuaire International de la Fonction Publique* (Paris, 1970–1971).

29. The sources of the figures are as follows: for Senegal—Veronique Campion-Vincent, "Systeme d'enseignment et mobilite sociale au Senegal," *Revue Francaise de Sociologie* 11, 2; for Ghana—Philip E. Foster, *Education and Social Change in Ghana*, (London: Routledge and Kegan Paul, 1966), p. 241; for southern Nigeria—David B. Abernethy, *The Political Dilemma of Popular Education* (Stanford Calif.: University Press, 1969), p. 245; for Zambia—Dr. Philip Kingsley's unpublished research paper, Lusaka, University of Zambia, 1972. For Professor Foster's general survey, see Philip E. Foster, "Education and Social Inequality in Sub-Saharan Africa," *Journal of Modern African Studies* 18, 2 (Cambridge).

30. The following classical social background studies of the civil service in First World countries may be cited as examples: for Britain:—R. K. Kelsall, *Higher Civil Servants in Britain* (London: Routledge and Kegan Paul, 1955): for France—Alain Darbel and Dominique Schnapper, *Les Agents du Systeme Administratif* (Paris: Mouton and Co. and Ecole Pratique des Hautes Etudes, 1969); for the United States—W. L. Warner et al., *The American Federal Executive* (New Haven, Conn.: Yale University Press, 1963); for Sweden—Landstrom Sten-sture, *Svenska Ambetsmans Sociala Ursprung* (Uppsala:

Almquist och Wiksells Boktryckeri AB, 1954): for Holland—A. Van Praam, *Ambetnaren en Bureaucratie in Nederland* (The Hague: W. De Haan, N.V., 1957).

There are several unpublished and ongoing studies in several other countries. I have collected comparative social background material for thirty countries, three of which—India, Australia, and Zambia—I researched myself.

31. Published research material on middle-class overrepresentation in schools and universities in the First World is enormous. The UNESCO volumes on Access to Higher Education and the OECD studies on education in various member countries give detailed evidence of this wealth of sources. A bibliography of published research on the facts of middle-class overrepresentation will occupy a volume by itself. The reasons for over-representation have also been researched all over the First World. It is impossible, however, to list the primary or even the secondary sources concerned with social class, family, and education. Philip E. Vernon's *Intelligence and Cultural Environment* (London: Methuen, 1969), Part II, "Factors Influencing the Mental Development of Children," provides a good summary of the more important research, for example, Bernstein on middle-class verbal ability, J. W. L. Douglas on the home and the school, Stephen Wiseman on education and the environment, Frazer on secondary school boys in Aberdeen, and several American studies. Another good secondary source is Maurice Craft, *Family, Class and Education: A Reader* (London: Longmans, 1970).

The relative ineffectiveness of the expansion of educational facilities through the 1944 Education Act (and subsequent reforms) in the United Kingdom in increasing working-class representation in the universities and even higher secondary education has been the subject of comment in the Robbins Report and the 1966 White Paper on education, nicknamed the Black Paper. For a concise summary of the factors inhibiting the use of educational facilities by the working classes, see John Westergaard and Alan Little, "Educational Opportunity and Social Selection in England and Wales: Trends and Policy Implications," in Maurice Craft, *Family, Class and Education*.

Again, a thorough cohort study of the 17,000 babies born in the week of 3–9 March 1958 in Britain by Ronald Davies, Neville Butler, and Harvey Goldstein in *From Birth to Seven* (London: Longmans, 1967) makes clear the increasing disadvantages of the non-middle-class child as the years pass by.

32. A considerable amount of research on the continuing advantages of the middle-class home and the disadvantages of the well-off working class in regard to home education has come out in the last two decades from Hungary, Czechoslovakia, and Poland. These studies were regularly summarized in the 1960s in *Revue Francaise de Sociologie* (Paris). The studies conclude that working-class families, even with increased income, spend it on things other than increasing educational facilities for their children.

33. V. Subramaniam, "Three Converging Factors Promoting Social Stratification in Newly Independent Countries: the Zambian Case," paper presented at the ninth World Congress of Sociology, Uppsala, 1978.

34. Marx's views on the parasitical, oppressive European bureaucracies are expressed directly in his *18th Brumaire of Louis Napoleon*.

Tocqueville, in his classic work on America, contrasts the humble bearing of the American public servant with the self-importance of the French *fonctionnaire*. But Gogol's short story, "The Overcoat," is probably the most powerful caricature of the self-important Russian civil servant of the nineteenth century.

35. For a summary of such criticism of the British civil service, see Kelsall, *Higher*

Civil Servants in Britain. See also Kenneth Robinson, "Selection and the Social Background of the Administrative Class," *Public Administration* 35 (London), p. 388.

36. For a more detailed discussion of the geographical origins of the middle class, see V. Subramaniam, "Coastal Colonialism and Educational Opportunity," paper presented to the meeting of the Research Committee on Social Stratification, International Sociological Association, at the University of Texas at Austin, February 1980.

37. For example, the presidential address of Rahmattullah Sayani to the Indian National Congress in 1896 discussed this Muslim demand most of the time. See A. C. Banerjee, *Indian Constitutional Documents* 2 (Calcutta: A. Mukherjee and Co., 1950), p. 179.

38. Madras Legislative Council Proceedings, Vol. 2, p. 425. For a concise history of communal representation in Madras, see *Sunday Observer* (Madras), Special Annual number 1953.

39. See Subramaniam, *Social Background of India's Administrators*, Chapter 6, "Scheduled Castes and Women."

40. The Sarkaria Commission was virtually flooded with representations from nearly a hundred castes and group organizations claiming backwardness and demanding special treatment. But the released summary of their report gives no recognition to these demands.

41. For a detailed discussion of the politicization of administration, See V. Subramaniam, "Politicized Administration in Africa and Elsewhere," *International Review of Administrative Sciences* 43, 4.

42. V. Subramaniam, "The Evolution of Minister-Civil Servant Relations in India," *Journal of Commonwealth Political Studies* 1, (London).

43. Subramaniam, *Transplanted Indo-British Administration*, Chapter 10.

APPENDIX: THE DERIVATIVE MIDDLE CLASS

V. Subramaniam

We have noted in Chapter 15 the close relation between an educated middle class and public administration in the Third World, particularly in countries formerly under Western colonialism. Taking shape during the colonial period, this class led the nationalist movement and at independence took over the reins smoothly. It has continued to use colonial administrative structures in the field and has borrowed practices of central administration from the metropolitan system. The middle class dominates secondary and university education through the interactional and motivational advantages of the middle-class family and is thereby overrepresented in the civil services. Its essentially nonentrepreneurial, managerial inclinations are at least partly responsible for the large role of public enterprises in Third World economies. To sum up, the characteristics of this class and of Third World public administration are related in a mutually compatible and supportive way, displaying Weberian elective affinity. A deeper exploration of this class is therefore necessary for a better understanding of Third World societies in general and Third World public administration in particular.

Most discussions of this class, guided excessively by ideology or emotion, have produced only limited insights. The dominant Marxist interest in the "nationalist bourgeoisie" of colonial countries was for a long while instrumentalist in encouraging them as partners in the communist confrontation with capitalist colonial powers.[1] After the colonies had won independence, the attitude of various communist parties to the "national bourgeoisie" spanned a wide spectrum of ambivalence and expediency.[2] A fresh start was later made by Rene Dumont in his *False Start in Africa* and Frantz Fanon in his *The Wretched of the Earth*.[3] Credit goes to Dumont for his blunt recognition of the para-Marxist nature of this class in his insightful observation: "A new type of bourgeoisie is forming in Africa which Karl Marx would hardly have foreseen."[4] But Dumont does not ask why, nor does he wait for an answer as he is preoccupied with immediate criticisms. Fanon goes to greater extremes in criticism but no further in analysis.

Thus, Dumont gives several instances of the privileged character and ostentatious living style of the middle class in his *False Start in Africa*. He discusses the disproportion between the enormous salaries of the small numbers of civil servants and politicians and the earnings of the peasant, and the large share of administrative salaries in governmental expenditure.[5] Fanon goes much further, lumping together businesspeople and civil servants, reinforcing the charge of parasitic consumption, and compiling a long list of sins such as corruption, cowardice, regionalism, and utter uselessness.[6] The reason, he explains, is: "The national bourgeoisie of underdeveloped countries is not engaged in production nor invention nor building nor labour; it is completely canalized into activities of the intermediary type. Its innermost vocation seems to be to keep in the running and to be part of the racket."[7] He goes on almost volcanically for several pages—sometimes suggesting planned extinction and sometimes total transformation of the class as a remedy.

Dependencists have long emphasized the economic mediation of this class in the exploitation of Third World countries by international capitalism, calling it "*comprador* bourgeoisie," without enough sociohistorical interest in the colonial origins of the "middle class" in Afro-Asia.[8] This was partly due to their preoccupation with the question of persistent nondevelopment in the Third World. Neo-Marxist neglect of this class is partly attributable to the inhibitions of orthodox Marxist theorizing in delineating the bureaucracy as a class.[9] The belated recognition of the "bureaucratic bourgeoisie" as a "class" by a few was again not accompanied by any search for comparative sociohistorical explanation. It is this missing link we explore. Research on this class has generally been piecemeal from different angles.[10] Here we will make an effort to integrate them conceptually and inductively into a general explanation.

The Western bourgeoisie of Marx was a product of a natural evolution, whereas the colonial bourgeoisie is derivative, that is, derived as a reaction to, and a product of, colonial rule. All its other characteristics emerge from this derivative character. This evolution needs to be interpreted afresh as it is substantially different from the European.[11]

The rise of the capitalist, middle, and working classes in Europe was a natural process in the sense that it did not happen under external compulsion of conquest or occupation. It was the result of internal factors generally understood and partly controlled by local groups in power. The discovery of other lands, the overseas expansion of Europe, the Protestant Reformation, European commercial expansion, and the Industrial Revolution, together with the rise of the entrepreneur, all these ultimately produced the class system which Marx observed and analyzed. A significant feature of this development was the internal equilibrium established from time to time between different actors. We may take note of two major aspects of this equilibrium in relation to the middle class. The professional class existed in embryo even before the rise of capitalism, but with its rise, there was more need for its services—as teachers, lawyers, doctors, and engineers. The greater availability of such professional skills indirectly released more capital and organizing energy, which then created more salaried jobs for professionals in industry and commerce. For example, expanding export trade needed a new corpus of commercial law and insurance law, and the availability of such lawyers encouraged international commerce. In other words, the professional classes helped the economy grow, and a growing economy absorbed more professionals.

Second, apart from large-scale capitalism, plenty of self-employed economic intermediaries emerged from small-scale manufacturers of spare parts and owners of service establishments to distributors, traders, and rentiers who formed an economic wing of this middle class. The professional salaried wing and this economic wing grew together in a complementary way with the economy. They had some common features and some differences too, based on their different attitudes to education and security.[12] These historical features of the development of the Western middle class are discussed briefly here to highlight, in the following paragraphs, the opposite features of the derivative middle class that arose in the countries of Asia and Africa under Western occupation. It arose first in India in the nineteenth century under British rule, and the pattern therein was repeated with local variations in other Asian and African countries.

Historically, it was quite a new phenomenon. Conquest of one country by another had led to several interactions between the conquerors and the conquered in previous centuries. They ranged from utter genocide, intermarriage or religious conversion, or complete noninterference in culture as a reward for political subjection. Some intermediaries were also used such as tributary princes or tribunes or the Herodian type of kings. But after the eighteenth century the conquering West posed a totally different problem. Racial differences and the small number of the militarily superior conquerors ruled out physical absorption as a meaningful reaction. The secularizing West was not interested in religious conversion to the same extent as Islam was. The more important difference between the conqueror and conquered lay in technological areas and even more in social organization. The conquered societies of Asia and Africa were organized on the basis of earlier natural communities (*Gemeinschaft*) such as caste, region, tribe, or village. The conquering West was progressively being organized on the basis of formal associations or *Gesellschaft*. This important difference made conquest easier but contact difficult. Going native or excluding all use of natives proved equally unsatisfactory. Ultimately, a new type of intermediary in the form of a "class" arose in Bengal in India and was already significant in numbers by the 1830s. It grew faster with the introduction of Western education by Macaulay in the 1850s under the general influence of British Utilitarian philosophy.[13]

The new derivative middle class exhibited its own special characteristics fairly early. It was derived from the external compulsion of conquest and the need for minimum conqueror-conquered contacts, unlike the natural middle class of Europe which arose out of internal factors. As a result, only those middle-class groups necessary for this contact came into being, namely, the professional and salaried groups, to carry out mediating functions such as clerical services, legal work, and the like to run an occupied society. The commercial intermediaries became less important after the East India Company gave up its trading activities. In fact, the old-fashioned Indian commercial groups began to evolve in their own way in isolation. This derivative middle class, as it emerged from the 1850s, was essentially a class of professionals such as lawyers and doctors and salary earners such as clerks and teachers without an economic wing of servicing industries or distributors.

The middle class was naturally imitative of some outward manners of the rulers. This came about partly as a result of contact with the rulers as a reference group and partly as a result of the need to impress the mass of subjects with their closeness to the rulers. The entrepreneurs and the manufacturers of the metropole barred the new middle class from various economic activities to reduce competition, thus making it more and more lopsided. Thus, a third characteristic, lopsidedness, grew out of the colonial situation.

The professionals and the salariat could offer only secondary services as needed by the economy. When economic development was limited in the interests of the metropolitan country, the need for their services was also limited. Such parasitic dependence on a deliberately limited economy led to economic frustration, denial of participation in the political-administrative process brought about political frustration, and racial and social discrimination created psychological frustration.

Thus, in every colonial situation involving the conquering West, a middle class arose with these four attributes of being derivative, imitative, lopsided, and frustrated. In this way, it was fundamentally different from the Western middle class, which was created by internal factors and balanced in its two wings. Sooner or later in every colony before independence it took shape with all these four characteristics. Its evolution in different colonies varied according to local conditions, but one can discern a general pattern of three stages.

India went through all these stages in great detail. In the first stage, from the Macaulayan educational reforms of the 1850s and for three decades or so, the rising middle class got on quite well with the British administrators with whom it threw its lot in the 1857 rebellion. But tensions were already developing as a result of British racial aloofness, on the one hand, and the demands of the middle class for a share in administration and political control, on the other. These tensions culminated in the second stage in which the British and the Indian middle class were clearly ranged against each other from the 1890s.[14] The anti-middle-class mood of British administrators was expressed in a hundred ways in speeches, minutes, memoranda, and actual policies. They tried to encourage the Maharajahs, the old feudal nobility, and landed proprietors, and poured contempt on the "inefficiency" of the middle class. Not unexpectedly, the middle class was stimulated to show a strong reaction as a way of demonstrating its worth. It did so successfully in several fields—in politics through agitation and the organization of the Indian National Congress; in business and banking through new ventures; and in education through founding many new institutions. It re-created the ethic of selfless action, or Karma Yoga, that animated the nationalist movement and all social activity.[15]

A third stage grew out of the second in response to the British administrators' implicit claim that they were more attuned to India's rural masses than the middle-class politician ways. The limited agitational methods of the middle class now gave place to the promotion of mass contact under Mahatma Gandhi. From then on, it was just a question of time as to when they would take over from the British.

During these long second and third stages which lasted about a century, the Indian middle class was able partly to work itself out of its four original sins through a series of dialectical reactions. Imitation gave rise to revivalism, particularly as the British spurned the imitators as intruders; and this situation generated a functional radicalist revivalism and self-discipline. Frustration produced the nationalist movement, and ultimately, lopsidedness was made up partly by the resurgence of the old commercial classes, and the rise of groups oriented to Western management.

In Africa, the evolution of the middle class included the same four characteristics and the same three stages, but in a jumbled and telescoped manner. In British West Africa, indirect rule was inaugurated in an anti-middle-class climate of opinion prevailing in British ruling circles around the turn of the century, triggered by the rise of Indian nationalism.[16] One of its implicit objectives was the postponement of the rise of an African middle class and the downgrading of the already emerging Creole middle class. The Creole intelligentsia felt bitter about their resultant downgrading, and the new West African middle class was equally bitter as it grew up. The results were mixed: the middle class was discouraged from the start and sought to be smothered at a young age, but at the same time, the facade of indirect rule reduced African confrontation with the British authorities. Ultimately, when the middle class sprouted and gathered some strength, disciplined itself, made mass contact, and challenged the British, its self-discipline was limited to political organization. It had all the other characteristics of the derivative middle class, being imitative, parasitic, and frustrated. It began to give up imitation and to assert its Africanness only after independence. It is still going through its own dialectic.

The Francophone West African middle class had even less occasion for self-discipline.[17] French colonial policy was Janus-like; the philosophy of assimilation encouraged educated Africans to go Gaelic, but colonial practice closed avenues of political agitation in their own country while inviting them to join colonial administration to a limited extent in Africa or to treat France as their stamping ground as qualified professionals. The French African middle-class leadership was not therefore driven too early to seek support from the masses as the Indian and Anglophone African middle classes were forced to do. Its self-discipline was acquired together with fallen France during the Second World War and from French left-wing groups in the postwar period, but this did not amount to political mobilization. Moreover, African politicians negotiated and won independence through expedient alliances using the multiparty system prevailing in the French National Assembly. This improved negotiating ability but not self-discipline. All told, under the French assimilative policy of encouraging the educated African, the emerging African middle class was given few opportunities for self-discipline throughout French colonial history. The class was derivative, imitative, and lopsided, but its frustration was limited. After independence, generous French aid sustained its unrealistic standards of conspicuous consumption for many years. The criticisms of Dumont and Fanon were based on this extreme case of an undisciplined, parasitic middle class which rarely tried to escape its characteristics, through a creative dialectic as in India.

Several African leaders with socialist leanings, like Nyerere of Tanzania or Kaunda of Zambia, have frequently proclaimed their intentions to control the emergence of a privileged middle class. Their success has been severely limited, however, as three sociohistorical factors have persistently combined to promote its emergence and entrenchment.[18] In the first place, a nucleus of this class already takes shape in the colonial period, and its members retain their advantages in education through the interactional and motivational advantages of the middle-class home, though these may be initially weaker than in the West. Second, secondary and postsecondary educational systems in Third World countries are organized to replicate the system of the respective metropole, building up the same motivation for white-collar professional or salaried jobs. Third, most post-colonial states compulsively build up a substantial tertiary sector of management and other services very rapidly after independence for reasons related to building up a modern state apparatus and expanding developmental activities, all of which need the services of an educated middle class. The three factors act so quickly and concertedly that political leadership can exercise little control over it.

This general pattern of evolution of the derivative middle class in the colonial and postcolonial context was modified in the case of Third World countries, that were not under modern colonialism. Examples of such countries are Latin American countries freed from an earlier medieval colonialism a century ago or Turkey and Iran which were never under colonial rule. There is not enough secondary research material available for us to theorize about a general pattern for non-colonial Third World countries.[19] In the case of Latin American countries, external control of capital investment in industry and an internal commitment to an elaborate state apparatus, a network of public enterprises, and an advanced social welfare system well ahead of its economic viability seem to have generated an unbalanced salaried cum professional class similar to the derivative middle class in the colonial and postcolonial context.[20] In general, one can say that Third World countries that were not directly under Western colonial rule were conscious of some threat and confrontation and reacted in ways similar to societies under colonial rule. Therefore, the resulting middle class was pretty similar.

We started this exploration by highlighting the close relation between the educated middle class and public administration in the Third World, approximating Weberian elective affinity. We then sought to explain the merits and shortcomings of this class through a critical sociohistorical exploration of its origins and development. In conclusion, we need to refer all too briefly to the parallel ongoing discussion about the middle class, management, and public administration in the First World in both neo-Marxist and non-Marxist circles.[21]

Karl Marx was critical of European bureaucracies as oppressive instruments of absolutist regimes but would not concede them the status of a class with a definite relation to the mode of production. For Marx the bureaucracy was simply an instrument of the exploiting bourgeoisie who controlled the state apparatus. Orthodox Marxists have clung to this view for decades. Marx was aware of the emergence of salaried managers and their powers of control but would not call them a class as yet. From the days of the October Revolution in Russia, however, bureaucracy began to pose a knotty question to Marxist theoreticians. Lenin began with an almost anarchist aversion to it and ultimately, with resignation and regret settled down with a large tentacular bureaucracy. Trotsky condemned it more freely as a betrayal of the Revolution but was still not prepared to call it a class. Finally, James Burnham, a former Trotskyite, ostentatiously shed his Marxist label and described the salaried managers in business and government not only as a class, but also as the ruling class that has displaced the owners of capital in the United States as well as the Soviet Union and Western Europe. Milovan Djilas in his *The New Class* echoed this view years later in the context of Yugoslavia.

Although this stream of thought has been loudly disowned by most Marxists, it has also set in motion a whole new train of inquiry and theorizing about the middle class in capitalist democracies of the First World and has generated a fast growing literature on this theme. We cannot attempt to discuss this literature here, but we must note some trends therein. The persistence of the capitalist state, rejuvenated by Keynesian manipulation and welfare legislation, first attracted critical Marxist attention. Simultaneously, the entrenchment and enlargement of the middle class of professionals and the salaried, contrary to Marxist prediction, compelled attention. Along with that, certain other tendencies were noted such as the large-scale bureaucratization of the world and of Western societies in particular, the much faster growth of public bureaucracies, and the decline of independent professionals. All these related and complicated developments have been subjected to diverse interpretations and explanations, but the crucial importance of the middle class and bureaucracy and their interrelationship is now acknowledged to be a major component of the explanation. Neo-Marxists like Nicos Poulantzaas and G. Carchedi have devoted much attention to placing the managers in the production process in a ''contradictory'' class location instead of ignoring them altogether. Weberian social scientists are equally eager to relate public administrators to social formations in some other way. It is clear to this writer that a general relation between this middle class defined para-Marxistically and public administration interpreted sociohistorically is the best foundation for a broadbased global study of comparative public administration.[22]

NOTES

1. Right from the 1917 October Revolution, the Comintern has encouraged nationalist movements to revolt and resistance. This was openly conceived as a call to self-liberation of the world's oppressed and exploited, but the benefits to the USSR itself from it in containing enemy powers was equally important, if unstated.

2. The Communist party of India (CPI) alone, over forty years from 1940 onwards, has spanned the whole spectrum of attitudes from cooperation with the national bourgeoisie to total opposition. The thesis in every annual meeting of the CPI changed from one to the other dramatically. The European Communist parties have also wavered from one to the other over the years.

3. Rene Dumont, *False Start in Africa,* Sphere paperbacks (1967), and Frantz Fanon, *The Wretched of the Earth* (London: MacGibbon and Kee, 1965).

4. Dumont, *False Start*, p. 68.

5. Ibid., p. 74.

6. Fanon, *The Wretched of the Earth*, p. 122 ff., p. 144 ff.

7. Ibid., p. 122.

8. For a general view of the ''bourgeoisie'' in dependent economies in dependency theory, see Magnus Bloomstrom and Bjorn Hettne, *Development Theory in Transition* (London: Zed Books, 1984), especially Chapter 3.

9. Regarding Marxist difficulties in accepting bureaucracy as a class, see V. Subramaniam, ''Western Marxist Approaches to Management and Organization Theory,'' *Indian Journal of Public Administration* 28, 4 (October-December 1982), for major references.

10. The earliest seminal work on the new middle class was B. B. Misra, *The Indian Middle Classes* (London: Oxford University Press, 1963), in which he clearly identified it as a purely salaried and professional class without direct creative involvement in trade, commerce, or industry. But he did not go beyond this empirically sustained conclusion either to theorize about it in terms of related characteristics or to compare it with similar ''classes'' in Africa. Much more work flowed from others on this new class, and the Utilitarian influence on Indian nationalism and their interrelationship. But for a long time research work on Africa was far too oriented to standard topics such as indirect rule and ''uhuruo.'' When research finally began to concentrate on economic development, classes, and the like, it was too ideologically oriented to produce much empirical work on the emerging salaried and professional classes, while the non-Marxists were stuck with the concept of elites. But much good work emerged as a byproduct of the research of educational sociologists. Latin American empirical work was again isolated and took little note of work in Africa or India. For a number of reasons associated with specialized regional research, or ideological orientations, work on the educated middle classes has continued piecemeal without attempting comparison and inductive theorizing.

My own initiative in this regard is partly derived from my penchant for wider comparisons and partly from accident. After a year of close contact with Professor B. B. Misra in Delhi in 1967, I took up a chair at the University of Zambia, Africa, and was getting acquainted with the work of Fanon and Dumont and witnessing the delayed emergence of an educated middle class right under my nose in Zambia. This concatenation of stimulating contacts generated my theorizings on the derivative middle class.

11. I have developed the theory of the derivative middle class in several conference papers and articles. I am drawing freely from the following in particular: "The Derivative Middle Class: A Colonial Residue," East African Universities Social Science Conference, Dar-es-Salaam, Tanzania, December 1970; "Three Converging Promoters of Social Stratification in Newly Independent Countries," Ninth World Congress of Sociology, Uppsala, Sweden, August 1978; "Formal Education and Social Stratification: The Contribution of Coastal Colonialism to the Relationship." Research Committee 28 on Social Stratification of the International Sociological Association, Meeting at University of Texas at Austin, February 1980; "Indirect Rule and the Indian Middle Class," Chapter 10 of V. Subramaniam, *Transplanted Indo-British Administration* (New Delhi: Ashish Publishing House, 1977).

12. In particular, electoral studies show the commercial "petite bourgeoise" voting right and the professionals voting left.

13. The influence of British Utilitarians on India and elsewhere has been studied from different angles. For a typical work, see Amartya Kumar Sen and Bernard Williams, *Utilitarianism and Beyond* (Cambridge, Eng.: Cambridge University Press, 1982).

14. Subramaniam, *Transplanted Indo-British Administration*, Chapter 10, "Indirect Rule and the Indian Middle Class."

15. V. Subramaniam, "Hindu Revivalism and a Westernized Middle Class Reinterpretation of the Bhagavadgita," paper presented to the ninth world Congress of Sociology, Uppsala, Sweden, August 1978. Reprinted as Appendix I in V. Subramaniam, *Cultural Integration in India* (New Delhi: Ashish Publishing House, 1979).

16. Subramaniam, *Transplanted Indo-British Administration*, Chapter 10, "Indirect Rule and the Indian Middle Class."

17. Edward Mortimer, *France and the Africans 1944–1960: A Political History* (London: Faber and Faber, 1969). The general account and even the introduction makes it clear how close the French-speaking African elite was to France and less interested in local nationalism.

18. Subramaniam, "Three Converging Promoters of Social Stratification."

19. The one general work of relevance is Karl Polanyi, *The Great Transformation: The Political and Economic Origins of Our Times* (Boston: Beacon Press, 1968), dealing with secondary induced social change, which Metin Heper uses to analyze the "modernization" of Turkey. But Polanyi's work is too general and not sharply focused on the middle class.

20. See Jorge Nef, Chapter 14 in this volume.

21. For more details and references, see V. Subramaniam, "Western Marxist Approaches to Management and Organization Theory," *Indian Journal of Public Administration* 28, 4 (October-December 1982), particularly pp. 756–57. Nicos Poulantzaas in *Political Power and Social Classes* (London, 1974) and G. Carchedi, "On the Economic Identification of the New Middle Class," in *Economy and Society* (London), struggle with this question at some length.

22. Apart from some of my own doctoral students who have used this approach, David C. Potter explicitly claims to have derived help and stimulation from my theorizing; see David C. Potter, *India's Political Administrators* (Oxford: Clarendon Press, 1986), pp. 10–11. I am completing a manuscript, "A Fresh Approach to Comparative Public Administration," posed on the sociohistorical class-oriented method developed in this appendix.

BIBLIOGRAPHICAL GUIDE

Any claim that one has compiled a bibliography of public administration in the Third World is grossly misleading for several reasons. There is a large amount of unprocessed primary material consisting of official files and confidential documents in each Third World country, and there are obvious difficulties in making a functional bibliography out of published and accessible secondary material. Any such bibliography needs to be focused and comprehensive. Neither criterion can be reasonably satisfied, as we have already suggested in our introduction.

Western interest in the study of public administration in the Third World originated in an attempt to supervise the administration of foreign aid to that part of the world from the 1950s onward, followed by an effort to understand the local structures and processes of public administration. This effort was colored in two ways. First, American or European institutions, practices, techniques, and remedies were applied, and when they proved inadequate or counterproductive, there was an attempt to explain this ultimately in terms of overall system theories, relating administration, politics, society, culture, and religion to everything else. The work of F. W. Riggs and those who followed his line of thinking illustrates this problem. In general, most published work on comparative public administration followed this approach. Others concentrated on short-term visible results for specific aid projects for development and produced a considerable amount of management-oriented literature on specific areas of public administration in the Third World such as planning or agricultural extension. Both the system-oriented comparativists and project-oriented pragmatists took an instrumental view of public administration, with "development" as the end product. The fairly substantial literature on administration which they have generated seems to lack a sharp focus in public administration, for its primary concerns are system-based theorizing or micro-project managing. Dependency theory shifts the focus even further away from administration onto international capitalism and its internal agents. Its attitude to public administration is either to rule it out as irrelevant or to study the administrators as culpable roadblocks to development as the "bureaucratic bourgeoisie." As explained in some detail in the introductory chapter, these factors have hindered the development of literature with its primary focus on public administration in the Third World.

There is, of course, a slowly growing literature on the Third World, and even more on specific regions such as Africa, Latin America, the Middle East, and South and Southeast Asia. Works of this genre treat public administration as part of government or the political system without too much emphasis or analysis. Also pointed out in the Introduction is the lack of interregional comparisons or integrated analysis. It took years before French- and English-speaking Africa were compared, and comparisons of Asian and African states started more as illustrations of the possibilities of Marx's *18th Brumaire* as an analytical tool. In summary, it would be easy enough to compile an impressive list of works on the Third World or developing countries or countries with a "dependency" relation to the world economy, but it would be misleading the reader to characterize that bibliography as focused on public administration in the Third World.

The paucity of published secondary literature with a sharp focus on public administration is in fact reflected in several chapters of this book in which the authors have drawn considerably on unpublished doctoral work, as well as their own earlier work and personal involvement in advisory or training roles. This is not entirely unfortunate, as it presents both opportunities and difficulties.

Having presented this caveat, we divide our modest bibliographical guide into three unequal parts, namely, journals, on-line information retrieval, and books. In regard to books, a list of references under each country actually used and cited by the respective authors is included with just a few additions. The journal articles they used are not listed or indexed as they can be easily picked up by the curious scholar from the chapter end notes. Instead, we have provided a classified list of journals that are devoted largely to Third World public administration or that publish occasional articles on the subject. A short note on on-line search is also included.

JOURNALS

Very few journals are devoted solely or even largely to public administration in the Third World, and usually they identify the Third World with development in some form. The following are the most useful. *Public Administration and Development* (London), continuing the work of *The Journal of Administration Overseas,* is now published by the Royal Institute of Public Administration and is almost wholly devoted to empirical studies of public administration practices and problems in the Third World, with some infrequent articles on developmental or dependency theories. The *I.D.S. Bulletin,* published by the Institute of Development Studies at Sussex University, complements this work through greater emphasis on theory and analysis. To this periodical we may add those journals devoted to developing countries in general such as the *Scandinavian Journal of Development Alternatives* (Stockholm), *The Journal of Developing Areas* (Ann Arbor), and the *Journal of Developing Societies* (Ottawa) and a more popular bimonthly *Development and Cooperation* (Bonn). More specifically, several journals published from the educationally advanced Third World countries focus on public administration in their own country or area and the Third World in general. The most notable among these are *The Indian Journal of Public Administration* (New Delhi), *The Philippine Journal of Public Administration* (Manila), *Quarterly Journal of Administration* (Ife), *African Administrative Studies* (Tangier, CAFRAD), *Bulletin d'Institut International d'Administration Publique* (Paris), *Journal of the Pakistan Academy of Administration* (Islamabad), *Politics,*

Administration and Change (Dhaka), and *Middle East Management Review* (Cairo). To these, one must add the journals in Spanish on administration in the more advanced Latin American countries such as Mexico, Argentina, and Chile.

Among the established journals devoted to public administration in general, some publish more articles on the Third World than others. Thus, *Public Administration* (London) and *La Revue d'Administration Publique* (Paris) publish such articles more frequently because of their former colonial connections and current liaison with them through the Commonwealth or French community. Similarly, the *International Review of Administrative Sciences* (Brussels), *Journal of Commonwealth and Comparative Politics* (London), and *Administration and Society* (Calgary), formerly the *Journal of Comparative Administration*, publish more on Third World administration because of their comparative orientation. Other journals devoted to public administration, such as *Public Administration Review* (Washington), *Administrative Science Quarterly*, the *Australian Journal of Public Administration* (Sydney), the *New Zealand Journal of Public Administration* (Wellington), *Canadian Public Administration* (Toronto), and *Administration* (Dublin) publish the odd article on public administration in the Third World.

Among the more regular publications on Third World administrative problems should be included particularly the annual *World Bank Report*. Although these reports concentrate on economic problems as such, they spill over very quickly into analyzing administrative problems, particularly those of public enterprises in Third World countries. In addition to these, (1) there are International Monetary Fund and World Bank reports on specific projects for which aid was requested (which branch out into a general evaluation of the administrative system of the country concerned); (2) reports by local United Nations Development Program (UNDP) offices in each country reporting on specific projects or issues, and (3) reports by various specific U.N. agencies such as the World Health Organization, UNICEF, or the Food and Agriculture Organization on specific problems and projects, many of which discuss public administration in the country or region concerned. Most of these are included in the list of publications issued by the U.N. Information Office in New York from time to time. The empirical information therein is substantial and as factual as possible in the context, but one must bear in mind the unstated major premises of each report.

Journals devoted to regional and comparative studies quite often contain perceptive articles on public administration. *Third World Quarterly* (London) is the one most sharply focused on the Third World. But in this class may be included some leading journals on Africa and the African economy, namely, the *Journal of Modern African Studies* (Cambridge University Press), *African Political Studies* (African Political Studies Association, Harare), *Africa* (London), *Africa and the World* (London), *African Development*, and *Review of African Political Economy* (London). The journals on Asia are less administration-oriented, but the following may carry the odd article on public administration: *Journal of Modern Asian Studies, Asian Survey, Pacific Affairs, Middle Eastern Studies, Comparative Studies in Society and History*, and *Economic Development and Cultural Change*.

We can add to this list some more journals devoted to development studies, such as *Planning and Administration, Third World Planning Review, Administration and Change, Asian Development Review, Development and Change, Development Policy Review, Journal of Development Studies*, and *World Development*.

Few journals focus as sharply on Third World public administration as *Public Admin-*

istration and Development. There is obviously room for another Third World administration quarterly, with more balance between theory and empirical accounts.

BIBLIOGRAPHIES AND ON-LINE SEARCH

Several institutions and aid agencies, apart from U.N. agencies, have been compiling
bibliographies of the literature on various sectors of public administration and development
in the Third World. The more important of these are the Organization for Economic
Cooperation and Development (Paris), Overseas Development Administration (London),
Institut Internationale d'Administration Publique (Paris), International Development Research Centre (Ottawa), and the Stanford Research Institute of the International Development Centre (Stanford). Most of the available bibliographies, however, belong to the
1970s except Nat J. Colleta's bibliography on human resource development of 1982.

Researchers, librarians, and information managers nowadays pin a lot of faith on on-
line search of databases, which are expected to be kept up to date by continuous feeding
in of information on published and on-going research. This faith is exaggerated, if not
misplaced, in regard to public administration in the Third World. The major databases
in the social sciences are the following (as discussed in William A. Katz, *Introduction
to Reference work, Vol. II Reference Services and Reference Processes* (New York:
McGraw-Hill series in Library Education, 1982), pp. 177–84: *Social Scisearch* (Social
Sciences Citation Index) (Philadelphia: Institute for Scientific Information, 1972 onward);
Sociological Abstracts (New York: Sociological Abstracts Inc., 1963 onward); and *PAIS*
International (New York: Public Affairs, Information Service, 1972 onward).

The other databases which Katz recommends relate mainly to education and information
science, that is, Education Resources Information Center (ERIC), Library Information
Science Abstracts (LISA), and National Information Center for Educational Media (NI-
CEM) or to psychology, that is, Psychological Abstracts and National Institute of Mental
Health (NIMH). The three databases that deal directly with the social sciences include,
of course, all the social sciences, with only a subordinate place given to public administration. In terms of retrieving information, there is no separate vocabulary for it, and
one has to use the thesaurus for political science. Besides this subordination, two other
factors make on-line search from these databases difficult, particularly in regard to Third
World public administration. The first applies to all social sciences, namely, the low
specificity of descriptors, that is, descriptive words and phrases to locate articles and
information, partly because of the uncontrolled growth of jargon, and partly because
many new, relevant developments in interdisciplinary areas are not recognized and fed
into the databases in time. The other factor related in particular to the Third World has
been the subject of complaint by librarians for many years, namely, the nonaccession
and nonaccessibility of research in Third World institutions for several reasons. On the
whole, the existing social science databases are less than satisfactory in regard to Third
World public administration, and there is a strong case for separate databases for (1)
public administration and business management in general and (2) public administration
in the Third World in particular.

1. INTRODUCTION

Blomstrom, Magnus, and Hettne, Bjorn. *Development Theory in Transition.* London:
Zed Books, 1984.

Dumont, Rene. *False Start in Africa*. London: Sphere Paperbacks, 1967.

Fanon, Frantz. *The Wretched of the Earth*. London: McGibbon and Kee, 1965.

Frank, A. G. *Capitalism and Underdevelopment in Latin America*. New York: Monthly Review Press, 1967.

Gant, George F. *Development Administration: Concepts, Goals, Methods*. Madison: University of Wisconsin Press, 1979.

Geertz, Clifford (ed.). *Old Societies and New States: The Quest for Modernity in Asia and Africa*. New York: The Free Press, 1963.

Geertz Clifford (ed.). *Politics and State in the Third World*. London: Macmillan, 1979.

Goulborne, Harry (ed.). *Politics and State in the Third World*. London: Macmillan, 1979.

Heady, Ferrel. *Public Administration: A Comparative Perspective*. Englewood Cliffs, N.J.: Prentice-Hall, 1986 (latest edition).

Horowitz, Irving Louis. *Three Worlds of Development*. New York: Oxford University Press, 1966.

Ilchman, Warren. *Comparative Public Administration and Conventional Wisdom*. Beverly Hills, Calif.: Sage Publications, 1971.

Kautsky, John H. (ed.). *Political Change in Underdeveloped Countries, Nationalism and Communism*. New York: John Wiley, 1962.

Kohli, Atul (ed.). *The State and Development in the Third World*. Princeton, N.J.: Princeton University Press, 1986.

Leys, Colin. *Underdevelopment in Kenya: The Political Economy of Neo-Colonialism*. London: Heineman, 1975.

Myrdal, Gunnar. *Asian Drama*. 3 vols. New York: Pantheon Books, 1968.

Riggs, F. W. *Administration in Developing Countries*. Boston: Houghton Mifflin, 1964.

Rodney, Walter. *How Europe Underdeveloped Africa*. Dar-es-Salaam: Tanzania Publishing House, 1972.

Schmitt, David E. *Dynamics of the Third World*. Cambridge, Mass.: Winthrop Publishers, 1974.

Shils, Edward. *Political Development in the New States*. The Hague: Mouton, 1968.

Shivji, Issa. *The Silent Class Struggle*. Dar-es-Salaam: Tanzania Publishing House, 1973.

Sigmund, Paul E. (ed.). *The Ideologies of the Developing Nations*. New York: Praeger, 1963.

Smith, Anthony D. *State and Nation in the Third World*. Brighton: Wheatsheaf Books, 1983.

Somjee, A. H. *Political Capacity in Developing Societies*. London: Macmillan, 1982.

Subramaniam, V. *Transplanted Indo-British Administration*. New Delhi: Ashish Publishing House, 1977.

Sutlive, Vinson H. et al. *The Rise and Fall of Democracies in the Third World*. Williamsburg, Va.: Studies in the Third World Series, 1984.

Wesson, Robert G. *Modern Governments: Three Worlds of Politics*. Englewood Cliffs, N.J.: Prentice-Hall, 1981.

Worsley, Peter. *The Third World*. London: Weidenfeld and Nicolson, 1964.

2. BANGLADESH

Ahamed, E. *Development Administration: Bangladesh*. Dhaka: Centre for Administrative Studies (CENTAS), 1981.

Ahmed, S. G. *Public Personnel Administration in Bangladesh*. Dhaka: University of Dhaka, 1985.

Campbell, Colin, S. J., and Peters, B. Guy. *Organizing Governance: Governing Organizations*. Pittsburgh: University of Pittsburgh Press, 1988.

CMLA's Secretariat, Establishment Division, Government of Bangladesh. *Report of the Committee for Examination of Irregularities in Appointment and Promotion of Officers and Staff in the Government* (CEIAPOSG), April 1983, pp. ii, iv, 19.

Khan, M. M., and Throp, J. P. (eds.). *Bangladesh: Society and Bureaucracy*. Dhaka: CENTAS, 1984.

Khan M. M., and Zafarullah, H. M. *Recruitment and Selection in the Higher Civil Services in Bangladesh: An Overview*. SICA Occasional Papers Series, Second Series, no. 6, Washington, D.C., 1984.

Muhith, A. M. A. *Bangladesh: Emergence of a Nation*. Dhaka: Bangladesh Books International, 1978, pp. 243–44.

Siddiqui, K. (ed.). *Local Government in Bangladesh*. Dhaka: National Institute of Local Government, 1984.

3. INDIA

Maheshwari, S. R. *State Governments in India*. New Delhi: Macmillan, 1979.

Maheshwari, S. R. *Indian Administration*. New Delhi: Orient Longman, 1984.

Maheshwari, S. R. *Local Government in India*. Agra: Lakshmi Narain Agarwal, 1984, 3d ed.

Maheshwari, S. R. *The Administrative Reform Commission*. Agra: Lakshmi Narain Agarwal, 1972.

Misra, B. B. *The Administrative History of India, 1843–1947*. New Delhi: Oxford University Press, 1976.

Misra, B. B. *Government and Bureaucracy in India*. New Delhi: Oxford University Press, 1986.

Potter, David C. *India's Political Administrators*. Oxford: Clarendon Press, 1986. (Potter's book in particular contains the most useful, comprehensive, up-to-date bibliography of secondary sources on Indian public administration, while the two books by B. B. Misra have a more complete reference guide to primary sources.)

Puri, B. N. *History of Indian Administration*. Vol. 1. *Ancient India;* Vol. 2, *Medieval Period*. Bombay: Bharatiya Vidya Bhavan, 1975. (Both of Puri's books contain detailed references to most secondary sources on the history of administration down to the British period.)

Sastry, R. Shama. *Kautilya's Arthasastra*. Mysore: Mysore Printing Publishing House, 1967, 7th ed.

Subramaniam, V. *Social Background of India's Administrators*. New Delhi: Publications Division, Government of India, 1971.

Subramaniam, V. *Transplanted Indo-British Administration*. New Delhi: Ashish Publishing House, 1977.

Subramaniam, V. *Cultural Integration in India*. New Delhi: Ashish Publishing House, 1979.

N.B. This bibliography includes only the works actually referenced in the chapter, but an enormous amount of published literature is coming out on different aspects of Indian public administration, which cannot be even selectively listed. We therefore refer the reader to the major bibliographical listings in the books of Potter, Misra, and Puri, as indicated earlier. In addition, the Indian Institute of Public Administration periodically publishes bibliographies and special issues on aspects of Indian public administration.

4. PAKISTAN

Ahmad, Muneer. *The Civil Servant in Pakistan*. Karachi: Oxford University Press, 1964.

Ahmad, Muneer. *Aspects of Pakistan's Politics and Administration*. Lahore: South Asian Institute, 1974.

Ahmad, Muzaffar. *Public Enterprises in South Asia*. Lujubljana: International Center for Public Enterprises, 1982.

Anwar-ul-Haq. *Commission on Administrative Reform: Report*. Government of Pakistan, 1978.

Birkhead, Guthri (ed.). *Administrative Problems in Pakistan*. New York: Syracuse University Press, 1966.

Braibanti, Ralph. *Asian Bureaucratic Systems Emergent from the British Imperialist Tradition*. Durham, N.C.: Duke University Press, 1966.

Burki, S. J. *Pakistan Under Bhutto, 1971–77*. New York: St. Martin's Press, 1980.

Burki, S. J. *Pakistan: A Nation in the Making*. London: Oxford University Press, 1986.

Burki, S. J., and Laporte, R., Jr. (eds.). *Pakistan's Development Priorities*. Karachi: Oxford University Press, 1986.

Chapman, Brian. *British Government Observed*. London, 1967.

Finkle, J. L., and Gable, Richard W. (eds.). *Political Development and Social Change*. New York: John Wiley, 1971.

Galadieux, Bernard L. *Report of Reorganization of Pakistan Government for National Development*. Karachi: Planning Commission, 1955.

Goodnew, Henry F. *The Civil Service of Pakistan*. New Haven, Conn.: Yale University Press, 1964.

Hussain, Asaf. *Elite Politics in an Ideological State: The Case of Pakistan*. Folkstone, Kent: Dawson, 1979.

Inayatullah (ed.). *Bureaucracy and Development in Pakistan*. Peshawar: Pakistan Academy for Rural Development, 1970.

Kochanek, Stanley A. *Interest Groups and Development: Business and Politics in Pakistan*. Karachi: Oxford University Press, 1983.

Laporte, Robert, Jr. *Power and Privilege: Influence and Decision Making in Pakistan*. Berkeley: University of California Press, 1975.

Mahbub-Ul-Haq. *The Poverty Curtain: Choices for the Third World*. New York: Columbia University Press, 1976.

Nazim. *Babus, Brahmins and Bureaucrats*. Lahore: People's Publishing House, 1973.

Papanek, Gustav F. *Pakistan's Development: Social Goals and Private Incentives*. Cambridge, Mass.: Harvard University Press, 1967.

Sayeed, Khalid B. *Pakistan: The Formative Phase*. Karachi: Pakistan Publishing House, 1960.

Sayeed, Khalid B. *Politics in Pakistan*. New York: Praeger, 1980.

Shifel, Lawrence D., et al. (eds.). *Education and Training for Public Sector Management in Developing Countries*. New York: Rockefeller Foundation, 1977.

Syed, Reza H. *Role and Performance of Public Enterprises in the Economic Growth of Pakistan*. Karachi: Investment Advisory Center, 1977.

Ziring, Lawrence. *Pakistan: The Enigma of Political Development*. Folkstone, Kent: Dawson-Westview, 1980.

5. THE PHILIPPINES

Abueva, Jose V. (ed.). *Perspectives in Government Reorganization*. Manila: University of the Philippines, College of Public Administration, 1969.

Bello, Walden, Kinley, David, and Elinson, Elaine. *Development Debacle: The World Bank in the Philippines*. San Francisco: Institute for Food and Development Policy, 1982.

Carino, Ledivina V., and Vineza, Emma B. (eds.) *The Indang Experience: Lessons from the First Barrio Immersion of the Career Executive Service Development Program*. Makati, Philippines: Development Academy of the Philippines, 1980.

Chenery, Hollis. *Redistribution with Growth*. London: Oxford University Press, 1974.

Constantino, Renato, and Constantino, Letizia R. *The Philippines: The Continuing Past*. Quezon City: Foundation for Nationalist Studies, 1978.

Corpuz, Onofre D. *The Philippines*. Englewood Cliffs, N.J.: Prentice-Hall, 1965; Philippine edition, 1970.

De Guzman, Raul P., and Tancangco, Luzviminda G. *An Assessment of the May 1984 Batasang Pambansa Elections*. Manila: University of the Philippines, College of Public Administration, 1986.

De Guzman, R. P., and Tancangco, L. G. *An Assessment of the February 1986 Special Presidential Elections: A Study of Political Change Through People Power*. Manila: University of the Philippines, College of Public Administration, 1986.

Dubsky, Roman. "Development and Technocratic Thought in the Philippines." Unpublished Ph.D. dissertation submitted to the University of the Philippines, 1981.

Feder, Ernest. *Perverse Development*. Quezon City, Philippines: Foundation for Nationalist Studies, 1983.

Golay Frank (ed.). *Philippine American Relations*. Manila, Bombay, and New York: Solidaridad Publishing House, 1966.

Illo, Jeanne Frances, and Chiong-Javier, Ma. Elena. *Organizing Farmers for Irrigation Management: The Buhi-Lalo Experience*. Naga City: Research and Service Center, Ateneo de Naga, 1983.

International Labour Organization, World Employment Programme. *A Study of Labour Based/Equipment Supported Road Construction in the Philippines*. Report prepared for the Ministry of Local Government, Republic of the Philippines, Regional Office for Asia and the Pacific, Bangkok and the ILO Office in Manila, August 1983.

Lee, Hahn-Ben, and Samonte Ahelardo G. (eds.). *Administrative Reforms in Asia*. Manila: Eastern Regional Organization for Public Administration, 1970.

Soriano, Emanuel V., Licuanan, Patricia B., and Cariño, Ledivina V. *Understanding People Power: A Collection of Papers Presented at a DAP Symposium on People Power*. Manila, 1986.

6. EGYPT

Ayubi, Nazih. *Bureaucracy and Politics in Contemporary Egypt.* London: Ithaca Press, 1980, p. 447.

Badran, Mogha A. *Co-ordination in Multiactor Programmes: An Empirical Investigation of Factors Affecting Co-ordination Among Organizations at the Local Level in Egyptian Family Planning Program.* Stockholm: Department of Business Administration, University of Stockholm, 1984.

Baker, Raymond W. *Egypt under Nasser and Sadat.* Cambridge, Mass.: Harvard University Press, 1978.

Farid, Samir. "Administrative Reforms in Developing Countries: The Case of Egypt 1952–1978," Ph.D. thesis, Department of Politics of the University of Wales, University College, Cardiff, 1983.

Gabr, Ibrahim Abdel. "Participation in the Decision-making Process in the Egyptian Public Sector." M.A. thesis, College of Commerce, Tanta University, Tanta, 1979.

Helmy, Amr Abbas. "Management of Training in State Audit Organizations: A Case Study of Central Audit Organization of Egypt." MPA thesis, Cairo, American University in Cairo, 1986.

Ikram, Khalid. *Egypt: Economic Management in a Period of Transition.* Baltimore: Johns Hopkins University Press, 1980.

Ikram, Khalid. *Egypt: Economic Management in a Period of Transition.* Published for the World Bank, Baltimore: Johns Hopkins University Press, 1980.

Mabro and Radwan. *The Industrialization of Egypt, 1939–73.* Oxford: Clarendon Press, 1976.

Marino, Joseph. "Decentralization and Public Participation in Urban Egypt." MPA thesis, Cairo, American University of Cairo, 1986.

Moore, Clement Henry. *Images of Development: Egyptian Engineers in Search of Industry.* Cambridge, Mass.: MIT Press, 1980.

Plum, Margaret Suzanne. "Decentralization as Public Policy: The Government of Egypt/US Agency for International Development Experience in Egypt." MPA thesis, Cairo, American University of Cairo, 1985.

Sinker, A. P. *Report on Personnel Questions of the Egyptian Civil Service.* Cairo: Ministry of Finance, Government Press, 1951.

Waterbury, John. *The Egypt of Nasser and Sadat: The Political Economy of Two Regimes.* Princeton, N.J.: Princeton University Press, 1983.

World Bank. *World Development Report, 1985.* New York: Oxford University Press, 1985.

Youssef, Samir Mohamed. *System of Management in Egyptian Public Enterprise.* Cairo: American University of Cairo Press, 1983.

7. IRAN

Abrahamian, Ervand. *Iran Between Two Revolutions.* Princeton, N.J.: Princeton University Press, 1982.

Afkhami, Cholam R. *The Iranian Revolution: Thanatos on a National Scale.* Washington, D.C.: Middle East Institute, 1985.

Afshar, Haleh (ed.). *Iran: A Revolution in Turmoil.* Albany, N.Y.: State University of New York Press, 1985.

Algar, Hamid. *Religion and State in Iran, 1785–1906.* Berkeley: University of California Press, 1966.

Amuzegar, Jahangir. *Iran: An Economic Profile.* Washington, D.C.: Middle East Institute, 1977.

Arasteh, Reza. *Man and Society in Iran.* Leiden: E. J. Brill, 1964.

Avery, Peter. *The Reign of the Ayotollahs: Iran and the Islamic Revolution.* New York: Basic Books, 1984.

Banuziazi, Ali, and Weiner, Myron C. (eds.). *The State, Religion, and Ethnic Politics: Afghanistan, Iran and Pakistan.* Syracuse, N.Y.: Syracuse University Press, 1986.

Bashiriyeh, Hossein. *The State and Revolution in Iran: 1962–1982.* New York: St. Martin's Press, 1984.

Bayat, Assef. *Workers and Revolution in Iran.* London and New Jersey: Zed Books Ltd., 1987.

Bernard, Cheryl, and Khalilzad, Zalmay. *"The Government of God"—Iran's Islamic Republic.* New York: Columbia University Press, 1984.

Bill, James, and Leiden, Carl. *The Middle East: Politics and Power.* Boston: Allyn and Bacon, 1974.

Bill, James, and Leiden, Carl. *Politics in the Middle East.* Boston: Little, Brown, 1984, 2d ed.

Binder, Leonard. *Iran, Political Development in a Changing Society.* Los Angeles: University of California Press, 1962.

Bonine, Michael E., and Keddie, Nikki R. (eds.). *Modern Iran: The Dialectics of Continuity and Change.* Albany, N.Y.: State University of New York Press, 1981.

Eisenstadt, S. N. *The Political Systems of Empires.* New York: Free Press, 1963.

Farazmand, Ali. *The State, Bureaucracy, and Revolution in Modern Iran: Agrarian Reforms and Regime Politics.* New York: Praeger, 1989.

Fischer, Michael M. J. *Iran: From Religious Dispute to Revolution.* Cambridge, Mass.: Harvard University Press, 1980.

Frye, Richard. *Iran.* New York: Henry Holt, 1953.

Frye, Richard. *The Heritage of Persia.* London: Weidenfeld, 1962.

Frye, Richard. *The Golden Age of Persia.* New York: Harper and Row, 1975.

Ghirshman, R. *Iran: From the Earliest Times to the Islamic Conquest.* Baltimore: Johns Hopkins University Press, 1954.

Graham, Robert. *Iran: The Illusion of Power.* New York: St. Martin's Press, 1979.

Halliday, Fred. *Iran: Dictatorship and Development.* New York: Penguin Books, 1979.

Hiro, Dilip. *Iran Under the Ayotollahs.* London: Routledge and Kegan Paul, 1985.

Hooglund, Eric J. *Land and Revolution in Iran, 1960–1980.* Austin: University of Texas Press, 1982.

Hoveyda, Fereydoon. *The Fall of the Shah.* London: Weidenfeld and Nicolson, 1980.

Hussain, Asaf. *Islamic Iran: Revolution and Counter-Revolution.* New York: St. Martin's Press, 1985.

Inlow, E. Burke. *Shahanshah: A Study of Monarchy.* Delhi: Motilal Banarsidas, 1979.

Jazani, Bizhan. *Capitalism and Revolution in Iran.* London: Zed Press, 1980.

Katouzian, Homa. *The Political Economy of Modern Iran: Despotism and Pseudo-Modernism, 1926–1979*. New York: New York University Press, 1981.

Kazemi, Farhad. *Poverty and Revolution in Iran: The Migrant Poor, Urban Marginality and Politics*. New York: New York University Press, 1980.

Keddie, Nikki R., and Hooglund, Eric (eds.). *The Iranian Revolution and the Islamic Republic*. Syracuse, N.Y.: Syracuse University Press, 1986.

Lambton, Ann. *Landlord and Peasant in Persia*. London: Clarendon Press, 1953.

Lambton, Ann. *Theory and Practice in Medieval Persian Government*. London: Variorum Reprints, 1980.

Nashat, Guity. *The Origins of Modern Reform in Iran, 1876–80*. Chicago: University of Illinois Press, 1982.

Parson, Anthony. *The Pride and Fall: Iran 1974–1979*. London: Jonathan Cape, 1984.

Ramazani, R. K. *Revolutionary Iran: Challenge and Response in the Middle East*. Baltimore: The Johns Hopkins University Press, 1986.

Sharan, P. *Government and Politics of Persia*. New Delhi: Metropolitans Publisher, 1983.

Stempel, John D. *Inside the Iranian Revolution*. Bloomington: Indiana University Press, 1981.

Tabari, Azar, and Nahid Yeganeh. *In the Shadow of Islam: The Women's Movement in Iran*. London: Zed Press, 1982.

Zabih, Sepehr. *Iran Since the Revolution*. Baltimore: The Johns Hopkins University Press, 1989.

8. SAUDI ARABIA

Al-Awaji, Ibrahim Muhammad. "Bureaucracy and Society in Saudi Arabia." Ph.D. dissertation, University of Virginia, 1971.

Al-Farsy, Fouad. *Saudi Arabia: A Case Study in Development*. London: Stacey International, 1978.

Al-Islami, al-Ma'had. *Memorandum Submitted to the Islamic Secretariat for the Celebration of the Fourteenth Hijirah Century*. Riyadh: Islamic Institute, 1979.

Al-Mazyed, Sulayman. "The Structure and Function of Public Personnel Administration in Saudi Arabia," Ph.D. dissertation, Claremont Men's College, Claremont, Calif., 1972.

Bader, Fayez. "Developmental Planning in Saudi Arabia: A Multi-Dimensional Study," Ph.D. dissertation, University of Southern California, 1968.

Bill, James A., and Leiden, Carl. *Politics in the Middle East*. Boston: Little, Brown, 1979.

The Impact of Petroleum on the Economy of Saudi Arabia. Riyadh: Ministry of Information, 1979.

Philby, H. St. John. *Saudi Arabia*. Beirut: Librairie du Liban, 1968.

Sayegh, Kamal S. *Oil and Arab Regional Development*. New York: Praeger Publishers, 1968.

Solaim, Soliman. "Constitutional and Judicial Organization in Saudi Arabia." Ph.D. dissertation, Johns Hopkins University, 1970.

Sulayman, Abd al-Hamid Abu. "The Islamic Theory of International Relations: Its Relevance, Past and Present." Ph.D. dissertation, University of Pennsylvania, 1973.

Tawil, Mohammad A. "The Procedures and Instruments of Administrative Development in Saudi Arabia," Ph.D. dissertation, University of Pittsburgh, 1970.

Wahbah, Hafiz. *Arabian Days*. London: Arthur Barker., 1964.

9. TURKEY

Armaoglu, Fahir, and Birkhead, Gutherie. *Siyasal Bilgiler Fakultesi 1946–1955 Mezunlar Hakkinda Bir Arastirma*. Ankara: Turkiye ve Orta Dogu Amme Idaresi Enstitusu Yayini, 1956.

Bozkurt, Omer. *Memurlar: Turkiye'de Kamu Burokrasisinin Sosyolojik Gorunumu*. Ankara: Turkiye ve Orta Dogu Amme Idaresi Enstitusu Yayini, 1980.

Davison, Roderic H. *Reform in the Ottoman Empire, 1856–1976*. Princeton: Princeton University Press, 1963.

Dincer, Nabi, and Ersoy, Turan. *Merkezi Hukumet Teskilati Arastirma Projesi (Mehtap) Tavsiyelerinin Uygulanma Durumunu Degerlendirme Arastirmasi*. Ankara: Turkiye ve Orta Dogu Amme Idaresi Enstitusu, 1974.

Guran, Sait. *Memurlar Hukukunda Kayirma ve Liyakat Sistemleri*. Istanbul: Fakultet Matbaasi, 1980.

Heper, Metin. *The State Tradition in Turkey*. Walkington, England: Eothen Press, 1985.

Heper, Metin. *Dilemmas of Decentralization: Municipal Government in Turkey*. Bonn: Friedrich-Ebert-Stiftung, 1986.

Heper, Metin. *Democracy and Local Government: Istanbul in the 1980s*. Walkington, England: Eothen Press, 1987.

Heper, Metin. *Governing Greater Istanbul: Domination or Cooperation?* London: Routledge, in press.

Heper, Metin, and Berkman, A. Umit. *Development Administration in Turkey: Conceptual Theory and Methodology*. Istanbul: Bogazici University Publications, 1980.

Heper, Metin, and Evin, Ahmet (eds.). *State, Democracy and the Military: Turkey in the 1980s*. Berlin and New York: Walter de Gruyter, 1988.

Lewis, Bernard. *The Emergence of Modern Turkey*. London: Oxford University Press, 1961.

Paneth, Philip. *Turkey, Decadence and Rebirth*. London: Richard Madley, 1943.

Roos, Leslie L., Jr., and Roos, Noralou P. *Managers of Modernization: Organizations and Elites in Turkey (1950–1969)*. Cambridge, Mass.: Harvard University Press, 1971.

Tutum, Cahit. *Turkiye'de Memur Guvenligi*. Ankara: Turkiye ve Orta Dogu Amme Idaresi Enstitusu, 1972.

Weiker, Walter F. *The Modernization of Turkey: From Ataturk to the Present Day*. New York: Holmes and Meier, 1981.

10. GHANA

Africa: General

Adu, A. L. *The Civil Service in Commonwealth Africa*. London: Allen and Unwin, 1969.

Arrighi, Giovanni, and Saul, John S. *Essays on the Political Economy of Africa*. New York: Monthly Review Press 1973.

Ayandele, E. A. et al. *The Growth of African Civilization*. Vols. 1 and 2. London: Longman, 1971.

Bretton, Henry L. *Power and Politics in Africa*. Chicago: Aldine, 1973.

Canale, Jean Suret. *Afrique Noire: L'ere Coloniale*. Paris: Editions Sociales, 1964.

Herskovitz, Melville J. *The Human Factor in Changing Africa*. New York: Vintage Books, 1962.

Lewis, William H. (ed.). *French-Speaking Africa: The Search for Identity*. New York: Walker and Co., 1965.

Markovitz, Irving Leonard. *Power and Class in Africa*. Englewood Cliffs, N.J.: Prentice-Hall, 1977.

Tordoff, William. *Government and Politics in Africa*. Bloomington: Indiana University Press, 1984.

Ghana

Alexander, H. T. *African Tightrope*. London: Pall Mall Press, 1965.

Amonoo, Ben. *Ghana: The Politics of Institutional Dualism*. London: Allen and Unwin, 1981.

Apter, David. *The Gold Coast in Transition*. Princeton, N.J.: Princeton University Press, 1955.

Austin, Dennis. *Politics in Ghana 1946–60*. London: Oxford University Press, 1970.

Black, J. E., Coleman, J. S., and Stiffel, L. (eds.). *Education and Training for Public Sector Management in Developing Countries*. New York: Rockefeller Foundation, 1977.

Bretton, Henry. *The Rise and Fall of Kwame Nkrumah*. New York: Praeger, 1967.

Caiden, Naomi, and Wildavsky, Aaron. *Planning and Budgeting in Poor Countries*. New York: John Wiley, 1974.

Chazan, Naomi. *Political System of Ashanti: A Study of the Influence of Contemporary Social Changes on Ashanti Political Institutions*. London: Oxford University Press, 1951.

Chazan, Naomi. *An Anatomy of Ghanaian Politics*. Boulder, Colo.: Westview Press, 1983.

Foster, Philip, and Zolberg, Aristide R. (eds.). *Ghana and the Ivory Coast*. Chicago: University of Chicago Press, 1971.

Heady, F., and Stokes, S. (eds.). *Papers in Comparative Administration*. Ann Arbor: University of Michigan Press, 1962.

Hill, John Raven (ed.). *Africa in Economic Crisis*. London: Macmillan, 1986.

Hyden, Goran. *No Shortcuts to Progress*. Berkeley: University of California Press, 1983.

Killick, Tony. *Development Economics in Action*. London: Heinemann Educational Books, 1978.

Lyon, P., and Manor, J. (eds.). *Transfer and Transformation: Political Institutions in the New Commonwealth*. Leicester: Leicester University Press, 1983.

Nkrumah, Kwame. *Consciencism: Philosophy and Ideology for De-Colonization*. New York: Monthly Review Press, 1970.

Nkrumah, S. A. "Atrophisation of Rural Ghana." Ph.D. dissertation, New York University, 1979.

Oquaye, Mike. *Politics in Ghana 1972–1979*. Accra: Tornado Publications, 1980.

Price, Robert M. *Society and Bureaucracy in Contemporary Ghana*. Berkeley: University of California Press, 1975.

Rawlings, Jerry John. *The Process of Consolidation*, Vol. 3, *Selected Speeches and*

Interviews of Flt.-Lt. Jerry John Rawlings, January 1, 1984-December 31, 1984. Accra: Ghana Publishing Corp., 1985.

Younger, Kenneth. *The Public Service in the New States.* London: Oxford University Press, 1960.

11. NIGERIA

Adamolekun, L. *Public Administration, A Nigerian and Comparative Perspective.* London: Longman, 1983.

Adamolekun, L. (ed.) *Nigerian Public Administration 1960–1980; Perspectives and Prospects.* Ibadan: Heinemann, 1985.

Adamolekun, L. and Osunkunle, E. L. *Nigeria's Ombudsman System: Five Years of the Public Complaints Commission.* Ibadan: Heinemann, 1982.

Adamolekun, L., and Rowland, L. (eds.). *The New Local Government System.* Ibadan: Heinemann, 1979.

Ayeni V., and Soremekun, K. (eds.). *Nigeria's Second Republic.* Lagos: Daily Times Publications, 1988.

Baker C., and Balogun, M. J. (eds.). *Ife Essays in Administration.* Ile-Ife: University of Ife Press, 1975.

Balogun, M. J. *Public Administration in Nigeria, A Developmental Approach.* London: Macmillan, 1983.

Dike, C. *The Nigerian Civil Service.* Owerri: Alfa Publishing Co., 1985.

Ekpo, M. U., (ed.). *Bureaucratic Corruption in Sub-Saharan Africa: Toward a Search for Causes and Consequences.* Washington, D.C.: University Press of America, 1979.

Federal Republic of Nigeria. *Presidential Task Force on the Implementation of Civil Service Reforms, Main Report and Summary of Recommendations.* Lagos: Federal Government Printer, 1988.

Federal Republic of Nigeria. *Implementation Guidelines on Civil Service Reforms.* Lagos: Federal Government Printer, 1988.

Federal Republic of Nigeria. *Dotun Philips Report—The Nigerian Civil Service in the mid–80's and Beyond.* Lagos, Mimeo, 1988.

Iluyonade, B. O., and Eka, B. U. *Cases and Materials on Administrative Law in Nigeria.* Ile-Ife: University of Ife Press, 1980.

Laleye, O. M. "The Role of Public Enterprises in the Development of Nigeria." Ph.D. thesis, University of Ife, 1986.

Murray, D. J. (ed.). *Studies in Nigerian Administration.* London: Hutchinson, 1978.

Nigerian Economic Society. *Public Enterprises in Nigeria.* Proceedings of the 1973 Annual Conference. Ibadan: University of Ibadan Press, 1975.

Nigerian Economic Society. *Structural Adjustment Programme and the Nigerian Economy.* Ile-Ife: Obafemi Awolowo University, 1988.

Odekunle, F. (ed.). *Nigeria: Corruption in Development.* Ibadan: Ibadan University Press, 1986.

Olowu, D. (ed.). *The Nigerian Federal System.* Ibadan: Evans, 1988.

Orewa, G., and Adewunmi, J. *Local Government in Nigeria: The Changing Scene.* Benin: Ethiope Publishing Co., 1983.

Panter-Brick, K. (ed.). *Soldiers and Oil: The Political Transformation of Nigeria.* London: Frank Cass, 1978.

Sanda, A. O., Ojo, O., and Ayeni, V. (eds.). *The Impact of Military Rule on Nigeria's Administration*. Ile-Ife: Faculty of Administration, University of Ife, 1986.

Stolpher, W. *Planning Without Facts, Lessons in Resource Allocation from Nigeria's Development*. Cambridge, Mass.: Harvard University Press, 1966.

12. ZAMBIA

Adu, A. L. *The Civil Service in Commonwealth Africa*. London: Allen and Unwin, 1975.

Dresang, Denis L. *The Zambian Civil Service*. Nairobi: East Africa Publishing Co., 1975.

Gann, L. H. *The Birth of a Plural Society: The Development of Northern Rhodesia 1894– 1914*. Manchester: Manchester University Press, 1958.

Kapotwe. *Edwin, The African Clerk*. Lusaka: Neczam, 1980.

Kaunda, Kenneth D. *Humanism in Zambia—Part I*. Lusaka: Zambia Information Services, 1967.

Kaunda, Kenneth D. *Humanism in Zambia—Part II*. Lusaka: Zambia Information Services, 1973.

Mwanakatwe, John M. *The Growth of Education in Zambia since Independence*. Lusaka: Oxford University Press, 1971.

Pettman, Jan. *Zambia: Security and Conflict*. Sussex: Julian Friedman, 1974.

Republic of Zambia. *Commission for Investigations Act 18 of 1974 and No. 22 of 1975*.

Republic of Zambia. *Decentralised Government: Proposals for Integrated Local Government Administration*. Lusaka: Government Printers, 1978.

Republic of Zambia. *Local Administration Act No. 15 of 1980*.

Republic of Zambia. *The Constitution of the Republic of Zambia*. Lusaka: Government Printers, 1982.

Republic of Zambia. *The Constitution of the United National Independence Party*. Lusaka: Government Printers, 1983.

Tordoff, William (ed.). *Politics in Zambia*. Manchester: Manchester University Press, 1972.

Waldo, D. *The Study of Public Administration*. Garden City, N.Y.: Doubleday, 1955.

13. THE ENGLISH-SPEAKING CARIBBEAN

Armstrong, Aubrey B. *A Survey of Management Development Training Resources and Priority Needs in the Commonwealth Caribbean*. Barbados: Caribbean Centre for Development Administration, 1980.

Barnett, L. G. *Constitutional Law of Jamaica*. London: Oxford University Press, 1977.

Demas, W. C. *The Economics of Development with Special Reference to the Caribbean*. Montreal: McGill University Press, 1965.

Green, Phyllis, Gordon, Derek, and Jones, Edwin. *Employee Morale in the Jamaican Civil Service*. Jamaica: Administrative Staff College, 1983.

Hamilton, B. St. J. *Problems of Administration in an Emergent Nation: A Case Study of Jamaica*. New York: Praeger 1964.

Jones, Edwin. "Pressure Group Politics in the West Indies." Ph.D. thesis, Manchester University, 1970.

Lewis, Gordon. *The Making of the Modern West Indies*. London: McGibbon and Kee, 1968.

Lewis, G., and O'Neill, J. (Chairmen). *The Role and Status of the Civil Service in the Age of Independence*. Report of Working Party, Trinidad and Tobago, September 1964.

Lewis, Selwyn. *Race and Nationalism in Trinidad and Tobago*. Toronto: University of Toronto Press, 1972.

Lewis, V. A. (ed.). *Size, Self-Determination and International Relations: The Caribbean*. University of the West Indies, ISER, 1976.

Ryan, Selwyn. *Issues and Problems in Caribbean Public Administration: A Reader* (2 vols.). St. Augustine, Trinidad: University of the West Indies, Department of Government, November, 1977.

Singham, A. W. *The Hero and the Crowd in a Colonial Polity*. New Haven, Conn.: Yale University Press, 1968.

Stone, Carl. *Democracy and Clientelism in Jamaica*. Transactions Publishing House, Rutgers University, 1980.

United Nations. *Report on Public Administration in Guyana*. Georgetown: Government Printer, 1966.

Wight, Martin. *The Development of the Legislative Council (1606–1945)*. London: Faber and Faber, 1946.

Young, Paul Chen. *Report on Private Investment in the Caribbean*. Kingston: Atlas Publishing Co., 1973.

14. LATIN AMERICA: THE SOUTHERN CONE

Alisky, Marvin. *Uruguay: A Contemporary Survey*. New York: Praeger, 1969.

Ascher, Louis. "Planners, Politics and Technology in Argentina and Chile." Ph.D. thesis, Yale University Department of Political Science, 1975.

Banks, Arthur S. (ed.). *Political Handbook of the World, 1984–1985*. Binghampton: Centre for Social Analysis, 1985.

Black, Jan (ed.). *Latin America: Its Problems and Its Promise*. Boulder, Colo.: Westview Press, 1984.

Daneau, Marcel (ed.). *Violence et conflits en Amérique latine*. Quebec: Centre Québécois des Relations Internationales, 1985.

Delpar, Helen (ed.). *Encyclopedia of Latin America*. New York: McGraw-Hill, 1974.

Furtado, Elso. *Economic Development of Latin America—Historical Background and Contemporary Problems*. London: Cambridge University Press, 1970, 2d ed.

Glade, William. *The Latin American Economies: A Study of Their Institutional Evolution*. New York: Van Nostrand Reinhold, 1969.

Hopkins, Jack (ed.). *Latin America and Caribbean Contemporary Record*. New York: Holmes and Meiser, 1985.

Jaguaribe, Helio. *Economic and Political Development. A Theoretical Approach and a Brazilian Case Study*. Cambridge, Mass.: Harvard University Press, 1968.

Linowitz, Sol. *The Americans in a Changing World*. New York: Quadrangle Press, 1975.

Malloy, James (ed.). *Authoritarianism and Corporatism in Latin America*. Pittsburgh: Pittsburgh University Press, 1977.

O'Brien, Philip, and Cammack, Paul. *Generals in Retreat: The Crisis of Military Rule in Latin America*. Manchester: Manchester University Press, 1985.

Oszlak, Oscar. *Diagnostice de la Administracion Publica Uruguaya*. San Jose: ICAP, 1975.

Petras, James. *Politics and Social Forces in Chilean Development*. Berkeley: University of California Press, 1969.

Rockefeller, Nelson. *The Rockefeller Report of a United States Presidential Mission to the Western Hemisphere*. Chicago: Quadrangle Press, 1969.

Stallings, Barbara. *Class Conflict and Economic Development in Chile, 1958–73*. Stanford, California: Stanford University Press, 1978.

Valenzula, Arturo. *Political Brokers in Chile: Local Government in a Centralized Polity*. Durham, N.C.: Duke University Press, 1977.

Weinstein, Martin. *Uruguay, the Politics of Failure*. Westport, Conn.: Greenwood Press, 1975.

Zeitlin, Maurice. *The Civil Wars in Chile (or Bourgeois Revolutions That Never Were)*. Princeton, N.J.: Princeton University Press, 1984.

CONCLUSION AND APPENDIX

Abernethy, David B. *The Political Dilemma of Popular Education*. Stanford, Calif.: Stanford University Press, 1969.

Adie, Robert, and Thomas, Paul G. *Canadian Public Administration: Problematical Perspectives*. Scarborough: Prentice-Hall, Canada, 1987 2d ed.

Albrow, Martin. *Bureaucracy*. London: Pall Mall Press, 1970.

Armstrong, John. *The European Administrative Elite*. Princeton, N.J.: Princeton University Press, 1973.

Barker, Ernest. *The Development of Public Services in Europe*. Hamden, Conn.: Archon Books, 1966.

Berg, Robert J., and Whitaker, Jennifer Seymour (eds.). *Strategies for African Development*. Berkeley: University of California Press, 1986.

Berger, Morroe. *Bureaucracy and Society in Modern Egypt*. Princeton, N.J.: Princeton University Press, 1957.

Butlin, N. G. *Investment in Australian Economic Development*. London: Cambridge University Press, 1964.

Canale, Jean-Suret, *L'Afrique Noire: L'ere Coloniale 1900–1945*. Paris: Editions Sociales, 1964.

Chapman, Brian. *The Prefects of Provincial France*. London: Allen and Unwin, 1955.

Chodak, Szymon. *Etatized Society*. Berkeley: University of California Press, 1988.

Craft, Maurice. *Family, Class and Education: A Reader*. London: Longmans, 1970.

Darbel, Alain, and Schnapper, Dominique. *Les Agents du Systeme Administratif*. Paris: Mouton and Co. and Ecole Pratique des Hautes Etudes, 1969.

Deschamps, Hubert. *Methodes et Doctrines Coloniales de la France*. Paris: Armand Colin, 1953.

Dumont, Rene. *False Start in Africa*. Sphere Paperbacks, 1967.

Fanon, Frantz. *The Wretched of the Earth*. London: McGibbon and Kee, 1965.

Finer, Herman. *Theory and Practice of Government*. 2 vols. London: Methuen, 1946, 2d ed.

Foster, Philip E. *Education and Social Change in Ghana*. London: Routledge and Kegan Paul, 1966.

Gant, George F. *Development Administration: Concepts, Goals, Methods*. Madison: University of Wisconsin Press, 1979.

Hopkins, Raymond. "Political Roles in a New State." Ph.D. dissertation, Yale University, 1968.

Ionescu, Ghita (ed.). *Between Sovereignty and Integration.* London: Croom Helm, 1974.

Kelsall, R. K. *Higher Civil Servants in Britain.* London; Routledge and Kegan Paul, 1955.

Landstrom, Sten-sture. *Svenska Ambetsmans Sociala Ursprung.* Uppsala: Almquist och Wiksells Boktryckeri AB 1954.

Lowi, Theodore. *The End of Liberalism.* New York: W.W. Norton, 1979, 2 ed.

Marx, Karl. *The 18th Brumaire of Louis Napoleon.* New York: International Publishers, 1963.

Miliband, Ralph. *The State in Capitalist Society.* London: Weidenfeld and Nicolson, 1969.

Misra, B. B. *The Indian Middle Classes.* London: Oxford University Press, 1963.

Mortimer, Edward. *France and the Africans 1944–1960: A Political History.* London: Faber and Faber, 1969.

Polanyi, Karl. *The Great Transformation: The Political and Economic Origins of Our Times.* Boston: Beacon Press, 1968.

Poulantzaas, Nicos. *Les classes sociales dans le capitalisme Aujourd'hui.* Paris: Editions de seuil, 1974 [*Political Power and Social Classes*, London, 1974].

Praam, A. Van. *Ambetnaren en Bureaucratie in Nederland.* The Hague: W. De Haan, N. V., 1957.

Rose, Richard (ed.). *Challenge to Governance: Studies in Overload Politics.* London, 1985

Rowat, Donald C. (ed.). *International Handbook on Local Government Reorganization.* Westport, Conn.: Greenwood Press, 1980.

Sarkaria Commission Report, (Summary). Government of India, 1988.

Shastri Indo-Canadian Institute. *Issues in Public Sector Analysis.* Calgary, 1986.

Shivji, Issa. *The Silent Class Struggle.* Dar-es-Salaam: Tanzania Publishing House, 1973.

Subramaniam, V. *Social Background of India's Administrators.* New Delhi: Publications Division, 1971.

Subramaniam, V. *Transplanted Indo-British Administration.* New Delhi: Ashish Publishing House, 1977.

Subramaniam, V. *Cultural Integration in India.* New Delhi: Ashish Publishing House, 1977.

Vernon, Philip E. *Intelligence and Cultural Environment.* London: Methuen, 1969.

Warner, W. L., et al. *The American Federal Executive.* New Haven, Conn.: Yale University Press, 1963.

NAME INDEX

This index includes personal names in the text alone and does not include names in the Notes and Bibliography.

SUBJECT INDEX

ABOUT THE EDITOR AND CONTRIBUTORS

V. SUBRAMANIAM is Professor of Political Science, Carleton University, Ottawa. His distinguished appointments include the Simon Senior Fellowship at Manchester University (England) and visiting appointments at Heidelberg, Leningrad, and several other universities. He has published ten books in public administration and political science and numerous articles in well-known readers. He is the author of *Cultural Integration of India: A Socio-Historical Analysis* (1983) and *Transplanted Indo-British Administration* (1977). He is also an internationally known classical composer of dance dramas in Sanskrit on Buddhist themes.

Ladipo Adamolekun, Professor of Public Administration at the Obafemi Awolowo University, Ile-Ife, Nigeria, is currently a Senior Public Sector Management Specialist at the Economic Development Institute of the World Bank. He is author and editor of a dozen books and monographs, as well as many articles in learned journals, on politics and public administration in Africa with emphasis on Nigeria. Among his most recent publications are *Politics and Administration in Nigeria* (1986) and *Issues in Development Management in Sub-Saharan Africa* (1989).

Syed Giasuddin Ahmed is Professor of Public Administration at the University of Dhaka and was also University Registrar in 1986–87. He has authored five books on public administration and political science and has published several articles in journals such as *International Review of Administrative Sciences*, *Indian Journal of Public Administration*, *Asian Profile*, *Administrative Change*, *South Asian Studies*, and *Pakistan Administration*.

Ayman Al-Yassini, originally from Syria, has taught for several years at Concordia University, Montreal, and was Visiting Professor at the University of Riyadh in the College of Administrative Sciences. He has worked with the Canadian Bureau of International Education and the Department of External Affairs and is now Director of Policy and Corporate Affairs, World University Service of Canada. He is the author of *Religion and State in Saudi Arabia* and several articles in journals.

Victor Ayeni is a Senior Lecturer in Public Administration at the Obafemi Awolowo University, Ile-Ife, Nigeria. His research interests are focused on organization theory and Nigerian and comparative public administration. He is a leading scholar of the Nigerian ombudsman system. His articles have appeared in *Public Administration and Development* and *Quarterly Journal of Administration*. He is co-editor of *Nigeria's Second Republic* (1988).

J. M. Bwalya is Senior Lecturer at the President's Citizenship College, Kabwe, Zambia.

Ledivina V. Cariño is Professor of Public Administration at the University of the Philippines and was Dean of the College of Public Administration for two years and Director of the Local Government Centre for one year. Cariño has received several distinguished research awards and has served as a consultant for USAID, UNFPA, and the Asian and Pacific Development Centre. She was President of the Philippine Sociological Society and Secretary-Treasurer of the Philippine Social Science Council. She has published eight books (as editor or co-editor), of which *The Indang Experience* received the Book Development Association of the Philippines award. She has published numerous articles in learned journals and was editor of the *Philippine Journal of Public Administration* and *Philippine Sociological Review*.

Chibwe Chibaye was successively lecturer and head of Political and Administrative Studies and Dean of Humanities and Social Sciences at the University of Zambia and has been Principal at the President's Citizenship College, Kabwe, since 1983. He has published several articles on Zambian and African public administration and is co-author with K. Woldring of *Beyond Political Independence: Zambia's Development Predicament in the 1980's* (1984).

Ali Farazmand was born and educated in Iran and has served there as a senior administrator. He is director of the public administration program at the University of Pittsburgh. He has published several articles on politics and administration in Iran and authored *The State, Bureaucracy and Revolution in Modern Iran* (1989).

E. Gyimah-Boadi is a Lecturer in Political Science at the University of Ghana, Legon. Previous collaborations with Donald Rothchild on Ghanaian politics and development have appeared in *Africa Today*, *Issue*, *Current History*, and John Ravenhill, ed., *Africa in Economic Crisis* (1986).

Metin Heper is Professor of Political Science at Bilkent University, Ankara, Turkey. He taught earlier at the Middle East Technical University (Ankara) and Bogazici University (Istanbul) and had been a Research Associate at Harvard University, Visiting Professor at the Southwest Texas State University, Lester Martin Fellow at the Hebrew University of Jerusalem, Visiting Professor and Fulbright Scholar at the University of Connecticut, and Simon Senior Fellow at Manchester University (England). His books include *Islam and Politics in the Modern Middle East* (co-editor), *State, Democracy and the Military: Turkey in the 1980s* (co-editor), *Dilemmas of Decentralization: Municipal Government Turkey* (editor), *Democracy and Local Government: Istanbul in the 1980s* (editor), *Local Government in Turkey: Governing Greater Istanbul* (editor), *The State and Public Bureaucracies: A Comparative Perspective* (editor), and *The State Tradition in Turkey*.

Nasir Islam is an Associate Professor at the Faculty of Administration, University of Ottawa and has served as Assistant Dean and Director of the M.B.A. Program. He has been consultant for the UNDP, the International Development Research Centre, and the Canadian International Development Agency, and has been a Visiting Professor in Haiti and Sri Lanka. His recent research interests are focused around implementation of policy and programs, administrative reform, and mid-career training. He has published numerous articles in *Etudes Internationales*, *Gestion Internationale*, *International Review of Administrative Sciences*, *Canadian Journal of Development Studies*, *Canadian Public Administration*, *International Journal of Middle Eastern Studies*, *International Journal*, and *International Perspectives*.

Mohammad Mohabbat Khan is Professor of Public Administration at Dhaka University, Bangladesh, and Chairman, Center for Public Affairs. He was Chairman of the Department of Public Administration from 1983 to 1986. He is the author or editor of eight books including *Personnel Management* (1978), *Bureaucratic Self-Preservation* (1980), *Participative Management in Industry (1980)*, *Administrative Reform* (1981), *Rural Development in Bangladesh* (1981), and *Bangladesh Studies* (1986) and four monographs, and has contributed chapters to ten books. He has published extensively in such journals as *Public Administration and Development*, *Development Policy Review*, *Community Development Journal*, *International Review of Administrative Sciences*, *Asian Survey*, *Indian Journal of Public Administration*, *Asian Thought and Society*, and *Asian Profile and Regional Studies*. He is the co-editor of *Politics, Administration and Change* and is on the editorial board of a number of journals.

Shriram Maheshwari is Professor of Political Science and Public Administration at the Indian Institute of Public Administration, New Delhi, and President of the Indian Public Administration Association (1989). Maheshwari was a member of the administrative reforms committee of the state of Uttar Pradesh in India. An author of over twenty-five books and numerous papers, his more important publications include *The Higher Civil Service in France* (in press), *The Higher Civil Service in Japan* (1986), *Rural Development in India* (1985), *Political Development in India* (1984), *Administrative Reform in India* (1981), *Open Government in India* (1981), and *Indian Administration* (1989, 4th ed.), *State Governments in India* (1979), and *Local Government in India* (1984, 3rd ed.).

Gladstone Mills, after two decades of distinguished work in the Jamaican Civil Service, joined the University of the West Indies, where he was Head of the Department of Government and Dean of the Faculty of Social Sciences. He was Simon Professorial Fellow at Manchester University for 1978. He has simultaneously served on several statutory and enquiry commissions of the government of Jamaica and is currently representing CARICOM in negotiations with the EEC. He has published numerous papers in well-known journals of public administration and has been honored recently by the government of Jamaica with the highest national honor, the Order of Jamaica (O.J.).

Jorge Nef is Professor of Political Studies and International Development at the University of Guelph. He has taught at the universities of Chile, California at Santa Barbara, and McGill and has been Visiting Professor in various Canadian and foreign universities and institutes. Between 1981 and 1983 he was President of the Canadian Association of Latin American and Caribbean Studies. He has published numerous articles in journals such as *Latin American Perspectives*, *Interamerican Review*, *North/South*, *The Canadian Journal of Development Studies*, *Latin American Research Review*, *New Scholar*, *The Nation*, *The Indian Journal of Public Administration*, *Public Administration and Development*, *Etudes Internationales*, *Relaciones Internacionales*, *Revista Centroamenica de Administracion Publica*, *Konflicternes Verden*, *Internationalist*, *The Canadian Journal of Latin American and Caribbean Studies* and in over twenty edited collections. He is also the author, editor, or co-editor of several books, including *Canada and the Latin American Challenge* (1978), *Repression and Liberation in Latin America* (1981), *Administracion Publica: Perspectivas Criticas* (1985), *Food Security and Insecurity in Latin America and the Caribbean* (1989), and *Ethics and Technology* (1989). In addition, he has worked as a consultant or cooperant with the Pan American Health Organisation, the Canadian International Development Agency, and the International Development Research Centre. He also represented the latter in the South Commission.

Donald Rothchild is Professor of Political Science at the University of California, Davis. Among various appointments to universities in Africa, he has been a

Visiting Professor in Political Science at the University of Ghana, Legon, in 1975–77 and in the winter of 1985. He is a frequent contributor to professional journals, and his recent books include *Scarcity, Choice, and Public Policy in Middle Africa; State Versus Ethnic Claims; Eagle Resurgent?; Afro-Marxist Regimes; The Precarious Balance;* and *Politics and Society in Contemporary Africa.*

E. H. Valsan is Professor of Management and Public Administration and Director of the Public Administration Program of the A. L. Jameel Center for Middle East Management Studies of the American University in Cairo, Egypt. He was an International Development Research Fellow at the East-West Center, University of Hawaii, and his research findings are published in *Community Development Programs and Rural Local Government: Comparative Case Studies of India and the Philippines* (1970). He has published several articles in international periodicals and chapters on India, Egypt, and Belgium. Valsan has worked as a consultant to UNDP and USAID assisted projects in Egypt, particularly in the fields of management of family planning programs and agriculture.

LIBRARY
OF
MOUNT ST. MARY'S
COLLEGE

JUL 0 5 1991